Philip Shenon, the bestselling author of *The Commission: The Uncensored History of the 9/11 Investigation*, was a reporter for the *New York Times* for more than twenty years. As a Washington correspondent for *The Times*, he covered the Pentagon, the Justice Department and the State Department. As a foreign correspondent for the paper, he reported from more than sixty countries and several war zones. He lives in Washington, DC.

'[A] masterful piece of modern history ... Even [Shenon's] asides reek of deep reporting ... a sober, gripping study of one of history's most overstudied moments, a work fit to rank alongside the previous masterpiece of the murder, William Manchester's *The Death of A President*' *Independent*

'A very thorough and well-researched book ... this is a valuable contribution to the oeuvre and should help lay [JFK's] ghost to rest' Toby Young, *Mail on Sunday*

'Philip Shenon's rollicking new book ... one part *Mad Men* and one part James Bond' *Washington Post*

'Meticulous rigour and the sure-handed storytelling of a gifted thriller writer ... Shenon's careful delineation of the limits of the facts is more necessary than ever' *Metro*

'Fifty years after the act, [Shenon] has, through *actual, on the ground, person-to-person investigation*, through nonstop digging, tugging at the tangled heart of the mystery, brought us to the brink of answer. An achievement that, I believe, merits the Pulitzer Prize and the thanks of a grateful nation ... Shenon paints a compelling picture' *Slate*

BY PHILIP SHENON

The Commission:
The Uncensored History of the 9/11 Investigation

A Cruel and Shocking Act:
The Secret History of the Kennedy Assassination

A CRUEL AND SHOCKING ACT

THE SECRET HISTORY OF
THE KENNEDY ASSASSINATION

PHILIP SHENON

ABACUS

First published in the USA in 2013 by Henry Holt and Company, LLC
First published in Great Britain in 2013 by Little, Brown
This paperback edition published in 2015 by Abacus

13 5 7 9 10 8 6 4 2

Photograph credits: p.15: Courtesy Everett Collection. p.65: Courtesy of
The Sixth Floor Museum at Dealey Plaza. p.397: © Bettmann/CORBIS. p.491:
© Rene Burri/Magnum Photos.

Maps by Gene Thorp
Photo research by Laura Wyss and Wyssphoto, Inc.
Designed by Meryl Sussman Levavi

A CIP catalogue record for this book
is available from the British Library.

ISBN 978-0-349-14061-2

Printed and bound in Great Britain by
Clays Ltd, St Ives plc

Papers used by Abacus are from well-managed forests
and other responsible sources.

MIX
Paper from
responsible sources
FSC   FSC® C104740
www.fsc.org

Abacus
An imprint of
Little, Brown Book Group
100 Victoria Embankment
London EC4Y 0DY

An Hachette UK Company
www.hachette.co.uk

www.littlebrown.co.uk

To the memory of my father,
Peter Warren Shenon,
whose kindheartedness and sense of fair play
were nurtured in the California
that Earl Warren created.

"The assassination of John Fitzgerald Kennedy on November 22, 1963, was a cruel and shocking act of violence directed against a man, a family, a nation, and against all mankind."

The final report of the President's Commission
on the Assassination of President John F. Kennedy,
September 24, 1964

QUESTION: Did he tell you anything about his trip to Mexico City?

MARINA OSWALD: Yes, he told me that he had visited the two embassies, that he had received nothing, that the people who are there are too much—too bureaucratic.

QUESTION: Did you ask him what he did the rest of the time?

MRS. OSWALD: Yes, I think he said that he visited a bull fight, that he spent most of his time in museums, and that he did some sightseeing.

QUESTION: Did he tell you about anyone that he met there?

MRS. OSWALD: No. He said that he did not like the Mexican girls.

Testimony of Marina Oswald
to the President's Commission,
February 3, 1964

Contents

A CRUEL
AND
SHOCKING
ACT

Prologue

There is no way to know exactly when Charles William Thomas began to think about suicide. Who could really know such a thing? Years later, congressional investigators could offer only their strong suspicions about what had finally led Thomas, a former American diplomat who had spent most of his career in Africa and Latin America, to kill himself. On Monday, April 12, 1971, at about four p.m., he put a gun to his head on the second floor of his family's modest rented house, near the shores of the Potomac River, in Washington, DC. His wife, downstairs, thought at first that the boiler had exploded.

Certainly two years earlier, in the summer of 1969, Thomas had reason to be disheartened. He was forty-seven years old, with a wife and two young daughters to support, and he knew his career at the State Department was over. It was official, even though he still could not fathom why he was being forced out of a job that he loved and that he thought—that he *knew*—he did well. The department long had an "up or out" policy for members of the diplomatic corps, similar to the military. Either you were promoted up the ranks or your career was over. And since he had been denied a promotion to another embassy abroad or to a supervisor's desk in Washington, Thomas was "selected out," to use the department's Orwellian terminology for being fired. After eighteen fulfilling, mostly happy years wandering the globe on behalf of his country, he was told he had no job.

At first, he thought it must be a mistake, his wife, Cynthia, said. His personnel records were exemplary, including a recent inspection report that described him as "one of the most valuable officers" in the State Department, whose promotion was "long overdue." After he was formally "selected out," however, there was no easy way to appeal the decision. And Thomas, a proud, often stoical man, found it demoralizing even to try. He had already begun boxing up his belongings in his office and wondering if, at his age, it would be possible to begin a new career.

He did have one piece of unfinished business with the department before he departed. And on July 25, 1969, he finished typing up a three-page memo, and a one-page cover letter, that he addressed to his ultimate boss at the department: William P. Rogers, President Nixon's secretary of state. Colleagues might have told Thomas it was presumptuous for a mid-level diplomat to write directly to the secretary, but Thomas had reason to believe that going to Rogers was his only real hope of getting some-one's attention. Thomas was not trying to save his job; it was too late for that, he told his family. Instead, the memo was a final attempt to resolve what had been—apart from the puzzle of his dismissal—the biggest, most confounding mystery of his professional life. Rogers was new to the State Department, sworn in only six months earlier along with the rest of Nixon's cabinet. Thomas hoped Rogers might be willing to second-guess the career diplomats at the department who—for nearly four years—had ignored the remarkable story that Thomas kept trying to tell them.

At the top of every page of the memo, Thomas typed—and underlined— the word "CONFIDENTIAL."

"Dear Mr. Secretary," he began. "In winding up my affairs at the Department of State, there is a pending matter which I believe merits your attention."

The memo had a title: "Subject: Investigation of Lee Harvey Oswald in Mexico."

His tone was formal and polite, which was certainly in character for Charles William Thomas, who used his middle name in official correspon-dence to avoid confusion with another Charles W. Thomas who worked at the department. He wanted to be remembered as a diplomat—to be diplomatic—to the end. He knew his memo outlined potentially explosive national-security information, and he wanted to be careful not to be perceived as reckless. He had no interest in leaving the State Department with a reputation of being some sort of crazy conspiracy theorist. At the end of the 1960s, there were plenty of craven, headline-grabbing "truth-seekers" peddling conspiracies about President Kennedy's assassination. Thomas did not want to be lumped in with them in the history books—or in the classified personnel archives of the State Department, for that matter. His memo contained no language suggesting the personal demons that would lead him to take his life two years later.

Secretary Rogers would have had easy access to the details of Thomas's career, and they were impressive. Thomas was a self-made man, orphaned as a boy in Texas and raised in the home of an older sister in Fort Wayne, Indiana. He served as a navy fighter pilot in World War II, then enrolled at Northwestern University in Evanston, Illinois, where he earned both a bachelor's and a law degree. Foreign languages came easily; he was fluent in French and Spanish and, over the years, developed a working knowledge of German, Italian, Portuguese, and Creole; the last had been valuable during a diplomatic posting in Haiti. After Northwestern, he studied in Europe and received a doctorate in international law at the University of Paris. In 1951, he joined the State Department and served initially in hardship posts in West Africa, where, despite several severe bouts of malaria, he was remembered for his good humor and enthusiasm. His friends said he was "the diplomat from central casting"—six feet tall, blond, preppy handsome, articulate, and charming. Early in his career, colleagues assumed he was destined to achieve the rank of ambassador, running his own embassy.

In 1964, Thomas was named a political officer in the United States embassy in Mexico, where he was posted for nearly three years. Mexico City was considered an especially important assignment in the 1960s since the city was a Cold War hot spot—Latin America's answer to Berlin or Vienna. There were big Cuban and Soviet embassies, the largest in Latin America for both Communist governments. And the activities of Cuban and Soviet diplomats, and the many spies posing as diplomats, could be closely monitored by the United States with the assistance of Mexico's normally cooperative police agencies. The CIA believed that the Russian embassy in Mexico was the KGB's base for "wet operations"—assassinations, in the CIA's jargon—in the Western Hemisphere. (It would have been too risky for the KGB to run those operations out of the Russian embassy in Washington.) Mexico City had itself been the scene of Kremlin-ordered violence in the past. In 1940, Soviet leader Joseph Stalin dispatched assassins to Mexico City to kill his rival Leon Trotsky, who was living there in exile.

Mexico City's reputation as a center of Cold War intrigue was cemented by the disclosure that Lee Harvey Oswald had visited the city only several weeks before the assassination of President John F. Kennedy in Dallas on Friday, November 22, 1963. Details about Oswald's Mexico trip were revealed in news reports published within days of the president's murder, giving birth to some of the first serious conspiracy theories about foreign involvement in the assassination. Everything about Oswald's stay in Mexico, which had reportedly lasted six days, was suspicious. A self-proclaimed Marxist, Oswald, who did not hide his Communist leanings even while serving in the U.S. Marine Corps, visited both the Cuban and Soviet embassies in Mexico City. It appeared he had gone there to get visas that would allow him, ultimately, to defect to Cuba. It would be his second defection attempt. He had tried to renounce his American citizenship when he traveled to the Soviet Union in 1959, only to decide to return to the United States from Russia three years later, saying that he had come to disdain Moscow's brand of Communism, with its petty corruptions and mazelike bureaucracy. He hoped Fidel Castro and his followers in Havana would prove more loyal to the ideals of Marx.

In September 1964, the presidential commission led by Chief Justice Earl Warren that investigated Kennedy's assassination, known to the public from the start as the Warren Commission, identified Oswald as the assassin and concluded that he had acted alone. In a final report at the end of a ten-month investigation, the seven-member panel said that it had uncovered no evidence of a conspiracy, foreign or domestic. "The commission has found no evidence that anyone assisted Oswald in planning or carrying out the assassination," the report declared. While the commission could not establish Oswald's motives for the assassination with certainty, the report suggested that he was emotionally disturbed and might have decided to kill the president because of "deep-rooted resentment of all authority" and an "urge to try to find a place in history."

And in the final days of his employment at the State Department in the summer of 1969, those were the conclusions that Charles Thomas wanted someone in the government to revisit. Was it possible that the Warren Commission had it wrong? Thomas's memo to Secretary of State Rogers outlined information about Oswald's 1963 Mexico visit that threatened to "reopen the debate about the true nature of the Kennedy assassination and damage the credibility of the Warren Report. . . . Since I was the embassy officer who acquired this intelligence information, I feel a responsibility for seeing it through to its final evaluation," he explained. "Under the circumstances, it is unlikely that any further investigation of this matter will ever take place unless it is ordered by a high official in Washington."

The details of what Thomas had learned were so complex that he felt the need to number each paragraph in the memo. He enclosed several other documents that were full of references to accented Spanish-language names and obscure locations in Mexico City; they offered a complicated time line of long-ago events. His central message, however, was this: the Warren Commission had overlooked—or never had a chance to see—intelligence suggesting that a plot to kill Kennedy might have been hatched, or at least encouraged, by Cuban diplomats and spies stationed in the Mexican capital, and that Oswald was introduced to this nest of spies in September 1963 by a vivacious young Mexican woman who was a fellow champion of Castro's revolution.

The woman, Thomas was told, had briefly been Oswald's mistress in Mexico City.

As he wrote the memo, Thomas must have realized again how improbable—even absurd—this might all sound to his soon-to-be former colleagues at the State Department. If any of his information was right, how could the Warren Commission have missed it?

In the body of the memo, he identified, by name, the principal source of his information: Elena Garro de Paz, a popular and critically acclaimed Mexican novelist of the 1960s. Her fame was enhanced by her marriage to one of Mexico's most celebrated writers and poets, Octavio Paz, who later won the Nobel Prize in Literature. A sharp-witted, mercurial woman, Garro, who was in her midforties when she met Thomas, spoke several languages and had lived in Europe for years before returning to Mexico in 1963. She had done graduate work at both the University of California at Berkeley and, like Thomas, the University of Paris.

The two had become friends on Mexico City's lively social circuit and, in December 1965, she offered the American diplomat a tantalizing story. She revealed—reluctantly, Thomas said—that she had encountered Oswald at a party of Castro sympathizers during his visit in the fall of 1963.

It had been a "twist party"—Chubby Checker's hit song was wildly popular in Mexico, too—and Oswald was not the only American there, Garro said. He had been in the company of two young "beatnik" American men. "The three were evidently friends, because she saw them by chance the next day walking down the street together," Thomas wrote. At the party, Oswald wore a black sweater and "tended to be silent and stared a lot at the floor," Garro recalled. She did not talk to any of the Americans or learn their names. She said she learned Oswald's name only after seeing his photograph in Mexican newspapers and on television after the assassination.

A senior Cuban diplomat was also at the party, she said. Eusebio Azque, who held the title of consul, ran the embassy's visa office. (In the memo, Thomas said that Azque's other duties included espionage; the U.S. embassy believed he was a high-ranking officer in Castro's spy service, the Dirección General de Inteligencia, or DGI.) It was Azque's consular office in Mexico City that Oswald had visited in hopes of obtaining a Cuban visa.

Garro, a fierce anti-Communist, loathed the Cuban diplomat. Before Kennedy's assassination, she said, she had heard Azque speak openly of his hope that someone would kill the American president, given the threat that Kennedy posed to the survival of the Castro government. The October 1962 Cuban missile crisis, and the bungled CIA-sponsored Bay of Pigs invasion a year before that, would have been fresh in Azque's memory. Garro recalled a party at which she and other guests overheard a "heated discussion" in which Azque supported the view that "the only solution was to kill him"—President Kennedy.

Also at the party, Garro said, was a notably pretty twenty-five-year-old Mexican woman who worked for Azque at the consulate: Silvia Tirado de Duran, who was related to Garro by marriage. Duran was an outspoken Socialist and a supporter of Castro, which helped explain how she had gotten a job working for the Cubans. Thomas found a copy of the Warren Commission report in the embassy's library and could see that Duran's name appeared dozens of times in its pages; the commission determined it was Duran who had dealt with Oswald during his visits to the Cuban mission in Mexico. She had helped him fill out his visa application, and it appeared that she had gone out of her way to assist him. Duran's name and phone number were found in a notebook seized among Oswald's belongings.

Garro told Thomas that she never liked Duran, both because of Duran's left-wing politics and because of what Garro described as the younger woman's scandalous personal life. Duran was married to Garro's cousin, but it was widely rumored in Mexico City that she had had a torrid affair three years earlier with Cuba's ambassador to Mexico, who was also married; the ambassador had offered to leave his wife to be with Duran. "Garro has never had anything to do with Silvia, whom she detests and considers a whore," Thomas wrote. (It would later be determined that the CIA had both Duran and the ambassador under surveillance in Mexico; the agency would claim it could document the affair.)

It was only after the Kennedy assassination, Garro said, that she learned that Duran had briefly taken Oswald as a lover. Garro told Thomas that Duran had not only bedded Oswald, she had introduced him around town to Castro's supporters, Cubans and Mexicans alike. It was Duran who had arranged Oswald's invitation to the dance party. "She was his mistress," Garro insisted. She told Thomas that "it was common knowledge that Silvia Duran was the mistress of Oswald."

Thomas asked Garro if she had told this story to anyone else. She explained that, for nearly a year after the assassination, she had kept quiet, fearing her information might somehow endanger her safety, as well as the safety of her twenty-six-year old daughter, who also remembered seeing Oswald at the party. In the fall of 1964, however, just after the Warren Commission had ended its investigation, she found the nerve to meet with American embassy officials in Mexico City and tell them what she knew. To her surprise, she said, she heard nothing from the embassy after that.

In his memo to the secretary of state, Thomas was careful to acknowledge this might all be fiction, offered up to him by an exceptionally talented writer of fiction. Garro, he admitted, had a reputation for a vivid imagination, and her politics might color her perceptions; it was possible that she had simply mistaken another young man at the party for Oswald. "I knew Garro to be something of a professional anti-Communist who tended to see a Communist plot behind any untoward political event," Thomas wrote. "A careful investigation of these allegations could perhaps explain them away." Still, there was a need for another review of her story, he said. "It would be easy and convenient to sweep this matter under the rug by claiming that Miss Garro is an unreliable informant since she is emotional, opinioned and artistic," he wrote. "But on the basis of the facts that I have presented, I believe that, on balance, the matter warrants further investigation."

According to his memo, Thomas's senior colleagues in the embassy knew all about Garro's claims because he had told them. He wrote them long reports after each of his conversations with her in 1965. He set aside part of Christmas Day that year to write a memo—it was dated December 25—recounting what he had heard that morning from her at a holiday party. He made sure his memos went straight to Winston "Win" Scott, the CIA's station chief in Mexico. The courtly, Alabama-born Scott, then fifty-six years old, had sources at the highest levels of the Mexican government, including a series of Mexican presidents who sought his protection and whose top aides became some of the CIA's best-paid informants in the country. Many Mexican officials saw Scott, who took up his post in 1956, as far more powerful than any of the American ambassadors he had worked with. His deputies knew he also wielded extraordinary influence back at CIA headquarters in Langley, Virginia, in part because of his decades-long friendship with James Jesus Angleton, the CIA's counterintelligence director—the agency's chief "mole hunter." Both men had been with the CIA since its founding in 1947.

In his memo to Rogers, Thomas said that Scott and others in the embassy did not pursue the information tying Oswald to the Cubans. After initial expressions of interest, Scott essentially ignored what Thomas had learned, even when Thomas tried to raise the questions again in 1967, as he prepared to leave Mexico for a new posting in Washington.

Thomas acknowledged that "even if all the allegations in the attached memo were true, they would not, in themselves, prove that there was a conspiracy to assassinate President Kennedy." But he concluded his letter to Rogers by warning of the danger to the government if Garro's allegations, unproven but uninvestigated, became known outside the State Department and the CIA. "If they were ever made public, those who have tried to discredit the Warren Report could have a field day in speculating about their implications," Thomas wrote. "The credibility of the Warren Report would be damaged all the more if it were learned that these allegations were known and never adequately investigated."

Thomas's last day of employment at the State Department was July 31, 1969, only six days after the date on his memo to Secretary Rogers. It is not clear from the department's records if Thomas was immediately informed about what happened next with his memo, but the department did pass on his information—to the CIA. On August 29, in a letter stamped CONFIDENTIAL, the State Department's Division of Protective Security wrote to the CIA and asked for an appraisal of Thomas's material. It provided the agency with Thomas's memo, along with several supporting documents.

A little less than three weeks later, the CIA sent back its curt reply. It read, in full: "Subject: Charles William Thomas. Reference is made to your memorandum of 28 August 1969. We have examined the attachments, and see no need for further action. A copy of this reply has been sent to the Federal Bureau of Investigation and the United States Secret Service." The memo was signed by Angleton, the CIA counterintelligence chief, and one of his deputies, Raymond Rocca. Thomas was notified of the CIA's rebuff and, as far as he knew, that was where the paper trail stopped; apparently, nothing more was to be done.

After his suicide two years later, the *Washington Post* published a 186-word obituary that made only a passing reference to how Thomas had died: "Police said the cause of death was gunshot wounds." (Actually, his death certificate identified only one gunshot wound—to his right temple.) After pleas from his family, congressional investigators reviewed his personnel files and determined that Thomas had been "selected out" from the State Department in error. A clerical mistake had cost him his career, or so it appeared; an important job performance report endorsing his promotion had been left out of his personnel files for reasons that were never fully explained.

Congressional investigators later suspected that there had been other factors in the decision to force Thomas out, including his persistent, unwelcome effort to get someone to follow up on Garro's allegations. "I always thought it was linked, somehow, to his questions about Oswald," said a former investigator for the House of Representatives. "It was impossible to prove, though. If he was forced out because of Mexico City, it was all done with a wink and a nod." There were rumors in Mexico that one of Win Scott's deputies at the embassy there had mounted a whispering campaign intended to damage Thomas's reputation—for reasons that Thomas's many Mexican friends could never fathom.

Former senator Birch Bayh of Indiana, chairman of the Senate Select Committee on Intelligence from 1979 to 1981, helped Thomas's family obtain some of the pension benefits they were initially denied after his suicide. Bayh said he intervened, at first, because Thomas had such strong family roots in Indiana. In a 2013 interview, he said he remained perplexed by Thomas's dismissal. "It never made sense," said Bayh, who insisted that he was never informed of any link between Thomas and the investigation of the Kennedy assassination. The former senator said that he could not necessarily draw a connection between Thomas's ouster from the department and what he had learned—and tried to expose—in Mexico City. "But something happened to Charles Thomas," Bayh said. "He was harassed to death by his government."

Late one afternoon in the spring of 2008, the phone rang at my desk in the Washington bureau of the *New York Times*. The caller was someone I had never met—a prominent American lawyer who had begun his career almost half a century earlier as a young staff investigator on the Warren Commission. "You ought to tell our story," he said. "We're not young, but a lot of us from the commission are still around, and this may be our last chance to explain what really happened." His call was prompted, he said, by the generous reviews I had received that year after the publication of my first book—a history of the government commission that investigated the September 11, 2001, terrorist attacks. My caller offered to do all he could to help me with a similar history of the Warren Commission, so long as I did not identify him to his former colleagues as the man who had suggested the idea. "I don't want to take the blame for this when you find out the unflattering stuff," he said, adding that the backstory of the commission was "the best detective story you've never heard."

And so began a five-year reporting project to piece together the inside story of the most important, and most misunderstood, homicide investigation of the twentieth century—the Warren Commission's investigation of the assassination of President Kennedy. Chief Justice Warren and the other six members of the commission died long before I began work on this book—the last surviving member, former president Gerald Ford, died in 2006—but my caller was right that most of the then young lawyers who did the actual detective work in 1964 were still alive. And I'm grateful that almost all of them have been willing to speak with me.

Sadly, time has begun to catch up with my sources, too. Some of the commission investigators and other key figures who granted me interviews for the book have died, most notably former senator Arlen Specter of Pennsylvania, who had been a junior staff lawyer on the commission. This book is therefore their last testament about the work of the commission and about the Kennedy assassination. I was the last journalist to interview former FBI special agent James Hosty, a central witness before

the Warren Commission because he had Lee Harvey Oswald under surveillance in Dallas for months before the assassination. Hosty faced
obvious questions about why he and his colleagues at the FBI had not
been able to stop Oswald. In interviews shortly before his death in June
2011, Hosty insisted that he became the scapegoat—both within the FBI
and for the Warren Commission—for the incompetence and duplicity of
others in the government.

The title of this book is drawn from the first line of the introduction
to the commission's final report: "The assassination of John Fitzgerald
Kennedy on November 22, 1963, was a cruel and shocking act of violence
directed against a man, a family, a nation, and against all mankind." But
while *A Cruel and Shocking Act* began as an attempt to write the first
comprehensive inside history of the Warren Commission, it has become
something much larger and, I believe, more important. In many ways,
this book is an account of my discovery of how much of the truth about
the Kennedy assassination has still not been told, and how much of the
evidence about the president's murder was covered up or destroyed—
shredded, incinerated, or erased—before it could reach the commission.
Senior officials at both the CIA and the FBI hid information from the
panel, apparently in hopes of concealing just how much they had known
about Lee Harvey Oswald and the threat that he posed. As this book will
reveal for the first time, important witnesses to events surrounding the
assassination were ignored or were threatened into silence. The reporting
for this book has taken me to places and introduced me to people I would
never have imagined would be so important to understanding President
Kennedy's death.

I became a victim of the dual curse faced by anyone who tries to get
closer to the truth about the assassination—of too little information and
too much. I made the astonishing, nearly simultaneous discovery of how
much vital evidence about President Kennedy's murder has disappeared
and also of how much has been preserved. There is now so much material in the public record about the assassination, including literally millions of pages of once-secret government files, that no reporter or scholar
can claim to have seen it all. Whole collections of evidence have still not
been adequately reviewed by researchers, almost exactly fifty years after
the events they describe. I was the first researcher, for example, to be
given full access to the papers of Charles Thomas, including the record of

his struggle to get colleagues to pay attention to the astonishing story of Oswald and the "twist party" in Mexico City, and I did not see the material until 2013.

The records of the Warren Commission—its formal name was the President's Commission on the Assassination of President Kennedy—fill up 363 cubic feet of shelf space in well-guarded, climate-controlled storage rooms at a National Archives facility in College Park, Maryland, just outside Washington, DC. Thousands of the commission's physical exhibits are there, including Oswald's 6.5-millimeter Italian-made Mannlicher-Carcano rifle, the murder weapon found on the sixth floor of the Texas School Book Depository, as well as the nearly intact three-centimeter copper-jacketed, lead-core bullet that was discovered near a stretcher at Parkland Memorial Hospital in Dallas on the afternoon of the assassination. The commission's staff—although significantly, not the commission itself—concluded that the bullet, fired from Oswald's $21 mail-order rifle, passed through the bodies of both President Kennedy and Texas governor John Connally in a scenario that became known as "the single-bullet theory."

The rose-pink suit worn by Jacqueline Kennedy in the motorcade is also stored in the modern, fortresslike complex in suburban Maryland. The suit, an American-made Chanel knockoff that was a favorite of the president's (Mrs. Kennedy "looks ravishing in it," he told a friend) is preserved in an acid-free container in a windowless vault. The vault is kept at a temperature of between 65 and 68 degrees Fahrenheit (between 18.3 and 20 degrees Celsius), the humidity set at 40 percent. The filtered air in the vault is changed at least six times every hour in order to help preserve the delicate wool fabric, which remains stained with the president's blood. The whereabouts of Mrs. Kennedy's iconic pink pillbox hat is a mystery; it was last known to be in the custody of her former personal secretary. A separate vault, kept at a constant temperature of 25 degrees Fahrenheit (−4 degrees Celsius), is used for the storage and preservation of a small strip of celluloid that is believed, by the National Archives, to be the most watched piece of film in the history of motion pictures. It was on those 486 frames of Kodachrome-brand 8mm color film that a Dallas women's wear manufacturer, Abraham Zapruder, captured the terrible images of the assassination on his Bell & Howell home-movie camera.

Much of Warren's personal paperwork from the commission that bore his name is stored at the Library of Congress, just a few minutes' walk down First Street from his former chambers at the Supreme Court. Warren, who died in 1974, might be startled to know that millions of Americans know of him principally because of the commission, not because of his history-making sixteen-year tenure as chief justice.

The decision to preserve the vast library of investigative reports and physical evidence gathered by the Warren Commission, and now retained at the National Archives and the Library of Congress, was meant to be reassuring to the public—proof of the commission's transparency and of its diligence. At the National Archives alone, there are more than five million pages of documents related to the assassination. But the truth about the Warren Commission, as most serious historians and other scholars will acknowledge, even those who fully support its findings, is that its investigation was flawed from the start. The commission made grievous errors. It failed to pursue important evidence and witnesses because of limitations imposed on the investigation by the man who ran it, Chief Justice Warren. Often, Warren seemed more interested in protecting the legacy of his beloved friend President Kennedy, and of the Kennedy family, than in getting to the full facts about the president's murder.

On the subject of the assassination, history will be far kinder to the commission's surviving staff lawyers, as well as its former in-house historian, who reveal in this book what really happened inside the Warren Commission. Much of this book is their story, told through their eyes. The lawyers, mostly in their twenties and thirties at the time of the investigation, were recruited from prestigious law firms, law schools, and prosecutors' offices around the country. Most are now at the end of long careers in law or public service. For several, being interviewed for this book was the first time they have talked in this much detail, certainly to any journalist, about the commission's work. Many have kept their silence for decades, fearful of being dragged into ugly, and often unwinnable, public debates with the armies of conspiracy theorists. Without exception, all of these men—the one woman among the lawyers, Alfredda Scobey, died in 2001—retained pride in their individual work on the commission. Many, however, were outraged to discover how much evidence they were never permitted to see. It is evidence, they know, that is still rewriting the history of the Kennedy assassination.

PART 1
NOVEMBER 22–29, 1963

President Kennedy's coffin in the Capitol rotunda,
November 25, 1963

1

Within hours of the return of the president's body to Washington, evidence about the assassination began to disappear from the government's files. Notes taken by military pathologists at the autopsy, as well as the original draft of the autopsy report, were incinerated.

Navy Commander James Humes, MD, said later he was appalled that his handling of the hospital paperwork on the night of Saturday, November 23, might be portrayed as the first act of a government-wide cover-up. Still, he admitted, he should have known better. "What happened was my decision and mine alone," he recalled. "Nobody else's."

At about eleven that night, the thirty-eight-year-old pathologist took a seat at a card table in the family room of his home in Bethesda, in the Maryland suburbs of Washington, and prepared to read through his notes from the morgue. He assumed he would be there for hours, writing and editing the final autopsy report. He had lit a fire in the fireplace, which provided some warmth on an early winter night.

The night before, he had led the three-man team of pathologists who conducted the president's autopsy at Bethesda Naval Medical Center. There had been no time during the day on Saturday to finish the paperwork, he said. So now he sat alone, hoping to find the energy to complete the report in peace. He needed to present a final copy to his colleagues for their signatures; they were under orders to deliver the report to the White House by Sunday night.

Humes was exhausted. He had managed a few hours of sleep that afternoon, but he had not slept at all Friday night. "I was in the morgue from 7:30 in the evening until 5:30 in the morning," he said later. "I never left the room."

It was on Friday afternoon, with the terrible reports still pouring in from Dallas, that Humes, Bethesda's highest-ranking pathologist, learned that he would oversee the postmortem of the president. He was told to expect the arrival of the corpse in a few hours' time. Jacqueline Kennedy had initially resisted the idea of having an autopsy; the vision of her husband's body lying on a cold, steel dissecting table seemed one more horror in a day already full of them. "It *doesn't* have to be done," she told the president's personal physician, Admiral George Burkley, as they flew in Air Force One from Dallas to Washington. She was sitting with the president's casket in the rear compartment of the plane. Burkley, who had proved himself a loyal and discreet friend to the Kennedy family, gently convinced her that there had to be an autopsy. She had always taken comfort from the fact that he was a fellow Roman Catholic, and an especially devout one, and at this moment she would trust his advice above almost all others'. He reminded her that her husband had been the victim of a crime and that an autopsy was a legal necessity. He offered her the choice of the Walter Reed Army Medical Center in Washington or the navy's hospital in Bethesda. The two hospitals were only eight miles apart. "Of course, the president was in the navy," Burkley reminded her.

"Of course," she said. "Bethesda."

The selection was a decision that even some navy doctors questioned. The veteran army pathologists at Walter Reed had far more experience with tracing bullet wounds than did their counterparts in the navy. (It was a simple fact that soldiers were more likely than sailors to die from gunshots.) Commander J. Thornton Boswell, another Bethesda pathologist, was assigned to assist Humes, and he thought it "foolish" to do the autopsy at the navy hospital given the other resources nearby. He thought the president's corpse should have been taken to the Armed Forces Institute of Pathology in downtown Washington, a Defense Department research center that handled complex medical-legal autopsies from all branches of the military. Neither Humes nor Boswell had credentials in forensic pathology, the branch of pathology that focuses on violent or unexpected deaths, so a third member was added to the team: Dr. Pierre Finck, a forensic pathologist from the Armed Forces Institute. Finck was a lieutenant colonel in the Army Medical Corps.

What might recommend Bethesda was the autopsy room itself. The whole morgue had just been renovated and outfitted with sophisticated medical and communications equipment. "We had just moved into it a couple of months before," Humes recalled. "It was all brand new." The autopsy room was spacious by the standards of military hospitals, about twenty-five by thirty feet, with a steel dissecting table fixed to the floor in the center. The room also functioned as an auditorium, with a viewing stand along one wall that allowed as many as thirty people—usually medical residents or visiting doctors—to view procedures. There was, in addition, a closed-circuit television camera so audiences across the street at the National Institutes of Health and down the road at the medical clinic at Andrews Air Force Base could observe at a distance. (Humes said later he wished someone had switched on the camera that night, to end the "ludicrous speculation" about what had gone on.) The morgue included large refrigerated closets able to store as many as six corpses, as well as a shower area for the doctors. The night of the president's autopsy, the pathologists would need every square inch of space.

The president's body arrived at about seven thirty p.m. The bronze casket was wheeled in from a loading ramp off the street. The corpse was gently removed from the casket and—after X-rays and photos of every part of the body—was placed on the autopsy table, where it would remain for most of the next ten hours. The wounds to the skull were not immediately visible since the head had been covered with sheets in Dallas. After removing the blood-soaked cloth, Humes ordered that all the sheets be laundered immediately. "We had a washing machine in the morgue, and he stuck those in," Boswell recalled. Humes worried from the start that something taken from the autopsy room would turn up as a grizzly souvenir in some rural sideshow—"he didn't want those appearing in a barn out in Kansas sometime."

The autopsy was a "three-ring circus," Boswell complained. Dozens of people—navy doctors and orderlies, X-ray technicians and medical photographers, Secret Service and FBI agents, military officers and hospital administrators—were either in the morgue or pressing at the door to be let in. The pathologists said the Secret Service agents who had accompanied the body to Bethesda, including some who had been in Dallas that day, were frantic with nervous energy. The man they had sworn to protect, even at the cost of their own lives, was dead. What were they protecting now? "Those people were in such an emotional state that they were running around like chickens with their heads off, and we understood their situation," Boswell said later.

Burkley, the president's physician, had accompanied the body to Bethesda, and initially he tried to take control of the autopsy. As a rear admiral, he would normally have been in a position to give orders to the lower-ranking navy pathologists, but his medical training was as an internist and cardiologist, and his recommendations met with angry resistance from Humes and the other pathologists. At first, Burkley tried to argue that a full autopsy was unnecessary. He said that since the presumed assassin, Lee Harvey Oswald, was under arrest in Dallas and there seemed little doubt about his guilt, there was no need for procedures that might severely disfigure the president's corpse. He knew the Kennedy family was weighing whether to leave the casket open for a viewing of the body before burial. Burkley wanted to limit the autopsy to "just finding the bullets," Boswell said.

Humes rejected the admiral's idea as absurd, given the danger that something important might be missed in a hasty postmortem, and Burkley backed down, although he insisted they move quickly. "George Burkley, his main concern was, let's get this over with as fast as we could," Humes said later, recalling his annoyance. Burkley appeared worried above all about the delay's effect on Mrs. Kennedy, who was waiting with Robert Kennedy and other family and friends in the hospital's VIP suite on the seventeenth floor. She had announced she would not leave Bethesda until she could take her husband's body with her. Humes said he cringed at the thought of what she must be going through; he knew she was still wearing the bloodstained pink suit he had seen on television. (She had refused to change out of the clothes, in fact. "Let them see what they have done," she had told Burkley defiantly.) Still, much as he felt sympathy for Mrs. Kennedy, Humes felt rushed by her presence in the hospital. "It did harass us and cause difficulty," he remembered.

Burkley had another request of the autopsy doctors, and on this point he was insistent. He asked Humes to promise that the pathologists' report would hide an important fact about the president's health, unrelated to the assassination. He wanted no mention of the condition of Kennedy's adrenal glands. The White House physician knew an inspection of the adrenals would reveal that the president—despite years of public denials—suffered from a chronic, life-threatening disorder, Addison's disease, in which the glands, which sit on top of the kidneys, did not produce enough hormones. Kennedy might have given the appearance of ruddy good health, but Burkley knew that was often a result of makeup and other staging for the cameras. The president survived because of daily hormone supplements that included high doses of testosterone.

Humes, eager to begin, agreed. "He promised George Burkley that we would never discuss the adrenals until all of the then-living members of the Kennedy family were dead, or something like that," said Boswell, who went along with the plan, even though it was a blatant violation of protocol. Days after the autopsy, Burkley returned to Humes with another secret request, this one about the handling of the president's brain, which had been removed from the skull for analysis after the autopsy. As Burkley had asked, Humes delivered the brain, which had been preserved in formalin in a steel pail at Bethesda, to the White House so that it could be quietly interred with the president's body.* "He told me flat out that the decision had been made and that he was going to take the brain and deliver it to Robert Kennedy," Humes recalled.

Humes's work on the night of the autopsy was hampered for other reasons. In the hours after the president's death, the fear that the assassination was the work of a conspiracy, and that the conspirators might strike again, was a topic of fevered discussion in the hallways at Bethesda. As Humes and his team set to work, they overheard colleagues talk about how the Russians or the Cubans might be behind the murder, and how Lyndon Johnson, sworn in hours earlier as president, could be the next target.

The doctors began to worry for their own safety. If there was a conspiracy, the killers might want to hide the truth of exactly how the

---

* The whereabouts of the president's brain became yet another mystery. In 1979, a special congressional panel that reinvestigated the president's murder, the House Select Committee on Assassinations, said it had learned from Dr. Burkley that he had transferred a sealed stainless-steel bucket containing the brain to Kennedy's former secretary, Evelyn Lincoln, who then stored it for a time in 1964 at the National Archives. The committee could not track the brain with certainty past that point. In its final report, the committee said it was told by former Yale Law School professor Burke Marshall, who represented the executors of Kennedy's estate, that he suspected Robert Kennedy ultimately obtained the brain and other autopsy evidence and "disposed of these materials himself, without informing anyone else." Marshall said, "Robert Kennedy was concerned that these materials would be placed on public display in future years in an institution such as the Smithsonian and wished to dispose of them to eliminate such a possibility." (House Select Committee on Assassinations, vol. VII, "Medical and Firearms Evidence," March 1979.)

president had died. Was it possible the Bethesda pathologists might also be silenced, or their evidence seized and destroyed? "It seemed like there might be some sort of cabal" behind Kennedy's death, Boswell remembered thinking. "Anybody was likely to be killed." Humes's superior officer was so alarmed by the potential threat that he ordered Boswell to make sure that Humes, who had taken responsibility for writing the autopsy report, got back to his house safely. "So I got in my car behind Jim Humes, and I followed him home," Boswell said.

When Humes finally walked through his front door at about seven a.m., he had no opportunity to collect his thoughts, let alone sleep. He was scheduled to drive his son to church that morning for the boy's First Communion—Humes was determined to be there—and he knew he needed to return to Bethesda within a few hours for a telephone call with the doctors at Parkland Memorial Hospital in Dallas who had tried, futilely, to save Kennedy's life. Humes later conceded he should have left the autopsy room and spoken with the Parkland doctors at some point Friday night, but he was under too much pressure to finish. "There was no way we could get out of the room," Humes said later. "You have to understand that situation—that hysterical situation—that existed. How we kept our wits about us as well as we did is amazing to me."

The call on Saturday to Dr. Malcolm Perry, the chief Parkland doctor to attend to Kennedy, resolved a central mystery for Humes. There had been no question among any of the doctors in Dallas or Bethesda about Kennedy's cause of death—the massive head wound from a bullet that blew away much of the right hemisphere of his brain, an image captured in awful photographs. The mystery was over what appeared to be the first bullet to hit the president, which entered his upper back or neck and should have remained relatively intact as it passed through soft tissue. Where had it gone? The Bethesda pathologists could find no obvious exit wound.

Humes and his colleagues struggled with the question for hours; it was one reason why the autopsy took so long. "I x-rayed the president's body from head to toe for the simple reason that missiles do very funny things occasionally in a human body," Humes said. Bullets often zig and zag once they strike flesh, even if fired from a direct angle, he explained. "It could have been in his thigh or it could have been in his buttock. It could have been any damn place." As they worked, Humes and the others talked about the unlikely possibility that the bullet had fallen back out of the entrance wound as the president's heart was massaged to try to

Air Force One, moments after returning to
Andrews Air Force Base, Maryland,
from Dallas, November 22, 1963.

President Lyndon Johnson rejected the advice of Secret Service agents who wanted him to depart Dallas's Love Field airport the instant he boarded Air Force One. The plane remained on the ground for an extra 35 minutes as Johnson waited for the arrival of Jacqueline Kennedy and the casket bearing her husband's body. Mrs. Kennedy boarded shortly after the casket was loaded onto the plane. Johnson was then formally sworn in, a scene witnessed by Mrs. Kennedy—still in the blood-caked clothes from the motorcade—and Lady Bird Johnson.

Art Rickerby/Time Life Pictures/Getty Images

Chief Justice Earl Warren and his wife, Nina, seen the day after the assassination outside the White House, where they had gone with other members of the Supreme Court for a viewing of the president's casket in the East Room. On Sunday, November 24, Warren stood before Mrs. Kennedy and her daughter, Caroline, and offered a eulogy for Kennedy in the Capitol Rotunda, where the casket had been on public display.

AP Photo

restore a beat—speculation that made its way into the report of FBI agents observing the autopsy.

During the phone call, Perry had an explanation for the missing bullet. The Parkland doctors had performed a tracheotomy, cutting into the president's badly damaged windpipe to allow him to breathe, exactly where there had been a small wound in front of the throat, near the knot of his tie. Perhaps that was where the bullet had exited? "The minute he said that, lights went on and we said, a-ha, we have some place for our missile to have gone," Humes said. The tracheotomy, he assumed, had destroyed evidence of the exit wound. The doctors could never be certain where that bullet had finally landed, but at least they now thought they knew where it had gone—out of the president's throat.

That Saturday night, as Humes sat at his card table near the fireplace in his family room, he noticed the streaks of blood—the president's blood—that stained each page of his notes from the autopsy room, as well as each page of the draft autopsy report. He later recalled being repulsed by the stains.

Slowly, carefully, he began transferring the information from his notes to clean sheets of paper. "I sat down and word for word copied what I had on fresh paper," Humes said later. It took hours. His well-thumbed copy of *Stedman's Medical Dictionary* was at his elbow: he wanted no spelling errors on the report that he would give to the White House.

Only Humes knew what motivated him to do what he did next. Were there embarrassing errors in the original autopsy report and in his notes that he wanted to correct? Did he adjust the location of the entry and exit wounds of the bullets? Beyond his promise to Burkley to eliminate any reference to the president's adrenal glands, did he leave out other information? Was he ordered to? Whatever the reason, Humes decided—as he sat there at the card table—to destroy every piece of paper in his custody, except the new draft. He was determined, he said, to keep the bloodied documents from falling into the hands of "ghouls."

Years later, he admitted that he did not fully understand the implications of his actions, and he acknowledged that they might have helped feed the conspiracy theories that dogged him the rest of his career. He tried to reconstruct his thinking: "When I noticed these bloodstains were on these documents that I had prepared, I said, nobody's going to ever get these documents."

Humes gave the original notes and autopsy report a final look before standing up and walking to the fireplace. He dropped the bloodstained pages of the original draft autopsy report into the fire and watched as the flames turned the paper to ash. He pushed his handwritten notes from the examination room into the fire as well.

"Everything that I had, exclusive of the final report, I burned," he said. "I didn't want anything to remain. Period."

EXECUTIVE INN
DALLAS, TEXAS
SATURDAY, NOVEMBER 23, 1963

In the city where the president had been killed, the destruction of evidence began within a day of the assassination. On Friday, hours after learning of her husband's arrest, Marina Oswald remembered the "stupid photographs" that she had taken of Lee in the yard of the shabby Dallas home where the couple lived earlier that year. The photos showed a smirking Lee, dressed in black, holding his mail-order rifle in one hand; in the other, he held recent issues of two leftist newspapers, the *Militant* and the *Worker*. There was a pistol in a holster around his waist.

On Friday night, after hours of initial questioning by the FBI and the Dallas police, Marina was allowed to return to the home of Ruth Paine, a local friend who spoke some Russian. Marina, the strikingly pretty twenty-two-year-old Russian who had married Oswald during his failed defection to the Soviet Union, had lived in the Paine home for several weeks that year while Oswald lived elsewhere, first in New Orleans, as he looked for a job.

When she got back to the house, Marina found the photos, which she had hidden in an album of baby pictures, and showed them to her mother-in-law, Marguerite Oswald. The two women barely knew each other—Oswald had always claimed to hate his mother and so refused to see her—and the two Mrs. Oswalds had been reunited only because of the assassination. Marina spoke just a few words of English.

"Mama, Mama," Marina said, showing her mother-in-law the photos.

Mrs. Oswald appeared shocked by the image of her young son with the weapons and replied, without hesitation, "Hide them," according to her daughter-in-law's account.

Marina said she did as she was told, putting the photos in her shoe.

The next day, Saturday, after hours of additional police questioning, she was approached by her mother-in-law and asked where the photos were hidden.

Marina said she pointed to her shoes. "Burn them," Marguerite told her daughter-in-law, according to Marina's account. "Burn them now."

Again, Marina said, she did as she was told. That evening, she and her mother-in-law were moved by the Secret Service to a small motel, the Executive Inn, near Love Field airport. Marina said she found an ashtray in the motel room, placed the photos in it, and then lit a match, touching the flame to the corner of one of the pictures. The heavy photographic paper was difficult to burn, she recalled, so it took several matches to do the job. Her mother-in-law would later insist that the decision to destroy the pictures had been Marina's alone. But Marguerite Oswald did admit that she was in the room and watched as her daughter-in-law destroyed the photos. And Marguerite admitted that she—not Marina—took the ashtray and emptied it into the toilet. "I flushed the torn bits and the half-burned thing down the commode," Mrs. Oswald later explained. "And nothing was said."

DALLAS FIELD OFFICE
THE FEDERAL BUREAU OF INVESTIGATION
DALLAS, TEXAS
SUNDAY, NOVEMBER 24, 1963

Evidence was also beginning to vanish that weekend from the files of the FBI. At about six p.m. Sunday, FBI Special Agent James Hosty was called to the office of his boss, Gordon Shanklin, the special agent in charge of the Dallas field office. Hosty said that Shanklin pushed a piece of paper across the desk.

"Get rid of this," Shanklin ordered. "Oswald is dead now. There can be no trial." Seven hours earlier, Oswald had been gunned down by Jack Ruby in Dallas police headquarters, a shocking scene captured live on national television.

Shanklin nodded to the piece of paper and repeated the order to Hosty, a square-jawed thirty-nine-year-old who had joined the FBI a decade earlier as an office clerk, a traditional career route for the bureau's field agents. "Get rid of it," Shanklin said again.

Hosty didn't need to be told a third time. He recognized the piece of paper—a handwritten note that Oswald had delivered in person to the FBI office in early November, apparently warning the bureau to stop disturbing his Russian-born wife.

"If you don't cease bothering my wife, I will take appropriate action," Oswald had written, according to Hosty's later account. The FBI receptionist who took the note from Oswald said she thought he sounded "crazy, maybe dangerous."

Hosty and Shanklin could well imagine what would happen if J. Edgar Hoover learned of the note's existence. It was proof that the bureau had been in contact with Oswald only days before the assassination; that there had been face-to-face contact between the bureau and Oswald's wife; that Oswald had actually stood there, in person, in the Dallas office. Simply put, the note could be read as proof that the bureau—in particular, Hosty and Shanklin—had missed the chance to stop Oswald before he gunned down the president.

And the note only hinted at the extent of the FBI's months-long pursuit of Oswald. The truth, Hosty and Shanklin knew, was that the bureau's Dallas office had maintained an open file on Oswald as a potential national-security threat since March. Oswald had returned to the United States the previous year after his aborted defection to Russia, and the FBI suspected that he might have come back to spy for the Soviet Union.

Shanklin continued to stare down at the note, waiting for Hosty to pick it up.

Hosty had a lot to protect—a wife and eight children at home who depended on his $9,000-a-year salary. At the FBI, orders were followed, no questions asked, even an order as grave and almost certainly illegal as destroying a vital piece of evidence involving the man who had just killed the president.

Hosty picked up the note and left Shanklin's office, walking a few feet down the hallway to the men's room. He entered one of the stalls and closed the door. He began to tear up the note, dropping the pieces into the white porcelain toilet bowl. When he was done, he pulled the heavy wooden handle on the metal chain to flush the toilet. He waited a moment and pulled the chain again. He said later he wanted to make certain every scrap of paper was gone.

2

THE JUSTICES' CONFERENCE ROOM
THE SUPREME COURT
WASHINGTON, DC
FRIDAY, NOVEMBER 22, 1963

The knock on the heavy oak door to the conference room was unexpected. It was rare for the justices of the United States Supreme Court ever to be interrupted during their weekly Friday conference. By tradition, the court's staff could interrupt the justices only in an emergency, or something close to it, and information could be passed to the justices in the conference room only in the form of a note handed through the door.

Chief Justice Earl Warren, then in his eleventh year on the court, had come to see the value of this and so many other seemingly arcane traditions, if only because they imposed a polite order on a group of nine strong-willed men—some of whom disliked one another to the point of hatred—who had agreed to spend the rest of their working lives in this place.

On Friday, November 22, 1963, shortly after one thirty p.m., the justices heard a knock. By tradition, the door was answered by the court's most junior member, and so Associate Justice Arthur Goldberg, who had joined the court a year earlier, stood up silently, went to the door, and opened it. He took the one-page note, shut the door, and handed it to the chief justice. Warren read the typewritten message from his personal secretary, Margaret McHugh, in silence. Then he stood and read it out loud to the others:

"The President was shot while riding in a motorcade in Dallas. It is not known how badly he is injured."

The members of the court, Warren later recalled, were "shocked beyond words" and adjourned to their own offices. "There was little said, but I believe each of us, stunned by the news, repaired to a place where he could receive radio reports of the tragedy." (Actually, some of the justices and their staffs gathered in the chambers of Justice William Brennan, who had a television set and was watching Walter Cronkite's coverage on CBS.) Warren went to his chambers, where he listened to the radio "until all hope was lost," he remembered. "In perhaps half or three-quarters of an hour, the news came that the president was dead—it was almost unbelievable."

Warren and the other justices had special cause to be shocked: only thirty-six hours earlier, they had been the guests of the president and Mrs. Kennedy at a reception in the First Family's private living quarters on the second floor of the White House. "We could not forget how friendly and happy the occasion was," Warren said. "It was a delightful occasion." He recalled how the justices had engaged in a lively conversation about Kennedy's imminent trip to Texas, which was scheduled to begin the next morning.

The two-day, five-city fund-raising trip was the talk of much of official Washington because, to many, it seemed politically risky. The president had been warned that he might face protests from right-wing demonstrators, especially in Dallas. "The Big D," as the city's boosters liked to call it, was home to several far-right extremist groups and had a reputation for discourteous, even disgraceful, treatment of prominent political visitors. Only a month earlier, Kennedy's UN ambassador, former Illinois governor Adlai Stevenson, had been heckled outside his Dallas hotel by anti-UN protesters, including a scowling Texas homemaker who hit him over the head with a cardboard placard that read: DOWN WITH THE UN. During the 1960 campaign, then Senate majority leader Lyndon Johnson of Texas, Kennedy's vice presidential candidate, and his wife, Lady Bird, were swarmed by dozens of screeching anti-Kennedy protesters as they tried to cross the lobby of the Adolphus Hotel in Dallas to reach the hotel's ballroom for a luncheon rally. One protester carried a defaced copy of a Johnson campaign poster with the words SMILING

JUDAS scrawled across it, while another spat on Mrs. Johnson. She described the nearly thirty minutes it took to cross the lobby as among the most frightening of her life.

At the White House reception, Warren recalled, "we jokingly admonished the President to be careful 'down there with those wild Texans'—of course, the thought of a real disturbance of any kind was far from our minds."

After receiving confirmation of the president's death, Supreme Court colleagues remembered how tears welled up in the eyes of the chief justice and how he remained close to tears for days. It was no secret around the court that Warren adored John Kennedy, even though that opened him up to charges of partisanship by the president's Republican opponents. Warren's affection was almost paternal, he admitted. The assassination was "like losing one of my own sons," he said. "The days and nights following were more like a nightmare than anything I had ever lived through."

A generation separated the president and the chief justice. Kennedy died at the age of forty-six; on the day of the assassination, Warren was seventy-two. In the younger man, Warren had seen the farsighted, progressive leadership—on issues of social justice, especially—that he had hoped to bring to the White House himself when he ran for president in 1952. Warren had been the wildly popular governor of California from 1943 until 1953, and, although he was a lifelong member of the Republican Party, his popularity in his home state had always stretched across party lines. He took pride in the fact that his landslides in three gubernatorial elections had included the votes of a huge share, if not most, of the state's Democrats.

As governor, he pursued policies that outraged many conservative, antitax Republicans. Warren was responsible for massive investments in higher education and transportation, and he raised gasoline taxes by more than $1 billion over ten years—an almost unheard-of sum at the time for a state government—to pay for construction of California's futuristic highways, which became the model for a national system. After World War II, he created statewide New Deal–like public works projects to address unemployment, especially among veterans. His attempt to establish universal health care for Californians was foiled by an aggressive lobbying campaign by the California Medical Association, which labeled the plan "socialized medicine."

Throughout the 1940s, Warren's star kept rising; in 1948, he was selected to run for vice president on the Republican ticket with New York governor Thomas E. Dewey. After Dewey's unexpected defeat by incumbent Harry Truman, Warren returned to California and began to consider his own run for the Oval Office. He launched a bid in 1952, only to be undermined by another prominent California Republican, Senator Richard M. Nixon, who led a revolt among the state's GOP leaders in favor of General Dwight D. Eisenhower. Nixon's move helped seal the nomination for Eisenhower, who went on to a decisive victory that November, with Nixon on the ticket as vice president. The relationship between Warren and Nixon remained poisonous for the rest of their lives. The chief justice was delighted by Kennedy's election victory in 1960, not least because it meant Nixon's defeat.

Still, Warren had reason to be grateful to Eisenhower, who placed him on the Supreme Court. It was the fulfillment of a pledge made by Eisenhower shortly after the 1952 election, apparently as thanks to Warren for what seemed to be his full-throated public support for the Republican ticket. Eisenhower came to regret the decision; he was later widely quoted as describing Warren's nomination to the court as the "biggest damn fool mistake I ever made." The president was reported to be furious over the Warren Court's far-reaching rulings in support of civil rights and civil liberties, beginning with the *Brown v. Board of Education* decision in 1954, in which the court ordered the desegregation of the nation's public schools.

For Warren, the election of John Kennedy changed everything. The new president reached out personally to the chief justice, attempting to nurture a genuine friendship. Warren and his wife, Nina, found themselves invited to glittery receptions and dinners at the White House, where they were introduced to Kennedy's celebrity friends from Hollywood and Palm Beach. Raised in the gritty, sunbaked town of Bakersfield, California, Warren, the son of a railroad worker, could often seem starstruck in Kennedy's presence.

The president's support went well beyond dinner invitations. He spoke out often in public to express his admiration for Warren and for the rulings of the court. The chief justice was grateful, especially given the heated, often hateful response to the court's civil rights decisions. Warren was scorned personally by much of the country; he had grown used to the regular death threats that would arrive at the court in the mail or by phone. By the time of Kennedy's assassination, a national campaign to bring impeachment charges against Warren had been under way for years. In Dallas, IMPEACH EARL WARREN posters and bumper stickers were a common sight on the day the president was killed there.

Within hours of the assassination, Warren had his staff release a public statement that reflected his assumption that the president had been killed because he, like Warren, had dared to stand up to the evils of racism and other injustice. "A good and great president has suffered martyrdom as a result of the hatred and bitterness that has been injected into the life of our nation by bigots," Warren wrote. The statement was handed out to reporters before the announcement later that day of the arrest of twenty-four-year-old Lee Harvey Oswald, a Dallas man who worked in a school-book warehouse on Dealey Plaza.

That afternoon, Warren was notified that the new president, Lyndon Baines Johnson, was headed back to Washington aboard Air Force One; the presidential jet also bore the bronze casket containing his predecessor's body. The White House invited the chief justice, along with congressional leaders and members of Kennedy's cabinet, to be at Andrews Air Force Base in Maryland, a few miles southeast of Washington, to receive the new president. Warren was chauffeured to the base by one of his Supreme Court clerks, and the chief justice looked on somberly as the plane touched down at about six p.m. He watched as President Johnson emerged from the plane, followed by Jacqueline Kennedy, still in the pink suit from the motorcade. Warren later wrote that he found it a "heart-rending sight to see a saddened new president and the fallen president's widow, still in the bloodstained clothes she wore after her mortally wounded husband had slumped in her lap." He remained at the side of the plane as the casket was lowered slowly from a rear passenger door.

The next morning, he and the other justices were invited to the White House for a private viewing of the casket in the East Room. Warren was joined by his wife, Nina, at the viewing, and afterward she stood in tears in the north portico of the White House, waiting for a car to take her home. Warren did not go home with her. From the White House, he went instead to the court, where he stayed much of the day "waiting for some information about what was to happen." The city had effectively shut down. "The entire government plant was closed," he wrote. "It was as though the world had stopped moving."

Many of the capital's residents recalled that their mourning was mixed with fear. The Pentagon and other military installations around Washington were on high alert, out of concern that the president's murder had been carried out by agents of the Soviet Union or Cuba—an act of war that could mean a nuclear exchange was imminent. For some in Washington, including President Johnson, the jittery, even apocalyptic feeling that weekend was similar to what they had been through only a year before, during the Cuban missile crisis.

Much of the rest of the weekend was a blur for Warren. He remembered returning home Saturday evening to his apartment in the residential wing of the Sheraton Park Hotel, in a leafy neighborhood of northwest Washington, and watching television for hours and "listening to the wild stories and rumors which permeated the air." Like millions of Americans, he was experiencing—for the first time—a national tragedy unfold on a flickering television screen. He found it "sickening" to sit there, numbly, and take in the black-and-white images—the repetition, over and over, of scenes from the president's murder and of the first images of Oswald under arrest. "But there didn't seem to be anything else to do." At about nine that evening, the phone rang. He picked up the receiver and was startled to hear the feathery, but now intensely solemn, voice of Mrs. Kennedy, calling from the White House. She asked if he would offer a short eulogy to her husband in the Capitol rotunda the following afternoon; the casket was being moved to the rotunda for its public viewing before burial. "I was almost speechless to hear her voice personally asking me to speak at the ceremony," Warren recalled. "I, of course, told her I would do so."

He grabbed a yellow legal pad and tried to draft a tribute to the slain president, but he quickly gave up. He was too tired and overwhelmed to write anything of value. "It was simply impossible for me to put thoughts on paper," he said. He went to bed around midnight, hoping to find inspiration in the morning. He rose before seven a.m. and went back to work, worried that he would not finish the tribute in time. The ceremony was scheduled to start at one p.m. At about eleven twenty, he was still writing when his daughter Dorothy rushed into the room where he was working.

"Daddy, they just killed Oswald!"

Warren was annoyed at the interruption. "Oh, Dorothy, don't pay any attention to all those wild rumors or they will drive you to distraction."

"But Daddy," she said, "I saw them do it."

Warren rushed to the television set and watched a replay of footage of the handcuffed Oswald, surrounded by police officers as he was being marched to a squad car, being shot by Dallas nightclub impresario Jack Ruby. It was not clear if Oswald would survive his injuries.

Despite this new shock, Warren forced himself back to his legal pad. He had less than an hour to finish the eulogy and have Nina type it up before they hurried out the door for the drive across town to Capitol Hill. With the help of policemen who recognized the chief justice and cleared the crowded city streets, the Warrens managed to arrive at the Capitol in time. The chief justice was one of three speakers at the ceremony; the others were chosen to represent the two houses of Congress: House Speaker John W. McCormack of Massachusetts and Senate majority leader Mike Mansfield of Montana, both Democrats.

All three eulogies were short. Warren's was by far the most pointedly worded and, it seemed, personally felt.

"John Fitzgerald Kennedy—a good and great President, the friend to all people of good will; a believer in the dignity and equality of all human beings; a fighter for justice; an apostle of peace—has been snatched from our midst by the bullet of an assassin," he began. "What moved some misguided wretch to do this horrible deed may never be known to us, but we do know that such acts are commonly stimulated by forces of hatred and malevolence such as today are eating their way into the bloodstream of American life. What a price we pay for this fanaticism!

"If we really love this country; if we truly love justice and mercy; if we fervently want to make this nation better for those who are to follow us, we can at least abjure the hatred that consumes people," he continued. "Is it too much to hope that the martyrdom of our beloved President might even soften the hearts of those who would themselves recoil from assassination, but who do not shrink from spreading the venom which kindles thoughts of it in others?"

Warren was proud of the eulogy, publishing it in full in his memoirs, but his effusive, unqualified praise for Kennedy struck some listeners as inappropriate for a chief justice, given his responsibility to rise above partisanship. Would he have offered similar praise in a eulogy for Eisenhower? Almost certainly not.

* * *

Robert Kennedy told friends later that he did not like the tone of Warren's remarks. "I thought it was inappropriate to talk about hate," he said. Others in Washington were even more offended. Warren's words denouncing "the forces of hatred" and their "venom" were instantly seen by many prominent Kennedy critics in Congress, particularly southern segregationists who had opposed the president on civil rights legislation, as an attack on them. They were all the more outraged after it become clear that Lee Harvey Oswald was a product of political forces that had nothing to do with them. If the early news reports were right, Oswald was a Marxist who had once tried to defect to Russia and openly admired Fidel Castro.

Senator Richard Brevard Russell Jr., the Georgia Democrat who was chairman of the Armed Services Committee and widely seen as the most powerful man in the Senate, told colleagues that he seethed when he heard Warren's eulogy. Russell, almost certainly the most brilliant legislative tactician of his generation, was a staunch segregationist. Most days, he memorialized his thoughts with jottings on a pad of tiny pink notepaper that he kept in his suit pocket; the pads were later gathered up by his secretary and filed away. In a handwritten note to himself about the eulogy, Russell described it as "Warren's blanket indictment of the South."

Russell could grow furious simply at the mention of Warren's name. That had been true since 1954 and *Brown v. Board of Education*, which Russell saw as the start of a campaign by the Supreme Court to undermine what he had always called the "Southern way of life." Russell felt very differently about the fallen president. Whatever their differences over civil rights, he had always liked Kennedy. On the afternoon of the assassination, reporters recalled seeing Russell in a lobby off the Senate floor, hunched over a cabinet that contained the "tickers" that printed out the news reports of the Associated Press and United Press International. He was reading the bulletins from Dallas aloud to his colleagues as tears streamed down his face.

If the sixty-six-year-old Russell could find anything of comfort that day, it was that he knew—and loved—the man who would now occupy the Oval Office. Lyndon Johnson was arguably his closest friend; the new president had been Russell's most devoted protégé in their years together in the Senate. Johnson called Russell "the Old Master" and treated him like a beloved uncle. He owed the Georgian much of his success in Congress and, as Senate majority leader, he had sometimes stood with Russell in opposing major civil rights bills.

Soon, however, Russell would have cause to be bitterly disappointed by his former protégé. In one of his first acts as president, Johnson chose to coerce his old Senate colleague—to blackmail him, really—into working with the man who, more than any other in Washington, Russell openly despised: Earl Warren.

THE HOME OF ATTORNEY GENERAL ROBERT KENNEDY
MCLEAN, VIRGINIA
FRIDAY, NOVEMBER 22, 1963

For a man who was only thirty-eight years old, Robert Kennedy had accumulated an extraordinary number of powerful enemies. In a horrible twist of fate, he learned of his brother's murder from one of them—FBI director J. Edgar Hoover.

Seconds after receiving word from the FBI's Dallas field office of the shooting in Dealey Plaza, Hoover picked up the telephone in his office and was patched through to Hickory Hill, Kennedy's sprawling six-acre, Civil War–era estate in the Virginia suburbs of Washington. Ethel Kennedy, the attorney general's wife, answered the phone as Kennedy and his guest, Robert Morgenthau, the United States attorney in Manhattan, lunched on tuna fish sandwiches on the patio. They had been discussing Kennedy's war on organized crime. It was a surprisingly warm November afternoon—so warm that the attorney general had earlier taken a swim in his pool as Morgenthau chatted with Ethel.

Ethel held the white telephone receiver and motioned to her husband. "It's J. Edgar Hoover."

Kennedy walked to the phone; he knew this must be important since Hoover never called him at home. "Yes, Director," he said.

"I have news for you," Hoover said. "The president has been shot." Hoover said he believed the president's injuries were serious and that he would call back when he had more to report. Then the phone went dead, Kennedy said. Years later, Kennedy could still recall the coldness in Hoover's voice, as if he had been calling on the most routine sort of Justice

Department business. Hoover's tone, Kennedy remembered bitterly, was "not quite as excited as if he was reporting the fact that he found a Communist on the faculty of Howard University."*

Morgenthau recalled later that Kennedy's response to the news was one of horror and stark, inconsolable grief. After Hoover's call, Kennedy crumpled into his wife's arms, his hand over his mouth as if to silence a scream.

John Kennedy was his older brother and best friend, and the fact that Robert Kennedy was also the attorney general of the United States—the nation's chief law-enforcement officer—seemed an afterthought in those first minutes. Ethel took her husband to wait in their upstairs bedroom for final word from Texas. She directed Morgenthau to a television set on the first floor.

Kennedy's closest aides flooded to Hickory Hill that afternoon. After the formal announcement of his brother's death at about two p.m. Washington time, the attorney general emerged from the bedroom and came downstairs. Slowly he began to move among his aides and friends, accepting their condolences and thanking them for their contributions to his brother's presidency. To a few, he offered hushed remarks suggesting that he was overwhelmed by a sense of guilt—that he was somehow responsible for this. He seemed to believe that some vicious, powerful enemy of the Kennedy administration—and, specifically, of Robert Kennedy's Justice Department—was behind his brother's murder. "There's been so much hate," he told one of his most trusted deputies, Ed Guthman, the department's press spokesman. "I thought they would get one of us. I thought it would be me." Recalling the exchange, Guthman said that Kennedy did not specify who "they" were.

Kennedy later confided to a handful of friends that he had initially feared that the assassination was the work of some element of the Central Intelligence Agency. It was a shocking thought, but he knew that there were people at the spy agency who had never forgiven his brother for the disaster at the Bay of Pigs in 1961, when CIA-trained Cuban exiles failed in their attempt to invade Cuba and oust Castro's government. Although

---

* At Hoover's direction, the FBI had been hunting for years for evidence of Communist sympathizers on the faculties of major American universities; a few were uncovered on the faculty of Howard University, the historically black university in Washington, DC.

CIA bungling was ultimately to blame for the fiasco, agency veterans were outraged by the president's decision not to order up American air power to save the guerrillas when the operation started to go wrong. After the debacle, Kennedy ousted Director of Central Intelligence Allen Dulles and reportedly vowed to an aide that he would "splinter the CIA into a thousand pieces and scatter it to the winds."

Within an hour of the assassination, Robert Kennedy telephoned the CIA and asked that John McCone, the former California industrialist who was Dulles's successor, come immediately to Hickory Hill. McCone arrived minutes later—the CIA's headquarters in suburban Langley, Virginia, was only a short drive away—and Kennedy took McCone for a somber walk on the lawn. McCone offered his condolences, only to be startled by the question that the attorney general asked him: Had the CIA killed the president?

"I asked McCone . . . if they had killed my brother, and I asked him in a way that he couldn't lie to me," Kennedy later recalled.

McCone assured Kennedy that the CIA had nothing to do with the assassination, a pledge he said he made as a man of faith—as a fellow Roman Catholic.

Kennedy said he accepted McCone's denial. But if the CIA didn't kill the president, then who, or what, did? The list of Robert Kennedy's sworn enemies might actually be longer than his brother's, and many had the motive and the ability to dispatch an assassin to Texas. The assassination had not required a sophisticated plot or a professional sniper; that much was already clear. Initial reports suggested that his brother and Texas governor Connally, who had been seriously injured in the gunfire as he rode in the president's limousine, had been easy targets in the slow-moving motorcade.

Could it have been the Mafia, which Robert Kennedy had made his target for so much of his professional life—first as a congressional investigator, now as attorney general? Or could the president's murder have been ordered up by a corrupt union boss, perhaps the thuggish Teamster head Jimmy Hoffa, another target of Kennedy's Justice Department? Or was the assassination carried out by southern racists, angered over the Kennedy administration's civil rights policies?

There was also the possibility that the president had been killed by a foreign enemy. In those first hours, Kennedy's friends recalled hearing nothing from him to suggest that he had any strong suspicion that the

Soviet Union was behind the assassination; Moscow would know that any successor administration in Washington was unlikely to treat the Kremlin differently. A more likely suspect was Cuba. The United States had almost been drawn into a nuclear war over Cuba during the missile crisis the year before. And Robert Kennedy knew better, maybe even better than his brother, that Fidel Castro might have reason to want to see John Kennedy dead.

Rather than wait for others to investigate the assassination, and perhaps sensing the political danger that an independent inquiry might pose, Kennedy launched his own private investigation that very afternoon. He picked up the telephone at Hickory Hill and called friends and well-connected political allies around the country, asking for their help to determine the truth behind his brother's murder. He called Walter Sheridan, a trusted Justice Department investigator who was an expert on labor racketeering and the Teamsters, and asked him to try to find out if Hoffa was involved. He phoned Julius Draznin, a prominent Chicago labor lawyer who had valuable sources within organized crime, to see if Draznin could find a Mafia link to the assassination.

From the start, Robert Kennedy seemed unable to accept the idea that Lee Harvey Oswald could have acted alone.

ABOVE: Attorney General Robert Kennedy loathed President Johnson but agreed to remain in his cabinet. The two men, shown at the White House in October 1964, were the highest-ranking government officials not called to testify before the Warren Commission. BELOW: Kennedy and wife, Ethel, leave the new Georgetown home of Jacqueline Kennedy after helping her move in on December 6, 1963.

ABOVE: The Kennedys aboard the Coast Guard yacht *Manitou*, sailing in Narragansett Bay, on September 8, 1962. Mrs. Kennedy can be seen reading William Manchester's respectful biography of Kennedy, *Portrait of a President*, as she smokes. LEFT: Although Kennedy demanded the resignation of Director of Central Intelligence Allen Dulles as a result of the Bay of Pigs disaster in 1961, he remained friendly with Dulles, seen here (*left*) on September 27, 1961, at the announcement of Dulles's successor at the CIA, California industrialist John McCone (*right*).

ABOVE: Ambassador to the United Nations Adlai Stevenson (*center*) is surrounded by police officers after he is struck on the head by a placard carried by an anti-U.N. demonstrator in Dallas on October 25, 1963. The incident, a month before the assassination, was another example of the hostility faced by prominent political visitors to conservative Dallas. BELOW: On the morning of his assassination, Kennedy told his wife that they were "heading into nut country" after seeing a black-bordered ad in the *Dallas Morning News* headlined: "Welcome Mr. Kennedy," in which the Kennedy administration was accused of "going soft on Communists, fellow travelers, and ultra-leftists in America." Leaflets appeared in the streets that portrayed Kennedy in a mock mug shot and said he was "Wanted for Treason."

The president appears to practice "the Johnson Treatment" on his political mentor, Senator Richard Russell of Georgia, in the White House Cabinet Room on December 12, 1963, three weeks after the assassination.

President Johnson meets with Supreme Court Chief Justice Earl Warren in an undated photograph. Johnson convinced the reluctant Warren to lead the commission by warning him that he might otherwise be responsible for a nuclear war in which tens of millions of Americans would die.

Johnson is interviewed on the White House lawn on April 16, 1964, by the powerful muckraking columnist Andrew "Drew" Pearson, a close friend of Chief Justice Warren's.

3

Lyndon Johnson had a conspiratorial mind. It had proved valuable in an unlikely political career that had taken him from the scrubby flatlands of central Texas to Capitol Hill and now, shockingly, into the Oval Office as the new president. His old colleagues in the Senate thought the cagey, power-hungry fifty-five-year-old Texan could see around corners, and God help anyone who might lurk around those corners and dare to conspire against him. Johnson would do almost anything—lying was the least of it—to deal with his enemies. He had always seemed to sense when plots were being hatched against him, which helped explain the brooding, ever-present paranoia and pessimism that he managed, usually, to keep hidden from the public. He had often felt humiliated during his three years as vice president, but he masked his despondency beneath layers of what some of Kennedy's aides cruelly described as his "Uncle Cornpone" persona—the crude, chaw-spitting, bigger-than-life Texan who seemed so out of place among the Massachusetts sophisticates.

Often as not, his instincts about conspiracies proved right. Now, in his first panicky minutes in Dallas as the thirty-sixth president of the United States, he was convinced that his predecessor's murder might be the first step in a foreign-born Communist conspiracy to overthrow the government. He feared his presidency would last only long enough to see him launch the nuclear warheads that would end the world. "When would the missiles be coming?" he recalled thinking to himself that afternoon. "What raced through my mind was that if they had shot our president, who would they shoot next?"

He was scared that he was the second target. He and Lady Bird Johnson had been in the motorcade, after all, in an open-air limousine just two cars behind the president's. One stray bullet, and they could have been hit, too. Johnson's close friend and protégé John Connally was a passenger in Kennedy's limousine and had been severely wounded. In the first hours, it was not clear Connally would survive the damage done by a 6.5-millimeter rifle bullet that had pierced his back and erupted from his chest.

One of Johnson's first orders as commander in chief was intended, specifically, to prevent himself from being killed, too. After Kennedy was declared dead at about one p.m., Johnson ordered the traveling White House press secretary, Malcolm Kilduff, to withhold the news from reporters until after the Johnsons had safely left Parkland Hospital for Dallas's Love Field airport, where Air Force One had been waiting since Kennedy's arrival late that morning. Johnson worried that whoever had killed Kennedy was still on the streets, hunting for him. "We don't know whether it's a Communist conspiracy or not," he told Kilduff. The assassin may be "after me as well as they were after President Kennedy—we just don't know."

After a frantic drive across Dallas in an unmarked police car, its sirens switched off on Johnson's order to avoid drawing attention to the passengers hunched down in the backseat, the new president arrived at the airport and scrambled up the steps into Air Force One at about one forty p.m., Dallas time. (It was an hour later, about two forty p.m., in Washington.) It had been approximately seventy minutes since the shots rang out at Dealey Plaza. Fearful of snipers hiding at the airport, Secret Service agents "rushed through the interior ahead of us, pulling down the shades and closing both doors behind us," Johnson said later of the scene aboard the plane.

He recalled a slight sense of relief at being aboard the regal presidential jet, surrounded by the familiar trappings of power, including the telephones and other communications equipment that would allow him to reach almost anyone in the world in a matter of minutes. As always, the simple presence of a telephone was a comfort to Johnson. Few politicians ever conducted so much business over phone lines as Johnson; a telephone receiver was alternately his instrument of political seduction and his weapon. In his years as president, many of those conversations were tape-recorded and transcribed—a secret that few of his callers knew.

Although Secret Service agents wanted to depart the instant Johnson arrived at Love Field, he would not allow the plane to take off until Jacqueline Kennedy was also on board. Mrs. Kennedy, then still at the hospital, had refused to leave without her husband's body, which had created a struggle between Secret Service agents and the Dallas coroner. (Initially, the coroner demanded that the president's corpse remain in the city for an autopsy, as required by local law; in the end, the agents all but shoved him aside.) The Johnsons would wait at Love Field another thirty-five tense minutes before a powder-white Cadillac hearse bearing Mrs. Kennedy and the bronze casket pulled up alongside the Boeing jet.

Minutes before departure, Federal District Judge Sarah Hughes of Dallas, a family friend of the Johnsons whose nomination to the federal bench had been arranged by the then vice president, rushed aboard to perform a swearing-in ceremony. Johnson took the presidential oath standing alongside a stricken Mrs. Kennedy. The White House photographer who captured the scene scrambled from Air Force One seconds before the doors were sealed; he had been told to get the photo to the Associated Press and other wire services as quickly as possible as proof to the world of the transition of presidential power. Minutes later the plane raced down the runway and climbed into the sky at what passengers remembered as a near-vertical angle. Two hours and eleven minutes later, it landed at Andrews Air Force Base in Maryland.

That night, as Jacqueline and Robert Kennedy waited at Bethesda Naval Hospital for the autopsy to be completed, Johnson was already moving decisively to assume command. His aides later marveled at how comfortable he seemed in those first hours in power. After a seven-minute helicopter ride from Andrews to the White House, he made only a brief appearance at the door of the Oval Office, perhaps sensing that it was presumptuous for him to be there so soon after the assassination. Then he walked across a blocked-off street and into the Executive Office Building, where his vice presidential offices were located and where he would conduct his meetings and make a string of phone calls.

He received a military briefing from Defense Secretary Robert McNamara. The initial news was reassuring. There was no evidence of a military advance by the Soviet Union or other foreign adversaries in the wake of the assassination, although American military forces would remain on high alert indefinitely.

The report from Dallas was not so comforting. Although there was no immediate evidence that Oswald had accomplices, both the FBI and CIA had troubling details about his past, including his attempt to renounce his U.S. citizenship and defect to Russia four years earlier. Since his return to the United States in 1962, the FBI had, sporadically, been tracking Oswald and his Russian-born wife as possible Soviet agents. The CIA reported that it had placed Oswald under surveillance when he had traveled to Mexico City in September; the reasons for his trip to Mexico were not entirely clear.

In his meetings that night and the next day with senior Kennedy aides, Johnson pledged continuity with the policies of the Kennedy administration and suggested that he intended to retain Kennedy's entire cabinet; he wanted people to know their jobs were secure. Johnson used the same words again and again: "I need you more than President Kennedy needed you."

From his first hours in office, Johnson made what he felt were valiant efforts to comfort—and seek guidance from—Robert Kennedy. But if the new president had any hope that the shock of the events in Dallas might ease their relationship, he was mistaken. The attorney general had always loathed Johnson, and that would not change, even after Kennedy accepted the new president's offer to stay on at the Justice Department. Unlike his older brother, who always seemed so remarkably even-tempered, so willing to make peace with former adversaries, Robert Kennedy was capable of bitter, even irrational hatreds. He seemed almost energized by blood feuds with men like Jimmy Hoffa, J. Edgar Hoover, and, maybe most of all, Johnson. He privately described Johnson as "mean, bitter, vicious—an animal in many ways." He was appalled, he said, that Johnson—a man "incapable of telling the truth"—had taken his brother's place in the White House.

At about seven p.m. on his first night as president, Johnson called J. Edgar Hoover. This was hardly surprising: Johnson would have expected the FBI director to have the latest information about the investigation in Dallas. And there were other good reasons for Johnson to reach out to Hoover that night—and to remind the FBI director of their years of loyal friendship. In the decades that followed, it would often be forgotten that in

November 1963, Johnson's political survival was in grave doubt because of a fast-moving corruption investigation involving a Washington lobbyist who had once been one of Johnson's closest aides in the Senate. The FBI was overseeing parts of the inquiry.

Bobby Baker, the lobbyist, was known as "Little Lyndon." He was accused of bribing lawmakers and running a so-called social club on Capitol Hill—the "Quorum Club"—that doubled as a de facto prostitution service for members of Congress and White House officials. The Baker scandal had threatened to ensnare President Kennedy as well as Johnson. Kennedy's extramarital activities were no secret to Hoover, and the director was closely monitoring the allegations against Baker, including charges that the lobbyist had helped arrange liaisons between Kennedy and an East German-born beauty who was rumored to be a Communist spy.

In the week before the assassination, Baker began spilling some of his secrets about Kennedy and Johnson to Washington's most famous and feared muckraking newspaper columnist, Andrew "Drew" Pearson. Pearson's syndicated column—the Washington Merry-Go-Round, written with his deputy, Jack Anderson—was a mix of serious political scoops and salacious, often flat-wrong gossip about the powerful. Pearson had sources everywhere, including senior White House aides, cabinet officers, and others at the highest reaches of government. Some of his sources leaked information to him because they feared him; others talked to him because they genuinely admired his bravery in exposing corruption and hypocrisy in Washington. To his credit, Pearson had been an early critic of Senator Joseph McCarthy.

Among Pearson's admirers was Chief Justice Earl Warren. In fact, the sixty-six-year-old columnist counted Warren among his closest friends— and boasted in print of the friendship. At a time when the Warren court was under attack in much of the country for its rulings on civil rights and civil liberties, the chief justice could count on Pearson to defend him. They were so close that they regularly vacationed together. In columns that September, Pearson wrote about his yachting holiday that summer with Warren and his wife in the Mediterranean and the Black Sea. During what was a working vacation for Pearson, Warren sat in as the columnist interviewed Soviet premier Nikita Khrushchev, and, later, the Yugoslav leader, Marshal Josip Tito.

On the afternoon of Thursday, November 21, less than twenty-four hours before the assassination, Pearson met with Bobby Baker in

Washington. It was their first face-to-face conversation, and the Senate-aide-turned-lobbyist had dirt to share. "Bobby confirmed the fact that the president had been mixed up with a lot of women," Pearson wrote in his personal diary. One of Kennedy's women—a prominent aide to Jacqueline Kennedy—"had her bed wired for sound by her landlady when Jack was sleeping with her," the columnist wrote.

Johnson was in Pearson's crosshairs in the Baker story. That very Sunday—November 24—Pearson's column was due to target the vice president over his financial ties to the lobbyist. In his diary, Pearson wrote that it would be "quite a devastating story" involving Johnson, Baker, and possible corruption in a $7 billion fighter-jet contract handed to General Dynamics, a Texas firm.

If Johnson was going to survive the Baker scandal and whatever else Pearson had tucked away in his notebooks, he could be certain—both before and after he became president—that he would need Hoover's help.

Johnson and Hoover were close friends, at least by the cynical standards of political friendships in Washington. Throughout his career, Johnson had courted the FBI director; as well as anyone in Washington, the Texan understood the value of Hoover's support. The FBI director was seen by millions of Americans as the face of law and order; opinion polls showed that Hoover remained one of the most popular men in the country, more popular than most of the presidents he had served.

Johnson understood the danger, too, that Hoover could pose to a politician with something to hide. He was well aware that the sixty-eight-year-old Hoover trafficked in the secrets of public figures—political, financial, sexual—and there was a constant threat that the secrets might be disclosed at Hoover's direction or whim.

Over the years, Johnson's attempts to befriend Hoover were fawning, sometimes comically so. In 1942, he bought a home on the same block as Hoover's—a coincidence, Johnson insisted—in a comfortable neighborhood of the capital known as Forest Hills. The two men were neighbors for nearly twenty years. Hoover saw Johnson's two daughters grow up, and often joined the Johnson family for Sunday breakfast. "He was my close neighbor—I know he loved my dog," Johnson said. The president and Hoover's mutual love of dogs remained a theme of their friendship. When one of Johnson's beagles died in 1966, Hoover gave him a new one. The president named his new pet "J. Edgar."

In May 1964, six months after he was thrust into the presidency, Johnson would sign an executive order exempting Hoover from compulsory retirement when the FBI director turned seventy the following year. "The nation cannot afford to lose you," the president said. Johnson's motives were not fully patriotic, he admitted privately, acknowledging that he kept Hoover in his job in part because "it's better to have him inside the tent pissing out, than outside the tent pissing in."

Over the course of several conversations in the weeks following the assassination, Johnson would remind Hoover—again and again, almost to the point of obsession—of his friendship. "You're more than the head of the Federal Bureau," he told Hoover during a call in late November. "You're my brother and my personal friend, and you have been for twenty-five, thirty years. . . . I've got more confidence in your judgment than anybody in town."

Late on the night of the assassination, Johnson returned to his family's home and slept—less than four hours, he recalled—before heading back downtown to the White House the next morning. Unlike the previous evening, he went to work in the Oval Office—a move that outraged Robert Kennedy, who felt that it was too early for Johnson to occupy what he still considered his brother's workspace. Johnson asked President Kennedy's secretary, Evelyn Lincoln, if she could vacate her desk within thirty minutes that morning to make way for his own secretarial pool. Lincoln agreed, but the request left her in tears.

Johnson received a briefing at about nine fifteen a.m. on Saturday from the director of Central Intelligence, John McCone, who had more alarming news about Oswald: the CIA's detailed surveillance of Oswald's mysterious visit to Mexico City revealed that he had made contact with diplomats in both the Soviet and Cuban embassies. That evening, McCone placed a call to Secretary of State Dean Rusk to alert Rusk to the situation in Mexico, including the possible diplomatic consequences of the arrest of a young Mexican woman, Silvia Duran, who worked in the Cuban consulate and had met face-to-face with Oswald. Her arrest had been requested by the CIA.

At about ten a.m., Johnson talked again with Hoover, and this time the conversation was recorded on the Oval Office taping system that Kennedy had also used as president. For reasons that were never made clear to the National Archives, which later compiled an inventory of

Johnson's White House recordings, the tape of the call with Hoover that morning was erased, leaving only an officially sanctioned transcript.

As he took the phone, Johnson could only assume that Hoover had mastered all the available information about the assassination. After all, this was the director of the FBI briefing the president of the United States about the murder—the day before—of his predecessor. In fact, the transcript of the call, published decades later, showed that Hoover's briefing was a jumble of misinformation. As many of Hoover's deputies knew, the FBI director was never as well informed as he pretended to be; he did not always bother to learn all the facts, since almost no one was brave enough to correct him. Hoover was so determined to present himself as all-knowing that he would often fall back on speculation or half-truths. He seemed incapable of uttering the words: "I don't know."

"I just wanted to let you know of a development which I think is very important in connection with this case," Hoover began. He said that "this man in Dallas"—Oswald—had been charged overnight with the president's murder but "the evidence that they have at the present time is not very, very strong." He added, "The case as it stands now isn't strong enough to be able to get a conviction."

The evidence wasn't strong? It was Hoover's first misstatement in the conversation, seemingly an effort to convince Johnson that—whatever the truth—the local police in Dallas could not be trusted to handle the investigation without strict oversight by the FBI. As Hoover's agents on the scene knew, the Dallas police and the FBI had already gathered overwhelming evidence of Oswald's guilt. Oswald was in custody, and several witnesses could identify him—possibly as the man with a rifle in the window at the Texas School Book Depository, certainly at the scene of the murder of a local policeman shortly after the president's assassination. The Italian-made rifle identified as the assassination weapon—purchased by mail order from a Chicago gun shop by "A. Hidell," an alias frequently used by Oswald, including on his application for a Dallas post-office box—had been found in the book depository. Moreover, Oswald had been taken into custody with a pistol bought by "A. Hidell" from a mail-order gun shop in Los Angeles. The preliminary evidence suggested the pistol had been used to kill the policeman, J. D. Tippit. In Oswald's wallet was a phony identification card for "A. Hidell" that bore a photo of Oswald.

Hoover told Johnson—correctly—that the mail-order rifle had been bought with a money order for $21. "It seems almost impossible to think that for $21 you could kill the president of the United States," he said. Then he launched into a series of false statements. He told Johnson that paperwork containing the Hidell alias had been found in "the home in which he was living—his mother's." (Wrong: Oswald had not seen his mother in more than a year.) The rifle, Hoover said, was "found on the sixth floor in the building from which it had been fired" (correct), but that "the bullets were fired from the fifth floor" (wrong), and that "three shells were found on the fifth floor" (wrong). He also reported that after the assassination Oswald fled to a movie theater across town "where he had the gun battle with the police officer" and was captured. (Wrong: Tippit had been killed blocks away from the theater.)

Johnson asked: "Have you established any more about the visit to the Soviet embassy in Mexico in September?"

Hoover answered with an assertion that, when revealed years later, would help launch a generation of conspiracy theories. Even though the evidence that the CIA would have passed to Hoover was incomplete and contradictory, the director told the president that someone had been impersonating Oswald in Mexico City and then suggested that Oswald might have had an accomplice. Specifically, Hoover said the Mexico trip was "one angle that's very confusing for this reason: we have up here the tape and the photograph of the man who was at the Soviet Embassy using Oswald's name." Hoover was referring to a photo taken by a CIA surveillance camera that showed a man—the CIA had said it initially thought this might be Oswald—outside the Soviet embassy in Mexico City. "That picture and the tape do not correspond to this man's voice, nor to his appearance. In other words, it appears that there is a second person who was at the Soviet embassy." Based on what he should have known was sketchy information, Hoover was hinting to the president that there had been a conspiracy to kill Kennedy that involved an Oswald double who had recently been in and out of a large Soviet embassy and dealing with Soviet agents.

Though Hoover had many of his facts wrong, he was right about one thing. The FBI had plenty of reason to doubt the competence of the Dallas police. The next day—Sunday, November 24—their bungling allowed Oswald to be killed as he was about to be transferred from police headquarters downtown to the county jail. The attempted transfer in the basement garage of police headquarters was witnessed by a crush of reporters, photographers, and television camera crews. Although both the FBI and the Dallas police had received telephone death threats overnight directed at Oswald, the security precautions were so inadequate that Jack Ruby was able to slip in among the reporters while carrying a .38-caliber Colt Cobra revolver. He shot Oswald from only inches away, in full view of television cameras broadcasting live.

Oswald was rushed to Parkland Hospital and wheeled into the same emergency room where President Kennedy had died two days earlier. At 1:07 p.m., Oswald was pronounced dead.

Among the tens of millions of Americans who witnessed Oswald's televised execution that day was the dean of the Yale Law School, Eugene Rostow, an influential Democrat whose brother, Walt, had been Kennedy's deputy national security adviser. Dean Rostow decided he had to act. He sensed—instantly, he said later—how Oswald's murder would undermine public confidence in the government, possibly for generations. The public, he said, would be deprived of the "catharsis and the emotional protection" of a trial to settle questions about Oswald's guilt and the all-important question of whether he had accomplices. Already television commentators were speculating that Oswald had been killed in order to silence him before he could expose a conspiracy.

Just before three p.m., Rostow telephoned the White House to speak with Bill Moyers; the twenty-nine-year-old Moyers, an ordained Baptist minister from Texas who had left the pulpit to go into politics, was one of Johnson's closest aides. Rostow urged Moyers to pass word to the president of the need to set up a high-powered commission to investigate "the whole affair of the murder of the President." In the tape-recorded conversation, Rostow referred to Oswald only as "this bastard."

"In this situation with this bastard killed, my suggestion is that a presidential commission be appointed of very distinguished citizens in the near future, bipartisan and above politics—no Supreme Court justices, but people like Tom Dewey," Rostow said, referring to the former Republica 1 g vernor of New York. He suggested that former vice president Richard Nixon might be considered. Rostow recommended "a commission of seven or nine people—maybe Nixon, I don't know."

Rostow told Moyers that a commission might be the only way the public could be convinced of the truth about what had happened—what was *still* happening. "Because world opinion, and American opinion, is just now so shaken by the behavior of the Dallas police that they're not believing anything." Moyers agreed with Rostow, and he promised to pass the suggestion on to the president.

Johnson initially dismissed the idea of a federal commission; his instinct was to leave the investigation in the hands of state officials in Texas. (Officials at the White House and the Justice Department were startled to learn that the assassination of a president was, at the time, not a federal crime. Had Oswald lived, he would have faced prosecution under Texas state homicide laws.) As a Texan, Johnson had more confidence than his aides in the ability of law-enforcement officials in his home state to deal with the aftermath of the assassination. He told a friend that he did not like the idea of "carpetbaggers" from Washington appearing in Texas to determine who was responsible for a murder on the streets of Dallas.

It took four more days, but Johnson changed his mind. The conspiracy theories, he knew, were beginning to spread wildly. With Oswald dead, Johnson later wrote, "the outrage of a nation turned to skepticism and doubt. . . . The atmosphere was poisonous and had to be cleared." In the end, the president adopted Rostow's model for a commission, with one notable difference. The Yale dean felt strongly that Supreme Court justices should not be involved in the inquiry; it was generally accepted among legal scholars and historians of the court that its reputation had been tarnished in the past when its members became involved in outside investigations. Johnson, however, insisted otherwise. He said he considered only one candidate to lead the commission: the chief justice, Earl Warren.

"The commission had to be bipartisan, and I felt that we needed a Republican chairman whose judicial ability and fairness were unquestioned," Johnson wrote. He barely knew Warren, but he knew the chief justice was a Republican who was respected, even beloved, by many of the president's Democratic allies, as well as by much of the Washington press corps, and that included the powerful, ever-threatening Drew Pearson. "I was not an intimate of the Chief Justice," Johnson wrote. "We had never spent 10 minutes alone together, but to me he was the personification of justice and fairness in this country."

4

Her youngest son was accused of killing the president of the United States, but what struck so many of the reporters and police officers who encountered Marguerite Oswald in the hours after the arrest of Lee Harvey Oswald was not her shock, or her grief. It was her excitement. They remembered how energized she was to have a role in this great drama.

In those first few days, it might have been unkind for reporters in Dallas to suggest that Mrs. Oswald, a fifty-six-year-old practical nurse from neighboring Fort Worth, was actually enjoying the situation in which she found herself. Suddenly, she was a global celebrity and had the opportunity to sell her son's story to the highest of many bidders from distant, exotic places like New York City and Europe. She did seem to have moments of true anguish: at times, often on camera, Mrs. Oswald would break into tears when questioned about her son or about her own circumstances. Lifting her thick prescription glasses to dab at her eyes, she would gently pat her head to make sure no strands had escaped from that tight bun of gray hair.

Still, if she was not actually finding pleasure in the attention, Mrs. Oswald was animated by the knowledge that people everywhere would soon know her name. They would see her picture and remember it. Like her youngest son, she had a powerful desire to make a mark on the world, to get people to stop and pay attention. "I am an important person," she told reporters in the days after the assassination, offering not a hint of doubt about the truth of that statement. "I understand that I will go down in history, too."

Mrs. Oswald was less eager to talk about her alienation from all three of her sons, especially Lee. In the year before he was charged with the president's murder, Lee had cut off all contact with his mother. He had also cut off her access to June, her one-and-a-half-year-old granddaughter—Lee and Marina's first child. It was only on the afternoon of her son's arrest that Mrs. Oswald learned that Marina had given birth to a second daughter, Rachel. Mrs. Oswald found it cruel that she first discovered Rachel's existence when Marina brought the one-month-old baby to Dallas police headquarters.

Lee Oswald seemed to feel that his mother had, over the years, gotten what she deserved—abandonment by children who had never had any reason to love her. Abandonment was an experience Mrs. Oswald was familiar with; it was a theme of her life. Two of her three husbands had divorced her, one on grounds of mental cruelty. The other, Lee's father, Robert, an insurance premium collector, died of a heart attack two months before Lee's birth in 1939. And when her sons were young, she had abandoned them for long stretches. At the age of three, Lee had joined his two older brothers in a Lutheran-run orphanage in New Orleans, the Bethlehem Children's Home, while Mrs. Oswald sought nursing work and pursued her search for a new husband. The three boys were not actually put up for adoption—she said she intended to bring them back to live with her when money allowed—even though that might have been difficult for three-year-old Lee to understand.

In the years before the assassination, Mrs. Oswald had almost no contact with her oldest son, John Pic, Lee's half brother, who in 1963 was stationed with the air force in San Antonio. She also had little contact with her middle son, Robert, even though he and his wife lived in nearby Denton, Texas. When Robert first encountered his mother at Dallas police headquarters in the hours after his brother's arrest, the twenty-nine-year-old was struck by his mother's lack of "any emotional strain at all" over the possibility that Lee had just killed the president. Her overwhelming concern, he said, was about herself.

"It seemed to me that Mother felt that now, at last, she was about to get the kind of attention she had sought all her life," Robert recalled. "She had an extraordinary idea of her ability and her importance." His mother "seemed to recognize immediately that she would never again be treated as an ordinary, obscure, unimportant woman."

Even in those first hours, Robert sensed the danger that his mother posed to any effort to learn the truth about Lee's guilt or innocence. From the start, Robert admitted to himself that there was a strong possibility that Lee was the president's assassin. His younger brother, Robert knew, was a delusional, violent, attention-seeking man. Their mother, however, would never allow herself to be burdened with the facts about Lee. The assassination, Robert sensed, would now give her an international stage to spout—and at some point, sell—her delusional conspiracy theories about Lee and his work as a government "agent."

It had always been infuriating to Robert how his mother could sound rational, even articulate, in short bursts of conversation. He feared that government investigators and journalists, not knowing any better, might actually believe what she told them.

On the afternoon of the assassination, Mrs. Oswald was driven from her home in Fort Worth to Dallas by Bob Schieffer, a twenty-six-year-old reporter for the *Fort Worth Star-Telegram*. She had called the newspaper's city desk, asking for help in getting to Dallas.

"Lady, this is not a taxi service," Schieffer told the woman on the phone. "And besides, the President has been shot."

"I know," the caller replied, almost matter-of-factly. "They think my son is the one who shot him."

Schieffer and a colleague grabbed a car and rushed to Mrs. Oswald's home on the west side of Fort Worth.

"She was a short, round-faced woman wearing enormous black horn-rimmed glasses and a white nurse's uniform," Schieffer recalled of his first glimpse of Mrs. Oswald. "She was distraught—but in an odd way." For most of the trip, he said, "she seemed less concerned with the death of the President or her son's role in it than with herself." She spoke obsessively about her fear that her daughter-in-law Marina "would get sympathy while no one would 'remember the mother' and that she would probably starve. I chalked it up to understandable emotional overload, and I couldn't bring myself to use her self-serving remarks in the story I filed later that day. I probably should have." Later, Schieffer, who went on to a long career in television news, concluded that Oswald's mother was "deranged."

Arriving at police headquarters in Dallas, Mrs. Oswald and Schieffer were ushered into a small room—perhaps an interrogation room, Schieffer thought—to wait to speak to the police about her son. Later that afternoon, Marina Oswald was also brought into the room. The two women had not seen each other in more than a year, and because Marina still spoke almost no English, they had—literally—almost nothing to say to each other.

Marina had just undergone a first round of questioning by the police and the FBI; as she admitted later, she was terrified. She was fearful, above all, that she would be separated from her children and arrested, even though she had insisted to her interrogators—through a translator— that she knew nothing about any plan by her husband to assassinate the president. Her fear of arrest was understandable: she knew she would have been taken into custody if she'd been back home in the Soviet Union. "That's how it would have been in Russia," she explained later. "Even if your husband was innocent, they would arrest you until it was straightened out."

Marina admitted that it might be natural for suspicion to fall on her: it was hardly implausible that she would know about, if not actually participate in, any plot by her husband to kill the president. Here she was, Marina Nikolaevna Prusakova, still newly arrived from the Soviet Union, who had entered the United States after a hasty marriage to an American turncoat who had never hidden his embrace of Marxism. There might be additional suspicion of Marina because of her family ties to Russian intelligence: an uncle worked in St. Petersburg, the city then officially known as Leningrad, in the Russian Interior Ministry.

Among those with early suspicions about Marina was her brother-in-law, Robert. On the day of the assassination, he considered, at least momentarily, that she was part of a plot to kill Kennedy, although the more he thought about the idea, the less likely it seemed. It was a matter of logic. If the Russians had launched a conspiracy to kill Kennedy, would they enlist the help of this tiny, seemingly petrified young woman who barely spoke English? And why would they have married her off to his misfit brother who soon saddled her with two small children?

In the days after the assassination, Robert's suspicions turned else-where—to Ruth Paine, the soft-spoken, thirty-one-year-old New York City–born woman who had given shelter to Marina, and to Ruth's estranged husband, Michael Paine, a thirty-five-year-old aircraft engineer. The Paines had separated a year earlier, although they remained friendly, if only for the sake of their own two children. Ruth, a Russian-language teacher who had been introduced to Marina through the local Russian expatriate community, lived in Irving, Texas, just outside Dallas, and she had welcomed Marina and her daughters into her home. In accordance with the charitable tenets of her Quaker faith, Ruth said, she did not ask Marina to pay any rent.

Robert Oswald admitted later that he had no evidence—because, he conceded, there was none—to show that the Paines had anything to do with the assassination. Still, there was something about the couple that troubled him, especially about Michael, who was introduced to Robert at Dallas police headquarters in the hours after the assassination. "Nothing really to put my finger on, but I just had a feeling. I still do not know why or how, but Mr. and Mrs. Paine are somehow involved in this affair," he told investigators. "His handshake was very weak and what I might term a live fish handshake. His general appearance, his face, and most partic-ularly his eyes to me had what I would term a distant look to them, and that he wasn't really looking at you when he was." On the basis of little more than a weak handshake and a distant stare, then, Robert Oswald decided to cut off all contact—forever, as it turned out—between Marina and the Paines. It deprived his sister-in-law of a loyal Russian-speaking friend, Ruth Paine, who might have helped Marina navigate the troubles to come in the language of her birth; Marina would never fully com-mand English.

Robert Oswald was the first of many men to enter Marina's life in the days after the assassination—some to help her, others to prey on a young woman whose fragile beauty was often remarked on. In photographs, she could be film-star pretty, so long as she avoided smiling; she was a victim of inadequate Soviet dentistry.

After her husband's murder by Jack Ruby, Marina and her children—as well as her mother-in-law and Robert—were hastily moved to a motel on the outskirts of Dallas, the Inn of the Six Flags, where it was thought they could be kept safe. The motel's dapper resident manager, thirty-one-year-old James Martin, readily agreed to take them in. It was the off-season for the motel, which was adjacent to the newly opened Six Flags Over Texas amusement park, and there was plenty of space for the Oswalds and the team of Secret Service agents protecting them.

Martin did not recall that he was ever actually formally introduced to Marina, but he quickly befriended the young widow. The following Thursday was Thanksgiving, so he invited the Oswalds to his home for a holiday dinner with his family; Martin and his wife had three children. (Martin did not invite Marguerite Oswald—an oversight, he said later—because she had returned to her own home in Fort Worth.) "They weren't going to have a very happy Thanksgiving, and living in those rooms was pretty cramped," Martin recalled. Marina and Robert accepted.

A few days after the holiday, Martin—without consulting his wife, he acknowledged—proposed to Marina that she and the children move in with the Martin family in their three bedroom house. "I know the Secret Service made a statement that they were quite concerned as to where Marina would go after she left the inn. They had no place to put her and they had no idea where she was going to go," Martin said. "I told them that if they couldn't find any place for her that I would be glad to take them into my home."

Marina soon moved into one of the Martin children's bedrooms, which adjoined the bedroom of Martin and his wife. He did not ask Marina to pay any rent or compensate the family in any way, at least initially. Two weeks later, however, Martin proposed that he become Marina's full-time business manager, in exchange for 10 percent of the tens of thousands of dollars in contracts she was offered—in late November alone—to sell her story to news outlets and book publishers. Marina agreed. Martin also found a local lawyer to represent her; the lawyer took another 10 percent.

Marina would later say she was naive and that she had welcomed help from these friendly American men who seemed to know what they were doing. She believed they could help her establish a new life without her husband. Her inability to speak English made her all the more dependent on them.

Quickly, Martin made it clear that he hoped for a different sort of relationship with Marina Oswald—he wanted to be her lover. He had pursued her romantically almost from the day they met, Marina said later. She remembered that on New Year's Day 1964, when his wife was out of the house, Martin put a record of songs by the crooner Mario

Lanza on the phonograph and professed his love. The advances continued for weeks. "He always hugged me and kissed me when his wife or children or the Secret Service agents were not around."

New people were finding their way into Marguerite Oswald's life as well. In early December, Mrs. Oswald, who had a listed phone number and welcomed calls from reporters and almost anyone else who had the patience to listen to her, picked up the receiver and heard the voice of Shirley Harris Martin. Mrs. Martin introduced herself as a forty-two-year-old homemaker and mother of four from Hominy, Oklahoma, who had become fixated on the idea that there had been a conspiracy to kill President Kennedy. (She was no relation to James Martin in Dallas.)

Within days of the assassination, the garage of Mrs. Martin's home had begun filling up with stacks of newspapers and magazines with articles about the assassination—everything she could find, she said. She had a passion for the mysteries of Agatha Christie, and she had decided that she had a mystery of her own to solve: who had really killed the president. Soon she began to meet and hear from people from all over the country who shared her obsession.

"In December 1963, I called Mama for the first time—Mama Oswald," she remembered. "At that time, she was very rational. She's such a character." After introducing herself, Mrs. Martin had a question: Had Mrs. Oswald read an article about her son that been published that month in the *National Guardian*, a self-proclaimed radical leftist weekly in New York?

The piece was a ten-thousand-word analysis of the case—or rather, the lack of a case—against her son. Headlined "Oswald Innocent? A Lawyer's Brief," the author was Mark Lane, a New York City criminal defense lawyer and former state legislator. Mrs. Oswald had not read the article but she was eager to see it. After a copy arrived in the mail from Oklahoma, an excited Mrs. Oswald tracked down Lane by phone. "Mrs. Oswald called and asked if I could meet her in Dallas to consider representing her and her son," Lane said later, recalling that Mrs. Oswald had described him as "the only person in America who is raising any questions" about her son's guilt. He was surprised—and naturally intrigued. Within days, Lane was on a plane to Texas, where he met with Mrs. Oswald and offered to join her campaign to prove that Lee Harvey Oswald was an innocent man.

In Lane, Mrs. Oswald had found her champion. And in Lee Oswald's mother, Lane had found his ideal client.

5

Lyndon Johnson knew, from the first days after the assassination, that some people would suspect he had something to do with Kennedy's murder. He seemed to take it as a given. There were simply too many ugly, obvious questions. After all, Kennedy had been gunned down in the streets of a Texas city, his alleged assassin was murdered in that same city two days later, and the hyper-ambitious former vice president—a Texan—now occupied the Oval Office. Already, the State Department had begun reporting that some foreign capitals were rife with rumors that Johnson had ordered his predecessor's death.

In truth, Johnson's outrageous bad taste over the years had invited some of the suspicion. As vice president, he had liked to joke about the odds of Kennedy dying in office—how an assassination or accident would clear the way for him. Clare Booth Luce, the former congresswoman and the wife of Time, Inc., founder Henry Luce, recalled asking Johnson at the 1960 inaugural ball why he had accepted the offer of the vice presidency. She remembered his cheery reply: "Clare, I looked it up; one out of every four presidents has died in office. I'm a gamblin' man, darlin'." He had made similar comments to others.

It pained Johnson to realize that Dallas would long be remembered as the place where the handsome young president was killed, and that the public image of his beloved Texas had been blackened, probably for years. The night of the assassination, Lady Bird confided to her husband that what might salvage their home state's reputation—perversely—was the fact that their good friend Governor Connally had also been hit. His grave injuries would dampen some of the talk of a Texas-based conspiracy. Lady Bird said she would have been willing to take the bullet herself, instead of Connally, to spare the good name of Texas. "I only wish it could have been me."

All this was just more proof to Johnson of why Chief Justice Warren had to run the investigation. His name would give instant credibility to the commission. The chief justice had many critics in Washington and around the country, but he also had a reputation for personal honesty and political independence that could help convince the public that the truth was not being hidden from them. "We had to bring the nation through this bloody tragedy," Johnson said. "Warren's personal integrity was a key element in assuring that all the facts would be unearthed and that the conclusions would be credible."

On the afternoon of Friday, November 29, Johnson dispatched Deputy Attorney General Nicholas Katzenbach and Solicitor General Archibald Cox to meet with Warren in his chambers in the court and convince him to lead the commission. As solicitor general, Cox, on leave from his teaching post at Harvard Law School, argued regularly in front of Warren and the other justices, and he had the chief justice's admiration. The feeling was mutual. Cox described Warren as the "greatest Chief Justice after John Marshall."

The conversation was over almost before it began. The words were barely out of his visitors' mouths before Warren rejected the president's request: "I told them I thought the president was wise in having such a commission, but that I was not available for service on it."

He reminded Katzenbach and Cox of the unfortunate history of court members taking on outside government assignments. There had been harsh criticism of Associate Justice Owen Roberts as chairman of the commission that investigated the Pearl Harbor attacks, and of Associate Justice Robert Jackson, who left the court for a year in 1945 to oversee the Nuremberg war-crimes trials. Former chief justice Harlan Fiske Stone described the trials as a "fraud" and accused Jackson of participating in a "high-grade lynching."

Warren thanked his guests for their visit and sent them back out the door to deliver the bad news to the White House. "Katzenbach and Cox went away, and I thought that that settled it," the chief justice remembered.

But nothing was settled, as Warren was about to discover; Johnson was determined to change his mind. "Early in my life, I learned that doing the impossible frequently was necessary to get the job done," the president said later. "There was no doubt in my mind that the Chief Justice had to be convinced that it was his duty to accept the chairmanship."

At about three thirty that afternoon, the president had a secretary phone the Supreme Court to ask Warren to come to the White House immediately. Warren was not told the purpose of the meeting, although the issue was "quite urgent," Warren recalled. "I, of course, said I would do so." The White House dispatched a limousine.

The chief justice was about to be subjected—in full force, for the first time—to what had long been known in the Capitol as "the Johnson Treatment." A potent mixture of flattery, pleading, deceit, and menace, it was a kind of salesmanship that Johnson had perfected in Congress to bend others to his will. It worked because it was so audacious—so unexpected, even undignified—that its targets were often too startled to do anything but give in.

Many times in the past Johnson had shown that, if necessary, he was prepared to reduce a proud man to weeping. In Warren's case, he was ready to make the case that the chief justice was all that stood between the people of the United States and Armageddon.

"I was ushered in," Warren said, recalling his arrival in the Oval Office. "With only the two of us in the room, he told me of his proposal."

The president said he needed Warren to change his mind. The assassination investigation had to be led by someone of Warren's stature, the president explained. Johnson said he was concerned about the "wild stories and rumors that were arousing not only our own people but people in other parts of the world."

Johnson mentioned the other six men he expected to name to the commission, and it was an impressive group. There were two senators: Democrat Richard Russell, the "Georgia Giant," and Republican John Sherman Cooper of Kentucky, a respected moderate who had been ambassador to India. There were two House members: Democrat Hale Boggs of Louisiana, the assistant majority leader, who had been close to

Kennedy, and Republican Gerald R. Ford of Michigan. And there were two high-profile appointees who, Johnson said, had been recommended to him by Robert Kennedy: former director of Central Intelligence Allen Dulles and former World Bank president John J. McCloy.

According to Warren, the president said that he had already talked with the others and that "they would serve if I would accept the chairmanship." The word "if" was important, Johnson made clear; all six had apparently said they would sign on only if Warren agreed to lead them. The president was suggesting that Warren would put the whole membership of the commission in jeopardy if he turned down the job. As Johnson recalled telling Warren, "All these appointments were conditioned on the Chief Justice being chairman."

Warren was flattered and startled by the suggestion that Russell—the Senate's most powerful segregationist—was willing to see beyond their differences and insist that he run the commission. Still, Warren declined. He explained his reasoning, repeating the arguments he had made that afternoon to his visitors from the Justice Department.

Johnson listened—and then turned up the pressure on the chief justice as far as it could go. It came down to this, he said: Was Warren willing to risk World War III? More than that, was he willing to be responsible for World War III? The president's wording was that stark, Warren remembered.

"I see you shaking your head," Johnson told him. "But this is something which is just as important to your country now as fighting for it was in World War I," reminding Warren of his wartime service in the army. "I am not going to order you to take this, as you were ordered to duty in 1917. I am going to appeal to your patriotism."

Johnson later recalled telling the chief justice: "Now these wild people are chargin' Khrushchev killed Kennedy, and Castro killed Kennedy, and everybody else killed Kennedy." If there was any truth in the allegations of a Communist plot, or if the investigation of the assassination was mishandled and false charges were made against a foreign government, the result could be nuclear war. He told Warren about rumors coming out of Mexico City that Oswald had received a payoff of $6,500 from Castro's government to kill Kennedy. "You can imagine what the reaction of the country would have been if this information came out," the president said.

Johnson told the chief justice that he had just spoken to Defense Secretary McNamara, who warned that a nuclear exchange between the United States and the Soviet Union would leave tens of millions of American dead in just the first strike. "If Khrushchev moved on us, he could kill 39 million in an hour, and we could kill 100 million in his country in an hour," he said, suggesting that the chief justice was now responsible for the fate of those people. "You could be speaking for 39 million people. Now I just think you don't wanna do that."

He called on Warren's patriotism. "You were a soldier in World War I, but there was nothing you could do in that uniform comparable to what you can do for your country in this hour of trouble," Johnson said. "The President of the United States says that you are the only man who can handle the matter. You won't say, 'no,' will you?"

Johnson remembered that Warren "swallowed hard and said, 'No, sir.'"

With a little cruel pride, Johnson later recalled that he made Warren cry: "Tears just came into his eyes. . . . They just came up. You never saw anything like it."

There is no known recording of the Oval Office meeting with Warren, but if the accounts offered by Johnson and the chief justice are accurate, the president lied outright in claiming that the other commissioners had agreed to serve only if Warren was in charge. The truth was that, with the exception of Russell, Johnson had not even talked to the others.

Johnson talked to Russell by phone at about four p.m., shortly before the Warren meeting, and tried to persuade him to serve on the commission. Russell rejected the idea outright. He was too busy with his Senate duties, he said. And his health was not good; Russell had been plagued for years by emphysema.

In that first call, Johnson asked Russell for suggestions of other candidates. The president said he might try to recruit a member of the Supreme Court to join the commission, although he suggested that it would probably prove fruitless. Warren's name was never mentioned in the call. "I don't think I can get any member of the court, but I'm going to try to," he said to Russell, neglecting to mention that the chief justice—at that very minute—was being summoned to the White House to be convinced to take the job.

Hours later, at about nine p.m., Johnson made his second call to Russell. He would be delivering two pieces of unwelcome news. First, that Russell would serve on the commission despite his protests. Second, that the commission would be led by—of all people—Earl Warren, a man Russell had long portrayed to his fellow Georgians as a villain.

Taking no chances, Johnson decided to force Russell's hand. Before making the call, he ordered the White House press office to issue a public statement announcing the creation of the commission and listing its members, including Russell.

Johnson reached Russell at his home in Winder, Georgia, where the senator was spending a few days after Thanksgiving.

"Dick?" Johnson began in a gentle, apologetic tone of voice.

"Yes?"

"I hate to bother you again, but I just wanted you to know that I'd made that announcement."

Russell: "Announcement of what?"

Johnson: "Of this special commission."

The president began reading from the press release and soon came to the names of the commission's members. Russell heard Warren's name as chairman and then heard his own.

He sounded flabbergasted by Johnson's duplicity. "Well now, Mr. President, I know I don't have to tell you of my devotion to you, but I just can't serve on that commission. . . . I couldn't serve there with Chief Justice Warren." This was personal, he said. "I don't like that man. I don't have any confidence in him."

Johnson cut him off. "Dick, it's already been announced, and you can serve with anybody for the good of America. This is a question that has a good many more ramifications than's on the surface." As he had with Warren, Johnson noted McNamara's estimate of the nearly forty million Americans who might be killed in a nuclear exchange, if the assassination led to war.

"Now the reason I asked Warren is because he's the chief justice of this country, and we've got to have the highest judicial people we can have," he said. "The reason I ask you is because you have that same kind of temperament, and you can do anything for your country. And don't go to givin' me that kinda stuff about you can't serve with anybody. You can do anything.

"You never turned your country down," Johnson continued. "You're my man on that commission. And you gonna do it. And don't tell me what you can do and what you can't. I can't arrest you. And I'm not gonna put the FBI on you. But you're goddamned sure gonna serve. I'll tell you that."

Russell: "Well, I know, but Mr. President, you oughta told me you were gonna name Warren."

Johnson then lied to Russell, just as he had lied to Warren a few hours earlier. "I *told* you," the president said. "I told you today I was gonna name the chief justice, when I called you."

Russell knew it was a lie, as transcripts of Johnson's phone calls would show. "No, you did not," he said.

Johnson: "I did."

Russell: "You talked about getting somebody on the Supreme Court. You didn't tell me you was gonna name *him*."

Johnson: "I begged him as much as I'm begging you."

Russell: "You haven't had to beg me. You've always told me, all right."

Johnson: "No, it's already done. It's been announced . . . hell."

Announced? Russell finally understood what Johnson had done: the press release with his name on it had already been given to the White House press corps.

Russell: "You mean you've got out that . . ."

Johnson: "Yes, sir, I mean I gave it. . . . It's already in the papers, and you're on it, and you're gonna be my man on it."

Russell: "I think you're sort of takin' advantage of me, Mr. President."

Johnson: "I'm not takin' advantage of you."

Johnson suddenly seemed to remember who he was talking to—his political mentor, a man who was closer to him than many members of his family. He pleaded with Russell to keep in mind how much he could do for Russell now that he was president: "I'm gonna take a helluva lot of advantage of you, my friend, 'cause you made me and I know it, and I don't ever forget. . . . I'm a Russell protégé, and I don't forget my friends."

Russell: "Hell, I just don't like Warren."

Johnson: "Well, of course you don't like Warren, but you'll like him 'fore it's over with."

Russell: "I haven't got any confidence in him."

Johnson: "You can give him some confidence, goddamnit! Associate with him. Now. . . . Now by God, I wanna man on that commission. And I've got one."

Russell gave up the fight: "If it is for the good of the country, you know damned well I'll do it, and I'll do it for you. I hope to God you'll be just a little bit more deliberate and considerate next time about it. But this time, of course, if you've done this, I'm gonna do it and go through with it and say I think it's a wonderful idea." He uttered those last few words—"it's a wonderful idea"—in a tone heavy with sarcasm.

Before hanging up, Russell admonished Johnson a last time. "I think you did wrong gettin' Warren, and I know damn well you got it wrong getting me, but we'll both do the best we can."

"I think that's what you'll do," the president replied. "That's the kind of Americans both of you are. Good night."

At the Supreme Court the next week, Warren had to explain himself to his fellow justices—why he had agreed to lead the commission after insisting, for years, how wrong it was for members of the court to take outside assignments.

He later told his friend Drew Pearson that the other justices reacted with outrage, with the exception of Justice Goldberg, the court's newest arrival. "Every member of the court except Arthur Goldberg gave him hell," Pearson wrote in his diaries. Justices William Brennan and John Marshall Harlan pointed out Warren's hypocrisy, reminding him that he had long argued that "members of the court should stick to their knitting and not assume extra-curricular duties." Warren knew his colleagues were right to be angry with him. He was, he admitted, angry with himself.

PART 2
THE INVESTIGATION

Frame #371 from the Zapruder film, November 22, 1963

6

The chief justice feared it would be a miserable Christmas—and a terrible new year. Warren's children said the Kennedy assassination had shaken him and their mother like no other event in their parents' lives. "The assassination was just unbelievable to both of them," said Robert, the youngest of their six children. "It changed them." Another son, Earl Jr., said that for the first time in his father's life, the "strain really, really showed." By agreeing to run the commission, "he was living that tragic event over every moment. . . . It was really quite cruel for him to have to go through it again and again."

That year especially, the chief justice would have welcomed the chance to escape the capital and spend the holidays back home in Northern California, surrounded by his children and grandchildren and his old friends, enjoying the sunny, sometimes warm December weather of the San Francisco Bay Area; the harshness of winters in Washington could still startle him. Traveling to California for the holidays had been his routine since joining the court, but now, having yielded to President Johnson, he suspected that he would be forced to remain in Washington. He needed to organize the commission, even as he prepared himself for a busy winter docket at the Supreme Court. The cases to be decided the following year included a momentous First Amendment case, *The New York Times v. Sullivan*, that was scheduled for argument on January 6. Several other major cases argued in late 1963 were set for rulings. Just nine days before the assassination, the court heard arguments in a landmark voting-rights case, *Reynolds v. Sims*; that case would allow the court to force all fifty states to adopt one-man, one-vote rules for elections of their state legislatures.

Luckily for Warren, he was still in good health at the age of seventy-two. He was proud that he was still vigorous, still hard at work at the court, even as so many of his old colleagues from the district attorney's office in Oakland and at the governor's offices in Sacramento were heading into retirement. Sadly, a few of his old California friends had recently gone to their graves.

By agreeing to run the commission, Warren had assumed two full-time jobs. He decided he would try not to limit, in any way, his activities on the court. After a decade on the bench—in October, he had marked his tenth anniversary as chief justice—Warren could see that the court under his leadership was remaking the country, pushing the United States into the future, making it fairer and freer. The court was defeating the bigots and the reactionaries who, he sensed, had somehow created the atmosphere that had resulted in Kennedy's murder. His legacy as chief justice might be far greater than anything he could have achieved had he realized his earlier dreams of winning the White House.

Johnson and his aides had pledged to Warren that he would have unlimited resources to run the commission. He would have all the money he needed to hire a staff, find offices, and pay for whatever investigation was necessary. But somebody had to hire that staff, and somebody had to find those offices, and now all those responsibilities rested on Warren's shoulders. He was being asked to run the court even as he set up and directed what amounted to a small federal agency to investigate the president's murder—an agency that, if it did its job poorly, might cause the nation to stumble into war.

Warren knew he needed help fast, and he immediately reached out to Warren Olney, his most trusted aide throughout his career in county and state government back in California. Olney, fifty-nine, another native Californian, had first gone to work for Warren in 1939 in the district attorney's office in Oakland. He was typical of Warren's closest deputies—loyal, discreet, progressive, but essentially apolitical, someone who saw in Warren an ideal of what a public servant could be. The chief justice considered

Olney "a man on whom I could bet my life for integrity." Olney had followed Warren to Washington. From 1953 to 1957, he was assistant attorney general in the Justice Department's criminal division; in effect, he was the Eisenhower administration's chief criminal prosecutor. At the department, Olney made his mark—like his mentor Warren, across town at the court—on civil rights. He helped draft the 1957 Civil Rights Act, the first major civil rights legislation approved by Congress since Reconstruction. In 1958, he became the director of the administrative office of the U.S. Courts, the agency responsible for the logistics of running the federal court system; the job kept him in close touch with the chief justice.

After his meeting with Johnson in the Oval Office, Warren called Olney and asked him to join the commission to run its day-to-day investigation, with the title of general counsel. It would be a full-time job for however long the investigation lasted—two or three months, Warren estimated. To his relief, Olney said yes.

Warren had not yet met his fellow commissioners, but he seemed confident the other six would respond enthusiastically to the appointment. Olney was a well-known figure in Washington legal circles; he was certainly admired by many of his former Justice Department colleagues. Warren apparently thought it would all be a formality.

FBI director Hoover had other plans, however. Exactly how he got word of Warren's intention to appoint Olney is not clear from FBI files. But within days of the chief justice's conversation with Olney, the FBI was aware of Olney's selection, and the bureau launched an aggressive, behind-the-scenes campaign to block it. The stop-Olney campaign was designed to remain a secret from the chief justice.

Olney had made enemies at the FBI. At the Justice Department, his zeal for civil rights enforcement was not shared by the bureau; Hoover, in particular, saw many civil rights leaders, especially Martin Luther King, as subversives, if not Communists. Hoover had come to consider Olney as "hostile" to the FBI and disparaged him as "Warren's protégé"—the description used in FBI files.

The campaign against Olney reflected how much the relationship between Hoover and Warren had deteriorated in the quarter century they had known each other. As California's governor in the 1940s, Warren had a close relationship—a friendship, he thought—with Hoover, earning him a place on the FBI's coveted "special correspondents list" of public officials entitled to the bureau's help. When Governor Warren traveled to Washington, he took advantage of the FBI's offer of a car and driver. The relationship with Hoover was once so close that Warren reportedly asked the FBI to conduct a background investigation of a young man who was courting one of the governor's daughters.

But when Warren arrived at the Supreme Court in 1953 and the court began to rein in the powers of the FBI, especially as the justices broadened the rights of criminal suspects, the relationship with Hoover chilled—and never recovered. By the time of Kennedy's assassination, it was one of mutual contempt. Warren later told Drew Pearson he believed that Hoover's FBI had been engaged for years in "gestapo tactics," including illegal wiretapping in high-profile criminal investigations—practices that were ended in part because of the actions of the court.

"I remember J. Edgar Hoover when he had 700 men before the war and was doing a fine job," Warren told Pearson in 1966 for what was supposed to be an authorized profile of the chief justice for *Look* magazine. "Now he has 7,000 men and power has gone to his head. He gets all the money he wants from Congress and there is no check on him whatsoever." He said he feared that if the FBI and the CIA were ever combined into one agency, "we will really have a police state." (Warren apparently realized he had spoken too freely to Pearson and convinced the columnist to abandon the article.)

Hoover had initially been opposed to the creation of an independent commission to investigate Kennedy's murder. It would be a "regular circus," he told Johnson in a phone call on Monday, November 25, three days after the assassination. His opposition was understandable. The FBI was not used to outside scrutiny of any sort; Congress offered little oversight of the bureau, routinely bowing to Hoover's requests for larger and larger budgets to be spent mostly at his discretion. But with the creation of a commission, the FBI could expect a deluge of questions about why it had failed to detect the threat posed by Oswald, who had been under the surveillance of the bureau's field offices in both Dallas and New Orleans in the months before the assassination. Hoover told his deputies he feared a commission might cause the bureau's operations to be second-guessed in ways that could threaten the FBI's very survival.

Still, he did not protest when, on November 29, Johnson called to announce that he had changed his mind and decided to create a commission. The recording of the call showed that Hoover accepted the decision without complaint, perhaps reflecting his trust in the new president to protect the FBI's interests. There is no evidence that he complained to Johnson directly about the choice of Warren as chairman.

It was the selection of Olney, however, that caused Hoover to act. Quietly Hoover's deputies contacted the members of the commission—apart from Warren—to warn them of Olney's reputation at the bureau as a man who had not supported Hoover's concept of law and order. As FBI assistant director Cartha "Deke" DeLoach wrote later, it was "necessary for a number of sources to confidentially brief members of the presidential commission, other than Warren, as to Olney's background" and his "miserable personality."

Warren scheduled the first meeting of the President's Commission on the Assassination of President Kennedy—the panel's formal name—for ten a.m. on Thursday, December 5. The setting was an ornate, wood-paneled conference room at the National Archives on Pennsylvania Avenue; the archives had agreed to make space for the commission to meet until it found offices of its own. Walking into the meeting that day, the chief justice was apparently unaware that his first key decision in running the investigation had already been undermined by the FBI.

Even before the meeting, there was evidence that the commission's relationship with the FBI would be difficult. Hoover peevishly refused to grant the commission's request that he send a senior FBI official to the meeting to answer questions about the state of the bureau's investigation in Dallas. The FBI argued that it would be more appropriate for Deputy Attorney General Nicholas Katzenbach, who was due to attend the meeting, to represent the bureau.

There appeared to be a much more significant act of defiance by the FBI with a series of leaks to some of the bureau's favorite reporters. On December 3, two days before the meeting, the Associated Press reported that the FBI was close to completing an "exhaustive report" that would identify Oswald as "the lone and unaided assassin of President Kennedy." The AP report, attributed to unnamed "government sources," said the FBI had determined that Oswald—"without accomplices"—fired three bullets at the president's limousine from the Texas School Book Depository. The FBI report would find that the first and third bullets hit Kennedy, while the second struck Connally. Similar stories were leaked to other news outlets.

To several of the commissioners, the articles amounted to an orchestrated effort by the FBI, and probably by Hoover personally, to cement public opinion around the idea that there had been no conspiracy to kill the president—certainly no conspiracy that the FBI might have been able to foil. The bureau was trying to force them to reach conclusions before they had weighed any of the evidence, it appeared.

"It is the most outrageous leak I have ever seen," Congressman Boggs, the Louisiana Democrat, told the other commissioners. "It almost has to come from the FBI." Deputy Attorney General Katzenbach was convinced Hoover and his deputies were leaking the stories: "I can't think of anybody else it could have come from."

The meeting that Thursday opened with a round of handshakes among the seven commissioners and Katzenbach. They took their seats at a long, handsome, wooden table; the only other person in the room was a court reporter hired to transcribe the proceedings. Most of the transcripts of the commission's executive sessions, classified as top secret, would remain locked away for decades.

"This is a very sad and solemn duty that we are undertaking," Warren began. "I am sure there is not one of us but what would rather be doing almost anything else that he can think of than to be on a commission of this kind. But it is a tremendously important one." President Johnson "is right in trying to make sure that the public will be given all of this sordid situation, so far as it is humanly possible," he continued. "I feel honored that he would think that I, along with the rest of you, are capable of doing such a job, and I enter upon it with a great feeling of both inadequacy and humility because the very thought of reviewing these details day by day is really sickening to me."

He then set out his view of the commission's assignment. He said he believed the scope of the investigation should be limited and that the commission should finish its work as quickly as possible. In fact, "investigation" was really not the word for what he proposed. He argued that the commission should simply review the evidence about the assassination that had been gathered by the FBI, the Secret Service, and other agencies; it would be the commission's responsibility to make certain that their investigations were adequate. Whatever he might privately think of Hoover, Warren seemed to believe that the FBI, in particular, could be trusted to get to the facts.

"I think our job here is essentially one for the evaluation of evidence, as distinguished from being one of gathering evidence, and I believe that at the outset, at least, we can start with the premise that we can rely upon the reports of the various agencies," he said. According to Warren, there should be no public hearings, nor should the commission seek subpoena powers, which would require approval from Congress. He said he saw no need to hire a separate staff of investigators. "I don't see any reason why we should duplicate the facilities of the FBI or the Secret Service."

If the commission had subpoena power and public hearings, Warren argued, it might be overwhelmed by mentally ill people "who believe they know of great conspiracies" and would demand to testify. "If we have the subpoena power, people are going to expect us to use it. Witnesses are going to have the right to come in and say, 'here, I've got this testimony I want to give.' . . . And if they are cranks, if they are nuts, we are in a bind." If the commission then failed to call the "nuts" to testify, "they are going to go out and say we have suppressed the evidence." Warren's mailbag at the court was already full of letters and postcards from disturbed people—some of them threatening, many written in tiny, scrawled handwriting, his files showed—who claimed they were ready to reveal the hidden truth about the president's murder.

With that, Warren sat back to hear the thoughts of the others. He seemed confident that his fellow commissioners—most nearly as busy with their lives as he was—would see the logic of his proposal.

Instead, the others pushed back, some to the edge of rudeness. He might be chief justice, deferred to in every other setting, but Warren was about to learn that many of these men intended to treat him as an equal. Several—Senator Russell, John McCloy, and Allen Dulles, especially—had been exercising power in Washington for decades, long before Warren arrived in the capital. And Warren had special reason to be wary of Gerald Ford, first elected to Congress in 1948, because of the friendship between the Michigan Republican and Richard Nixon.

McCloy, a sixty-eight-year-old lawyer, diplomat, and banker who had been a valued adviser to presidents since Franklin Roosevelt and was dubbed "The Chairman of the Eastern Establishment" a year earlier by *Esquire* magazine, was the first to stand up to the chief justice. He suggested Warren was downright foolish to trust government agencies to investigate their own shortcomings. McCloy did not use the word "coverup" in describing what the FBI and Secret Service might do, but he came close.

"There is potential culpability here on the part of the Secret Service and even the FBI," he said. "Human nature being what it is," the agencies might submit "self-serving" reports about what had happened.

Warren was wrong about subpoena power, too, McCloy declared. The commission needed to be able to compel witnesses to testify, and to force agencies to turn over evidence. Without subpoena power, he said, the commission risked being seen as toothless. The investigation had an obligation beyond "the mere evaluation of the reports of agencies. . . . I think that if we didn't have the right to subpoena documents, the right to subpoena witnesses if we needed them, that this commission's general standing might be somewhat impaired." Boggs and Ford agreed.

Seemingly startled to be challenged so openly at the commission's first meeting, Warren put up no real fight. "If the rest of you think that we ought to have subpoena power, it is perfectly all right with me," he said.

Next, Russell objected to Warren's suggestion that the commission go without a staff of investigators. "We are going to have to have somebody" to review the flood of paperwork from the FBI, the Secret Service, and elsewhere, he said. "I hope that we can get a staff—not an army, but a staff of exceedingly capable men that will be able to formulate a report that will stand the most exacting scrutiny of any fair-minded person."

He reminded Warren of the danger that the investigation posed to all seven of them—that if they did not have adequate resources to get the truth about the assassination and lay out the evidence clearly to the public, history would not forgive them. Whatever else they accomplished in their long careers, this might well be the work they would be remembered for. "The reputations of all of us are at stake in this thing," Russell said, sharing with the others his anger with Johnson. "Frankly, I don't know if I will ever feel the same to the president for putting me on this commission. . . . I told him I didn't want to serve, and wouldn't serve, but I couldn't figure any way out of it."

McCloy suggested that the commission find a "rattling good" lawyer to direct the staff as the commission's general counsel, giving Warren the opportunity to offer his candidate: Warren Olney. The chief justice spent several minutes describing Olney's career in California and in Washington, asserting that "there isn't a man in my acquaintance who is any more honorable." Olney, he said, was "a fellow with real ability. . . . I just don't believe I could find anyone in the country who has comparable experience in this field for that kind of job."

His praise was so effusive that anyone who chose to challenge Olney's appointment might have sounded impertinent, even insulting, to the chief justice. But that is what happened, and Ford led the attack. Olney might be "an excellent recommendation," Ford said, but the close relationship between Warren and Olney was well known—the FBI had quietly made sure of that—and "with your long relationship with him, there can be some, unfairly perhaps, who would then say the Chief Justice is dominating the commission and it will be seen as his report rather than the report of all of us."

"I don't want the commission to be divided," Ford said. "I don't want it to be your commission or the commission of half of us or otherwise."

McCloy made no judgment on Olney's qualifications, but he agreed with Ford that there should be a broad search for a general counsel to oversee the investigation. "I have a feeling that we ought to look and pick out the best damned man," he said. "Personally, I would like to take a look myself at Olney."

The collegial Boggs seemed to sense that Warren was offended by the questions about Olney, and the Louisianan rose to defend the chief justice. "I think the chairman needs a counsel with whom he can be completely at ease," he said. "The Chief Justice should have someone that he has total, absolute confidence in."

Warren made a final pitch for Olney—and if not Olney, someone else of talent and experience who would be available in a hurry. The chief justice said he needed someone who understood the inner workings of law-enforcement agencies and the rest of the government and would not require "months and months to learn their way around" the capital. He put the plea in personal terms: "If I don't have a counsel that I know very well with whom I can work from the very first day, I know I won't even see my family Christmas day," he said. "I'm going to have to stay here every day, because a man just doesn't drop into Washington, no matter how good a man he is, and know his way around."

The meeting ended at twelve forty-five, after nearly three hours, with the commissioners scheduled to meet again the next afternoon.

The FBI's quiet lobbying campaign had worked, and when the commissioners gathered the next day—Friday, December 6—the appointment of Olney was a dead issue. Ford, Dulles, and McCloy informed Warren that they all had reservations about Olney, with McCloy revealing that he knew Olney was "at swords-point with J. Edgar Hoover." Warren had given up.

"I would not want to have anyone here that would not have the full confidence of the commission," he said. "So as far as I'm concerned, the question of Mr. Olney for counsel before the commission is closed."

Overnight, McCloy had called friends in Washington and on Wall Street, asking for the names of other experienced lawyers for the job. Several people, he said, had recommended J. Lee Rankin, who had been solicitor general in the Eisenhower administration and was then practicing law in New York. "Rankin seems to be a man of high character, high integrity," he said.

The mention of the name came as a relief to Warren. A fifty-six-year-old Nebraskan, Rankin was a familiar, friendly face to the chief justice. As solicitor general, he had represented the government before the court in many of the most important cases of the 1950s. In an earlier job, he had argued for the Justice Department on behalf of the young children and their parents in Topeka, Kansas, who had sought the desegregation of their local schools in *Brown v. Board of Education*. "We saw a great deal of him over in the Supreme Court because he argued all of the top ones himself," Warren said. "He's a splendid man in every respect. . . . He's a human being." Rankin, he said, was "not political in any sense."

Russell recommended that, if Warren and McCloy were agreed, the commission should hire Rankin. The other commissioners voiced no objection. Warren made plans to call Rankin that night.

Before the meeting ended, McCloy raised another question. The discussion among the commissioners had focused so far on the FBI and the Secret Service and the information those two agencies would be asked to provide to the commission. But what about the Central Intelligence Agency? Had the chief justice or anyone else been in touch with the CIA to determine what it knew about the assassination—and about Oswald and his travels in Russia and Mexico?

"No, I have not," Warren replied, "for the simple reason that I have never been informed that the CIA had any knowledge about this."

"They have," McCloy shot back, seeming to scoff at the chief justice's naïveté in suggesting the CIA would know nothing of value about Oswald. Pressing Warren, McCloy said, "Don't we have to ask them?"

"Of course we do," the chief justice replied, seeming to realize his earlier answer had been foolish. "I think we have to ask them."

Gerald Ford asked for the meeting. He invited FBI assistant director Cartha "Deke" DeLoach, the bureau's chief congressional liaison, to stop by his offices on Capitol Hill on the morning of Thursday, December 12, a week after the first meeting of the assassination commission. Ford had an offer to make to the bureau. "Upon arriving, he told me he wanted to talk in the strictest of confidence," DeLoach wrote to Hoover later that day. "This was agreed to."

Throughout his congressional career, Ford, like Lyndon Johnson and so many others on Capitol Hill, had gone out of his way to stay close to the FBI. Over the years, the bureau had come to see Ford as a reliable friend, especially when it came time to round up support each year for the FBI's budget requests. Ford was a member of the powerful House Appropriations Committee, which decided how the federal budget was divided up among agencies. Now, in his work for the commission, Ford would seize on a new opportunity to demonstrate his loyalty to the bureau.

Fifty year old "Jerry" Ford of Grand Rapids, Michigan, presented himself to his constituents as one of them—another modest, polite, amiable midwesterner. On Capitol Hill, he was known for his level head and good humor, and Democrats admired his internationalist approach to foreign policy. But his congressional colleagues saw a side of Ford that was not often on display to Michigan voters—that of a fiercely ambitious, sometimes ruthless politician who knew how to choose friends and allies who might help advance his career. In 1948, he had defeated a Republican incumbent to enter the House. From his first days in Congress, Ford surprised his staff by speaking openly about his dream of being elected Speaker someday. In early 1963, he was named chairman of the House Republican Conference—the Republican Party's third-highest leadership post in Congress—after ousting the veteran incumbent. In the 1960 general election, his friend Richard Nixon, the Republican presidential nominee, was reported to have come close to choosing Ford as his running mate.

Ford reached out to the FBI within weeks of arriving in Washington in 1949. He used one of his maiden speeches on the House floor that winter to call for a pay raise for Hoover, announcing that he was the author of a newly introduced budget amendment that would increase the FBI director's salary by 25 percent—from $14,000 to $17,500 a year—which would keep Hoover among the best-paid officials in the federal government.* The director, he said, was a national hero who deserved every penny: "The monetary reward proposed by my amendment, after long years of faithful and devoted service, is small compensation for his invaluable contribution."

Almost fifteen years later, Ford saw his appointment to the Warren Commission as a way to establish a national reputation—and also to further his alliance with Hoover. Over the years, Ford repeatedly insisted that he had resisted President Johnson's invitation to join the commission, citing his heavy duties in the House. But the release of Johnson's White House phone recordings decades later showed that in fact Ford had accepted Johnson's offer eagerly and without hesitation.

For the FBI, Ford's appointment meant that the bureau had a valuable contact—and a defender, if needed—on the investigation. In an internal memo shortly after the commission's membership was announced in late November, Hoover wrote that Ford could be expected to "look after FBI interests."

It turned out that Ford was willing to go even further to help, as he

---

* Given inflation, Hoover's new $17,500 annual salary would be equivalent to about $171,000 in 2013.

explained to DeLoach when the two men took a seat in the congressman's office. Ford said he was willing to be the bureau's secret source on the commission—in particular, to help the bureau keep an eye on the chief justice. It was the bureau's decision to make. Did the FBI want him to serve as an informant?

"Ford told me he was somewhat disturbed about the manner in which Chief Justice Warren was carrying on his chairmanship," DeLoach wrote in a memo later that day that went straight to Hoover. "He explained that the first mistake that Warren made was his attempt to establish a 'one-man commission' by appointing a chief counsel, Warren Olney, that was his own protégé."

Ford told DeLoach that during the commission's initial discussions, he and others objected to Warren's idea of installing Olney. "Warren put up a stiff argument" to try to rescue Olney's appointment, Ford informed DeLoach, but "a compromise was made when the name of Lee Rankin was mentioned." The memo suggested that Ford was unaware—or at least unwilling to acknowledge that he knew—that the FBI had organized a behind-the-scenes campaign to block Olney.

He then made his offer to DeLoach. "Ford indicated he would keep me thoroughly advised as to the activities of the Commission," DeLoach wrote. "He also asked if he could call me from time to time and straighten out questions in his mind concerning the investigation. I told him by all means he should do this. He reiterated that our relationship would, of course, remain confidential. We have had excellent relations with Congressman Ford for many years."

Hoover had reason to be elated, and not just by Ford's offer. The FBI director now had early evidence that Ford and some of the other commissioners were ready to put up a fight against the chief justice.

"Well-handled," he wrote at the bottom of DeLoach's memo.

The FBI's former number-three official, Assistant Director William Sullivan, who broke with Hoover years later and was forced into early retirement, recalled Hoover's excitement over Ford's offer to feed information. Over time, he said, Ford protected the FBI by "keeping us fully advised on what was going on behind closed doors. . . . He was our man, our informant, on the Warren Commission."

The investigation of Kennedy's assassination would be the largest criminal inquiry in the bureau's history, up to that time, as measured by the number of agents and man-hours devoted to the inquiry. The investigation was centered in Dallas, where scores of agents had been temporarily deployed from around the country. Extra agents were dispatched to New Orleans, where Oswald had been born and where he lived for part of 1963; to New York, where he had spent part of his childhood; and to Mexico City. Even so, just days after the assassination and certainly by early December, Hoover seemed ready to declare that Oswald—and Oswald alone—was responsible for the president's murder.

On Sunday, November 24, the day of Oswald's murder and two days after Kennedy's assassination, Hoover told Walter Jenkins, one of Johnson's top aides at the White House, that the FBI intended to prepare a report that would "convince the public that Oswald is the real assassin." Hoover appeared willing to overrule deputies to make a public declaration that Oswald had acted alone. On Tuesday, November 26, one of his senior deputies wrote to the director to say it was wrong to make any quick judgments about the assassination, including a final determination that Oswald was the lone gunman. "We must recognize that a matter of this magnitude cannot be fully investigated in a week's time," he argued.

Hoover disagreed and made his annoyance clear in a handwritten note he jotted at the top of the memo: "Just how long do you estimate it will take? It seems to me that we have the basic facts now." Three days later, on November 29, Hoover told President Johnson in a telephone call that "we hope to have the investigation wrapped up today, but probably won't have it before the first of the week."

That estimate proved much too optimistic, but on Monday, December 9, the FBI presented the Warren Commission with a five-volume, four-hundred-page report that, as promised, effectively identified Oswald as the lone killer. "Evidence developed in the investigation points conclusively to the assassination of President Kennedy by Lee Harvey Oswald, an avowed Marxist," the report said. The FBI did not completely rule out the possibility of a conspiracy involving Oswald, but the report offered no hint of anyone else involved in Kennedy's murder. There was the clear suggestion that although the FBI had Oswald under surveillance earlier that year as a possible Soviet spy, the bureau had never had reason to believe he posed a threat to the president. It was the findings of that report that had been leaked to reporters a week earlier.

THE NATIONAL ARCHIVES
WASHINGTON, DC
MONDAY, DECEMBER 16, 1963

Warren and the other commissioners gathered at the National Archives for their third meeting, which would center on a discussion of the FBI report.

Lee Rankin, newly arrived as general counsel, attended the session, and the chief justice said how pleased he was that Rankin could assume much of the burden of organizing the investigation. "He's been with me most of the time since our last meeting and we have been trying to tend to the housekeeping part of this thing," Warren said.

The chief justice opened the meeting with other good news—he had found office space for the commission at the newly opened headquarters of the Veterans of Foreign Wars, the national veterans group, on Maryland Avenue. Conveniently, the five-story, marble-facade building was just two blocks from the Supreme Court and a few minutes' walk from the Capitol. The commission could occupy the entire fourth floor of the building—about ten thousand square feet—and its members had been invited to use the VFW's large, ground-floor conference room for important witness interviews and other gatherings. "We have everything we need over there," Warren said.

The commission had been assigned its own phone number and would soon have its own telephone operators and receptionists, he announced. That news would be a relief to the bank of phone operators at the Supreme Court building who had grown alarmed by the bizarre, sometimes threatening calls from people who claimed to know dark secrets about the assassination.

Warren also reported that he was receiving good cooperation elsewhere. The General Services Administration, the federal logistics agency, had found an office administrator to organize the commission's payroll system and other bookkeeping. The National Archives had dispatched an archivist to help organize a filing system for what would soon be a flood of documents, many classified as top secret and higher. "We're in business over there," Warren said.

The conversation then turned to the FBI report. The appraisal by most of the commissioners was harsh. Warren and several others said they found the report incomplete and confusing—astonishingly so—and so badly written that it was hard to follow from one sentence to the next; parts of it were written in something like shorthand. "The grammar is bad and you can see that they did not polish it up at all," McCloy said.

Their alarm about the report was matched by their annoyance that so many details had been leaked—apparently by the FBI—before anyone at the White House or the commission had had a chance to read it. "Gentlemen, to be very frank about it, I have read that report two or three times and I have not seen anything in there that has not been in the press," Warren complained.

"I couldn't agree with that more," Russell said. "Practically everything in there has come out in the press at one time or another, a bit here and a bit there."

While the report left no doubt that the FBI considered Oswald the lone gunman, it was full of gaps about the medical findings and about the physical evidence gathered in Dealey Plaza. McCloy said he had read—more than once—the sections about Oswald's rifle and the trajectory of the bullets fired at the president's limousine, and he could not make sense of the ballistics evidence. "This bullet business leaves me confused," he said. "That is very unsatisfactory."

"It's totally inconclusive," Warren agreed.

Boggs was surprised that the report said almost nothing about Governor Connally and his near-fatal injuries. It left Boggs with "a million questions."

The report also failed to provide basic information about Oswald's biography and his foreign travels, including his trip to Mexico that fall. It offered only a brief description of his firearms training in the Marine Corps. "There are all kinds of questions in my mind," Boggs said. "He was such an expert marksman, for instance. Where did he do his practicing?"

The commissioners questioned why the report had only sketchy information about Ruby, who, it was rumored in Texas, might have known Oswald. "They have obviously done a lot to establish the life and habits of Oswald," Boggs said, "but there is still little on this fellow Ruby, including his movements, what he was doing, how he got in there—it's fantastic."

Even Ford, the FBI's reliable defender, admitted that the report "did not have the depth that it ought to have."

The report's glaring inadequacies had changed Warren's mind about the scope of the commission's investigation. It would need to be much bigger, and it would take longer, he admitted reluctantly. He told the other commissioners that he now believed they needed to issue a government-wide demand for all "raw materials" about the assassination. In the FBI's case, the commission would need to see all of the thousands of witness statements and evidence reports that its agents had already prepared in Dallas and Washington, as well as all the reports they would prepare in the future.

"It will take quite a while to digest that mass of material," Russell warned. "I think it will take a truck."

"Yes," Warren conceded. "I have no doubt."

Warren was also now ready to begin to assemble a staff to work under Rankin. He recommended that the commission hire "perhaps half a dozen" experienced lawyers from around the country—in some cases, veteran trial lawyers drawn from nationally prominent law firms—and then match them up with promising, younger lawyers who would do most of the actual digging.

The young lawyers would be hired full-time, with their senior partners asked to contribute whatever time they could; they would be divided into two-man teams, each given responsibility for some part of the investigation. One team would do a complete investigation of Oswald's life—"traced from the day of his birth right down to the time he was assassinated," Warren said. A separate team would do the same for Ruby.

The other commissioners supported the concept. They raised no objection to Warren's plan to hire lawyers—and for the moment, only lawyers—to conduct the initial investigation. The seven commissioners, all of them lawyers too, seemed to assume from the start that a law school degree was the essential credential for members of the commission's staff.

In the wake of the shoddy FBI report, Russell was brave enough to say what some of the other commissioners might have been thinking—that the commission's staff would need to consider the possibility that the FBI was getting this wrong. He said there was a chance that the bureau, innocently or intentionally, would misstate the facts about the assassination. Someone on the staff, Russell said, should act as "a Devil's Advocate who would take this FBI report"—and whatever reports were eventually turned over by the CIA and other agencies—and "go through it and analyze every contradiction and every soft spot in it, just as if he were prosecuting them." There should be at least one staffer who would evaluate the evidence "as if he were going to use them to prosecute J. Edgar Hoover."

Ford raised a different issue. He said he wanted to be certain that lawyers hired for the staff would have no strong political views that might influence the investigation. "This is a serious concern I have, and I think we've got to be scrupulously careful in this regard," he said. The commission's staff members should not be "involved in one extreme or the other."

"I don't believe we should have ideologists either," Warren agreed. "We're looking for lawyers, not ideologists."

The conversation turned to other questions that had been raised, but not answered, in the FBI report. The commissioners had questions, especially, about Marina Oswald and Ruth Paine. The FBI report said that Oswald, although he was not living with his wife and children at the time, had stored his rifle in the Paine home until the morning of the assassination.

Boggs suggested that Marina might be tempted to flee home to Russia. "She's a Russian citizen, and she might just take off and leave," he said. Dulles said he was also "rather worried about that," given reports that Marina had written to the Soviet embassy in Washington before the assassination to ask about returning home to Russia.

McCloy had questions about another woman who, he thought, was central to the commission's investigation—Jacqueline Kennedy. It might be seen as distasteful, he acknowledged, but the panel needed to interview her as quickly as possible. The former First Lady was, in many ways, "the central witness" in the investigation. "She's the chief witness as to how those bullets hit her husband," McCloy said. "I don't think you should cross-examine her, but after all she was a witness right alongside of her husband when the bullet struck." She might have information that was available nowhere else. Wasn't it possible that the president had shared—only with her—some concern about dangers he might face in Dallas, and from whom? "I just think it's going to look strange if we don't" interview her, McCloy said.

McCloy traveled in many of the same social circles in New York and Washington as the Kennedy family, and he knew that Mrs. Kennedy had begun talking to friends—freely—about the assassination. The young widow seemed to find it cathartic to share even some of the gruesome details of what had happened. "I think it's a very delicate thing to do, but

I'm told that she's quite prepared to talk about it," McCloy told his fellow commissioners. "I've talked to one of the members of the family about it."

Warren hesitated, as he would so often do when the panel discussed the Kennedy family. The commission was just getting organized, the chief justice pointed out; it did not have enough information to "question witnesses in the formal way," especially the former First Lady. "When you're going to talk to someone like Mrs. Kennedy, I think we ought to know exactly what we want to find out from her."

McCloy questioned Warren's judgment; the delay in interviewing Mrs. Kennedy was a mistake, he said. "I think a month is going to go by before you're in that position and I think that is dangerous."

"Do you think she'll forget, Jack?" Warren asked.

"Yes," McCloy replied. "Your mind plays tricks on you. She's got it very definitely in mind now, and I'm told that she's physically in a position where she can do it." He suggested the commission ask Robert Kennedy for guidance on how to approach his sister-in-law. "You can talk to Bobby about that. He might have an idea."

Warren made no commitment on how—or when—Mrs. Kennedy would be interviewed. Years later, McCloy would look back on this exchange as evidence that the chief justice would be much too protective of Jacqueline Kennedy and her extended family.

There was a final item on the commission's agenda that day—how to deal with the crush of reporters waiting outside the meeting room at the archives, all of them hoping for some scrap of news about the commission's deliberations. Russell, now in his fourth decade of dealing with the Washington press corps, said it would be dangerous to allow the reporters to leave without giving them something. "You have to feed them a little because they expect it."

The chief justice agreed, and after the meeting ended the reporters were called into the room. Warren announced the opening of the commission's offices in the VFW building and briefly described the panel's plans to recruit a staff of lawyers. He told the journalists that the commission had just begun to review the FBI report and could not comment on its contents, although he noted that the commission would now request all of the evidence and witness statements the FBI had gathered. "You understand that reports we are receiving are merely summary reports of what happened—and in more or less skeleton form," he told the reporters. "We will have to see some of the materials upon which those reports are based."

He called an end to the impromptu news conference after a few minutes and finished by wishing the reporters a Merry Christmas.

That afternoon, the Associated Press and other wire services carried articles about the chief justice's comments. The articles were read within hours by FBI director Hoover, who was outraged to discover that Warren considered the multivolume FBI report as "merely" a summary of evidence in "skeleton form." The commission's inquiry was barely two weeks old, and the chief justice was engaged in "carping criticism" and "endeavoring to find fault with the FBI," Hoover said. The next day, he called in Inspector James R. Malley, a veteran FBI supervisor who had been named as the bureau's day-to-day liaison to the commission, to give him new orders. If Warren and the commissioners now wanted all of the bureau's raw information about the investigation, they would get it— every bit of it, including every report about every tip from every "nut" who claimed to have an answer to the assassination; Hoover's order to Malley meant the commission would be choked within days with tens of thousands of pieces of paper. "I want all reports, whether of substantial nature or so-called 'nut' reports to be sent" to the commission, Hoover told Malley. "I want nothing to be withheld irrespective of what the volume might amount to. . . . Since the Chief Justice had asked for it, we should give it to him."

THE OFFICES OF REPRESENTATIVE GERALD R. FORD
THE HOUSE OF REPRESENTATIVES
WASHINGTON, DC
TUESDAY, DECEMBER 17, 1963

The day after the meeting, Ford invited FBI assistant director DeLoach back to his offices on Capitol Hill, this time to share details of Warren's plans to complete the commission's investigation and release a final report "prior to July 1964, when the presidential campaigns will begin to get hot."

The two men also discussed the advance leaks of the conclusions of the FBI's report—the leaks that other commissioners were convinced had been orchestrated by the bureau. "I again went over very carefully with

Congressman Ford the fact the FBI had not had any 'leaks' whatsoever," DeLoach wrote later. He suggested to Ford that the leaks were coming from elsewhere—"from Deputy Attorney General Katzenbach and from the Justice Department, as well as from within the commission." DeLoach suggested that Warren himself was leaking information through his friend Drew Pearson. "I told Congressman Ford in strict confidence that apparently Chief Justice Warren was quite close to Drew Pearson and obviously used Pearson from time to time to get thoughts across to the general public."

Ford ended the conversation with a request. He and his family were about to leave for a skiing vacation in Michigan. "He wanted to take the FBI report with him yet he had no way of transporting it in complete safety," DeLoach wrote. "I told him I felt the Director would want him to borrow from us one of our agent briefcases that contains a lock. He stated this would be ideal and he would appreciate the loan of a briefcase very much." The FBI-issue briefcase was delivered to Ford the next day, with Hoover's compliments.

8

Lee Rankin was not the sort of man to draw attention to himself. In the 1960s, when remembering his years at the Justice Department, he was much more likely to salute the hard work of his colleagues than to boast about his own role as solicitor general. It was Rankin's family, not Rankin, who talked about the threats he had faced as a result of his work at the department, including a frightening incident in the late 1950s when they discovered a burning cross outside their home in the Virginia suburbs of Washington.

His teenage son Roger, who had left the dinner table to check on the family's dogs, first saw the flaming wooden cross that someone had planted in the yard. "It was probably six feet tall," he recalled years later. "There it was—a big, burning cross."

He remembered that even as they rushed out the front door to douse the flames with a garden hose, he saw nothing like fear on his father's face, even though his family was now almost certainly under threat by the Ku Klux Klan or some local band of racists. "He never expressed that kind of emotion—of fear or of worry," his daughter, Sara, said years later. "I can't remember him worrying about anything. He seemed to be always in control. He was reserved, self-effacing, quiet."

The cross-burners were never caught, although Rankin's colleagues were sure that he was being threatened because of his work at the department to expand the reach of federal civil rights laws. For several days after the incident, FBI agents were assigned to protect the family; the agents sat in an unmarked car on the street outside as the Rankins slept.

J. Lee Rankin—he had not used his first name, James, since childhood—had been recruited to the Justice Department by Attorney General Herbert Brownell, a fellow Nebraskan who had run Eisenhower's 1952 presidential campaign. Rankin, forty-five years old when he arrived in Washington, was first given the position of assistant attorney general for legal counsel, a prestigious post in which he acted as the department's top in-house lawyer. In 1956, he was named solicitor general, a job that made him the administration's chief lawyer in cases before the Supreme Court.

In both jobs, Rankin found himself in the front lines of the Justice Department's efforts to enforce the nation's civil rights laws in the face of violent opposition by segregationist groups. He helped draft the administration's legal briefs in support of black Kansas schoolchildren in the *Brown v. Board of Education* case. Chief Justice Warren had always been impressed by Rankin's no-nonsense, unflappable style during his appearances at the Supreme Court, especially when Rankin—a thin man whose thick glasses gave him an owlish, professorial look—argued for expansion of civil rights and civil liberties protections. In 1962, after Rankin left for private practice in New York, he returned to the court to argue on behalf of the American Civil Liberties Union in the landmark case known as *Gideon v. Wainwright*, in which the court agreed with the ACLU and ordered that criminal defendants had to be provided with a defense lawyer if they could not afford one.

On December 6, 1963, Warren telephoned Rankin in New York and offered him the job of general counsel on the assassination commission, and he asked Rankin to begin immediately. Later, both men remembered that Rankin put up a brief struggle over accepting the assignment, telling the chief justice that he was just starting to build his private law practice and that it would be difficult to leave New York. He warned Warren that some members of the commission might not want him, likely a reference to Senator Russell and Rankin's role in *Brown v. Board of Education* and other civil rights cases. But Warren was insistent, saying that he already had the approval of the full commission. He assured Rankin that the job would not require an extraordinary time commitment. "He said it would not last more than two or three months," Rankin recalled.

Warren and Rankin were Republicans of a similar stripe—progressives who took special pride in the history of the GOP as the party of Abraham Lincoln. They had both admired President Kennedy. "My dad was heartsick over the assassination," remembered Sara Rankin. The two men also shared a similar pride in their humble backgrounds; neither man was born to anything resembling privilege.

Rankin, a graduate of the University of Nebraska Law School, had always worked hard, sometimes obsessively so. His wife, Gertrude, urged him to reject Warren's offer. She told her children she feared the job would consume her husband to the point of endangering his health. She had seen it before during their years in Washington, when he would return home every night with a briefcase bulging with paperwork; he disappointed his children by setting aside every Sunday afternoon to read legal briefs and prepare himself for the workweek ahead at the Justice Department.

Rankin was a perfectionist who would ask a secretary, very politely, to retype a letter or a legal brief if there was the smallest typographical error; he did not like the appearance of correction fluid. "If you made a typo, you'd begin all over again," said his daughter, who sometimes helped him with secretarial work. "He wanted the letter to look right, even if you had to type it four or five times."

Warren and Rankin had a friendly but formal relationship during Rankin's years as solicitor general. That appeared to reflect Rankin's modesty and shyness more than anything else; he seemed unwilling to presume to consider himself a possible intimate of the chief justice, a man he revered. Now, at the commission, Rankin intended to work *for*—not so much *with*—Warren and the other commissioners. He was their employee, the attorney they had hired for this job. "The substantive decisions were all made by the commission," Rankin said later. "I didn't have authority to execute on my own." (His deference to authority and exquisite manners might explain why he—unlike Warren Olney, his former colleague at the Justice Department—had not made an enemy of J. Edgar Hoover.)

Within hours of Warren's call, Rankin sat down with a yellow legal pad in his apartment on Sutton Place on the East Side of Manhattan and began to outline how the investigation might be organized. Warren had agreed to allow him to divide his time between Washington and New

The hostility between FBI Director J. Edgar Hoover and Attorney General Robert Kennedy was no secret to their aides. It was Hoover who—in a brief telephone call minutes after the shots rang out in Dealey Plaza—notified Kennedy that his brother had been shot. In this photograph, the two men are seen at a White House ceremony on May 7, 1963.

President Johnson meets in the Oval Office with Richard Helms, the career intelligence operative named by Johnson to run the Central Intelligence Agency. Helms would later admit there were caveats to his promise of full cooperation with the Warren Commission; he admitted he told the commission nothing about the CIA's plots to kill Castro.

A formal portrait of the members of the Warren Commission, taken in the hearing room in the Washington, DC, headquarters of the Veterans of Foreign Wars, where the commission had its offices. *Left to right*: Representative Gerald R. Ford of Michigan, Representative Hale Boggs of Louisiana, Senator Richard B. Russell of Georgia, Chief Justice Earl Warren, Senator John Sherman Cooper of Kentucky, former World Bank president John J. McCloy, former Director of Central Intelligence Allen W. Dulles, and commission general counsel J. Lee Rankin.

LEFT: J. Lee Rankin, the commission's general counsel and a former United States solicitor general, led the commission's staff lawyers, who were divided into two-man teams made up of a "senior counsel" and a "junior" partner. In most cases, the junior lawyers did the bulk of the work. RIGHT: Norman Redlich, a New York University law professor, was the central editor and author of the final report. Rankin's decision to hire Redlich, linked by the FBI to left-wing groups the bureau considered subversive, would create a furor among the commissioners.

York, with the understanding that Rankin would conduct the commission's work by phone when he was back in Manhattan. Rankin quickly developed a routine and became a regular on the Eastern Airlines shuttle. "On Monday mornings, he was on the first shuttle out of New York down to Washington," his eldest son, Jim, remembered, "and then he would work all day Monday, all day Tuesday, and then Wednesday night he would come home, with tons of stuff in his briefcase."

Rankin got to work quickly in Washington, establishing his base at the newly opened Madison Hotel, a few blocks from his old offices at the Justice Department. He would work out of his hotel room until the commission was ready to move into its new offices on Capitol Hill.

Warren had given authority to Rankin to hire a staff of young lawyers, subject to the chief justice's veto. "He may have asked me about people sometimes, but I left it to Rankin," Warren said later. The chief justice did urge Rankin to look for young men—there appears to have been no discussion of hiring women—from different parts of the country, not just from the Boston–New York–Washington corridor that produced most of the government's top lawyers. (Warren did not need to remind Rankin that the Boston-to-Washington corridor had produced neither of them.) The chief justice told Rankin that he "wanted the men to be independent and not to have any connections that might later be embarrassing."

Rankin recruited one of the staff's first lawyers from the Justice Department. For weeks after the assassination, Robert Kennedy had been away from his offices at the department's headquarters building on Pennsylvania Avenue; his staff could see that he was too deep in mourning to carry out any but his essential duties. That left Deputy Attorney General Nicholas Katzenbach in charge, and he assigned a promising young lawyer from the department's criminal division, thirty-two-year-old Howard Willens, to serve as the department's liaison to the commission. Willens, a Michigan native who had graduated seven years earlier from Yale Law School, was told that the assignment would last several months and that he would remain on the department's payroll.

Willens arrived at the commission's office on Tuesday, December 17. Rankin was immediately impressed by the take-charge young lawyer, and he asked Willens if he would consider working for the commission full-time—both as the Justice Department's representative and also as a senior member of its staff. Three days later, with Katzenbach's approval, Willens signed on.

Challenged years later about whether his dual roles had posed a conflict of interest, Willens insisted there had been none, even though a central question before the commission was whether the assassination was somehow linked to foreign policy decisions of the Kennedy administration—decisions in which Robert Kennedy had a central role, especially about Cuba. "No one could seriously maintain that the Department of Justice headed by Attorney General Kennedy had any interest in this investigation other than the most thorough and honest canvassing of all the available facts," Willens said. Later, some of the commission's critics would maintain precisely that.

Rankin asked Willens to help him search for other young lawyers, and Willens called friends and colleagues at the Justice Department, as well as prominent law firms and law school deans around the country, to ask for the names of candidates. The search quickly reflected his ties to Yale, as well as to his many friends and associates who were graduates of his alma mater's great rival, Harvard Law School, and a handful of other elite law schools. "I do concede that there is here a predominance of lawyers from Yale and Harvard," he said later in reviewing the staff list.

Rankin was eager to hire a prominent black lawyer. Given how much he valued his reputation as a civil rights advocate, Rankin understood how hypocritical he—and the chief justice—might look if the commission did otherwise. He thought there was an obvious candidate: William Coleman of Philadelphia, and Warren said he was delighted by the suggestion. Coleman, forty-three, a magna cum laude graduate of Harvard Law School, had become the first black law clerk in the history of the Supreme Court when he was hired in 1948 by Justice Felix Frankfurter. Even while establishing himself as one of the nation's most sought-after corporate litigators—his client list would eventually grow to include many of the nation's most powerful corporations, including Ford Motor Company—Coleman had become a key behind-the-scenes figure in the civil rights movement. He was coauthor of the key legal brief filed on behalf of the black schoolchildren in *Brown v. Board of Education*.

Rankin also decided that he wanted his friend Norman Redlich, a thirty-eight-year-old law professor at New York University, to join the staff as his chief deputy. Redlich had befriended Rankin two years earlier, when he invited Rankin, then newly arrived in New York, to join the NYU faculty to teach part-time.

Rankin thought that Redlich was precisely what he needed in a deputy, and he seemed untroubled that the Bronx-born Redlich had no background in criminal law or in anything that could be labeled as investigative work; Redlich's specialty was tax law. Within days, he was on his way to Washington—the law school was closed until January for the winter holiday—at which point he would also begin to commute between Washington and New York.

In his early hiring decisions, Rankin said later, he was well aware of Ford's insistence—and Warren's agreement—that the staff members hired by the commission have no extreme political ties. And from what he knew of Redlich, there was no problem. Rankin saw a man much like himself—and like the chief justice, for that matter. Redlich, yet another graduate of Yale's law school, was deeply committed to civil rights and civil liberties. His involvement in social justice issues had begun early: as an undergraduate at Williams College in Williamstown, Massachusetts, in the 1940s, he organized a protest against the one barbershop on the main commercial street in Williamstown over its refusal to cut the hair of black students. The shop abandoned the policy.

Rankin would later insist that he had known nothing about Redlich's ties in the 1950s and early 1960s to civil liberties and civil rights groups that J. Edgar Hoover believed were fronts for the Communist Party. Rankin said he learned—too late and much to his dismay—that the FBI maintained a thick file on Redlich and his links to organizations that the bureau had labeled as "subversive."

9

The sealed envelope containing the autopsy photographs was forwarded from the Bethesda Naval Hospital to the chief justice at his chambers at the Supreme Court. An FBI inventory prepared on the night of the autopsy reported that all of the photos were four inches by five inches—twenty-two of them in color, eighteen in black and white.

In his fourteen-year career as a county prosecutor in Oakland, California, how many autopsy photos had Warren seen—hundreds, thousands? Back in the homicide squad in the DA's office in Alameda County, it was a routine part of the job—best done on an empty stomach—to review autopsy and crime-scene photos and decide which of them could be shown to a jury without risk that some of the jurors would be so revolted that they would rush from the courtroom.

Now, all these years later, Warren thought he still had a strong stomach. But the photos of the president's autopsy were awful in a way he could not have imagined. "I saw the pictures when they came from Bethesda Naval Hospital, and they were so horrible that I could not sleep well for nights," he later wrote. The worst, he told a friend, were of the president's head, which was "split almost wide open." The skull was "disintegrated."

Warren had been appalled by news reports, beginning only weeks after the assassination, about plans in Dallas and elsewhere to establish "museums" to commemorate the president's death. "The president was hardly buried before people with ghoulish minds began putting together artifacts of the assassination," the chief justice wrote. Some of the museum promoters—"these sideshow barkers," as he described them—announced their intention to try to purchase Oswald's weapons from the government for the central display cases. Warren remembered reading that the museum promoters "offered as much as ten thousand dollars for the rifle alone. . . . They also wanted to buy from the family the clothes of Oswald, his revolver with which Officer Tippit was murdered, various things at the Depository and they were even making inquiries about the availability of the clothes of President Kennedy They also, of course, wanted pictures of his head."

Now that he had seen the photos for himself, Warren said he did not struggle about what to do with them.* It was an easy decision: they would be locked away, forever, unless the Kennedy family decided otherwise. No one outside the family had the right to see them—and that included the other members of the commission and its staff, Warren decided. He ordered all of the autopsy photos, as well as all of the X-rays, be sent to the Justice Department, where Robert Kennedy would have control over them.

Warren convinced himself that the commission did not need the photos and X-rays, since the navy doctors who had conducted the autopsy were available to testify and the commission had full access to the written autopsy report, which contained hand-drawn diagrams of the wounds to the president's body. The photos and X-rays were of no special value, Warren declared. The commission, he said, would have "the convincing testimony of the Naval doctors who performed the autopsy to establish the cause of death, entry, exit and course of the bullets."

Other horrifying images from the day of the assassination were beyond Warren's control. The public had already begun to see portions of the astonishing amateur film taken by a Dallas women's wear manufacturer, Abraham Zapruder, who had captured the assassination on his Bell & Howell Zoomatic home-movie camera. The fifty-eight-year-old Zapruder had been

---

* In his memoirs, which were published posthumously in 1977, Warren revealed that he had reviewed the photos during the commission's investigation, although he did not disclose exactly when in 1963 or 1964 the review had taken place.

standing near a grassy bit of Dealey Plaza a few feet from the Texas School Book Depository, a spot that reporters covering the aftermath of the assassination quickly began to refer to as the "grassy knoll."

On Monday, December 9, Warren's press officer at the Supreme Court, Bert Whittington, got a call from a representative of *Life* magazine, which had bought the film from Zapruder. In its "John F. Kennedy Memorial Issue," the week before, *Life* had reproduced thirty frames of the film, beginning with an image of the president's limousine as it began to move slowly down Elm Street in front of book depository. Published in black and white, the frames captured images of the president being struck by a bullet, apparently in the neck, and then dropping into his wife's lap; later frames showed the First Lady trying to climb onto the trunk of the car in what the magazine's editors described in a caption as a "pathetic search for help."

In that issue, *Life* did not explain to its readers what it had left out— that the full twenty-six seconds of film were far more horrifying and that the film was in color. The magazine chose, in particular, not to publish the frame that captured the moment a bullet struck the president's head, blowing away much of the right side of his brain in a halo of pinkish, bloody mist. "We felt that publishing that grisly picture would constitute an unnecessary affront to the Kennedy family and to the president's memory," recalled Richard Stolley, the *Life* correspondent who bought the film from Zapruder on behalf of the magazine.

In his memo to Warren, Whittington wrote that the magazine was offering the commission a copy of the entire film, in color. Warren returned the memo to Whittington with a handwritten note asking him to contact *Life* immediately and thank them for their cooperation. "We will undoubtedly want to see it and will advise," he wrote.

A few days later, a copy of Zapruder's film arrived in Washington, and Warren had a chance to see for himself what the magazine had chosen not to show its readers.

THE OFFICES OF THE COMMISSION
WASHINGTON, DC
DECEMBER 1963

By late December, Rankin and Willens—the younger man's authority grew by the day—decided on a final structure for the staff, which would initially total fifteen lawyers. Most of them would be assigned to two-man teams led by a "senior counsel" whose partner—a younger, less experienced lawyer—would have the title of "junior counsel."

With Warren's approval, Rankin and Willens settled on six areas of investigation. Area 1 would reconstruct a time line of everything that happened from the moment President Kennedy departed the White House on Thursday, November 21, to begin his Texas trip, until the moment his corpse returned to lie in state at the White House in the predawn hours of Saturday, November 23. Area 2 would gather evidence to establish—conclusively, it was hoped—the identity of the president's assassin, presumably Oswald. Area 3 would reconstruct Oswald's life. Area 4 would study the possibility that there had been a foreign conspiracy, with a focus, it was assumed, on the Soviet Union and Cuba. Area 5 would construct the biography of Jack Ruby and look for any possible connection between him and Oswald. Area 6 would investigate the quality of the protection provided to President Kennedy by the Secret Service, as well as the history of law-enforcement efforts to protect other presidents from harm.

Warren had little trouble coming up with the names of prominent, well-established lawyers for the "senior counsel" jobs. They were the sorts of lawyers the chief justice and Rankin had worked with every day of their careers for decades. William Coleman was asked to lead Area 4—the "conspiracy" team—since he had experience in foreign policy issues. That year, Coleman had become an adviser to the government's newly created Arms Control and Disarmament Agency, so he already had a government security clearance.

Rankin recommended Francis Adams, fifty-nine, a Manhattan litigator who had been New York City's police commissioner in the mid-1950s, while Warren offered the name of Albert Jenner, fifty-six, who was a name partner of a powerhouse Chicago law firm, Raymond, Mayer, Jenner & Block, later renamed simply Jenner & Block. Both men agreed to serve. Adams, who obviously had experience with crime scenes, was assigned to Area 1, which would reconstruct the events of the day of the assassination. Jenner was given responsibility for Area 3 and the investigation of Oswald's past.

Warren was eager to hire an old friend from California, sixty-one-year-old Joseph Ball of Long Beach, who was among the state's most successful criminal-defense lawyers and also taught at the law school at the University of Southern California. To Warren, Ball was a living rebuttal to the many lawyers in the East who still assumed their counterparts on the Pacific Coast were somehow less talented or sophisticated. Ball was put in charge of the Area 2 team, which would determine if Oswald was in fact the assassin.

With lawyers hired from the East, West, and Midwest, Warren also wanted representation from the South. Congressman Boggs came up with the name of a fellow Louisianan: fifty-two-year-old Leon Hubert, the former district attorney of New Orleans and a law professor at Tulane University who was then in private practice. Hubert was put in charge of Area 5 and the effort to reconstruct Ruby's life story.

THE OFFICE OF THE DISTRICT ATTORNEY
PHILADELPHIA, PENNSYLVANIA
TUESDAY, DECEMBER 31, 1963

Arlen Specter was a young man on the rise in Philadelphia, his adopted hometown. In 1963, the year he turned thirty-three, he was an assistant district attorney, and that June he became a local hero—certainly a hero in the district attorney's office—after obtaining the conviction of several of the city's most powerful Teamsters officials on racketeering charges. He was so impressive in the case that Attorney General Robert Kennedy called Specter to Washington for a face-to-face meeting to try to recruit him to join the Justice Department to assist in the prosecution of Jimmy Hoffa, the Teamsters' national leader. Specter turned down the offer, in part, he said, because he hoped to run for local office in Philadelphia.

Colleagues in the district attorney's office, as well his adversaries on the defense table, saw Specter as unusually self-confident, often to the point of being cocky and arrogant. Specter did not necessarily disagree with the description.

The recruiting call from the commission came on New Year's Eve. It was about five thirty that afternoon, and Specter was still at his office, "trying to concoct an excuse for arriving home so late," he remembered. His wife, Joan, was planning a New Year's Eve party that night with some friends. The caller was Howard Willens, a classmate from Yale Law School. Now in his second week working for Chief Justice Warren on the assassination commission, Willens urged Specter to come to Washington to join the investigation.

Specter turned down the offer, citing the appeals court battles to come in the Teamsters case. At the party that night, however, he was convinced to change his mind. He mentioned Willens's call to his wife and their guests and—to his annoyance, he insisted later—their response was unanimous: it was his duty to take the job. "They were all very excited about me going off to war—to fight to the last drop of Arlen Specter's blood," Specter said. He called Willens back and accepted the job.

Two weeks later, Specter arrived in Washington to discover the city buried under heavy snow. He trudged to the VFW building on Capitol Hill, where he was greeted by Willens and introduced to Lee Rankin, who, he remembered, was "paternal and soft-spoken, with a light humor." Rankin explained the organization of the staff and told Specter that, given his youth, he would be the junior member of whichever two-man team he joined. Since he was among the first lawyers hired, Specter was given his choice of assignments. He selected Area 1, which would focus on Kennedy's activities in the final hours of his life—and on the murder itself. "It seemed the most compelling," Specter said. He did not want to spend that night in Washington—he wanted to sleep in his own bed in Philadelphia—so he filled his briefcase with some of the early investigative reports about the assassination and returned to Washington's Union Station for the train ride home. "The paperwork would keep me busy for much of the week ahead," he figured. He told Rankin he planned to return to Washington—full-time—in several days.

In the train, he sat down next to an empty seat "so I could read some of the material, taking care to shield it from other passengers." He remembered that he turned quickly to the autopsy report from the Bethesda Naval Hospital and found it sickening to read, especially the description of Kennedy's head wound. "As I read through the grisly details of the president's wounds, I felt nauseated and depressed."

And the autopsy report was, apart from a few crude anatomical drawings, just words on paper. Specter could only imagine how he would react when he had the chance—shortly, he assumed—to see the actual autopsy photos, as well as the X-rays of the president's body. As a career prosecutor, he understood from the start how valuable those photos and X-rays would be.

10

In the first days of January 1964, David Slawson, a thirty-two-year-old associate at one of Denver's most prominent law firms, found himself busy with clients' work. Not overwhelmed, just busy: partners at Davis, Graham & Stubbs admired Slawson's ability to focus, almost totally, on the complicated corporate work in front of him and to get it done in a hurry. Unlike some of the other associates, the Harvard-educated Slawson did not need to stay at his desk late into the night to keep clients satisfied; he liked to get home at five if he could. He had not allowed his work to suffer even in the first days after Kennedy's assassination. Slawson had loved the president and was shattered by his murder. He had worked in Kennedy's 1960 campaign, initially at the urging of his law firm's star partner, Byron "Whizzer" White, Slawson's first mentor at Davis Graham. White, a lifelong Democrat, had managed the Kennedy campaign in Colorado. Within days of the election, White left Denver to become deputy attorney general under Robert Kennedy at the Justice Department; in 1962, he was named to the Supreme Court.

Slawson had hoped to follow White to Washington. With Kennedy in the White House, the nation's capital had glamour and star power it had not known in Slawson's lifetime; for many young, ambitious lawyers,

Washington had suddenly become the place to be. It would take Kennedy's death, however, to get Slawson his invitation to the capital.

The call came in early January, when Slawson picked up his office phone and heard the voice of a man he did not know—Howard Willens, who identified himself as a Justice Department lawyer assisting Chief Justice Warren in organizing the investigation of the president's assassination. Willens had been directed to Slawson by a mutual friend, a State Department lawyer who had been a classmate of Slawson's at Harvard. Willens asked if Slawson would be interested in joining the commission, and Slawson jumped at the offer; the only condition, he told Willens, was that his partners at the law firm would need to approve a leave of absence. There was no second-guessing about this, Slawson remembered. It would be thrilling to be part of the investigation to determine "what the hell really happened" in Dallas.

To Slawson's relief, the firm's partners quickly gave their permission, with the understanding that he would be gone no more than two or three months. He made plans to leave for Washington immediately. There was no reason for delay: he was unmarried and had no steady girlfriend, so nothing except work tied him to Denver.

Before departing, he began reading everything he could find in the local papers about the assassination and about the commission. He turned up copies of the *New York Times*—a precious commodity in faraway Denver at the time—and read about the commission's plans to create teams of investigators, each focusing on a different aspect of the assassination. He was especially intrigued to read about the team that would investigate the possibility of a foreign conspiracy.

For many of his new colleagues, the "conspiracy" team seemed an unappealing assignment. The FBI appeared insistent that Oswald, and Oswald alone, had killed the president, and so the conspiracy team would probably be off on a wild-goose chase. Slawson, however, thought he was ideally suited for the work. He imagined it would be, at heart, a logic puzzle, in which investigators would have to tease out answers on the basis of little or no concrete information. He knew little about the Cold War beyond what he read in the paper each morning, but he assumed that if the Russians or the Cubans had been involved in the assassination, they would have tried to hide every bit of evidence pointing to their guilt.

Since his childhood in Grand Rapids, Michigan, Slawson had been good at puzzles. He had the ability, in the quiet of his mind, to sort through a complicated math or science problem. He did not necessarily need to see pictures or diagrams to work his way through a puzzle; he could do it in his head. That explained why mathematics and science had come so easily for him. He had originally dreamed of becoming a physicist. It was the career path he had first pursued at Amherst College, where he graduated first in his class, in 1953. Despite the shyness that would define him all his life, he was as popular with his classmates as he was smart—one classmate remembered him as Amherst's "golden boy"—and he was elected president of his class. Slawson then arrived at Princeton for graduate studies in physics. He planned to focus on quantum mechanics, the branch of physics that explained the behavior of the tiniest elements of the universe—subatomic particles that could never be seen by the most powerful microscope, let alone by a human eye. He remembered the thrill at catching a glimpse of the world's most famous physicist, Albert Einstein, who had lived in Princeton since fleeing Nazi Germany in the 1930s. "Sometimes you'd be walking by, and there he was," Slawson said.

What changed Slawson's life—and pulled him away from science—was what he saw on a television screen in his apartment building at Princeton in 1954. Between classes he sat, transfixed, by the live coverage of what would become known as the Army-McCarthy hearings—the Senate hearings that effectively signaled the end of the Red-baiting McCarthy era. Slawson found a hero in Joseph Welch, the army's chief lawyer, whose testimony before Senator Joseph McCarthy turned into a showdown over the senator's claim that the military employed Communists in defense plants. In his bravest moment, Welch turned to McCarthy and asked: "Have you no sense of decency, sir?" This, Slawson decided, was what he really wanted to do—to be a lawyer who, like Welch, took on bullies while engaging in the great issues of the day. "This is the life I want," he remembered thinking. He had already begun to worry that a career in physics would separate him too much from the rest of the world. "It wasn't that I didn't love physics," he said. "It was because the life I could foresee in physics was one of cloistered work, doing long, difficult mathematical equations—analyzing the size of galaxies and stuff—and I thought no, no, I don't want to do that."

A year later, after earning a master's degree, Slawson left Princeton to join the army; he decided to enlist rather than wait to be drafted. While in uniform he applied to Harvard Law School and was accepted. He paid for Harvard through the GI Bill and graduated near the top of his class, which earned him an editor's post on the law review. After that, Slawson could have had his pick of jobs at law firms in New York, but he was intrigued by the idea of working for a small firm, in a smaller city, especially one where the outdoors beckoned. Denver, he thought, was an obvious choice since he loved mountain sports.

At Davis, Graham & Stubbs, Byron White had an eye for young talent, and he asked that Slawson be assigned to work for him. It was a heady thing to be associated with White, who had been a celebrity in Colorado for decades, first as an all-American halfback at the University of Colorado. After playing professional football for the Pittsburgh Pirates (the name was later changed to the Steelers), White won a Rhodes scholarship to Oxford University and then enrolled at Yale Law School. As a football player and as a lawyer—in almost everything he did, in fact— "Byron was a superstar," Slawson recalled. It was White who turned Slawson into a Kennedy supporter. In the 1960 election, Slawson had planned to vote for Adlai Stevenson, but White pressed him to reconsider. "He gave me a bunch of stuff to read about Kennedy, and I read it, and I said, yes, I'll switch." White then made an arrangement with the firm that allowed his young protégé to work part-time on the Kennedy campaign.

Slawson was in the firm's offices on November 22, the day of the assassination; a startled secretary broke the news to him. After the announcement of Kennedy's death, the firm shut for the day. "Everyone was told they could go home," said Slawson, whose apartment was walking distance from the firm. "I was tremendously moved. I think I went home in tears." When Oswald was murdered two days later, Slawson watched the scene on television, thinking to himself that it was almost too much to comprehend. It did not occur to him that some larger conspiracy—first to kill the president, then to kill the president's assassin— might explain what was happening. "I just thought, The world is going crazy."

Within a week of the call from Willens, Slawson was on his way east to Washington, driving across the country from Colorado in a Buick sedan that his father had lent him. "It was one of those huge things, with fins, so inappropriate for me." He wanted to reach Washington as quickly as possible. "I didn't have much money, so I would drive as far as I could each day." He arrived in Washington on Sunday night, January 19—it was the first time he had ever been in the capital—and found a room at a cheap motel. The next morning, he pulled on a coat and tie and showed up at the commission's offices, where he was introduced to Willens and Rankin. He did not remember being asked what assignment he wanted. Instead, he was told that he would be the junior member of the "conspiracy" team, working under William Coleman. Slawson was delighted; it was exactly the assignment he wanted.

Slawson did not know Coleman's name, although he was impressed when he learned that his new partner had also graduated at the top of his class at Harvard and that he had been involved in *Brown v. Board of Education*. It was the first time that Slawson had worked closely with a black lawyer. He did not recall feeling intimidated by the assignment that he and Coleman were given. They were being asked to determine if a foreign government—most likely, the Soviet Union or Cuba—had just killed the president of the United States, an act that might easily lead to a nuclear war. "I wasn't overwhelmed," Slawson said, "I was thrilled." That was true of many of his new colleagues. "I don't think I ever doubted my intellectual ability," Slawson said. "I don't think any of us did."

He got to work immediately. That afternoon he was asked to go to the lobby of the VFW building to meet someone who claimed to have evidence that would point to a conspiracy in the assassination. Slawson went downstairs and encountered a white-haired, well-dressed man—in coat and tie—who appeared to be in his late forties. At first, the man seemed reasonably articulate and coherent. "I didn't want to cut him off, because maybe the guy had something," Slawson recalled. Two hours later, an exasperated Slawson realized that "I had a paranoid nut on my hands." The secret of the Kennedy assassination, the man said, could be found in a message written on a piece of paper that had been buried beneath a rock somewhere in Switzerland. "He wanted us to fly him to Switzerland, where he would point out the rock," Slawson said.

After the man finally left, Slawson kicked himself for having wasted so much time listening to the man's delusions. Later, he realized that the experience had been valuable. In his first hours on the commission's staff, he had learned that many people who, at first, seemed sober witnesses with important information to share about the assassination were in fact "nutty as a fruitcake."

Slawson recalled being introduced to Coleman that Friday, when

Coleman made what would become his one-day-a-week visit from Phila-delphia. The two men formed a close, frictionless partnership. Like sev-eral of the "senior" lawyers, Coleman planned to work only part-time on the investigation. He had warned Warren and Rankin that his appear-ances in Washington would have to be sporadic because of his caseload back at his firm. It was Slawson who would do most of the digging and writing, and that suited Slawson fine.

Early on, Slawson kept an open mind on whether the president had been killed in a foreign conspiracy. Coleman, however, was more suspicious. "At the beginning, I really thought it was the Russians or the Cubans," he said, remembering how he feared the investigation might turn up evidence that would force the United States to go to war.

For several weeks, Slawson rarely left his small office on the fourth floor of the VFW building. He had thousands of pages of documents to read. He and his new colleagues were being flooded with classified files—many of them stamped TOP SECRET—from the FBI and CIA. Given his focus on possible foreign conspiracies, Slawson knew that he, more than most of the other staff members, would need to understand the CIA and how it oper-ated. He was excited to realize that he would soon meet some real spies.

In dealing with the CIA, Slawson believed the commission might have an extraordinary resource in one of its members: Allen Dulles, who had led the CIA from 1953 until his ouster in 1961 after the Bay of Pigs fiasco. Dulles's forced retirement produced surprisingly few hard feelings between him and President Kennedy. "He dealt with his ouster with a great deal of dignity, and never attempted to shift the blame," Robert Kennedy said later. "The President was very fond of him, as was I." It was Robert Ken-nedy, President Johnson said, who had recommended Dulles's appoint-ment to the Warren Commission.

Slawson assumed that if the CIA had information tying Oswald to a conspiracy, Dulles would know how to ferret it out. But that was before he actually met Dulles. When the two men were finally introduced, Slawson found the former spymaster to be surprisingly doddering and fragile. He still resembled a "boarding-school master," in the words of Richard Helms, his former deputy at the CIA, with "parted gray hair, care-fully trimmed moustache, tweeds and his preferred rimless, oval glasses." But by early 1964, Slawson thought, Dulles had the look of a schoolmaster in ill health and well past retirement.

He seemed much older than his seventy years. It had been that way since the Bay of Pigs. Robert Kennedy recalled that Dulles had "looked like living death" in his final days at the CIA: "He had gout and had trouble walking, and he was always putting his head in his hands." The gout lingered into his service on the Warren Commission. He often came into the offices of the commission and padded around in bedroom slippers because shoes were too painful. Years later, after learning how much Dulles had known—and possibly withheld—from the commission, Slawson still wanted to believe the best about him. He suspected that Dulles, after the humiliation of his ouster from the agency and in the haze of his final years, had simply forgotten many of the most important secrets he had once known.

11

In the first hours after the assassination, the CIA's number-two official, Deputy Director Richard Helms, decided he had to bring some order to the frantic search at CIA headquarters for information about the president's murder. Director of Central Intelligence John McCone, who had no real background in intelligence issues before joining the CIA in 1961, was content to leave major decisions about the investigation to Helms, a career officer who was the agency's real spymaster. On November 23, the day after the assassination, Helms created a team of about thirty analysts gathered from around Langley to search for evidence about Oswald and any possible foreign conspiracy. At a meeting of his deputies that morning, Helms announced that John Whitten, a forty-three-year-old CIA veteran who had often handled special projects for Helms, would lead the team.

Whitten's real name would not have been recognized by some of his colleagues, at least not by those who knew him through the paperwork that his office produced. He was known on paper by one of his agency-approved pseudonyms, John Scelso; the Scelso name appeared on internal cables in which the agency wanted to keep the number of people who knew his real identity to a minimum.

When President Johnson created the assassination commission a week after the president's murder, Whitten, a sometimes abrasive man who started his intelligence career as an army interrogator, was given the additional responsibility of day-to-day contact with the commission's staff. At the time, he was chief of the agency's covert operations in Mexico and Central America, a job he had held for about eight months. His branch was known as WH-3—the third branch of the Western Hemisphere division of the CIA's Clandestine Services—and was responsible for all American espionage operations in the area that stretched from the U.S.-Mexican border to the southern borders of Panama.

Like so many of his colleagues, Whitten did not go home at all on the night of November 22. He remained at the agency until the next day, as the CIA gathered up intelligence about Oswald. Whitten discovered what he said was a modest agency file on Oswald as a result of his attempted defection to the Soviet Union in 1959 and his return to the United States three years later. Far more intriguing, Whitten thought, were the reports from his CIA colleagues in Mexico who had conducted surveillance of Oswald during his mysterious trip there in September.

At the meeting on November 23, Helms told the others that Whitten would have "broad powers" and that all information about the assassination should be directed to him, even if that broke traditional lines of reporting. As Whitten recalled it, Helms announced that Whitten "was to be in charge of the investigation, that no one in the agency was to have any conversations with anyone outside the agency, including the Warren Commission and the Federal Bureau of Investigation, concerning the Kennedy assassination without my being present." Whitten thought Helms had entrusted him with the assignment because "I had investigated a number of other giant operations of absolutely critical importance for him over the years and had come up, you know, with the right answers."

Among the others in Helms's office for the Saturday meeting, Whitten recalled, was James Jesus Angleton, the agency's counterintelligence director—the "mole hunter" who was responsible for detecting the efforts of foreign spy agencies to infiltrate the CIA with double agents. Angleton's presence in a room was always troubling to Whitten. The two men had clashed repeatedly over their careers, especially when Whitten reviewed spy operations that somehow involved Angleton. "None of the senior officials at the agency were ever able to cope with him," Whitten said.

Angleton, then forty-six, was as eccentric and secretive a figure as anyone who worked at the agency. Whitten thought of him as a sinister force, a man with a hawk-like stare who was driven by paranoid suspicion of Communist infiltration of the CIA. Inside the agency, it was understood that Angleton's paranoia was the result of the treachery of his once-close friend Kim Philby, the high-ranking British spy who turned out to be a KGB mole. Angleton had a "sense of dread of foreign conspiracies and an over-suspiciousness" that was simply "bizarre," Whitten recalled. The Yale-educated Angleton, who was raised in Europe, reveled in his reputation for Anglophilic eccentricity, including his dedication to the hobby of orchid growing and his love of poetry. He also reveled in secrecy, so much so that no one—not even Helms, his supposed boss—seemed to know what Angleton was actually up to. It was obvious he enjoyed the confusion—or, in Whitten's view, the chaos—that he created. Drawing on the words of the poet T. S. Eliot, Angleton was fond of describing the work of counterintelligence as a "wilderness of mirrors."

"Everything that Angleton did was so secret," Whitten remembered. "Several times in my career, I was appointed to investigate or handle or look into investigations that Angleton was running. This always caused bitter feelings—the most bitter feelings." When he was asked by Helms or others to confront Angleton, Whitten did it with trepidation. "I used to go in fingering my insurance policy, thinking about notifying my next of kin."

Angleton had a portfolio of responsibilities that went beyond counterintelligence. Part of his power derived from his close friendship with FBI director Hoover. Whatever the rivalry between the CIA and the bureau, the two men shared a similar fixation on the dangers of Communism, and the Soviet Union in particular. "He had enormously influential contacts with J. Edgar Hoover," Whitten said of Angleton. In turn, Angleton was "extremely protective of the FBI" and "would not allow any criticism of them or any kind of rivalry." Whitten figured that was part of the reason why he, not Angleton, was given responsibility for the Oswald investigation. Initially, Helms may have feared that Angleton would help his friends at the FBI cover up blunders they had made in their surveillance of Oswald before the assassination. "One of the reasons that Helms gave me the case in the first place was that Angleton was so close to the FBI," Whitten said. "The FBI could be extremely clannish and protective of their own interests. I think that J. Edgar Hoover and others wanted to make very, very sure that they could not be criticized, and they wanted all the facts before they would let anybody else know anything."

Angleton's influence also extended to several of the CIA's most important overseas spy stations, which were run by his friends and protégés, including Winston Scott, the station chief in Mexico City. And both Angleton and Scott were close to Allen Dulles.

Whitten admitted he took some pleasure from Angleton's discomfort about the Oswald investigation. "In the early stages Mr. Angleton was not able to influence the course of the investigation, which was a source of great bitterness to him," Whitten recalled. "He was extremely embittered that I was entrusted with the investigation and he wasn't."

Believing that he had Helms's full support, Whitten went to work to piece together Oswald's life story and to understand his possible motives for killing Kennedy. Much of Whitten's time was spent reading through stacks of paperwork that related to the assassination. "We were flooded with cable traffic, with reports, suggestions, allegations from all over the world, and these things had to be checked out," he said. "We dropped almost everything else and I put a lot of my officers to work on tracing names, analyzing files." Much of it was "weirdo stuff," tying Oswald to every sort of coconspirator, including space aliens, he recalled.

Whitten said he knew nothing about Oswald, including his name, before Kennedy's murder. Although the Mexico City station answered to Whitten's staff at the WH-3 branch and had dispatched several cables to headquarters that fall about the surveillance of Oswald during his trip to Mexico, Whitten did not recall seeing any of them. That was not surprising, he said, since at the time Oswald appeared to be just another of the "small-potatoes defectors" and "kooks" who turned up occasionally in the Mexican capital.

According to Whitten, several American soldiers and defense-industry workers approached the Russian embassy in Mexico City in the 1950s and early 1960s to defect or sell secrets. They were detected so frequently by the CIA's Mexico City station that Hoover, who was routinely briefed on the cases so the FBI could track potential spies when they returned to the United States, "used to glow every time he thought of the Mexico [City] station—this was one of our outstanding areas of cooperation with the FBI," Whitten said.

Whitten shared Hoover's admiration for the Mexico City station—and especially for Scott, who "was as good a station chief as we had, and you could fairly say that he had the best station in the world." Under Scott, the station had developed a network of paid informants throughout the Mexican government and among the country's major political parties. According to Whitten, Scott also oversaw the CIA's most extensive and sophisticated electronic surveillance operation in the world. Whitten said that every phone line going in and out of both the Soviet and the Cuban embassies in Mexico City was tapped by Scott's station—about thirty lines in all. There were banks of CIA surveillance cameras around both embassies.

Whitten thought that explained why some of the information about Oswald had been slow to reach CIA headquarters in the weeks after Oswald's visit. Scott and his staff were victims of their own success. The Mexico City station was overwhelmed by a backlog of surveillance tapes—tapes that needed to be translated into English and transcribed—and photographs.

Whitten recalled that he immediately began to pursue a question that he knew the Warren Commission and other investigators would want answered: Given the bizarre circumstances of his aborted defection to the Soviet Union, had Oswald ever worked for the CIA? The answer, Whitten said he quickly discovered, was no. "Oswald was a person of a type who would never have been recruited by the agency to work behind the Iron Curtain or anywhere else. . . . Oswald's whole pattern of life was that of a very badly, emotionally unbalanced young man."

Whitten said he was told by Helms to cooperate fully with the Warren Commission, except when it came to divulging the details of how the CIA actually gathered information—"sources and methods," in the agency's jargon. He said the commission was kept ignorant about the CIA's electronic surveillance programs in Mexico City and elsewhere, at least at the start. "We were sure to give them everything when we thought we could do that without revealing how, exactly, we got the information," Whitten recalled. He said the CIA was particularly concerned that the existence of the wiretapping and photo-surveillance programs in Mexico City might become public, which would tip off the Soviets and Cubans and destroy the programs' value. "We wondered whether divulging this to them might not unnecessarily compromise forever our capability," Whitten said. "There was no nefarious reason for our not giving it to them.

It was simply that we did not consider it vitally relevant and we wanted to protect our sources."

The frenzy at CIA headquarters in the hours after the assassination was matched by that of the agency's Mexico City station, then housed on the top floor of the U.S. embassy on the Paseo de la Reforma, a central thoroughfare in the heart of the Mexican capital. Scott seemed to understand instantly the questions he would face from Langley and from Washington. Just a few weeks earlier, his station had conducted a supposedly intensive surveillance operation on the man who had apparently just killed the president of the United States. The station had secretly recorded telephone calls made by Oswald—and about Oswald—during several days that fall, and the agency was trying to determine if its surveillance cameras had caught Oswald's image during his visits to the Soviet and Cuban embassies. Some of the wiretap transcripts had been marked "urgent" and sent straight to Scott's desk, his files showed. Could the CIA—and its Mexico City station, in particular—have done anything to stop Oswald?

Scott was a force unto himself at the CIA. A mathematician by training, he had begun a PhD program at the University of Michigan before being pulled away from the scholar's life in the 1940s by the FBI, which recruited him to apply his mathematical talents to cryptography. During World War II, Scott had joined the Office of Strategic Services, the spy agency that was the predecessor of the CIA. At the OSS, he would establish lifelong friendships with several fellow spies—among them Angleton, Dulles, and Helms—who would all go on to join the CIA when it was created in September 1947.

Among his deputies in Mexico, few were closer to Scott than Anne Goodpasture. She had also begun her spying career at the OSS. During World War II, she was posted in Burma with a fellow OSS agent, Julia McWilliams, who later gained fame as a cookbook writer under her married name, Julia Child. In later years, Goodpasture denied she was ever close to Angleton, but it was understood inside the agency that Angleton had actually dispatched her to Mexico; he had been impressed by her diligence in an earlier counterintelligence operation. Scott, Angleton's friend, agreed to add her to his staff in 1957, a year after his own arrival.

Goodpasture was sometimes confused for a secretary or a typist in the CIA offices in Mexico City, and the sexism of that assumption always bothered her, she said. She was, in fact, a key deputy—Scott's "Girl Friday" or "right-hand woman," as she put it. She was not a street spy—most of her work was done within the confines of the U.S. embassy—but she knew spycraft, including how to open a sealed envelope so no one would notice, a technique known as "flaps and seals." Her friendship with Scott was made easier by their common roots in the South; Goodpasture was a Tennessean. Both were courtly and soft-spoken. (Among the secrets kept by Goodpasture was her exact age, which does not appear on many of her key personnel files. At the time of the Oswald investigation, she appeared to colleagues to be, like Scott, in her midfifties.) "He was a southern gentleman," she said of Scott. "I felt he fancied himself as an intellectual. . . . He was particular about his dress, and he always wore dark suits and white shirts."

Despite their mutual respect, there was never any doubt who was in charge and who, ultimately, kept the secrets—Scott. Within the station, information flowed to and through Scott exclusively, to the point of obsessiveness, she remembered. "He maintained his own set of classified files, separate from those of the station, that he stored in several different combination safes in his office, and a large one at his home," she said. "Win never trusted anyone." Scott had several other deputies, she recalled, but they were "deputies pretty much in name only because Win was there all the time" and made "every decision."

Goodpasture liked and respected Scott, although she did not believe he always told the truth when he reported back to Langley. In her view, that explained why he spent long days at his desk—he needed to be there to control the flow of information and make sure that no one had the chance to detect his dishonesty. "They would find out that he was probably exaggerating things," Goodpasture would tell the Washington author Jefferson Morley. "There were numerous instances in which he changed figures. Somebody would describe a crowd of 500 in the newspaper; he would add another zero."

According to Goodpasture, Scott became especially anxious—paranoid, even—after the Kennedy assassination, and especially after the creation of the Warren Commission. He made it clear to Goodpasture and his other deputies that he would take control of every detail of the interactions between the station and the commission. Over time, he went a step further, largely sealing himself off from Goodpasture and her colleagues whenever the subject of Oswald came up. She said that the topic was simply not discussed after the assassination: when the commission began to address questions to the CIA that needed to be answered in Mexico City, Scott would deal with them himself. He did not share the questions with Goodpasture, nor ask her or her colleagues to review the station's files for information. Instead, when the questions came in, he would ask for the Oswald files to be brought to him, search for an answer, then report back to Langley himself. There was never any discussion of Goodpasture testifying before the Warren Commission or being questioned by its staff, even though she had been part of the surveillance operation aimed at Oswald. Scott, she knew, intended to answer all of the commission's questions himself.

12

By early December, Whitten and his thirty-member team at the CIA believed they had a basic understanding of Oswald's life story. They even had a preliminary sense for what might have motivated him to kill the president.

Whitten put together a report—he recalled that it was about twenty pages—for distribution within the agency, summarizing what was known. By this point, he believed Oswald was some kind of "pro-Castro nut" who had probably acted alone. Despite Oswald's contacts with the Cuban embassy in Mexico City, Whitten saw no evidence that Castro's government had anything to do with the assassination. Whitten's specialty was Latin America; he knew a lot about Cuba, and he doubted that Castro would risk his regime's survival by recruiting a disturbed young man like Oswald as an assassin. Whitten seemed to trust that if there was anything more to be found in Mexico City, Scott would find it.

As he finished the report, Whitten was outraged—but not surprised, he said—to hear from CIA colleagues that Angleton was pursuing his own, informal investigation of Oswald and discussing the case with his friends at the FBI. "It was in total defiance of Helms's orders," Whitten said. He confronted Angleton, who, to Whitten's astonishment, readily confirmed that the rumors were true, as if Helms's rules simply did not apply to him. He acknowledged that his FBI contacts updated him daily on the assassination investigation. Without Whitten's knowledge, Angleton had also begun meeting regularly with their old boss, Allen Dulles, now on the commission. Whitten complained to Helms, who made clear he did not want to get involved in a dispute between his two deputies. Whitten said that Helms never wanted to confront the always difficult Angleton. If Angleton was making trouble, "you go tell him" to stop, Helms told Whitten.

Whitten began to worry that Angleton, given his close ties to Hoover and others at the FBI, was receiving different and perhaps better information than the bureau was sharing with him. His fears were realized when he was invited to the office of Deputy Attorney General Nicholas Katzenbach in December to review the initial, four-hundred-page FBI report on Oswald. As he read, Whitten was furious to discover how much he did not know—how much the FBI had withheld from him. The bureau had passed along tidbits about Oswald, but Whitten's team knew few of the most important details in the FBI report, including the fact that Oswald had apparently tried to assassinate someone else that year: Retired Army Major General Edwin Walker, a prominent right-wing extremist, who had been shot at from outside his home in Dallas in April.

Whitten was also startled to discover that Oswald had kept some sort of diary and that the FBI had evidence of his ties to pro-Castro activists in the United States, including a prominent pro-Castro group known as the Fair Play for Cuba Committee. Oswald had claimed to run the committee's New Orleans branch when he lived in Louisiana earlier that year. In August, he had been arrested in New Orleans during a streetside scuffle with several anti-Castro Cubans.

As he read on, Whitten remembered, he felt humiliated. He had just turned in a report to the CIA that was supposed to be a detailed portrait of Oswald. But as he sat there at the Justice Department, paging through the "vast amount of information" in the FBI document, he realized that his own report was so full of gaps that it was "simultaneously outdated and made redundant by the FBI's report." His report was "useless."

The situation provided Angleton with his opportunity to push Whitten aside. At a meeting of Helms and his deputies, Angleton savaged Whitten, describing his earlier Oswald report as "so full of errors that we couldn't possibly send it over to the FBI." Whitten found the comment bizarre, since the report "was never supposed to be sent to the FBI." As Helms listened, Whitten tried for a moment to defend himself, explaining that the FBI had obviously hoarded information about Oswald that it should have shared from the start. Angleton ignored the explanation and continued his attack. "He sandbagged me," Whitten said.

Angleton urged that the Oswald investigation be taken away from Whitten and handed over, at once, to his own counterintelligence staff—in particular, to one of Angleton's most trusted deputies, Raymond Rocca. And Helms agreed. Without further discussion, Helms announced in his characteristically matter-of-fact tone that the entire Oswald investigation would be moved into Angleton's office, and that Angleton would now be responsible for the agency's dealings with the Warren Commission.

Whitten was struck that Helms had apparently overcome his earlier concern about Angleton's close friendship with Hoover. Indeed, Helms suddenly seemed eager to have the FBI and CIA work closely together on the Oswald investigation. "Helms wanted someone to conduct the investigation who was in bed with the FBI," Whitten recalled bitterly. "I was not, and Angleton was."

Within the CIA, Helms depicted the transfer of the Oswald investigation to Angleton as routine—as if anything involving the assassination could be considered routine. Whitten's specialty was Mexico and Central America, and by the time Angleton took over, the Oswald investigation had expanded well beyond Latin America—to the Soviet Union and parts of the world that Angleton better understood. "We could see this investigation broadening far beyond Mexico City and it didn't make much sense to have it in the hands of someone who was running the Mexico City desk," Helms said years later.

Richard McGarrah Helms had always had the ability to make the extraordinary seem routine—dull, even. As deputy director for plans, he was responsible for all covert CIA operations around the globe. With his slicked-back hair, well-tailored suits, and careful diction, the fifty-year-old looked and sounded the part of a dapper spy. The son of an aluminum industry executive, he attended high school in Switzerland and was fluent in French and German. He was introduced to spying when he served in naval intelligence during World War II, which brought him into the OSS, and then the CIA. He was known for his no-nonsense style and dry wit. He typically ended conversations with the phrase: "Let's get on with it."

Helms told colleagues that he intended to cooperate fully with Warren and the commission. "The whole thrust of the agency was to be of as much help as we possibly could and to go over the edge, if necessary." But his definition of full cooperation had an important caveat. The CIA would respond to any request made by the Warren Commission—"when they asked for something, we gave it to them"—but he said he felt the CIA had no responsibility to volunteer information unless it directly involved Oswald and the assassination. Full cooperation, to Helms's mind, did not mean that the CIA had to open up all of its files to the Warren Commission about its most secret operations. He might be criticized for the decision someday, he knew, but so be it. "It is an untidy world," he said.

David Slawson, still new to his work at the commission, knew nothing about the internal strife at the CIA over the Oswald investigation. As it was, he had plenty to do. With Coleman planning to be in Washington only one day a week—and given a prohibition on phone calls to Coleman to discuss classified information—Slawson knew he would do much of this work by himself.

He was struck by how much of the material that was being handed to him was stamped SECRET or TOP SECRET. It was especially surprising since he, like the other young lawyers, did not have a security clearance at first. The decision had been made, presumably by Warren and Rankin, that he and the other lawyers could see classified documents without a full background check. Slawson and the others were happy not to question the decision.

Even though he was reading through CIA material that had been gathered inside the agency by John Whitten, Slawson later said he had no memory of ever meeting Whitten or even hearing his name. Nor did he ever hear Angleton's name or learn that the CIA's counterintelligence chief was responsible for determining what information the commission saw. Instead, he was introduced within days of his arrival in Washington to Raymond Rocca.

Slawson thought the CIA had done itself a favor by assigning the hard-charging forty-six-year-old Rocca as its liaison to the commission; Rocca would appear in the commission's offices almost every day.

"I came to like and trust him," Slawson said. "He was very intelligent and tried in every way to be honest and helpful." If the CIA withheld information from the commission, Slawson came to believe, it was because it had been withheld from Rocca, too.

Rocca, a San Franciscan who had a bachelor's degree and a master's degree in history from the University of California at Berkeley, was typical of many CIA officials who dealt with the commission. They tended to be smart, well educated, and articulate. They were very different from their more hardscrabble, blue-collar counterparts at the FBI and the Secret Service. Slawson said he found himself amused—not disturbed—by Rocca's fervid anti-Communism, a belief that "the Communists were behind everything" that went wrong in the world. Rocca, Slawson recalled, became apoplectic when discussing Castro. "One day we were talking about Cuba, and he was on one side of the table and I was on the other, and he jumped up and almost screamed, 'Fidel Castro?' he said. 'That man is evil. Evil.'"

Slawson realized early on that he had little choice but to trust Rocca and his colleagues at the CIA. The commission had almost nowhere else to turn for most of the information it would need regarding questions involving the Soviet Union, Cuba, and other foreign adversaries that might have had something to do with Kennedy's death. "There was no way that I could imagine carrying on an investigation of foreign intelligence operations like this, other than through the CIA," Slawson recalled. Even so, he tried to devise strategies that would allow him to double-check what he was being told by the spy agency. Early on, he established a policy of requesting the same government document from every agency that might have received it. If a report had been prepared for the CIA and the State Department, he would request it from both agencies. If one agency failed to produce a copy of a document, the other might turn it over. Slawson admitted that it was exciting to be exposed to spies and learn some of the secrets of the CIA. Spy novels and movies—*Dr. No*, the first film based on Ian Fleming's James Bond character, had opened in 1962 and been a worldwide hit—were then at the heart of American popular culture.

In January, the CIA offered, and Slawson eagerly accepted, a briefing on the KGB and its history of assassination attempts. The briefing led him to believe that Kennedy's murder would have been completely out of character for the KGB. "They gave us background material on how Russian spies killed people when they wanted to," including a history of all known KGB murders outside the Soviet Union, "and none of them fitted the pattern of Lee Harvey Oswald," Slawson remembered. "When the Russians did something, they tried to make sure they were never detected. They would make it appear like a natural death or in some way an accident."

Seemingly true to their promise to share all information in CIA files that might involve the assassination, Rocca and others at the agency began to volunteer eye-popping, top secret information to Slawson. In the early weeks of the investigation, Rocca told Slawson that he had a piece of information that the young lawyer could share with no one else, including members of the commission, at least not at first. Tantalized, Slawson agreed. "There has been a defection," Rocca told him somberly. "It may be a very important defection." He explained that a mid-ranking KGB officer, Yuri Nosenko, had just defected to the West and was now in the CIA's custody. Nosenko claimed that he had read through the complete files maintained by the KGB on Oswald during his years in the Soviet Union and that the files proved that Oswald had not been recruited by the KGB—that he was not a Soviet spy. The Russian was still being interrogated, Rocca said, but if his information could be verified, it would exonerate the Soviets from involvement in the assassination.

Back at Langley, all information about Oswald and the assassination was now being funneled into Angleton's office, including the information being gathered in Mexico City by Winston Scott. Angleton, like Whitten, considered Scott to be a model spy.

The focus of the investigation changed dramatically under Angleton. For reasons he never fully explained, he turned the investigation away from the hunt for clues about a Cuban conspiracy. Instead, he wanted to focus almost exclusively on the possibility that the Soviet Union was behind the assassination, an idea that reflected his decades-long obsession with the Soviet threat. In his colleagues' view, Angleton believed that while Castro was dangerous, Cuba was still a sideshow in the larger Cold War struggle between Moscow and Washington. From Angleton's staff, three other counterintelligence analysts were chosen to work with Rocca; all were KGB specialists.

Whatever Angleton's view, Castro had never stopped being the obsession of others at the CIA. During the Kennedy administration, the agency established a special unit, the Special Affairs Staff, or SAS, to direct secret operations to overthrow Castro. The SAS had its own counterintelligence analysts who, although they did not answer to Angleton, were supposed to work with his staff. In dealing with the Warren Commission, congressional investigators would later show, Angleton bypassed the SAS almost entirely; its analysts were never asked to look for evidence of a possible Cuban conspiracy in the president's death.

On February 20, Angleton received what would seem to be troubling news. One of his deputies sent Angleton a memo reporting that at least thirty-seven documents had disappeared from the internal file the CIA had maintained on Oswald before the assassination. The missing documents included seven memos from the FBI, two documents from the State Department, and twenty-five CIA cables. Several weeks later, when the Warren Commission's staff was invited to the CIA to review the file, Angleton's team insisted that the file was complete. The commission's records suggest its investigators were never told that, for at least some period of time, dozens of documents about Oswald had vanished.

13

For a brief moment, Earl Warren thought Oswald might have been part of a foreign conspiracy. In the hours immediately after the assassination, when the chief justice heard the first reports about Oswald's aborted defection to the Soviet Union, he thought there might be a plot involving the Soviets. "The only thing that gave me any pause about a conspiracy theory was that Oswald had been a defector to Russia," he recalled.

But in the days that followed, especially after the initial police reports from Dallas seemed to establish that Oswald was the sole assassin, Warren's instincts as a veteran criminal prosecutor overwhelmed any suspicion about a conspiracy. He was convinced that Oswald acted alone in Dealey Plaza. Although the crime was monstrous and had changed the course of history, Warren sensed that Oswald actually had much in common with the violent, impulse-driven, often mentally ill young thugs he had prosecuted in homicide cases back at the district attorney's office in Oakland in the 1920s. Warren believed he knew how criminal minds worked and that Oswald had not needed anyone's help to assassinate the president.

Within a week of Kennedy's murder, Warren concluded that there was no conspiracy in Dallas or anywhere else. "I never put any faith in a conspiracy of any kind," Warren said later. "As soon as I read about Oswald working at the Texas School Book Depository and leaving it as he did—the only employee to disappear—and after the gun was found, with the cartridges, it seemed to me that a surface case was established." Warren insisted that he never shared these thoughts with the commission's staff because he did not want to prejudice their investigation. Rankin said he never heard Warren rule out a conspiracy: "I never heard anything from him except find out what the truth was."

Many of the commission's newly hired young lawyers agreed later that they heard nothing at the start of the investigation to suggest that Warren had reached an early conclusion that Oswald acted alone. Several would have been disappointed to know it—because they had come to Washington determined to find a conspiracy in the president's death. "I assumed conspiracy," said David Belin, a thirty-five-year-old lawyer from Des Moines, Iowa, who had been hired on the recommendation of a classmate from the University of Michigan law school who was then working in the Johnson administration. (The classmate, Roger Wilkins, would go on to become a prominent journalist and civil rights activist.) Belin suspected that the conspiracy might have involved Castro, eager for revenge against Kennedy for the Bay of Pigs and the Cuban missile crisis. Oswald's murder might well have been the conspiracy's second act, he thought. "I felt it was highly probable that there was a conspiracy, that Lee Harvey Oswald might not be the real assassin, despite the claims of the FBI, and that Ruby had killed Oswald to silence him." He was thrilled by his assignment as the junior partner on the two-man team for Area 2, responsible for proving the identity of the assassin or assassins. The assignment would put Belin and his partner, Joseph Ball, the California lawyer, at the heart of the search for accomplices.

Burt Griffin, thirty-one, a former federal prosecutor in Cleveland, also suspected a conspiracy before joining the commission's staff. He thought some group of racists, determined to put an end to Kennedy's advances on civil rights, might have been responsible. "My initial reaction was it was some segregationist southerners," he said years later. Willens had recruited Griffin, who also had a Yale law degree, to join the commission's staff at the suggestion of a mutual friend from Ohio. Unlike so many of his young colleagues, Griffin had experience in Washington, having worked in the capital three years earlier as a clerk to a federal appeals court judge. He and his wife loved Washington and were excited to return. "I called home to tell my wife that we were going to Washington, and she was packing before I got off the phone."

When he entered law school, Griffin had planned to apply his degree to a career in journalism or in politics, but he was diverted to the law because he was so successful at Yale. He actually hated the law school: "I didn't think the faculty members were very interested in education; they were interested in indulging their egos with this old type of Socratic method." Still, he excelled, and his grades earned him a job on the law review, "so I thought I must have some knack for it," he said. After graduation, he found himself drawn further down a career path in the law, including a two-year stint in the United States attorney's office in Cleveland, his hometown. He loved the job, he said; it allowed him to ferret out wrongdoing like the investigative reporter he had once planned to be, albeit with the advantage of subpoena power.

When he arrived in Washington in January, Griffin was struck by how few of his new colleagues had been prosecutors or had any other experience in law enforcement. He was the only one of the junior lawyers who had ever had significant contact with the FBI, and he warned the others that they needed to be wary of the bureau's competence, and its honesty. As a federal prosecutor in Ohio, he had worked closely with agents from the FBI's Cleveland field office, and he came away with little respect for J. Edgar Hoover and the bureau. "They were a bunch of bureaucrats," he said. "They have a great myth about their ability." If there had been a conspiracy to kill the president that was the least bit sophisticated, Griffin was not convinced the FBI had the investigative skills to uncover it. "They could only stumble on it."

And Griffin had darker suspicions about the bureau. From the start, he worried that the FBI might try to hide the full truth about the assassination, to cover up its own mistakes with Oswald in Dallas. Griffin thought that the bureau, in a frantic effort to shield itself from the allegation that it had missed evidence of a conspiracy, would try to pin the blame solely on Oswald, whatever the evidence actually showed. "I thought the FBI might be trying to frame Oswald," he said. Others on the commission's staff, Griffin remembered, felt the same way. Several of the young lawyers were "downright excited" by the possibility that the commission would uncover a conspiracy, if only because it might disgrace Hoover, a man many of them already disdained. "We were determined, if we could, to prove that the FBI was wrong—to find a conspiracy

The commission's staff gathers for a group portrait in the offices in the national headquarters of the Veterans of Foreign Wars. *Front row, left to right:* Alfred Goldberg, Norman Redlich, J. Lee Rankin, David Slawson (with glasses), Howard Willens (no glasses), David Belin. *Second row:* Stuart Pollak, Arlen Specter, Wesley Liebeler (with cigarette), Samuel Stern, Albert Jenner, John Hart Ely, and Burt Griffin.

ABOVE: David Slawson, one of the junior lawyers, stands next to Chief Justice Warren. Slawson was the commission's key investigator on the question of a possible foreign conspiracy. RIGHT: Arlen Specter, who was effectively abandoned by his "senior" partner in reconstructing the events of day of the assassination, would become known as the "father of the single-bullet theory."

TOP LEFT: David Belin was the junior partner on the team responsible for identifying the assassin—Oswald, presumably. TOP RIGHT: Burt Griffin was the junior lawyer on the team investigating Jack Ruby's background. CENTER (*left to right*): Alfred Goldberg, an air force historian, helped outline and write the report; Melvin Eisenberg, Redlich's deputy, became the commission's in-house expert on the science of criminology and could knock down many of the conspiracy theories; Joseph Ball, the senior lawyer on the team to determine the assassin's identity, was praised for his hard work. BOTTOM: Richard Mosk prepared studies on Oswald's marksmanship and his surprisingly sophisticated reading habits.

if we possibly could," Griffin said. "We thought we would be national heroes."

Griffin was assigned to work as the junior lawyer on Area 5, investigating the background of Jack Ruby, and shared an office with Leon Hubert, the courtly Louisianan who would be his senior partner. Their office was cramped, about ten feet square; the two lawyers worked at desks placed side by side. As he introduced himself around the office, Griffin was impressed to encounter a former college classmate, David Slawson, who had been a year ahead of him at Amherst. Griffin remembered feeling intimidated: "I was in awe of Slawson—Phi Beta Kappa, president of the student body. I felt honored to be there with Slawson."

Staff meetings could resemble an Ivy League reunion, reflecting Wil lone's preference for graduates of a handful of elite law schools. If the commission's staff botched the investigation, they joked, their law professors back at Harvard and Yale would have some explaining to do. Griffin and the other three Yale graduates were matched by an equal number from Harvard, and many other lawyers with Harvard law degrees would arrive at the commission as the months passed. The Harvard graduates: Slawson and Coleman; Samuel Stern, a thirty-four-year-old Washington lawyer who had been a law clerk to Chief Justice Warren and was now a member of the law firm of Wilmer, Cutler & Pickering; and Melvin Eisenberg, who graduated first in the Harvard Law class of 1959 and worked at a large New York firm, Kaye Scholer.

Stern became the one-man team responsible for Area 6. He would evaluate the Secret Service and its performance in Dallas, as well as research the larger history of how presidents had been protected from assassins over the years. He was the only junior lawyer without a senior partner. Warren felt that the subject matter could be handled by a single lawyer, and he trusted the quality of Stern's work.

Even though Eisenberg was still new to Kaye Scholer and knew that even a temporary absence might endanger a climb to partner, he jumped at the invitation to join the commission. "It was like meeting my wife," Eisenberg recalled. "From the moment I met her, I wanted to marry her." Besides, he had grown disenchanted with life in a big law firm. "At Harvard and the law review, you're the center of the world, and then all of a sudden, I found myself writing memos" for older lawyers he barely knew. He had already been thinking about leaving the law for a career as an English professor.

Eisenberg was assigned to work as Redlich's deputy, a recognition that Redlich might otherwise be buried under a mountain of paper, given his decision to volunteer to read every document that entered the commission's offices and then decide how the paperwork should be divided among his colleagues. For his first major assignment, Eisenberg was asked to make himself an expert on the science of criminology—fingerprints, ballistics, acoustics, eyewitness testimony—and determine which evidence the commission should pay most attention to and which it could ignore. Since he had no background in law enforcement, Eisenberg turned to books. The Library of Congress was two blocks away, and he requested a collection of its best works on criminal science.

It was no secret among the junior lawyers that most of them shared the same political leanings; they were registered Democrats, considered themselves liberals, and had supported President Kennedy. The odd man out was Wesley James Liebeler, known to his friends as Jim, a thirty-two-year-old New York litigator who was a graduate of the University of Chicago law school and was recommended to the commission by the school's dean. Born in Langdon, North Dakota, and raised on the farmlands of the Great Plains, Liebeler was a fiercely outspoken Republican who liked to boast about his intention to vote for Arizona senator Barry Goldwater in the presidential election that November. He made it clear that his conservatism did not extend to his private life, however, and, to the amusement of his new colleagues, he liked to boast about this, too. Within days of arriving in Washington, he told his colleagues—he told almost anyone who would listen, in fact—that he intended to use his time in the capital to meet women. That he was married and had two children back in New York seemed no hindrance at all.

Liebeler was named the junior lawyer on Area 3; he and his senior partner, Albert Jenner, would be responsible for investigating Oswald's life. From the start, Liebeler was less respectful than his colleagues in dealing with Rankin, Redlich, and Willens. He told Specter that he worried Willens had been brought onto the commission's staff from the Justice Department as a "stoolie" for Robert Kennedy—a stool pigeon who would protect the attorney general's interests, whatever they might be.

Rankin was struck by the wariness of Warren and some of the other commissioners to speak—even privately, among themselves—about the possibility that there had been a foreign conspiracy to kill Kennedy. There was no similar fear, Rankin said, among the young lawyers, who were ready to follow the facts. He recalled conversations among the lawyers about what would happen "if we find a conspiracy with the Soviet Union involved or Cuba" and how that could lead to a nuclear showdown. And they seemed unfazed by that prospect, even of war, Rankin remembered. "They were eager to get the information and get it out and didn't care who it hurt or helped," he said. "Maybe that is youth and a lack of recognition of all the hazards." He also saw a determination by the staff lawyers—especially the young ones, at the start of their careers—to get to the truth about the president's murder because they knew their "reputations would be destroyed" if they participated in anything that could be labeled a cover-up.

Slawson remembered a few early, nervous conversations among the lawyers about rumors that some rogue element of the CIA might be behind the assassination, or that President Johnson was involved. The conversations were "mostly humorous," he said. Still, would the lawyers find their lives at risk if they unearthed a conspiracy within the U.S. government? Slawson remembered thinking that if he and his colleagues found evidence that the assassination was the result of some sort of coup d'état, they should expose it as quickly as possible, if only to keep themselves safe from an effort to silence them. "It was my theory that if you made it public, then they wouldn't dare rub you out, because it would only solidify the evidence that it was true."

On Monday, January 20, Warren called the first meeting of the staff. Years later, several lawyers remembered the excitement they felt to be in the presence of the chief justice, whose talents as a politician were still obvious. He charmed the young lawyers, speaking with "great warmth and sincerity," Griffin recalled. According to memos of the meeting prepared by Willens and Eisenberg, the chief justice told the staff that their duty was "to determine the truth, whatever it might be." He told them about his encounter with President Johnson in the Oval Office, and how Johnson had convinced him to take the job. The commission, Warren said, had a responsibility to put an end to the rumors that were sweeping the country—including rumors that Johnson himself had something to do with the murder. "The President stated that rumors of the most exaggerated kind were circulating in this country and overseas," Warren said of his meeting with Johnson. "Some of those rumors could conceivably lead the country into a war which would cost 40 million lives."

Warren offered a time line for the commission's final report. It would be difficult to issue a report, he said, before the trial of Jack Ruby had been completed in Dallas; it was scheduled to begin in February. But Warren said he wanted to finish the report before the presidential campaign that fall "since once the campaign started it was very possible that rumors and speculation would gin up again." He proposed a target date of June 1, less than five months away.

14

Hugh Aynesworth of the *Dallas Morning News* was searching for a conspiracy, too. In the weeks after the assassination, no reporter in Texas had landed as many scoops about the president's murder as Aynesworth, a thirty-two-year-old West Virginian who had been earning a paycheck as a newspaperman since he was a teenager. Over time, the Warren Commission would be forced to deal, repeatedly, with the aftermath of one of Aynesworth's exclusives.

At first, Aynesworth said, he doubted Oswald could have carried out the assassination by himself. He guessed it was probably a conspiracy involving the Russians. His suspicion grew after he learned how Oswald had been permitted to leave the Soviet Union in 1962 and return home to the United States with his pretty young Russian wife. "I thought there was no way that this guy could get out of Russia with a Russian wife that fast," he said. Aynesworth admitted that his suspicions were fueled by an assumption—felt nowhere more strongly than in ultraconservative Dallas—that the Kremlin's leaders were evil enough to assassinate Kennedy. "We were all scared to death of the Russians."

His competitors would have been loath to admit it, but Aynesworth was running circles around them on what would likely be the biggest story of their lives. He had managed to witness every major moment of the assassination drama, beginning on the day of the murder. He was in Dealey Plaza when the shots rang out; he had been inside the Texas Theatre when Oswald was captured and arrested later that afternoon; and he had been a few feet away from Oswald on Sunday morning in the basement of Dallas police headquarters when Ruby pushed through the crowd and killed him.

Aynesworth understood the risk that Kennedy had taken by visiting Dallas: the reporter felt the city deserved its reputation as a hateful place that was full of racists and right-wing extremists. Before the president's trip, he assumed Kennedy might face some kind of ugly protest in the city. "I never dreamed they would shoot him, but I thought they would embarrass him by throwing something at him."

Aynesworth was ashamed of his employer, a newspaper that he felt brought out the worst in its readers. In his view, the *News* fostered a spirit of intolerance in the city that might have helped inspire the assassination. "I felt badly because the editorial page of my newspaper had really caused it, as much as any other single thing," Aynesworth said later. The paper's "shrilly right-wing political slant appalled and embarrassed many people in the newsroom, including me."

The paper was controlled by the radically conservative Dealey family—the small urban park where the president was shot was named for George Dealey, who bought the newspaper in 1926—and the *News* had criticized Kennedy mercilessly. In the fall of 1961, publisher Ted Dealey, George's son, was among a group of Texas media executives invited to a meeting with Kennedy in the White House. Dealey used the opportunity to read a statement attacking the president to his face. "You and your administration are weak sisters," he said. The nation needed "a man on horseback to lead the nation and many people in Texas and the Southwest think that you are riding Caroline's tricycle."

On the morning of the assassination, the paper had run a black-bordered, full-page advertisement placed by a group of right-wing extremists who identified themselves as the American Fact-Finding Committee. The ad accused Kennedy of allowing the Justice Department "to go soft on Communists, fellow travelers and ultra-leftists." Jacqueline Kennedy remembered that, as they prepared to drive into Dallas in the motorcade, her husband showed her the ad and remarked, "We're heading into nut country."

Aynesworth had many gifts as a reporter, including a phenomenal

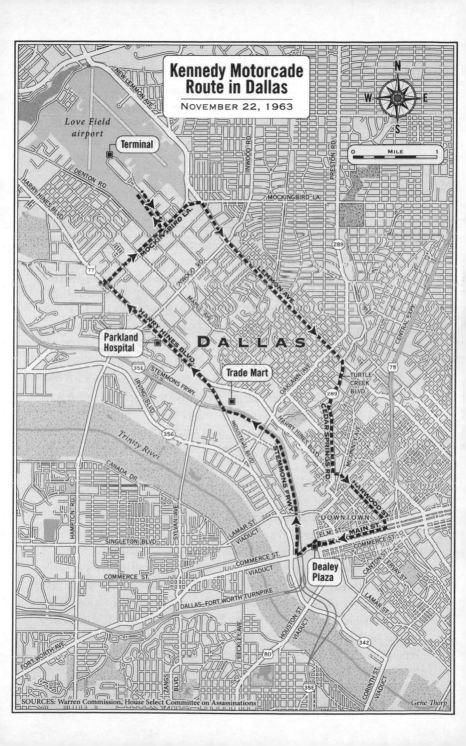

memory, a polite, aw-shucks manner, and a slow, soft speaking style that encouraged people to trust him. Despite a boyish face, he was a big man who knew how to defend himself. He had a scar that ran from his throat to one ear, the result of an encounter with a knife-wielding assailant who broke into his home in Denver when he worked there as a reporter for United Press International. An admiring Texas reporter once said that the scar made Aynesworth "look like a cross between Andy Hardy and Al Capone."

On the day of the assassination Aynesworth was not supposed to be in Dealey Plaza. He was the paper's aviation and space correspondent—seen as the most prestigious reporting job on the paper, given the proximity of the new NASA space center in Houston—and originally he had no part in covering the president's visit. He went to the plaza as a spectator, excited to see Kennedy and his glamorous wife. The moment shots rang out, however, he found himself in the middle of the mayhem. He immediately went to work. "My God, this is really happening," he said to himself.

He had no notepad, so he grabbed a utility bill from his back pocket. He had no pen either, so he paid a child on the street 50 cents for his "fat jumbo pencil, like the ones kids used to use in early grade school." A tiny plastic American flag dangled from the eraser.

"I was a reporter and I knew to start interviewing people," Aynesworth said. And it was clear from the first minutes that the shots—he distinctly heard three of them—had probably been fired from the Texas School Book Depository. "I remember three or four people pointing toward the upper floors of the Book Depository."

He saw police gathering around a frightened man on the street outside the book warehouse and overheard the man offer what appeared to be an eyewitness description of the assassin. The witness—Howard Brennan, a forty-four-year-old steamfitter who was still carrying his helmet from work—was telling the police officers that he had been across the street from the depository when he saw a man with a rifle lean from the window of one of the upper floors of the building. "I knew he was scared to death," Aynesworth said of Brennan, who had noticed that reporters were listening in on the conversation, which made him even more upset. "He asked the police to get rid of us."

About forty-five minutes after the assassination, Aynesworth heard a police radio crackle with a bulletin that a policeman, Officer J. D. Tippit,

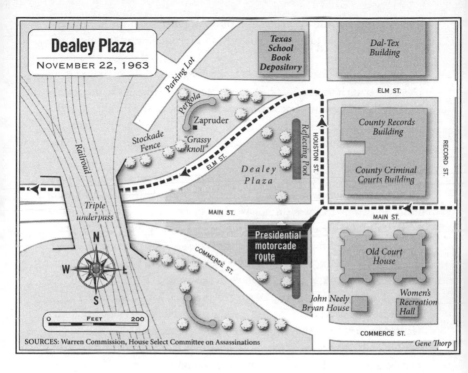

Dealey Plaza
NOVEMBER 22, 1963

Parking Lot

Pergola

Zapruder

Stockade Fence

"Grassy knoll"

Railroad

Triple underpass

ELM ST.

Dealey Plaza

Reflecting Pool

HOUSTON ST.

MAIN ST.

Presidential motorcade route

COMMERCE ST.

N W E S

0 FEET 200

John Neely Bryan House

Texas School Book Depository

ELM ST.

County Records Building

County Criminal Courts Building

MAIN ST.

Old Court House

Women's Recreation Hall

COMMERCE ST.

Dal-Tex Building

RECORD ST.

SOURCES: Warren Commission, House Select Committee on Assassinations

Gene Thorp

had been gunned down across town—in the Oak Cliff neighborhood of Dallas. Aynesworth sensed, instantly, that the shooting must be connected to the assassination, so he jumped in a car and rushed to Oak Cliff, where he found several people who said they had witnessed Tippit's murder.

Helen Markham, a forty-seven-year-old waitress at the nearby Eatwell restaurant, had seen the killer—she later identified Oswald in a police lineup—pull a gun on Tippit and shoot him as the officer stepped from his squad car. "Strangest thing," Aynesworth quoted her as saying of Oswald. "He didn't run. He didn't seem upset or scared. He just fooled with the gun and stared at me." Then, Markham said, Oswald jogged away.

Several minutes later, Aynesworth followed police when they entered the nearby Texas Theatre, which was in the middle of a matinee showing of the film *War Is Hell*. Witnesses had reported a man resembling Oswald darting into the theater without buying a ticket. Aynesworth watched as the police entered the theater, turned up the lights, and grabbed Oswald, who initially resisted the arrest and pulled a pistol from his hip. After a scuffle, Oswald was taken into custody, yelling out, "I protest this police brutality."

Aynesworth woke up on Sunday, November 24, to hear the news on television that Oswald would be transferred within minutes to the county jail. He rushed from the house without shaving or eating breakfast, arriving just in time at Dallas police headquarters. He was about fifteen feet away when Jack Ruby pushed through the crowd and shot Oswald in the stomach.

Aynesworth knew—and disliked—Ruby, a self-promoting strip-club operator who was always trying to befriend police officers (in hopes of protection) and reporters (in hopes of publicity). "He was a nut," Aynesworth said. "Ruby was a showboat—always trying to get his picture in the papers, pictures of the strippers." At the *News*, he was considered a "noxious presence" and a "loser." Aynesworth recalled how, in the newspaper's cafeteria, Ruby would "cut a peephole in his paper to keep up his surveillance as he pretended to read"—surveillance of what, it was never clear. Ruby was notoriously violent and always carried a gun. "I saw him twice beat up on drunks," Aynesworth said. Ruby's Carousel Club had a steep set of stairs that he turned into another weapon. "I remember him beating up this one guy and throwing him down the stairs, hurting the guy bad."

Aynesworth was horrified by Oswald's murder, but he was not surprised that Ruby was the killer. "If I had to pick out the one guy in all of Dallas, Texas, who would do something like this, I would think Ruby would be on the top of the list."

Within hours of Kennedy's assassination, Aynesworth started hearing from strangers who claimed they had secret information about a conspiracy to kill the president. He had encountered such people before on the space beat—"loonies, tin-foil people"—but never more than two or three a year. Now, "I was inundated with them." The first, he said, showed up on the night of the assassination at his home—"an odd, bedraggled little man sitting on my doorstep." The man was delusional and claimed the conspiracy involved an unlikely alliance of H. L. Hunt, the right-wing Dallas billionaire, and the Soviet Union. The second showed up the next morning, "a tall, painfully thin man who stank something awful" who managed to get into the newsroom. "I've got the story for you," he told Aynesworth, claiming he knew the secret behind Kennedy's murder. The man rolled up his trouser leg to reveal a huge abscess, which he claimed was somehow related to the conspiracy. "That's how my leg got torn up."

Over time, Aynesworth saw the conspiracy theorists fall into two categories. There were those who hoped to cash in on the murder by selling a wild story. "That makes money," Aynesworth said. "Nobody pays for the truth. They pay for a conspiracy." And there were others who wanted to enjoy, or at least embrace, the fantasy that they had played some part in this terrible drama. In that category he placed Carroll Jarnagin, a Dallas lawyer who claimed he had seen Oswald and Jack Ruby together in deep conversation in the Carousel Club days before the assassination. Aynesworth remembered Jarnagin, who was probably in his midforties, as a "bad alcoholic who always wanted to be somebody. . . . He just wanted attention." The newspaperman knew better than to pay attention to Jarnagin, who also told his story about Oswald to the Dallas police. Later Jarnagin took a police polygraph examination about his claims and "failed miserably," Aynesworth said.

Sometime in December, Aynesworth got a phone call from Mark Lane, the New York lawyer who had already begun to attract national attention with his conspiracy theories. Aynesworth had read Lane's *National Guardian* article suggesting that Oswald might be innocent, and he knew it was riddled with errors. "He told me he was representing Oswald because Oswald had nobody to represent him," Aynesworth remembered. "He told me he was this great lawyer and had done all of these important things." Despite his skepticism about Lane's motives, Aynesworth agreed to meet with the lawyer the next night at his home.

"He came by my house and started telling me what had really happened" and how Oswald had been framed. Aynesworth recalled being startled by Lane's brash attempt to pretend he knew more about the assassination than Aynesworth did; in effect, Lane argued that Aynesworth should not believe what he had seen with his own eyes in Dealey Plaza. Aynesworth was angry. "You don't take it too kindly when somebody tells you you didn't see some of what you saw."

Sitting at Aynesworth's kitchen table, Lane claimed that there was "no doubt" that Ruby and Oswald knew each other. He said he had an interview scheduled for the next day with a secret witness with an "impeccable memory" who had seen Oswald and Ruby together at the Carousel Club—a source Aynesworth was certain was the drunken lawyer Jarnagin. "I talked with him on the phone and he sounded like the real thing," Lane said of his secret witness.

Increasingly irritated, Aynesworth explained, point by point, how Lane was misstating the facts of the assassination and how he was misleading the public about the president's death.

"How do *you* know the truth?" Lane demanded.

"*How* do I know?" Aynesworth asked. "I'll tell you how I know. I know because I have their statements, I know exactly what the witnesses said on the day of the assassination, where they were, who they were, everything."

He was referring to a stack of classified witness statements taken by police officers on the day of the assassination; the statements had been leaked to Aynesworth, and he had taken them home for safekeeping. He grabbed them to show to Lane, whose eyes widened at the sight. "The only reason I'm showing you these," Aynesworth said, "is that you made many, many misinterpretations in your article. If you are truly interested in giving Oswald a fair shake from a historical standpoint, I think you need to know what the investigation shows so far."

Lane asked if he could borrow the witness statements for a few days. "Will you help me find the truth?" he asked. "I have to go back to New York in a day or so, and I was wondering if I could borrow these statements."

Aynesworth agreed, a decision he would soon regret. Within days, he said, Lane would begin brandishing the witness statements at news conferences as proof that he had secret sources who, when their identities became public, could vindicate Oswald.

"I was very naive," Aynesworth said later. "I made mistakes. I helped create the monster of Mark Lane. There's no doubt about it."

Other, less talented reporters in Texas sought Aynesworth's help in covering the aftermath of the assassination; he was considered a walking encyclopedia on the story. Among the most persistent was Alonzo "Lonnie" Hudkins of the *Houston Post*, who telephoned constantly. Whatever his failings as a reporter, Lonnie was the "nicest guy in the world," Aynesworth said. "Everybody liked him. He wore a little Homburg hat."

Hudkins had made up his mind early on about the assassination. "He had decided it was a conspiracy, and he was going to set out to prove it."

For a time, Aynesworth put up with Hudkins's calls for help. "I thought he'd go away eventually," Aynesworth said. "And then I didn't hear from him for a while."

Late in December, though, the calls resumed, and Aynesworth decided he would play a trick on his friend from Houston. Hudkins was pursuing a widely circulating rumor that Oswald had been an FBI informant, a rumor that Aynesworth found no evidence to support.

"You hear anything about this FBI link with Oswald?" Hudkins asked.

Mischievously, Aynesworth replied that he had heard the rumors, and they were true. Oswald, he said, was indeed on Hoover's payroll. "You got his payroll number, don't you?" he asked Hudkins in a tone that suggested it was a widely known piece of information.

Aynesworth remembered that he reached, at random, for one of the telegrams on his desk—he was also filing assassination stories, by telegram, to *Newsweek* magazine and the *Times* of London—and read out a sequence of numbers from across the top.

"Yeah, yeah, that's it," Hudkins replied, apparently thinking he had bluffed Aynesworth into giving up a world-class scoop. "That's the same one I got."

Aynesworth said he forgot about the telephone call—and his joke on Hudkins—until the *Post* ran a front-page story on January 1, 1964, alleging that Oswald may have worked for the FBI. The byline was Hudkins's. The headline: "Oswald Rumored as Informant for U.S."

Only later would Aynesworth learn, to his astonishment, that his practical joke on a competitor created the Warren Commission's first great crisis—and forever ruptured the commission's relationship with the FBI.

If Aynesworth had a counterpart in Washington for early scoops about the assassination, it was the muckraker Drew Pearson, Chief Justice Warren's friend.

In his column for Monday, December 2—published just three days after the creation of the Warren Commission—Pearson lobbed out a bombshell for his millions of readers: six Secret Service agents who had been part of the squad protecting the president in Texas had, the night before the assassination, gone out drinking, a direct violation of the agency's rules of conduct. Some of the agents remained out "boozing" until nearly three a.m., and "one of them was reported to have been inebriated," Pearson reported. "Obviously men who have been drinking until nearly three a.m. are in no condition to be trigger-alert or in the best physical shape to protect anyone."

The column also targeted the FBI, which, Pearson reported, had failed to notify the Secret Service about the danger posed by Oswald, who had been under surveillance by the bureau's office in Dallas for months. Pearson declared it outrageous that a man "who had professed Marxism and whose record showed a mixed-up, unsteady emotionalism, should not have been kept under careful watch on the day the president entered his city—one of the most lawless and intolerant cities in the United States." Pearson blamed the FBI's failure to alert the Secret Service to the bureau's "long-standing jealousy" of the Secret Service as the protectors of the president. "They should stop squabbling over jurisdiction and headlines at least where the life of the president is concerned."

The column created a firestorm at the Secret Service—because the essence of what Pearson wrote was true. Several agents had in fact gone out drinking the night before the assassination, a fireable offense. The agency's regulations barred agents from using alcohol at all times when traveling with the president. The director of the Secret Service, James Rowley, insisted later that he knew nothing about the drinking until he read Pearson's column, and he immediately dispatched a deputy to Texas to investigate. In the meantime, Rowley decided, he would take no action, even tentatively, against the agents. Any move to discipline them might lead the public to "conclude that they were responsible for the assassination of the president—I didn't think that was fair."

In his diary, Pearson disclosed that the information about the Secret Service agents had come to him from Thayer Waldo, a reporter at the *Fort Worth Star-Telegram* who apparently feared that his editors would never publish such a controversial story. "Thayer said he would lose his job if it were known that he had spilled this," Pearson wrote.

Later in December, Pearson again took aim at J. Edgar Hoover and the FBI, and his second column was even more scathing. He accused the FBI of a "cover-up" of what it had known about Oswald before the assassination. "The FBI neither kept Oswald under scrutiny when President Kennedy passed through Dallas, nor did it give his name to the Secret

Service. These are some of the amazing facts about the preliminary probe of the Dallas tragedy which explain why the FBI wanted to get its version of the story out to the newspapers ahead of the study by the presidential commission." Pearson accused the FBI of leaking copies of its four-hundred-page preliminary report on Oswald—the report that essentially exonerated the FBI of mishandling its investigation of Oswald before the assassination—to preempt the findings of Warren's commission.

The same column praised Pearson's friend, the chief justice, and revealed the heavy pressure that President Johnson had used in the Oval Office to convince Warren to accept the job of running the commission; they were details that only Johnson and Warren should have known. Pearson did not identify Warren as his source for the column, but Hoover and his colleagues at the FBI would say later they had no doubt that the chief justice was leaking to Pearson. Warren, Pearson wrote, "was not about to let J. Edgar Hoover decide the facts in the tragedy of Dallas even before the presidential commission could start work."

15

By the time many of the newly hired staff members arrived in Washington, there was already an outline of what the commission's final report would say. Before Christmas, Lee Rankin had asked Howard Willens to draw up the ten-page outline, and it was attached to the welcome-to-Washington memo that was given to each of the lawyers on his first day of work. The outline was crafted largely on the basis of the initial reports from the FBI, the Secret Service, and the CIA and reflected the assumption that Oswald was the assassin and that his past, and his possible motives, would be the focus of the investigation. "We have an important job to do," Rankin wrote in his memo. "I know you share my desire to accomplish it with thoroughness, imagination and speed." The memo asked each of the five two-lawyer teams, plus Sam Stern, to prepare a summary of the facts already known in their parts of the investigation and to suggest what needed to be done.

Rankin admitted in his memo that the offices were "in disarray," with stacks of additional classified documents pouring in almost by the hour. He promised to bring some order to it. The commission, he said, had begun recruiting secretaries from around the federal government, as well as an archivist who would run a file room. He said the commission was also seeking assistance from a psychiatrist, the recently retired superintendent of St. Elizabeths Hospital in Washington, the capital's large public psychiatric hospital, to offer perspective on the mental states of Oswald and Ruby. The commission would also hire a historian to help draft the final report.

The memo made clear the central role of Norman Redlich, whose office was the clearinghouse for all documents and evidence. He had also taken on the responsibility of preparing for the testimony of Marina Oswald, who was expected to be the first witness when the commissioners began taking testimony in February. The commission had already received extensive background information from the FBI on Oswald's widow, and it was now waiting for a detailed report from the bureau on Ruth and Michael Paine. It had also sought a full FBI background check on George de Mohrenschildt, an eccentric, Russian-born petroleum engineer who had befriended the Oswalds in Dallas.

Rankin's memo asked that all staff lawyers attend a screening later that month of the film taken in Dealey Plaza by the Dallas dressmaker Abraham Zapruder. Most of the lawyers had seen only the individual frames published in *Life* magazine, so it would be their first chance to see Zapruder's full, grisly film.

The seven commissioners convened again on the afternoon of Tuesday, January 21. It had been more than a month since their last meeting, and it was their first in the new offices in the VFW building.

Warren opened the session with a progress report on the hiring of the staff lawyers; he also described the assignment of two Internal Revenue Service agents to the commission who would "trace every dollar that we can in the possession of Oswald and every dollar that he spent, because we don't know where his money came from."

Gerald Ford said he was pleased to hear that the commission had hired one of his former Michigan constituents, David Slawson of Grand Rapids. "His father," Ford declared, "is a fine lawyer in my home town." Warren said he had not yet met Slawson, but reported that he had been approached at lunch at the court that day by Justice Byron White with congratulations. "White came up to me and said, 'You took one of the finest young men in Colorado from my old firm.'"

John McCloy asked about Slawson's partner on the staff, William Coleman: "Is he the colored fellow?" Warren said nothing about Coleman's race, simply replying that Coleman was "a tremendous lawyer" and that the commission was lucky to have him.

The chief justice then turned to the issue that seemed never far from his thoughts—when to end the investigation. "It is not too early for us to start thinking about when we anticipate quitting," he said. "If this should go along too far and get into the middle of a campaign year that would be very bad for the country." As he had already told the staff, he said he wanted to set a June 1 deadline. "Things can drag on if you don't have a target date."

One problem, he acknowledged, was Ruby's impending trial. The commissioners agreed that an intensive on-the-ground investigation in Dallas would have to wait until after the trial was over. Warren feared the presence of the commission's staff in Dallas might interfere with Ruby's defense.

For related reasons, he said he wanted to bring Marina Oswald to testify before the commission in Washington rather than in Dallas, where the presence of the commissioners might create a media circus that would intimidate the young widow. She could be better protected in Washington, he said. He asked Russell, in his capacity as chairman of the Senate Armed Services Committee, if he could arrange a military plane to bring "that little woman with her babies" to Washington. If she took a commercial flight, "she will be subjected to flashbulbs and everything, and she will be embarrassed and maybe she will be hostile." Warren's feelings toward the young widow—long before he had met her—had become almost paternal. Russell, who wielded more power at the Pentagon than most four-star generals, said there would not be "the slightest difficulty" in arranging a military jet.

Marina Oswald was swiftly emerging as the key witness against her dead husband; in interviews with the FBI and the Dallas police, she had left little doubt that she believed her husband had killed the president and that he had acted alone. It was a story she had begun to sell to news organizations, a situation that did not seem to bother Warren; he suggested she had had no other obvious way to support herself. She had already sold magazines a fifty-page handwritten summary of her life; it was being translated from Russian to English. "Her attorney is apparently cooperating very well with us," the chief justice told the other commissioners. "She intends to sell her story to one of the magazines, but we got him to agree to send the story to us, and let us see it and let us examine her before the thing goes to the printer."

Rankin suggested that Marina's credibility with the commission had grown because of her refusal to work with Mark Lane, who had approached her in Texas in hopes of representing Oswald's legal interests. "She didn't want any part of him," Rankin said. The commissioners knew they would still have to deal with Lane, though, since by then he had announced that he was representing Oswald's mother.

When Rankin joined the commission, he believed he could work well with J. Edgar Hoover. He still respected the FBI director, despite all the vicious criticism directed at Hoover by Rankin's growing circle of liberal friends in his new home in New York. Hoover liked Rankin, too. He told aides in December he welcomed the news that Rankin had been hired as the commission's general counsel. Hoover said he had "the closest and most amiable working relationship with Mr. Rankin during the Eisenhower administration."

Rankin understood from the start why the FBI would be anxious about the commission's investigation, and he suspected that the bureau might delay turning over witness statements or evidence that might somehow reflect badly on the FBI's performance; Hoover would probably want to review that material personally before it was turned over. Even so, Rankin said, he joined the commission believing that Hoover and his deputies would never engage in any sort of cover-up. "I never believed he would withhold information or have it withheld," Rankin said later. "I thought the FBI would never lie about anything."

It took only weeks for Rankin to realize just how wrong he had been. "To have them just lie to us," he said later, angrily, of the FBI. "I never anticipated that."

The relationship between the commission and the FBI began to sour in December with the bureau's apparently well-orchestrated leaks of its initial report on Oswald. After that, Rankin said, the commissioners took a more skeptical view of the FBI and decided that "we had to be careful about anything that they gave us."

The relationship was damaged much more seriously on Wednesday, January 22, when the phone rang in Rankin's office shortly after eleven a.m. The caller was the state attorney general of Texas, Waggoner Carr. Rankin remembered the excitement in Carr's voice. "He said he thought he had some information that he should get to us immediately," Rankin said later. "Carr said that he had received information from a confidential source that Lee Harvey Oswald was an undercover agent for the Federal Bureau of Investigation, and had been paid $200 a month by the FBI since September 1962."

Carr told Rankin that Oswald had an FBI informant number—179—and was apparently still in the pay of the FBI in November; indeed, he was supposedly working with an FBI agent in the Dallas office on the day of the assassination. "Carr indicated that this allegation was in the hands of the press and defense counsel for Ruby" and that its source appeared to be the office of Dallas district attorney Henry Wade.

Carr sounded as if he knew what he was talking about, Rankin remembered. If the allegation proved to be true, the FBI was engaged in a massive cover-up of its relationship with the man who had killed the president. Rankin recalled years later that the question raced through his mind: Was it possible that someone at the FBI knew of Oswald's plans for the assassination and could have stopped him?

He immediately called Warren, who shared his alarm. They agreed that Carr and Wade should be summoned to Washington as quickly as possible. The chief justice called an emergency meeting of the commission for five thirty that afternoon.

Ahead of the meeting, Rankin spoke to Carr again. "He told me the source of the information was a member of the press" whose name he did not know. "He said he was trying to check it out to get more definite information."

Ford was in a hearing of the House Appropriations Committee when he got a message that he was needed urgently at the commission's offices on Capitol Hill. He tried to imagine what the emergency might be. When he walked into the offices that afternoon, he said, the tension in the conference room was overwhelming. In all his years in Washington, "I cannot recall attending a meeting more tense and hushed," Ford said later. The commissioners took their seats around the eight-foot oblong table, and Warren somberly asked Rankin to give a summary of what he had heard that morning. Ford said he and the other commissioners listened with "amazement" to Rankin's account of how the president's assassin might have worked for the FBI.

The troubling news from Dallas came at a time when Ford, despite his relationship with the FBI, was already beginning to have private doubts about the bureau's conduct of the investigation. These new rumors about Oswald only added to his suspicion that Oswald had been some sort of government agent—for the CIA, if not the FBI, despite the agencies' adamant denials. Ford had closely read through the biographical material about Oswald, and he was struck in particular by how much exotic foreign travel he had completed before he died at the age of twenty-four—Japan and the Philippines when he was in the Marine Corps, then Europe and his nearly three years in the Soviet Union, and then Mexico briefly that fall. To Ford, "it sounded more like the journeys of a well-heeled globetrotter than the restricted life of a sometimes employed laborer without a skill." Could they be the journeys of a young secret agent? Ford kept this speculation to himself at the time, but he wondered whether Oswald's supposed defection to Russia was in fact a ploy by handlers at the CIA or the FBI to allow him to spy on the Soviet Union. And had Oswald then returned home to begin spying on leftists who were part of the Fair Play for Cuba Committee? "Perhaps he was a CIA agent, trained by the FBI, who had then been used to penetrate Fair Play for Cuba," Ford recalled thinking to himself. "He could have made a perfect counteragent to spy on Castro's supporters."

Others at the meeting scoffed at the suggestion that Oswald could have been anyone's spy. Allen Dulles said he doubted the FBI would ever consider working with someone like Oswald, given his emotional instability. "You wouldn't pick up a fellow like this to do an agent's job," he explained. "What was the ostensible mission?" he asked. "Was it to penetrate the Fair Play for Cuba Committee? That is the only thing I can think of where they might have used this man."

Rankin told the commissioners he had begun to fear it would be impossible to find the truth. If Oswald had been an FBI informant, he said, the bureau might simply deny it. Perhaps that explained why the FBI had been so eager to label Oswald as the sole assassin—it wanted to shut down the commission's investigation before it uncovered evidence that would damage or destroy the bureau. "They found their man," Rankin said, his skepticism about the bureau's credibility now on full display. "There is nothing more to do. The commission supports their conclusions, and we can go home and that is the end of it."

Rankin said he and Warren agreed on the danger posed to the commission's work if the allegations, true or false, became public: "You would have people think there was a conspiracy to accomplish this assassination that nothing the commission did—or anybody—could dissipate."

"You are so right," Hale Boggs said. "The implications of this are fantastic." The implications were "terrible," Dulles agreed. At about that moment some of the commissioners realized to their alarm that their words, including their speculation about a possible FBI cover-up, were being recorded. "I don't even like to see this being taken down," Boggs said, nodding to the stenographer at the table.

Dulles agreed: "Yes, I think this record ought to be destroyed. Do you think we need a record of this?"

Rankin noted that the commission, in a spirit of transparency, had promised to keep records of its meetings. If that was the case, Dulles insisted, the transcripts should never be allowed to leave the commission's offices. "The only copies of this record should be kept right here."

The commissioners adjourned for the day, agreeing there was nothing more to be done until Warren and Rankin met with the Texas officials.

On Friday, January 24, the delegation from Texas, including Attorney General Carr and Dallas District Attorney Wade, arrived in Washington to meet with the chief justice and Rankin. The Texans warned them that the Oswald rumor was spreading quickly in Dallas, and the details—the $200-a-month payment, the FBI informant number—were surprisingly consistent. Wade said he had also heard allegations that Oswald was an informant for the CIA. Carr and Wade declared that several reporters in Texas knew about the rumors and were spreading them, although they named only one: Lonnie Hudkins of the *Houston Post*. Now even more alarmed, Warren called a meeting of the commission for the following Monday.

Over the weekend, the possible ties between Oswald and the FBI had become national news, with the reports of major newspapers and magazines feeding off each other. The *New York Times* reported the rumors, noting the FBI's flat denial of any connection to Oswald. The *Nation* ran a detailed article listing unanswered questions about Oswald, including his possible relationship with the FBI; the article cited the reports by Hudkins in the *Houston Post*. *Time* magazine was also pursuing the story; McCloy had been called by the magazine for comment.

At the meeting on Monday, Rankin said gravely that the commission needed to decide how to confront the rumors, which meant deciding how to confront Hoover. "We do have a dirty rumor that is very bad for the commission," Rankin said. "It must be wiped out insofar as it is possible to do so."

Warren and Rankin had considered asking Robert Kennedy, as Hoover's superior in the chain of command at the Justice Department, to intervene. But the attorney general seemed intimidated by Hoover as well. The word of Kennedy's reluctance to confront the FBI director came from Willens, who continued to answer to the department. He reported to Warren and Rankin that Kennedy would be uncomfortable asking Hoover about the rumors because "such a request might be embarrassing" and make it "very much more difficult for him to carry on the work of the department for the balance of his term."

Rankin suggested there were two options. One, he could meet Hoover privately as the commission's representative. "I would be frank and tell him" that the FBI had to conduct an internal investigation of the rumors and that Hoover needed to provide the commission with "whatever records and materials they have that it just couldn't possibly be true." Rankin said that "a simple statement by Hoover" that the rumors were false would not be enough. The alternative, he said, was for the commission to investigate the rumor itself, before confronting Hoover. They would begin by interviewing Hudkins, the Houston reporter, and then question FBI officials "right up the line" to the director.

The chief justice said he preferred the second option. "My own judgment is that the most fair thing to do would be to try to find out if this is fact or fiction" before a showdown with the FBI director.

Boggs realized the commissioners had an expert in their midst on the subject of government informants: Dulles, who had spent his career at the CIA dealing with information from secret sources. Boggs turned to the former spymaster and asked if the CIA had sources who were so well protected that there was no paper trail at all to show they worked for the agency. "Do you have agents about whom you had no record whatsoever?"

"The record might not be on paper," said Dulles, explaining that the commissioners simply had to accept that Oswald could have been an FBI informant, that the bureau might lie and deny it, and that there would be no way to establish the truth. At the CIA, he said, he had always been prepared to lie himself, even to cabinet officers, to protect a valuable source. As the nation's top spy, he owed the full truth only to the president. "I am under his control," Dulles said. "He is my boss. I wouldn't necessarily tell anyone else, unless the president authorized me to do it. We had that come up at times."

Hoover, he said, might now feel he was in a similar position. "You can't prove what the facts are," Dulles continued. The commission, he suggested, had no choice but to accept Hoover's word. "I would believe Mr. Hoover. Some people might not."

Even in the supposed privacy of the commission's conference room, Russell seemed to realize that he needed to choose his words carefully when it came to the FBI director. "There is no man in the employ of the federal government who stands higher in the opinion of the American people than J. Edgar Hoover," he began, as if to protect himself should the transcript of the meeting ever become public. But he agreed with Warren and others that the commission had to conduct its own investigation of the rumors. "We can get an affidavit from Mr. Hoover and put it in this record," he said. But the commission risked a harsh verdict from history if it relied simply on that. "There still would be thousands of doubting Thomases who would believe" that Hoover was lying and that the commission missed its chance "to clear it up."

Rankin acknowledged his concern about how Hoover would react; the director might believe "we are really investigating him."

Warren: "If you tell him we are going down there to do it, we *are* investigating him, aren't we?"

Rankin: "I think it is inherent."

The discussion left the commissioners struggling directly, for the first time, with the question of whether they could trust the FBI to conduct so much of the commission's essential detective work, given the bureau's determination to prove that Oswald had acted alone.

"They have decided that it is Oswald who committed the assassination, they have decided that no one else was involved," Rankin said.

Russell: "They have tried the case and reached the verdict on every aspect."

Boggs: "You have put your finger on it."

Warren now supported sending Rankin in to confront Hoover directly. He outlined what he expected Rankin to do: "Go to Mr. Hoover and say, 'Mr. Hoover, as you know, there are rumors that persist in and around Dallas, and it is getting into the national press, to the effect that Oswald was an undercover FBI agent.'" Rankin, he said, would ask for a vow from Hoover that "you will give us all the information that you have which will enable us to ferret this thing out—to the very limit." The commission voted unanimously to dispatch Rankin to talk to Hoover the next day.

16

Rankin was ushered into Hoover's suite of offices in the Justice Department building at three p.m. on Tuesday, January 28. He had been to these offices before, many times, during his years at the department in the Eisenhower administration.

Some of Hoover's deputies thought his offices were surprisingly unpretentious, with beaten-up, overstuffed couches for visitors. Assistant Director Cartha DeLoach described the choice of furnishings as intentional; they were meant to be a symbol of Hoover's "stern rejection of frivolity." In an outer office, behind the desk of Hoover's longtime secretary, Helen Gandy, sat the two standard-issue gray file cabinets that housed the so-called Official and Confidential files that were considered too sensitive for routine storage elsewhere. They contained derogatory private information on hundreds of politicians and other public figures, including—it would later be discovered—several members of the Warren Commission.

The effect of opening the door to the inner office to discover the unsmiling, bulldog-faced Hoover seated at his desk, on a platform slightly elevated from the floor, was like encountering "the Great and Powerful Oz," DeLoach said. That, too, was intentional. FBI employees "never felt at ease in his presence," DeLoach said. "Agents viewed him with awe and terror. You were a cog in the vast machinery of the universe. You existed at his whim, and if he chose to, he could snap his fingers and you'd disappear."

Rankin took a seat, and within minutes he realized that if there had ever been any sort of friendship between Hoover and himself, it was over. Like Chief Justice Warren, Rankin was now perceived as one of Hoover's enemies—"hostile to him and to the FBI," Rankin said.

He began by explaining the reason for his visit. He told Hoover that the commission was eager for the FBI to disprove the rumors that Oswald had been an FBI informant, and to do it as quickly as possible. The commission was trying to deal with the issue delicately to avoid any embarrassment to the bureau, especially any perception that "the commission was investigating the FBI," he said.

Hoover's response was blunt and chilly, his notes from the meeting would suggest. He appeared insulted by the implication that the FBI would ever have a relationship with a man like Oswald. The idea, he said, was preposterous. "I told Rankin that Lee Harvey Oswald was never at any time a confidential informant, undercover agent and even a source of information for the FBI, and I would like to see that clearly stated for the record of the commission and I would be willing to do so under oath," Hoover wrote in a memo to deputies.

He used the meeting to launch a wider attack on the commission and what he saw as thinly veiled public criticism of the FBI by the chief justice. Hoover was still angry over Warren's description of the initial FBI report in December as containing only "skeletal" information. He reminded Rankin of the extraordinary demands that the commission was making of his agents in Dallas and elsewhere. Every day, sometimes several times a day, Rankin dispatched letters—directly to Hoover—that effectively demanded that the bureau pursue some new witness or lead. Hoover "commented upon all the man hours that we were demanding of him, and how it was a burden to the FBI," Rankin noted. He left the meeting with a depressing realization that from now on and for months to come he would have to struggle to avoid "an open fight" with the FBI. The bureau's attitude would be "surly" and "reluctant," even as the commission continued to depend on the FBI for much of its basic detective work.

*　*　*

Within the bureau, Hoover's critics—and even some of his most loyal deputies—marveled at the director's ability to marshal the same set of facts to make different arguments in front of different audiences. It was a skill that Hoover had first mastered as a student at Central High School in Washington, DC, where he was champion of the school's undefeated debate team. Decades later, he would talk with gratitude of what he had learned in debate class.

This remarkable dexterity was on full display after the Kennedy assassination. In public, Hoover could argue persuasively that the FBI was offering full cooperation to the Warren Commission. The bureau had nothing to hide, he insisted, because it had done nothing wrong in its surveillance of Oswald before Kennedy's murder. He told the commission—and the White House and the Washington press corps—that the FBI had made no serious mistakes. Since Oswald did not appear to be a threat, there had been no need for the FBI to alert the Secret Service to his presence in Dallas ahead of Kennedy's visit. "There was nothing up to the time of the assassination that gave any indication that this man was a dangerous character who might do harm to the president," Hoover later told the commission under oath.

Behind closed doors at the FBI, however, Hoover's view, shared with his deputies, was precisely the opposite. Within days of the assassination, he determined that the FBI had, in fact, bungled its investigation of Oswald before the assassination—and that many bureau agents and supervisors needed to be disciplined as a result. In late November, he directed the bureau's Inspection Division, its internal watchdog, to determine whether there were "any investigative deficiencies in the Oswald case." The answer came on December 10, when the division's head, Assistant Director James Gale, known internally as "The Barracuda," reported that serious errors had indeed been made by several employees, including agents in Dallas and New Orleans who had failed to keep a close watch on Oswald.

Gale recommended disciplinary action, although he cautioned Hoover about the risk of punishing anyone until after the Warren Commission had finished its investigation. If the punishments became known outside the FBI, it would undermine Hoover's insistence that the bureau had done nothing wrong. Hoover waved Gale's concerns aside. He would go forward with the punishments because "such gross incompetency cannot be overlooked, nor administrative action postponed," he wrote to Gale.

DeLoach urged Hoover to reconsider. If news of the disciplinary actions leaked outside the bureau, it would be seen "as a direct admission that we are responsible for negligence which might have resulted in the assassination of the president," DeLoach wrote. Hoover's mind was made up, however. "I do not concur," he wrote back.

DeLoach could tell Hoover was looking, desperately, for a scapegoat; he needed someone to blame for the indisputable fact that a man under FBI surveillance in the fall of 1963 had eluded the bureau long enough to gun down the president of the United States. "Rain clouds had formed in his office," DeLoach remembered. "He wasn't about to shoulder the blame. He decided to spread it around."

Within days, seventeen bureau employees in Dallas, Washington, and elsewhere were notified—privately—that they were being disciplined for "shortcomings in connection with the investigation of Oswald." Included on the list was James Hosty, the agent who had been responsible for the Oswald investigation in Dallas. The disciplined employees were told their failures included the decision not to place Oswald on the FBI's internal Security Index, a roster that would have been shared with the Secret Service ahead of Kennedy's visit to Dallas.

Despite his public assurances to the contrary, Hoover determined that Oswald's name should have been on the index. The failure to do so "could not have been more stupid," Hoover wrote. "Certainly no one in full possession of all his faculties can claim Oswald didn't fall within this criteria."

There was another issue at the heart of the investigation on which Hoover was consistent in his comments, publicly and privately. He was adamant that Oswald had acted alone. As he told the commission, he believed there was "not a scintilla of evidence showing any foreign conspiracy or domestic conspiracy" in the president's murder.

Hoover's view of Oswald as the lone gunman took hold internally during the weekend after the assassination. On Saturday, November 23, the day after the president's murder, the FBI dispatched a Teletype to its field offices nationwide declaring that Oswald was "the principal suspect in the assassination" and that FBI agents could "resume normal contacts with informants and other sources." In other words, with the assassin in custody, agents not directly involved in the assassination investigation could resume all regular duties; there was no need for their help.

Hoover's files suggest that, after his first confused calls with President Johnson in late November, the FBI director never seriously considered the possibility that the Soviet Union was involved in the assassination. Like his old friend James Angleton at the CIA, the FBI director seemed even less suspicious about a Cuban tie, despite the many unanswered questions about Oswald's trip to Mexico City and his links to pro-Castro activists in the United States. The pattern established at the CIA was also seen at the FBI. While the question of possible Soviet involvement in the assassination was at least raised within the bureau, few questions were asked about the Cubans. The FBI's Domestic Intelligence Division, which oversaw the Oswald inquiry, asked a squad of the bureau's Washington-based intelligence specialists on the Soviet Union and the KGB to review evidence about Oswald's years in the Soviet Union and his possible ties to Russian agents operating in the United States, and they found nothing to support the idea of a Soviet conspiracy. But congressional investigators later determined that no similar requests were made of the FBI's counterintelligence analysts who specialized in Cuba; the bureau's Cuba experts were effectively cut out of the investigation.

Questioned years later, the FBI supervisor reputed to be the bureau's top analyst on Fidel Castro and the Cuban government in 1963 said he was never asked to attend a single meeting at FBI headquarters to discuss the assassination. And he did not pursue the questions himself. He admitted later that he never bothered to go back and review news coverage of Castro in the weeks leading up to the assassination, to see if there were clues the FBI might have missed. He had no memory of having ever read an alarming article published by the Associated Press on September 8, 1963, by an AP reporter in Cuba who interviewed Castro briefly at a reception at the Brazilian embassy in Havana. In the interview, Castro suggested that he knew the Kennedy administration was trying to assassinate him and that he was ready to respond in kind. "U.S. leaders should think that if they are aiding terrorist plans to eliminate Cuban leaders, they themselves will not be safe," Castro was quoted as saying. The story was given prominent play in the *New Orleans Times-Picayune*, a newspaper that Oswald was known to have read avidly when he lived in the city at the time. The FBI supervisor would acknowledge years later that "in retrospect, that certainly looks like a pointed signal," less than three months before the assassination, that Kennedy's life might have been in danger.

Word of Hoover's insistence that Oswald was the lone assassin reached Mexico, where the bureau had a staff of nearly a dozen agents and other employees operating out of the U.S. embassy. As a result, the FBI investigation of Oswald's trip there that fall was limited from the start. The FBI's top official in the embassy, Clark Anderson, a twenty-two-year veteran of the bureau who held the title of legal attaché, had known about Oswald's presence in Mexico within days of his arrival in September. Anderson had received a detailed report in October prepared by his CIA counterpart, Winston Scott, about Oswald's contacts in Mexico City with both the Cuban and Soviet embassies. Anderson recalled that he asked no questions at the time about how Oswald's visits to the embassies had been detected by the CIA. In fact, Anderson, who had a cordial but not close relationship with Scott, later claimed that at the time of the assassination he knew nothing at all about the CIA's elaborate photo-surveillance and wiretapping operations in Mexico City. That was the CIA's business, not his, he said.

FBI headquarters had known about Oswald's trip weeks before the assassination. On October 18, Anderson sent a memo to Washington in which he outlined what was known about Oswald's stay in Mexico, including his September 28 meeting in the Soviet embassy with a diplomat, Valeriy Vladimirovich Kostikov, who was known to be a top KGB operative. The CIA believed Kostikov was a member of the KGB's thirteenth directorate, which was responsible for overseas assassinations and kidnappings; he operated undercover as a regular member of the Soviet diplomatic corps.

The question of how much the CIA knew about the conversations between Oswald and Kostikov, and why that information was not shared immediately by FBI headquarters with its field agents in Dallas in advance of Kennedy's visit, would never be fully answered. Some of the answers were likely to be found in the sclerotic bureaucracy of the FBI; sensitive information often moved slowly within the bureau.

Just days after the assassination, FBI headquarters seemed to lose interest in Mexico City entirely, at least as measured by the requests it made to Anderson and his colleagues in the embassy. Anderson could recall few explicit orders, of any kind, from Washington about what should be investigated in Mexico. Nor did he feel pressure to work closely with the CIA to follow up leads about Oswald. In fact, Anderson said that he and Scott did not have a single private conversation about the assassination, apart from their joint meetings with the U.S. ambassador, Thomas Mann. "I don't think there was ever any sort of sit-down session where we took all of it and put it together," Anderson said of his contacts with Scott. "I don't recall Scott outlining any specific investigation they were conducting." As for the FBI's investigation in Mexico, he said, it was mostly limited to determining where Oswald had traveled during his days in Mexico City and whether he had been accompanied by anyone; even that limited investigation left questions unanswered.

"I don't recall that we were able to establish where he was every day while he was in Mexico," Anderson admitted years later. His agents did determine with certainty the date that Oswald entered Mexico (Saturday, September 26) and the day he crossed the border back into the United States (Saturday, October 3), as well as the name and location of the Mexico City hotel, the Hotel del Comercio, where Oswald took a room for $1.28 a day. "We were able to get him in, get him out, where he stayed," Anderson said.

Anderson, who had worked outside the United States for much of his career, including as the FBI's representative in the American embassy in Havana from 1945 to 1955, said that if there were ominous connections between Oswald and Cuban or Soviet agents in Mexico, it would have been a subject for investigation by the CIA, not the FBI.

Anderson and his FBI colleagues might not have harbored much suspicion about an assassination plot hatched in Mexico City, but others in the American embassy did, especially Ambassador Mann. In December, Anderson told FBI headquarters that he needed help to "calm down" the ambassador, a fifty-one-year-old career diplomat who would later become close to President Johnson; reportedly it was Johnson who pressed President Kennedy to name Mann, a Latin American specialist and fellow Texan, to the Mexico City embassy in 1961.

Almost from the moment of the assassination, Mann said, he was convinced that Castro was behind the president's murder and that Oswald's trip to Mexico was somehow tied to the conspiracy. Mann seemed perplexed that the FBI and CIA did not share his suspicions—or, at least, that they did not seem eager to act on them. He called in Scott and Anderson repeatedly to outline his theory of a Cuban conspiracy. He wrote them that he wanted to know much more about the "promiscuous" young Mexican woman, Silvia Tirado de Duran, who worked in the Cuban consulate and had dealt with Oswald. (Mann knew about the reports of an affair between Duran and the former Cuban ambassador to Mexico.)

Mann had praised Scott when the CIA station chief requested that Mexican authorities arrest and interrogate Duran on the day of Kennedy's assassination. The ambassador told colleagues that he had an "instinctive feeling" that Duran was lying when she claimed she dealt with Oswald only on questions about his visa application for Cuba. Anderson relayed Mann's alarming theories to FBI headquarters. In a memo to Washington two days after the assassination, he reported Mann's belief that the Soviet Union was "much too sophisticated" to be involved but that Castro was "stupid enough to have participated." The ambassador speculated that Oswald had visited Mexico to establish a "getaway route" after the murder. According to Anderson's memo, Mann wanted the FBI and CIA to do everything possible in Mexico "to establish or refute" a Cuban connection. At Mann's urging, Anderson proposed to FBI headquarters in a cable that the bureau consider "polling all Cuban sources in [the] U.S. in [an] effort to confirm or refute" the ambassador's theory that Castro was behind the assassination. The proposal was quickly rejected by headquarters. "Not desirable," an FBI supervisor in Washington wrote on his cable. "Would serve to promote rumors."

On November 26, Mann received startling information that, he believed, proved that his fears were justified. A twenty-three-year-old Nicaraguan government spy, Gilberto Alvarado, had telephoned the U.S. embassy with a story that, if true, meant Oswald had been paid off by Castro's government. Alvarado, who had contacts in the past with the CIA, claimed that he had been in the Cuban embassy in Mexico City in September when he saw a "red-haired Negro" man hand over $6,500 in cash to Oswald, presumably an advance payment for the assassination. Alvarado said he had been in the embassy on an undercover assignment for the fiercely anti-Communist Nicaraguan government.

In an urgent cable to the State Department, Mann said he was impressed by the details in the Nicaraguan's account, including the description of the "almost lackadaisical way in which the money is alleged by Alvarado to have been passed to Oswald." That fit in with Mann's contemptuous view of Castro as "the Latin type of extremist who acts viscerally rather than intellectually and apparently without much regard for risks."

Mann received more news that he considered alarming. On November 26, the CIA had secretly recorded a telephone conversation between Cuban president Osvaldo Dorticós and Cuba's ambassador to Mexico, Joaquin Armas, in which Armas described the questions that had been asked of Silvia Duran during her interrogation by the Mexicans, including whether she had "intimate relations" with Oswald and whether Oswald had received money from the embassy. "She denied all of that," Armas said in the call, seemingly relieved. Still, Dorticós sounded anxious about why the Mexicans were asking questions about the money, as if there might be some truth to the allegation that Oswald had been paid off. In a cable to Washington, Mann said he thought Dorticós's anxiety "tends to corroborate Alvarado's story about the passing of the $6,500."

Word of Alvarado's allegations, and Mann's growing suspicions, spread beyond the State Department, ultimately reaching the Oval Office. (President Johnson said later he cited the rumor about the $6,500 payment to Chief Justice Warren in their Oval Office meeting.) The questions about Alvarado's truthfulness would consume the U.S. embassy in Mexico City for days, and led Ambassador Mann, who worried that he was not being fully briefed by the FBI, to request that the bureau dispatch a senior Washington supervisor to Mexico City. He wanted the bureau to take the investigation in Mexico much more seriously.

Back in Washington, Hoover dismissed Mann and his concerns. The ambassador, Hoover wrote to a deputy, was "one of those pseudo investigators, a Sherlock Holmes" who was trying to tell the FBI its business. Still, Hoover had reviewed the raw intelligence about Alvarado, and he could not deny that the Nicaraguan's allegations would have to be investigated. If true, they would "throw an entirely different light on the whole picture" of the assassination, Hoover conceded. He agreed to dispatch an FBI supervisor from the bureau's training academy in Quantico, Virginia, Laurence Keenan, who knew nothing about the Oswald investigation but who spoke Spanish.

Keenan, who had been with the FBI a dozen years, would look back on the assignment as the most bizarre and troubling of his career. He did not realize it at the time, he said, but he came to understand years later that he had been part of a charade to avoid discovering the full truth about Oswald in Mexico. It was a charade intended to avert the possibility of a nuclear war over Cuba, he believed. "I realized I was used," Keenan said.

He was given the assignment at about eleven a.m. on Wednesday, November 27, and put on a plane to Mexico at four that afternoon. Before he left, he was given a "very short briefing" in Washington about the assassination investigation and about the Alvarado allegation. "I was completely in charge of the full investigation there in Mexico.

"I didn't even have a visa or a passport," he said, recalling that his wife met him at the office with a suitcase and fresh clothes before he sped to Dulles International Airport, outside Washington, for his flight.* "I got in a car that rushed me off to Dulles and was escorted with a siren through city traffic."

He arrived in Mexico City late that night and was met by Anderson, an old friend. According to Keenan, he and Anderson talked into "the wee hours of the morning" about the investigation. Keenan decided he had two responsibilities in Mexico. First, he would try to interview Alvarado to gauge his credibility. Second, he would protect the bureau's reputation "from any future allegation that the investigation was shoddy," given Ambassador Mann's alarm that something had been missed. He was there, as he put it later, to "cover ourselves, to pacify the ambassador."

In the ambassador's office the next morning, Keenan met with Mann and Scott. The ambassador "expressed his opinion that he felt that this was definitely a conspiracy and that we must turn over the last stone to find out if there is any overt conspiracy on the part of the Cubans," Keenan recalled. Mann noted the Associated Press article from September in which Castro had seemed to threaten Kennedy's life.

Keenan then made his presentation, telling the ambassador what he had been told the day before in Washington: the FBI believed there was no conspiracy. "Every bit of information that we had developed in Washington, in Dallas and elsewhere, indicated that this was a lone job," he explained. "This appeared to be a lone job—a one-in-a-million shot."

---

* The airport was named for John Foster Dulles (1888–1959), secretary of state under President Eisenhower and the brother of Allen Dulles, the former director of Central Intelligence and a member of the Warren Commission.

Still, Keenan said he wanted to talk to Alvarado "to go the last mile, to turn the last rock over." He turned to Scott, who was holding the Nicaraguan spy in one of the CIA's safe houses in Mexico City. "We would like very much to set up a conference or an interview with Alvarado," he said. Keenan could not remember how Scott replied. "He was not particularly communicative," he said of the CIA station chief.

Keenan had another message for the ambassador from FBI headquarters. He wanted the embassy to understand that the bureau did not consider the investigation of Oswald's activities in Mexico City to be its responsibility. It was a job for the CIA.

That afternoon Keenan got a shock. Within hours of his meeting, he was told that the CIA had decided to turn Alvarado over to the Mexican government immediately for further interrogation—before the FBI was given its chance to talk to him. The CIA's decision was "very definitely" peculiar, Keenan remembered. "I have no way to specifically say this was CIA's attempt to torpedo my investigation."

Keenan soon found himself with little to investigate, especially after the CIA reported that the allegations made by Alvarado had fallen apart. On November 30, the Mexican government reported that Alvarado had recanted, claiming that he made up the story about the Cuban payments to Oswald because "he hates Castro and thought that his story, if believed, would help cause the U.S.A. to take action against Castro," according to a CIA report. With Alvarado's reversal, "the pressure was off," Keenan recalled. "There was really nothing for me to coordinate or do at this point." He left Mexico on December 2, five days after he arrived, and had nothing more to do with the Oswald investigation. (The day of Keenan's return to Washington, Alvarado, now officially discredited by the Mexicans and the CIA, reversed himself again, returning to his original story about seeing Oswald receiving money from the Cubans. The Nicaraguan claimed he had recanted only because his Mexican interrogators had threatened to torture him by hanging him "by the testicles.")

Waiting in Keenan's office mailbox when he returned was a memo announcing his immediate reassignment as a supervisor in the bureau's field office in San Juan, Puerto Rico. It was, he said, a "wonderful job," one he had coveted, especially with the harsh winter weather on the East Coast fast approaching. He was expected in San Juan four days later.

Keenan left Washington so quickly that he did not even have time to brief FBI headquarters officials involved in the Oswald investigation about what he had learned in Mexico City, including tantalizing information about Silvia Duran, the young Mexican woman. Duran, he had been told, was a low-level spy for the Mexican government "and possibly the CIA." As Keenan put it years later, Duran was not "very, very high" in the hierarchy of the Cuban embassy. "I don't believe she ever had access to classified information." He did not recall hearing allegations suggesting a relationship between Oswald and Duran outside their meetings at the Cuban consulate. Nor did he recall ever thinking that the CIA had not interrogated Duran itself—and did not allow the FBI to—because she might work for the agency.

Mann also left Mexico City in a hurry. On December 14, President Johnson promoted him to the job of assistant secretary of state for Latin American affairs, as well as to an additional post in Washington as special assistant to the president. Before departing Mexico, Mann expressed his frustration about the assassination investigation; he suggested to embassy colleagues that he had given up trying to get to the bottom of what had happened in Mexico City. At least he would be well placed at the president's side in Washington if new evidence about a conspiracy emerged.

In one of his final cables to the State Department from Mexico, Mann wrote in December that he was not optimistic that "we shall be able to find anything definitive on the central issue" of a Cuban conspiracy to kill the president. He was quoted by an American reporter years later as saying that the seeming lack of interest by the CIA and the FBI in getting to the bottom of what had happened in Mexico City was "the strangest experience of my life."

17

Francis Adams, the former New York City police commissioner, towered over the other staff lawyers. The fifty-nine-year-old Adams was well over six feet tall. And Arlen Specter, his junior partner on the team responsible for reconstructing the events of the assassination, said it was not just Adams's height that made him seem big; it was Adams's sense of his own importance in the world. He was "the picture of the high-powered Wall Street lawyer," always convinced he could bend anyone to his will, Specter remembered.

Specter came to like Adams, despite the older lawyer's arrogance. Adams had an outspoken contempt for all places that were not New York City, and Specter, a native of Kansas, found his partner's big-city chauvinism funny, not insulting. In their first meeting, Adams looked over Specter's résumé and noted that the younger lawyer, the son of a Ukrainian émigré fruit peddler, was born in Wichita.

"Wichita?" Adams asked drily. "Where was your mother on her way to at the time?"

Adams showed up in Washington a few days after Specter had begun work in the commission's office. He explained that he felt the investigation could move quickly, since Oswald was so obviously guilty. "He said, 'It's just another simple murder case,'" Specter recalled.

Adams deserved some of his self-regard, Specter knew. During his tumultuous eighteen-month tenure as New York's police commissioner, beginning in January 1954, Adams took what were remembered as historic steps to root out corruption on the police force. He targeted a budding crime wave in the city by forcing hundreds of reluctant police officers out of desk jobs and putting them on street patrols, earning the public's gratitude. After leaving the police department, he established himself as one of the city's most sought-after and best-paid courtroom lawyers.

Specter remembered going to lunch with Adams near Lafayette Square, a few blocks from the White House, at an expensive French restaurant ("Frank Adams did not dine at any other sort of restaurant"), and Adams insisted on picking up the tab. He boasted to Specter that he could better afford the meal since "his daily charge for trial work was $2,500." Specter gulped at what he considered "a giant sum of money." Adams earned more in a day than Specter would earn in a month on the commission's staff.

Almost from the start, Adams seemed uncomfortable at the commission. It was going to be a difficult assignment. He and Specter would have to produce a detailed, second-by-second chronology of the events of the assassination, as well as review and understand much of the medical and ballistics evidence. Adams, however, had "no drive for detailed work," Specter said. At his law firm, he supervised five or six associates when preparing a case, he told Specter. But at the commission, he and Specter were on their own. "He was unused to working on a prolonged project with only one junior associate, and especially with one so young," Specter said.

Adams soon established a routine. He usually arrived after eleven a.m. "He chatted briefly, fingered some files and phoned his New York office before finding some reason to leave," Specter recalled. Adams had a pressing caseload back in New York that winter, he warned his partner in early January. "Adams told me right from the start that he had to work on a major antitrust case by mid-February—five weeks away—and he implied that he expected to finish the work by then." Adams's firm had a Washington office, and he spent many days there, rather than on Capitol Hill in the cramped office he shared with Specter.

After a few weeks, Adams disappeared altogether, essentially abandoning the commission. He came down to Washington on a handful of days that winter and spring, including the day in March that Specter had scheduled for the deposition of the navy pathologists who had conducted the president's autopsy. Specter was introducing the doctors to Chief Justice Warren that day when Adams entered the room. He was such a stranger in the commission's offices that Warren did not recognize him.

"Good afternoon, Doctor," Warren said to Adams, who stood there, mortified not to be recognized by the chief justice.

"And that was the last we saw of Frank Adams," Specter said.

Adams's disappearance was fine with Specter, who was described by many of his colleagues as the single most self-confident young man they had ever met. "I thought it was an advantage not to have to work with anybody," he explained. "I didn't have to share the work. All I had to do was do it."

After the initial staff meeting in January, Warren had little contact with the young staff lawyers, which disappointed many of them. He delegated responsibilities through Rankin and through Rankin's two increasingly influential deputies—Redlich and Willens. Warren also met frequently with a few of the "senior" lawyers, especially his old friend Joseph Ball. The two men liked to swap stories about their early adventures in the law back home in California. "He was one of the finest men I ever knew," Ball said of Warren. "He was strong physically, morally and mentally, and he had a great soul."

Warren's routine was to arrive in the commission's offices early each morning, usually by eight, and then leave about an hour later for the Supreme Court, two blocks away. At about five, he would return, often remaining in the commission's offices for several more hours.

Among the young lawyers, only Specter had frequent face-to-face dealings with the chief justice—the result of Adams's disappearance. As effectively the sole member of his team, Specter was left to conduct many of the commission's most important witness interviews by himself, often with Warren listening in. Specter established a courteous, if sometimes chilly, relationship with the chief justice. Warren was used to people being intimidated in his presence; he clearly enjoyed being at the center of, and usually directing, conversations. Specter, however, would insist that he was never intimidated by the chief justice and that he stood up to him when necessary.

"It was a thrill to work for Warren," Specter said years later. "We felt we were in the presence of history. But what was there to be intimidated about? I was not intimidated by him. I was aggravated by him sometimes."

Specter formed an early bond with David Belin, the Iowa lawyer—in part, Belin believed, because he and Specter were Jews raised in stretches of the Midwest where Jews were a novelty, and often an unwelcome one. Belin made friends easily; he was ebullient, full of energy and ambition, and he relished his standing as the "Iowa country boy" and "hayseed" suddenly working among lawyers from New York and Washington. He was appalled by Adams's disappearance from the investigation, and he urged Specter to protest. "Adams should have been asked to resign when it became apparent that he was not going to undertake his responsibilities," Belin said later. He was grateful that his own partner, Joseph Ball, was so fully committed to the commission's work. Ball had taken a leave of absence from his firm in Long Beach, and the Californian's sweet charm and capacity for hard work made him popular throughout the commission's staff. Specter remembered Ball as "cherubic, with a twinkle in his eye," who "made women swoon, even at 62."

Ball and Belin, responsible for finding evidence to prove that Oswald was the assassin, became so close that their names were often uttered together as a single word—"Ball-Belin"—by Rankin and his deputies. Early on, Ball, Belin, and Specter saw how their investigations would overlap, and they hit upon a way to divide up their duties. Ball and Belin "would handle all witnesses at the assassination scene except for those in the motorcade, whom I would handle," including Governor Connally and the Secret Service agents, Specter said.

Specter took responsibility for the medical evidence, including the analysis of the results of the autopsy at the Bethesda hospital. Determining the source of the bullets—presumably, Oswald's rifle—remained a subject for investigation by Ball and Belin. As for the scientific analysis of the ammunition, "we decided that the bullet in flight was the dividing point," Specter said. "Before the bullet left the barrel, it was the responsibility of Ball and Belin. After striking the president, it was my responsibility."

For all three men, the early days of the investigation were consumed by reading. Ball and Belin took nearly a month to read through all of the paperwork from Dallas produced by the FBI and the Secret Service.

Belin established an index-card system that allowed the three men to cross-index the information they were receiving from different agencies "so we didn't have to read everything twice," Ball said.

They were all struck by the FBI's apparent certainty about the number and sequence of shots in Dealey Plaza, especially since the three of them found the ballistics evidence so confusing. According to the FBI, Oswald fired three shots: the first hit Kennedy in the upper back or lower neck, the second hit Connally, and the third struck the president in the head—the fatal shot. But the FBI's reports did not make clear how the bureau had arrived at those conclusions.

Down the hallway in the VFW building, Norman Redlich was preparing for the commission's interview of Marina Oswald, and his research was exhaustive to the point of obsession. He outlined hundreds of questions that Oswald's widow could be asked. He prepared a mammoth typed chart in which he laid out, chronologically, every significant moment of her life, beginning with her birth in the northern Russian city of Molotovsk on July 17, 1941, and continuing through the president's murder in Dallas. He listed questions that could be addressed to her about every major event of those twenty-two years, with the questions divided into subcategories, based on information that she had given to other investigators. She could be challenged on everything she had already told the FBI and the Secret Service, as well as what others had said about her.

Redlich's questions reflected his suspicion that Marina was something other than the innocent, bereaved young woman she claimed to be. As his questions showed, he believed she might in fact be some sort of Russian agent who had recruited her husband into espionage for the Soviet Union, or who had duped an unknowing Oswald into taking her to the United States for some sinister purpose. "If Lee was as unpleasant as he appears to have been in the U.S., it is hard to understand Marina's ready agreement to leave her friends and family for a strange land with a difficult husband," Redlich noted on one page of questions. "I feel we should attempt to discover whether Marina is the simple 'peasant' girl that everyone thinks she is."

He wanted to challenge Marina's portrayal of herself as "the suffering wife trying to help this disturbed man" when, in fact, both the FBI and the Secret Service had developed a portrait of her as an emotionally cold woman who disparaged her husband to his face, in front of friends—even about his sexual performance. Redlich had detailed questions about Marina's relationship with Ruth Paine. "There have been various suggestions that Mrs. Paine's role in this story is not an innocent one," he wrote, adding that suspicions had arisen, in part, because Paine's in-laws were tied to "radical" left-wing politics. Michael Paine's father had been prominent in the Socialist Workers Party of the United States.

Rankin and Redlich invited the other lawyers to submit questions to be posed to Marina. In a memo attached to his list, Specter suggested that whatever questions were going to be asked of Oswald's widow, they needed to be asked quickly; he thought she might soon be dead. "She could be the object of foul play herself if someone would want to silence her to hide something," Specter warned. If there had been a conspiracy and it had already ended in the deaths of the president and his alleged assassin, Marina Oswald's life was almost certainly in danger, too.

Given the size of the egos involved, several of the lawyers were surprised they got along so well. Friendships were formed that, for some, would last the rest of their lives. "Nearly every day, we would be in and out of each other's offices learning facts, questioning theories, arguing and questioning any preliminary conclusions or findings made as we went along," Belin recalled. Several ate lunch together most days at the cafeteria in the national headquarters of the United Methodist Church, two blocks away from the VFW building. Often they would go out to dinner at nearby restaurants for what Specter remembered as "skull sessions" about the investigation.

Warren asked the director of the National Archives, Wayne Grover, for advice on recruiting a historian to the staff, and Grover said that some of the best in the government came from the Defense Department. He recommended two historians from the Pentagon—one from the army, the other from the air force. After interviewing both candidates, Rankin recommended the air force historian, forty-five-year-old Alfred Goldberg, a man of dry humor who had the instincts of a reporter. Goldberg had launched his career as a military historian while in uniform in Europe in World War II and later earned a PhD in history at Johns Hopkins University.

He was invited to meet Warren in his chambers at the Supreme Court and found the chief justice "very easy to talk to—friendly, pleasant, and I got to asking him questions. I asked him, why do you want to hire a historian?" Goldberg remembered. "And he said—and this is a direct quotation—'I don't trust all those lawyers.'"

Goldberg had assumed Warren wanted him to write a history of the commission and that his job would be to document the work of the investigation as it went along. No, Warren said. He wanted Goldberg to bring a historian's eye to the events of the assassination itself and to be a writer and editor of the commission's final report. The chief justice, he said, wanted a report that read like something other than a cold legal brief.

Goldberg was given an office on the fourth floor of the VFW building, adjacent to one occupied by a pair of senior IRS inspectors who were trying to reconstruct Oswald's finances. Goldberg found their work fascinating. The tax agents, Edward A. Conroy and John J. O'Brien, were excited to explain to Goldberg what they were doing. They were in search of the slightest bit of evidence that might suggest Oswald had received money from foreign agents or some other group of conspirators. Goldberg said he was convinced that if Oswald had spent a penny more than he earned from his assortment of menial jobs, Conroy and O'Brien would find it; there was a reason why taxpayers feared an IRS audit, Goldberg now knew. "They got Oswald's grocery receipts, they got everything," he recalled. "It was remarkable."

Goldberg received a less friendly reception from some of the commission's other staffers. "A lot of the lawyers looked rather askance at having somebody else, other than a lawyer, involved in the investigation," he said. He got a particularly frosty reception from Redlich, who planned to be the central author and editor of the final report and who was territorial about his authority. "I had the impression he was holding me at arm's length," Goldberg said. "He could be arrogant and high-handed."

Then there was Rankin's fearsome secretary, Julia Eide, who had worked for him at the Justice Department. Eide looked on herself as Rankin's protector and enforcer. "She was not easy to get along with," Goldberg remembered. "Once I sized her up, I was careful not to get in her way."

Still, Eide was intelligent and hardworking, which could not be said for many of the other secretaries who were dispatched to the commission from elsewhere in the government. Many were sent over from the Pentagon, which had a large pool of secretaries with the necessary security clearances. It seemed to many of the commission's lawyers that the Defense Department and other agencies had taken advantage of the opportunity to move out their worst secretaries and dump them on the investigation; a few could barely type. "They were incompetent, the dregs," David Slawson remembered.

Most of the lawyers shrugged off their annoyance, thinking there was nothing they could do. But not Jim Liebeler, the young North Dakotan. As David Slawson remembered fondly, Liebeler had quickly proved himself to his new colleagues to be "fun, brave—and obnoxious." Liebeler marched into Rankin's office and demanded that the incompetent secretaries be removed. "We can't work with these idiots," declared Liebeler, who knew he was quietly being cheered on by the other lawyers.

From what he had seen of the secretaries, Rankin could not disagree. At Liebeler's urging, he placed a call to the White House and left a message with McGeorge Bundy, President Johnson's national security adviser. Slawson was in Rankin's office when Bundy returned the call. "Rankin told him about the secretaries," Slawson recalled, "and Bundy said, 'Okay, just hold.'" As Rankin waited on the line, "Bundy apparently picked up another phone and called the Defense Department and then got back on the line to Rankin." The national security adviser had good news: "I just told the Defense Department to have twenty of the best secretaries over there tomorrow morning."

The new secretaries appeared the next day as promised, ready for work. Slawson marveled at what Liebeler had managed to accomplish: "From that point on we had good secretaries." To no one's surprise among his new friends on the staff, Liebeler managed to have one of the best, and the prettiest, assigned to him.

TOP LEFT: William Coleman, senior lawyer on the "conspiracy" team, was a key legal strategist in the civil rights movement and is shown standing next to Martin Luther King. TOP RIGHT: Francis Adams, former New York City police commissioner, effectively abandoned the investigation. CENTER (*left to right*): Leon Hubert, former district attorney of New Orleans, left the commission's staff early, angry that little attention was being paid to his investigation of Jack Ruby; Albert Jenner was the senior lawyer in investigating Oswald's life story; Samuel Stern was the sole investigator assigned to study the history of presidential protection and the performance of the Secret Service. BOTTOM: Julia Eide was Rankin's intelligent and intimidating secretary.

CERTIFICATE OF SERVICE
ARMED FORCES OF THE UNITED STATES

THIS IS TO CERTIFY THAT

ALEX JAMES HIDELL

HONORABLY SERVED ON ACTIVE DUTY IN THE

United States Marine Corps

FROM TOP LEFT (*clockwise*): Marina Oswald in Minsk; Marina and Lee in Minsk; the Oswalds with infant June in Texas; Oswald's falsified Marine Corp ID card (in the name of alias Alex Hidell); Oswald with rifle and pistol in New Orleans, 1963.

18

It was Marguerite Oswald on the phone again, which was never good news in the commission's offices. A call from Oswald's mother led, invariably, to a wave of rolled eyes and silent snarls among the staff members who were forced to deal with her, especially the unfortunate telephone receptionists and secretaries who were the first targets of her abuse.

The collect calls from her home in Fort Worth began in January, shortly after Mrs. Oswald obtained the commission's phone number. The calls might have been treated as comical had it not been for Mrs. Oswald's ability to manipulate the press corps in Dallas and Washington to pay attention to her. Her attacks on the commission were considered headline news, so her threatening calls had to be taken seriously.

As the mother of the man accused of killing the president, Mrs. Oswald was, for many reporters, a good story. She was always available and always quotable. Even reporters for powerful newspapers and magazines who should have known better—or, at least, signaled to their readers that she spouted easily refuted nonsense—wrote about her endlessly, lending credibility to her claims that she had evidence that could prove her son innocent.

On January 14, Mrs. Oswald became an even bigger threat. At a news conference in Fort Worth, she announced her decision to retain Mark Lane to represent her son's interests. Lane, she said, had generously agreed to work without a fee, and with his help she would "fight to my last breath" to vindicate her son. The meeting with reporters gave Mrs. Oswald and Lane the chance to announce that they had rented a post office box in Fort Worth—No. 9578—so that anyone with evidence pointing to her son's innocence could write in. Well-wishers were invited to mail in cash donations.

At the news conference, she pleaded again, as she had for weeks, for her daughter-in-law Marina to resume contact with "Mamma." Mrs. Oswald said she had sent a written message to Marina through the Secret Service, which was continuing to protect the young widow. She said she had put the message in simple English so that her Russian daughter-in-law might understand it: "Marina, Mamma grieves. Marina, Mamma needs to see you and the grandchildren. Mamma *has* to see you and the grandchildren."

Mrs. Oswald used the news conference to accuse the Secret Service of blocking her access to her son's family: "They have no right to keep me from speaking to my daughter-in-law and granddaughters." Lane went further, suggesting that the Secret Service was attempting to "brainwash" Marina Oswald to incriminate her husband; cutting off communication between Mrs. Oswald and her daughter-in-law was part of the agency's plan. Mrs. Oswald appeared unaware that it was her surviving son Robert, not the Secret Service, who had insisted that Marina end all contact with his "irrational" mother.

No one posed more of an obstacle to Mrs. Oswald's campaign to prove her son innocent than his widow. Marina had continued to say openly that she was convinced that her husband had killed the president and that he had almost certainly done it alone. In January, she authorized James Martin, her business manager, to tell the *New York Times* that she was so certain of her husband's guilt that she had decided against bringing a negligence lawsuit against the city of Dallas over her husband's death.

Marina, Martin, and her lawyer, James Thorne, arrived in Washington on Sunday, February 2, a day ahead of her scheduled testimony before the commission. She settled into the Willard Hotel, one of the city's finest, with spectacular views up Pennsylvania Avenue toward the Capitol dome;

the hotel was a few minutes' drive from the VFW building. Marina had brought her daughters to Washington: June Lee, called Junie, who would turn three that month, and four-month-old Rachel.

Reporters got wind of Marina's arrival and thronged the hotel. She did not resist their efforts to follow her. In fact, she seemed amused by the crush of reporters and photographers who had managed to turn her into a global celebrity. "Silly men, silly men," she said, smiling, when the photographers turned up in the lobby of the Willard. Everywhere she went, she was also trailed by Secret Service agents. She had come to see them as her protectors—her friends, even.

A reporter from *Time* magazine found Marina at a table at Parchey's Restaurant and noted the glamorous makeover she had undergone since the assassination. Her hair had obviously been set in a beauty parlor—"something her late husband would not have allowed," the magazine noted—and she wore touches of makeup and smoked a cigarette while sipping, first, a vodka gimlet, before rejecting it in favor of a cherry cordial. Although she said she was not hungry, she ate a little of her filet mignon with mushroom sauce.

On Monday, February 3, at ten thirty, the commission met in the ground-floor conference room of the VFW building. Warren and four of the other commissioners were present; Senator Russell and John McCloy missed the start of the session. Under the commission's rules, a witness could request a public hearing, but there had been no such request from Oswald's widow or her lawyer, so the press had to wait outside.

"Mrs. Oswald, did you have a good trip here?" Warren said as he opened the session, his words translated into Russian by an interpreter. She nodded yes. With that, he asked her to rise from her chair and be sworn in.

Rankin oversaw the questioning, which would last for four days, and began by asking her full name.

"My name is Marina Nikolaevna Oswald. My maiden name was Prusakova."

Rankin noted that, as best he could tell, this was the forty-seventh time that Marina had been questioned by government agencies since the assassination—by the FBI, the Secret Service, and the Dallas police, mostly. Rankin did not say it, but he and many of the commissioners were well aware that, in many of those earlier interviews, Marina had not told the truth. The list of her lies was long and disturbing, beginning with her initial claim to the FBI that she knew nothing about her husband's attempt to kill the right-wing extremist Edwin Walker in Dallas in April, seven months before the president was assassinated. In fact, she later admitted, he had told her about the Walker attack in considerable detail on the night it had occurred; it resulted, she said, in a furious argument in which she threatened to go to the police if he tried anything like it again. She had also initially insisted that she knew nothing about her husband's trip to Mexico. Later she confessed that she knew about the trip as he was planning it; he had even asked her what gift she would like him to bring back. She had requested a traditional Mexican silver bracelet.

Rankin asked if she wanted to correct anything she had said previously: "Do you know of anything that is not true in those interviews that you would like to correct?"

"Yes," she answered, "I would like to correct some things because not everything was true."

In the earlier interviews, she said, she had not been under oath and so felt that she could be "less exact." She explained that, at first, she had wanted to believe that her husband was innocent of killing the president, and she did not want to implicate him—or implicate herself—in other crimes, including the Walker shooting. Her lies, she said, were also explained by her dislike for the FBI agents who did much of the questioning. "I didn't want to be too sincere with them."

Rankin led her through hours of questioning about her marriage. He asked her what she had initially found attractive about the young American defector she had reportedly met in March 1961 at a community dance in the central Soviet city of Minsk, where Oswald was working at an electronics factory. "You don't meet Americans very often," she said, recalling her husband-to-be as "very neat, very polite . . . it seemed that he would be a good family man." After the dance, he asked to see her again, and she agreed.

Oswald soon told her how disillusioned he had become with the Soviet Union, she said. "He was homesick, and that perhaps he was sorry for having come to Russia." She recalled that "he said many good things" about the United States. "He said that his house was warmer and that people lived better."

At the end of April 1961, only weeks after their first meeting, they married. About a month after that, Marina said, Lee proposed that they go together to the United States. A year later, after tangling with bureaucrats in the Russian government and the State Department, the couple received permission to leave the Soviet Union. In June 1962, they arrived in the United States and settled in Fort Worth, near the homes of Oswald's mother and brother Robert.

It was then, Marina said, that she discovered how dysfunctional her husband's family was: he hated his mother and wanted little contact with his two brothers. He had difficulty finding a job and, once he did, holding on to it. He found most work boring, she said. Their marriage quickly began to unravel, with Oswald becoming distant and delusional, as well as violent, she said. He beat her regularly, leaving her with purplish bruises on her pale skin and, on one occasion, a black eye. "I think that he was very nervous and . . . this somehow relieved his tension."

Raised in a culture in which wife-beating was not uncommon, Marina said, she thought that perhaps she had brought some of the violence on herself. "Sometimes it was my own fault," she explained. She had given Oswald reasons for jealousy; he intercepted a letter she had written to an old boyfriend in Russia in which she said she should have married him instead of Oswald.

Her husband had never abandoned the commitment to Marxism that had taken him to Russia—far from it. He insisted to her that he was searching for a purer form of Communism and thought he had found it in Castro's Cuba. He told her that he was planning to defect again, this time to Havana. "Lee wanted to get to Cuba by any means."

He purchased a rifle and began practicing with it, suggesting to her that he would use it to hijack a plane to Cuba. He proposed that Marina join him, perhaps carrying a gun onto the plane herself. She rejected the idea as crazy. "I told him that I was not going with him—I would stay here."

He had gone to Mexico City, she said, to get visas that would allow the family to travel to Cuba. His plan, it appeared, was to lie to the Russian embassy in Mexico, pretending that he wanted to return to the Soviet Union. With a new Soviet visa in hand, he could obtain travel papers from the Cuban embassy, supposedly to transit through Havana on the way to Moscow. In fact, Marina said, Oswald intended to stay in Cuba if he could get there. "He wanted to go to Cuba," she said. "I know he had no intention of going to Russia."

Rankin pressed her on other details of her husband's trip to Mexico, asking what else he had told her about how he had spent his time there.

She remembered he talked about attending a bullfight and doing other sightseeing. Was there anything else? Although her husband had never expressed any interest in other women during their marriage—"he doesn't like other women"—he had specifically noted his distaste for women in Mexico. "He said he didn't like Mexican girls," she said, a comment that drew no follow-up from Rankin.

During her testimony, she insisted, as she had consistently since the day of the assassination, that she had no advance knowledge of Oswald's plans to kill the president. In fact, she thought her husband liked Kennedy. "I had never heard anything bad about Kennedy from Lee." Even so, she said she was convinced of her husband's guilt in the assassination. She knew almost from the minute she visited him at Dallas police head-quarters on the afternoon of the murder. "I could see by his eyes that he was guilty," she said. And she was convinced that he had acted alone—that there was no conspiracy.

She thought that he killed the president because he was consumed by the idea of making a mark in history, she said. He was a voracious reader; he spent hours each week at the public library near their homes in Dallas and New Orleans, and he often checked out biographies of important figures from world history, including Kennedy. Lee Oswald wanted to be remembered, too. "I can conclude that he wanted, in any way, whether good or bad, to do something that would make him outstanding, that he would be known in history."

She suggested sadly that she might have prevented the assassination if she had only been more understanding the night before the president's murder, when Oswald had visited Marina and the children at the home of Ruth Paine. The Oswalds had been separated for several weeks, and Marina said he pleaded for her to reconcile and to go with the children to live with him in Dallas. At one point that night, she said, he was in tears. He "just wanted to make up."

Although she intended to reconcile with him eventually, she had refused to give in that night, she said. "I gave the appearance of being very angry. . . . When he went to bed, he was very upset." He left the next morn-ing, taking the rifle he had stored, hidden in a blanket, in Ruth Paine's garage.

Marina knew that her mother-in-law was scheduled to be the next witness to testify before the commissioners, and she expressed her con-dolences to Warren and the others for what they were about to endure. "I am sorry that you will devote your time to questioning her, because you will only be tired and very sick after talking to her," Marina said. "When you get to know her, you will understand why."

Her mother-in-law, she said, had seized on the assassination as an opportunity to make money. "She has a mania—only money, money, money." Marina knew how angry her mother-in-law was over her conclusion that Lee had murdered the president. If given a chance, Marina said, she "would scratch my eyes out."

At five fifty p.m. on Thursday, February 6, after four days and twenty hours of testimony, the commission ended its questioning of Oswald's widow.

"Mrs. Oswald, you have been a very cooperative witness," Warren said warmly. "You have helped this commission."

"It is difficult to speak the truth," she said. "I am very grateful to all of you, I didn't think among Americans I would find so many friends."

"You have friends here," Warren assured her.

The chief justice told reporters after her testimony that Mrs. Oswald was "a very brave little woman." Marina in turn told reporters that she had become fond of Warren. She said he reminded her of one of her grandfathers in Russia.

In Texas, Marguerite Oswald was outraged by the sympathetic coverage of her daughter-in-law's trip to Washington and her testimony to the commission, and she decided to strike back.

On February 3, the first day of Marina's testimony, Mrs. Oswald called Secret Service headquarters in Washington to offer to reveal what she said was damaging information about her daughter-in-law. The Secret Service did not return the call, but instead passed word to the Warren Commission that Mrs. Oswald was agitated.

Rankin, busy questioning Marina, had Norman Redlich call Mrs. Oswald in Texas the next day. Redlich had a secretary listen in on an extension and make a transcript.

"Hello Mrs. Oswald," said Redlich, identifying himself as Rankin's deputy. "I am calling you because of your call to the Secret Service."

"Yes," she replied.

"You indicated that you had some information which you would like to give about which we might question Marina. I am calling and would like to know if you would like to give this information to me."

Mrs. Oswald began by saying how outraged she was to have to deal with a midlevel staffer like Redlich. "I will give the information only to Mr. Rankin or one of the officers on the commission. I am tired of being pushed around, no offense to you. I will talk directly to Mr. Rankin, Mr. Warren or the president of the United States." She explained that after hearing nothing back from the Secret Service the day before, she had called a radio station that morning to report that she was being stonewalled in her effort to expose the truth about the assassination. "The only course I have is to make this public."

She then claimed, as she often would, that "I think my life is in danger," before launching into a mostly incoherent rant about the sacrifices she had made for her children and her country, and how no one would listen to her. "If you could know what a woman alone has had to take, I've been pushed around," she said. "I want to have a voice in this, and the public and the foreign public wants me to have a voice in this." She warned darkly that the truth about Marina was not being told and that only she knew it. "When my daughter-in-law says anything, I should be there. I am not accusing her of anything. I hope she is innocent, but I have no proof that anyone is innocent."

Redlich listened for several more minutes before trying to end the conversation. "Do you have anything else you wish to say?"

"I think I have said everything at this particular moment," she said. "This important information I am keeping in my heart. How long I can do it, I don't know."

Redlich hung up the phone and tracked down Rankin, warning him of what seemed to be Mrs. Oswald's threat to go public with some devastating allegation against her daughter-in-law. Rankin and Warren quickly agreed to invite Mrs. Oswald to come to Washington immediately. Rankin called her the next day and asked her to testify the following Monday.

"Well, I will have to call Mr. Lane and discuss it with him," she replied.

"You are welcome to come by yourself or with your attorney," Rankin said.

With no additional prompting, Mrs. Oswald then launched into a seventeen-hundred-word stream-of-consciousness monologue about the mendacity of her daughter-in-law. She accused Marina of vanity and laziness, suggesting she might have deserved the battering she had taken from her husband. "I saw Marina with a black eye," she said. "I certainly don't approve of men beating their wives but there are some times when I believe a woman should be beaten."

The venom kept pouring out, until finally Mrs. Oswald revealed the extraordinary allegation that she intended to make. She would accuse Marina and her friend Ruth Paine of involvement in the president's assassination. "Marina and Mrs. Paine are in this together," she said. "I believe in my heart that Marina and Mrs. Paine set Lee up. There is a high official involved in this, and I would say that there are two Secret Service men involved."

Lane, she said, "has a lot of documents—affidavits—proof almost that my son is not guilty of killing President Kennedy."

Rankin could only imagine the furor that would result if the allegation—Oswald's mother accusing his widow of involvement in the assassination—made its way to reporters. "We want anything you have," he said, trying to placate her. He urged her to call him, collect, when she decided to travel to Washington. The next day, he sent her a telegram, formally asking her to appear in Washington the following Monday, all expenses paid.

She told reporters in Fort Worth how excited she was to go to Washington and how much work she had to do to prepare herself. She began gathering up documents—the letters, the phone bills, the yellowing newspaper articles—that she insisted would demonstrate that her son was innocent.

On Monday morning, February 10, she arrived at the VFW building in Washington accompanied by Lane and by John F. Doyle, a Washington lawyer retained by the commission to represent her; Doyle had been recommended by the local bar association. To the relief of the commissioners, she asked to be represented in the hearing by Doyle, which meant that Lane had to remain outside.

Congressman Ford recalled that Mrs. Oswald made her "presence felt from the moment she entered" the conference room. He was impressed at first. "If I saw her walking down the street, I would have said, 'Here is a strong, purposeful woman.'" He remembered she clutched an "oversized black handbag which proved to be her portable filing cabinet. It bulged with letters, documents and clippings."

Her testimony began with a promise from Warren of fairness. "I am going to ask you if you would like first, in your own way, and in your own time, to tell us everything you have concerning this case," he began.

"Yes, Chief Justice Warren," she replied. "I would like to, very much."

And with that, she began talking, almost nonstop, for three days, her answers usually unrelated to the question she was asked. Her monologue was often punctuated by the statement, "This is important." She seemed to revel in this. She had been given what her sons knew she always wanted: a captive audience of powerful men, foremost among them that day the chief justice of the United States, who would be forced to listen to her every word. Ford said later that "our job was to sit patiently and listen," even though her testimony was "confused bordering on incoherence." He later concluded that she was, simply, "kooky."

She launched into her life story, and that of her sons, before getting to her central allegation—that her daughter-in-law had a role in the assassination and that two of the Secret Service agents who protected Marina after the assassination were part of the plot.

The Secret Service was involved? Warren asked incredulously. "With who?"

Mrs. Oswald: "With Marina and Mrs. Paine—the two women. Lee was set up, and it is quite possible these two Secret Service men are involved."

Rankin: "What kind of a conspiracy are you describing that these two men are engaged in?"

Mrs. Oswald: "The assassination of President Kennedy."

Rankin: "You think that two Secret Service agents and Marina and Mrs. Paine were involved in that, in the conspiracy?"

Mrs. Oswald: "Yes, I do." The proof, she said, would be found in the details of Marina's financial arrangements to sell her life story, as if the young widow knew in advance that she would be rewarded with magazine covers and book contracts if her husband was blamed for killing the president. "Marina is going to be fixed—you know, she is fixed financially and otherwise."

Her rambling again veered toward self-pity. "But I am nothing," she said. "What is going to become of me? I have no income. I have no job. I lost my job. And nobody thought about me."

Rankin pressed again, insisting that she explain what proof she had of a conspiracy.

"I do not have proof, sir," she finally admitted. "I do not have proof of an agent. I do not have proof my son is innocent. I do not have proof."

Rankin: "You don't have any proof of a conspiracy?"

Mrs. Oswald: "Of anything."

Rankin might have thought he was getting somewhere until, a few minutes later, Mrs. Oswald reversed herself and restated her allegations against Marina.

Ford said he left the sessions exhausted, even though there was value in what he had witnessed. "The commission now had a lucid understanding of the volatile relationships between members of the family" that might explain why Lee had been so troubled since childhood, Ford said. The Oswalds were "a family in fragments" whose ties to one another were "a relatively meaningless accident of birth."

In a statement released to the press, Warren dismissed Mrs. Oswald's testimony, saying it "produced nothing that would change the picture." He made no mention of her allegations against her daughter-in-law.

When asked later what she had told the commission, Mrs. Oswald was coy with reporters. She still wanted to sell her story. "I have to have something left to write about, don't I?" she said. She said she planned to meet with New York publishers about a book contract and was hoping for an advance of $25,000 to $50,000.* "I don't even think I'll have to have a ghostwriter," she said. "No, I don't want one. I believe I can write the book by just dictating."

The next day, Mrs. Oswald and Lane flew from Washington to New York, and Lane revealed to reporters waiting at LaGuardia Airport that he had obtained copies of more than twenty documents from the files of the Dallas district attorney's office that, he said, bolstered Mrs. Oswald's campaign to prove her son's innocence. He did not explain how he got the documents, except to say that "someone was kind enough to secure them for me" and "I like to think he secured them legally." He made no suggestion that his source was Hugh Aynesworth, the Dallas reporter.

Lane and Mrs. Oswald had traveled to New York to hold a public rally at the Town Hall, the landmark theater on West Forty-Third Street in Manhattan, to raise support for the campaign. The *New York Times* reported that more than fifteen hundred people packed into the theater, paying a total of more than $5,000 for tickets, and that they cheered loudly for Mrs. Oswald as she demanded justice for her son. Dressed in black, she told the audience that hers was a lonely struggle. "All I have is humbleness and sincerity for our American way of life."

Lane tantalized the crowd, claiming he would soon reveal the evidence

---

* Given inflation, $25,000 in 1964 would be equivalent to about $188,000 in 2013.

to prove that Mrs. Oswald was right. He called for a government investigation of a "two-hour meeting" that he believed had occurred about a week before the assassination in Jack Ruby's Carousel Club between J. D. Tippit, the slain Dallas police officer, and others who may have had a role in Kennedy's murder.* Lane declared that he had found other witnesses who heard shots being fired toward Kennedy's limousine from the front of the motorcade—from the so-called grassy knoll—and not from the Texas School Book Depository behind it.

Back in Washington, another woman was taking steps that same week to tell her story—Jacqueline Kennedy. She was at the center of early efforts to establish an untarnished legacy for her husband's presidency. It had begun on Friday, November 29, a week after the assassination, when she gave an interview to the famed journalist Theodore H. White for *Life* magazine, in which she compared her husband's White House years to the mythical Camelot. In December, she arranged for a plaque to be placed in the Lincoln Bedroom, engraved with the words: "In this room lived John Fitzgerald Kennedy, with his wife Jacqueline, during the two years, ten months and two days he was President of the United States." (Years later, President Richard Nixon would have the plaque removed.)

Robert Kennedy had joined in her campaign to burnish the record of the Kennedy administration, and he had recruited Chief Justice Warren, then at the start of his work on the commission, to participate. On January 9, Kennedy sent a telegram to Warren, asking him "on behalf of the family" to serve as a trustee of the John F. Kennedy Presidential Library, which would be built in Boston and "maintained as a permanent and active library and memorial to the late president." Warren eagerly accepted the invitation, sending a reply the next day, saying he was "greatly honored."

The next month, the Kennedy family took a more dramatic step to

---

* Lane would later say that he did not talk to anyone who claimed to have witnessed the Carousel Club meeting. The information, he said, had instead come to him secondhand from the late Thayer Waldo, a reporter for the *Fort Worth Star Telegram*—the same reporter who told Drew Pearson about how Secret Service agents had gone out drinking the night before the assassination. Asked if he believed the meeting had actually taken place, Lane told the author of this book in 2011, "I have no idea now, and I had no idea then." (Lane interview.)

FROM TOP LEFT
(*clockwise*): Oswald in
Marine Corps uniform;
Oswald's falsified ID
(in name of alias Alex
Hidell); Oswald and
friends in Russia,
including Ella German,
who refused to marry
him, seen top right;
Oswald with coworkers
in Minsk; Oswald hands
out "Hands off Cuba"
leaflets in New Orleans
in 1963.

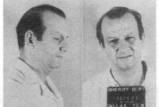

ABOVE LEFT: Jack Ruby, "host" of the Carousel Club burlesque house, was known in Dallas for his aggressive effort to court the police and reporters. Ruby poses with three of the club's performers. ABOVE RIGHT: Ruby's business card; a mug shot taken after his arrest for Oswald's murder; the ramp that Ruby was believed to have used to reach the basement of Dallas police headquarters to kill Oswald. BELOW: On Sunday, November 24, Ruby murdered Oswald on live national television, pushing through a crowd of reporters and cameramen to fire his pistol at point-blank range.

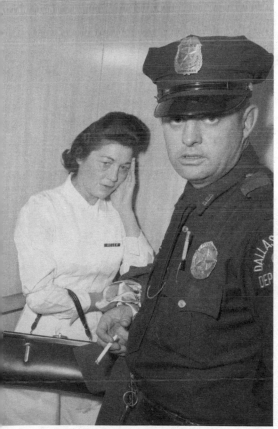

LEFT: The cold-blooded murder of Dallas police officer J. D. Tippit, shown in uniform, was seen by commission lawyer David Belin as the "Rosetta Stone" in understanding that Oswald was obviously guilty of the president's assassination, too. BELOW LEFT: Tippit's murder was witnessed by restaurant waitress Helen Markham, seen next to an unidentified policeman; she identified Oswald in a police lineup later that day. BELOW RIGHT: Shortly after Tippit's killing, Oswald was arrested as he tried to hide in the darkened auditorium at the nearby Texas Theatre. In his pocket was a bus transfer (shown with key), which Belin suspected that Oswald intended to use to reach another bus that would allow him to escape to Mexico.

Dallas Police Department

Dallas Municipal Archives

Dallas Municipal Archives

Courtesy of The Sixth Floor Museum at Dealey Plaza

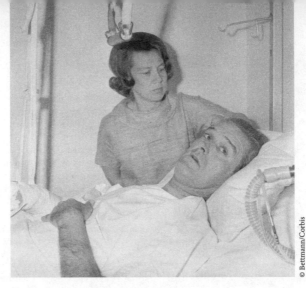

ABOVE: Texas Governor John Connally is comforted by his wife, Nellie, at Parkland Hospital in Dallas, as he recovered from the bullet wounds suffered as he rode in the president's limousine in Dealey Plaza. BELOW: *Dallas Morning News* reporter Hugh Aynesworth interviewing Marina Oswald, while daughter June Oswald plays on the floor.

Courtesy of The Sixth Floor Museum at Dealey Plaza

cement how history remembered John F. Kennedy. On February 5, the journalist and author William Manchester was in his office on the campus of Wesleyan University in Middletown, Connecticut, when the phone rang. The caller was Pierre Salinger, who had been Kennedy's White House press secretary and had continued in the job under President Johnson, relaying a message from Mrs. Kennedy that she wanted Manchester to consider writing an authorized history of the assassination.

Manchester remembered turning to his secretary and asking, "Mrs. Kennedy wants me to write the story of the assassination. How can I say no to her?"

"You can't," she replied.

A former foreign correspondent for the *Baltimore Sun*, Manchester, forty-one, had written a highly respectful biography of President Kennedy, *Portrait of a President*, which had been published two years earlier. Kennedy had granted Manchester interviews for the book; after the biography's publication, the president praised it. Manchester was flattered when he saw a photograph of the president and Mrs. Kennedy sailing aboard a Coast Guard yawl sometime in 1962, with Mrs. Kennedy seated and reading his book as she smoked a cigarette.

Manchester said later that he believed Mrs. Kennedy selected him "because she thought I would be manageable." He had submitted galleys of *Portrait of a President* to the White House before publication, allowing the president to alter quotations attributed to him. "He requested no changes, but Jackie may well have concluded that the incident proved that I would be infinitely obliging," said Manchester. "It was a natural mistake."

Three weeks after Salinger's call, Manchester met with Robert Kennedy in Washington. "I was shocked by his appearance," Manchester said of the attorney general, who still seemed inconsolable over the death of his brother. "I have never seen a man with less resilience. Much of the time he seemed to be in a trance, staring off into space, his face a study in grief."

Kennedy explained that he had been directed by his sister-in-law to work out the logistics of a deal with Harper & Row, the publisher that had brought out John Kennedy's Pulitzer Prize–winning book *Profiles in Courage* in 1956. Ultimately, the agreement between the Kennedy family and Manchester provided him with an advance of $36,000; all other author's earnings after the first printing would be donated to the Kennedy

Memorial Library.* Manchester would also receive the proceeds from any magazine serialization of the book, which was likely to provide him with much more money than the advance.

Manchester requested an early meeting with Mrs. Kennedy, in preparation for the extensive interviews she would give him later. But Robert Kennedy said the preliminary meeting was not necessary. She would be ready to talk to him—in detail—within a few weeks.

Manchester also scheduled an early interview with the chief justice. The writer said he wanted to assure Warren that he did not want to interfere with the commission's work, even though Manchester intended to pursue what was in many ways a parallel investigation. Knowing that Manchester was operating with the full endorsement of the Kennedy family, Warren was eager to help. He was so enthusiastic, in fact, that he initially agreed to Manchester's request for access to the commission's supposedly top-secret investigative reports. A few days later, Rankin quietly talked to Manchester and urged him to withdraw the request, saying it could complicate the commission's work. Graciously, it appeared, Manchester did so.

---

* Given inflation, $36,000 in 1964 would be equivalent to about $271,000 in 2013.

19

For weeks, Senator Richard Russell had gritted his teeth and tried to work with the chief justice, and it had not been easy. To his fiercely segregationist constituents back in Georgia, it was awkward to explain how he could serve on a commission led by Earl Warren. How could he even be in the same room with a man so many of Russell's fellow white Georgians believed was determined to destroy their way of life?

Russell's estimation of Warren as chief justice had not improved, he assured friends. Away from the commission, Russell continued to dismiss the court under Warren's leadership as the "so-called Supreme Court." He reminded his colleagues that he had not volunteered to serve on the commission; he had been ordered by President Johnson to join the investigation, a duty he could not shirk.

Russell was polite and deferential to Warren in the commission's early meetings, and the other commissioners thought he offered wise advice to the chief justice, especially over the struggles with Hoover and the FBI. Russell had mostly kept his silence about some of the commission's management decisions, including the hiring of what he considered radical young northern lawyers. "For some reason, Warren is stacking his staff with extreme liberals," Russell wrote to himself in his diary in

January. He also noted that he had not been consulted before the commission hired that "negro lawyer" from Philadelphia, William Coleman.

By midwinter, Russell was exhausted, and the commission was only part of the reason why. As he had predicted to President Johnson, he was overwhelmed by his Senate duties in 1964—mostly *because* of Johnson. Russell was leading the effort in Congress to block far-reaching civil rights legislation that Johnson, eager to establish an early legacy on civil rights, had championed from his first days in the White House as a fitting tribute to Kennedy. On February 10, the House passed the Civil Rights Act of 1964, a landmark bill that outlawed most forms of discrimination based on race, religion, or gender. The bill then headed to the Senate, where Russell would try—and ultimately fail—to stop it. (It was a tribute to the intense personal ties between Johnson and Russell that the friendship survived mostly intact.)

Finally, in late February, it all became too much, and Russell decided he had to quit. He began to draft a letter of resignation. The final straw, he said, was the commission's failure to keep him informed about the schedule for testimony from Robert Oswald, Lee Oswald's brother. Russell had missed the first two days of Oswald's testimony, on Thursday, February 20, and Friday, February 21. But he woke up on Saturday to read in the newspaper that the testimony would continue that morning in an unusual weekend session. His Senate staff had not been notified about the meeting, but Russell assumed reporters would not get such a basic fact wrong. He dressed himself and went to his Senate office, a few minutes' walk from the commission's offices, and had an aide call over to determine when the testimony would start. The puzzled staffer reported back to Russell that the commission's offices were closed—no one was picking up the phone. Russell went home, annoyed that he had interrupted his weekend for no good reason.

He was furious, then, when he learned that Oswald's testimony had in fact continued Saturday but that, because it was a weekend, no receptionist had been on duty to answer the phones.

In his resignation letter to the president, Russell cited the incident: "I do not think it reasonable to expect anyone to serve on any commission that does not notify all its members definitely as to the time of the meetings and as to the identity of the witness that will appear." He continued: "Since I cannot possibly attend a majority of the sessions of the commission and discharge my legislative duties, I feel constrained to request you to accept my resignation and relieve me of the assignment. Please be assured of my desire to serve you, your administration and our country in every possible way."

After finishing the letter, Russell let his temper cool, and he decided not to send it, at least not right away. He kept a draft in his files.

Word of his anger reached the chief justice, who had been worried for weeks about Russell and his increasing absence from the commission's meetings. Russell had been absent for most of the testimony of Marina and Marguerite Oswald, and now he had missed all of Robert Oswald's. "The only person who did not come regularly was Dick Russell," Warren said later. "I was disturbed about it." He was even more disturbed, however, about the possibility that Russell would try to find an excuse to leave the investigation entirely. If Russell stepped down, "it might appear there was disharmony on the commission."

Warren dispatched Rankin to see Russell in his Senate office and convince him to stay, and Rankin listened to Russell's long list of complaints. "He was completely frank," Rankin recalled. Russell said he was so overtaxed in his Senate duties that he barely had time to read the transcripts of the commission's hearings late at night before he went to bed, let alone attend the hearings.

He assured Rankin that he did not intend to embarrass the commission with his resignation. He planned to issue a statement in which he made it clear that he was not leaving because of any differences over Warren's leadership or the direction of the investigation, but simply because he did not have the time.

Rankin reasoned with him: "I told him about the problem that if he should leave the commission, how it might be misunderstood by the country and by people regardless of what he said." And he had come with an offer, approved by Warren, to hire a lawyer who would do little but help Russell keep up with the commission's work.

Grudgingly, Russell gave in. "Well, then I will stay on if you do that," he told Rankin.

Russell was invited to choose the lawyer, and he selected Alfredda Scobey, a fifty-one-year-old legal researcher on Georgia's state court of appeals who had been recommended to him by his nephew Robert, a justice on the Georgia court. Scobey was a lawyer with no law degree. She managed to pass the Georgia state bar examination without attending law school; she taught herself the law as she helped her husband study for his own bar exam. In March, Scobey moved to Washington and found herself the only woman lawyer on the commission's staff. Her arrival meant that Russell would disappear almost entirely from the offices of the commission. She would be his eyes and ears.

Another proud southerner was fast becoming disgruntled with the commission that winter: Leon Hubert, the former New Orleans district attorney who was overseeing the investigation of Jack Ruby. He told his new colleagues that he could not understand why Warren and Rankin seemed so uninterested in the intriguing evidence that he and his junior colleague, Burt Griffin, kept turning up.

Ruby's murder trial had begun in Dallas on February 17, and it had become the embarrassing spectacle that the city had feared. Dallas and its leaders were being alternately condemned and ridiculed in the reports of the hundreds of journalists who had flooded in from around the world. Columnist Murray Kempton of the magazine the *New Republic* found himself feeling sorry for Ruby—a "pathetic" figure who seemed to be another victim of this "shabby," violent city. "Ruby turns out to be a pallid man with a bald spot down to the back of his neck, sitting in a courtroom whose chartreuse walls turn his flesh sickly green," Kempton wrote. "We look at him and understand the ultimate failure of Dallas: It was not merely incapable of protecting John F. Kennedy from what was done to him and of protecting Lee Oswald from what was thereafter done to him, but was not even capable of protecting Jack Ruby from what he did. He sits there, trapped."

The lowest moment for the city's law-enforcement agencies came two weeks into the trial, when seven prisoners in the city jail used a dummy pistol made of soap and shoe polish to try to make their escape; at least two rushed past the courtroom where Ruby was on trial. Television cameras posted outside captured some of the scenes of the jailbreak and the panicky evacuation of the courthouse that followed. For the press corps, it was a fresh reminder of the incompetence that had permitted Ruby to saunter past dozens of police officers and kill Oswald.

Ruby was represented by Melvin Belli, a talented, publicity-hungry lawyer from San Francisco known nationally as the "King of Torts" because of the tens of millions of dollars he had won for clients in personal-injury cases. Belli had attempted to move Ruby's trial out of Dallas; when that was denied, he tried to turn the proceedings into a trial of the city itself. He alleged that Dallas's "oligarchy" of oilmen and bankers had dictated that Ruby would be convicted and then sentenced to death, to exact revenge on him for having embarrassed the city by murdering Oswald. According to Belli, rampant anti-Semitism in Dallas also explained the city's desire to punish Ruby, who had changed his name from Jacob Rubenstein and was the fifth of eight children born to Polish-Jewish émigrés in Chicago.

Belli used an insanity defense, arguing that his client suffered from brain damage—he had a long history of violent outbursts that grew worse after he suffered a concussion in his thirties—and that the murder could not have been premeditated. The lawyer offered testimony from a clerk at the downtown office of Western Union who testified that his time stamp showed he sold Ruby a money order on Sunday, November 24, at exactly 11:17 a.m., four minutes before Oswald was murdered across the street at Dallas police headquarters. If the murder had been planned, Belli argued, Ruby would not have been in the Western Union office only moments earlier, wiring $25 to "Little Lynn," one of his strippers, at her home in Fort Worth. And there was other evidence to suggest that Oswald's murder was unplanned. Ruby had left his favorite dog, Sheba, in his unlocked car outside the Western Union office. His friends said it was unimaginable that Ruby would abandon the dachshund—he referred to the dog as his "wife"—to be found by strangers. Ruby's bizarre relationship with Sheba and his other dogs would later be seen by Warren Commission investigators as evidence of serious mental illness.*

In his closing argument, Belli portrayed his client as a loud-mouthed, but generally well-intentioned, Damon Runyon character who got a thrill from spending time among police officers and reporters. "A village idiot, a village clown," he said of Ruby. But the defense strategy failed, and Ruby was convicted on March 14 and sentenced to death in the electric chair. Belli stood and sneered at the jurors: "May I thank this jury for a verdict that is a victory for bigotry." He described his client as the victim of a "kangaroo court, a railroad court—and everybody knows it."

---

* Ruby's acquaintances offered stomach-churning stories to the FBI about his relationship to his pets. One witness described watching as Ruby casually masturbated one of his dogs in front of visitors. Another described Ruby allowing his dogs to lick blood from his hand after a deep cut with a kitchen knife.

* * *

Back in Washington, news of Ruby's conviction meant that the commission's staff could finally get to work on the ground in Dallas; as Warren had insisted, they had stayed out of Texas until then to avoid prejudicing the trial. Hubert and Griffin were among the first to travel to Dallas, where they began to interview witnesses about Ruby.

From the FBI reports and witness statements they had been reading for weeks, the two lawyers thought that Belli was, in many ways, correct in his description of Ruby. The circumstances of Oswald's murder suggested Ruby was anything but a cold-blooded assassin dispatched to silence Oswald—the description some conspiracy theorists had tried to apply to him. "The fact that he would go forward and shoot some guy in the basement with a whole crowd of reporters around?" Griffin said years later. "What does that say about Ruby?"

The tumultuous lives of Ruby and Oswald had similarities, beginning with their tortured relationships with their mothers. Ruby's mother was institutionalized repeatedly in mental hospitals during his childhood, and she and Ruby's father were so neglectful of their children that Ruby was never sure of his exact age because his parents never bothered to record his birth date. As adults, both Ruby and Oswald had troubled dealings with women. The FBI questioned many witnesses about the possibility that Ruby—who never married and had a middle-aged male roommate in Dallas—and Oswald might have had "homosexual compulsions," in the FBI's terminology of the era.

Still, Hubert and Griffin worried that there was some part of Ruby's biography they did not fully understand—that he might in fact have been motivated by more than a sudden, uncontrollable impulse to kill Oswald. They wondered, in particular, if someone might have encouraged Ruby, possibly gangsters from his past who knew he was susceptible to impulsive acts and who wanted him to silence Oswald. Ever since his youth in rough Chicago neighborhoods, Ruby had counted criminals among his friends. As an adult, he befriended gamblers and low-level associates of Italian-American crime families, as well as the families' corrupt allies in the labor movement, especially in Jimmy Hoffa's Teamsters Union. Phone records obtained by the commission showed that Ruby had placed long-distance phone calls to a "known muscleman" for Hoffa in the weeks before Kennedy's assassination.

Hubert and Griffin were also interested in Ruby's connections to

Cuba. During his trial, Ruby confirmed that he had tried to do business there after Castro's victory in 1959. FBI reports showed that Ruby traveled to Cuba that year and met in Havana with an associate of the Gambino crime family in Chicago; Ruby said he had hoped to sell fertilizer and jeeps on the island but that the venture "never got to first base."

In the opening weeks of their investigation, Hubert and Griffin put together a detailed time line of Ruby's activities in the weeks before Kennedy's assassination. The chart began with dates in mid-September 1963, when the White House made a final decision that Kennedy would travel to Texas. It was the logical place to start. "That's the first moment that anybody in Dallas or anywhere else could have decided that they were going to assassinate Kennedy," Griffin recalled. "That was the demarcation point." The chart was divided into vertical rows, with days of the week down one side of the page, matched up against FBI documents and witness statements that had some reference to Ruby's activities on each day.

Hubert and Griffin also began to flesh out the rest of Ruby's odd, complicated life dating back to his childhood. It occurred to them that they might have a much larger workload than the staff lawyers focused on the biography of Oswald, a man less than half Ruby's age who had few real friends or associates. "Hell, there are two of us doing what eight other guys are doing on Oswald," Griffin protested later.

In mid-March, Hubert and Griffin put together a detailed memo that outlined all of Ruby's ties to organized crime and to Cuba, and they analyzed how those ties might possibly be linked to the murders of Kennedy and Oswald. The memo noted how Ruby had appeared intentionally to misstate the number of times he visited Cuba. He claimed to have gone only once, in 1959, for about ten days. But immigration records showed that he had been in Havana at least one more time that same year. The FBI found evidence that he might have had contacts with Cuban exiles in the United States who, like some of Ruby's friends in organized crime, were eager to see Castro ousted. The Communist victory in Cuba meant the end of lucrative gambling and liquor operations long controlled on the island by American mobsters.

Hubert and Griffin were also struck that, immediately after the assassination, Ruby had publicly demonstrated a more-than-routine knowledge of Cuban affairs. At a police news conference on the night of Kennedy's murder, Ruby, sitting among reporters and pretending to be a reporter himself, had spoken up after Dallas district attorney Henry Wade mis-stated the name of the pro-Castro group that Oswald had claimed to join earlier that year. Wade described it as the "Free Cuba Committee." Ruby corrected him, blurting out, "Henry, that's the Fair Play for Cuba Commit-tee." Why, Hubert and Griffin wondered, had he known that?

They also questioned whether Ruby was telling the truth when he insisted that he had not known Oswald. There was at least one intrigu-ing, if indirect, tie between the men. The housekeeper in the Dallas rooming house where Oswald lived at the time of the assassination, Earlene Roberts, had a sister who was close to Ruby. Roberts's sister had been asked by Ruby in the 1950s to invest in one of his nightclubs. The sister told the FBI that she had met with Ruby as recently as November 18, four days before the assassination, to discuss a different investment.

Hubert and Griffin were excited by the idea that there might be much more to Ruby's story—a possible connection, even, between Ruby and Oswald before the assassination. If there had been a conspiracy to murder Kennedy, it might be unraveled by understanding Ruby, not Oswald. And yet, from the first weeks of the investigation, the two lawyers felt ignored by the commission—especially by Rankin, who had so much control over what information gathered by the staff was shared with Warren and the other commissioners. "Hubert and I were totally on the periphery," Griffin said.

Rankin did not invite conversation with Hubert and Griffin or praise their work. "Hubert was there every day, but Rankin ignored him," Griffin said. "He didn't think Rankin respected him." While Rankin would regularly step into the offices of some of the other staff lawyers to ask for updates on their work, he "seldom came in to talk to us." The situation was made worse by Hubert's debilitating shyness. He seemed intimi-dated. He may have been a powerful figure in legal circles in Louisiana, but here in Washington he was working with young men drawn from the Ivy League and the nation's finest law schools, and from powerful institutions like the Supreme Court and the Justice Department.

"He was a nervous guy," Griffin said of his partner. "He was a chain-smoker who started the day with a cold Coca-Cola and drank Coke all day," growing jittery from the caffeine. "He treated me with total respect," Griffin said later. "I felt he put me on a pedestal, which is maybe why I thought he was naive."

Hubert locked in a perception that he was not up to the job with a ponderous, awkwardly written memo to Rankin in February in which he asked that the commission compile a list of every person who crossed the border into the United States in the months before the assassination and everyone who had left the country in the weeks that followed—hundreds of thousands, if not millions, of names that would have to be checked, by hand, against lists of possible suspects. Hubert acknowledged that the move might be "totally impractical," but "even if the job is not done, the final report must show that it was considered and must show why it was not done." The memo dismayed Rankin and his deputies, who saw it as a needle-in-the-haystack request that would waste the commission's time.

After the request was denied, Hubert wrote again to Rankin, urging that the full commission be made aware that the proposal for the massive name-check was suggested—and turned down. He defended the request again, arguing that the list might, in fact, turn up the name of an assassin. "A culprit would want to get out of the U.S.," he said. He questioned whether "Americans not yet born" would accept the fact that the commission had not reviewed every bit of evidence that might point to a conspiracy, even if gathering the information was onerous.

In the case of Ruby, he warned, the available evidence did not allow for any firm conclusions about his motivations for killing Oswald, and the commission would be wrong to suggest otherwise. "The fact is that so far, the Ruby materials on hand are not sufficient either to exclude the possibility of a conspiracy or to warrant a conclusion that there was none." In the weeks that followed, Hubert grew more bitter over the way he was being ignored, to the point where he began to consider resigning. "He was demoralized," Griffin said.

20

In late February, the commissioners decided it was time for a face-to-face confrontation with Mark Lane, the New York lawyer who had emerged—seemingly from nowhere—as their biggest public critic. Warren was furious about Lane. The investigation was "plagued" by him, the chief justice said later. He found it difficult to believe that a previously obscure civil rights attorney and one-term New York state legislator had managed to turn himself into a national celebrity in just a matter of weeks, with what Warren believed were absurd claims about the assassination. Lane was taking advantage of the commission's decision to conduct its hearings in private and limit its public statements, allowing Lane to make outlandish claims that the commission had little ability to correct. "Pure fabrication," Warren said of the conspiracy theories spread by Lane. "Absolutely nothing to do with it."

This was personal for Warren, since Lane was trying to convince the public that the chief justice was complicit in a conspiracy to hide the truth about the president's murder, even to blame the assassination on an innocent man. Warren told friends he could not understand why respectable journalists gave any credibility to either Lane or his client, Marguerite Oswald. And yet there Lane and Mrs. Oswald were, day after day, on the front page of major newspapers, spreading their "outrageous" theories about the assassination. Lane was also becoming a celebrity in Europe: he was embraced by a number of left-wing intellectuals, including the British philosopher Bertrand Russell, who established a London-based group to support Lane's work. (Russell's group called itself The British "Who-Killed-Kennedy?" Committee, and its other members included the writer J. B. Priestley and Oxford historian Hugh Trevor Roper.)

Secretly, the commission became so worried about Lane that it began to have his movements followed closely by the FBI. The bureau had already begun conducting limited surveillance of Lane's appearances around the country when, on February 26, Howard Willens prepared a memo that outlined the commission's options in having the FBI step up the monitoring of Lane. Within days, apparently at the commission's urging, the bureau's surveillance operation was expanded. Through the winter and spring, Lane was trailed by the FBI almost everywhere he went in the United States. The bureau reported back regularly, often daily, about Lane's whereabouts and the details of his attacks on the investigation.

In a separate memo in late February, Willens proposed that the commission also call Lane to Washington to testify. It would be a way of blunting Lane's ability to argue, as he did regularly, that the commission was ignoring evidence that could vindicate Oswald. If Lane had evidence, he could present it to the commission directly. If he had nothing, that would be evident, too. "We are aware that Mr. Lane is making numerous speeches to the effect that he has information indicating that Lee Harvey Oswald is not the assassin of President Kennedy, and that the commission has not requested that information," Willens wrote. In calling him in to testify, "I think we should make an explicit request for all documents possessed by Mr. Lane regarding the assassination." The commission agreed, and the invitation to Lane went out.

Lane's unofficial investigation of the Kennedy assassination had become his full-time job. He looked everywhere for witnesses or evidence pointing away from Oswald as Kennedy's assassin. He had a road map in locating the witnesses from Dealey Plaza and from the scene of Tippit's murder thanks to the stack of police witness statements from Hugh Aynesworth in Dallas.

One early victim of his methods was Helen Markham, the forty-seven-year-old Dallas waitress who said she had watched Oswald gun down

Tippit and then identified Oswald in a police lineup. She appeared to have been the witness closest to the murder scene—only about fifty feet away. Lane telephoned Markham and, without telling her, tape-recorded the interview. When he was promised immunity from prosecution later that year in exchange for the tape, the recording would be seen by the commission's staff as proof of Lane's efforts to bully unsophisticated witnesses into saying things they did not believe.

According to a transcript of the phone call, Lane briefly introduced himself before launching into questions.

"Could you just give me a moment?" he asked Markham, claiming that he had heard from Dallas reporters that she had described Tippit's killer as "short, stocky and had bushy hair"—descriptions that did not match Oswald. Oswald's autopsy report showed that he was of normal height (five feet, nine inches) and thin (about 150 pounds), with thinning hair.

"No, no, I didn't say this," Markham replied, sticking to her original description of Oswald.

Lane tried again. "Well, would say that he was stocky?"

Markham: "Uh, he was short."

Lane: "And was he a little bit on the heavy side?"

Markham: "Uh, not too heavy."

Lane saw an opening: "Not too heavy, but slightly heavy?"

Markham: "No, he wasn't, he didn't look too heavy, un-huh."

Lane: "He wasn't too heavy, and would you say that he had rather bushy hair?"

Markham: "Yeah, just a little bit bushy." (She would later say that she was confused by Lane's insistent questioning and meant to say that Oswald's hair was unkempt, not bushy.)

After turning for a moment to another set of questions, Lane tried again: "Do you say that he was short and a little bit on the heavy side and had slightly bushy hair?"

Markham: "Uh, no, I did not. They didn't ask me that."

Despite Lane's badgering, the unsophisticated Markham mostly stuck to the account she had given the police. She continued to believe that Lee Oswald had killed Tippit, she said.

That was not how Lane would portray the conversation, however. In public appearances in the weeks that followed the phone call, he announced that he had talked to Markham and that she was now backing away from her description of Tippit's killer. "She gave to me a more detailed description of the man who she said shot Officer Tippit—she said he was short, a little on the heavy side, and his hair was somewhat bushy," Lane said, twisting Markham's words.*

The commission's staff lawyers shared Warren's contempt for Lane. David Belin thought that Lane used a "carefully cultivated mask of sincerity" to turn the Kennedy assassination into a "lifetime meal ticket." Jim Liebeler compared Lane's tactics to the "old legend about frogs jumping from the mouth of a perfidious man every time he speaks." The frogs represented the man's lies "and you have to run in all directions to grab them."

Lane accepted the commission's invitation to testify, and the hearing was scheduled for Wednesday, March 4. Lane was the only witness ever called before the commission to request a public hearing, which was granted; reporters were invited into the hearing room on the ground floor of the VFW building. "I think that there are matters here of grave concern to all the people of our country, and that it would, therefore, be fruitful and constructive for the sessions to be conducted in a public fashion," Lane said. He clearly sensed how valuable it would be to have the Washington press corps witness this moment; by allowing him to face down the chief justice and the other gray-haired commissioners, Lane might win newfound credibility as the commission's leading critic.

Rankin led the questioning: "Do you have some information concerning the matters being investigated by this commission that you would like to present to the commission?"

Lane launched into a long, detailed monologue intended to pick apart the evidence that the Dallas police and the FBI—and, it now seemed, the

---

* Years later, Lane would insist that he had not harassed Helen Markham, suggesting instead that he had done a service by revealing that such a seemingly important witness before the Warren Commission could be confused about what she had seen. He noted, correctly, that Markham's credibility had been damaged by the fact that she initially claimed to the commission under oath that she had never talked to him. "It's not badgering," said Lane, adding that he remains convinced that Oswald did not kill Tippit despite the many other witnesses who said otherwise. "It's only what every lawyer in the world always does" in cross-examination. "No lawyer will look at that and say I did anything wrong." He acknowledged that he had taped the call without notifying Markham, although he said that was legal so long as he did not divulge the contents, which he did not do; it was the commission that released the transcript. In its final report, the commission would describe Markham's testimony as "reliable" and that "even in the absence of Mrs. Markham's testimony, there is ample evidence to identify Oswald as the killer of Tippit." (Lane interview; Warren Report, p. 168.)

commission—were presenting to the public to suggest Oswald's guilt. As it had been from the beginning, his method was to suggest a cover-up whenever he could identify even small discrepancies in the public record and in press reports.

He began by focusing on the many photographs that had appeared in the weeks since the assassination that purported to capture an image of Oswald holding the Italian-made Mannlicher-Carcano rifle that had been identified as the murder weapon. A photo that had been published on the cover of *Life* magazine—the photo that Marina Oswald said she had taken in the yard of their home in New Orleans in the spring of 1963—showed the rifle equipped with a telescopic sight. But a seemingly identical photograph distributed by the Associated Press and published in the *New York Times* and other newspapers showed the rifle without the scope. That, Lane said, suggested that the photos had been doctored, which in turn could well be evidence of a "crime" to hide a conspiracy. (The truth, the commission quickly determined, was nothing of the sort. In some cases, photo editors altered the photo to create the sharpest possible silhouette of the rifle—a technique that had long been widespread, if ethically questionable, among American newspapers and magazines.)

Lane then cited witness statements in the records of the FBI and the Dallas police—statements that the commission had in its own files—that contradicted the official story that three shots had been fired from the Texas School Book Depository, hitting Kennedy and Connally from the rear. Some witnesses, Lane pointed out, heard four or more shots, while others insisted that the gunfire had come from in front of the limousine— from the so-called grassy knoll on the west side of Dealey Plaza or from the freeway overpass ahead of the motorcade. Lane argued that the witness statements, along with the medical evidence, offered "irrefutable evidence that the president had been shot in the front of the throat."

Rather than challenge Lane, the chief justice and Rankin mostly sat back and let him talk for almost three hours, just as they had permitted Lane's client, Marguerite Oswald, to offer her confused testimony the month before, mostly unchallenged. Warren's strategy, it seemed, was to rob Lane of the ability to argue that his evidence had gone unheard by the commission. "We asked you to come here today because we understand that you did have evidence," Warren told Lane. "We are happy to receive it. We want every bit of evidence that you have."

During his testimony, Lane repeated a request that he had been making publicly for weeks: He wanted to serve as Oswald's defense attorney before the commission, and to see all the evidence gathered by the investigation. "The fact that Oswald is not going to have a real trial flows only from his death," Lane said. "Every right belonging to an American citizen charged with a crime was taken from him, up to and including his life." He said Oswald deserved "counsel who can function on his behalf in terms of cross-examining evidence and presenting witnesses."

Warren listened patiently before turning him down. "Mr. Lane, I must advise you that the commission, as you already know, has considered your request and has denied it. It does not consider you as the attorney for Lee Oswald." He noted that Marina Oswald, his closest survivor, had not requested a lawyer to, essentially, defend her husband's ghost. "We are not going to argue it," Warren said.*

On the commission's staff, no one could poke as many holes in Lane's claims about the evidence as Redlich's deputy, Melvin Eisenberg. The young lawyer had become the commission's in-house expert on the science of criminology, and he could see how ridiculous many of Lane's claims were, especially about the scientific evidence; he assumed others could see through Lane, too. "It would be ridiculous to be obsessed with Mark Lane," he told himself. He was less bothered than others on the staff by Lane's implication that they were all part of a conspiracy to hide the truth about Kennedy's murder. "I thought that as long as we offered honest answers, nothing could happen to us," he said. "Our reputations were safe."

With the diligence that had led him to graduate first at Harvard Law School five years earlier, Eisenberg had finished poring through the thousands of pages of criminology textbooks that had been sent over from the Library of Congress. The science, he believed, showed that Oswald was guilty beyond any reasonable doubt: the ballistics and fingerprint evidence conclusively demonstrated that he had fired the bullets that killed Kennedy and nearly killed Governor Connally. Eisenberg could

---

* Warren would later insist that the commission had been fair to Oswald, even in death, through an arrangement made in February with the president of the American Bar Association, Walter E. Craig, who agreed to evaluate the commission's work "in fairness to the alleged assassin and his family." Although Craig was invited to cross-examine witnesses and offer the names of witnesses who should be called, the records shows that he and two associates had little involvement in the investigation. (See Warren Report, pp. XIV–XV)

not rule out the possibility that Oswald had accomplices, but he was certain that Oswald had pulled the trigger that day at Dealey Plaza. "There couldn't be any rational doubt that Oswald had at least shot the bullets that entered the president's body," he argued.

Eisenberg had not found it difficult to understand the science, which he outlined to the commission in a series of memos that winter. It came down to some very basic physics, chemistry, and biology. "It was easy," he said. "This wasn't rocket science." He thought the ballistics evidence was especially straightforward. It could be proved with almost 100 percent certainty that the bullets that passed through the bodies of Kennedy and Connally had been fired from Oswald's mail-order rifle. As Eisenberg learned from his reading, a rifle would leave distinctive grooves and other markings on bullets that traveled through its barrel. By examining the spent bullets under a microscope, an investigator could identify Oswald's rifle as the murder weapon "to the exclusion of every other rifle on earth," Eisenberg said.

In arguing for Oswald's innocence, Lane was relying on witness statements and other types of evidence that deserved little, if any, credibility, Eisenberg now knew. It was disturbing for Eisenberg, who had never practiced criminal law, to discover that serious criminologists placed little value in the testimony of so-called eyewitnesses. Hollywood and popular crime novels might want to suggest that the best possible proof of a crime came from the accounts of people who had seen it take place, but from what Eisenberg was reading, eyewitnesses routinely got their facts wrong. It was common for people who saw the same crime to offer completely different accounts of what had happened, sometimes resulting in the conviction—and even the execution—of the innocent.

Even less credible, Eisenberg learned, was testimony from witnesses about what they had *heard* at a crime scene—so-called ear-witness testimony. It was often flatly wrong, especially in a relatively closed-in space like Dealey Plaza, where the sound of gunfire had ricocheted wildly and where witnesses had panicked and paid little attention to what they were hearing because they were running for their lives. In one of his memos, Eisenberg wrote that it was not surprising that some witnesses had heard only two or three shots, while others heard four or five or more, and that some witnesses insisted that they had heard the shots fired from the grassy knoll and other locations in front of the president's motorcade rather than from the Texas School Book Depository.

As part of his assignment, Eisenberg met with scientists from the FBI's crime laboratory, and he was impressed with their technical expertise and their intelligence. Still, he felt the commission should not rely solely on the bureau for the scientific analysis, so he asked permission to hire outside experts to review the physical evidence. To review the fingerprints, he proposed that the commission seek experts from the crime laboratory of the New York City police department. For the firearms, he suggested that the evidence be reviewed by nationally renowned specialists at the Illinois state Bureau of Criminal Identification. The commissioners, already so skeptical of the FBI, readily agreed.

Burt Griffin took time away from his study of Ruby's life to bolster Eisenberg's findings. After searching through FBI and Dallas police files, Griffin wrote a memo on March 13 that identified four men in and around Dallas who closely resembled Oswald and who had been mistaken for him on the day of the assassination. A fifth look-alike, Billy Lovelady, who worked with Oswald at the book depository, was photographed on the steps of the book warehouse minutes after the shots rang out. The commission's lawyers were not surprised that even after Lovelady publicly identified himself as the man in the photographs, Mark Lane continued to insist it was Oswald on the steps—proof, Lane suggested, that Oswald must have been innocent of the president's murder because he did not flee the scene of the crime.

21

Several weeks into the investigation, the commission's staff lawyers continued to assume the best about the CIA. The officials they dealt with were smart and often charming, and they seemed sincere in their assurances that the agency would share whatever information it had about Oswald. That was in sharp contrast to the attitude of much of the staff, and certainly of the commissioners, toward Hoover and the FBI; the bureau was now widely viewed as obstructing the commission's work, probably to hide the bungling in its surveillance of Oswald before the assassination.

Then, in February, came the first disturbing evidence that the CIA might be withholding something, too. That month the staff learned from the Secret Service that, in the hours immediately after the president's assassination, it had been provided with CIA reports detailing what had been known about Oswald's visit to Mexico City. The commission double-checked its files and determined that those reports had never been handed over to the commission; the CIA had never acknowledged that the reports even existed. The Secret Service declined to turn the reports over to the commission, saying that would be a decision for the spy agency since the reports were so highly classified.

Since joining the commission, Rankin had dealt with the CIA mostly through Deputy Director Richard Helms, a man he had come to like and respect. Rankin recalled years later that he had believed at the time that Helms and other top officials at the CIA were cooperating fully. But the discovery of the missing CIA reports about Mexico City alarmed Rankin, and in this case he thought that he needed to go over Helms's head. In February, he wrote directly to Helms's boss, Director of Central Intelligence John McCone, insisting that the agency turn over copies of the reports that it had given to the Secret Service about Oswald's Mexico trip. And just so there was no confusion in the future, Rankin asked in the letter that the CIA be prepared to gather up and hand over its complete files on Oswald, including a copy of every communication it had with other government agencies about him before and after the assassination. After the mix-ups and ill will between the commission and the FBI, Rankin was—politely, he thought—putting the CIA on notice.

The commission received the CIA's reply on Friday, March 6, when the agency turned over a thick file that, it said, contained all of the information the agency had ever gathered on Oswald, beginning with his attempted defection to Moscow in 1959. Willens, Rankin's deputy, and others went through the file, and they could detect almost instantly how much was still missing. The file contained none of the paperwork or cable traffic about Oswald that the agency's Mexico City station had sent to CIA headquarters that fall, for example.

Willens called Helms, who admitted that some material was still being withheld because of "certain unspecified problems." Willens recalled in a memo to Rankin that Helms tried to offer an explanation. "He stated that some of the information referred to has already been passed on to the commission in a different form and other of the material included irrelevant matters or matters that had not checked out." This was unacceptable, Willens said; the commission needed to see everything. Helms pushed back, seeming to suggest—cryptically—that the young lawyer did not fully understand the implications of forcing the CIA to share everything it had on Oswald. The agency "would prefer not to comply," he said. Unlike Rankin, Willens felt he had no authority to insist that Helms do anything, and so he and Helms agreed to discuss the issue at a meeting tentatively scheduled for the following week, when Helms planned to visit the commission's offices in Washington.

The following Thursday, at about eleven a.m., Helms sat down with Rankin and several of the other lawyers, including Willens, Coleman, and Slawson. Their questions for Helms were direct, including what was in many ways the central one for the spy agency: Was the CIA certain that Oswald had never worked for the agency as some sort of undercover agent, possibly during his years in the Soviet Union?

Helms assured the lawyers that Oswald had never worked for the CIA in any capacity and that he and other senior CIA officials, including McCone, were ready to sign sworn affidavits, under penalty of perjury, to confirm it. But he was pressed: If the CIA had nothing to hide, why was it continuing to withhold information about Oswald's trip to Mexico? Helms acknowledged that the agency had held back some specific reports because they might reveal the agency's spying methods in Mexico City, including the wiretapping operations and surveillance cameras targeting the Cuban and Soviet embassies.

Rankin still wanted to believe the CIA was telling the truth, and he and the other lawyers were impressed by the need to keep secret the CIA's spycraft in Mexico. So he offered a compromise that Helms accepted. In the future, the agency would offer a sanitized summary of any report prepared for its files about Oswald, with the understanding that a commission staff member could go to CIA headquarters to review the full, original documents.

There was more discussion of Mexico, including the commission's concern about the many holes in the CIA's knowledge of exactly where Oswald had gone in Mexico City, and the people he had met there, especially at night. He was registered at a small hotel near the bus station, but he could have been almost anywhere in the city after dark, apparently unobserved. "The evenings of his entire trip were unaccounted for," Slawson remembered telling Helms, who responded with a suggestion: the commission's lawyers should go to Mexico City themselves in search of answers. They would be in "a good position to bypass ordinary government channels and get things done," Helms said, vowing that the CIA's Mexico City station would do all it could to help. Slawson was excited by the idea.

In the days following the meeting with Helms, the CIA did begin turning over more material, including the reports that the agency had provided to the Secret Service about the Mexico trip. Among them was a report, dispatched by the CIA at ten thirty a.m. the day after the assassination, that alerted the Secret Service to the fact that the CIA's Mexico City station had a surveillance photograph of a man who might be Oswald. The photograph had still not been turned over to the commission, however, and, in a separate letter to Rankin, Helms explained why;

the agency had felt no need to turn over the photo since the agency had quickly determined after the assassination that it was not of Oswald. The CIA, he suggested, had not wanted to burden the commission with unnecessary leads, since the photo apparently had no value. He invited Rankin to send a staff investigator over to the agency to see the photo, which captured the image of a full-faced man with Slavic features who appeared to be much taller and heavier than Oswald.

In what seemed to be a new spirit of openness, the CIA also gave permission to the State Department in March to turn over two cables that the then U.S. ambassador to Mexico, Thomas Mann, had sent to the department and the CIA in late November about his suspicions of a Cuban conspiracy in Kennedy's assassination. Helms admitted to deputies that he "brooded" over whether to allow the cables to be given to the commission. Slawson read them and realized—to his dismay—how much more the commission still did not know about what had happened in Mexico. He was struck by Mann's almost panicked tone, and the ambassador's conviction that Castro was somehow behind the president's murder. The cables also hinted at evidence that the commission had not seen, including detailed transcripts of CIA recordings of Oswald's phone calls in Mexico. Slawson found the memo in which Mann referred to the embassy's reports of an affair between the former Cuban ambassador to Mexico and Silvia Duran, the "promiscuous-type" Mexican woman who had dealt directly with Oswald. Slawson worried about what else might be in the embassy's files.

In a memo to Rankin on April 2, Slawson said the commission needed to get copies of the transcripts of all intercepted phone calls in Mexico City that might be tied to Oswald. Beyond that, "we should see the entire Embassy file on the whole Kennedy assassination including copies of all correspondence to other government agencies." And the commission, he said, needed to know much more about that young Mexican woman: "We would like more information on Silvia Duran—for example, the evidence that she was a 'promiscuous type.'"

In late March, Samuel Stern drove to CIA headquarters in suburban Virginia to begin to review the full Oswald files. He later remembered being impressed by the CIA's sophisticated filing rooms, as well as its new data-processing system known as Lincoln, which made use of some of the federal government's first computers.

Stern was handed an inventory of all the Oswald documents, and he was then allowed to go—document by document—through the actual files to make sure they were complete. He found the cables prepared by the CIA's Mexico City station about Oswald—the ones the commission had originally been denied. As best he could tell, nothing was missing from the Oswald "jacket," as the collection of files was called. It was such a cynical, unsubstantiated thought that Stern did not repeat it in a memo he sent to Rankin about his visit, but he distinctly recalled thinking that day how easy it would have been for the CIA to have forged all this material or to have altered the inventory and removed documents from the "jacket" that it did not want to share. The CIA was in the business of keeping secrets, and if the agency chose to keep some secrets about Oswald and the assassination, the commission would not be able to detect it. "There was no way for us to get the ultimate, absolutely reliable certainty about anything," Stern said.

It slowly dawned on David Slawson that winter that the CIA might be trying to recruit him. Later he became convinced of it. There was never a direct offer, but his conversations with Ray Rocca and other CIA officials would sometimes turn to Slawson's plans after the commission went out of business, with the obvious suggestion that he might want to give up his legal career and join them. "They let it be known that if I was interested, they'd be interested."

He was flattered by their approach, he said, and at the time he did not see it as an effort to influence his work on the commission. The CIA was then a much-admired institution, Slawson said later. He had actually considered the idea of joining the agency years earlier, after learning that some of his Amherst classmates had become CIA officers. "They had seemed to hire high-caliber people," he said. Slawson had left his graduate studies in physics at Princeton because he believed the law would be a more exciting career; perhaps, he thought, the CIA might be an even bigger adventure. For now, though, he had little time to ponder his next career move. In just a matter of weeks, he had been expected to turn himself into the commission's in-house expert on the daunting question of whether there had been a foreign conspiracy to kill the president, and he was doing much of this work alone. Coleman, his partner on the "conspiracy" team, continued to come into Washington from Philadelphia only one day a week, and there were weeks he said he could not come in at all.

Certainly Slawson felt he did not have time to focus obsessively on what else the CIA might be trying to keep him from knowing. Despite the flap over the Mexico City documents, he said, "I thought basically that the CIA was being honest." He especially valued Rocca's willingness to share with him the latest news about the debriefings of Yuri Nosenko, the former KGB agent. Years later, Slawson said he never had any sense of the turmoil that the case had created—that almost from the day of the defection, Nosenko's case pitted some of the agency's Soviet analysts, as well as the FBI, against James Angleton, Rocca's boss. Angleton was convinced that Nosenko was a double agent who had been dispatched to the United States to try to exonerate the Soviet Union of any involvement in the Kennedy assassination.

Yuri Ivanovich Nosenko, thirty-six years old when he defected, had been in contact with the CIA since 1962, when, traveling undercover for the KGB in Switzerland, he said he was robbed of $200 by a prostitute. According to the CIA's account, Nosenko approached an American diplomat he knew in Geneva and asked for a loan, saying he feared that if he did not account for the $200, his sexual indiscretions would be exposed to his KGB bosses. The incident became an opportunity to recruit Nosenko to spy for the United States.

In February 1964, three months after the Kennedy assassination, Nosenko contacted the CIA again and said he needed to defect immediately and that he had important information about Lee Harvey Oswald. Nosenko's defection was worldwide news—it was a front-page story in the *New York Times*—before he vanished, for years, from public view. Nosenko told his CIA handlers that he had personally reviewed the KGB files on Oswald and that they proved Kennedy's assassin had never been a Russian agent. The Soviet spy agency considered Oswald too mentally unstable— "a nut," as the English-speaking Nosenko put it—to be considered for intelligence work. It had abandoned any thought of recruiting him, Nosenko said, when Oswald attempted suicide in October 1959, shortly after his arrival in Moscow.

The FBI believed Nosenko. J. Edgar Hoover and his counterintelligence deputies at the bureau, responsible for tracking down Communist spies on American soil, concluded that he was a bona fide defector. In earlier years, Hoover's support might have provided the Russian with all the credibility he would need to be treated like a hero in Washington. But Nosenko had too powerful an adversary in Angleton, and it was Angleton who controlled the flow of information from the CIA to the commission—to Slawson, in particular. Angleton asked his staff to look for holes in Nosenko's story that might prove he was a double agent. He worried, especially, that Nosenko had been sent from Moscow to discredit an earlier KGB defector then living in the United States, Anatoly Golitsin. For years, Golitsin had been feeding Angleton's paranoia about KGB infiltration of the CIA; Golitsin insisted Nosenko was a double agent dispatched to the United States specifically to discredit him.

Who to believe? If Nosenko was telling the truth, it would seem to rule out any Soviet involvement in the assassination. If he was lying, it suggested that the KGB was trying to cover up its relationship with the man who had just killed the president.

Rocca insisted to Slawson that the best-informed people at the CIA believed Nosenko was a phony, and Slawson remembered seeing the logic of it. "The information that Nosenko brought over was just too convenient" in vindicating the Kremlin, Slawson said. Nosenko "had all the hallmarks of a plant."

Within the commission, the case files on Nosenko were treated with such secrecy that some of the other lawyers never even heard his name. In the commission's files, he was often referred to simply as "N." Slawson knew the commission would have to make a decision about how much, if any, of Nosenko's information could be made public in its final report. If the CIA was right that Nosenko was a double agent, the commission would only serve the interests of the Kremlin by promoting Nosenko's claims. "It would be basically exonerating Moscow." On all of this, Slawson would, again, have to trust the CIA, which refused to allow him or anyone else from the commission to meet with Nosenko to try to verify his claims. "I asked to see him, and the answer I got was 'no way.'"

Slawson recalled that he was told little at the time about how Nosenko was being treated by his CIA interrogators. He did know that the Russian was being kept in solitary confinement, and Slawson remembered being troubled at the other harsh conditions that Nosenko might face; he had long assumed that solitary confinement, if it went on for long, could amount to "psychological torture."

It was far worse than Slawson imagined. Congressional investigators and even some CIA officials would later agree that Nosenko was subjected, for years, to torture. He was held in solitary confinement for 1,277 days—more than three years. Much of that time, he was housed at a CIA training site near Williamsburg, Virginia, in a specially built, uninsulated cell, lit by a single bulb that remained on twenty-four hours a day. He had no one to talk to apart from his interrogators. He was given nothing to read and denied basic comforts, including a toothbrush and toothpaste, for months at a time. "I had no contact with anyone," Nosenko said later. "I could not read, I could not smoke, I even could not have fresh air."

The Justice Department was complicit in the decision to treat Nosenko harshly. In April 1964, the department secretly signed off on all elements of the Russian's confinement when a delegation of CIA officials visited Deputy Attorney General Nicholas Katzenbach at his offices at the department. Katzenbach would later insist under oath that he could not recall the meeting, but CIA records confirmed that it had taken place. The documents showed that Katzenbach approved the CIA's plans to confine Nosenko indefinitely, without any legal process or appeal.

In other ways, the CIA had continued to be quietly helpful to Slawson. It helped him prepare a request to the Cuban government for copies of all documents in its embassy and consulate in Mexico City involving Oswald. The request would have to go through the government of Switzerland, which served as a diplomatic go-between for Washington and Castro's government, and Slawson requested permission from the commission to begin drawing up the paperwork.

The request "went up through channels to Earl Warren, and his first response was no," according to Slawson. "The reason he gave was that he did not want to rely upon any information from a government which was itself one of the principal suspects" in the assassination. Slawson was baffled. The commission, he thought, had the responsibility to gather evidence wherever it might be found, and then, when possible, to try to authenticate it. But the chief justice was apparently willing to block some important evidence from being gathered at all.

Warren *had* allowed the commission to approach the Russian government to ask for its records on Oswald's two-and-a-half-year stay in the Soviet Union. But for the chief justice, Russia and Cuba were very different types of countries. He saw a distinction between the long-established, gray-haired Communist leaders in Moscow—he had met Khrushchev only the summer before, during his vacation with Drew Pearson—and the angry, bearded young revolutionaries led by Castro who had taken control in Havana in 1959.

Slawson did not see the difference, at least not when it came to collecting the evidence he needed to do his work, and so he did something that he admitted was totally out of character—he decided to ignore Warren. "Any information that we could get we ought to get," he remembered thinking. He might be risking his job, but "I simply disobeyed orders and went ahead and made the request to the State Department."

An approach to Castro's government was considered so sensitive that the letter to the Swiss government had to be signed personally by Secretary of State Dean Rusk. Slawson could only hope that Warren, unaware of any of this, did not bump into Rusk on the Washington social circuit that spring and begin discussing the commission's work. Slawson's request got results: Havana produced the paperwork, including copies of what appeared to be Oswald's visa application, as well as the passport-sized photographs that Oswald had submitted.

Weeks later, in one of his rare face-to-face encounters with the chief justice, Slawson was asked for an update on his efforts to gather evidence from foreign governments. Slawson noted, sheepishly, that a package of material about Oswald had arrived from Cuba—the material that Warren had specifically ordered him not to request.

Warren was outraged. "I thought I told you we didn't want it," he said.

Slawson had to lie. "I am sorry," he told Warren. "I didn't understand it that way."

Once the Cuban files were in hand, Slawson was grateful that Warren did nothing to block their use. "He accepted the fact that we had it," Slawson said. "He did not make any effort to suppress it." With additional help from the CIA, much of the material, including Oswald's signature on the visa form, was authenticated.

22

True to his word to read every piece of paper that came into the commission's offices, Norman Redlich spent much of February paging through the FBI files that had been flooding in, and he was the first to notice a crucial deletion.

It was sometime early that month when he came across an intriguing document: the FBI's typewritten, word-for-word accounting of what Oswald had written down in an address book found by Dallas police among his belongings. The typewritten document was supposedly prepared by the bureau as a courtesy to the commission and other investigators, since Oswald's handwriting could be difficult to read.

Redlich, characteristically, took the next time-consuming step, something he knew others on the staff might not bother with. He decided to compare—page by page—what was in the address book with what the FBI's typewritten account showed. Redlich was not a trained prosecutor, but he lived by the conviction that a good lawyer reviewed every bit of raw evidence gathered for a case, no matter how tedious that might be. He wanted to be sure the FBI had not unintentionally misstated any of what Oswald had written down.

The handwritten and typewritten accounts matched up, at least for the first twenty-four pages of the FBI report. Then he came to page 25. He turned to what should have been the corresponding pages of Oswald's address book and saw what was missing. On that page, Oswald had written "AGENT JAMES HASTY," a misspelling of the name of James Hosty, the FBI agent in Dallas. Beneath the agent's name, Oswald had noted Hosty's office address and, it appeared, the license plate number of his FBI car. The entry was dated November 1, 1963—three weeks before the assassination.

Yet neither the agent's misspelled name nor any of the other information about Hosty had been transferred to the FBI report. Redlich immediately suspected that this might be a crude attempt by the bureau to hide evidence about its ties to Oswald. He rushed to find Rankin, who was also alarmed. It was one thing for the commission weeks earlier to try to tamp down loosely sourced newspaper reports suggesting that Oswald might have been an FBI informant. Now, it seemed, the bureau might actually be doctoring evidence.

Rankin called a staff meeting on February 11, 1964, to announce what Redlich had discovered and to ask their advice. Several of the lawyers felt that the deletions were the final straw. At the very least, it seemed, the FBI was trying to obscure the fact that it had the president's killer under such close surveillance just weeks before the assassination that Oswald had written down an FBI's agent's name, address, and license-plate number. "Of course we thought they were covering up," Slawson recalled. Specter was also convinced this was no innocent oversight: "It was self-protection at its worst—it raised the obvious question of what else was withheld that the commission never found out." Griffin saw it as the moment when the commission's lawyers became convinced that they could not trust the FBI—ever.

This time, Rankin would not offer Hoover the courtesy of a face-to-face meeting. Instead, he wrote the director, demanding an explanation of how and why the deletion had occurred. "Needless to say, we would like a full explanation," he told Hoover. The letter asked Hoover to identify, by name, all of the agents and supervisors who had prepared the report or "made any decision to omit information from the report."

Hoover responded in kind: he, too, was outraged. He insisted in a letter to Rankin that the information about Hosty had not been included in the typewritten report simply because it did not offer an "investigative lead" of any value. In other FBI documents describing the contents of

Oswald's address book, he noted, there was a clear reference to the Hosty entry—just not in this particular document. "This bureau, from the beginning of this investigation, has developed and reported all relevant facts and it will continue to do so," he declared.

Hosty himself knew that what Hoover had written was untrue. He was later told that the Dallas FBI agent who prepared the typewritten report—a friend named John Kesler—had intentionally left out the information about Hosty to try to protect him from even more harsh scrutiny from FBI headquarters. As Hosty described it, "Kesler had simply been trying to save me from Hoover's wrath."

It was too late for that, as Hosty already knew. In December, he had received his formal, possibly career-killing reprimand signed by Hoover. Without making any direct reference to the assassination or to Oswald, Hoover wrote that "your recent handling of a security-type case was grossly inadequate." Hosty could only assume the letter was referring to his failure to interview Oswald that fall and his failure to alert the Secret Service about Oswald's presence in the city. "It should have been apparent to you that he required a status which would have insured further investigative attention," the letter continued.

Hosty had begun to think of himself as a victim. It was better for the FBI to criticize the supposed errors of a single field agent in Dallas than to question whether the FBI as a whole had made much larger mistakes before and after the assassination. "I was the classic scapegoat for J. Edgar Hoover," Hosty said later. "Following the assassination, Oswald had whined to the press that he was just the patsy. Now, I knew who was the real patsy." Several of his colleagues agreed. "You're going to be the goat," he was told by another Dallas agent, Vince Drain.

Hosty could not deny that he did have moments of doubt, asking himself: "Could I have prevented President Kennedy's assassination?" Over time, though, he became convinced that he had done nothing wrong; nothing he had learned before the assassination suggested Oswald was violent. In fact, Hosty thought the record showed he had been diligent in his investigation. The national-security case file on Oswald, opened after he returned from Russia in 1962, had actually been closed by another FBI agent in Texas; that agent thought Oswald posed no obvious threat. It was Hosty who had reopened the file.

He sensed, almost from the start, that FBI headquarters was determined to end the investigation of the assassination quickly—with Oswald identified as the sole assassin—whatever the facts. There was no eagerness to search for a possible foreign conspiracy, which made Hosty suspect that something was being hidden from him. "I didn't know what was going on back in Washington," he said. "But something was afoot." He recalled an astonishing order from Gordon Shanklin—the agent in charge of the FBI's Dallas field office and "a man who wouldn't blow his nose unless he cleared it first with someone"—on November 23, the day after the assassination. Shanklin told his agents that "Washington does not want any of you to ask questions about the Soviet aspect of this case. Washington does not want to upset the public." And it was Shanklin who, the next day, ordered Hosty to destroy Oswald's note—the note that Hosty had ripped up and flushed down a toilet. (Although Shanklin would deny years later that he had ordered the note's destruction, other FBI employees in the Dallas field office distinctly remembered that the order had come from him.)

Despite Hoover's reprimand, Hosty was assigned to work on the assassination investigation. Excluding him might have been seen as a public admission that the Dallas field office had done something wrong in its surveillance of Oswald before the president's murder. But he said he was told to keep his name off any paperwork that would be forwarded to Washington and might end up on Hoover's desk. "My name had brought public embarrassment to Hoover and the FBI."

In the months after the president's murder, Hosty's central goal was to do what he could to hold on to his job. He had eight children, the youngest of them only three months old on the day of the assassination; his three-year-old son, Dick, had been born with cerebral palsy and required intensive, and expensive, physical therapy four times a week. The way to survive within the bureau, he knew, was to follow orders. "In 1942, when I joined the Army as an 18-year-old, one of the first lessons I learned was that in battle, a private had to blindly obey orders," he wrote. "In many ways, the FBI was like the military."

In mid-December, he was ordered to follow up on an urgent lead. He was asked to try to determine if there was any truth to a perplexing story being told by a seemingly credible young Cuban-American woman who lived in the Dallas area. The woman, Silvia Odio, claimed she had met Oswald weeks before the assassination in the company of two anti-Castro activists who came to her door late one night. Odio, the twenty-six-year-old daughter of two prominent anti-Castro activists then imprisoned in Cuba, had other witnesses to back her up, including a teenage sister who said she was in the apartment the night of Oswald's visit.

Hosty interviewed Odio on December 18. She was, he recalled, "a strikingly beautiful woman who had fled Cuba when her father was imprisoned by Castro for disloyalty." She appeared to be part of the Cuban elite that fled to the United States in the aftermath of Castro's rise to power— "the pampered Cuban upper class," as Hosty described it. She was clearly intelligent and well educated; her law school studies in Cuba were interrupted by Castro's revolution, she said.

Her story, if true, indicated either that Oswald had aligned himself with anti-Castro Cubans shortly before the assassination or—more likely, in Hosty's view—that he had tried to infiltrate the anti-Castro movement in a demonstration of his support for Castro's revolution. Hosty knew that earlier that year, while living in New Orleans, Oswald had tried to infiltrate an anti-Castro group known as the DRE, possibly to gather information for the pro-Castro Fair Play for Cuba Committee.

As Odio described the encounter, she was at home in her apartment one night in late September when three strangers arrived at her door and introduced themselves as anti-Castro activists passing through Texas. Two of the men were Latinos, possibly Cubans, and spoke Spanish; one of the Latinos went by the "war name" of Leopoldo. She said the third man was clearly not Latino, spoke no Spanish, and was introduced as "Leon Oswald," an American who was "very much interested in the Cuban cause." Leopoldo said the three men had come to ask for Odio's help in raising money and buying weapons for the anti-Castro movement—a request often made of Odio because of her father's prominence among exile groups. "We are very good friends of your father," Leopoldo said. He seemed to be telling the truth, she said, because he knew "so many details about where they saw my father and what activities he was in." Leopoldo claimed that he and the other two men had just come from New Orleans—why New Orleans, he did not explain—and were about to leave on a trip. "I didn't ask where they were going," Odio said. The next day, she got a call from Leopoldo. She thought he was trying to flirt with her—another common experience for Odio, given her beauty—and he asked what she had thought of "the American."

"I didn't think anything," Odio replied.

"You know our idea is to introduce him to the movement in Cuba, because he is great, he is kind of nuts," he told her.

Leopoldo described the American as a former marine who was an expert rifleman and who thought President Kennedy deserved to be assassinated. "He told us you don't have any guts, you Cubans, because President Kennedy should have been assassinated after the Bay of Pigs, and some Cubans should have done that."

She heard nothing more about "Leon Oswald" until after the assassination, when she and her sister, Annie, saw television pictures of the man accused of killing President Kennedy—the same man who had appeared at her apartment a few weeks earlier.

Annie, a student at the University of Dallas, asked the question first, Odio remembered. "She said, 'Silvia, you know that man?' And I said, 'Yes,' and she said, 'I know him. He was the one that came to our door.'"

The Odios had been too frightened to go to the FBI or to the Dallas police after the assassination because they worried that their father's anti-Castro movement might be blamed for Kennedy's murder, Silvia said. Instead, it was a friend of hers who contacted the FBI, without her knowledge.

During the interview with Hosty, Odio freely admitted something that, she knew, might affect the way the FBI evaluated her story. She was, as she put it, "emotionally disturbed" and suffered from fainting spells. Her mental troubles had begun after her husband abandoned her in Cuba, leaving her with four children to support; at the time of the assassination she had been under the care of a Dallas psychiatrist. But, as she reminded Hosty, someone else saw Oswald at the door: her sister. And there were others who would vouch for her credibility. She said she had, before the assassination, told her psychiatrist in detail about the odd visit from the three men, including the "Anglo."

Hosty was intrigued by Odio's story, although he understood the risk—given Hoover's determination to prove that Oswald had acted alone—in pursuing evidence of a possible conspiracy. He contacted Odio's psychiatrist, Dr. Burton Einspruch, who confirmed that she had told him about the late-night visit by the three men, shortly after it occurred. Einspruch told Hosty he thought she was being truthful.

Years later, Hosty said he never doubted Odio's truthfulness; she seemed to believe what she was saying. "She's not a phony," he commented. "It made sense to her. I really believe she believes she saw Oswald." But he had encountered this many times before—witnesses who became confused after a shocking crime and who believed they had seen something they could not have seen. Ultimately, Odio's psychiatric problems led him to discount her story. Einspruch told Hosty that Odio suffered from "grand hysteria, a condition he found to be prevalent among Latin American women from the upper class." And Hosty thought that might explain Silvia Odio's confusion. He thought Annie might have confirmed her sister's account in a demonstration of family solidarity, not because it was true.

In the weeks after the assassination, Hosty had too much other work to do, and he put Silvia Odio's claims out of his mind. "I had a stack of other leads to pursue." After filing her witness statement, "I more or less forgot about Odio."

23

The reports from the FBI's Dallas field office about Silvia Odio were directed to the "conspiracy" team—David Slawson and William Coleman. The reports were not flagged by the bureau as especially important, but Slawson, in particular, seized on them. He recalled reading about the young woman in Dallas and being excited by the idea that a credible witness could place Oswald in the company of anti-Castro Cubans shortly before the assassination. It fit in with one of the conspiracy theories that Slawson treated most seriously.

If the commission determined that Castro had no hand in the assassination, he wondered, was it possible that Castro's most passionate opponents—anti-Castro Cuban exiles in the United States—were involved, possibly as revenge against Kennedy for not having done more to oust the Communist government in Havana? He tried to imagine the web of conspiracy that might tie Castro's opponents to Kennedy's murder. His theory of that conspiracy was so complicated that Slawson, despite all of his years of training as a physicist and his ability to put the scientific mysteries of the universe into layman's terms, found it difficult to explain to colleagues on the staff. It would involve layers of duplicity—double crosses and triple crosses both by Oswald and by the anti-Castro exiles he might have met.

One possibility: knowing that Oswald was in reality an outspoken champion of Castro's revolution, anti-Castro exiles might have set him up to take the blame for the assassination by killing Kennedy themselves and then framing Oswald by planting his rifle at the Texas School Book Depository. Another, even more complex scenario: anti-Castro Cubans had lied to Oswald and convinced him that they, too, were Castro supporters, and that he could best support the Cuban government by killing Kennedy. After the assassination, some anti-Castro exile groups had tried to argue that Oswald was in fact an agent of Havana and that Kennedy's murder needed to be answered with an immediate American invasion of Cuba. "That was my major suspicion—the anti-Castro community, largely centered in Florida, wanted to effectively frame Castro for the assassination, so they could trigger a war," Slawson recalled. "That's what made the Silvia Odio story so interesting to me."

For the commission, there were now "The Two Silvias," as they became known around the offices. There was Silvia Odio in Dallas, and there was Silvia Duran in Mexico City. The fact that both Silvias were exotic, strikingly attractive young Latin women was not lost on Slawson and his male colleagues.

At first, Slawson could do little to pursue Silvia Odio's allegations on his own; he could only hope that the FBI would continue to press the investigation in Dallas, especially by establishing the identity of the two Latino men who were reported to be traveling with Oswald. Slawson said years later that he never focused on Hosty's continued involvement in the investigation and how that might have been a conflict of interest. He said he did not recall ever noticing Hosty's name on the paperwork about Odio. Slawson and the rest of the commission's staff were ignorant of Hoover's move to discipline Hosty and several other FBI employees over their failures before the assassination.

There was more that Slawson could do to follow up on Silvia Duran. He had seen her early on as a key witness in his part of the investigation— "perhaps *the* essential witness"—given her repeated interactions with Oswald in Mexico. As Helms had recommended, Slawson and Coleman planned to go to Mexico that spring; during the visit, they could press for an interview with Duran. Slawson read the full CIA reports about her, and he was aware of the rumors that she was an intelligence operative— possibly for the Mexican government, possibly even for the United States.

Slawson said he was never told directly why CIA and FBI officials in Mexico City made no request to interrogate Duran themselves, leaving her to be questioned instead by the Dirección Federal de Seguridad, or DFS, the brutal Mexican spy agency. It complicated his investigation, since the Mexicans had not provided the United States any sort of transcript of Duran's interrogation. Instead, the Mexicans offered only a summary of what they said she had told them. For Slawson, the summary raised as many questions as it answered.

When it came to imagining conspiracy theories about the assassination, Slawson knew he was "an amateur," he joked later. Spinning those theories was becoming a business, in fact, and a lucrative one. Marguerite Oswald and Mark Lane were in the midst of their national speaking tour that spring, raising money as they went, and Lane planned to travel across Europe to spread his message of Oswald's innocence. Like his colleagues, Slawson said he never troubled himself with Lane. "He was lying so blatantly, I couldn't imagine anyone taking him seriously."

In Europe, Lane would find a rapt audience for conspiracy theories, even more so than in the United States. The popular French newsmagazine *L'Express* had begun running a series of articles by an American expatriate journalist, Thomas Buchanan, who suggested—on the basis of what was later found to be confused, scant evidence—that Kennedy had been murdered in a conspiracy by right-wing Texas industrialists and oilmen. Over time, Buchanan would claim that Oswald and Ruby had known each other and that Ruby had loaned Oswald the money he needed to pay back the State Department for his travel costs to return to the United States in 1962. By late winter, Buchanan was writing a book titled *Who Killed Kennedy?* and he had lined up publishers on both sides of the Atlantic.

In the United States, a more serious writer, Harold Feldman of the *Nation*, continued to suggest that Oswald might have been an FBI informant. In February, Redlich prepared a detailed memo suggesting that Feldman's reporting was "sufficiently accurate to warrant consideration." Redlich, who had written for the *Nation* himself, felt the magazine raised valid questions about the seeming ease with which Oswald had received a new passport when he returned to the United States after his failed defection to the Soviet Union, a fact that might suggest some secret, long-standing tie between Oswald and the State Department or the CIA. "In general, it is wise to study articles such as this one rather than dismiss them because of their inevitable factual inaccuracies," Redlich wrote. "They may contain the germ of an idea which we might otherwise overlook."

Redlich would soon find himself the target of conspiracy theories. On February 12, *Tocsin*, a small, right-wing newsletter based in Oakland, California ("The West's Leading Anti-Communist Weekly"), published a front-page article about Redlich's work on the commission. The headline: "Red-Fronter on Death Probe." The article began: "A prominent member of a Communist front is a member of the staff of the Warren Commission investigating the slaying of President Kennedy. He is Norman Redlich, a professor at New York University Law School." The article suggested that Redlich was a leftist plant, noting his past membership in the Emergency Civil Liberties Committee, a New York–based lawyers' group that had been labeled a Communist front by the FBI. The committee was organized in the early 1950s to defend people targeted as Communists by the House Un-American Activities Committee.

Within days, Congressman John F. Baldwin, a Northern California Republican, forwarded a copy of the *Tocsin* article to Gerald Ford, his GOP colleague in the House. "I am quite concerned about this article about a man who has been employed as assistant counsel to the Warren Commission, of which you are a member," Baldwin wrote in a scolding letter on February 12. "You may possibly want to do something about this."

The next day, an agitated Ford replied to Baldwin: "I share your concern about the allegations . . . We are having this matter investigated." He noted to his colleague that when the commission was formed, "I insisted, among other things, that no member of the staff have any past association with extremist groups of any kind." If Ford was angry, he felt he had good reason to be; despite his insistence that the commission's staff members have no extreme political ties, left or right, Redlich had been hired anyway. Now, Ford could see, he risked being embarrassed over this among his own conservative colleagues in Congress.

Ford decided to do some digging of his own. He contacted the House Un-American Activities Committee, then led by Congressman Edwin Willis, a staunchly conservative Louisiana Democrat, and asked for a full report on Redlich. Ford was sent a two-page memo that listed Redlich's ties to civil liberties and civil rights groups that the committee considered subversive. It was no surprise that Redlich had earned the wrath of the Un-American Activities Committee since he had appeared at several rallies in New York to denounce the committee and its work.

The discoveries about Redlich were the latest frustration for Ford in dealing with the chief justice and the commission. Just days earlier, he had been forced to respond to a furor sparked by Warren's baffling public comments on the first day of Marina Oswald's testimony. Asked by reporters gathered at the VFW building if the commission would make public the information she and other witnesses revealed, the chief justice replied: "Yes, there will come a time. . . . but it might not be in your lifetime. I am not referring to anything especially, but there may be some things that would involve security. This would be preserved but not made public." He was quoted separately by the Associated Press as saying that if Mrs. Oswald's testimony revealed national-security secrets, they might have to be suppressed for decades—"and I say that seriously."

His remarks produced an uproar, since they seemed to support the arguments of conspiracy theorists that the commission intended to hold back the full truth about the assassination. The alarm spread to the commission's staff, with several of the young lawyers wondering what the chief justice was talking about. Arlen Specter said he knew, the minute he heard about Warren's comments, that the chief justice had "seriously damaged the commission's reputation" and threatened "to cast a pall on everything the commission did." From what he now knew about Warren, Specter thought he understood what had happened: the chief justice had become flummoxed by the reporters' questions and blurted out something he did not mean, to stop the journalists from pressing him further. This was Warren's "spontaneous way of avoiding the questions," Specter recalled. The chief justice was not "a man who could think quickly on his feet."

The blunder resulted in angry editorials in conservative newspapers that had been hostile to Warren for years. The *Columbus Enquirer* of Columbus, Georgia, said the chief justice had "injected a new sinister note" into the investigation. "Warren's remarks could undermine public confidence," the paper said in an editorial, calling on the commission to "issue an immediate statement on what he meant." The chief justice was denounced on the House floor by Representative August Johansen, a Michigan Republican whose congressional district was near Ford's. He charged that Warren's comments "struck at the very heart of the all-important factor of public confidence" in the investigation.

In a letter sent to angered constituents, Ford wrote that he, too, was startled by what Warren had said—and that the chief justice was simply wrong. "I can assure you as one member of the commission that all information relative to the solemn responsibility of the commission will be made public at the time the report is published."

Friends of Warren's began to worry that he had done serious damage to the investigation. A senior editor at *Newsweek* magazine, Lester Bernstein, was so alarmed by the gaff that he asked Katherine Graham, the president of the Washington Post Company, the magazine's owner, to forward a letter to him at the Supreme Court. He knew she was a good friend of the chief justice's. In a tone that might be read as condescending, Bernstein urged Warren to stop talking to reporters entirely. "It seems to me that you are courting an undesirable—and unnecessary—impression by publicly discussing the investigation, however guardedly, while it is in progress," he wrote. "To deal casually on a day-to-day basis with reporters invites risks of misquotation, misunderstanding and sensational exploitation, all of which, I believe, played a part in the recent clamor of whether or not you said that some evidence in the case would be withheld 'in our lifetimes.'" He urged Warren to hire an experienced public spokesman.

In a separate letter to Warren that began "Dear Chief," Mrs. Graham did not disagree with her editor's judgments. "I think him very intelligent and he was worried," she wrote of Bernstein. "I apologize, as he does, for burdening you further. This was something he felt he must say."

Warren wrote back to Graham, telling her Bernstein's suggestions were "quite appropriate." To Bernstein, he admitted in a letter that "you were as right as anyone could be" and that he had decided to change "my relationship with the press, which has been a delicate one at best. The commission was really between the devil and the deep blue sea. We desired no publicity whatsoever, but for a time, the pressure was almost hysterical." He said that his words had been misunderstood, although he was not specific how. "I was quoted as saying that some of the testimony would not be released in our lifetime. I assure you that nothing is further from our desires or intentions."

There were, in fact, secrets that Warren intended to keep—possibly forever, certainly while the commission's investigation was under way. Many of them involved the private life of Marina Oswald.

On Monday, February 17, Hoover sent a classified letter to Rankin with a bizarre—and, it was quickly determined, incorrect—report that the young widow might have been raped while she was in Washington to testify to the commission. The FBI had learned from a "confidential informant" that she might have been "subjected to sexual intercourse by force" by her business manager, James Martin, in her room at the Willard Hotel, Hoover wrote. The story had apparently originated with her brother-in-law, Robert, who had heard it from Marina herself after she returned to Dallas.

Rankin reacted instantly, calling a meeting that day with Secret Service inspector Thomas Kelley, who was serving as the agency's liaison to the commission. The implications for the Secret Service were dire, since Mrs. Oswald had been under its protection in Washington. How could she have been sexually assaulted with its agents outside her hotel room door?

Rankin told Kelley that the Secret Service needed to determine immediately whether there was any hint of truth in this. Kelley was shocked, too, and "stated categorically that he had no knowledge" of anything like it, Rankin recalled. As Rankin watched, Kelley picked up the phone and called the Secret Service's field office in Dallas and ordered that an agent drive out to Martin's home that instant to see if Marina Oswald was still there.

The answer from Dallas came back quickly: Marina had left the Martin house and moved in with Robert Oswald. Two days later, FBI agents in Dallas interviewed her, and she insisted there had been no rape. Instead, she said, she had consummated, once and only once, a weeks-long romance with Martin. It occurred on Friday, February 7, in her hotel room, after she dismissed her Secret Service detail for the night. Martin, she said, had then slipped into her room. "I took a bath and was partly dressed when I reentered the bedroom. Jim finished undressing me, and thereafter we had sexual intercourse. It was with my consent, and I did not resist." She said she had told Martin in Washington that while she would continue to refuse his proposal of marriage, she would be his mistress, even as she continued to live with Martin and his wife in their family home.

Marina and Martin returned to Dallas—and to Martin's home—that weekend. On Sunday, during a visit to her husband's grave, Marina told Robert about her sexual encounter with Martin. Appalled, her brother-in-law insisted that she break off her business relationship with Martin immediately and move in with him, and she agreed. She then went a step further and insisted that Martin's wife be informed of everything that had happened. "His wife should know the whole truth," she decided. She telephoned Mrs. Martin that night; with Martin listening in on an extension, Marina told Martin that she was "ending his services as my business manager and my lover."

Her account to the FBI was relayed back to the Warren Commission, where Rankin was alarmed that the young widow—whose credibility seemed so essential to the case the commission was making against her husband—might now be the subject of scandal. He knew the story, if it ever became public, could easily demolish the commission's portrayal of her as the guileless, shattered woman who had bravely identified her husband as the president's killer. Now she might be portrayed instead as a conniving home-wrecker.

Marina's morals, and her truthfulness, were about to come under even closer, more substantive scrutiny. Robert Oswald was the next witness scheduled to testify before the commission in Washington and, in advance of his appearance, he had provided the panel with a copy of a handwritten diary he had kept since the assassination. The diary contained an alarming entry from a month earlier—Sunday, January 12. On that day, Robert wrote, he and Marina planned to visit Lee's gravesite, and he went to James Martin's home to pick her up. Before the drive, he said, Martin pulled Robert aside to reveal something Marina had just told him—that her husband had plotted to kill former vice president Richard Nixon when Nixon visited Texas sometime in 1963. In the car, Robert asked Marina about the Nixon story and she confirmed it.

To several of the commissioners, the disclosure was a shocking new blow to Marina's credibility. She had told no one else about a plot to kill Nixon; certainly she had not mentioned it in her appearance before them in early February.

Ford was dumbfounded when he heard about the Nixon plot. "Could it be possible that Marina had simply forgotten this incident?" he asked himself. Or could she have some sinister reason to keep this secret? "The many-sided Marina now had another side," he said.

During his testimony to the commission, Robert Oswald was composed and to the point. He impressed the commissioners with his intelligence. "Here was a young man, conservatively dressed, soft-spoken, conscientiously trying to recall incidents of his family's history of many years ago," Ford recalled. "I wondered whether I could have been as precise if asked similar questions concerning my own family."

Robert testified that he had reluctantly come to the conclusion that his brother had killed the president and that he had done it alone. He believed Lee had the skills with a rifle to kill Kennedy, especially since the president's motorcade passed slowly in front of the Texas School Book Depository. Like his brother, Robert had served in the Marine Corps, and he knew that Lee had been rated as a competent marksman by his military trainers. Both brothers liked to hunt, and Robert said that Lee had told him about bird-hunting trips he had taken while living in Russia.

He was asked in detail about the Nixon threat, and repeated what he had written in his diary. He recalled how Marina had told him on the day of the graveyard visit that "Lee was going to shoot Mr. Richard M. Nixon" when Nixon was in Dallas one day in 1963 and that she had "locked him in the bathroom all day" to stop him. Robert had no explanation for why she had failed to share the story with the commission.

Despite the weeks of tension between Rankin and Hoover, the two men now shared a common concern—about Marina Oswald and her secrets.

On February 24, Rankin called Hoover to discuss the new revelations about Oswald's widow. Rankin said he was worried both about the disclosure of her illicit relationship with Martin and about whether her continued dishonesty—he was apparently referring to the belated discovery of the Nixon plot—meant she might still try to flee the country. He said he wanted the FBI to place her under aggressive, round-the-clock surveillance.

Hoover provided his deputies with a detailed memo about the phone conversation: "Mr. Rankin said he would hate to have her run out on us, which is always a possibility, particularly down in Dallas, and he was wondering about a stakeout on her in which we would watch her and see who is visiting her for a while." Rankin, Hoover said, asked for the FBI director's opinion of Marina's character and "if I didn't think it was odd that Marina considered being willing to be Martin's mistress. . . . I said that I did. It shows certainly the complete lack of character." Marina before and after the assassination "were like two different people," Hoover said. Before the president's murder, she was "sloppy and unattractive, but somebody got a hold of her and got her fixed up and all that probably put ideas into her head." The two men agreed on the danger of a leak to news organizations about her dalliance with Martin, and how that would undermine her credibility. "People are talking down there in Dallas," Hoover warned.

Rankin and the director had a common contempt for Martin and for Marina's former lawyer, James Thorne. The two Texas men had refused to accept her decision to dismiss them; they continued to insist on their cut of the rights to her story. Rankin told Hoover he understood that she already had signed contracts with publishers and news organizations that guaranteed her "an excess of $150,000, so it can be seen how much money is involved."

"This is just a nasty shakedown," Hoover replied. "These two individuals are doing everything in their power to make as much money out of her."

Rankin told Hoover to use his own judgment in determining how long to maintain surveillance of Marina. The commission, he said, wanted to determine "what kind of people are visiting her when she does not know she is under surveillance." Hoover recommended her phones be tapped. The wiretaps would carry little legal or public-relations risk since there would never be a trial in which their existence would be revealed, he said. Within days, eight FBI agents were assigned to the surveillance operation, which would monitor Marina at her home and as she moved around Dallas. Her phone was tapped. The FBI also secretly entered her new rented home and placed microphones in light fixtures that looked down on her living room, her kitchen, and her bedroom.

The next witness before the commission was Martin, her spurned lover and former business manager. He used his testimony to describe the young Russian widow as craven and greedy. He admitted that he had been part of a sham publicity campaign on Marina's behalf "to create in the public mind an image of a bereaved widow and a simple lost girl. The image is not true."

Warren had made the decision in advance that Martin would not be asked about his romance with Mrs. Oswald or about their sexual encounter in Washington. Even so, the chief justice allowed Martin to offer a full, damning indictment of her character. "She is too cold," he said, telling the commissioners that Marina showed little grief over her husband's death. The grief she did express "didn't ring true," he said. "The closest I ever saw her to really showing any emotion, at all, was when—it was about a week after she had been there—she saw a picture of Jackie Kennedy." At the sight of the president's widow, Marina teared up.

Martin recalled how Marina tried to portray herself in interviews as a devout Christian and that, as a result, gifts of Russian-language bibles began to arrive in the mail. "To my knowledge she has never read the first page of one of them," he said. "She never cracked a bible." More offensive, he suggested, was the way she mocked well-meaning donors who sent in small amounts of money to help her and her children: "Someone would send a dollar—I don't know, maybe it was their last dollar—and she would look at it and throw it aside and say, 'Oh, it's just a dollar.'" She was lazy around the Martin household, often leaving his wife to care for Marina's children, he said. "She got up between 10 and 11 o'clock every day. . . . The only household chores she did was wash the evening dinner dishes, and occasionally she would vacuum."

Martin admitted that he had known about the Nixon threat and that he had advised her to stay silent. "'Don't go around telling people something like that,'" he said he told her. He worried that her credibility might be damaged further if investigators learned—after all of her other lies—that she had withheld information about yet another of her husband's plots to assassinate a prominent public figure.

Norman Redlich sat in on the questioning of Martin. Whatever contempt he felt for the witness, Redlich suspected he might be telling the truth—that Marina Oswald was not who she appeared to be. "As Martin's testimony indicates, there is a strong possibility that Marina Oswald is in fact a very different person—cold, calculating, avaricious, scornful of generosity, and capable of an extreme lack of sympathy in personal relationships," he wrote in a February 28 memo to Rankin. He said that might help the commission understand why Oswald killed Kennedy. "If Lee Oswald was the assassin, the character and personality of his wife must be considered relevant in our determination of motive. There are many possible explanations for the assassination—a foreign or domestic plot, Oswald's insanity or Oswald's political motivations." Another possibility, he wrote, was that "Oswald was a mentally disturbed person with delusions of grandeur who was driven to commit this act by a wife who married him for selfish motives, degraded him in public, taunted him about his inadequacies and drove him to prove to her that he was the 'big man' he aspired to be."

"Neither you nor I have any desire to smear the reputation of any individual," he told Rankin. "We cannot ignore, however, that Marina Oswald has repeatedly lied to the Secret Service, the FBI, and this commission on matters which are of vital concern to the people of this country and the world."

The FBI was also continuing its surveillance operation against Mark Lane, at the commission's request. Through his FBI sources, Ford gathered his own information on Lane. On February 12, he had another meeting with Cartha DeLoach, Hoover's deputy, to discuss the commission's work. Two days later, DeLoach wrote back to Ford enclosing an "attached memorandum, which you specifically indicated an interest in." The three-page memo, typed on plain paper, not on FBI stationery, was a summary of what the FBI knew about Lane, including his ties to left-wing groups that the bureau labeled as Communist fronts. There were details on his marital history and sex life. "It was reportedly general knowledge in local New York political circles that Mark Lane and a young single girl had maintained an intimate sexual relationship during 1960 and 1961 and had lived together," the memo said. In Hoover's FBI in 1964, an unmarried man's affair with an unmarried woman was a fact worth recording.*

---

* Lane said he knew the FBI and other government agencies had placed him under surveillance and that they were trying to gather derogatory information about his private life. After he began to speak out about the Kennedy assassination, he said that he was routinely stopped by U.S. immigration authorities when returning from speaking trips abroad. He suggested he was most offended when he was temporarily detained in 1964 at New York's newly renamed John F. Kennedy International Airport—"I was not allowed into the city where I was born" without harassment. As for the FBI effort to compile derogatory information and share it with members of the Warren Commission, Lane suggested he wore it as a badge of honor. "They did the same thing with Martin Luther King," he said. (Lane interview.)

24

As the commission's chief investigator on the Secret Service, Sam Stern did not need much time to figure out that President Kennedy had been a "sitting duck" in Texas and that the Secret Service had not done nearly enough to protect him in a city where violence might have been expected. Stern went back and read the newspaper clippings about UN ambassador Adlai Stevenson's trip to Dallas that October, when Stevenson was hit over the head with a placard by a woman in a mob of anti-UN protesters. He read about the 1960 incident in which Lyndon Johnson and Lady Bird Johnson were jeered and spat on in the lobby of the Adolphus Hotel. And yet in this same city, the Secret Service had organized a motorcade in which President Kennedy and the First Lady were driven slowly past crowds in an open-air limousine. The route took them past several tall buildings from which an assassin could easily position himself for a clear shot at the president; at least one assassin had apparently done just that.

Unlike some of the other young lawyers on the commission's staff, Stern was able to master his part of the investigation in only a few weeks. What he discovered in his research on the Secret Service was discouraging, but it was not difficult to understand. The agency was, as he put it, "old-school, not up-to-date," with agents protecting the president who had a "cop mentality" that was unsuited to outwitting even an unsophisticated assassin.

It didn't help that Kennedy had always courted danger in his public appearances. He insisted on remaining accessible to crowds, often alarming his Secret Service detail by walking outside security perimeters to shake the hands of well-wishers. When traveling in a slow motorcade, he preferred that Secret Service agents walk alongside his presidential limousine rather than stand on special foot rails on the sides of the vehicle. He did not want them so close that it gave the appearance he had something to fear.

It was darkly fitting that the legislation creating the United States Secret Service arrived on President Lincoln's desk at the White House on April 14, 1865—the day of his assassination. The Secret Service was established initially as the anticounterfeiting arm of the Treasury Department, which was then battling a flood of counterfeit currency after the Civil War. In 1901, a self-proclaimed anarchist gunned down President William McKinley, and the responsibilities of the Secret Service were quickly broadened to include presidential protection. At the turn of the century, no other federal law-enforcement agency was capable of carrying out the assignment; it would be another seven years before the federal government established the agency that would eventually become the FBI.

Stern was startled by much of what he discovered about the inadequacy of Secret Service procedures for out-of-town trips, beginning with its routine use of open-top limousines. The limousine used in Dallas—a 1961 Lincoln Continental four-door convertible that bore the Secret Service codename "X100"—offered its passengers no protection whatsoever from a gunman shooting from above. A plastic bubbletop roof could be attached to the limousine to allow crowds to see the president in bad weather, but the roof offered protection from precipitation and extreme temperatures—not from gunfire. "It was not designed to be and is not bulletproof," Stern wrote to Rankin. For at least three years before the assassination, the Secret Service had been trying, without success, to find a manufacturer to make a bulletproof plastic roof. (The proposed specifications called for "reasonably good protection against a .45 calibre sidearm fired at a distance of 10 feet.") The bubbletop plastic roof was transported to Dallas on November 22 but was not used. The forecast that day was for unseasonably warm, sunny weather.

Stern found it hard to know where to begin in listing the other failings of the Secret Service. The agency, he discovered, had no policy of inspecting buildings along motorcade routes, with one exception: buildings were inspected every four years along the route of the presidential inaugural parade in Washington, DC. Asked by Stern why building inspections were not done routinely everywhere, the Secret Service said it lacked the manpower to carry out inspections in each of the dozens of cities a president might visit each year. "Surveys of hundreds of buildings and thousands of windows is not practical," it told the commission.

But why, Stern asked, couldn't the Secret Service at least inspect the buildings on a motorcade route that "present the most favorable vantage points to an assassin"? And why couldn't a few agents conduct a "spot check of a random sample of buildings immediately preceding the motorcade"? A spot check at the Texas School Book Depository might have found Lee Harvey Oswald sitting with a rifle at the window on the sixth floor.

There were other simple precautions the Secret Service could have taken but didn't. Stern wondered why the agency did not station agents with binoculars along a route to keep watch on the buildings the president was about to pass. Why didn't the Secret Service ask the managers of buildings along a motorcade route to stay alert to the possibility of strangers or to seal windows temporarily?

He was appalled, he said, when he saw some of the television footage from the day of the assassination. Like the crowds lining the streets, Dallas police officers were caught up in the excitement of catching a glimpse of the president and First Lady; they were not looking up to see if there were threats, especially from the buildings above. "It was horrible," Stern said. "If you look at the newsreels, the Dallas cops along the way are looking at Kennedy. There's nobody checking the rooftops. Nobody is looking at the buildings. And yet there was Oswald, sitting in an open window."

Back in Washington, the methods used by the Secret Service to identify potential assassins were almost laughably inadequate. Within the agency, a special unit, the Protective Research Section, or PRS, was supposed to maintain an elaborate, nationwide checklist of people who might pose a danger to the president when he traveled. Stern discovered that the list, which at the time included fifty thousand names, was made up almost entirely of the people who had sent threatening letters or packages to the

White House or who had made threatening phone calls to the White House switchboard. The PRS maintained a separate "trip file" of about one hundred people who were considered especially dangerous, but a search of the file before Kennedy's trip to Texas found no Dallas-area resident on the list—a surprise, Stern thought, given the attack on Stevenson the month before. It was absurd, he thought. "If some illiterate in Dallas didn't bother writing a hate letter to the White House—but was out there beating Adlai Stevenson over the head—he wouldn't make the list."

The Secret Service did make contact with the FBI when the president traveled. Local FBI field offices were routinely asked to alert the Secret Service if they were aware of threats in cities the president planned to visit, and that happened ahead of Kennedy's visit to Dallas. The FBI's Dallas field office provided the Secret Service with the names of local residents who met the bureau's criteria for a potential risk; Oswald's name was not among them.

On the commission's staff, it would be left to Stern to make the initial judgment as to whether the FBI's Dallas office—and more specifically, Special Agent James Hosty—had violated the bureau's guidelines in withholding Oswald's name from the Secret Service. Not surprisingly, the Secret Service seemed eager to blame the FBI for what had happened. On March 20, Stern interviewed Robert Bouck, the director of the Protective Research Service; Bouck said that the FBI should have known to alert the Secret Service about Oswald, especially given his aborted defection to Russia and his weapons training in the marines. Stern was not so convinced. Whatever his radical politics, Oswald had no history of violence, and there was no record of him making any sort of threat against Kennedy or any other political figures. Hosty had known before the assassination that Oswald worked at the Texas School Book Depository, but Stern thought it understandable that the FBI agent had not made an instant connection between the book depository and the motorcade route that Kennedy followed on November 22. The route had been made public on the evening of November 18.

Stern felt sorry for Hosty, whose career in the FBI was obviously in tatters. "I didn't think Hosty should be condemned over this," he said later. "I could understand how a busy local FBI agent would not see Oswald as an immediate threat." Stern also didn't believe that the Secret Service agents in Texas who had gone out drinking the night before the assassination should be subjected to harsh, career-ending discipline. Drew Pearson,

Warren's friend, and other muckraking journalists in Washington were trying to make a scandal of it. "But I don't remember being shocked or thinking it was so awful, or that Kennedy would have minded if he had known about it," Stern said. He certainly did not think the drinking incident deserved special attention in the commission's final report. "I think the story tells itself, it doesn't need hyperbole," he said.

Chief Justice Warren would come to a different conclusion.

As a former clerk to the chief justice, the thirty-five-year-old, Philadelphia-born Stern had a special perspective on Warren, and he was often quizzed by the commission's other lawyers about what it was like to work for him at the Supreme Court. After getting his law degree at Harvard in 1952, Stern had been a clerk to a federal appeals court judge in Washington and then was hired by Warren in 1955. Stern and another of Warren's clerks were put in an office that adjoined the conference room, which meant they could hear the justices deliberating cases next door. After the initial thrill of being hired at the court, Stern was disappointed that he did not have more opportunity to interact with Warren. Unlike other justices, the chief justice tended not to form lifelong bonds with his clerks. "He was very warm, but it was a kind of political warmth," Stern said. "I never felt close to him personally." Warren came closest to opening up to his clerks when they all came into the office on weekends to catch up on paperwork. "Warren would sometimes wander in Saturday afternoon and sit down and tell us war stories about California politics in the old days." During these conversations, Stern remembered, Warren made clear his loathing for Richard Nixon, who in Warren's view had cost him any chance at the White House.

Stern had a sense of how strongly Warren felt about Kennedy. Early in the Kennedy administration, Stern attended a reunion of Warren and his former clerks. The party was held at the Metropolitan Club, an elite men's club close to the White House, and the president had turned up as a surprise guest. "Kennedy came and shook hands with everybody and told the chief justice how much he respected his work, and Warren just beamed," Stern recalled. "He basked in it."

Warren, Stern came to think, "would have made a fabulous president" himself. Whatever his legacy on the court, it was "sort of a waste" that Warren had finished up there, instead of at the White House. He was not a great legal thinker or scholar, but he was an extraordinary politician—

a true leader, Stern believed. Warren had magnetism, and a sense of purpose and dignity, that made people eager to compromise and to sacrifice to help him. "He had the ability to bring antithetical groups together."

As he had expected, Stern had little contact with the chief justice at the commission. From a distance, though, he became concerned about Warren's health. He would catch a glimpse of the chief justice in the commission's offices at the VFW building and "he was sick, rheumy," Stern remembered. "I was worried." He could see how Warren's dual roles at the court and on the commission had begun to take a physical toll, even as the chief justice continued to appear in the commission's offices each morning like clockwork, before walking down the street and pulling on his black robes to begin a full day at the court.

25

Gerald Ford wanted to get tough on Marina Oswald. Certainly Ford was being encouraged by his political advisers and by some hawkish anti-Communists on his staff not to rule out a conspiracy involving the Soviet Union or Cuba, and the many lies of Oswald's widow raised new concerns that she was hiding evidence of a plot. He knew that some of the commission's investigators suspected that Marina might, in fact, be a sleeper agent for Moscow. Perhaps she didn't actually know about her husband's plans to kill Kennedy, but she might have been sent to the United States to provide cover and support for Oswald while he carried out whatever secret plan the Kremlin had devised for him. That would explain why they had married so quickly after meeting and why they had been allowed to leave Russia.

In March, Ford wrote to Rankin to recommend that Oswald's widow be questioned again, this time connected to a polygraph machine in hopes that she would be intimidated into finally telling the full truth. "A polygraph test for her on a voluntary basis would go a long way in satisfying the public's interest in the whole matter," Ford wrote. "We already know that she did not 'volunteer' a number of matters which have since come up. . . . Perhaps she is not 'volunteering' all she knows about Lee Oswald's schools, activities and relationships with the Soviets." Like several of the staff lawyers, he was worried that the commission did not know the truth about the reasons for Oswald's visit to Mexico City—but that Marina did. "She appears to know something more about the Mexico visit than she told us." He recommended that other witnesses be polygraphed "where there appears from the record certain inconsistencies or a failure to be completely frank."

Ford continued to chafe under Warren's leadership of the commission. The chief justice was never impolite with Ford and the other commissioners, but he was "brusque," never treating them as equals, Ford said. "He made a number of decisions that, at least in the original few months, were unilateral." Warren "delegated too much power to himself" and "there was no deviation from his schedule and his scenario." A star football player at the University of Michigan in the 1930s, Ford used a football analogy to describe the chief justice: "He treated us as though we were on the team, but he was the captain and the quarterback."

Whatever their differences, the chief justice had to admit that Ford was among the most diligent members of the commission, perhaps the most hardworking apart from Warren himself. Senator Russell had essentially disappeared from the investigation, and the other two lawmakers—Senator Cooper and Representative Boggs—had spotty attendance records. Ford, however, made a point of being present to hear the testimony of almost all important witnesses. His questions were consistently well thought-out and reflected his close reading of the evidence.

He had assembled a team of outside advisers to help him prepare those questions, a fact that Ford's records suggest he never shared with the commission. The chief justice and the other commissioners might well have been disturbed to learn that Ford allowed a group of friends and advisers—some without security clearances—to read sensitive documents from the commission's files.

Ford asked three men, in particular, to back him up. John Stiles, one of his oldest friends from Grand Rapids, Michigan, and his campaign manager in his first race for the House in 1948, tracked the commission's work on a day-to-day basis, preparing long lists of questions for Ford to ask witnesses. Ford also asked for help from former Republican congressman John Ray of New York, a Harvard-trained lawyer who had chosen to step down from his House seat the year before. Later, he recruited a young constituent from Grand Rapids who was then a student at Harvard Law School, Francis Fallon, to review the evidence.

Ford shared commission documents with his three advisers almost as soon as the material landed on his desk in his House office. When the commission's lawyers traveled to Dallas after Ruby's trial and started taking witness depositions there, Ford asked that copies of all the transcripts be shipped to his office "in order for me to keep fully abreast of the developments." He then shared the depositions with his trio of advisers.

The memos to Ford from his advisers were often not signed or initialed, suggesting how close he was to them. He took their advice seriously, often converting their memos wholesale into letters that he sent under his own name on congressional stationery to Rankin, with long lists of tasks for the commission's staff. In March, Ford passed to Rankin a list of scores of detailed questions that he wanted asked of witnesses who were at Dealey Plaza and at the scene of Officer Tippit's murder.

Ford's advisers also prepared lists of follow-up questions for the staff, prompted by witness testimony. After Mark Lane appeared before the commission in March, Ford was provided with a three-page list of all of Lane's cover-up allegations, taken page by page from a transcript of Lane's testimony. Next to each allegation was a box for Ford and his staff to check if Lane's facts could be verified. (A copy of the checklist maintained in Ford's files showed that not a single box had been checked.)

Ford also sought expert advice from House colleagues who were doctors or had other medical training, and who could give him some perspective on the hospital records from Dallas and on the autopsy report. Representative James D. Weaver of Pennsylvania, a retired air force surgeon who had begun a second career in Republican politics, reviewed the medical evidence at Ford's request and wrote back to say that given Kennedy's massive head wounds, "there was nothing that could have been done in any way that would have saved the life of the late president." He also shared with Ford, politician to politician, why he thought there had been so much confusion about the medical evidence—why the Parkland doctors, for example, had initially suggested that an exit wound in Kennedy's throat might have been an entrance wound. The doctors had faced "harassment" by irresponsible reporters—"press or alleged press," as Weaver put it—to say things they did not intend to say.

The memos from Stiles and Ford's other advisers reflected their consistent worry that the commission was overlooking evidence of a conspiracy. A memo to Ford dated March 17 warned that Chief Justice Warren might "arbitrarily rule out the possibility of the assassination involving a conspiracy—and particularly one which has international implications or involves a foreign power." Stiles reminded Ford of the disturbing news reports from Cuba in the weeks before the assassination, including the wire service interview with Castro in September in which Castro seemed to threaten Kennedy's life. The memo noted the continuing mysteries over Mexico: "Has the commission been able to account for all of the time spent by Oswald in Mexico City?"

All winter, Ford continued to be swamped with letters from House Republican colleagues, and from conservative constituents, demanding that Norman Redlich be fired from the commission's staff. "How did it happen that this goat was sent to guard the cabbage patch?" Representative Richard Poff, a Virginia Republican, asked Ford in a letter. A Texas doctor wrote in with a threat to make political trouble for Ford among voters back home in Michigan: "As a member of Congress, don't tell me you can't do anything about Pro Commies in the Warren Commission like Redlich. If you don't expose them and remove them, we will let the Michigan press know."

On April 3, Rankin wrote to Ford to bring his attention to a provocative article that Redlich had written eleven years earlier for the *Nation*. The article, an attack on Senator Joseph McCarthy, argued in support of the right of witnesses appearing before McCarthy to cite their Fifth Amendment rights to silence. Rankin's belated discovery of the article, headlined "Does Silence Mean Guilt?," was just more evidence for Ford of why Redlich should never have been hired. McCarthy might have died in disgrace in 1957, but there were still members of Congress, including friends of Ford's, who quietly cheered at the mention of his name.

It had not been announced publicly, but Ford and the other commissioners knew the FBI was quietly conducting a new, intensive background investigation on Redlich in response to the public attacks. Ford wrote Rankin in April to say that the belated discovery of the *Nation* article was proof of why the FBI investigation "should be expedited to the maximum" and "I believe the full commission should meet to discuss the situation and take whatever action appears appropriate." In a separate letter to Rankin on April 24, Ford passed along a copy of an editorial from the *Richmond Times Herald*, the influential, archconservative Virginia newspaper, with the headline, "Who Hired Redlich?" The editorial said that the "apparent close affinity of Communist front-ers with a key member of the investigation does not inspire confidence in the Warren Commission."

Ray, the former congressman advising Ford, speculated that Redlich might somehow be connected to Mark Lane and other left-wing conspiracy theorists. He prepared a handwritten chart to see if he could determine if Redlich and Lane had been members of the same "Communist Fronts," as Ray labeled them—left-wing civil rights and civil liberties groups that the FBI listed as subversive. Down the left-hand column, he listed groups that both Redlich and Lane had been affiliated with, including the New York–based Emergency Civil Liberties Committee. Next to each group, he put the years of Redlich's and Lane's affiliations, as best as Ray could determine it. Ray wrote Ford to say that he dropped the inquiry after determining "there is less overlapping than I had expected to find." Under "Communist Party Membership," Ray wrote—for both Redlich and Lane—"No evidence."

An unsigned staff memo to Ford in April outlined ways that the commission could force out Redlich. The author admitted that Redlich's position on the commission was not actually "dangerous" to its work. "He is not in a position to be that important, nor is there any reason in his work thus far to find fault," the memo said. "However, the fact that he remains on the commission will be—and has been—criticized." The memo urged that Redlich not be fired outright, since that might create public confusion and lead some people to assume there was "even more basis for 'plot' theories" about the assassination. Instead, Redlich could be kept on the payroll "but simply excluded in the future from the important work of the commission." He should be moved to a "harmless job" and, to limit his grounds to protest, allowed to keep his salary.

Prominent conservatives around the country saw Ford as their voice on the commission, and they considered him their best defender against the persistent rumors, especially in Europe, that right-wing groups had a role in the assassination. Articles in left-wing newspapers and magazines in Europe often mentioned H. L. Hunt, the ultraconservative Dallas oil magnate, as a potential paymaster for the murder plot. One of Hunt's sons had helped pay for the black-bordered ad published in the *Dallas*

Morning News on the morning of the assassination that accused Kennedy of abandoning anti-Castro guerrillas in Cuba. Kennedy, the ad said, had adopted the "Spirit of Moscow." Radio scripts prepared by a far-right Hunt-backed group, Life Line, were found in Jack Ruby's car on the day of the assassination.*

In January, Ford's Washington office received a cryptic letter from Hunt in which the oilman questioned whether Ford and Senator Russell had become unwitting tools of a larger left-wing conspiracy to hide the truth about Kennedy's murder. "I know of many favorable things about you, but do not know the extent of your awareness of the conspiracy," Hunt wrote, without explaining what the conspiracy was. "It may be that you and Senator Russell are only being used on the commission to investigate the assassination to lend prestige and respectability to others in public life who are considered by many astute anti-Communists to be pro Socialist or pro Communist." Hunt enclosed several copies of recent Life Line newsletters that he said might be helpful to Ford in pursuing "the cause of Freedom."

Word of Ford's behind-the-scenes attacks on Redlich began to circulate among the other young lawyers on the staff, and they worried that Ford might actually try to oust Redlich from the investigation. "When I heard about this, I thought it was absurd," said Alfred Goldberg, the air force historian. "I thought it was a pure political ploy by Ford." The attacks had begun to poison Ford's reputation among Redlich's friends on the staff. Many said later that they had assumed the Michigan congressman was trying to use the commission as a stepping-stone to greater power in the House; they feared that Redlich was about to become a victim of Ford's ambition.

In his hard work on the commission, Ford may have been motivated by something other than pure public service. He and his old friend Stiles had quietly decided to write a book about the investigation—the "inside story" of the commission—and they thought it had the potential to be a bestseller. They intended to publish the book as quickly as possible after the commission issued its final report, possibly within weeks of the report's release. That spring, they went in search of a book agent in New York, and

---

* Ruby denied any connection to Hunt and insisted he was given the scripts at a local trade fair at which Hunt family companies were promoting their Texas-made food products.

a publisher. Warren and several other commissioners said later that they had known nothing about the book project until the final weeks of the investigation. The chief justice told friends he considered Ford's book an appalling betrayal, creating the appearance that Ford was going to profit from a national tragedy. "Warren was still angry about it many, many years later," recalled Alfred Goldberg, who became close to the chief justice after the investigation. "It certainly added to his distaste for Ford." Goldberg said the chief justice felt that Ford was "simply untrustworthy—he had contempt for Ford."

26

David Belin could not help himself. It was a clear violation of the commission's rules, which barred the staff from discussing the details of the investigation with outsiders, but he felt he had to tell friends back in Iowa about his great, history-making adventure in Washington. He sent home regular updates about the commission's work in a series of open letters to his partners at the Des Moines law firm of Herrick, Langdon, Sandblom & Belin.

Belin, thirty-five years old and a proud native of the Cornbelt, liked to refer to himself as a "country lawyer," albeit one who had graduated Phi Beta Kappa from the law school at the University of Michigan. He could have had his pick of jobs at prestigious law firms in Chicago or at one of the big car companies in Detroit, but Iowa was his home and he returned there to begin his law career.

In January 1964, though, the "country lawyer" found himself transplanted to the nation's capital—a city he thought had been made so glamorous by John Kennedy—and called upon to work with Chief Justice Earl Warren, one of Belin's heroes, to resolve the mysteries surrounding Kennedy's death. Despite the horrible event that had prompted the investigation, he was exhilarated. It was one thing to be celebrated back in

Iowa for one's accomplishments; it was another to achieve that sort of recognition in Washington.

His first letter to the firm went out in late January, just days after he arrived in Washington. "First, a big 'hello' to everyone at HLS&B!" he began. While he might be known back at the firm in Des Moines for a desk covered with stacks of clients' paperwork, "I have had to somewhat alter my habits here in Washington, because the material which we are going over has been labeled 'Top Secret' and we have a safe in each office where we have to lock everything up at night." His senior partner on the commission's staff, Joe Ball, was surprised by how little of what they were reading deserved to be classified at all, Belin wrote. "He cannot understand why this material is labeled 'Top Secret,' and as to most of it, I tend to agree." Both men were getting an education in the tendency of self-important federal bureaucrats, especially at the FBI and CIA, to pretend that routine information was somehow secret.

It was a thrill to work for Warren, Belin said. The chief justice has been "extremely personable," and Belin was excited when Warren recognized him on the street and "immediately smiled at me and said 'Hello.'" At the first staff meeting in January, Belin wrote, Warren spoke darkly of the "rampant rumors in countries around the world" about whether there had been a conspiracy to kill Kennedy. "According to Warren, President Johnson said the situation could become such a tinderbox that it could conceivably lead to war with all of the ramifications of atomic destruction." Belin knew how tantalizing this would be to his colleagues back home—how excited they would be to hear what was happening behind the closed doors of the assassination commission in faraway Washington. And his letters were the talk of the firm for days after they arrived.

Belin had always known how to satisfy an audience. Raised in a music-loving home in Sioux City, he was a violin prodigy who was so talented that he won admission to New York's Juilliard School of Music. His family had little money, however, and he bypassed Juilliard to join the army; he planned to take advantage of the GI Bill to pay for college later. He brought his violin with him and performed at military hospitals in the Far East and on armed forces radio; for the radio performances, he always preferred compositions by Dvořák, which he thought he played particularly well.

Another letter to Des Moines followed on February 11. As an Iowan, he mocked the inability of the city government in Washington to plow the streets after what was, by the standards of the Hawkeye State, a mild dusting: "Washington is completely disorganized today, for overnight there has been three inches of snow." He then went on to share details of the recent closed-door testimony by Oswald's mother. "One of the more cynical of the lawyers here has suggested that Marguerite be nominated for 'Mother of the Year' in light of her great protestations in defense of her offspring," he wrote, adding that Warren had demonstrated remarkable patience in sitting and listening to her babble. "If some of us had gambling instincts, which of course I do not, we would start a pool in an effort to determine how long the Chief Justice will sit back and listen to all of the irrelevancies that are coming forth."

By late winter, Belin had read through most of the hundreds of witness statements gathered in Dallas by the FBI, the Secret Service, and the Dallas police. He had never worked in law enforcement, but he had plenty of experience in cross-examining witnesses, and he insisted to colleagues on the commission's staff that he was not worried about the many discrepancies he noted in the witness accounts of what had happened at Dealey Plaza and at the scene of the murder of Officer J. D. Tippit. Discrepancies among important, well-meaning witnesses were common in the civil cases he handled back in Des Moines, and so it was here. "When there are two or more witnesses to a sudden event, you will always get at least two different stories about what happened."

Some of the discrepancies from Dallas were almost funny. For instance, Oswald's fellow workers at the book depository—although clearly trying to testify honestly—could not agree on even the most basic details about his appearance. Asked how Oswald dressed, one coworker, James Jarman Jr., swore that he always wore a T-shirt. Another, Eugene West, said exactly the opposite: "I don't believe I ever seen him working in just a T-shirt." Belin thought both men were telling what they believed was the truth, even if one of them had to be wrong. There were far more jarring discrepancies elsewhere, especially in the witness statements of the two Secret Service agents who were in the president's limousine in Dallas. Agent Roy Kellerman, who was riding in the front passenger seat, insisted that after the first shot, he heard Kennedy yell out, "My God, I am shot!" Kellerman was asked how he could be so certain it was Kennedy, not Connally, who shouted. "It was his voice," Kellerman said. "There is only one man in that backseat that was from Boston, and his accent carried very clearly."

Yet the agent who was driving the limousine, William Greer, insisted that Kennedy said nothing after the first shot. Connally and his wife, Nellie, also in the limousine, agreed with Greer: the president remained silent. (The commission's staff determined that Greer and the Connallys were almost certainly right, since the first bullet passed through Kennedy's voice box, making it impossible for him to say anything.) Yet while their accounts were completely contradictory, Belin asked, would anyone suggest that either Kellerman or Greer was lying?

Belin's letters to his colleagues became more somber in March, when he and Ball made their first trip to Dallas. They saw Dealey Plaza for themselves and drove the length of the route of Kennedy's motorcade. "I really was not prepared for the emotional experience of actually seeing the building for the first time," Belin wrote, adding:

> With a Secret Service man at the wheel, we drove the presidential parade route down Main Street in Dallas and followed it directly to Houston Street where the car turned to the right and there, one block ahead, standing in stark reality, was the TSBD Building, about which I had read so much over the past sixty days. In a matter of seconds, I put myself in the actual parade procession with the colored moving pictures that we actually have that were taken on the day of the assassination. The car drove slowly north on Houston Street one block to its intersection with Elm, and my eyes froze on the window at the southeast corner of the sixth floor. We turned to the left—a reflex angle of about 270 degrees, and we started down the diagonal entrance into the Expressway. This is where the shots struck the president.

It was at that moment, Belin wrote, that his mind was overcome with a "flash" of memories of the grisly evidence he had reviewed back in Washington—the autopsy report, the Zapruder film, the photographs of the bullet fragments and of bits of the president's skull found in Dealey Plaza.

While in Dallas, Belin retraced what the FBI believed was Oswald's journey, by taxi and then by foot, after the assassination—first, to his rooming house in the Oak Cliff neighborhood, and then to the scene of the murder of Officer J. D. Tippit. Belin thought it was cruel that Tippit's name and his murder were often forgotten in discussions of the

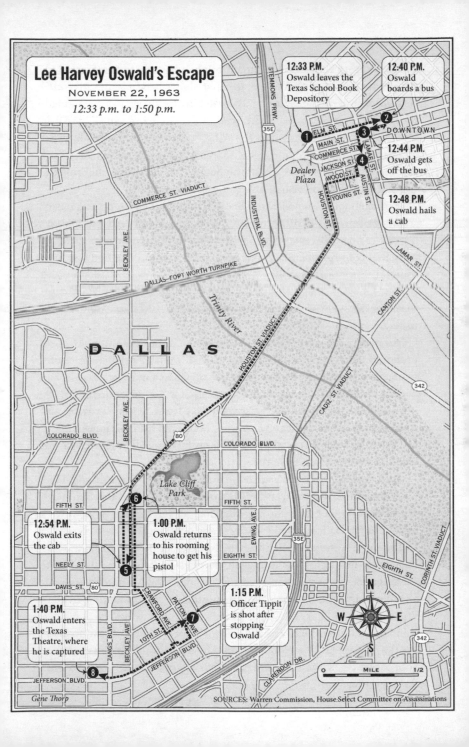

Lee Harvey Oswald's Escape

November 22, 1963

12:33 p.m. to 1:50 p.m.

12:33 P.M. Oswald leaves the Texas School Book Depository

12:40 P.M. Oswald boards a bus

12:44 P.M. Oswald gets off the bus

12:48 P.M. Oswald hails a cab

12:54 P.M. Oswald exits the cab

1:00 P.M. Oswald returns to his rooming house to get his pistol

1:15 P.M. Officer Tippit is shot after stopping Oswald

1:40 P.M. Oswald enters the Texas Theatre, where he is captured

DOWNTOWN

Dealey Plaza

DALLAS

Lake Cliff Park

Trinity River

Gene Thorp

SOURCES: Warren Commission, House Select Committee on Assassinations

assassination, as if the policeman's death had been an insignificant foot-note to the events of that day. Friends on the police force described the thirty-nine-year-old Tippit—he told friends his initials, "J.D.," stood for nothing in particular—as a fine man. An army paratrooper in World War II, he had participated in the Allied crossing of the Rhine in 1945 and earned a Bronze Star. In 1952, he was hired by the Dallas police as a $250-a-month apprentice. He left behind a wife and three children, the youngest of them five years old.

Belin thought the evidence that Oswald had killed Tippit was incon-trovertible. Driving in his patrol car, the officer had noticed Oswald walk-ing on the side of the road; Tippit tried to stop and question him, thinking he matched the description of the president's assassin that had just been broadcast on the police radio. As he stepped from his car, Tippit was hit by four bullets—three in his chest, one in his head—and cartridge cases found at the scene were a precise match for Oswald's Smith & Wesson pistol.

As part of his tour, Belin also visited the Texas Theatre (its owners preferred the European spelling of "theatre") on West Jefferson Boule-vard, a few blocks away from the scene of Tippit's murder. Oswald had been arrested in the movie house—initially for Tippit's murder, not the president's—after he ducked past the ticket booth without paying and tried to hide in the darkened audience. Belin told his colleagues back in Iowa that he made a special point of plopping himself down "in the seat where Oswald was apprehended."

Belin and Ball set aside hours to inspect the book depository and inter-view Oswald's coworkers, including three men who said they had been on the fifth floor of the building, watching out the window as Kennedy's motorcade passed by, when the shots rang out. The coworkers agreed in earlier police interviews that they had heard the bolt of a rifle moving back and forth just above them; they also said they had heard the sound of empty cartridge cases hitting the floor. Belin wanted to test out whether that could be true. The warehouse had cement floors that were thick enough to bear the weight of tons of school textbooks, and Belin wondered if it would really be possible for someone a floor below to make out the relatively subtle sound of a rifle bolt and of cartridges striking the floor above. Perhaps, he thought, Oswald's coworkers had imagined what they said they heard.

For the test, Belin and Ball placed a Secret Service agent with a bolt-action rifle on the sixth floor, at the southeast corner window where Oswald had been seen. Ball stayed with the agent while Belin went downstairs to the fifth floor with Harold Norman, one of the depository employees. "I then yelled for the test to begin," Belin wrote later. "I really did not expect to hear anything. Then, with remarkable clarity, I could hear the thump as a cartridge case hit the floor. There were two more thumps as the two other cartridge cases hit the floor above me." He said he could also hear the Secret Service agent move "the bolt of the rifle back and forth—and this too could be heard with clarity."

"Joe, if I had not heard it myself, I would never have believed it," Belin told Ball.

Belin conducted another test designed to see how quickly Oswald could have gotten from the sixth floor to the second floor, where Oswald had encountered his supervisor, Roy Truly, and Dallas police officer Marrion Baker within seconds of the shots. Baker said he had stopped his motorcycle and run into the building when he heard the gunfire because he believed it had come from the book depository. Belin ran behind Baker with a stopwatch as Baker re-created his movements, jumping again from his motorcycle outside the depository and then rushing in and climbing to the second floor. The test left Belin panting for breath. (In joining the commission, "no one told me that there would be physical exertion involved," he joked to his friends in Iowa.) The test proved to Belin that Oswald had the time to descend to the second floor before the police officer arrived there.

Belin was surprised that he was the first investigator to conduct these tests. For all their claims of an exhaustive investigation in Dallas, the FBI, the Secret Service, and Texas authorities had left gaping holes in the record. He was astonished to come across an important witness who had been all but ignored by other investigators: Domingo Benavides, an auto repairman who stopped his 1958 Chevy pickup when he saw Tippit gunned down near the corner of Tenth and Patton Streets. "I could hardly believe what the man was telling me," Belin said. Benavides said he had not only witnessed the policeman's murder, he had then gone to Tippit's car and tried desperately "to use the police radio to tell the department that an officer had been shot." He found two empty cartridge shells that the man he identified as Oswald had thrown into the bushes, and he turned them over to police.

Yet while Belin had managed to track down Benavides easily enough, his name did not appear in any of the witness statements prepared by the FBI and the Dallas police on the day of the assassination. The police had not bothered to take Benavides to police headquarters on the afternoon of Tippit's murder to identify Oswald, as they did with other witnesses. Why, Belin asked, was it being left to the commission to discover such a critical witness?

After the Dallas trip, Belin returned to Washington to begin taking formal, sworn testimony from some of the same witnesses he had met in Texas. Among them was the man he considered to be "the single most important witness" at Dealey Plaza—Howard Brennan, the forty-four-year-old steam-fitter who had been sitting on a wall at the corner of Houston and Elm Street, directly across the street from the book depository, when the shots rang out. Brennan's spot on the wall was only about 110 feet from the sixth-floor window. Other, highly credible witnesses said they saw a rifle pointing out of one of the upper windows, including a photographer for the *Dallas Times-Herald* who was riding in the motorcade and who, after hearing the first shot, pointed up and yelled out to his colleagues, "There is the gun!" Brennan, however, provided by far the most detailed account, including a clear physical description of the shooter. In the minutes before the shots, he said, he had looked up at the windows of the book depository and "observed quite a few people in different windows" who seemed to be eagerly awaiting the chance to see the president. "In particular, I saw this one man on the sixth floor."

A moment after the president's limousine passed by, Brennan said, "I heard this crack that I positively thought was a backfire"—from a motorcycle engine, he thought. Then, Brennan said, he heard a second noise that sounded like a firecracker being thrown from the book depository. "I glanced up. And this man—that I saw previously—was aiming for his last shot." The man held "some type of a high-powered rifle" and was "resting against the left window sill, with the gun to his right shoulder, holding the gun with his left hand and taking positive aim and fired his last shot." That was the third shot, the one that hit the president in the head, Brennan said. The assassin, Brennan said, was white, about 160 to 170 pounds and wearing light-colored clothes—a reasonably accurate description of Oswald. In the chaos after the shots, Brennan approached police officers and told them what he had seen. Minutes later, police radios across town crackled with the department's description of the gunman, apparently based on Brennan's account.

That afternoon, a shaken Brennan was taken to police headquarters and shown a lineup that included Oswald. At that instant, Brennan admitted later, he made a decision to lie. Although he later said he knew the president's assassin was standing right in front of him, he looked over the lineup and claimed he could not pick out the gunman. He lied, he said later, because he feared that Kennedy had been killed as part of a foreign conspiracy—"a Communist activity"—and that he might be next to die. "If it got to be a known fact that I was an eyewitness, my family or I, either one, might not be safe."

Belin found it disappointing, but sadly understandable, that Brennan had not told the truth. At about the time of his testimony in Washington, newspapers around the country were reporting an appalling story about the murder that month of a New York City woman, Kitty Genovese, who was stabbed to death in her home in the borough of Queens—an attack supposedly overheard by thirty-eight people, none of whom did anything to respond to her pleas for help.* "In an age in which people in New York offer no help as a woman is murdered . . . perhaps it is to be expected that a person, fearing some sort of communist conspiracy, would not come forth and immediately identify the man who killed the President of the United States," Belin wrote later.

Belin needed to make sense of the confusing testimony from other, seemingly credible witnesses who believed the rifle shots did not come from the book depository but instead from the so-called grassy knoll in front of the president's limousine. The most compelling testimony about a possible grassy-knoll assassin came from Sterling M. Holland, a supervisor for the Union Terminal Railroad, who was inspecting signals on the highway overpass ahead of the motorcade. He said he had been watching the motorcade, trying to catch a glimpse of Kennedy, when he heard gunfire and saw the president slump over. Turning his head to the left

---

* Those news reports, especially in the *New York Times*, were later found to have been seriously exaggerated. In later years, others journalists and researchers determined that only a few witnesses near the scene of Genovese's murder would have been in a position to see or hear anything.

toward the grassy knoll, Holland saw a "puff of smoke" that "came out about 6 or 8 feet above the ground" under a group of trees. He said he then ran toward the area and saw twelve to fifteen policemen there who were looking "for empty shells," suggesting the gunman had just fled the grassy knoll.

Holland's statement was taken in Dallas in early April by Sam Stern, who had traveled to Texas to assist with witness interviews. Stern was so excited by what Holland was telling him—and the clear suggestion of a second gunman—that the young lawyer excused himself from the interview room for a moment to track down Belin, who was also in Dallas.

Holland's testimony was "gripping," Stern said later. "The puff of smoke? What did it mean?" Belin, however, was unimpressed. "Oh yeah," he said dismissively. "We know all about that."

Stern was annoyed that this seemingly important witness might be ignored, but he bowed to what was, by then, Belin's much more detailed knowledge of what had happened in Dealey Plaza. Long afterward, Stern said that Holland's testimony still nagged at him, and he wondered if it should have been given more attention. "Nobody was taking it seriously," he said. In the years after the assassination, Holland's testimony would be seized upon by conspiracy theorists as proof that the commission had ignored a key witness.

Belin said later that he had always understood the potential significance of Holland's account but that, in the end, the railroad supervisor fell into the category of honest, but mistaken, witnesses. As Belin knew, no physical evidence—spent cartridges or anything else—was ever found in the grassy knoll. And it seemed impossible to imagine that a gunman could have fired off rifle shots from there without anyone seeing him clearly; several spectators had been standing in the grassy knoll as the motorcade passed.

Belin and Ball were also trying to sort out problems involving another potentially key witness—Helen Markham, the waitress at the Eatwell restaurant who had witnessed Tippit's murder. Unlike Domingo Benavides, Markham had been taken to a police lineup within hours of the policeman's death, and she identified Oswald as his killer.

If Howard Brennan was the commission's most important witness in demonstrating Oswald's guilt, Markham would be remembered as "the most controversial," Belin said. Questions about her credibility would dog the investigation for months. When Markham arrived in Washington to give testimony, she was in a state of near panic at her sudden celebrity. Mark Lane had stepped up his public attacks on her credibility, claiming that he had interviewed her and that she had backed away from identifying Oswald as Tippit's killer. The commission needed to determine what, if anything, she had actually told Lane and why she might have changed her story.

The chief justice tried to put Markham at ease as she arrived in the commission's offices and took a seat in the conference room. Warren "seemed almost like a scholarly minister as he looked and smiled" toward Markham, Belin remembered. Warren passed a handwritten note to Congressman Ford: "This witness is likely to be hysterical."

Markham admitted that she was rattled: "I am very shook up."

Ball, who led the questioning, tried to calm her down. "Take it easy," he said. "This is a very informal little conference here." He led her through the events of a hardscrabble life—she was divorced, with five children to support—before asking her to describe what she had seen on the afternoon of November 22. She described Tippit's death as cold-blooded murder, with Oswald pulling the trigger of his pistol seconds after the officer stepped from his police car. After pumping the shots into the officer's head and chest, Oswald stared straight toward her, Markham recalled. "He looked wild," she said. "I put my hands over my face and closed my eyes, because I knew he was going to kill me. I couldn't scream, I couldn't holler. I froze." But instead of turning his gun on Markham and other witnesses who would be able to identify him, Oswald simply "trotted" away.

Markham said she ran to Tippit's side and listened as he tried—and failed—to utter some final words as blood pooled around him on the street. Later that afternoon, she identified Oswald in the lineup. "I would know that man anywhere," she said later. "I know I would."

Ball turned to the question of Lane, asking whether she had talked to him and why she would back away from any of her account. She denied that she had ever talked to anyone she knew as Mark Lane or that she had claimed to anyone that Tippit's shooter was "short, heavy and with bushy hair," as Lane had insisted. Since November, she said, she had been interviewed by a reporter from *Life* magazine, which published some of her comments, and by a man who represented himself as a French journalist and who spoke with an accent. She could not recall the Frenchman's name, but she said he had a "dark" complexion and a medium build and wore "horn-rimmed glasses"—a physical description that might match Lane's.

Could Lane have impersonated a French reporter? Norman Redlich, who was watching the testimony, left the room and found two newspaper photographs of Lane, which were then shown to Markham. "I have never seen this man in my life," she insisted. Ball and Belin were baffled, since Lane had given sworn testimony that he had talked to Markham. Lane might be duplicitous, Belin said, but he found it difficult to imagine that Lane would lie outright to the commission and risk a perjury charge.* The conflicts between Markham's account and Lane's would not be resolved for several more weeks, with the credibility of both of them damaged in the process.

It gnawed at Belin then and for years to come, he said. At least six credible eyewitnesses, other than Markham, had identified Oswald as Tippit's killer. That included Benavides, the witness Belin had tracked down himself. Increasingly, Belin thought of Tippit's murder as the "Rosetta Stone" of the Kennedy assassination—the event that explained everything else, since it proved that Oswald was capable of murder, and since he had no reason to kill Tippit other than to flee from police searching for the president's assassin. And yet Lane and his growing army of conspiracy theorists were able to convince gullible audiences that the entire case against Oswald was a sham because a single "flighty" witness like Helen Markham might have confused her words in a telephone conversation she said she could not remember.

Understanding the crime scene in Dealey Plaza would never be so easy. Although Belin was certain that Oswald had acted alone in killing Tippit, he continued to suspect that Oswald might not have acted alone in gunning down the president. Belin was convinced that the bullets aimed at Kennedy's limousine had all come from behind, ruling out a shot from the grassy knoll or some other location in front of the motorcade; but given the confusion about the ballistics and the conflicting witness testimony, he asked how the commission could rule out the possibility that Oswald had been joined in the book depository by an accomplice. Could another gunman have been positioned somewhere else behind the

---

* The commission would not learn until June that Lane had tape-recorded his telephone call with Markham.

motorcade? Belin had joined the commission believing there had been a conspiracy to kill Kennedy, and he was still eager to expose one. Beginning in January, Mel Eisenberg, Redlich's deputy, organized staff viewings of the Zapruder film. Eisenberg and several others, including Belin and Specter, watched the same sickening images hour after hour, analyzing the film frame by frame.

In late February, *Life* magazine finally, and reluctantly, agreed to provide the commission with the original film it had purchased from Abraham Zapruder. Up until then, the staff had depended on copies of the film made by the Secret Service and the FBI. The original film was far clearer and had "considerably more detail than any of the copies we had," Belin recalled. *Life* also agreed to provide the commission with 35mm color slides of each frame. Belin was excited by the opportunity to see the original film; it was his best hope of demonstrating a conspiracy, possibly by showing that Oswald did not have enough time to fire all the shots that hit Kennedy and Connally.

Zapruder's Bell & Howell home-movie camera was in the custody of the FBI, and the bureau's technicians determined that it operated at a speed of 18.3 frames per second. That calculation enabled the bureau to determine the average speed of Kennedy's limousine through Dealey Plaza—11.2 miles per hour. The FBI then matched the limousine's speed against the results of tests to determine how quickly a gunman could fire off shots from Oswald's Mannlicher-Carcano rifle. The tests showed that the minimum time needed to fire "two successive well-timed shots" from the rifle would be 2.3 seconds—equivalent to 42 frames of the Zapruder film. The FBI insisted that its evidence proved that Kennedy and Connally had been hit by separate bullets. So if Belin and his colleagues could prove from the Zapruder film that shots had been fired at the motorcade less than two and a quarter seconds apart, they would have proof of two gunmen at Dealey Plaza.

For several days over the course of the late winter and early spring, the staff lawyers sat in a conference room with Lyndal Shaneyfelt, a former newspaper photographer who was now the FBI's principal photography analyst. Together they watched the Zapruder film hundreds of times. The images haunted Belin for the rest of his life, he said. "I would wake up in the middle of the night seeing the president waving to the crowds and then, within a few seconds, seeing the fatal shot and the head of the president jerk and then slump over."

Shaneyfelt numbered every frame of the film. The most disturbing image, marked as frame No. 313, captured the moment when the president was shot in the head and the bloody mist rose over the limousine. Two identifiable fragments of that bullet, which appeared to be Oswald's third and final shot, were found inside the limousine. The other shots seemed to pose the bigger mystery. From the film, it was possible to determine that the first shot to strike Kennedy—the bullet that hit him in the upper back or lower neck—landed sometime between frames 210 and 224; it was not possible to be more precise, since Zapruder's view was obstructed by a freeway sign during that period. (Beginning at frame 225, when Kennedy became visible again, he was clearly hit, because his hands were moving toward his throat.)

Shaneyfelt and the staff lawyers agreed that Connally was almost certainly hit sometime between frames 207 and 225, given the location of his wounds and his position in the limousine. An analysis of the medical evidence about Connally, matched up against the location of his body at other moments, showed that the very latest he could have been struck by a bullet was frame 240.

The remaining math was not so complicated, Belin realized. Assuming the FBI and Secret Service were right, the first and third bullets hit Kennedy and the second hit Connally. So if the president was hit for the first time no earlier than frame 210 and Connally was hit no later than frame 240, there were a maximum of 30 frames of film between the two shots, or less than two seconds. That would not have been enough time for Oswald to fire both shots. And that, Belin thought, meant that he might have the answer he had been searching for—there was at least one more gunman in Dealey Plaza.

27

Arlen Specter faced an extraordinary workload. He had as much to do as any of the young lawyers on the staff and—after the abrupt disappearance of his senior partner, Frank Adams—probably more. "When will I get to see my family again?" he asked his colleagues, only half in jest. Of the ninety-three witnesses who gave formal testimony to the commission in Washington, twenty-eight were Specter's responsibility. He took the testimony of most of the government officials and others who rode in the motorcade in Dallas, and of virtually all the doctors and medical personnel from Parkland Hospital and from the autopsy room at Bethesda. Specter was responsible for understanding the smallest details of what his witnesses described, and the transcripts of the witness testimony show that he was consistently well prepared.

He also continued to impress his colleagues with his willingness to stand up to the chief justice and Rankin. Not that he always got his way: he had recommended that when commissioners began to take witness testimony in Washington, they start with the people who were physically closest to the president in the motorcade. The logical leadoff witness, Specter argued, was the president's widow: "Jacqueline Kennedy would have made an appropriate beginning," since no one had been closer to the president, physically or otherwise, at the moment of his death.

In the first weeks of the investigation, Specter had prepared a list of ninety questions he wanted to ask the former First Lady. He divided them into seven categories, beginning with "Events of November 22, 1963, Preceding the Assassination." He thought she should be asked about every element of her husband's murder, including what she remembered of his facial expressions after the first bullet pierced his throat. Question 31: "What reaction, if any, did President Kennedy have after the first shot?" He also wanted to resolve a lingering mystery about why Mrs. Kennedy had tried to climb onto the trunk of the limousine after the shots rang out. "That question is of historical interest and has caused some speculation," Specter wrote to Rankin, offering several possible explanations for what she did, including the possibility that she was simply trying to escape "the tragedy and danger in the car."

In March, Specter said he was disappointed but not surprised when told that Mrs. Kennedy would not testify early in the investigation and that she might not be called to testify at all because of Warren's reluctance to question her. "The Chief Justice had taken a protective stance toward Mrs. Kennedy," Specter said later. It set a terrible double standard, he thought. If this had been a homicide case back at the Philadelphia district attorney's office, police officers and detectives would have interviewed the victim's spouse—especially one who had been at the murder scene—within hours of the crime. "In a first-degree murder case, the Commonwealth is obliged to call all eyewitnesses," he said. "That's because they're that important to finding out the truth." In the investigation of the assassination of the president, however, his widow might be asked no questions at all. "My view is that no witness is above the reach of the law to provide evidence," Specter said. "I don't think that Mrs. Kennedy was above that one iota." He felt just as strongly that the commission needed to take testimony from President Johnson. The case for questioning the president was made stronger by the many conspiracy theories that he was somehow involved in the assassination. Specter insisted that he was ready to ask Johnson—"point blank"—if he had been part of a conspiracy. "Under other circumstances, he would have been considered a prime suspect," Specter said later. "I don't think President Johnson had anything to do with the assassination of President Kennedy, but I do not think that would have been an inappropriate question to ask."

* * *

When Specter finally began taking testimony in Washington, his leadoff witnesses were the two Secret Service agents who had been in Kennedy's limousine—first, Roy Kellerman, who had been riding in the right front seat, and then William Greer, the driver. Both were called to testify on Monday, March 9.

Kellerman struck Specter as "the casting model for the role" of a Secret Service agent. A former autoworker and Michigan state trooper, the soft-spoken Kellerman—so quiet that colleagues had jokingly given him the nickname "Gabby"—was "six feet four, weighed well over 200 pounds and was muscular and handsome." While Kellerman might look the part, however, Specter was not convinced that the agent did his job well on the day of the assassination. He struck Specter as surprisingly unemotional, even blasé, when discussing the final moments of the life of the president he had been sworn to protect. Specter questioned why Kellerman did not jump to the back of the limousine, where Kennedy and Connally were grievously wounded, after hearing the gunfire in Dealey Plaza, at least to shield their bodies from the possibility of additional shots on the drive to Parkland Hospital. Kellerman insisted there was nothing he could have done; he felt he was more valuable to the victims by remaining in the front seat, where he could pass radio messages to Greer. Specter concluded that Kellerman "was the wrong man for the job—he was 48 years old, big, and his reflexes were not quick."

Greer was a far more sympathetic witness. A fifty-four-year-old Irish-American immigrant who had arrived in the United States as a teenager, he still spoke with a slight brogue. He had joined the Secret Service after serving in the navy in World War II and then working for nearly a decade as a chauffeur for wealthy families in the Boston area. He made clear to Specter that he had been shattered by Kennedy's murder. "He clearly felt deep affection for Kennedy, which I sensed had been reciprocal," in part because of their shared Irish ancestry, Specter said. Greer was tormented by his actions in the motorcade, including his failure to hit the accelerator immediately after hearing the first shot. Photos and television film from the scene suggested he had actually hit the brakes after the first shot, turning around to see what was happening, possibly making Kennedy an easier target. When Jacqueline Kennedy learned those details later, friends said, she was furious, complaining that the Secret Service agents were no more capable of protecting the president than her children's nanny would have been. Later, when William Manchester published his history of the assassination, he would report that Greer wept as he apologized to Mrs. Kennedy at Parkland Hospital, saying he should have swerved the car to try to save the president.

The chief justice, who sat through most of the witness testimony conducted by Specter, thought the young lawyer's interrogation methods were methodical to the point of wasting time. Certainly, Warren thought, they were wasting *his* time. In the questioning of Kellerman and Greer, for instance, Specter asked the agents to give their best estimate of the time that passed between each of the shots, where each shot seemed to come from, and from how far away. He also asked them to mark on a map where they believed the motorcade had been when each of the shots was fired. Specter thought it was his obligation to ask about the most "minute details of the assassination," no matter how much time it took. Warren disagreed, and he signaled his annoyance to Specter by tapping his fingers, loudly. During Kellerman's testimony, Specter recalled, "the Chief Justice's finger-tapping reached a crescendo," and "he took me aside and asked me to speed it up."

Warren told Specter that it was "unrealistic to expect meaningful answers to questions about the elapsed time" between the shots, especially when the agents had no clear memory of hearing the individual shots. But Specter refused the chief justice's order to hurry up. "No, sir," he recalled telling Warren. "These questions are essential." Specter reminded Warren that people would "read and reread this record for years, if not decades, and perhaps over centuries." He had plenty of experience with appeals courts back home in Pennsylvania and he knew how appeals judges scrutinized trial transcripts, looking for a prosecutor's smallest error or inconsistency. The commission's transcripts would be more closely reviewed than any transcript of any case he would ever prosecute. Specter thought that Warren, who had spent so much of his law-enforcement career managing prosecutors instead of prosecuting cases himself, did not understand that. "I don't know if Warren had any comprehension of what a transcript would look like," Specter remembered. "This was my work, and I was going to do it right."

Warren was not pleased with Specter's defiance, "but he didn't order me to change my approach," Specter said. "Aside from drumming his fingers, Warren did not interfere with this examination."

The next Secret Service agent to testify, Clint Hill, was the true hero of the day of the assassination, Specter thought. He believed that anyone who closely reviewed the Zapruder film could see that Hill, a thirty-one-year-old North Dakotan who had been with the Secret Service for nine years, had saved Jacqueline Kennedy's life. Hill had been in the follow-up car directly behind the presidential limousine; when he heard the first shot, he jumped into the street and ran toward the Kennedys, climbing onto the trunk of the presidential limousine. "I was amazed every time I watched the Zapruder film and saw Hill dash to the limousine, barely grasp the handle of the left rear fender and leap on the small running board at the left rear just as the car accelerated," Specter said. The young agent pushed Mrs. Kennedy back in the limousine as she began to climb onto the trunk. Without his actions, Specter said, "Mrs. Kennedy would have tumbled into the street when the Lincoln accelerated, into the path of the speeding backup car."

Specter was forgiving of Hill's acknowledgment that he had broken Secret Service rules by going out drinking the night before the assassination; the agent admitted he had a Scotch and soda at the Press Club in Fort Worth and then went to another club, where he remained until he returned to his hotel at two forty-five a.m. Whatever the aftereffects of the alcohol, Specter believed that "Clinton Hill's reflexes could hardly have been quicker when they were needed to save Mrs. Kennedy's life."

Hill offered Specter a convincing, if horrifying, explanation, for why Mrs. Kennedy had attempted to climb onto the trunk. "She had jumped up from the seat and was, it appeared to me, reaching for something coming off the right rear bumper of the car," Hill said.

Specter: "Was there anything back there that you observed, that she may have been reaching for?"

Hill thought she had been reaching for bits of her husband's skull that had been blown off by the second bullet to hit him. The blast "removed a portion of the president's head and he had slumped noticeably to his left," Hill said, remembering the bloody mist and particles of flesh in the backseat of the limousine. "I do know that the next day we found the portion of the president's head" on the street in Dallas. He recalled that his only impulse was to get the First Lady back into the passenger compartment. "I grabbed her and put her back in the back seat, crawled up on the top of the back seat and lay there."

Specter was also responsible for reviewing the medical evidence, and much of it was a mess, he quickly discovered. The record created by the emergency-room doctors at Parkland Hospital and later by the autopsy-room pathologists at Bethesda Naval Hospital, was full of contradictory, inaccurate information. Specter sensed early on how the confusion might give birth to conspiracy theories. The problems began within hours of the assassination, when doctors at Parkland held an ill-advised news conference. Facing a crowd of frantic reporters, Dr. Malcolm Perry, who had attended the president in the emergency room, seemed to say that one of the bullets that hit the president had come from the front of the motorcade instead of from the Texas School Book Depository or some other point behind Kennedy's limousine. "Yes, it is conceivable," said Perry, a comment suggesting at least two gunmen. An alarmed reporter from *Time* magazine, Hugh Sidey, warned Perry, "Doctor, do you realize what you're doing? You're confusing us."

Perry later admitted he had not inspected the wounds closely enough to make any judgment about where the bullets had come from, but many news reports that afternoon treated his speculation as fact. No news organization may have created more confusion that day than the Associated Press, the nation's largest wire service, which stated in one of its early reports that Kennedy had been shot "in the front of the head." (The AP also had to correct reports that afternoon that Johnson had been slightly wounded in the gunfire and that a Secret Service agent in the motorcade had been killed.)

The autopsy report was also full of gaps, reflecting the Bethesda pathologists' rush to complete their work. The doctors did not have time even to trace the path of the bullets through the president's body, which would normally be routine in the autopsy of a gunfire victim. Two FBI agents who had observed the autopsy took down—and stated as fact—what the pathologists later described as their ill-informed speculation that the first bullet to hit the president had not penetrated deeply into his body but had instead fallen out of the hole in his back.

Before taking the formal testimony of the Bethesda pathologists, Specter went to the naval hospital outside Washington to interview the doctors on Friday, March 13. He asked Ball, perhaps the most experienced trial lawyer on the commission's staff, to join him. At the hospital, they tracked down Commander James Humes, the pathologist who had overseen the autopsy. An agitated Humes demanded that Specter and Ball show him identification. "He was very suspicious," Specter said, recalling that he dug out "the only credentials Ball and I could produce"—the building passes

Admiral George Burkley, the White House physician, insisted that military pathologists hurry Kennedy's autopsy at Bethesda Naval Hospital on the night of the assassination.

Robert Knudsen. White House photographs. John F. Kennedy Presidential Library and Museum, Boston

The autopsy-room pathologists. Navy Commander James Humes, M.D. (*center*), was in charge of the autopsy, assisted by Navy Commander J. Thornton Boswell, M.D. (*left*) and Army Lieutenant Colonel Pierre Finck, M.D. (*right*). Humes's decision to destroy the original autopsy report and his notes would spark conspiracy theories that he was trying to hide something. BOTTOM LEFT: Secret Service Director James Rowley would face some of the commission's harshest questioning after admitting that he had not disciplined agents in the Dallas motorcade who had gone out drinking the night before. BOTTOM RIGHT: FBI special agent James Hosty in Dallas would find his career derailed because he had Oswald under surveillance at the time of the assassination and had failed to detect the threat he posed.

TOP LEFT: Marguerite Oswald often appeared to delight in her celebrity. Smiling, she talks with Dallas Judge Joe B. Brown, who oversaw the trial of Jack Ruby for her son's murder. TOP RIGHT: She retained New York lawyer Mark Lane, who quickly established himself as a leading critic of the Warren Commission, to represent her. BOTTOM LEFT: During her trip to Washington to testify for the first time before the commission, Oswald's young widow, Marina, was joined by her business manager, Jim Martin, whose private relationship with Marina would come under scrutiny by the commission. BOTTOM RIGHT: Oswald's older brother, Robert, is shown in Washington on February 20, 1964, after finishing his testimony before the commission.

they used to enter the commission's offices in Washington. "My pass didn't look very official to begin with, even less so because the typeface used for my name didn't match the print on the card."

Humes was still not satisfied, and it took an order from a senior hospital administrator, a navy admiral, to make him cooperate. "He was scared to death," Ball remembered. "He didn't want to talk to us."

Specter and Ball pressed Humes first to explain why there had been so much confusion about the path of the first bullet. Humes told the two lawyers the path had not been obvious, since the doctors at Parkland Hospital had performed a tracheotomy to allow the president to breathe, masking the exit wound in the throat. Early in the autopsy, Humes said, word came from Dallas that the Parkland doctors had performed heart massage on the president and that a bullet had been found on a hospital stretcher. That led Humes and his colleagues to speculate out loud, over the autopsy table, about the possibility that the bullet might have been pushed out of Kennedy's body when his heart was massaged. But it was just speculation, and it was wrong, Humes said. As the autopsy continued, the pathologists could see that the muscles in the front of the president's neck had been badly bruised—proof, they thought, that the bullet had passed through his neck and then exited out the front.

Humes said he and his colleagues at Bethesda were startled when they learned weeks later that the FBI agents in the autopsy room had continued to promote the heart-massage theory in their formal reports. An FBI report issued in December stated flatly—and incorrectly—that "there was no point of exit" for the bullet that entered the president's back. A separate FBI report in January stated flatly—and incorrectly— that the bullet "penetrated to a distance of less than a finger's length."

Specter had brought a copy of the autopsy report with him, and he asked Humes to go through it, line by line, and to explain how the navy pathologists had reached their conclusions. He asked Humes to provide a chronology of the drafting and editing of the report. Where were the early drafts?

It was then, Specter said, that Humes admitted that he had destroyed all of his notes, as well as the original copy of the autopsy report, to prevent them from ever becoming public. He had burned them in the fireplace of his home in suburban Maryland, he said, because they were stained with the president's blood from the autopsy room and he was worried that they might become some sort of nightmarish museum exhibit. Specter was astonished at the disclosure, he said. He recalled thinking—at that moment, as he sat there in front of Humes—that this had the makings of a scandal if it became known outside the commission. In Philadelphia, Specter had spent enough time with trial judges and juries, not to mention cynical courthouse reporters, to know what the reaction would be to the discovery that such essential documents had been incinerated. It would "give people an opening to say there was a cover-up."

He said later he tended to believe that Humes had not tried to hide something significant by destroying the paperwork. "I concluded he was inexperienced and naive, not realizing how many people would be looking over his shoulder, but not malicious." Still, he feared that conspiracy theorists would assume that Humes had been "trying to hide his mistakes, or worse."

Humes had another revelation that afternoon, although this one was welcome. It involved the first bullet to strike Kennedy. Although Humes had not mentioned it in the autopsy report, he volunteered that the bullet would have exited the president's throat at high speed and remained largely intact; it hit nothing solid—no bones or thick tendons—as it passed through his neck. The bullet had certainly not fallen backward out of the president's body, as the FBI report had suggested.

So where was it? If it had been traveling at high speed when it left Kennedy's body and could not be found in the limousine, what did it hit next? The slug found on Connally's stretcher at Parkland Hospital had presumably been the one that struck Connally—and, according to the FBI and Secret Service, only Connally. Specter pondered the questions over the weekend, thinking he would pursue the issue again on Monday, when Humes was scheduled to give his formal testimony in Washington. Specter would have the chance to show Humes some of the physical evidence from Dallas that the pathologist had never seen, including frames from the Zapruder film.

Specter later remembered Humes's testimony in Washington as historic, certainly a turning point in the commission's investigation, because it was the first time anyone outlined the hypothesis that would become known as the single-bullet theory.

It came after Humes was sworn in and was shown the blown-up image of the frame of the Zapruder film that showed Kennedy's hands rising to his neck, apparently after he was struck by the first bullet. Humes stared at the photo for a moment, noting the location of the president in the backseat and how Connally was sitting in a jump seat just ahead of him.

"I see that Governor Connally is sitting directly in front of the late president," Humes said: "I suggest the possibility that this missile, having traversed the low neck of the late president, in fact traversed the chest of Governor Connally." In layman's terms, then, he was speculating that the first bullet to hit Kennedy also hit Connally.

Suddenly, Specter said, it all made sense. The FBI and Secret Service had been wrong in concluding that Kennedy and Connally were hit by separate bullets. They were hit by the same bullet, one that first passed through the president's neck, then struck Connally in the back. Humes's theory might resolve the commission's confusion over whether Oswald had enough time to fire the shots. The assassin might not have had time to pull the trigger three times in the period in which the Zapruder film showed both Kennedy and Connally were hit, but there would have been time to pull the trigger twice—one bullet hitting both men, another hitting Kennedy in the head. Many witnesses in the motorcade and in the crowd at Dealey Plaza were convinced they heard three shots, so the commission would still have to sort out what happened to the third bullet; Specter thought that shot might somehow have missed.

Humes was shown what would be remembered by Specter as the most important piece of physical evidence the commission recovered from Dallas—the flattened, but nearly intact, copper-jacketed lead-core 6.5-millimeter rifle bullet that had reportedly been found on Connally's stretcher at Parkland. As evidence was introduced during the commission's hearings, it was labeled with exhibit numbers, and Specter now affixed a small commission exhibit tag—"CE #399"—to the transparent plastic tube that held the bullet.

If Humes was correct, CE #399 had to be the bullet that had hit both Kennedy and Connally. Specter asked Humes to look at the bullet in the tube. Assuming it only hit soft tissue in Kennedy's neck, could this bullet have also caused all of Connally's wounds? Humes was skeptical at first. "I think that extremely unlikely," he said. He knew from Connally's medical records that metal fragments had been found in the governor's chest, thigh, and wrist. This bullet seemed too pristine to have left behind so many bits of metal.

Specter was not discouraged by the pathologist's response—that Humes was distancing himself almost instantly from the valuable theory he had just offered the commission. As Specter looked back at the blowup from the Zapruder film, he thought the single-bullet theory simply sounded right. Humes, he knew, had only limited ballistics experience—little experience in performing homicide autopsies, for that matter—and might not know how to judge the weight of the metal flakes in Connally's body. Specter suspected the flakes were so tiny that they might well have come from the same bullet—the one he was holding in his hands.

Specter was angry that he was being forced to take Humes's testimony without showing him the autopsy photos or X-rays from Bethesda—the ones that Humes himself had ordered taken.

Three months into the investigation, Specter had still not been permitted to see the photos or X-rays, reflecting what he understood was Warren's indulgence of the Kennedy family. Specter had pressed Rankin repeatedly about the issue, and Rankin kept putting him off, saying the commission first needed to reach a decision on how, and whether, the photos and X-rays would be presented in the panel's final report. For the time being, he was told, he should rely on the expert testimony of Humes and the other pathologists. For his testimony, Humes had tried to be helpful by bringing along diagrams of the president's wounds prepared by a navy sketch artist at Bethesda, but both he and Specter knew the drawings were based on Humes's imperfect memory.

Now, with Warren and other commissioners present in the witness room, Specter decided to put his alarm about the situation on the record— to remind the chief justice of the absurdity of discussing the president's autopsy report without access to all of the medical evidence.

Specter turned to Humes and asked how he could be certain that the sketches by the navy artist were accurate, since the artist had not seen the autopsy photos or witnessed the autopsy himself.

"If it were necessary to have them absolutely true to scale, I think it would be virtually impossible for him to do this without the photographs," Humes admitted, offering Specter the response he wanted. Humes explained that he had not seen the photos himself since the night of the autopsy, when the Secret Service took them away for safekeeping; they would be helpful in getting his own testimony right, he acknowledged. "The pictures would show more accurately and in more detail the character of the wounds," he said. They offered "a more graphic picture of the massive defect" to the president's head.

Specter said later he remembered Warren scowling as he listened.

And the chief justice interrupted, turning the tables on Specter with his own question for Humes: "May I ask you this, Commander? If we had the pictures here and you could look them over again and restate your opinion, would it cause you to change any of the testimony you have given here?"

Humes was understandably reluctant to suggest he was getting his facts wrong in front of Warren and the other commissioners: "To the best of my recollection, Mr. Chief Justice, it would not," he replied.

It was the answer that Warren had been looking for.

Specter shared his frustration with Belin and some of the other young lawyers. They were united in thinking how wrong it was for the commission to block their access to any evidence, and especially the most basic medical evidence of how the president had died. "It was dangerous," Belin believed. "It violated basic, elementary rules of evidence familiar to every law student in America." He said he was also offended by the commission's decision—or at least Warren's decision—to allow the Kennedy family to dictate what evidence could be seen. "It was special treatment to a favored few," Belin said. There was no similar restriction on the staff in reviewing the autopsy photos of Officer J. D. Tippit, some of which were nearly as horrifying as those of President Kennedy. "If Officer Tippit's widow wanted to keep photos and x-rays of her husband private, she would not" get her way, Belin declared. "So why should President Kennedy's family be treated differently?"

Specter eventually got a fuller explanation. The photos and X-rays, he was told, were in Robert Kennedy's custody at the Justice Department, and the late president's brother did not want to release them to the commission for fear that they might become public—a judgment Warren came to share. The Kennedy family worried that "those ghastly images might reach the public," Specter said. "They feared that the American people would then remember John F. Kennedy as a mutilated corpse with half his head blown away, rather than as the dashing young president." He also saw a political calculation by the Kennedy family. "It seemed that the family wanted to preserve the late president's image in part for the future political benefit of family members. Younger brothers Robert and Edward both closely resembled the late president. Any damage to John Kennedy's image could harm them."

28

Warren did not want Specter to wait before leaving for Texas. "The Chief Justice did not let grass grow under anyone's feet," Specter said. So on Monday, March 16, the same day the commission took the testimony of Humes and the other pathologists from Bethesda Naval Hospital, Warren asked Specter to leave for Dallas immediately to take testimony from the doctors and medical staff at Parkland Hospital.

"Well, Mr. Chief Justice, Passover is midweek, and I kind of have to do some preparation for these witnesses," said Specter, who wanted to be with his family for the Jewish holidays. "I think I can leave a week from today."

"I was hoping you'd leave this afternoon," Warren replied.

The two men compromised, with Specter agreeing to leave Thursday. He arranged for his wife and children to go to Kansas to spend the holidays with his family.*

Specter hoped his trip to Texas would clear up several mysteries about the medical evidence. Why, for instance, did the Parkland doctors ini-

---

* Although Specter offered this account in his memoirs and noted it in interviews with the author of this book, the Jewish holiday actually began later in the month. In 1964, the first day of Passover was Saturday, March 28.

tially suggest to reporters that the wound in the president's throat was an entry wound, not an exit wound, which would rule out a shot from the book depository? And what was the chain of evidence for the mostly intact bullet found in the hospital's first-floor hallway—the bullet, Specter now believed, that had passed through the bodies of both Kennedy and Connally? Ballistics tests proved that the bullet had been fired by Oswald's rifle.

Specter was curious to see Parkland for himself and to meet the emergency-room doctors who had been confronted on November 22 with the challenge of trying to save the life of the president of the United States. The hospital proved to be nothing like the luxurious, well-equipped military clinics back in Washington where a president and his family would normally receive their medical care. Parkland was a big, noisy, dingy medical center on the outskirts of a large city—"a rambling, dun-colored, 13-story teaching hospital," Specter remembered. He was given a small meeting room for his interviews, and he set to work immediately, asking the hospital to arrange appointments with "every staff member even tangentially involved" with the treatment of Kennedy and Connally. "I intended to take the sworn testimony of every doctor, nurse, orderly and bystander who had been involved." On Wednesday, March 25, he interviewed thirteen witnesses back to back.

Specter would say later that, under the circumstances, the performance of the Parkland staff on the day of the assassination was "superb." Dr. Charles Carrico, the surgery resident who was the first to treat Kennedy, told Specter that the president's heart was still beating when he arrived in the emergency room. "From a medical standpoint, I suppose he was still alive," Carrico said. But as Specter now knew, so much of Kennedy's brain had been blown away that the doctors' efforts were futile despite "every conceivable, desperate effort to save him."

The Parkland doctors had a logical explanation for the confusion about the president's throat wound and why they initially suggested the wound might have been an entry point. (The error had been memorialized in the hospital's paperwork, with one of the emergency-room doctors describing the hole in the president's throat as "thought to be a bullet entrance wound.") As the doctors explained it, they had simply never turned the president's body over, so they had not seen the entry wound in the back. After the president was declared dead, the doctors said, they left the emergency room without any further examination. "No one, at

The single-bullet theory

The commission's staff concluded that the first bullet to hit the president's limousine was fired by Lee Harvey Oswald from the sixth floor of the Texas School Book Depository and wounded both President Kennedy and Governor Connally. Critics would claim that a single bullet—they dubbed it the "magic bullet"—could not have done so much damage and remained relatively intact. Later scientific analysis backed the commission's theory.

Texas School Book Depository

1. Traveling at an estimated speed of about 1,700–2,000 feet per second, the bullet enters Kennedy's body from behind.

President Kennedy

2. Proceeding through his body in a slightly downward angle, it misses major bony structures and exits below his Adam's apple near the knot of his tie.

3. The bullet is now tumbling and enters Connally's back, shatters his fifth right rib, and exits beneath his right nipple, leaving a large ragged chest wound.

Governor Connally

4. Slowing as it continues to tumble, the bullet passes through Connally's right wrist, cutting a nerve and a tendon.

5. With most of its momentum spent, the bullet barely punctures Connally's left thigh about 5 or 6 inches above the left knee. The nearly intact bullet is found near a stretcher at Parkland Memorial Hospital.

Todd Lindeman and Gene Thorp SOURCES: Warren Commission, House Select Committee on Assassinations, ABC News.

that time, I believe, had the heart to examine him," Carrico said. In other cases, he and his colleagues might inspect a corpse "for our own education and curiosity." In this case, Carrico said, "I make no apologies. I just saw the president die." Specter suspected that if the doctors had any thought of turning the president's body over to inspect it, they abandoned it when they noticed Mrs. Kennedy standing nearby. "They didn't want to prod the body with the widow watching."

Specter took a tour through the hospital and examined the medical equipment that had been used on the president. He was shown the metal stretcher that had been used to move Connally. If the single-bullet theory was correct, the bullet would have fallen from this stretcher after Connally was transported to an operating table in the second-floor surgical wing. From other testimony, Specter knew that the stretcher used to move Kennedy was nowhere near the area where the bullet was found.

An orderly testified that after Connally was transferred to the operating table, the stretcher was placed in an elevator to be returned to the ground floor, where it would be wiped down and used again. The key testimony on the issue came from a hospital engineer, Darrell Tomlinson, who recalled that he had found the stretcher in the elevator on the ground floor and pushed it out into the hallway, setting it along the wall near another stretcher. He said he then heard the sound of a bullet hitting the floor; it had apparently been hidden under a rubber mat on one of the stretchers. Specter was frustrated by Tomlinson's testimony; the engineer was confused about several details and could not say for certain which of the two stretchers produced the bullet. Even so, Specter said that under the circumstances there could be only one conclusion about the source of the bullet: it had to have fallen from Connally's stretcher.

When he returned to Washington, Specter sat down with David Belin to talk through the single-bullet theory. In a sense, Specter knew that his friend from Iowa might be disappointed by the theory; it was Belin's detailed analysis that winter of the Zapruder film and the timing of the shots that suggested the presence of a second gunman—and therefore a conspiracy. But as Belin listened to Specter, he could not deny the logic of the single-bullet theory, and he said later that he quickly accepted that it was the truth. Oswald had not fired three bullets into the limousine; he had fired only two, one hitting both Kennedy and Connally. In the decades that followed, scientific studies, using methods unavailable to the Warren

Commission in 1964, would validate the single-bullet theory, although it would become perhaps the most controversial of the investigation's findings. On the staff, it was never so controversial; in fact, several of the lawyers would recall that they readily embraced the theory when they first heard it that spring; "It just seemed sensible," said Sam Stern.

That still left open the question of what had happened to the other shot that most of the witnesses in Dealey Plaza thought they had heard. If one hit the president in the head and another hit both Kennedy and Connally, where had the third one gone? The staff debated the question for weeks but could not come up with a final, conclusive answer, apart from deciding that the bullet had obviously missed the limousine. One strong possibility, cited in the commission's final report, was that the first shot missed. Oswald may have fired for the first time—and missed—just as Kennedy's limousine turned the corner onto Elm Street and approached a large oak tree that would have obstructed Oswald's view for a moment. That could have prompted him to fire too quickly in the knowledge that his target was about to be hidden by the tree branches. If Oswald missed the first shot, the explanation might also be nerves, some of the lawyers thought. In pulling the trigger that first time, Oswald might have been struck by the monstrous significance of what he was about to do.

John and Nellie Connally agreed to testify before the commission in April. Specter assumed he would handle the questioning, since he had taken the testimony of all of the other witnesses who had been in the Dallas motorcade; no one knew the medical evidence better. The Connallys' testimony had become all the more important with the discovery—astonishing to Specter—that the governor's mangled clothes from the day of the assassination had been dry-cleaned and pressed. The clothes were "totally ruined for evidentiary value," Specter said. The decision to clean them, it was later discovered, had been made by Mrs. Connally. "I couldn't bear to look at the blood," she said, insisting that "I told the cleaner to remove the stains as best he could but do nothing to alter the holes or other damage."

Specter was startled when he was told, a few days before the Connallys' testimony, that he would not conduct the questioning. Instead, at Warren's request, Rankin would do it. It was a decision, Specter assumed, that reflected Warren's annoyance at the detailed way he had questioned earlier witnesses. Rankin delivered the news to Specter, who tried to convince himself that he did not care. "It didn't make a good goddamn to me whether I questioned them or not," Specter said. "That's not my call."

Rankin asked for Specter's help, though. "Arlen," he said, "get me prepared."

Specter took the opportunity to remind Rankin—really, to warn him—how much detail he would have to understand before questioning such important witnesses. Specter was not going to "dress this up," as he put it, and he inundated Rankin with facts and figures, as well as the medical and ballistics terminology, that he would need to master quickly. "I pointed out to Rankin that the bullet had a muzzle velocity of approximately 2,200 feet per second; that by the time it reached the president, the bullet speed was about 2,000 feet per second and that the bullet would have had an exit velocity of about 1,900 feet per second." Rankin listened as Specter explained how the army had just completed ballistics tests to try to replicate the victims' wounds "with a gelatin solution and compressed goat meat" and that the bullet had slowed as it "entered slightly to the left of the governor's right armpit, exited beneath his right nipple, leaving a large exit wound, and entered the dorsal aspect of his wrist and exited the volar aspect, finally lodging in his thigh."

Years later, Specter chuckled while remembering the look on Rankin's face. "By the time I had finished, Rankin, knowing he had little time to immerse himself in such detail, shook his head in despair."

Rankin gave up on the spot. "You'll have to question Connally," he told Specter, who admitted that he took a little pleasure in effectively overturning the decision of the chief justice. "Warren wanted Rankin but he was stuck with me."

The Connallys' testimony was scheduled for the afternoon of Tuesday, April 21. That morning, the Texas governor and his wife were invited to the commission's offices to see, for the first time, the full Zapruder film. Specter, who had already viewed it hundreds of times, remembered being fascinated as he sat there, "watching Governor Connally watch himself get shot." Nellie Connally found it a "sickening experience, but strangely surreal" to see the film, "as if it all were happening to someone else at some other time and place." She was particularly disturbed, she said, by the image of the shot to the president's head, and of Jacqueline Kennedy's attempt to climb out of the passenger compartment. "I watched the grainy film in disbelief as it showed Jackie crawling onto the trunk. What on earth was she doing?"

Mrs. Connally's testimony was, in many ways, just as important as her husband's, since she had not been hit by the gunfire and had memories unhindered by the physical pain and shock her husband had suffered. And that was part of Specter's problem. The strong-willed, articulate First Lady of Texas was convinced that her husband and Kennedy had been hit by separate shots. She believed the first bullet had hit Kennedy in the throat—she knew this, she said, because she turned around after the first shot and saw the president reaching for his neck—and that a second bullet fired moments later hit her husband in the back. It was the third bullet, she said, that shattered the president's skull, by which time her husband was hunched down in her lap.

As the Connallys watched the film, Specter had a sense of the power that Nellie Connally could exert on her husband. The couple began to argue about whether she had pulled her injured husband into her lap or whether he fallen there. She insisted she had pulled him down.

"No, Nellie, you didn't pull me down," the governor said. "I fell into your lap."

"No, John," she answered. "You didn't fall—I pulled you."

Specter recalled that the argument lasted some time—they "shot back and forth, several times." David Belin, who was also watching this exchange, remembered that the Connallys ended the debate only when they realized that others were in the room listening to them argue. Mrs. Connally had the film stopped, and the couple left the room, Belin said. "When they returned, Nellie Connally and the governor were in agreement—on Mrs. Connally's version."

Specter was disturbed that Mrs. Connally had convinced her husband to alter his account, especially since the couple's seemingly consistent testimony might forever be seen as a credible attack on the single-bullet theory. She wrote later about her conviction that her husband could not have been hit by a bullet that also hit the president. She insisted that her husband had time to turn back and forth in the car after the first shot was heard and before he was hit. "Even 'magic' bullets don't hang in the air that long," she said.

After lunch, the Connallys returned to the VFW building for their formal testimony. The entire commission had gathered to hear from them. Specter said it was the first time he had ever seen Senator Russell in the commission's offices for witness testimony; he was there out of respect for a fellow southern governor, Specter assumed. (Russell had been Democratic governor of Georgia before his election to the Senate in 1932.) Specter was struck by what a lonely figure Russell seemed to be, a man with almost no life outside of the chambers of the Senate; he would never marry. "Russell was immaculately dressed in a blue suit and white starched shirt and tan socks that barely covered his ankles," said Specter. "He was a bachelor. Nobody took care of his socks."

Governor Connally testified first, and his testimony was stomach-churning in its description of what had taken place inside the president's limousine as the motorcade rounded the corner onto Elm Street and approached the book depository. "I heard a noise which I immediately took to be a rifle shot," he told Specter. "I instinctively turned to my right because the sound appeared to come from over my right shoulder. . . . The only thought that crossed my mind was this was an assassination attempt."

He said he had no memory of hearing the second shot—the one he believed hit him—but "I was in either a state of shock or the impact was such that the sound didn't even register on me." But he felt it: "I felt like someone had hit me in the back." Blood started to pour from his chest, he said, and he assumed he was moments from death. "I knew I had been hit, and I immediately assumed, because of the amount of blood . . . that I had probably been fatally hit."

"So I merely doubled up," he said. "And Mrs. Connally pulled me over to her lap. So I reclined with my head in her lap, conscious all the time, and with my eyes open."

Then he heard another shot, which he was later told was the third shot. He said he assumed it was aimed at Kennedy. "I heard the shot very clear. I heard it hit him," he said. "It never entered my mind that it ever hit anybody but the president."

Suddenly, he said, the passenger compartment was covered with blood and bits of human tissue. The tissue was "pale blue—brain tissue, which I immediately recognized, and I recall very well." On his trousers, Connally said, there was "one chunk of brain tissue as big as almost my thumb." He remembered yelling out: "Oh, no, no, no. . . . My God, they are going to kill us all."*

---

* Connally's remark that "they" were trying to kill the occupants of the limousine would often be cited by conspiracy theorists as proof that the Texas governor knew that there was more than one gunman. Connally said later he meant no such thing and that he accepted the conclusion that Oswald had acted alone.

Connally agreed with his wife that separate bullets hit him and Kennedy. "The man fired three shots, and he hit each of the three times he fired," he said. "He obviously was a pretty good marksman." He said the president was silent after the first shot. After the last shot, he heard Mrs. Kennedy cry out: "They have killed my husband. . . . I have got his brains in my hand."

Asked by Specter to describe his wounds, Connally suggested it would be easier for the commissioners to see for themselves. "If the committee would be interested, I would just as soon you look at it. Is there any objection?"

There was none, and Connally took off his shirt, pointing first to the entry wound just below his right shoulder blade, then turning around to show where the bullet had exited from his chest. Specter recalled "a large, ugly, four-inch-diameter scar under his right nipple." The scene produced the only moment of humor in the otherwise grim day of testimony. Specter remembered that he had to suppress a laugh when Rankin's secretary, Julia Eide, walked into the room and was shocked to see the bare-chested governor. "She walked in in the middle of the hearing and saw Connally with his shirt off and gasped and walked out."

Connally's testimony was useful to Warren and others who believed that Oswald acted alone—because the governor said he was convinced of it, too. "You had an individual here with a completely warped, demented mind who, for whatever reason, wanted . . . a niche in the history books of this country." He was also convinced that all of the shots came from the rear—from the direction of the Texas School Book Depository.

In his testimony, Connally speculated that Oswald might have been targeting him, as well as Kennedy. Before his election as governor in 1962, Connally had been the Kennedy administration's navy secretary, which gave him responsibility for the Marine Corps. While still in Russia, Oswald had written a letter to Connally, asking him to overturn the less-than-honorable discharge that Oswald had received from the marines after his attempted defection. (He had been given an "undesirable" discharge, one level less punitive than a dishonorable discharge.) The request was rejected. Perhaps the sting of the discharge was still on his mind in Dealey Plaza. It was possible, Connally said, that "I was as much a target as anyone else."

When Connally finished his testimony after nearly three hours and began to leave the room, Specter could see how upset Warren was—

agitated again at the detailed, time consuming questioning. When Mrs. Connally then entered the room and was sworn in, Warren took charge: "Mrs. Connally, would you mind telling us the story of the affair as you heard it, and we will be brief." Warren's promise—*"we will be brief"*— was directed at him, Specter knew.

Her testimony was equally chilling. In the moments after the shooting, she, like her husband, assumed he had been fatally wounded. "Then there was some imperceptible movement, just some little something that let me know that there was still some life, and that is when I started saying to him, 'It's all right. Be still.'" Then she heard the third shot. "It felt like spent buckshot falling all over us," she recalled. But it was not buckshot. "I could see the matter, brain tissue or whatever, just human matter, all over the car and both of us." She agreed with her husband that the shots had come from the rear—from the direction of the book depository. "From the back of us   to the right."

Warren tried to puzzle out the single-bullet theory in his own mind. Back in the district attorney's office in Oakland in the 1920s and 1930s, he had been involved in plenty of homicide cases in which bullets flew every which way into a body—and through one body into another—and so it made sense to him that the bullet that flew out of Kennedy's throat might then have hit Connally. He was convinced by the argument that the bullet that hit Kennedy in the neck "just went through flesh" and had more than enough velocity to hit the man sitting directly in front of him in the limousine.

Connally, Warren decided, was mistaken in believing that he was hit by a separate bullet—understandable, given the shock that his wounds had caused. "I didn't put much faith in Connally's testimony at all," the chief justice said later. He was bolstered in his view by another of the commissioners, John McCloy, a fellow army veteran from World War I. McCloy had fought in Europe and knew how confused soldiers could become on the battlefield after they were hit by bullets or shrapnel, often not realizing for several minutes that they had been grievously, and sometimes fatally, wounded. McCloy recalled to Warren that he knew of two soldiers struck by bullets who did not realize it "for a considerable time" and "then a few seconds later dropped dead."

29

Again and again, Stuart Pollak, a twenty-six-year-old Justice Department lawyer, watched a startled Lee Harvey Oswald grimace in pain, clutch his stomach, and begin to die. In March, Pollak, on loan to the assassination commission, was given the assignment of reviewing the films that captured the scene at Dallas police headquarters on Sunday, November 24, as Jack Ruby emerged from a crowd of reporters and cameramen and killed Oswald. "I must have watched that 1,000 times," Pollak said later. "I went over to the Pentagon, and they had a room there, a projection room, where they would play it for me, over and over and over again. All the footage taken from different television cameras of that shooting."

Pollak was asked to determine if the film offered any hint that Ruby had accomplices in the crowd—maybe a police officer who tried to make way for Ruby to reach Oswald. The young lawyer was told to determine if there was eye contact, or any other sign of recognition, between Oswald and Ruby, given the rumors in Dallas that they had known each other. "I was looking for other people moving, other sights. Is there eye movement? Is Ruby acting alone? Is he getting any help from the cops?" Pollak asked himself.

After watching the film so many times, he was able to pick out nearly the full cast of characters in each of the frames—the individual reporters and police officers who were in the crush around Oswald. But he could not see anything that suggested a conspiracy or that suggested that Ruby and Oswald recognized each other. "We learned that there was not much to learn."

Pollak was impressed by how much scrutiny was being given to every part of Oswald's life, including its final moments, as a result of his murder by Ruby. If Oswald had lived and gone to trial, Pollak believed, the public might have accepted that the most important facts of the assassin's life were revealed in the courtroom. Now, because he was murdered on live television and denied a trial, even the tiniest details of Oswald's life and his death—frame by frame, millisecond by millisecond—were being analyzed. "I was impressed we were doing one hell of a job," he said later.

Others had more success in picking out something significant in the newsreels from Dallas. Alfred Goldberg, the air force historian, was respon sible for reviewing film of Oswald's appearance at a late-night news conference at Dallas police headquarters on November 22, several hours after the assassination. The police wanted Oswald to make a public appearance before reporters to prove that he was not being mistreated in custody. After watching different versions of the film repeatedly, Goldberg noticed someone in the crowd of reporters and photographers who did not belong there—Jack Ruby, pretending to be a journalist. "There he was," Goldberg remembered. "Ruby was standing right there, just a few feet from Oswald." It was a valuable discovery, suggesting that Ruby had a chance to kill Oswald Friday night instead of waiting until Sunday; that argued against a conspiracy to silence Oswald, since the conspirators would seemingly want Oswald dead as quickly as possible, before he could spill any secrets.

Goldberg had taken on the larger assignment of gathering all of the television film from Dallas that captured images of the assassination—from the national television networks, as well as footage from their local affiliates in Texas and from independent channels. He eventually tracked down seventeen hundred pounds of film and, through his air force contacts, arranged to have it all flown to Washington aboard military planes.

Pollak was one of several young lawyers who passed in and out of the commission's office on temporary assignment. It was his second chance to work under the chief justice. After graduating from Stanford and then earning a law degree, magna cum laude, from Harvard in 1962, Pollak was immediately hired on as one of Warren's clerks. He shared a view that was similar to that of Sam Stern, the other former Warren clerk on the commission staff. "The Chief Justice was not an intellectual heavyweight, but he had uncanny common sense and decency," Pollak said. Warren was eager to have the court issue rulings that reflected what was best for the country, sometimes without worrying over legal technicalities or precedent. "He'd say, 'cut through the law.'"

Pollak joined the Justice Department's Criminal Division in the summer of 1963. On the day of the assassination, he was in the waiting room outside the office of Assistant Attorney General Herbert "Jack" Miller, the head of the division, when the first word arrived from Dallas. Miller, he remembered, emerged from his office, shaken. "He came out the door to tell me the terrible news, 'The President has been shot,'" Pollak recalled. "It wasn't clear if he was dead or alive."

Miller asked him to rush to the department's library "to find out what federal jurisdiction we have" to prosecute a presidential assassin. Pollak was gone for about an hour—Kennedy's death was announced while he was in the library—and he returned with what he thought was a startling discovery. "We had no jurisdiction," Pollak remembered. "Shooting the president was not a federal crime."

Pollak's immediate supervisor was Deputy Assistant Attorney General Howard Willens. After Willens joined the commission's staff, he invited Pollak to join him, an offer that Pollak turned down. Early in 1964, Willens tried again, this time offering Pollak the chance to help write the final report. This time Pollak agreed, and he shared an office with Alfred Goldberg. The next several months were, Pollak said, the most intense working experience of his life. "In my whole career, I never put in more hours—every night, every weekend."

There were days when Californians, beginning with the chief justice, Pollak, and Joseph Ball, seemed everywhere in the commission's offices. Richard Mosk, a Los Angeles native, had followed a year behind Pollak at both Stanford and Harvard Law School. The twenty-four-year-old Mosk knew Warren through his father, Stanley Mosk, then California's state attorney general. The younger Mosk wrote to the chief justice to ask for a job on the commission, and he was hired in February and given the title of associate.

Richard Mosk's first assignment was far from glamorous: he was asked to study the history of congressional subpoenas and create a subpoena form that the commission could use. The work quickly got more interesting, though, if somewhat quirkily so. In March, he was asked to determine who was behind a series of mysterious classified ads that appeared in the two major Dallas daily newspapers in the weeks before the assassination. The first, on October 15, appeared in the personal-ads section of the *Morning News*: "Running Man—Please call me. Please! Please! Lee." The second was published the next day. "I want Running Man. Please call me. Lee." Had Lee Oswald used the classifieds to make contact with a coconspirator in the assassination who had used the code name "Running Man"? After a few phone calls, Mosk was disappointed to discover that the ads were simply part of a publicity campaign for a new movie, *The Running Man*, starring Lee Remick. (The film also starred the British actor Laurence Harvey, and it became Hollywood legend that the film was a commercial failure because it opened at about the time of the assassination and starred someone named Lee and someone named Harvey.)

Mosk was also asked to list all of the books that Oswald had checked out of public libraries in Texas and New Orleans, to see if his reading offered any clues about a possible motive for the assassination. "He was pretty well read for an uneducated guy," Mosk said. "I don't think he had a high IQ, but at least he was trying to read this stuff." The list included several biographies of world leaders, including Mao and Khrushchev, as well as Kennedy. Oswald also liked spy novels, including Ian Fleming's James Bond thrillers.

One book on the list was worth special scrutiny—*The Shark and the Sardines* by former Guatemalan president Juan José Arévalo, an allegorical tract about the domination of Latin American nations ("the sardines") by the United States ("the shark"). In late April, Mosk wrote a memo to David Slawson to highlight a passage of the book in which Arévalo wrote that foreign "statesmen" involved in the suppression of Latin America should be "purged, possibly by armed rebellion." Mosk noted ties between the book's publisher and the Fair Play for Cuba Committee, the pro-Castro group that Oswald had claimed to support, and that the book's author and translator were "all intimately connected with the Castro government." The translator, June Cobb, an American woman then living in Mexico City, was later revealed to be a paid CIA informant, and she would later figure prominently in the investigation of Oswald's mysterious trip to Mexico.

Mosk shared an office with another young lawyer on temporary assignment to the commission: John Hart Ely, twenty-five, who had graduated from Yale Law School the year before and had just been hired as one of Warren's clerks on the court. Ely had agreed to work at the commission until his clerkship began. Two years earlier, he had worked as a summer associate at the elite Washington law firm of Arnold, Fortas & Porter. The firm asked him to write the first draft of a Supreme Court brief on behalf of a pro bono client, Clarence Gideon, the Florida prison inmate whose name would be memorialized in *Gideon v. Wainwright*, the landmark case in which the Warren court ruled that indigent criminal defendants were entitled to a free lawyer. Ely was justifiably proud of his part in the case, and he showed Mosk a copy of an issue of *Time* magazine that spring that noted his role in Gideon's brief. "He flips the magazine to me, and I put my feet up on my desk" to read the story, Mosk said. That produced a mortifying moment for Mosk, since just then Lee Rankin walked through the door of their office. "It was the first time Rankin had ever walked into our office, and there I was, with my feet upon the desk, reading *Time* magazine." Mosk would make a far better impression as the weeks went on.

Ely was about to have his own awkwardness with Rankin—over the discovery of a distasteful fact about Oswald's health. Ely had been assigned to do a thorough review of Oswald's service in the marines; he summarized what he found in a memo on April 22. He went through Oswald's personnel files, including his medical records, and he came across information that he thought should be brought to the attention of the other lawyers, including the fact that Oswald had a Japanese girlfriend while stationed in Japan in 1958 who was "possibly a prostitute" and that he was diagnosed that same year with gonorrhea.

Rankin, the commission's paperwork suggests, was appalled that Ely was willing to put on paper something so vulgar—even if it was true. The seemingly prudish Rankin spoke with Ely on May 5 to make his displeasure clear; later that day, Ely offered an abject apology, insisting in a memo that he had been misunderstood and that he was not recommending any further investigation of the matters. "I mentioned Oswald's venereal disease, just as I mentioned every other fact I had encountered," Ely wrote. "I tried to treat it like any other event in Oswald's life, and intended neither to suggest that it is probative of whether or not Oswald killed President Kennedy, nor to 'smear' Oswald." As Rankin had insisted, the commission's final report made no mention of Oswald's bout with a sexually transmitted disease or of his possible romance with a prostitute.

30

With each passing week, the commission's contempt for the Dallas police department grew stronger. It was not just the department's incompetence, especially when it came to the chaos that had allowed Oswald to be killed in police custody. Often it was the inability of Dallas police officers to tell the truth, even under oath.

Commission lawyer Burt Griffin was convinced, for example, that Dallas police sergeant Patrick Dean had lied repeatedly about the circumstances of Oswald's murder. An eleven-year veteran of the force, Dean had been responsible for security in the basement of police head-quarters on the morning that Ruby slipped in and gunned down Oswald. The fact that Ruby had managed to get into the supposedly secure basement was proof either that Dean and his colleagues had not done their jobs or, more alarmingly, that someone on the force had helped Ruby, maybe in the knowledge that he would kill Oswald. Griffin thought it was possible that the delusional Ruby had been encouraged to act by policemen who wanted vengeance for the damage that Oswald had done to the city's reputation.

Dean had told a number of seemingly contradictory stories about what happened in the basement and what he heard Ruby say immediately after his arrest. By the time Dean testified as a star prosecution witness in

Ruby's murder trial in March, however, he had settled on his account, one that would help put Ruby on death row.

According to Dean's testimony, Ruby claimed in his initial police interrogation, minutes after shooting Oswald, that he had slipped into the basement by walking down a ramp off Main Street, past an unsuspecting police guard. During the same interrogation, Dean said, Ruby made a statement that the murder was premeditated. Specifically, Dean said, Ruby blurted out that he had originally thought of killing Oswald two days earlier, when he attended the Friday night news conference at police headquarters. Prosecutors cited Dean's testimony in convincing a jury that Oswald's murder was two days in the planning—not the result of temporary insanity, as defense lawyers claimed—and that Ruby should die in the electric chair.

Griffin was not the only person in Dallas who believed Dean was lying. Ruby's defense lawyers said they were convinced of it, especially since no one else could back up the policeman's testimony. Griffin thought Dean was motivated to lie both to cover up his own "dereliction of duty" and to try to grab publicity for himself. Dean had proved himself remarkably publicity hungry. On the day of Oswald's murder—without permission from his superiors—he had granted several interviews about what he had seen in the basement and what he knew of Ruby. Also without permission, he drove across town that afternoon to Parkland Hospital, where he managed to attach himself to Oswald's family, even joining Oswald's widow and mother in viewing the corpse.

Griffin thought it was possible that Dean had actually seen Ruby walk down the ramp and had done nothing to stop him. The police officer had been friendly with Ruby for years and was an occasional patron at the Carousel Club; Dean might have assumed that Ruby simply wanted the thrill of being a witness to a moment of history when Oswald appeared in front of the cameras again. Griffin could understand why Dean would lie if he had let Ruby into the basement; he would want to save his job. "If somebody in the police department had either let him come in or was aware that he would come in, that guy is out of a job, and the Police Department is totally discredited," Griffin said later.

As for Dean's claim that Ruby had acknowledged that the murder was premeditated, Griffin believed it was probably motivated by the policeman's desire to help local prosecutors win an all-important conviction.

That lie, Griffin said, would have been even more "reprehensible" since it was the reason Ruby faced execution.

When Griffin took Dean's testimony in Dallas in late March, he wanted to confront him with what he thought were his lies. At the end of about two hours of questioning, he announced to Dean that he would like to continue the conversation "off the record" with the court reporter out of the room. The unsuspecting Dean agreed.

"I told Dean that he was not telling the truth," Griffin recalled. "I told him the two particular points in his testimony that I believed to be untrustworthy: that Ruby told him on November 24 that he had entered the basement through the Main Street Ramp and that he thought of killing Oswald on the night of Nov. 22."

Dean said he was shocked at the accusation of perjury. "I can't imagine what you're getting at," he said. "I quoted Ruby just about verbatim. . . . These were the facts and I couldn't change them."

Griffin tried to ease the blow, he said. "I took considerable pains to explain to Dean that I felt that I understood why he was coloring his testimony and that I believed him to be a basically honest and truthful person. I don't recall ever using the word perjury. . . . I most certainly did not tell him that he was going to be prosecuted for anything." He advised Dean to consider hiring a lawyer if he needed to make a "substantial amendment" to his testimony.

Dean insisted again he was telling the truth, and Griffin went back on the record without getting the confession he had hoped for. He tried to end Dean's testimony on a friendly note. The court reporter returned to the room and Griffin, speaking for the record, said: "I appreciate very much the assistance that Sergeant Dean has given us here this evening, and I hope, and I am sure, that if anything further comes to light which he thinks would be of value to the commission, that he will come forward with it voluntarily."

The confrontation with Dean quickly "blew up in my face," Griffin acknowledged later. The police sergeant walked out of the witness room and contacted Dallas district attorney Henry Wade, the prosecutor who had won Ruby's conviction. Dean warned that the Warren Commission seemed to be out to undermine his testimony and therefore reverse the conviction. Wade immediately contacted Rankin in Washington to protest.

Dean said later he understood that Wade also telephoned President Johnson, an old Texas friend of the district attorney's, to complain about the commission's tactics, and specifically about Griffin. The story leaked to the Dallas newspapers, which reported that Griffin was being "recalled" to Washington.

Griffin might have predicted what would happen next, given his belief that the Ruby investigation had always been treated as a stepchild of the commission's work. When he learned of the flap in Dallas, Chief Justice Warren sided with Sergeant Dean, not with Griffin. Whatever Warren's view of Dean's truthfulness, he did not want the commission caught up in a nasty public fight with officials in Dallas. In early June, Dean was invited to Washington to testify, and he received an apology directly from the chief justice. "No member of our staff has a right to tell any witness that he is lying or that he is testifying falsely," Warren said. "That is not his business."

The confrontation over Dean came at an already difficult moment for Griffin and Hubert, who were beginning to wonder if they could ever finish their part of the investigation. From the evidence they had gathered, it was impossible to rule out the possibility that—somehow, someway—Ruby had in fact been part of a conspiracy to kill Kennedy or Oswald, or both. Ruby had undeniable, if indirect, ties to mobsters who might have had reason to want to see the president dead because of the Justice Department's war on organized crime. "There were lots and lots of associations that he had with underworld types," Griffin said. And there was a Cuba connection. Over the years, Ruby had wanted to be part of those seemingly shady business deals in Cuba that might have put him in touch with Cubans—both supporters and opponents of Fidel Castro—who might be implicated in the president's assassination.

By late winter, Warren had abandoned any hope of meeting his original deadline of June 1 to finish the investigation. The commission's lawyers were then facing a new deadline of June 15 to prepare drafts of their contributions to the final report. But for Griffin and Hubert, that deadline was still wildly optimistic. In March, they sent a memo to Rankin to remind him how much of their basic detective work was not finished. There had still been no effort to check out all of the names, telephone numbers, and addresses found in Ruby's belongings, nor had anyone conducted a thorough analysis of the records of phone calls that Ruby and some of his associates had made in the days before Oswald's murder.

Immediately after a staff meeting on Friday, April 3, the two lawyers met with Rankin and asked for help. They estimated they would need three extra investigators, working with them for at least a month, to get their work done. The response they got was, in their view, insulting. Rankin told them that Warren's bodyguard might be able to help them; no one else was available.

The next day, Griffin and Hubert mounted something close to an insurrection. They sent a memo to Rankin and Willens, recommending that the commission leave questions about Ruby and about Oswald's murder out of the commission's final report entirely. "We do not think the Ruby aspects of the case should be included," they wrote. "There is no possibility that this work can be properly done so as to be useful in the final report."

They said the commission could offer the public a sensible explanation for why questions about Ruby were not addressed, given his continuing appeal of his murder conviction. "If Ruby's conviction is reopened and our report is in any way hostile to Ruby, the commission could be justly criticized for issuing a report which impaired his right to a fair trial," the two lawyers wrote. Including material about Ruby in the report could create a serious conflict of interest for the chief justice. "Is it proper," they asked, "for a commission of the high rank and prestige of this commission to comment extensively about a person whose case is on appeal and will surely get to the United States Supreme Court?"

Willens's response was blunt. He told them to finish the job as best they could and not to expect more help. It was not up to them to decide what information got into the commission's report. "We should proceed as though we were definitely going to publish something on this subject," he wrote.

Griffin and Hubert stepped up their protest, this time with an eleven-page memo to Rankin that listed all of their unanswered questions about Ruby. They cited the many gaps in the commission's evidence about Ruby's activities in the months before Kennedy's assassination. They also outlined an explosive theory about ties between Ruby and Oswald: "We believe that the possibility exists, based on evidence already available, that Ruby was involved in illegal dealings with Cuban elements who might have had contact with Oswald. We suggest that these matters cannot be left 'hanging in the air.' They must either be explored further or a firm decision must be made not to do so, supported by stated reasons for the decision."

The memo essentially called the bluff of their superiors, and it produced what Willens later called "substantial discussion" about what could be done to satisfy Griffin and Hubert. In a memo dated June 1, Willens told Griffin to "submit to me in writing in the next few business days every investigative request" that "was necessary to complete the investigation." That same day, Hubert announced to Rankin that he would leave the investigation by the end of the week. Bitter over how the commission had ignored his work, Hubert had been planning for weeks to scale back his work on the commission and return to New Orleans. Now, he wanted to leave entirely. He told Rankin he needed two days "to clean out my desk and also to vacate my apartment." He said he would be available to return to Washington on weekends, if needed, for special projects and that he would travel to Dallas if the commission finally took Ruby's testimony.

That, it was decided, would not be necessary. Days later, when the commission finally scheduled a trip to Texas to question Ruby, Hubert and Griffin were not invited, and Arlen Specter went in their place. Their colleagues felt badly for Hubert and Griffin. According to David Belin, they were "brilliant lawyers who were crushed that they were not allowed to be present at the interrogation of the man they had been investigating for so many months." Later, however, Griffin insisted he understood and accepted the decision to exclude him. After his confrontation with Sergeant Dean, "I had become an embarrassment," he said. His reappearance in Dallas might stir up local officials in protest.

The man who was at the center of so much turmoil inside the Warren Commission, Jack Ruby, had spent most of the winter and spring in a jail cell in Dallas—occasionally trying to hurt, if not kill, himself.

As defense lawyers prepared to appeal his conviction for Oswald's murder, Ruby was being held at the Dallas county jail. On April 26, just after midnight, he tricked guards into getting him a glass of water so he could try again to injure himself. When the guards stepped away, Ruby charged into the concrete wall of his cell, headfirst. He was found, bleeding and unconscious, and taken to a hospital for X-rays, which revealed no serious injury. In searching his cell, guards discovered that he had begun removing the lining from his prison clothes, apparently to make a noose.

The next afternoon, Ruby had a visitor—Dr. Louis West, a professor of psychiatry at the University of Oklahoma Medical Center, who had been hired as a consultant by lawyers handling Ruby's appeal. West met with Ruby in a private interview room and found him "pale, tremulous, agitated and depressed." He could see the large cut on Ruby's head. Why had he tried to hurt himself? the doctor asked.

Ruby said he felt guilty. "The Jews of America are being slaughtered," he replied. "Twenty-five million people." They were being killed in retaliation for "all the trouble" he had created by murdering Oswald. Ruby said his own brother, Earl, was among the victims of this genocide— "tortured, horribly mutilated, castrated and burned in the street outside the jail." Ruby said he could "still hear the screams" of the dying Jews. "The orders for this terrible 'pogrom' must have come from Washington, to permit the police to carry out the mass murders without federal troops being called out or involved," he told West. He was responsible for "a great people with a history of 4,000 years to be wiped out."

When West tried to assure him he was wrong, Ruby "became more suspicious of my sincerity and once or twice seemed about to attack me," the psychiatrist said.

"Don't tell me you don't know about it—everybody must know about it," Ruby snapped. He had smashed his head against the wall "to put an end to it."

In his report to defense lawyers, West said that Ruby referred frequently to Oswald, describing him as "the deceased" or "that person."

The next day, West went to see Ruby again, and he seemed in better condition. Still, as West watched, Ruby experienced hallucinations that caused him to "quickly rise, move to a corner of the room and stand with head cocked, eyes wide and darting about." At another moment, Ruby "crawled under the table to listen" to the voices he was hearing. "The hallucinations were of human groans and cries, sometimes of children or a child," West wrote. Ruby believed they were coming from "Jews under torture."

West said he was convinced this was not play-acting. "Ruby is technically insane at this time," he concluded. Ruby was "obviously psychotic— he is completely preoccupied with the delusions of persecution of the

Jews on his account. He feels hopeless, worthless and guilty because he is to blame for the mass-murders of his own people." Ruby did not belong in jail, West said. "This individual should be in a psychiatric hospital for observation, study and treatment."

Two weeks later, a Dallas psychiatrist, Robert Stubblefield, visited Ruby at the request of the judge in Ruby's trial, and he agreed that Ruby was severely mentally ill and in need of hospital treatment. Ruby readily acknowledged to Stubblefield that he had killed Oswald, and that he had done it—as he had claimed from the beginning—to help Jacqueline Kennedy. "I killed Oswald so Mrs. Kennedy would not have to come to Dallas and testify," he said. "I loved and admired President Kennedy."

Ruby insisted, again, that he had acted alone in murdering Oswald, Stubblefield reported. His enemies "think I knew Oswald, that it was a part of some plot," he told the psychiatrist. "It's not true. I want to take a polygraph test to prove that I did not know Oswald, that I was not involved in killing President Kennedy. After that, I don't care what happens to me."

31

In the final days of planning for their trip to Mexico City, David Slawson and William Coleman decided they had no higher priority there than to arrange an interview with Silvia Duran. Her importance to the investigation had only grown in the weeks since January, when the two lawyers heard her name for the first time. "Duran could be my most important witness," Slawson told himself. "Just imagine what she might know." At the request of the CIA, Duran was going to be cited, by name, as an essential source for information in the commission's final report about Oswald's visit to Mexico. The CIA was eager not to give away any details of its elaborate photo-surveillance and wiretapping operations in Mexico City. Instead, the agency wanted the commission, whenever possible, to attribute information only to Duran if her testimony overlapped with what the CIA had also learned through its spycraft. If the CIA had its way, what Duran disclosed to her Mexican interrogators—or, at least, what the Mexicans claimed she had disclosed—would be the only publicly available record of many of Oswald's activities in Mexico.

The day before their departure, Slawson and Coleman were invited to the State Department for a briefing by Assistant Secretary of State Thomas Mann, the former American ambassador in Mexico City; he had left

Mexico four months earlier. Slawson and Coleman were ushered through the lobby, past the rows of brightly colored foreign flags that decorated the hallways, and into Mann's offices. He invited the two lawyers to take a seat, and he apologized for the unpacked boxes; he was still settling back into Washington, and it had been a busy time. In his new job, he said, he oversaw all Latin American affairs for the State Department and, given his growing friendship with President Johnson, a fellow Texan, he was a frequent visitor at the White House.

Since Slawson had finally been given a chance only two weeks earlier to read through all of Mann's top secret cable traffic from Mexico from late November, he knew just how valuable Mann's perspective might be on the question of a foreign conspiracy. So Slawson and Coleman asked the question directly: Was Mann still convinced that the Kennedy assassination was a Cuban plot?

He was, he said, even if he still could not prove it. Mann felt "in my guts" that Castro was "the kind of dictator who might have carried out this kind of ruthless action, either through some hope of gaining from it or simply as revenge." The fact that Oswald had visited both the Cuban and the Russian embassies before the assassination "seemed sufficient . . . to raise the gravest concerns" that Oswald had acted at the direction of the Cubans, possibly with the tacit agreement of their Soviet backers. Mann said his suspicion of a Communist plot had only grown stronger after he learned about the Nicaraguan spy in Mexico City who claimed to have seen Oswald being paid $6,500 in the Cuban embassy, and after learning about the intercepted phone call between Cuba's president and the country's ambassador to Mexico, in which the two Cubans talked about the rumors that Oswald had been paid off.

Mann excused himself, saying he had to leave for another meeting, although he invited Slawson and Coleman to consult with him again after their trip. As he shook their hands good-bye, Mann turned to Slawson and asked if the commission felt he had overreacted to the evidence. Had he been "unduly rash" in suspecting a Cuban conspiracy in the assassination? No, Slawson replied. Although the evidence increasingly pointed away from any foreign involvement in Kennedy's death, the commission's investigators had "found nothing in what the ambassador had done to be unjustified."

In the days before the trip, Slawson received a separate briefing from the CIA on what to expect in Mexico City. "The CIA told me that Mexico

City was a spy headquarters, so to speak, for lots of countries—like Istanbul used to be in detective thrillers. The spies always met in Istanbul." In the early 1960s, Mexico City was a capital of Cold War espionage, and Slawson was excited to see it for himself.

On Wednesday, April 8, Slawson and Coleman, accompanied by Howard Willens, boarded an Eastern Airlines plane at Dulles Airport and flew to Mexico City, arriving that evening at six. They were met at the airport by Clark Anderson, the FBI's legal attaché in Mexico. Because of the color of his skin, Coleman was used to being harassed when he traveled, both at home and abroad, and an immigration officer tried to block his entry to the country, questioning whether he had proper vaccination papers. He was waved through after an Eastern Airlines manager noted "something to the effect that Mr. Coleman was a representative of the Warren Commission," Slawson wrote later.

Coleman was nervous throughout the visit, fearing his life was in danger because of the secrets he knew from the commission. He had known threats of violence in the past—they were common for anyone prominent in the civil rights movement—but it was more frightening to face that danger in the streets of a foreign capital. If there had been a conspiracy to kill Kennedy, it seemed possible to Coleman that some of Oswald's coconspirators were still in Mexico, eager to kidnap him and force him to share what he knew. "If the Mexicans were involved in the conspiracy, maybe they would kill me," he worried. That first night, he had trouble sleeping in his room at the Continental Hilton Hotel, especially after he heard a mysterious rustling.

"About three o'clock in the morning, I could hear scratching at the windows, and I thought, 'Oh, my God, somebody's come to kill me,'" Coleman remembered. "I'd better get the hell out of here. . . . I was scared as hell."

The next day, he asked a CIA official standing outside the hotel if there had been any threat. No, the CIA man assured him. "Don't worry, we watched you all night."

That morning, the commission's delegation arrived at the sprawling American embassy compound on Paseo de la Reforma, where they were introduced to Winston Scott, the CIA's station chief, and to the newly arrived ambassador, Fulton Freeman, who had been in the city only two days. At a meeting with Scott and the ambassador, Coleman explained

Lee Harvey Oswald in Mexico City

SEPTEMBER-OCTOBER 1963

Flecha Roja busline terminal
Oswald arrives, September 27, 9:45 a.m.

Hotel del Comercio
Oswald registers here throughout his stay.

Transportes del Norte busline terminal
Oswald departs, October 2, 8:30 a.m.

United States Embassy
Embassy's CIA Station detects Oswald's visit.

Chihuahuenses Travel Agency
Oswald purchases ticket home, September 30.

Chapultepec Park

MEXICO CITY

Cuban diplomatic compound
Oswald visits September 27 and perhaps later

Soviet diplomatic compound
Oswald visits September 27 and perhaps later.

Plaza Mexico arena
Oswald reportedly attends bull fight

Gene Thorp

SOURCES: Warren Commission, House Select Committee on Assassinations

that the commission lawyers planned to meet with Mexican officials and hoped to conduct depositions, especially with Duran. Freeman had been briefed enough to know how important Duran was, and how delicate a subject she was for the Mexican government. The ambassador said that "seeing Silvia Duran would be a highly sensitive matter and that it should be discussed fully" before anyone approached her, Slawson recalled. Freeman said he would give his approval for an interview with Duran "so long as we saw her in the American Embassy and made clear to her that her appearance was entirely voluntary."

Slawson and Coleman met separately with Anderson and his FBI colleagues in the embassy. Although Anderson would concede years later how limited the bureau's investigation in Mexico City had been, he left his visitors that day with the impression that the FBI had been aggressive in following up on leads about Oswald. Anderson gave off "a very good impression of competence," Slawson wrote later.

The commission lawyers asked Anderson what he made of Duran. He said he believed she was a "devout Communist" who, while married and the mother of a young child, had a reputation for a scandalous private life. As Anderson put it, she was a "Mexican pepperpot" and notably "sexy." He agreed with the ambassador that a request to interview her would be a "touchy point" for the Mexican government, although he said he would try to help. He had good news for them about Duran—just that morning, the FBI had finally obtained a copy of her signed statement to her Mexican interrogators about Oswald, a document the commission had previously known nothing about. Slawson and Coleman said they wanted a copy as soon as possible.

The two lawyers spent much of the afternoon with Scott, and they found that the CIA station chief lived up to his reputation for unusual intelligence. He impressed Slawson with his milky, southern-bred charm, and the two men bonded over the discovery of their shared love of math and science. Both talked about how they had almost ended up in academia—Slawson trained in physics at Princeton, Scott in mathematics at the University of Michigan. "It was common ground," Slawson remembered. "There was something simpatico between us." (Since Scott operated undercover for the CIA, identified officially to the Mexican government as an employee of the State Department, Slawson removed all references to his real name in his later reports about Mexico City, replacing it with the single letter "A.")

Slawson and Coleman were impressed when Scott took them downstairs in the embassy to a soundproof safe room for his initial briefing about Oswald. "It was way down in the basement—it may have even been in a subbasement," Slawson remembered. "Everything that was told to us in the safe room or shown to us was considered top, top secret." During the briefing, which was also attended by the embassy's number-two CIA officer, Alan White, Scott turned on a small radio; he said it would muffle the sound of their conversation, a precaution in case someone was trying to listen in. "It was all very cloak-and-dagger," Slawson said.

As he began the briefing, Scott went out of his way to convince the visiting lawyers that he and the agency intended to cooperate fully with the commission and that he intended to hold nothing back, even at some risk to the CIA. He said he understood that the lawyers had "been cleared for Top Secret and that we would not disclose beyond the confines of the commission and its immediate staff the information we obtained through him without first clearing it with his superiors in Washington," Slawson recalled. "We agreed to this."

Scott then described, in detail, how Oswald had been tracked in Mexico using some of the CIA's most sophisticated surveillance technology, including wiretaps of almost all phones at the Soviet and Cuban embassies, as well as with the banks of hidden cameras mounted outside the two embassies. The exhaustive surveillance had begun, he said, within hours of Oswald's first appearance at the Cuban embassy. He then described how the Mexico City station had responded to the assassination, immediately compiling dossiers on "Oswald and everyone else throughout Mexico" who might have had contact with the alleged assassin. He pulled out the transcripts of what he said were Oswald's phone calls to the Cuban and Soviet embassies. The lawyers raised Duran's name, and Scott acknowledged that she had been of "substantial interest to the CIA" long before the Kennedy assassination because of her affair with a senior Cuban diplomat, Carlos Lechuga, while he was Cuba's ambassador in Mexico; Lechuga had gone on to become his nation's ambassador to the United Nations in New York. After the assassination, Scott said, the CIA had worked closely with Mexican authorities, "especially on the Duran interrogations."

Slawson was impressed by how comprehensive this briefing was. But as he listened to Scott, the young lawyer also found himself alarmed to realize how much of this information he had never heard before. Scott offered details about Oswald's visit to Mexico that his colleagues back at CIA headquarters had never passed on to the commission, despite the agency's recent effort to reassure the investigation that nothing was being held back. Other information that had been previously shared by the CIA was filled with "distortions and omissions," Slawson now knew. He and Coleman had brought along their own chronology of Oswald's activities in Mexico, intending to show it to Scott for his comments. "But once we saw how badly distorted our information was, we realized that this would be useless."

Slawson asked Scott why, given the elaborate photo-surveillance system, the commission had not yet been provided with photos of Oswald. Unfortunately, Scott replied, there were no photos. "Photographic coverage was limited by and large to the daylight weekday hours, because of lack of funds and because there were no adequate technical means for taking photographs at night from a long distance without artificial light," he told the lawyers. The answer was clearly evasive, Scott's colleagues would say later. Oswald was not known to have visited the embassies at night, and the Mexico City station was one of the best-funded and -equipped in the CIA. But Slawson and Coleman accepted Scott's explanation, if only because they had no good way of challenging it. Slawson remembered being surprised to learn that there were no photos. "I remember being puzzled, I guess, but I was too innocent to think they would deliberately hide stuff," Slawson said later. "I think I was naive."

The lawyers moved on to the larger questions. They asked Scott and White if they personally believed that there might have been a foreign conspiracy in the assassination, and if Mexico City might have figured in it. No, both men said. They felt that "had there been such a conspiracy, they would at least by this time have had some firm indication of its existence."

As the briefing drew to a close, Slawson remembered, Scott made an offer: Would the commission lawyers like to hear the actual recordings of Oswald's calls? "We still have the tapes," he said. "Do you want to listen to the tapes?"

"I don't think I need to," Slawson said. "I don't think I'd learn anything."

But Coleman did want to hear them: "As a good trial lawyer, I want to see and hear all the evidence."

As Slawson headed upstairs to meet with a group of FBI agents, he said, he left his partner in the safe room, pulling on headphones as he prepared to listen to the recordings of Oswald's voice.

Years later, after Scott's death, Slawson was outraged when the CIA effectively declared that the scene he described in the agency's safe room in Mexico City was a figment of his imagination—that Coleman could not have listened to the tapes because they had been routinely destroyed before Kennedy's assassination. (Coleman added to the confusion when he later blamed a faulty memory and said he could not remember listening to the tapes, although he said he had no doubt about the quality of Slawson's memory. "If David says it's true, it's true.") The CIA's claim that the tapes had been destroyed before the assassination was "a goddamned lie," Slawson would say later.

On Friday, April 10, their second full day in Mexico City, Slawson and Coleman were taken by the FBI on a tour of the capital. They saw the exterior of the Cuban and Soviet embassies and consulates, the bus terminals where Oswald supposedly arrived in and departed from the city, and the Hotel del Comercio, the modest hotel where he had stayed. They saw the restaurant, next to the hotel, where Oswald ate many of his meals, always choosing the least expensive item on the menu. The restaurant's employees recalled that Oswald was so frugal that he always passed up dessert and coffee, not realizing that they were included in the price of the meal.

After the tour, Slawson, Coleman, and Willens were driven to the offices of Luis Echeverria, a powerful Mexican official then on the verge of being named the country's interior minister; he would later be elected Mexico's president. Echeverria, who had been close to Scott for years, led off the conversation by offering his "strong opinion that there was no foreign conspiracy involved" in Kennedy's assassination—"at least no conspiracy connected with Mexico," Slawson said. Coleman pressed Echeverria for permission to interview Mexican witnesses, especially Silvia Duran. An interview with Duran might be possible, the Mexican said, although it would have to be informal—labeled as a simple social occasion—and conducted away from the American embassy. The government could not allow the commission's investigators to "give the appearance of an official investigation being carried out by the American government on Mexican soil."

Coleman said the interview with Duran was "of the highest importance" to the commission, and Echevarria said he understood why. Her testimony, he said, "was of the greatest importance" to Mexico, as well. It was her statements to interrogators that led the Mexican government to conclude "that no conspiracy had been hatched during Oswald's visits to Mexico."

Echeverria apologized and said he had to end the meeting promptly because he was expected at a lunch with Queen Juliana of the Netherlands, then on a state visit to Mexico.

"*We* would like to have lunch with Silvia Duran," Coleman said jokingly.

Echeverria replied with a rude joke about Duran, suggesting that Mexican women were less attractive than their Cuban counterparts. The commission's lawyers would "not have as much fun as we thought because Duran was not a good-looking Cuban—only a Mexican."

That afternoon, Slawson and Coleman asked other American embassy officials for their advice on how to arrange an interview with Duran. The ambassador's top deputy, Deputy Chief of Mission Clarence Boonstra, said he doubted the Mexicans would ever allow them to see her, especially if it meant she had to be taken into custody again; she had already been arrested twice since the assassination, the first time at the request of the CIA. As Slawson remembered it, Boonstra "felt that the Mexicans were too politically sensitive to risk having her picked up a third time." And from what the diplomat knew about Duran (Boonstra called her "a Communist") and her husband ("a very militant Communist and a very bitter person in general"), he doubted she would agree to be interviewed voluntarily.

The commission lawyers said they still wanted to try, perhaps by inviting her to an informal meal, as Echeverria had suggested. Inspired by what they had come to learn about CIA spycraft, Slawson and Coleman proposed that they could arrange some electronic surveillance of their own, asking Duran to a lunch in a "private place" in Mexico City that could outfitted "with recording apparatus so that no notes would be necessary." Boonstra had another idea. He suggested the commission bring Duran to the United States for an interview—and throw the Mexican government off her trail by labeling the trip as something else, perhaps a cultural exchange or for medical treatment. Duran might be willing to cooperate, he said, so long as she created no more trouble for herself with her own government. "The idea was worth considering," Slawson replied, saying he would "bring it up at the highest levels of the commission after we returned to the United States."

With Duran in hiding and with so many other obstacles put in their way, Slawson and Coleman gave up on the idea of interviewing her before they left Mexico. When they got back to Washington, they decided, they would pursue Boonstra's idea of bringing her to the United States. Besides, Coleman wanted to return home to Philadelphia as quickly as possible, so he booked a flight out of Mexico City on Sunday. Slawson and Willens made reservations to return to Washington on Monday.

On Saturday night, the American embassy organized a reception for the commission's investigators, and it was the setting for an odd encounter between Slawson and Scott. Slawson remembered that Scott pulled him aside for a chat, and the conversation quickly took an uncomfortable turn, with Scott telling him some of his uglier duties at the CIA. He told Slawson how he was regularly required to set traps for his CIA colleagues in Mexico City to see if they would betray the United States for money or some other reward. "He said he had to test his best friends and associates in the CIA every two or three years by offering some kind of bribe to see if they would go over," Slawson recalled.

"It's the hardest thing I do," Scott said. "I wonder whether I would have joined the CIA if I'd known that was part of my work."

Scott's comments were so jarring—so out of place, in the middle of an otherwise relaxed embassy reception—that Slawson was certain that he was trying to send a message. He thought Scott was trying to do him a favor by convincing him not to give in to the agency's recruitment efforts back in Washington. "I read that as his warning to me—don't accept."

The embassy party was memorable for Slawson for another, unfortunate reason. "They served good champagne and—you know champagne—I got so high and thirsty that when I got back to the hotel, I drank the tap water" by mistake. He quickly began to feel ill, and his trip to Mexico came to an ignominious end. "Sunday I was wiped out," he said. "It was even difficult getting on the plane to go back to DC." He felt better in a day or two, and he returned to the commission's offices in Washington the next week with a mission. He was determined to find a way to bring Silvia Duran to Washington.

32

Jacqueline Kennedy was beaming. It was a few minutes before noon on Tuesday, April 7, four and a half months after the assassination, and this was William Manchester's first appointment to interview Mrs. Kennedy for the book she had authorized.

"Mr. Manchester," she said in that "inimitable, breathy voice," welcoming Manchester into the living room of her new home on N Street in Georgetown. She closed the sliding doors behind her "with a sweeping movement, and bowed slightly from the waist," he said later. She was wearing a black jersey and yellow stretch pants, "and I thought how, at 34, with her camellia beauty, she might have been taken for a woman in her mid-20s." The relationship between Mrs. Kennedy and Manchester would later sour, but at the start of their collaboration, he thought she could not have been more gracious or helpful.

"My first impression—and it never changed—was that I was in the presence of a very great tragic actress," he said. "I mean that in the best sense of the word."

Manchester was in the first stages of researching the book, which was meant to be, essentially, the family's authorized history of the assassination and its aftermath. In time, he came to believe that the project was an effort, above all else, to discourage other writers from attempting a similar project that the family could not control.

His five interviews with the president's widow, conducted between April and July, were, not surprisingly, the most wrenching he would conduct for the book. Mrs. Kennedy talked about everything, including exactly what had happened inside the limousine when the shots rang out at Dealey Plaza. "She would withhold nothing during our interviews," he said. "About half of the people I interviewed displayed deep emotional distress while trying to answer my questions, though none of the other sessions were as affecting as those with Jackie."

The interviews were taped by Manchester on a bulky but reliable Wollensak reel-to-reel recorder. Under his agreement with the Kennedy family, his ten hours of taped conversations with the former First Lady were to be handed over to the planned Kennedy presidential library in Boston when the book was finished. "Future historians may be puzzled by the odd clunking noises on the tapes," Manchester wrote. "They were ice cubes. The only way we could get through those long evenings was with the aid of great containers of daiquiris." Mrs. Kennedy and Manchester smoked throughout the interviews, so "there are also frequent sounds of matches being struck."

At the offices of the assassination commission, Arlen Specter and the other staff lawyers were well aware of Manchester's book—it was a topic of fevered gossip around Washington—and of what amounted to Manchester's parallel, Kennedy-family-approved investigation. It angered Specter that Manchester was interviewing Mrs. Kennedy even as the commission's staff was being denied access to her by the chief justice. Specter asked why it was acceptable for the president's widow to talk to a journalist about the assassination but not acceptable for her to be interviewed by the federal commission charged with explaining to the American public why their president had been murdered.

He did not know the extent of it, but Mrs. Kennedy was just one of several important witnesses who agreed to be interviewed by Manchester that spring. Robert Kennedy consented to a taped interview on May 14, although he proved to be far less forthcoming than his sister-in-law. "His replies are abrupt, often monosyllabic," Manchester said. In some cases, Manchester got access to important government witnesses long before the commission. Four days after meeting with Mrs. Kennedy for the first time, he interviewed Director of Central Intelligence John

McCone, who would not testify before the Warren Commission until mid-May. And unlike the commission, Manchester was allowed to question both President and Mrs. Johnson. The White House granted an interview with the First Lady on June 24. The president initially offered to meet for a face-to-face interview but "found he could not bear to do it," Manchester said. Instead, he provided written answers to a list of the author's questions.

Through the winter and early spring, Specter continued to press for interviews with the Johnsons, and he drew up long lists of questions to ask them, just as he had for Jacqueline Kennedy. Specter would be disappointed, again, by Warren. The chief justice raised no objection when the White House announced that President Johnson, instead of testifying to the commission, would prepare a written statement about his memories of the day of the assassination. The 2,025-word statement would not arrive at the commission's offices until July 10, and it was seen by some of the new president's political enemies—especially by aides to Robert Kennedy—as self-serving and inaccurate. Johnson portrayed himself as having done all he could in the hours after the assassination to comfort Mrs. Kennedy and to seek counsel by telephone from the attorney general—conversations that, in some cases, Robert Kennedy said never occurred.

The chief justice would later concede that he should have pushed for face-to-face testimony from Johnson, if only to avoid the appearance that the commission had left questions unanswered by such a key figure. "I think it would have been a little better if he had testified," Warren said years later. "But he sent word to us that he would give a statement and Mrs. Johnson would give a statement. So we didn't even discuss it with him."

For her part, Mrs. Johnson's testimony came in the form of a transcript of a tape recording she made on November 30, eight days after the assassination. Commission staff members remembered it as a beautifully rendered depiction of all she had witnessed. She described arriving at Parkland Hospital and looking back toward Kennedy's limousine as she was rushed into the emergency room: "I cast one last look over my shoulder and saw, in the president's car, a bundle of pink, just like a drift of blossoms, lying on the back seat. I think it was Mrs. Kennedy, lying over the President's body." Later, inside the hospital, Mrs. Johnson found herself "face-to-face with Jackie" in a small hallway. "I think it was right outside the operating room," Mrs. Johnson said. "She was quite alone. I don't think I ever saw anyone so much alone in my life."

With the Kennedy family's encouragement, the chief justice continued to offer his help to Manchester. Warren agreed to be interviewed himself about his memories of the events of the assassination and the days that followed. Manchester later recalled that Warren "was unfailingly polite to me and he recognized that, while the lines of the two investigations might occasionally intersect, they certainly did not run parallel to each other." Over the next several months, Warren and Manchester remained in contact, the writer said. "We exchanged some confidences, and inevitably we ran across each other's tracks." At the Kennedy family's request, Manchester was given access to almost all of the most important physical evidence from the scene of the assassination, including the full Zapruder film—images of the assassination that the public would not be permitted to see for decades. Manchester said he was allowed to screen the film "70 times" and inspect it "frame by frame."

He was given a tour of Air Force One by one of the plane's pilots and invited to inspect both the surgery wards at Parkland Hospital and the morgue at the Bethesda Naval Hospital. He was allowed to have the president's original coffin—it was not used for the burial because it was damaged during the trip from Dallas to Washington—uncrated for his inspection.

Manchester's book was only one element of the Kennedy family's campaign to shape how the public remembered the president and the day of his assassination. In his unpublished diaries from November 1964, the columnist Drew Pearson chronicled the often cruel backlash directed at the family, much of it the result of Mrs. Kennedy's efforts to frame her husband's legacy.

The Kennedys had always inspired a blend of envy and disdain among Washington's power brokers, and the gossip about them was not ended by the president's violent death. If Pearson shared any of what he was hearing with his friend the chief justice, it might help explain why Warren became so protective of the family. Pearson knew that the Kennedys' enemies had not been silenced by the assassination, even for a few hours. On Monday, November 25, the day of the president's funeral, Pearson recorded in his diary that Mrs. Kennedy's standing with the public could not have been higher: "Jackie has been reigning supreme, as of course she should." But in a diary entry for that same day, he recalled that after watching the president's funeral on television that morning, he went to lunch with friends at the Carlton Hotel, two blocks from the White House, "and I'm afraid we were not so kind to Jackie Kennedy as the crowds who mourn outside."

The main topic of the lunch conversation was the troubled Kennedy marriage. "We recalled the flagrant way in which Kennedy had played around with other women" and how Mrs. Kennedy had traveled to Greece earlier that year and spent time on the yacht of the Greek shipping magnate Aristotle Onassis "chiefly to spite her husband." Pearson noted that Onassis was in Washington for the funeral and was expected to spend time with Mrs. Kennedy's sister, Lee Radziwill, who had a well-publicized romance with Onassis that summer as she prepared to divorce her husband. "It will be interesting to see whether the Radziwill divorce and remarriage to Onassis now comes off," Pearson wrote.

The columnist had lunch four days later with an influential Washington lawyer, Joe Borkin, who warned that "the tide has begun to turn against Jackie on several points," especially after the disclosure that Mrs. Kennedy had insisted on many of the most dramatic flourishes of her husband's funeral service and burial, including the open-air procession in which President Johnson, French president Charles de Gaulle, and other world leaders had marched down Connecticut Avenue. The event had created a panic at the Secret Service; Johnson admitted to friends that he worried that he would be assassinated by a gunman in the crowd. "She demanded that the heads of state march behind the body in the funeral, which could have meant a heart attack for Lyndon, pneumonia for De Gaulle and risked the lives of the free world chiefs if an assassin had wanted to risk his own life," according to Pearson's diary.

Borkin told Pearson there were growing behind-the-scenes attacks on Mrs. Kennedy over her plans to install a gas line at the Arlington National Cemetery for a so-called eternal flame to mark the president's gravesite. The move was seen as presumptuous. "There's only one other eternal light in front of a grave, and that's at the Paris tomb of the unknown soldier," Pearson noted in his diary. "Some people think that Kennedy doesn't really rate this yet."

Several news accounts in the days after the funeral described Mrs.

Kennedy's effort to persuade President Johnson to rename the national space center in Florida for her husband—Cape Kennedy, instead of Cape Canaveral—and to put the Kennedy name on the new national cultural center that was being built on the Potomac River. "Lincoln didn't get a memorial for about 75 years and Teddy Roosevelt and FDR still don't have a memorial," Pearson wrote after the lunch with Borkin. "Yet already they want to name the Cultural Center the Kennedy Center."

In the weeks after the assassination, Pearson noted, there were uglier attacks on Mrs. Kennedy over her repeated, well-publicized visits to the Arlington cemetery, as if her displays of devotion were an attempt to rewrite the story of her marriage. "The ladies seem to think that Jackie's five visits to the grave were too much and also there has been a lot of comment about the fact that Bobby Kennedy, her brother-in-law, accompanied her on some of these trips," Pearson wrote in his diary.

Pearson knew that some of the venom being directed at Mrs. Kennedy came from people who were supposedly her most devoted friends, including Marie Harriman, the wife of former New York State governor and Democratic kingmaker Averell Harriman. The Harrimans had volunteered to move out of their palatial home in Georgetown temporarily to allow Mrs. Kennedy and her children to move in while they searched for a home of their own. But as Mrs. Harriman was packing up her things to move into a nearby inn to make way for the Kennedys, she called Pearson's wife, Luvie, to say she "regretted having given up her house to Jackie." According to Pearson's diary, Mrs. Harriman "talked to Luvie on the telephone today, complaining that she was now cleaning out her drawers, putting away her toilet articles and preparing to move to the Georgetown Inn, where, she said, the food is terrible. . . . Marie is wondering why Jackie couldn't have gone down to Virginia for one month of mourning and then come back and found a house for herself. But no, Jackie likes Georgetown and *has* to stay there."

Pearson was certainly not above trading in gossip about Mrs. Kennedy in his column. On December 10, he reported that a White House doctor had medicated Mrs. Kennedy and her children to help them get through the funeral. "TV viewers of the Kennedy funeral were impressed with the manner in which the president's widow stuck close to her brothers-in-law," the column said. "This was no accident. The doctor had dosed Jackie with tranquilizers and asked the two brothers to stay by her side in case she faltered. Caroline and John Jr. got children's tranquilizers in case they got too frisky."

The column produced an angry denial from Mrs. Kennedy through a friend, Washington socialite Florence Mahoney, "who telephoned me to say that Jackie Kennedy was very upset," Pearson wrote. "Florence says that Jackie claims it isn't true and was quite emotional about it." He admitted in his diary that he regretted publishing the item, at least in the form it had appeared. The story, he said, had come from Jack Anderson, his junior reporting partner. "I wish I had used better judgment in editing it," Pearson said. "I called Jack Anderson who had written the item and who swears it is true. I am not sure." The item also angered Robert Kennedy, who canceled a scheduled interview. Kennedy's spokesman, Ed Guthman, "telephoned me on behalf of Bobby Kennedy to say that he was sore at me and would not see me," Pearson said.

Under his contract with the publisher Harper & Row, William Manchester had three years to finish his book. He worried from the start, he said, that he could not get it done on time. By comparison, then, the deadlines facing the staff of the Warren Commission were brutal. There was constant pressure on the staff from the chief justice to get their work done. Warren always felt that the investigation was "taking too damn long," said Alfred Goldberg. "The commissioners all wanted to get back to their jobs. Warren wanted to get back to the court."

In April, Rankin asked Goldberg to prepare a final outline for the report, as well as a memo recommending a uniform writing style for the staff. He also wanted Goldberg to draft a brief introduction to the report that would establish its tone and purpose.

In his style memo, Goldberg recommended that the report be written for the general public: "It should aim to achieve the maximum of clarity and coherence through the use of simple, straightforward language." Much of the report, he thought, should take the form of a narrative—a well-documented chronology of the assassination and its aftermath. The report might well be hundreds of pages long, "and it seems to me that it is too much to expect the reading public, not all of whom will be lawyers, or even historians, to grope for the thread of a narrative through 500 pages of what will be chiefly analysis."

Goldberg had known since his Baltimore childhood that serious history was best presented as a compelling story, albeit with a rigorous adherence to the facts. His career as a historian was born, he said, in the pages of the books of G. A. Henty, the prolific nineteenth-century British novelist who wrote more than a hundred adventure stories for children that "covered the whole history of the world," beginning with Ancient Egypt. By the time he was twelve, he figured, "I'd probably read 50 or 60 of them."

He recommended to Rankin that the commission's report include a special section on "theories and rumors" to respond to the many conspiracy theories being spread by Mark Lane and others. "This part should demonstrate that the Commission was fully aware of these questions and took due notice of them," Goldberg said, cautioning, however, that the "rumors" chapter should be brief. "To explore these questions in detail would give them much more than their due."

On March 16, he provided Rankin with his first draft of an introduction:

The assassination of President John F. Kennedy in Dallas, Texas, on November 22, 1963, shocked and grieved the people of the United States and, indeed, most of the peoples of the world. Within a few hours of the deed the Dallas police arrested and subsequently charged as the assassin Lee Harvey Oswald, who had in the interim allegedly shot and killed Dallas policeman J.D. Tippit. On the morning, of November 24, 1963, Oswald was himself shot and fatally wounded while in the custody of the police in the Dallas police station. Oswald's murder loosed a flood of rumor, theory, speculation and allegation that threatened to becloud and distort the true facts surrounding the assassination of President Kennedy.

When Goldberg's outline was circulated within the commission, there was an angry response from some of the staff lawyers. They argued that the report should read more like a fact-filled judicial opinion or a law review article—the type of writing they understood best—and focus on scientific evidence and witness testimony that would presumably establish Oswald as the president's sole assassin. Goldberg had sensed that would be the reaction, especially among the younger lawyers. "They had all been law-school hot shots at the very best law schools, very full of themselves," he said. The lawyers had been trained how to write dry legal briefs, not the more easily digested history that Goldberg was proposing.

No one on the staff was more hostile to Goldberg's approach than David Belin. "From an overall standpoint, I take basic exception to the entire proposed outline," Belin wrote after reading the historian's drafts. "I believe that it is essential that the report be prepared by the lawyers who have been working in each area with the standards of a legal document, rather than the discussion of a historical approach. So far as possible, the report should be written on a fact-finding basis. There should be a minimum of opinions and conclusions other than those clearly shown by the facts."

Goldberg did not yield. On April 28, he completed a new memo to Rankin, with another impassioned plea for the commission's conclusions to be structured around an easy-to-follow narrative of the assassination. The memo took an unsubtle swipe at Belin and some of the other young lawyers: "This report should be a narrative and members of the staff should remind themselves that it is intended for the public and not for lawyers."

33

David Slawson understood why Silvia Duran might want to say nothing. If the reports from Mexico were accurate, the United States government bore responsibility for her rough treatment, since her first arrest had been requested by the CIA's Mexico City station. He heard that the bruises on her body might be the least of it; there were reports she had a nervous breakdown as a result of the harsh interrogations by the Mexican secret police. Slawson assumed that "she was tortured—we didn't know it for a fact, but we strongly suspected it." That was the reason, he guessed, that the Mexican government had tried to block the commission from interviewing her. "My own belief was that, simply, they had mistreated her and they didn't want that to come out."

After returning from Mexico City, Slawson began pressing the CIA for help to arrange an interview with Duran outside Mexico. He went through the new interrogation report on Duran that had been given to him by the FBI in Mexico City, but it was still full of gaps. The Mexican government had not provided a transcript of Duran's actual words. Instead, the best the Mexicans had offered was a summary, signed by Duran, of statements in which she insisted she knew nothing about a plot by Oswald to kill Kennedy. Slawson remembered thinking that he would have been more impressed had Duran written out the statement in her own hand. Instead, the summaries were typed, suggesting she was simply handed prewritten documents to sign. "It was all second-hand," Slawson recalled. "And that's not enough, obviously."

From a distance, Slawson and Coleman had a favorable impression of Duran. Whatever her political views, she was said to be smart and gutsy. "From what we heard about her, she was a woman of real character," Slawson said. "I can't remember whether it was reading between the lines or what, but Bill and I had some reason to see this woman was a straight-shooter." He thought she might say things in Washington that she had been too scared to say in Mexico. Even if she stuck by the account she had given to her Mexican interrogators, Slawson believed it was important for the commission to judge her credibility face-to-face. "There was obviously some chance of getting more detail from her, especially if she trusted us," Slawson said. "And if we weren't beating her up."

The first challenge, he said, was simply to determine where Duran was. Her protective husband, Horacio, had moved her into hiding and was blocking access. "We couldn't get to her, the CIA couldn't get to her, nobody could," Slawson recalled. "She was hiding out" and her husband was "mad as hell" about the way she had been treated.

Slawson could not recall exactly when he got the news, but within weeks of his return from Mexico, Ray Rocca reported that the agency had made contact with the Durans and believed Silvia Duran would agree to come to Washington. Slawson remembered that Rocca seemed excited by the news—"he was really eager"—and wanted to help with the logistics. Rocca asked if the commission wanted the agency to take the next step and make arrangements for Duran to travel, probably with her husband. "Bill and I didn't have to think two minutes to say, 'Yes, yes,'" Slawson recalled.

He was exhilarated to think he would now get a chance to talk to the woman who—more than anyone else, possibly including Marina Oswald—may have known Oswald's thoughts in the weeks before he killed Kennedy. Slawson suspected that to Oswald, Duran must have seemed a kindred spirit. She was a fellow Socialist and a fellow champion of Fidel Castro. She could speak with him in English, and she seemed genuinely to want to help him get his visa for a trip to Cuba. She had been "very, very sympathetic to him," Slawson said.

Slawson remembered telling Rankin about the CIA's good news on Duran and asking permission to begin organizing her travel. "And Lee said, 'I'll talk to the chief.'" It was typical of Rankin not to make a decision like this himself, no matter how obvious it seemed to be, Slawson recalled. "He made no decisions without the chief's approval."

And Rankin returned with Warren's unexpected, baffling reply. "The chief says no," he told the stunned Slawson. There would be no interview with Duran.

Slawson could not recall if Rankin offered a detailed explanation for Warren's reasoning, but the chief justice seemed to be suggesting that Duran's support for Castro and her self-declared Socialism—she denied to her Mexican interrogators she was a Communist—made her unacceptable as a witness. It was similar reasoning to Warren's earlier decision to block Slawson from seeking paperwork from the Cuban government about Oswald—the decision that Slawson had decided to ignore, at his peril.

In passing on Warren's decision about Duran, Rankin cushioned the blow by telling Slawson that "the decision wasn't final" and that he could appeal directly to Warren if he felt so strongly about the need to interview her.

Slawson was astonished at the idea that he might be denied the chance to talk to Duran. "It was stupid, stupid," he thought. Much as his colleague Arlen Specter felt he needed Kennedy's autopsy photos and X-rays to do his work in reconstructing the events in Dealey Plaza, Slawson needed to talk to Duran if the commission wanted to rule out any possibility of a conspiracy. The commission did not have to accept anything Duran had to say at face value, he reminded himself. "We didn't have to accept her word," Slawson said. "But we should talk to the enemy if we need to."

He told Rankin he wanted to see the chief justice as soon as possible, and he asked for help from Howard Willens, who was "totally supportive" of the plan to bring Duran to Washington. Increasingly, Willens was viewed by Slawson and some of the other lawyers as their best advocate—much more so than Rankin. There were reports that, behind closed doors, Warren was angry about what he saw as Willens's impertinence. "He thought Howard was disrespectful," Slawson said. "Howard was maybe the only guy who disagreed with him to his face." Warren, for his part, confirmed that years later, saying that Willens "was very critical of me from the time he came over to us" from the Justice Department.

Slawson was nervous as he prepared himself for the meeting. The chief justice appeared in the commission's offices virtually every day but continued to have little interaction with the young lawyers. He rarely invited conversation. "He was the chief justice of the United States, and you didn't go in there to shoot the breeze with him," Slawson said. "He would have given you short-shrift if you tried." Still, Slawson and Willens quickly got their appointment, and Slawson remembered that he was received graciously by Warren, who welcomed the two lawyers into his office with a smile. "He asked us to have a chair, and we did, and then we made our case to him."

Slawson explained why Duran might be such an important witness, since she might offer information about Oswald that she had not risked sharing with the Mexican police. He argued that there was the possibility that the Mexican police had intimidated, even tortured her into silence, so that she would not reveal details pointing to a conspiracy hatched on Mexican soil.

What was there to lose by talking to her? Slawson remembered asking Warren. "There might be something valuable to gain."

The chief justice did not hesitate with his answer: He had not changed his mind. There would be no interview with Duran. Slawson said he remembered Warren's exact words:

"You just can't believe a Communist," Warren said. "We don't talk to Communists. You cannot trust a dedicated Communist to tell us the truth, so what's the point?"

He invited no more argument. "He just gave us his opinion, and that was that," Slawson recalled. On the Supreme Court, the chief justice might have a reputation as a champion of the rights of the political left, including Communists, but in this case, "he accepted the stereotype of a Communist as someone close to evil," a category in which he apparently placed Silvia Duran.

Slawson walked out of Warren's office feeling defeated. He remembered turning to Willens and saying, "Jesus, that is a big disappointment and a big mistake." But short of resigning from the staff, which he never seriously considered, Slawson concluded there was nothing more he could do.

Decades later, Slawson said he remained mystified by the chief justice's decision on Duran: "It's crazy we didn't talk to her." He came to wonder if the decision was a political calculation; Warren might have worried that the commission's right-wing critics would criticize him for giving credibility to an alleged Communist. More troubling, Slawson said, was the possibility that Warren had been secretly pressured to leave Duran alone. In light of what he later learned about the CIA, Slawson suspected—but could not prove—that Warren had been asked by the spy agency not to interview Duran. Slawson believed Rocca was sincere in offering to help bring Duran to Washington. But he wondered if others, much higher in the agency, were frightened of what she might reveal about Oswald or about American intelligence operations in Mexico City.

Warren, he later learned, had given in to pressure from the CIA about another possible foreign witness, Yuri Nosenko, the Russian defector. In June, Warren met privately with Richard Helms to hear the CIA's plea that the commission drop any reference to Nosenko in its final report. Helms "took me aside and told me that the CIA had finally decided that the defector was a phony," Warren remembered. And the chief justice agreed to the request, even though the commission had never been given a chance to interview Nosenko or even to submit written questions to him through his CIA handlers. "I was adamant that we should not in any way base our findings on the testimony of a Russian defector," Warren said later. Nosenko, like Duran, could not be trusted to tell the truth.

As the commission began to consider how to organize and write its report, Willens sent out memos to the staff listing the "loose ends" of the investigations, many of which involved Slawson and questions about a possible foreign conspiracy. That was no criticism of the quality of Slawson's work, he said. It reflected, instead, the mammoth task of trying to prove or disprove a conspiracy with evidence that often seemed vague or conflicting.

Although the evidence clearly pointed away from any involvement by the Kremlin, Slawson decided in April to ask the FBI and CIA to gather more information about Oswald's stay in the Soviet Union, including evidence that might substantiate his claim in his "Historic Diary" that he attempted suicide shortly after he arrived there in October 1959. Oswald wrote that he tried to end his life after Soviet officials initially refused to allow him to stay in the country. "I decide to end it," he wrote in the entry for October 21. "Soak wrist in cold water to numb the pain. Then slash my left wrist. Then plunge wrist into bathtub of hot water." He was discovered by a Russian tourist guide an hour later and taken to the hospital "where five stitches are put in my wrist."

Slawson felt the commission could not ignore the possibility that Oswald was lying and that the suicide attempt had been concocted as part of a KGB cover story—possibly to allow him to disappear from the streets of Moscow for a time to receive training as a spy. Oswald's autopsy report showed there was a scar on his left wrist, but Slawson wanted to be sure it was deep and dramatic enough to suggest an actual suicide attempt. Specter was responsible for the medical evidence, so Slawson wrote him a memo, asking that he question Dallas pathologists about the scar: "If the suicide incident is a fabrication, the time supposedly spent by Oswald in recovering from the suicide in a Moscow hospital could have been spent by him in Russian secret police custody being coached, brainwashed, etc." Slawson knew the CIA was so interested in verifying Oswald's account of the suicide attempt that it had considered exhuming his body to inspect the scar. The FBI opposed the proposal and the CIA dropped the idea, fearing it might inspire even more wild conspiracy theories.

Mexico City was never far from Slawson's thoughts that spring. After his trip there in April, he drafted a letter to the FBI listing dozens of new questions that the commission wanted answered in Mexico. He asked the FBI to prepare itemized estimates of how much money Oswald might have spent in Mexico City, down to the cost of purchasing six picture postcards of the kind found in his possession after the assassination. Since Oswald had reportedly attended a bullfight, Slawson wanted the FBI to establish "the cost of a ticket of the bullfight for the section in which Oswald probably sat." The idea, Slawson said, was to determine if Oswald would have needed to accept money from someone to cover his travel costs.

Slawson also had many unanswered questions about "the other Silvia"—Silvia Odio, the Dallas woman who claimed to have met Oswald in the company of anti-Castro activists. Slawson was convinced that the FBI had been too eager to dismiss her story. In a memo to his colleagues on April 6, he said his research showed that "Mrs. Odio checks out as an intelligent, stable individual." He was increasingly convinced she was telling the truth, at least as she understood it. "There is a substantial chance that if Mrs. Odio backs down from her story, it will not be because she disbelieves it, but because she is frightened."

The FBI reported that it had been unable to find the two Latino men who had supposedly been seen with Oswald at Odio's door, but that did not surprise Slawson: he suspected the pair might have gone into hiding to avoid being accused of involvement in the assassination and that they might since have tried to intimidate Odio into silence. "They could by now very easily have brought pressure or threats to bear on Mrs. Odio to keep quiet."

Slawson planned a visit to Dallas that spring, in part to take Odio's testimony. In advance of the trip, his colleague Burt Griffin, already in Texas, was asked to interview witnesses who might corroborate Odio's story, including her psychiatrist, Burton Einspruch. Griffin tracked down Einspruch at his offices at Parkland Hospital, an institution that had already figured in so much of the investigation in Dallas. "Einspruch stated that he had great faith in Miss Odio's story of having met Lee Harvey Oswald," Griffin reported back. The psychiatrist recalled how she told him—before the assassination—of her troubling encounter with the three strangers, including the man she now identified as Oswald. "In describing Miss Odio's personality, Dr. Einspruch stated she is given to exaggeration but that the basic facts which she provides are true," Griffin wrote. "Her tendency to exaggerate is an emotional type, characteristic of many Latin-American people, being one of degree rather than basic fact."

Odio's claims intrigued several of the commission's other staff lawyers. Slawson was so consumed by other work in Washington that he did not object when Jim Liebeler, who had become a close friend, volunteered to take on the assignment of interviewing Odio during a trip he had scheduled to Dallas. Liebeler had special reason to look forward to the interview: the photographs of Odio forwarded to the commission from the FBI in Dallas showed that she was, as reported, as pretty as a fashion model. While in Dallas, Liebeler was also scheduled to interview Marina Oswald, and she was lovely, too.

34

Wesley "Jim" Liebeler was a force of nature. He was a true libertarian, ready to ignore—or better yet, outrage—anyone who tried to impose rules on him. When it came to politics, he was a conservative Republican. He was fiercely anti-Communist and talked about it, and there were rumors on the staff—apparently untrue—that he was a member of the ultraconservative John Birch Society. Rankin remembered Liebeler as an "extreme conservative in rather a hotbed of liberals on our staff, and he early on became disenchanted with some of the others." Liebeler's disdain was often directed at Norman Redlich, who was as liberal on political issues as Liebeler was conservative. "Mr. Redlich and I have quite profoundly different views of the world on political questions," Liebeler said later.

For many on the staff, Liebeler also fit the role of a charming rogue. Decades later, several would describe him as among the most memorable people they would ever meet; just the mention of his name would prompt a knowing smile. Slawson recalled him as "devil-may-care" in his attitudes toward authority, beginning with his demand that the commission's incompetent secretaries be replaced. Griffin said that he and Liebeler "wouldn't agree on anything" when it came to politics and that Liebeler would be vocal about their differences. "But even through all his aggressiveness, he had this tender quality to him," Griffin said. "Even if he were saying that you were an idiot on some subject, he did it in a way that you knew he didn't think you were an idiot." Liebeler, he thought, "cared deeply about people."

Others had less fond memories. Specter thought Liebeler was highly intelligent but also "prickly" and a "flake" who was prone to bizarre flashes of anger. He recalled going to lunch with Liebeler at The Monocle, a popular Capitol Hill restaurant near the commission's offices, and watching, amazed, as his colleague blew up because the egg on his corned beef hash was not runny enough. "In a demanding, insulting voice, he brings over the waiter and says, 'Goddamn it, when you cook the egg, it's supposed to bleed onto the corned beef hash.'"

Warren made it clear that he did not like Liebeler, several of the lawyers recalled. Months into the investigation, Liebeler did what would have been—in most major law firms or government agencies at the time—the unthinkable. He began to grow a beard. "It was a great, beautiful beard—all red," Rankin remembered. "It irritated the chief justice." Warren was so upset that he told Rankin to order Liebeler to shave it off. Rankin said he tried to talk Warren out of it. "I said, 'Look, he has a right to have his hair the way he wants it, and if he wants a beard, he has a right to that.'" Specter remembered thinking how hypocritical it was for Warren—the "great egalitarian and civil libertarian"—to be angered over Liebeler's decision to allow his whiskers to grow out. The chief justice exacted his punishment, Specter recalled, by "banishing" Liebeler for a time to a different floor of the VFW building.

Liebeler titillated his colleagues with stories about his exploits in Washington with different women, and he enjoyed long nights of carousing and drinking, often inviting the other lawyers to join him. The sexual revolution of the 1960s was well under way, and although he had a wife back in New York, he intended to be part of it. "He was a crazy, huge womanizer," Slawson remembered.

"He would do anything—absolutely anything," recalled Griffin, who happily went home to his wife each night. "I live a very puritanical life. But Liebeler, despite all of his political conservatism, was not conservative about anything else." With alcohol, "he had no restraint," Griffin said. His nightly exploits were no secret because "he talked about it all the time." Other staff lawyers saw no sign that Liebeler's nighttime activ-

ities affected his work, and he returned to the office in the morning energized by the adventures of the night before. The alcohol seemed to have
no effect, perhaps because he "was a big guy, maybe 6 foot 1 or 2, weighed
200, 220 pounds," Griffin said.

Whatever the state of his marriage, Liebeler made clear that he was
devoted to his two sons, who remained behind with their mother in New
York while he worked in Washington. Over the years, his younger son,
Eric, was willing to forgive his father for some of his failings because he
so admired him "as a man who wanted to live every single damned day"
as if it were his last. "He looked at every day as a day that he should do
something interesting, something intense, something valuable."

Liebeler was happiest and most productive when he disappeared to
the family's seventy-two-acre summer home in Vermont, on the outskirts
of the Green Mountains National Forest. In joining the commission, he
asked Rankin for permission to fly to Vermont every few weeks, at the
commission's expense, to work and clear his head. Rankin agreed, apparently not realizing that Liebeler would stuff his briefcase full of classified
documents to read on the trip—a fact that would later come back to
haunt them both.

Liebeler's senior partner on the commission's "Oswald team," as it became
known, was Albert Jenner, the high-powered litigator from Chicago. Their
relationship collapsed almost instantly. The two men came to despise each
other, and they barely talked after the first few weeks. "I finally decided to
do my own thing and basically went ahead and did most of the original
work myself," Liebeler said. According to Specter, the differences in personality between Jenner and Liebeler could not have been more stark.
While Liebeler was a modern-day Falstaff, "Bert Jenner was known
principally by his dry attitude," Specter said, remembering staff meals at
which Jenner would insist that his food have no seasoning. "He ate salad
with no dressing."

The team's responsibilities were eventually divided up so that the two
men did not have to cross paths. Liebeler focused on questions about
Oswald's possible motive, while Jenner looked for evidence of a domestic
conspiracy involving Oswald's contacts with people inside the United
States after his return from Russia in 1962.

Back in Chicago, Jenner was a much-admired figure. He was one of the nation's best-paid lawyers—he would be one of the first in the country to bill corporate clients $100 an hour—and clients did not quibble over the fees because of his success in the courtroom. He was also celebrated by civil liberties and civil rights groups for his commitment at the firm to offering free legal counsel to the poor and for championing pro bono appeals for death-row inmates. At the commission, he earned a reputation for hard work. Unlike other senior lawyers on the staff, Jenner spent most of his time in Washington until the investigation was over. Still, he baffled some of his new colleagues with his work habits and his obsession for detail. Alfred Goldberg recalled reading a draft report on Oswald written by Jenner that, at 120 pages, had almost twelve hundred footnotes, including one especially pointless footnote in which Jenner identified the exact geographical location of the Soviet city of Minsk, where Oswald had lived. Specter remembered a second "worthless" twenty-page report about Oswald that Jenner had written. "The word was that it was read and thrown in the waste basket."

Jenner fit a mold that some of the young lawyers had encountered at their own firms. He was a high-paid litigator who knew how to win over a jury and impress a judge but who left the task of gathering evidence, and making sense of it, to junior associates. Certainly Jenner seemed to have no ability to organize his thoughts on paper. "Jenner was a pain in the ass," Slawson remembered. "Everybody rolled their eyes." Like other lawyers on the commission, Slawson wondered if Jenner suffered from a learning disability because, rather than read transcripts of witness interviews, "he had his secretary read them out to him," hour after hour.

Liebeler and Jenner were both invited to call on the research services of John Hart Ely, the young lawyer who was about to go to work at the Supreme Court as one of Warren's clerks. Ely took on several research projects for Liebeler and Jenner, including a survey of every home where Oswald had lived through his childhood and teenage years, beginning with the New Orleans orphanage where his mother placed him in 1942 at the age of three. It was notable, Ely thought, that Mrs. Oswald had dropped her son at the orphanage on the day after Christmas. If there was any doubt that Oswald was entitled to feelings of rootlessness, it was dispelled by Ely's six-page memo, which listed seventeen different homes, in four different states, in places as far afield as Covington, Louisiana, and the Bronx, New York, in which Oswald had lived with his mother. Often,

Oswald and his brothers would stay in a house, and a school, for only a few weeks before their mother would move them, often on a whim about where a better life might be found.

Ely was next asked to take on a detailed reconstruction of Oswald's military career, which began on October 24, 1956, six days after Oswald's seventeenth birthday, when he enlisted in the marines. Ely went through the records of Oswald's training in boot camp, including his three-week instruction in the use of an M-1, the military's standard rifle. When Oswald was finally tested on his weapons skills in December 1956, he ranked as a "sharpshooter," the middle of the three rankings used in the Marine Corps. (The highest ranking was "expert" and the lowest passable ranking was "marksman.")

Ely interviewed many of Oswald's colleagues from the marines and got a consistent view of Oswald as withdrawn and antisocial—"loner" and "nonentity" were common descriptions. When drawn into conversations with other marines, Oswald readily acknowledged that he was a Marxist and hoped to visit the Soviet Union and perhaps live there. A fellow marine recalled that Oswald, who was studying the Russian language, "played records of Russian songs so loud that one could hear them outside the barracks." Another said Oswald referred to other marines as "comrades" and that he used the Russian words for yes and no—"*da*" and "*nyet*"—in regular conversation. As a result, some of the marines began to refer to Oswald, to his face, as "Oswaldovitch." One former marine recalled that Oswald had talked of wanting "to go to Cuba to train Castro's troops."

Ely heard differing recollections of Oswald's life away from the barracks. There were conflicting reports about his drinking habits—some recalled Oswald getting drunk, while others recalled no drinking at all—and his attitude toward women. There were persistent rumors that Oswald was homosexual, mostly because he was so rarely seen in the company of women off base. Other sorts of rumors, involving firearms and violence, stuck to him. He was court-martialed after he injured himself with an unregistered .22-caliber pistol that he had purchased privately; the pistol fell out of his locker and discharged, wounding him above the left elbow. He was court-martialed again as a result of a fight with one of his sergeants. Ely also reported allegations, never substantiated, that Oswald was involved in the death of another marine, Private Martin Schrand, who was killed by a shot from his own weapon in January 1958, when both men were stationed in the Philippines.

Ely was surprised by how little attention the commission's investigators—and the FBI and other law-enforcement agencies—were paying to Oswald's career in the marines, and he recommended that several of Oswald's marine colleagues be tracked down and questioned under oath about what they had witnessed during Oswald's nearly three years in uniform. "In the Marine Corps, Oswald was doing a great deal of serious thinking about Marxism, the Soviet Union and Cuba," Ely wrote.

Jenner took on the assignment of investigating the background of people in Dallas who had befriended Oswald and his family and who, it was initially suspected, might have been involved in the assassination. The commission had asked the FBI to conduct background investigations on three people in particular: Ruth Paine; her estranged husband, Michael; and George de Mohrenschildt, the fifty-two-year-old Russian-born geologist who was the closest thing that Lee Oswald had to a real friend in Dallas.

The Paines came under suspicion in part because of their liberal views on foreign affairs and civil rights, which isolated them from their neighbors in the conservative suburbs of Dallas. Ruth's interest in the Soviet Union received particular scrutiny. A Quaker, she had been studying Russian since 1959 and had participated in a Quaker pen-pal program with Soviet citizens. She said her interest in learning Russian had brought her into contact with Marina Oswald; the two women were invited to a party attended by several Russian expatriates, which ultimately led to a friendship.

The Paines' marriage had fallen apart in 1962, and Michael had moved out that fall. Early in 1963, Ruth invited Marina—then caring for her one-year-old daughter, June, and pregnant again—to move in. Newly unemployed, Lee was planning to leave Texas in April to find work in his hometown of New Orleans. So Ruth, who had two children of her own, proposed that Marina remain with her until Lee found a job and could afford to support the family in Louisiana. Ruth said she welcomed Marina's presence as a chance to improve her Russian.

Marina followed her husband to New Orleans in May; Ruth Paine drove her there. But Oswald had trouble holding a job in Louisiana, just as he had in Texas, and the Oswalds returned to the Dallas area that fall. Rather than live with her husband as he looked for work, Marina moved back in with Ruth and remained there until the day of the assassination. During the week, Lee lived in a boardinghouse in Dallas, commuting on the weekends to the Paine home in nearby Irving.

After the assassination, the Paines drew attention to themselves by their strangely placid reaction to the chaos around them. To some investigators, that seemed to suggest that the Paines might have known of Oswald's plans. A Dallas homicide detective, Guy Rose, told the commission he was startled when he arrived at the Paine home on the afternoon of the assassination, before Oswald's arrest was announced, and Mrs. Paine came to the door and said calmly, "I've been expecting you to come out—come right on in." Later, Oswald's mother, Marguerite, and his brother Robert fed the suspicion of the Paines as somehow being involved in the president's murder.

De Mohrenschildt had a background out of a Cold War thriller. Worldly and sophisticated, fluent or conversant in at least six languages, he was born in czarist Russia to an affluent family with ties to the nobility. His parents fled to Poland when the family faced persecution as the Communists came to power in Moscow. He entered the United States in 1938 despite suspicions, noted in State Department files, that he might be a spy for Nazi Germany. He denied any Nazi ties, and none was ever proved. He initially settled in New York and worked in several different jobs, including filmmaking; for a time, he was a polo instructor. He mingled easily in high society in Manhattan and spent summers on the beaches of Long Island. Jenner and other commission lawyers were startled to discover that de Mohrenschildt's Long Island friends included the family of Jacqueline Bouvier, the future wife of President Kennedy. "We were very close," de Mohrenschildt said of the Bouviers. "We saw each other every day. I met Jackie then, when she was a little girl." The future First Lady was "a very strong-willed child, very intelligent and very attractive."

He moved to Texas to try to make his fortune in the oil industry, first earning degrees in engineering and geology from the University of Texas. As an oilman, he then took on assignments in several countries, including Yugoslavia, France, Cuba, Haiti, Nigeria, and Ghana. He acknowledged that, while living in Texas at the start of World War II, he did some spy work—at the request of a French friend—on behalf of the French intelligence services. He was never an official employee of a French spy agency, he said, but "I collected facts on people involved in pro-German activity" and tried to outbid German firms for the purchase of Texas crude oil.

By 1962, he had settled in Dallas with his fourth wife, and it was there that he was introduced by other Russian expatriates to the Oswalds, who were then reduced to what de Mohrenschildt remembered as "dire poverty." He was especially concerned for Marina—"a lost soul, living in the slums, not knowing one single word of English, with this rather unhealthy looking baby—horrible surroundings." Over the next year, he estimated, he saw the Oswalds "10 or 12 times, maybe more." He helped Marina escape from her husband for a time in the fall of 1962 after discovering that Lee had beaten her, leaving her with a black eye.

De Mohrenschildt recalled a visit to the Oswalds' in the spring of 1963 during which Marina displayed a rifle that her husband had just bought. She mocked the purchase. "That crazy idiot is target-shooting all the time," she said. De Mohrenschildt recalled asking Oswald why he bought the weapon. "I like target-shooting," he replied. At the time, Texas newspapers were full of stories about the seemingly fruitless search by the police for a gunman who had attempted to kill retired army general Edwin Walker; the unidentified sniper, lurking outside Walker's home in Dallas, had fired at him through a window, missing by inches. Marina would later acknowledge that she had known, within hours of the attack, that her husband was responsible.

During the visit, de Mohrenschildt said, he tried to make a joke about the Walker shooting. "Are you then the guy who took a pot shot at General Walker?" he remembered asking. "I knew that Oswald disliked General Walker, you see."

Oswald did not answer, although a "peculiar" look came over his face. "He sort of shriveled, you see, when I asked this question."

After months of careful review of the FBI files on the Paines and de Mohrenschildt, Jenner said he believed they had nothing to do with the assassination. In many ways, he came to see the Paines and de Mohrenschildt—their lives upended, dogged for years by a lingering suspicion about their ties to the assassination—as some of Oswald's other victims. To be certain of their innocence, however, Jenner subjected all three to hours of questioning under oath, especially over evidence suggesting that they might have guessed what Oswald was about to do.

Jenner put it directly to Ruth Paine during her testimony in

TOP: Marina Oswald, shown in Washington for testimony before the Warren Commission, said she was convinced that her husband had killed the president and that he had acted alone. BOTTOM LEFT: Marina's friend Ruth Paine, shown in Washington with her estranged husband, Michael; the Paines became entangled in the investigation. BOTTOM RIGHT: George de Mohrenschildt, a Russian-born oil engineer who tried to help the impoverished Oswalds, said he broke off his friendship after Marina Oswald openly mocked her husband's sexual performance.

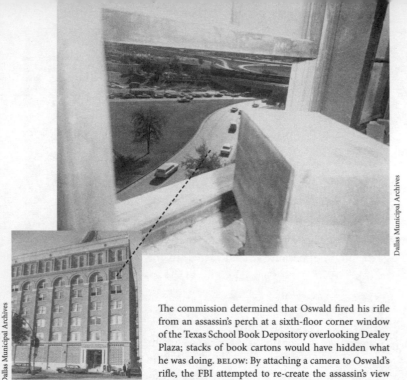

The commission determined that Oswald fired his rifle from an assassin's perch at a sixth-floor corner window of the Texas School Book Depository overlooking Dealey Plaza; stacks of book cartons would have hidden what he was doing. BELOW: By attaching a camera to Oswald's rifle, the FBI attempted to re-create the assassin's view from the window at the moment a bullet was fired at the president's head.

Washington: "Mrs. Paine, are you now or have you ever been a member of the Communist Party?"

"I am not now and have never been a member of the Communist Party," she said.

Jenner tried it a different way: "Do you now or have you ever had any leanings which we might call Communist Party leanings?"

"No," she replied. "On the contrary. . . . I am offended by the portion of the Communist doctrine that thinks violence is necessary to achieve its aims."

Her interest in the Russian language, she said, was the result of her faith. "God asked of me that I study language," she explained. She chose Russian, she said, because it coincided with the efforts of the Quaker Church to organize exchange programs in the Soviet Union.

She invited Jenner and the commissioners to ask blunt questions to prove her truthfulness, even awkward questions about why her marriage had fallen apart.

"Members of the commission have voiced to me some interest in that," Jenner admitted. "They are seeing to resolve in their mind who Ruth Paine is and, if I may use the vernacular, what makes her tick. . . . What was the cause of the separation between your husband and yourself, in your view?"

The answer, she said, was simple. Her husband was always kind and attentive, but he did not love her. Her tone was matter-of-fact. "We never quarreled, we never indeed have had any serious difference of opinion, except I wanted to live with him and he is not that interested in being with me."

She acknowledged that, months before the assassination, she worried that Oswald was capable of violence—she knew he beat Marina—and that he might have a troubling connection to the Soviet embassy in Washington. She had found a copy of a letter he had written to the embassy, referring to FBI surveillance of his activities in Dallas.

So why had she permitted him into her home at all? And why, given what she knew, did she then help him get a job at the Texas School Book Depository? Jenner thought Paine had reasonable answers to both questions. She had not wanted Oswald in her home for the weekend visits. "I would have been happier had he never come out." But she was eager to help Marina and excited at the chance to improve her Russian. She also welcomed the company that Marina offered. With her marriage over, "I was lonely." She readily acknowledged that she helped get Oswald his job at the book depository and explained, in detail, how it happened. She had been at a "coffee klatch" with a group of women friends, including Marina; one of the women mentioned that her brother worked at the book warehouse and that a job might be open there. Marina pleaded with Paine to call the warehouse. The job was available, and Lee was hired in October. Paine insisted she had no idea the warehouse was on Dealey Plaza.

Jenner spent most of two full days taking testimony from de Mohrenschildt, who required several hours just to get through a summary of his globetrotting life story, beginning with his childhood in Russia. He seemed to understand why people might assume the worst about his friendship with Oswald, given de Mohrenschildt's own unconventional, "bohemian" life. "All sorts of speculation have arisen from time to time," he admitted to Jenner. "I am very outspoken."

The more he answered Jenner's questions, the more his story about his unlikely friendship with Oswald made some sense. De Mohrenschildt said he found Lee Oswald a "sympathetic fellow" who seemed to want to improve himself even though he was "a semi-educated hillbilly." The Oswalds, he declared, "were very miserable, lost, penniless, mixed up." He said he found it laughable to imagine that the Soviet Union or any other foreign power would recruit Oswald as a spy. "I never would believe that any government would be stupid enough to trust Lee with anything important," he said. "An unstable individual, mixed-up individual, uneducated individual, without background? What government would give him any confidential work?"

He said he continued to feel sorry for Oswald even after discovering he beat Marina. "I didn't blame Lee for giving her a good whack on the eye." Marina, he said, openly mocked her husband in front of the de Mohrenschildts for his failings as a husband, including his lack of interest in sex. De Mohrenschildt said he sensed that Oswald was "an asexual person." Marina was "straightforward about it," telling the de Mohrenschildts, with her husband listening, that "he sleeps with me just once a month, and I never get any satisfaction out of it."

De Mohrenschildt said he and his wife were so uncomfortable with Marina's open complaints about her sex life that they cut off their friendship with the Oswalds in mid-1963, just as de Mohrenschildt was about to move to Haiti for a business venture. "This is really the time that we decided just to drop them," he said. "We both decided not to see them again because we both found it revolting, such a discussion of marital habits in front of relative strangers, as we were."

Although he found it impossible to believe that Oswald was a spy, he did say he worried at times that Oswald was somehow up to no good. "He had been to Soviet Russia—he could be anything," de Mohrenschildt said. He testified that he asked another Russian expatriate friend in Dallas, "Do you think it is safe for us to help Oswald?" The friend said he had been in contact with the FBI about Oswald and that the bureau had no concerns.

De Mohrenschildt said he believed he also mentioned Oswald's name in 1962 to another friend, Walton Moore, who was known to be "a government man—either FBI or Central Intelligence," and that Moore offered nothing to suggest Oswald was a risk. The commission later determined that Moore was, in fact, a CIA official based in Texas whose office was responsible for gathering information from Dallas-area residents who had recently visited or worked in Communist countries. The investigation found no evidence to show that Moore had ever been in contact with Oswald, although the commission's disclosure of a friendship between Moore and de Mohrenschildt would feed conspiracy theories about the assassination for decades to come.

35

At their late-night staff dinners, Specter and some of the other young lawyers began to mock the commissioners. They joked about "Snow White and the Seven Dwarfs," with Warren and the other commissioners in the role of the dwarfs. "Snow White was alternatively Marina or Jacqueline Kennedy," Specter said. "Warren was Grumpy," while Congressman Boggs of Louisiana was "Happy" because he sometimes arrived in the commission's office after "having had several cocktails late in the afternoon." Specter thought that Dulles qualified either as "Sleepy" or "Dopey," given the former spymaster's strange, sometimes barely coherent presence.

Slawson, the staff lawyer who worked with Dulles most closely, was increasingly convinced that Dulles, seventy-one years old, was demonstrating signs of senility, perhaps brought on by his humiliating public ouster from the CIA after the Bay of Pigs debacle. Dulles often dozed off at commission hearings, and his gout seemed to get no better over the months of the investigation. When Malcolm Perry, the emergency-room doctor from Parkland Hospital in Dallas, arrived in the commission's offices to give testimony in March, he was pulled aside by Dulles, who asked if Perry had any suggestions for his painful feet. "Sorry, it's not my field," the startled Perry told him.

Over time, Specter came to agree with Slawson that Dulles may have forgotten much of what he knew about American intelligence operations directed against Castro and other foreign adversaries who might have wanted to see Kennedy dead. And it was possible, he thought, that Dulles never knew some of the agency's most closely held secrets; his deputies could have kept the information from him, maybe even at his request, to allow him plausible deniability. When Dulles joined the commission, "everybody thought he was really smart," Specter said. "He turned out to be a nit."

Dulles did, unintentionally, bring lighthearted moments to some of the commission's otherwise most somber hearings. Specter recalled having to struggle to avoid laughing when, during an examination of vials that contained two metal fragments removed from Kennedy's body, Dulles stopped the proceedings with the startling announcement that actually the vial contained four fragments, not two. The FBI agent who attended the session "raced from one end of the table to the other to inspect the contents of the vials," Specter recalled. "The agent took two of the fragments and crushed them between his fingers."

"No, Mr. Dulles," the agent said in exasperation. "These are two flakes of tobacco that fell out of your pipe."

Specter was not the only one to snicker, he recalled, when Dulles became confused during the testimony of Dr. James Humes, the Bethesda pathologist. In discussing what became of Kennedy's clothes in Dallas, Humes explained how the president's tie had been cut off at Parkland Hospital to help him breathe. Following procedure, the fabric was cut to the left of the loop. "Dulles may have been distracted, or maybe he'd dozed off," Specter said, because when Humes held up the two pieces of the obviously expensive blue-pattered Christian Dior tie, Dulles, who spoke in the manner of an English school don, saw the knot and blurted out: "By Jove, the fellow wore a ready-made tie." Specter remembered that "we all found it funny that anyone, even for a moment," could think that the dashing John Kennedy "would wear a ready-made."

Dulles deserved credit for at least making the effort to attend the testimony of essential witnesses. That was not true for the majority of the commissioners. From what Specter could see, most of them remained ignorant of even the basic facts of the assassination: "I don't think the commissioners ever knew much about the case." Warren and the other commissioners never invited the junior lawyers into their executive sessions, and Specter said that in their few encounters with the staff, most of the commissioners "came and they sat there—they never asked any questions, made any suggestions. We ran the investigation ourselves."

Few among the staff lawyers were more critical of Warren than Specter. He tried always to qualify his criticism, describing Warren as a great chief justice. "He had a deep sense of decency . . . the moral conscience of the nation." But Specter felt that Warren lacked any similar intellectual depth. "Warren wasn't much of a lawyer. He wasn't brilliant. He wasn't even really smart." In running the commission, he said, Warren's stubbornness and impatience—and, most alarmingly, his unshakable loyalty to the Kennedys—damaged the investigation. Specter believed Warren was taking shortcuts in the investigation, rushing it in ways that threatened to create new conspiracy theories. Since Warren was convinced early on that Oswald acted alone, "it was all cut-and-dry for him." His's attitude was "let's get the goddamned thing over with," Specter said. "Warren wanted to get everything done in a hurry."

Specter felt that placed a grave burden on the staff, given Lee Rankin's unwillingness to stand up to the chief justice. The young lawyers felt obligated to try to block or overturn some of Warren's worst decisions—for the sake of the chief justice's own reputation. "We really felt we were the guardians of Warren," Specter said. "Warren was doing a lot of screwy stuff. We had to be sure he didn't get into trouble. Is that bad to say? It happens to be the truth."

Specter made harsh judgments, as well, about some of the other staff lawyers, especially those who had mostly disappeared from Washington. He did not know David Slawson well, but he knew that Coleman, Slawson's partner, was almost never there. "I don't know that Bill ever did anything."* To Specter's mind, almost all of the important detective work was being done by just four lawyers: "When it really came down to it, what you really had was Belin, Ball, Redlich and me." He also admired the work being done by Howard Willens, Rankin's deputy, despite the continuing whispers on the staff that Willens was there mostly to feed information back to Robert Kennedy at the Justice Department.

---

* Although commission records would show that Coleman worked substantially fewer hours than most of the lawyers, Specter appeared unaware before his death in 2012 that Coleman had taken on special assignments for the commission away from Washington.

* * *

None of Warren's decisions was worse, Specter thought, than his continuing refusal to allow the staff to review Kennedy's autopsy photos. In Specter's view, the crude artist's drawings from Bethesda Hospital that supposedly depicted the president's wounds were worthless. "They're inexact, they're misleading." Throughout the spring, Specter had continued to plead with Rankin to get Warren to reconsider the decision. "I raised hell with Rankin." One of Specter's colleagues recalled seeing him in tears as he left a meeting to discuss the subject. Specter insisted he did not cry, but "I recall long, bitter arguments."

David Belin remembered going to dinner with Specter one night at the restaurant The Monocle and suggesting that they both quit in protest over the photos. It would be an extraordinary step, they knew, possibly creating a scandal for the chief justice and the commission. Belin said he was as angry as Specter on the subject; he was offended that the chief justice seemed more determined to protect the Kennedy family's privacy than to allow the commission's staff to have access to vital medical evidence. The Kennedys, Belin said, were being treated as if "they were some sort of an elite, similar to the nobility of an eighteenth-century European monarchy."

Years later, Specter did not dispute Belin's memory of the dinner, although he insisted that he never thought of resigning. "I wasn't going to quit over that," he said. What he did instead was to make a formal protest—on paper, in a memo to Rankin—that would establish for the commission's permanent record how angry he felt. "It wasn't a cover-your-ass memo," Specter insisted later. It was, he said, a final plea for the evidence he needed to do his job in determining exactly how the president of the United States had been murdered. "It was a memo written to try to persuade Rankin to get the goddamned photos and x-rays."

The memo, dated April 30, began: "In my opinion, it is indispensable that we obtain the photographs and x-rays of President Kennedy's autopsy." He then listed the reasons why, noting that the commission took a terrible risk if it relied on the navy sketch artist's depiction of the president's wounds, instead of on the actual photos and X-rays; there was already discussion on the staff of reprinting the sketches in the commission's final report. Specter reminded Rankin that the navy artist had never seen the photos or X-rays himself; the accuracy of the sketches depended on the "hazy recollections" of the Bethesda pathologists who were also being denied access to the photos—the photos they had ordered taken.

Specter warned, presciently, that "someday, someone may compare the films with the artist's drawings and find a significant error which might substantially affect the essential testimony and the Commission's conclusions."

In the memo, Specter proposed a solution. He recommended that the commission ask Robert Kennedy to grant access to the autopsy photos and X-rays in exchange for a commitment that the evidence would "be viewed only by the absolute minimum number of people from the Commission for the sole purpose of corroborating (or correcting) the artist's drawings, with the film not to become a part of the Commission's records."

Specter's memo was timed to an executive session of the commission scheduled for that same day. It would be the panel's first meeting in more than a month. Rankin told Specter that he could make no promises but that he had been swayed by the young lawyer's arguments, and he agreed to make an appeal to the commission on his behalf. Rankin knew that the argument for reviewing the autopsy photos and X-rays had become much more compelling in the wake of Connally's testimony, which had been such a direct challenge to the single-bullet theory. If Connally continued to insist that he had been hit by a separate bullet, it might come down to the autopsy photos and X-rays to prove that the otherwise credible Texas governor was wrong.

At the commission meeting, Rankin did not mention Specter's name— that would have antagonized Warren, Specter assumed—and instead framed the request for the autopsy photos and X-rays as an appeal from the entire staff: "The staff feels that we should have some member of the commission examine these pictures." He acknowledged what the commissioners apparently already knew—that the photos and X-rays were in the custody of Robert Kennedy and that the attorney general did not want to release them to anyone. Rankin said he had initially shared Kennedy's concern. "I thought we could avoid having those pictures . . . being a part of our record, because the family has a strong feeling about them," Rankin said. "They don't want the president to be remembered in connection with these pictures. That is their basic thought."

But Rankin said he had changed his mind, especially given the confusion about the ballistics evidence. "A doctor and some member of the commission should examine them sufficiently so that they could report to the commission that there is nothing inconsistent with the other findings," he said, adding that the attorney general might now be agreeable to a compromise. "I think that he would recognize the need and permit that limited examination."

Warren, however, remained unconvinced. He agreed to allow Rankin to approach Kennedy to ask about a limited review, but the chief justice wanted it understood that "we don't want those in our record. . . . It would make it a morbid thing for all time to come." And those were Warren's last words to the commission on the subject of the autopsy photos and X-rays, at least according to the long-classified transcripts of the commission's executive sessions. Within weeks, Warren had declared, once and for all, that the photos and X-rays were off-limits to the commission's staff and that they would remain in the attorney general's custody indefinitely. "They were just too horrifying," he explained later. "I take full responsibility for it."

The April 30 meeting represented a surrender on a different question, one that had dogged the commissioners from the start: Could they state with absolute certainty that Oswald had never worked as some sort of agent or informer for the FBI or the CIA? Both agencies had insisted, repeatedly, that they had no relationship, formal or informal, with the president's assassin. But why, then, had the FBI apparently tried to cover up evidence of its contacts with Oswald in Dallas before the assassination? And why had the CIA held back, and then misstated, some of the evidence about its surveillance of him in Mexico?

The solution, Warren decided, was for the commission to say what it knew—that the investigation had found no evidence that Oswald had worked for either the FBI or the CIA—and then to place the men who ran the two agencies under oath to attest to it. J. Edgar Hoover and John McCone should be made to testify, under threat of a perjury charge, that Oswald had never been in their employ. Warren also wanted both men to state, under oath, that there had been no conspiracy to kill Kennedy: "I would like to take their testimony because of these statements— statements from the right and the left—that there *has* been a conspiracy," the chief justice said. Hoover and McCone needed to say under oath that they knew of no evidence "that there has been a conspiracy with anybody—government, individual or otherwise."

At the meeting, Warren said that the commission should also now consider taking testimony from Robert Kennedy, not so much as the head of the Justice Department, but as the brother of the slain president.

He argued that Kennedy's testimony would go a long way toward convincing the public about the truth of the commission's findings; it would be hard to imagine that he would hide information about a conspiracy to assassinate his own brother. "If he was to testify he had no information," Warren said, "I would think that with any reasonable person, it would have tremendous force." Rankin agreed: "It is hardly believable that the brother of the president would stand by if there was some conspiracy in the United States to dispose of his brother."

The commissioners continued to be deviled by the conspiracy theorists—and continued to monitor them secretly with the FBI's help. Beyond the surveillance of Mark Lane, they requested the FBI's background files on Thomas Buchanan, the Yale-educated American writer for the French magazine *L'Express*, who was continuing to press his theory that ultraconservative businessmen in Texas were behind the assassination. The bureau's files on Buchanan detailed how he had exiled himself to Europe after he was fired as a reporter by the *Washington Star* in 1948, when editors discovered his membership in the American Communist Party.

At their meeting in April, the commissioners passed around copies of an article published a week earlier by United Press International that focused on Buchanan. It began: "Millions of Europeans refuse to believe that the assassination of John F. Kennedy was not part of a larger conspiracy that has still not been exposed." Buchanan had become a media phenomenon in Europe, and he was about to find a new audience in the United States. His book, *Who Killed Kennedy?*, was scheduled to be published in English in May. He was being treated as credible by reputable news organizations across Europe, including, in Britain, the BBC and the *Manchester Guardian*. The UPI article noted that Lane was traveling across Europe that spring, giving well-attended speeches to argue for Oswald's innocence.

Warren told his fellow commissioners that he was so worried about the conspiracy theorists—Buchanan and Lane, in particular—that he wanted to open the commission's files to a handful of reporters in advance of releasing the final report. He proposed that the commission quietly invite UPI and its news-agency rival, the Associated Press, to begin to review the investigation's paperwork and speak with its staff. The agencies would then be asked to suggest avenues of inquiry that the commission might have missed—"anything that may be in their minds as to what should be investigated," Warren said. It would be a way of proving that the commission had nothing to hide. McCloy thought it was "an important suggestion," especially given how conspiracy theories had taken hold in Europe. "What with Mr. Lane's visits over there, there is a deep-seated feeling that there is a deep conspiracy here."

Thomas Kelley, the Secret Service inspector who served as his agency's liaison to the commission, traveled to Dallas with Specter in May for some final on-the-ground investigation. During the trip, Kelley pulled Specter aside and said he wanted to ease what he knew were Specter's concerns over not having seen the president's autopsy photos and X-rays. Kelley said he had a photo of Kennedy's corpse and that he would share it with Specter when they got back to their hotel. "When Kelley and I were alone in a hotel room," Specter recalled, "he showed me a small picture of the back of a man's body, with a bullet hole in the base of the neck, just where the autopsy surgeons said Kennedy had been shot."

He said he assumed that Kelley had been dispatched by Warren or someone else on the commission to show him the picture—possibly to calm him down before his protests about the medical evidence became public. "They knew they were having trouble with me," Specter remembered. "This was an era before whistleblowers," but still the commission wanted to placate him because of what it feared he might do. The photo resolved nothing in Specter's mind. He had no way of knowing that this was even the president's body. "It was a bunch of horseshit," he said later. "I know what evidence is."*

Back in Washington, Alfred Goldberg was shown what he believed were other unauthenticated Secret Service photos of Kennedy's body on the autopsy table. As he looked through them, he said, he understood more clearly than before why Warren had been determined to block the staff from seeing them. "I just remember seeing those photos and being appalled by them."

---

* Specter would finally be shown the autopsy photos in the National Archives in April 1996, when he was a United States senator from Pennsylvania. He described what he saw: "The photos are grue-some. John F. Kennedy is lying on an autopsy table, his handsome face discolored and distorted by the gaping bullet wound in his head. As I looked at the slain president, I was struck again by the same waves of nausea that had hit me when I first read the medical reports 35 years earlier. I was also struck by the president's clearly robust physical condition, which somehow made the photographs even more ghastly. Kennedy, at 47, had well-defined, muscular shoulders and arms, a flat stomach and a full head of hair." (Specter, *Passion for Truth*, p. 89.)

36

Norman Redlich was frightened, several of his colleagues could see. In April, Gerald Ford stepped up his behind-the-scenes attacks, hoping to convince the other commissioners that Redlich needed to be forced off the staff before his presence did lasting damage. Ford had new ammunition for his fight: the full FBI background report on Redlich had been completed in March, and it documented his years of involvement in civil liberties and civil rights groups that the FBI labeled as subversive.

Other, very public attacks were being made on Redlich by some of Ford's Republican colleagues in Congress, as well as by a group of powerful right-wing newspaper columnists and radio commentators. In a speech on the House floor, Representative Ed Gurney, a Florida Republican, called Redlich's appointment to the commission "an incredible violation of U.S. security," since he had been given access to top secret government documents. The fervid anti-Communist radio broadcaster and newspaper columnist Fulton Lewis Jr., once a close ally of Senator Joseph McCarthy, had taken up the campaign. Redlich was denounced in several newspaper editorials. "It is absolutely inconceivable that Chief Justice Earl Warren would hire, or permit to be hired, a key staff official with the left-wing and civil disobedience background of Norman

Redlich," the *St. Louis Globe-Democrat* thundered. "Having a man on the commission who advocates defiance of United States anti-Communist policy is beyond belief." In May, the *New York Times* ran a brief news story about the controversy under the headline, "Warren Panel Aide Held a Defender of Reds."

The commission received so many letters denouncing Redlich that Mel Eisenberg, his deputy, was asked to write a form letter that could be sent out in response, defending his colleague. "The commission knows of no evidence which would cause us to doubt Professor Redlich's integrity, loyalty and complete dedication to the work of this commission and the interests of the United States," the letter said. A script was prepared so that the commission's secretaries could read it out over the phone in answer to the many people who called in to attack Redlich.

The FBI's background investigation of Redlich focused on his membership on the executive board of the Emergency Civil Liberties Committee. The FBI files also documented his opposition to the death penalty—seen by the bureau as evidence of potentially subversive views—and his work in organizing legal appeals for death row inmates held in New York State prisons. His work with a group of other law professors and students was credited with saving five men from the electric chair between 1960 and 1963. *Life* magazine quoted Redlich as saying that his ultimate goal was to see the death penalty abolished in New York State. Until then, "when I've saved a man from the chair, at least I've abolished capital punishment for him."

The character witnesses interviewed by the FBI, including several of Redlich's colleagues at New York University, as well as his neighbors in a university-owned apartment building in Greenwich Village, were glowing. They portrayed a man who could be prickly and had a sizable ego but who had an inspiring commitment to justice. Even the few people interviewed who disliked Redlich offered the sort of criticism that his admirers would have seen instead as evidence of his strength of character. The manager of his apartment building complained to an FBI agent about his campaign to desegregate public areas by allowing maids to use passenger elevators at the front of the building.

Outraged by the attacks on Redlich, many of the commission's young lawyers protested to Rankin about what they saw as Ford's "McCarthyism" and "red-baiting"—the terms they recalled having used to describe Ford's actions. In 1964, McCarthyism was not a distant memory, and some of Redlich's colleagues thought his career, even his physical safety, might be in jeopardy if he were dismissed, especially in such a public fashion. Redlich might find it impossible ever to get another job in government that required a security clearance.

Eisenberg, as close to Redlich as anyone on the staff, said he never saw fear on Redlich's face—"he had a poker face." Others, however, remembered the situation differently. "Redlich was scared," David Slawson remembered. "And I was scared for him."

Redlich's wife, Evelyn, a Manhattan pediatrician, said that the attacks made for a "difficult period" for the family. The attacks were often tinged with anti-Semitism. She remembered how offended she was when, while visiting the family's country home in Vermont, she overheard someone refer to her husband as "Earl Warren's little Jew boy." There was a moment of panic that summer when she heard a shot ring out near the Vermont home. For a moment, she feared, it had been fired by someone targeting her husband as a result of the attacks in Washington. "I was pretty upset, and the police came out," she remembered. The police determined the shot had been fired by a local boy out hunting.

Rankin seemed undecided about how aggressively to defend Redlich. He had been responsible for hiring Redlich and giving him such a prominent role on the commission's staff, and so Rankin accepted responsibility for the controversy. It bothered him, he said later, that Redlich had never warned him about his ties to the Emergency Civil Liberties Committee and other controversial groups. He thought Redlich should have told him.

After reading through the FBI report, Ford did not want to compromise. He wanted the thirty-eight-year-old law professor off the commission's staff entirely. If Redlich refused to resign, Ford wanted him fired. He insisted that the commission hold a special meeting to discuss the issue, which Warren and Rankin scheduled for Tuesday, May 19. The situation was considered so grave that all seven commissioners showed up for the session.

Warren opened the meeting, then immediately turned it over to Rankin. The commission had gathered, Rankin said, to consider the results of the new, intensive FBI background checks on both Redlich and Joseph Ball. The reinvestigation of Ball had been prompted by complaints from right-wing activists in California who were still angry over his public criticism years earlier of the House Un-American Affairs Committee for its campaign to hunt down Communists among lawyers on the West Coast. Rankin reported that there was nothing in the FBI report to suggest Ball had any subversive ties, and the commissioners agreed that he should stay. "We need him very badly," Rankin said.

The real debate, the commissioners knew, was about Redlich. Rankin opened the discussion by admitting that he felt some guilt over the controversy since "I am the one who hired Norman." He reminded the commissioners of Redlich's stellar legal credentials, first as a student at Yale Law School, where he finished first in his class in 1950, and now as a professor of constitutional tax law at NYU. "All I knew of him is good." But Rankin's choice of the verb in the past tense—"knew"—might have been deliberate. Rankin said that while "personally I feel there is no question of Mr. Redlich's loyalty as an American citizen or his dedication to the commission," his involvement in controversial groups had come as an unwelcome surprise. "I did know that he was very much interested in civil liberties and civil rights," Rankin said. "I didn't know he was a member of the Emergency Civil Liberties Committee."

He warned the commissioners how difficult it would be to replace Redlich and how his departure would be a logistical disaster for the commission because Redlich was meant to be the principal writer and editor of the final report. "He has worked long hours, longer than anyone," Rankin said. "I think he is more familiar with our work than anybody else." Redlich had continued to read every investigative report that arrived in the commission's offices—tens if not hundreds of thousands of pieces of paper—and his firing would mean the loss of all that knowledge. Rankin also urged the commissioners to consider how Redlich's departure would damage morale. His colleagues were "very much disturbed about the attack on him. . . . They have worked intimately with him and are fully satisfied of his compete loyalty."

It was then Ford's turn, and he began by praising the man he wanted fired: "I would like to state for the record that I have been tremendously impressed with Professor Redlich's ability. I think he is a brilliant man. And in the work I have seen in the commission, I think he has contributed significantly to what we have done. He has been very diligent."

Ford insisted that he wanted to be fair to Redlich and not overstate the case against him: "As I read the report of the FBI, there is not a scintilla of evidence that he is a member of the Communist Party or has been a member of the Communist Party." But Redlich, he said, was still tied to many controversial, potentially subversive left-wing groups. "I think it is regrettable that somebody as intelligent as he, and as nice a person as he, appears to get involved in some of these causes." He reminded the others that he had attempted months earlier to head off just the sort of awkward situation the commission now faced—how he warned against hiring any staff member associated with "the radical right or the radical left." And yet Redlich was hired anyway. "I think the facts are clear that we shouldn't continue his employment," Ford said, calling for a formal vote to dismiss him. "I would move that under the current circumstances, that the employment of Norman Redlich be terminated as of June 1."

As the conversation moved around the table, Ford had reason to believe that he would win the vote. The three other lawmakers on the panel—Russell, Cooper, and Boggs—and Allen Dulles spoke up to suggest they agreed with Ford. Russell said the FBI files depicted Redlich as a "born crusader—and I think he is going to be controversial as long as he lives." He continued: "I am not saying anything against his character or patriotism . . . but he has been tied up with a lot of fellow-traveling groups. For my part, I don't want to take the responsibility of employing him." Boggs said he was hearing criticism of Redlich from Democrats and Republicans alike. "This has been a matter of concern to those of us who serve in the Congress," he said. "And it is not something that can be brushed aside. It has to be answered."

It was left to Warren, then, to rescue Redlich. Warren had a well-earned reputation—first in California politics, then on the Supreme Court—for forcing onetime opponents to his side, and he was about to demonstrate to the commissioners how he went about it. Years later, Rankin would still be marveling at his performance at the meeting.

Warren's disdain for Ford was well known to the other commissioners and to much of the staff. And so the chief justice began his defense of Redlich by feeding Ford's own words back to him. "I have observed Professor Redlich here, and I have the same opinion of him that Congressman Ford has expressed," Warren said. "I think he is an able man. And I have come to believe that he is a man dedicated to the work of this commission, also. I know the staff, every member of it, feels the same way about him, and they feel that a great injustice has been done by reason of this attack that has been made upon him in the Congress by a very few members." Warren did not need to remind the other commissioners that Ford was among those "very few."

If the commission gave in to pressure to fire Redlich, "it would be branding him as a disloyal individual—and that is a hurt that can never be remedied as long as a man lives," Warren continued. "It affects his wife, it affects his children. . . . I am told that one of the commentators, in reporting on what went on over in Congress, even gave his home address in New York, and I am just sure for the sole purpose of harassing his wife and his children. And I am told that they have been harassed by this thing, and they will be harassed, just as long as the injustice remains."

Warren then boxed in Ford. The chief justice declared that if Ford and the others really wanted to force out Redlich, the commission would hold a tribunal in which Redlich could defend himself. "The least we could do would be to give him a trial, where he can defend himself, and where he can show that he is a good American citizen and is not disloyal," Warren said. "That is the American way of doing things."

At first, only one commissioner stood with Warren—John McCloy. Characteristically, McCloy's argument was less passionate than practical. Redlich, he said, was "a man who is definitely somewhat addicted to causes," but he was no security risk. "I think if I had known about this at the beginning, I would have raised my eyebrows," McCloy admitted. "But there is no use crying over spilled milk." If the commission fired Redlich, it would be perceived as giving in to pressure from right-wing critics, which would then open the investigation to attacks from the left. "I don't see how it is going to help us one single bit to remove him," McCloy said. "This is a good man, he has an honest approach, even though he leans in this direction."

Then Rankin spoke up with a pair of additional warnings for the commissioners—both of them seemingly ominous. With Redlich gone, he said, the commissioners would face the prospect of having to write the report themselves, or finding someone as hardworking to do it as the man they had just fired. "I did not conceive that you wanted the task of trying to make the draft yourself," Rankin told the commissioners, as if that would be the only option left to them. The commissioners, he said, also needed to be reminded that if they dismissed Redlich as a security risk, they would effectively be admitting that they had allowed a possible subversive to spend months rifling through some of the government's most classified national-security files. Those allegations would be "the worst thing that could happen to this commission."

Russell was the first to back down. "We are in a predicament either way," he said.

And then a humbled Ford—not eager to take the job of chief prosecutor at the "trial" that Warren was now proposing for Redlich—withdrew his motion entirely. "I would not have employed anybody that was affiliated with any organization or any cause of one extreme or the other," he said. "But I don't want to belabor the question. I think I have rather extensively, on the record, expressed my view."

Warren hurriedly ended the meeting. Redlich's job was safe, and he would be at work within days drafting the commission's final report.

Word of the commission's decision was met with delight—and relief—among Redlich's colleagues. It quieted some of the criticism that was becoming common on the staff about the chief justice. Warren had redeemed himself; certainly it renewed some of the young lawyers' faith in the chief justice as a champion of fair play and decency.

Redlich's gratitude was evident in the way he now dealt with his job. Before then, he had usually been among the lawyers who pushed back against the commission's demands that they speed up their work and begin writing the final report. After his job was saved, however, some of Redlich's colleagues found him suddenly eager to do whatever the chief justice wanted—to meet Warren's demands for the commission to issue a conclusive final report within weeks. "Redlich's tone changed," Burt Griffin said. "It made a big difference. My sense was that once his job was safe, Redlich stopped resisting the pressure to get the job done more quickly than the rest of us" believed was possible. "Warren had saved his skin, and he knew it."

37

The phone rang at about ten thirty p.m. in the Dallas home of FBI Special Agent James Hosty. It was Thursday, April 23, and the late-night caller was Hugh Aynesworth of the *Dallas Morning News*. The reporter had unwelcome news.

"We're running a story tomorrow," Aynesworth said, "and I wanted to see if you wanted to make a comment."

The article would allege that Hosty had known, long before the assassination, that Oswald was potentially dangerous and capable of murdering Kennedy, and that Hosty and the FBI had shared none of that information with the Dallas police department or the Secret Service. The source of the story was Dallas police lieutenant Jack Revill, who claimed that Hosty had walked up to him on the afternoon of the assassination to report that Oswald had been under FBI surveillance for weeks and that the bureau was well aware of the threat he posed. Revill's account had been recorded in an internal memo that the police had shared with the Warren Commission.

Hosty would later insist that Revill's allegations were a lie and that he, Hosty, had said no such thing. But he could not tell that to Aynesworth. Under FBI policy Hosty needed permission to speak to a reporter. "No comment" was all he told Aynesworth before hanging up. He tried to go back to bed, hoping that the story was not as "god-awful" as it sounded.

A few hours later, the phone rang again, waking Hosty from a fitful sleep, and this time the caller was his boss in the Dallas field office, Special Agent in Charge Gordon Shanklin. "Listen, Aynesworth called me earlier to say they are running a story about you telling Revill you knew Oswald was capable of killing the president."

Shanklin ordered Hosty to come to the office that minute to prepare a message that could be sent overnight to headquarters in Washington to try to preempt some of the damage the article might do. Hosty rushed to get dressed. "Walking out to my car I looked at all my neighbors' homes, wondering what they would be thinking later this morning as they sat in their kitchens, drinking their coffee in their robes, reading the *Morning News*."

He arrived in the office at about three fifteen a.m. and noticed a copy of the first edition of the paper on Shanklin's desk. The bold-faced, front-page headline: FBI KNEW OSWALD CAPABLE OF ACT, REPORTS INDICATE.

"Oh, God," Hosty groaned. He hurriedly read through the article, convinced it had been planted by the Dallas police in an attempt to shift the blame to him—again—for the law-enforcement bungling that allowed Kennedy, and then Oswald, to be murdered. The information in the story was attributed to "a source close to the Warren Commission." According to Aynesworth, Hosty had told Revill that the FBI knew Oswald was capable of assassination "but we didn't dream he would do it." The police claimed that Revill's memo was filed within hours of his conversation with Hosty.

Hosty put down the newspaper and turned to Shanklin. "This article has got it all wrong. I don't understand how they can print crap like that." It was true, he said, that he had talked to Revill on the day of the assassination and suggested that Oswald was "the guilty party." But he insisted that he had said nothing about Oswald having a violent streak or being capable of killing the president. Before the assassination, Hosty said, he had no sense that Oswald posed a danger to Kennedy—or to anyone else. That was what he planned to tell the Warren Commission when he testified in Washington in early May, an appointment he already dreaded. Shanklin ordered Hosty to draw up a summary of his version of events, which they would immediately send by Teletype to Washington. They hoped it would land on Hoover's desk first thing in the morning, before he had a chance to see the *Morning News* article. Shanklin and Hosty could be sure that Hoover would be incensed about the story—furious with the Dallas police and furious with them.

The Teletype did the Dallas agents some good. To the relief of Shanklin and Hosty, Hoover came out fighting the next morning, seemingly on their behalf. With Hosty's denial in hand, the FBI director issued a statement in Washington that categorically denied the allegations being made by the Dallas police. Revill's assertions, he declared, were "absolutely false."

Hosty was grateful that "I had kept my job for another day," even if he was more convinced than ever that his future with the FBI was in doubt. Aynesworth's article was picked up and reprinted across the country.

Hosty spent much of the following week preparing for his testimony before the commission in Washington. He began what he remembered as the "tedious but thorough review of everything" that was in the bureau's Oswald files in Dallas. It was not long, he said, before he realized that two important documents were missing. Both had come from Washington that fall and involved Oswald's trip to Mexico. One was an October 18 report from FBI headquarters that outlined what the bureau knew about the CIA's surveillance of Oswald in Mexico. The other was a November 19 memo prepared by the FBI's Washington field office about the contents of a letter that Oswald had written to the Soviet embassy in Washington, referring to his Mexico trip and his contacts there with a Soviet diplomat; the diplomat had been identified as an undercover KGB agent. Hosty tried to imagine why someone had removed the two documents. Was someone trying to hide them, "hoping that I hadn't already seen them?"

He had no answer to that mystery when he flew to Washington on May 4, the day before his testimony. He had wanted to get there a day early, to try to get a good night's sleep before what could be one of the most difficult days of his life. The next morning, he pulled on a dark suit, a well-starched white shirt, and a neutral tie—"the uniform of an FBI agent"—and walked into the commission's offices at the VFW building on Capitol Hill with two other FBI agents who had also been called to testify. They were accompanied by FBI assistant director Alan Belmont, the bureau's number-three official, who oversaw all criminal investigations in the FBI. "I couldn't help that I was starting to sweat," Hosty recalled.

He was greeted by commission lawyer Samuel Stern, who said he needed to ask a few preliminary questions before Hosty went into the witness room to testify. Stern wanted to clear up confusion about exactly what Hosty had known about Oswald before the assassination. How much had he known about Oswald's Mexico trip? Hosty said he remembered reading two reports about the CIA's surveillance of Oswald in Mexico—the documents that had since disappeared from the files in Dallas.

Belmont looked stricken at the mention of the reports, Hosty said. "He leaned over and muttered in my ear, 'Damn it, I thought I told them not to let you see them.'"

Hosty was startled at the comment. "Here was the head of all FBI investigations admitting that FBI headquarters was deliberately trying to conceal matters from me." What had happened to Oswald in Mexico that the FBI did not want Hosty to know? "I understand the need-to-know policy, but what was going on?"

That afternoon, Hosty was escorted into the commission's hearing room, which resembled the sort of conference room "you would find in any prestigious law firm, nicely furnished, and against two walls were stacks of what looked like law books." Off to one corner, he could see the damaged windshield from President Kennedy's limousine, which the commission had been inspecting as evidence. "I shivered when I looked at it," he recalled.

Chief Justice Warren and several other members of the commission sat at a large wooden conference table, "all staring at me expectantly." He was invited to take a seat at the head of the table, with Stern to his left and, next to Stern, the chief justice. On Hosty's right was Congressman Ford. When the court reporter nodded to Warren that he was ready, the chief justice swore in Hosty and asked Stern to lead the questioning.

Hosty had anticipated most of the early questions—about the history of the FBI's investigation of Oswald, including the transfer of the investigation in 1963 from the FBI field office in Dallas to the field office in New Orleans and back again to Dallas, as Oswald moved between the two cities. Hosty became alarmed when the commissioners interrupted Stern with questions that seemed designed to show that the FBI had a responsibility before Kennedy's visit to Dallas—specifically, that Hosty had a responsibility—to warn the Secret Service about Oswald's presence there.

"Did it occur to you that he was a potentially dangerous person?" Senator Cooper asked.

"No sir," Hosty replied. "Prior to the assassination of the president of the United States, I had no information indicating violence on the part of Lee Harvey Oswald."

He had expected tough questions about Aynesworth's article, but he was relieved that the commission seemed just as skeptical about the story as he was. That was confirmed, Hosty said, when Warren asked to take the conversation off the record, so that the court reporter would not take down what was being said. The commissioners, Hosty said, told him they were "disgusted" with the Dallas police; they suggested that they, too, believed Revill's memo was a phony, written months after the assassination to create a paper trail that would allow the police to make a scapegoat of the FBI.

Hosty was relieved, too, at the questions that were not being asked. He faced no questions about the handwritten note that Oswald had delivered to the FBI field office in early November—the note that Hosty had torn up and flushed down a toilet. Maybe, he hoped, that meant the commission had never learned about the note's existence and its destruction. Stern did ask if Hosty had retained any of his own notes from the day of the assassination. Hosty replied that he, like most agents, routinely threw away handwritten notes after using them to prepare typewritten reports. He had kept no notes of his own about Oswald, he said.*

The questioning ended at five ten p.m. Hosty left the commission's offices thinking his testimony had gone well, or at least as well as he could have hoped. It was a warm spring day, and he took a walk down Capitol Hill and along the National Mall to FBI headquarters at Ninth and Pennsylvania. "Feeling better and glad this was over, my step became a little lighter, and I enjoyed the green grass and beautiful blooming trees on the Mall."

It was something less than an open-door policy, but all FBI agents knew they could request a private meeting with Hoover when they visited Washington. The FBI director sometimes granted the request, sometimes not. Hoover said he found the meetings a useful way of bolstering

---

* In fact, Hosty had kept his handwritten notes, a fact that he later insisted he had not remembered at the time of his testimony to the commission. "Several months after the Warren report was released, I discovered the notes among my papers in my desk. Realizing their significance, I chose to hang on to them, and I kept them safely stored away." (Hosty, *Assignment: Oswald*, p. 146.)

agent morale and gathering information that might not otherwise reach him.

Hosty had requested a meeting with Hoover while he was in the capital, and he took it as a good sign that Hoover agreed.

At about two p.m. on Wednesday, May 6, he found himself standing in Hoover's office, facing "the Old Man" himself. "Hoover had his head buried in foot-high stacks of paperwork," Hosty said. "Next to this desk was a single chair, which he waved for me to take when he looked up and saw me. I sunk into the low chair, descending significantly lower than Hoover. I am sure this was the desired effect."

Hoover put down his pen and swiveled in his chair toward him. As Hosty recalled it, "I just burst out with the only thing I wanted to say: 'Mr. Hoover, I just wanted to thank you in person for really standing by and publicly defending me on the Revill memo a couple of weeks ago.'"

"Oh, that was nothing," Hoover said, smiling.

Hosty had no chance to say much more, he remembered. Hoover took over the conversation, launching into a monologue that lasted several minutes in which he described his lunch that day at the White House with President Johnson, who had just decided to waive the mandatory retirement age for Hoover. "The president told me that the country just couldn't get along with me," Hoover said, obviously delighted. He went on to talk about his close friendship with Johnson and his loathing for Robert Kennedy. The attorney general, he said, "disgusted him."

He then referred to Chief Justice Warren and the commission. "He told me that the FBI had a source on the commission," Hosty recalled. "Hoover's information, which he considered reliable, was that the commission would clear the FBI of any mishandling of the Oswald case by a 5-to-2 margin." According to Hoover, only Warren and McCloy would vote against the FBI. "Hoover told me how Warren detested him," Hosty said.

Whatever his apparent self-confidence in front of a rank-and-file agent like Hosty, Hoover was actually in something like a panic that spring. He was convinced the Warren Commission and its staff were feeding stories to reporters in Washington, Dallas, and elsewhere that were designed to undermine his legacy—even to threaten the bureau's very survival. At the commission's insistence, Hoover had been reduced to answering to the reports of scandal-mongering tabloids. On May 5, Rankin wrote to

Hoover to demand the FBI's detailed response to a front-page story in the *National Enquirer*—the sensationalist weekly tabloid that billed itself as "The World's Liveliest Newspaper" and was best known for stories focused on sex and violence—that alleged the FBI had covered up evidence that Oswald and Ruby had known each other. The article claimed that the Justice Department had pressured the Dallas police to hold off arresting both Oswald and Ruby earlier in 1963 for their involvement in a supposed plot to kill General Walker. As a result of the article, FBI agents were ordered to interview the police chief in Dallas, Jesse Curry, who insisted that the *Enquirer* story was a fabrication and that the Dallas police had never heard of Oswald until the day of his arrest. On May 8, Hoover wrote back to Rankin to say there was no truth to the tabloid's article.

On Thursday, May 14, Hoover was himself called to testify before the commission. It appeared to be another sign of the ill will between Hoover and Warren that the chief justice offered no words of welcome or support to Hoover, usually treated with such deference before every other audience in Washington. After swearing Hoover in at nine fifteen, Warren got straight to business, outlining what the commission wanted from the FBI director: Hoover's unqualified statement, under oath, that the FBI was not hiding evidence about Oswald.

"Mr. Hoover will be asked to testify in regard to whether Lee H. Oswald was ever an agent, directly or indirectly, or an informer or acting on behalf of the Federal Bureau of Investigation in any capacity at any time, and whether he knows of any credible evidence of any conspiracy, either domestic or foreign, involved in the assassination of President Kennedy," Warren said. Hoover would not be above questions about even the most outrageous allegations in a gossip magazine. The commission, Warren said, wanted to know what Hoover "has to say about the article in the *National Enquirer*."

Rankin led the questioning, and Hoover provided, as promised, a flat denial that the FBI had ever had any sort of relationship with Oswald. "I can most emphatically say that at no time was he ever an employee of the bureau in any capacity, either as an agent or as a special employee, or as an informant." As for the possibility of a conspiracy: "I have been unable to find any scintilla of evidence showing any foreign conspiracy or any domestic conspiracy that culminated in the assassination of President Kennedy." Hoover testified that he believed that Oswald killed President

Kennedy and that he did it alone. It was true that the FBI had Oswald under surveillance at the time of the assassination, Hoover said, but the bureau had no indication that he was violent. "There was nothing up to the time of the assassination that gave any indication that this man was a dangerous character who might do harm to the president." The *National Enquirer* article, he said, was an "absolute lie."

That same day, immediately after Hoover's testimony, Director of Central Intelligence John McCone and his deputy, Richard Helms, walked into the witness room to give their testimony. Like Hoover, they insisted under oath that they had no evidence that Oswald had ever been any sort of government agent or that he had been part of any conspiracy to kill the president. They said that Oswald's trip to Mexico had been thoroughly investigated by the CIA and that the investigation had turned up nothing to indicate that Oswald had accomplices there or anywhere else.

In Dallas, Hugh Aynesworth had another big scoop in June. From sources he did not identify, he had obtained a copy of the "Historic Diary," Oswald's handwritten account of his aborted defection.

Marina Oswald said that much of the melodramatic "Diary," which was so full of misspellings and grammatical errors that it suggested to the commission's staff that Oswald was dyslexic, was actually written after they left the Soviet Union. It depicted Oswald's disenchantment and eventual despair with life in Russia; he described his suicide attempt in the Moscow hotel room, as well as his failed effort to court another Russian woman, Ella German, before settling for Marina. "I married Marina to hurt Ella," he wrote.

Two weeks after Aynesworth's scoop in the *Morning News*, the entire diary was published by *Life* magazine. David Slawson, who was responsible for analyzing the journal for the commission, said he was horrified by the leaks. He was convinced they would endanger the lives of several Russians named in the diary who had assisted Oswald in ways that the Soviet government might consider treasonous. Slawson worried, in particular, about a Russian woman, a government tour guide, who met Oswald shortly after his arrival in Moscow and who may have tried to warn him of the bleak future he faced in Russia. Official tour guides "are normally under the control of the KGB," Slawson knew. Her warning came in the form of a gift to Oswald—a copy of the Dostoyevsky novel *The Idiot*.

(Oswald referred to it in his diary as "IDEOT by Dostoevski.") The book, Slawson felt, was a "disguised warning that he was a fool and ought to turn back." The guide, he feared, may have committed "a serious offense, similar to an FBI agent here secretly warning a Russian defector to go back to Russia." Slawson also worried about the family of Alexander Ziger, who had befriended Oswald in Minsk; Ziger, too, had warned Oswald to return to the United States. "We have been informed that the Zigers for many years have been trying to escape from Russia" and that "they are probably more than usually susceptible to persecution" because they were Jews, Slawson wrote.

He had originally planned to cite only edited excerpts of the diary in the commission's final report, to prevent the names of Oswald's Russian contacts from being revealed. After the leaks, however, he felt the commission needed to "print the entire diary without any deletions whatsoever," if it printed any of it. If the commission published only excerpts, it would draw attention to the portions of the diary that had not been published; it would be easy enough for the KGB to cross-check the commission's report against what had appeared in the Dallas paper and *Life* to see what was missing.

The Dallas police and the FBI tried to determine who had leaked the diary. Marina Oswald was an obvious suspect, given her eagerness to sell other information, but she denied it. *Life* insisted that she was not its source, although the magazine reported that it had printed the diary "with her full permission" and had changed some names at her request "to prevent reprisals against Oswald's acquaintances."

Later that summer, a Dallas police detective, H. M. Hart, reported to his superiors that he identified a suspect in the leaks: Congressman Gerald Ford. In a July 8 memo, Hart wrote that a "confidential informant" had reported that Ford, who had access to the diary through the commission's files, sold a copy to the *Morning News* and that he had also offered it to both *Life* and *Newsweek*. Executives of the news organizations then paid $16,000 to Marina Oswald "for the world copyright of the diary," Hart wrote. Ford would insist that he had nothing to do with the leaks, and FBI investigators would later say that they determined that the source of the leaks was a supervisor in the Dallas police department. Still, Ford was so alarmed by the rumors that he requested that the FBI take a formal statement from him denying that he had sold information to news organizations from out of the commission's files. The statement was drawn up by FBI assistant director Cartha "Deke" DeLoach, Ford's long-standing contact at the bureau, during a meeting with Ford in his congressional office. Ford "desired to unequivocally state, and to furnish a signed statement if necessary, that he did not leak the information in question," DeLoach reported.

The truth, told years later, was that Ford had nothing to do with the leak. Hugh Aynesworth, the Dallas reporter, would eventually acknowledge that he had sold the diary to *Life* that summer, for $2,500. The sale was approved by his editor at the *Morning News*, with an understanding that the money would be paid to the reporter's wife, allowing Aynesworth to argue that—technically, at least—he had not taken money from *Life*, which might have been a violation of the newspaper's internal rules for its employees. Aynesworth said that *Life* had promised him that the *Morning News* would be credited in the magazine with the scoop, a promise that the magazine did not keep. Although he would never confirm or deny reports that he had obtained the diary from Marina Oswald, Aynesworth acknowledged that he arranged to have *Life* pay her a fee of $20,000 since "if anybody actually owned the diary, I believed it was probably Marina."*

---

* Given the effects of inflation, the $2,500 paid to Aynesworth in 1964 would be equivalent to $18,800 in 2013, while the $20,000 payment to Marina Oswald would be equivalent to $150,700.

38

Each week brought some new, exasperating decision by the chief justice, or so it seemed to Arlen Specter. Throughout the spring, Specter and others on the staff pushed to conduct on-site tests in Dallas, including a full reconstruction of the scene in Dealey Plaza. The staff lawyers proposed to capture the scene just as Oswald would have seen it out the sixth-floor window of the Texas School Book Depository. Oswald's rifle would be taken back to the building, and a camera would be attached to the top of it, allowing a photographer to capture the images as a limousine resembling Kennedy's was driven slowly past. Men of a similar size to Kennedy and Connally would be placed in the limousine, lined up as in the Zapruder film. It would be a valuable way of testing the theory that a single bullet fired from the sixth floor could have passed through the bodies of both victims.

To Specter's astonishment, though, Warren did not want any on-site tests at all; he did not feel they were necessary. "Warren was dead-set against it," Specter said. "He thought staff was making too big a deal of it." He recalled Warren saying, "We know what's happened. We've got the FBI report." Through Rankin, the staff pressed Warren to reconsider. And possibly sensing a rebellion led by Specter, the chief justice yielded.

The reconstruction, which was conducted with the help of the FBI, was set for the early morning of Sunday, May 24. Sunday was chosen in the hope of avoiding traffic disruptions downtown. Warren did not plan to be there himself; he would hold off going to Dallas until June, when he planned to take testimony from Jack Ruby.

The reconstruction went well, and Specter said he was even more confident about the single-bullet theory as a result. The FBI had done what the commission had requested. The camera attached to Oswald's rifle offered the images that Specter had hoped for, including a clear picture of how a single bullet fired from the sixth floor would have passed through Kennedy's neck before hitting Connally. Zapruder's camera, and two other home-movie cameras that had captured the scenes of the assassination in Dealey Plaza, were also brought to Dallas for the reconstruction, and the FBI was able to replicate the images from those cameras, as well.

Specter got other welcome news. New ballistics tests supported the single-bullet theory; they showed that the metal fragments in Connally's wrist were so tiny that they could have come from the same bullet that passed through the president's neck. The Parkland bullet would have weighed 160 or 161 grains before firing; it now weighed 158.6 grains. X-rays of Connally's wrist showed that the fragments left in his body probably weighed much less than the difference.

The trajectory of bullets fired from Oswald's rifle, and the damage they could do to flesh, were tested independently by both the FBI and the military. The army's Edgewood Arsenal in Maryland, a high-security Defense Department research center outside Washington, used Oswald's Mannlicher-Carcano rifle for a series of tests beginning in April. Army scientists were asked if they could confirm that the rifle could have produced the wounds suffered by Kennedy and Connally. The test results, described in an army report, made for grim reading. In trying to replicate the effect of bullets when they struck the two bodies, the scientists fired the rifle into a series of different targets, including gelatin-filled human skulls and the arms of human cadavers. Thirteen heavily anesthetized goats were also used as targets to re-create the wounds to Connally's chest; the goats were covered in layers of cloth resembling the suit jacket, shirt, and undershirt that the governor had been wearing. Animal lovers on the commission's staff cringed at the army photos of the tests, including one of the live goats strapped in place, waiting to be shot.

The army tests also largely supported the single-bullet theory. "The results indicated that the wounds sustained by the President and Governor Connally, including the massive head wound of the president, could be produced" by Oswald's rifle and the sort of bullets he used, the report stated. "The bullet that wounded the president in the neck had enough remaining velocity to account for all of the governor's wounds." In support of the single-bullet theory, the report raised an obvious question: Where did the bullet that hit Kennedy in the neck go—if not into Connally's back? There was no other sign of it in the limousine. If the bullet had struck something else in the vehicle, the report said, "the damage would have been very evident and much greater than the slight damage that was found on the windshield."

Like his colleagues and many of the doctors and scientists he interviewed, Specter said he had stopped being troubled by a disturbing phenomenon seen in the Zapruder film. the way the president's head snapped backward when he was hit by the second shot, as if the bullet had come from the front, not the rear. Doctors and ballistics experts explained to the commission's investigators that it was often difficult to guess how flesh reacted to a bullet strike; the wound could cause spasms of the nervous system that moved the body in unusual ways. The movements could seem to a layman to defy physics, they said. It was a grisly thought, Specter admitted, but he compared what he saw in the Zapruder film to what he had seen as a child back in Wichita, when his father killed a chicken for the family meal. After the bird's head was cut off, its body would continue to move uncontrollably, Specter recalled. "Just instinctively, I analogized it to the chicken," he said. "It's just spasms, just nerves."

David Belin could often seem like the commission's cheerleader, but for all of the Iowan's exuberance at the beginning of the investigation, he often found himself discouraged that spring. "As fascinating as the work was, there was almost an equal amount of frustration—frustration about secretarial help, frustration about not enough lawyers to do the investigation, frustration about the sham" of the commission's decision to treat Marina Oswald so delicately, even after it was clear that she had lied under oath. There was "frustration about the whole course of our work." He was angry with Rankin, who was supposed to be the go-between for the commissioners and the staff lawyers. "At no time was there a proper line of communication between the commission and its lawyers, nor for that matter was there a proper exchange of ideas between and among

Rankin and the lawyers," Belin said. He considered himself, along with Specter, a father of the single-bullet theory, yet the commissioners seemed to have no interest in discussing even that important subject.

Belin thought he had valuable suggestions for how the final report should be written. In a memo, he pressed for the central report to include long excerpts from the testimony of important witnesses, so readers could understand the full impact of what they had to say. That would require more than one volume, he believed. "I wanted to have a great amount of the testimony set out verbatim, which I felt would be the most effective way to show the truth." But he could not get an audience with Rankin and others even to discuss the proposal. "In this, as in almost everything else, I felt that I 'never had my day in court'—we were too busy with the trees to see the forest."

Like everyone else, Belin was exhausted. He calculated that he worked seventy hours a week—more even than Redlich, who never seemed to leave the office, even to sleep. And Belin was alarmed to realize that he would soon need to leave Washington, even with so much work left to be done on his part of the investigation. His partners at his law firm in Des Moines were insisting that he return. He planned to leave before Memorial Day and then commute to Washington for short stays when his firm allowed it.

One night Belin reflected on all of these frustrations in a conversation with Specter. The commission's report would not be good enough, Belin declared. "I expressed my disappointment that what could have been a monumental piece of investigation with an extremely talented group of lawyers and a potential A-plus job was instead turning into a mediocre Class B piece of work." The levelheaded Specter urged his friend to keep in mind that the investigation, whatever its failings, seemed to be establishing the facts about the assassination. "The most important thing is that we found the truth," he told Belin.

Belin smarted that so many of his other ideas were ignored. He had continued to argue that Marina Oswald, Jack Ruby, and other key witnesses should be questioned using a polygraph. He wrote several memos on the subject to Rankin. If Marina Oswald found herself strapped to a lie detector, he wrote, she might reveal secrets about her life with Oswald in Russia—a subject on which the commission otherwise had almost no way of testing her credibility. "If she would refuse our request, it might indicate she had something to hide." He felt almost as strongly about the need to polygraph Ruby, but that was rejected too, with "most of the staff lined up against me." The chief justice sided with the staff against Belin. Warren described polygraphs as "instruments of Big Brother."

Belin thought it was just one more bizarre coincidence in an investigation full of them—he was a friend of Jack Ruby's rabbi. He had met the handsome, dynamic young rabbi, Hillel Silverman, of Congregation Shearith Israel, a Conservative synagogue in Dallas, in the summer of 1963 during a religious study mission that both men had taken to Israel.

So on one of his first visits to Dallas, Belin went to see his friend Rabbi Silverman, who had continued to visit Ruby regularly in jail. Belin told Silverman he recognized that much of what was said between a rabbi and a congregant was privileged, "but I wondered if he had any question about the existence of a conspiracy." Did Silverman believe Ruby when he insisted he acted alone?

"Jack Ruby is absolutely innocent of any conspiracy," Silverman replied. "Without a doubt." Ruby had assured the rabbi that he had acted alone, and Silverman was certain he was telling the truth. Ruby told Silverman that if he had been acting on someone's orders, he would have gunned down Oswald when he first encountered him on Friday night, at the police news conference. "Had I intended to kill him, I could have pulled my trigger on the spot, because the gun was in my pocket," Ruby told Silverman. According to the rabbi, Ruby always offered the same explanation for why he killed Oswald: "to save Mrs. Kennedy the ordeal of having to come back for the trial."

Given Silverman's conviction that Ruby had acted alone, Belin had an important favor to ask, and he needed the rabbi to keep it a secret. "I told him that even though he was convinced that Ruby was not involved in an assassination conspiracy, the world would never be convinced unless Ruby took a polygraph examination," Belin recalled. "I also told him that the Warren Commission would never ask Ruby to submit to one, but that Ruby himself could request one." The polygraph might complicate Ruby's appeal of his death sentence, but it was hard to see how his predicament could be much worse.

Would Silverman try to convince Ruby to request a polygraph? Belin asked. Ruby was scheduled to be questioned by Warren sometime in June. He could make the request directly to the chief justice.

The rabbi agreed to try.

39

Robert Kennedy did not want to testify before the commission. It was a message relayed to the chief justice in early June by Howard Willens, in his seemingly awkward dual role as a senior member of the commission's staff and as the Justice Department's representative to the investigation.

Kennedy did not explain—at least not on paper—why he felt so strongly that he should not be required to testify. Warren decided not to press the issue; he seemed willing to accept that it would just be too painful for Kennedy to be questioned by anyone about his brother's murder. Not surprisingly, the chief justice did not bring the commission's young lawyers into the decision. Had they been asked, several said later, they would have pressed for the attorney general's testimony, especially about whether he suspected a conspiracy. Robert Kennedy knew who his brother's enemies were. He had been, almost without question, the president's closest adviser during the Cuban missile crisis in 1962 and in dealing with other threats from the Soviet Union, Cuba, and the nation's other foreign adversaries, as well as in battling domestic foes like the Mafia and corrupt union leaders. If there had been a conspiracy, he might at least have had a strong guess about who was behind it, and why. David Slawson knew how important Kennedy's testimony might be, especially with respect to Cuba. It was well known in foreign policy circles in Washington that after the Bay of Pigs, President Kennedy had put his brother in charge of the government's secret war against Castro. "He was the president's confidant on Cuba," Slawson said.

Instead of sworn testimony, Kennedy was willing to offer a brief written statement to the commission. After consulting with Kennedy and Deputy Attorney General Nicholas Kaztenbach, Willens sent a memo to Rankin that attached drafts of two letters. The first would be signed by Warren and sent to Kennedy, asking if the attorney general had any information that he wished to share with the commission. The second letter was for Kennedy's signature and was a response to the chief justice; the attorney general would confirm that he had no information to share. "The Attorney General would prefer to handle his obligations to the commission in this way rather than appear as a witness," Willens wrote.

In the memo, Willens said that Kennedy had made clear to him that he had not been closely following the commission's investigation, which helped explain why he had so little to add. "The Attorney General informed me that he has not received any reports from the Director of the Federal Bureau of Investigation regarding the investigation of the assassination, and that his principal sources of information have been the Chief Justice, the Deputy Attorney General and myself."

Warren's letter, which was dated June 11, read in full:

Dear General:

Throughout the course of the investigation conducted by this Commission, the Department of Justice has been most helpful in forwarding information to this Commission's inquiry.

The Commission is now in the process of completing the investigation. Prior to the publication of its report, the Commission would like to be advised whether you are aware of any additional information relating to the assassination of President John F. Kennedy which has not been sent to the Commission. In view of the widely circulated allegations on this subject, the Commission would like to be informed in particular whether you have any information suggesting that the assassination of President Kennedy was caused by a domestic or foreign conspiracy. Needless to say, if you have any suggestions to make regarding the investigation of these allegations or any other phase of the Commission's work, we stand ready to act upon them.

On behalf of the Commission, I wish to thank you and your representatives for the assistance you have provided to the Commission.

Given Warren's decision not to press him to testify, the commission expected a grateful Kennedy to sign his response letter quickly and send it back. Instead, to the surprise of Warren and the staff, it would take him months to reply.

Other than the attorney general, perhaps no one had more influence with President Kennedy than special assistant Kenneth O'Donnell, the wiry forty-year-old Massachusetts lawyer who was the heart of the circle of White House aides known as the "Irish Mafia." O'Donnell, who had been part of the planning for the Texas trip, had been in the motorcade in Dallas. He had been in a Secret Service car directly behind the president's limousine.

He told the commission he did not want to testify, either. He had his secretary at the White House inform Arlen Specter that another close Kennedy aide, Dave Powers, who had been seated next to O'Donnell in the motorcade, could be called instead, since Powers would offer identical testimony. Specter protested to Rankin, and O'Donnell was eventually convinced to testify, although he was not required to appear in the commission's offices. Instead, Specter and Norman Redlich went to the White House on Monday, May 18.

O'Donnell's account of the Dallas trip conformed to the testimony of others, although he had a remarkable story to tell about his final conversation with the president on the morning of the assassination. They had talked, he said, about how easy it would be for someone with a rifle to kill Kennedy. The setting for the conversation was the Hotel Texas in Fort Worth, as the president was preparing to leave for Dallas. "The conversation took place in his room, with Mrs. Kennedy and myself, perhaps a half hour before he left the hotel," O'Donnell said. "As I can recollect, he was commenting to his wife on the function of the Secret Service, and his interpretation of their role."

Kennedy, he recalled, said that "if anybody really wanted to shoot the president of the United States, it was not a very difficult job—all one had to do was get into a high building with a telescopic rifle, and there was nothing anybody could do."

Specter asked O'Donnell what Mrs. Kennedy had thought of her husband's bleak appraisal. "I think the general tenor of the conversation was that she agreed that this was—in this democracy—this is inherent."

In his testimony, O'Donnell let slip something that he quickly regretted telling the commission's lawyers, and it would give Specter a taste of how tightly the Kennedy family intended to control the narrative of the assassination. Specter asked O'Donnell to describe the trip back to Washington aboard Air Force One, and his conversations with Mrs. Kennedy in the plane. Characteristically, Specter focused on the smallest details.

"What did you talk about?" he asked.

"We reminisced," O'Donnell said.

"Did she have anything to eat on the trip back?"

"No, I think we both had a drink," O'Donnell said. "I tried to get her to take a good strong drink." She accepted the drink—a Scotch and water, it was later reported—but preferred to talk, he said.

After completing the interview, Specter returned to the commission's offices and was confronted by an agitated Rankin.

"Why did you ask O'Donnell about Mrs. Kennedy having a drink on the plane?"

"Lee, I didn't do that," Specter replied, explaining that O'Donnell had volunteered the information.

"Well, they've called us and they're madder than hell about it," Rankin said. "They're complaining."

Specter guessed that O'Donnell had panicked at the thought that the public might learn that the First Lady had sipped alcohol to settle her nerves on the day of her husband's murder, as if that had been a sign of weakness. "I think what happened to O'Donnell was that, after he blurted out that she had a drink, he got very goddamned nervous, and he wanted to shift the blame to me," Specter said later.

"It never happened," Specter told Rankin. "Check the transcript." The transcript proved that Specter was right.

By late spring, it appeared to the staff that Warren intended to finish the commission's investigation without taking testimony from Jacqueline Kennedy. He had never hidden his discomfort at the prospect of formally questioning her about the circumstances of her husband's death, and he had put off the subject for months, even after it was raised so insistently by Specter. Warren was as protective of the former First Lady "as he would have been of one of his own daughters," Specter said later. When he pressed Rankin about scheduling her testimony, he always got the same answer: "No decision had been reached."

Specter was told, but was never able to confirm conclusively, that Warren gave in and finally agreed to interview Mrs. Kennedy only at the insistence of fellow commissioner John McCloy. In conversations behind closed doors, McCloy was said to have become furious on the issue, telling Warren that the commission had no choice but to interview her. She had been in the motorcade; she was the closest eyewitness to her husband's murder. And besides, "she's talking about the assassination at all the cocktail parties in Washington," McCloy told Warren. Certainly it was known to both men that she was discussing the assassination with William Manchester for his book. Specter said he was told that during the argument, McCloy pointedly kept referring to Warren as "Mr. Chairman" instead of "Mr. Chief Justice," which McCloy would have known was a "cutting insult" to Warren, normally a stickler about being referred to by his title on the court.

If there was going to be an interview with Jacqueline Kennedy, however, Warren was going to conduct it himself, with none of the commission's young staff lawyers present. Specter, who had taken testimony from the other passengers in the Dallas motorcade, would be told nothing about the interview until after it occurred. Warren also decided that he would take Mrs. Kennedy's testimony at her home. He was not going to insist that she travel halfway across the capital to see him.

Shortly after four p.m. on Friday, June 5, Chief Justice Warren's official town car pulled up in front of 3017 N Street, the Colonial-era brick mansion that Mrs. Kennedy had purchased a few weeks after the assassination. Shaded by magnolia trees, the seventeen-room home was in the choicest part of Georgetown, just down the street from a much smaller town house where she and then senator Kennedy had enjoyed their first years of marriage.

This new home should have been Mrs. Kennedy's sanctuary, a place to make a new life for herself. But from the moment he drove up, Warren could see that the house had become a virtual prison for Mrs. Kennedy and her two children. There was a twenty-four-hour police guard to keep away the paparazzi—that word was still new to Washington, introduced to American audiences by a Fellini film in 1960—and fend off the parade of gawking tourists who wanted to catch a glimpse of the former First Lady. To the dismay of Mrs. Kennedy's new neighbors, street vendors had camped out at both ends of the street, selling popcorn and soda to the camera-clicking tourists. As he was ushered into Mrs. Kennedy's home, Warren, accompanied only by Rankin and a court reporter, was determined that this interview would be as quick and painless as possible for the young widow.

Robert Kennedy sat in on his sister-in-law's testimony, and he met Warren at the door. That she wanted her brother-in-law present would be no surprise to Mrs. Kennedy's family and friends. With the blessing of his wife, Ethel, the attorney general had been by Jacqueline Kennedy's side every day since the assassination, often spending long afternoons with her in Georgetown. "I'll share him with you," Ethel told her sister-in-law. They took seats around a table in Mrs. Kennedy's drawing room, the same room she had been using for her interviews with Manchester. Warren instantly tried to put her at ease. This would be no interrogation, he promised. "Mrs. Kennedy," he said, "the commission would just like to have you say in your own words, in your own way, what happened at the time of the assassination of the president. And we want it to be brief. We want it to be in your own words and want you to say anything that you feel is appropriate."

With that, he turned to Rankin, who would conduct the questioning.

"Please state your name for the record," Rankin began.

"Jacqueline Kennedy."

"And you are the widow of the former president Kennedy?"

"That is right."

Rankin: "Can you go back to the time that you came to Love Field on Nov. 22 and describe what happened there after you landed?"

Mrs. Kennedy: "We got off the plane. The then-vice president and Mrs. Johnson were there. They gave us flowers. And then the car was waiting. But there was a big crowd there, all yelling, with banners and everything. And we went to shake hands with them."

With his first few questions, Rankin led Mrs. Kennedy, gently, through the chronology of what happened in the hour before the assassination and what she remembered of the motorcade. He asked her where she had been seated in the car relative to her husband and to the Connallys.

Mrs. Kennedy recalled how hot it had been in Dallas that day, and how she welcomed the sight of a tunnel in the distance as the president's limousine made its turn onto Houston Street. The motorcade was headed toward the tunnel, which would lead them out of Dealey Plaza.

"I remember thinking it would be so cool under that tunnel."

Rankin: "And then do you remember as you turned off of Houston onto Elm right by the Depository Building?"

Mrs. Kennedy recalled how Mrs. Connally had pointed to the cheering crowds and turned back to the first couple to say, "You certainly can't say that the people of Dallas haven't given you a nice welcome."

Rankin: "What did the president say?"

Mrs. Kennedy: "I think he said, 'No, you certainly can't' or something. And then the car was very slow and there weren't very many people around. And then . . ."

There was a pause.

"Do you want me to tell you what happened?" she asked.

With her question, it was as if Mrs. Kennedy wanted to remind Warren and Rankin what they were now asking her to do—to offer up, on the public record, the details of what had happened inside the limousine when the shots rang out.

Rankin: "Yes, if you would, please."

And so she began: "I was looking this way, to the left, and I heard these terrible noises, you know? And my husband never made any sound. So I turned to the right. And all I remember is seeing my husband, he had sort of a quizzical look on his face and his hand was up. It must have been his left hand.

"And just as I turned and looked at him, I could see a piece of his skull and I remember it was flesh colored, with little ridges at the top. I remember thinking that he just looked as if he had a slight headache. And I just remember seeing that. No blood or anything. And then he sort of did this . . ."

She raised one hand to her head, explaining that her husband "put his hand to his forehead and fell in my lap. And then I just remember falling on him and saying, 'Oh, no, no, no,' I mean, 'Oh, my God, they have shot my husband.' And 'I love you, Jack,' I remember I was shouting. And just being down in the car with his head in my lap. And it just seemed an eternity. You know, then, there were pictures later on of me climbing out the back. But I don't remember that at all."

Rankin asked if she remembered Secret Service agent Clint Hill climbing onto the trunk and pushing her back into the passenger compartment.

Mrs. Kennedy: "I don't remember anything. I was just down like that. And finally I remember a voice behind me, or something, and then I remember the people in the front seat, or somebody, finally knew something was wrong, and a voice yelling, which must have been Mr. Hill, 'Get to the hospital,' or maybe it was Mr. Kellerman, in the front seat. But someone yelling. I was just down and holding him.

"I was trying to hold his hair on," she said, describing the large piece of his skull that had been blown off by the second bullet. "From the front, there was nothing—I suppose there must have been. But from the back you could see, you know, you were trying to hold his hair on, and his skull on."

Rankin: "Do you have any recollection of whether there were one or more shots?"

Mrs. Kennedy: "Well, there must have been two because the one that made me turn around was Governor Connally yelling. And it used to confuse me because first I remembered there were three and I used to think my husband didn't make any sound when he was shot. And Governor Connally screamed. And then I read the other day that it was the same shot that hit them both. But I used to think if I only had been looking to the right I would have seen the first shot hit him, then I could have pulled him down, and then the second shot would not have hit him. But I heard Governor Connally yelling and that made me turn around, and as I turned to the right my husband was doing this . . ."

She raised to a hand to her neck. "He was receiving a bullet," she said. "And those are the only two I remember. And I read there was a third shot. But I don't know. Just those two."

Rankin: "Do you have any recollection generally of the speed that you were going?"

Mrs. Kennedy: "We were really slowing turning the corner. And there were very few people."

Rankin asked if she thought the limousine had stopped at any time after the shots.

Mrs. Kennedy: "I don't know, because—I don't think we stopped. But there was such confusion. And I was down in the car and everyone was yelling to get to the hospital and you could hear them on the radio, and then suddenly I remember a sensation of enormous speed, which must have been when we took off."

Rankin: "And then from there you proceeded as rapidly as possible to the hospital, is that right?"

Mrs. Kennedy: "Yes."

Rankin: "Do you recall anyone saying anything else during the time of the shooting?"

Mrs. Kennedy: "No. There weren't any words. There was just Governor Connally's. And then I suppose Mrs. Connally was sort of crying and covering her husband. But I don't remember any words. And there was a big windshield between—you know—I think. Isn't there?"

Rankin: "Between the seats."

Mrs. Kennedy: "So you know, those poor men in the front, you couldn't hear them." She was referring to the two Secret Service agents in the front seat.

Rankin turned to the chief justice: "Can you think of anything more?"

"No, I think not," Warren said, drawing her testimony to a close nine minutes after it began. "I think that is the story and that is what we came for. We thank you very much, Mrs. Kennedy."

The transcript of Mrs. Kennedy's testimony was included in the published archives of the commission, although the commission chose to leave out, without an explicit explanation of why, three sentences in which Mrs. Kennedy described trying to hold the president's skull in place, beginning with the words, "I was trying to hold his hair on." In the official transcript, the commission replaced that passage with the phrase: "Reference to wounds deleted."

40

Earl Warren was not eager to go to Texas, even in the final weeks of the investigation, and his reluctance was understandable. If any large city in the United States was enemy territory to the chief justice, it was Dallas—the city where his friend the president had been murdered, and where he knew so many of the ultraconservative, segregationist leaders of the national Impeach Earl Warren movement lived and worked. The chief justice could be certain that on any trip to Dallas, he was likely to see several Impeach Earl Warren billboards. Warren claimed to friends that he was never angered by the signs; it was his wife, Nina, who was offended. "I could smile at it," he said. "It was not so easy, though, to convince my wife."

However reluctantly, he had agreed to go to Dallas to take the testimony of Jack Ruby, scheduled for Sunday, June 7. The trip would also give him the chance to see Dealey Plaza and the Texas School Book Depository for himself. With Specter's help, Rankin began to organize a full week's itinerary. Specter remembered that the trip was originally going to be "crammed with meetings and inspections." But Warren balked; he did not want to spend nearly that much time in Dallas. Rankin then proposed a long weekend, organized around Ruby's testimony, with Warren leaving Washington at lunchtime Friday and returning the following Monday in time to join arguments at the Supreme Court.

"I'll give you Sunday," Warren said, according to Specter. The trip would be limited to a single day. The chief justice would not agree to spend even one night in Dallas.

Specter felt badly for his colleague Burt Griffin, the commission's expert on Ruby; Griffin would be left behind in Washington because of his flap with the Dallas police. Specter would have happily turned down the trip if Warren and Rankin had given him the chance; he would have preferred to go home to Philadelphia and "spend the whole weekend with my wife and young sons."

Rankin asked Specter to help organize a Sunday morning tour of Dallas for the chief justice. It would focus on Dealey Plaza, as well as Oswald's route across town to the scene of the murder of Officer Tippit, and then to the Texas Theatre. When the tour reached the book depository, Rankin wanted Specter to make a full presentation to Warren about the single-bullet theory—"right from the assassin's perch on the sixth floor," Specter said.

On Friday, June 5, Specter did the last-minute planning in Washington for the trip. He had hoped to get out of the office early that afternoon to catch a train home to Philadelphia; he wanted to spend at least part of the weekend with his family before returning to Washington to join the flight to Dallas early Sunday. But he needed to speak to Rankin before leaving, and Rankin was nowhere to be found. So Specter waited. "I missed the four o'clock train and then the five."

It was that afternoon that Warren and Rankin, without telling Specter, had gone to Jacqueline Kennedy's Georgetown home to take her testimony. Rankin returned to the commission's office shortly after five p.m., and he ran into Specter in the men's room.

"Rankin said he'd heard I was looking for him," Specter recalled. "I said I had the details worked out for Sunday's trip to Dallas."

Rankin then revealed, reluctantly, where he had been, and Specter remembered that Rankin "braced" for the young lawyer's angry response.

And Specter was furious, he said. He had been pressing for months to interview Mrs. Kennedy, and now Warren and Rankin had gone to talk to her without even the courtesy of telling him in advance.

"I didn't say anything," Specter said later. "I didn't have to. Rankin knew I was livid."

Specter remembered taking a deep breath and deciding there was no point in mounting any larger protest, at least not at that moment. "What was done was done." He tried to put aside his anger and focus on his immediate priority—getting home to Philadelphia for the night.

Rankin was also in a bad mood. Warren had insisted that he join the Dallas trip, which meant that he would not be able to commute home to Manhattan that weekend to see his wife. Instead, he would be in Dallas, locked in an interrogation room with Jack Ruby and the chief justice. Like Specter, he was growing tired of spending so much time in Washington. "It looks like I'm going to have to have a damn bed in the skies," he complained.

On Sunday morning, Specter was back in Washington, and Warren offered to pick him up at his hotel for the ride to Andrews Air Force Base in Maryland, where they would board a small government JetStar plane for the flight to Texas. The chief justice was in an unusually good mood, Specter recalled. On the plane, the two men talked baseball. A game that afternoon between the San Francisco Giants, Warren's team, and Specter's hometown Philadelphia Phillies would decide first place in the National League. "So the battle lines were clear," Specter said.

They landed in Dallas mid-morning and got right to work. Congressman Ford and commission lawyer Joe Ball had traveled there separately and met up with Warren, Rankin, and Specter for the tour of the book depository. The presence of the chief justice and his delegation in the streets of Dallas attracted small, friendly crowds. Drawing on the political talents he had honed in California, "Warren chatted and kidded with a stream of passersby," Specter said.

At the book depository, Warren was taken to the sixth floor and shown what was believed to have been Oswald's perch. The scene from the day of the assassination had been re-created for Warren's inspection, including the stacks of boxes of children's wooden blocks—the blocks were known as "Rolling Readers," since each block contained letters and words that children could fashion into sentences—that Oswald had apparently assembled to hide what he was doing. Warren could not resist his politician's instincts and took some of the blocks out of the boxes to sign and give away as souvenirs when he got back outside; Specter got one with Warren's signature.

At about eleven a.m. Specter and Warren stood at the sixth-floor window. "Warren assumed a silent and thoughtful pose at the window, which I knew was my cue to start," Specter remembered. "For about eight minutes, the chief justice didn't say a word as I summarized" the single-bullet theory.

As he spoke, "Warren stood with his arms folded across his chest and studied Dealey Plaza," Specter recalled. "Except for the cheering crowds and the presidential motorcade, our view of Dealey Plaza, Elm Street and the Triple Underpass matched what Oswald had seen as he crouched at that window six and a half months before."

Specter opened the presentation by reminding Warren of "the incontrovertible physical evidence" of Oswald's guilt, including the discovery of his Mannlicher-Carcano rifle on the sixth floor—only inches from where Warren was standing at that moment—and the ballistics evidence that proved that the bullet found at Parkland Hospital had been fired from the same rifle. Oswald's fingerprints were on the rifle, and the spent cartridges found on the sixth floor matched the rifle and the fired bullets.

He reminded the chief justice of the findings in the autopsy report and how navy pathologists demonstrated that a bullet had entered the base of Kennedy's neck from behind and exited out his throat, nicking the knot of his tie. Specter then used his finger, pointing out the window, to show the bullet's trajectory in the instant after it struck the president's neck. He explained how the on-site tests done two weeks earlier showed that the bullet would then have entered Connally's back, exiting his chest before passing through his wrist and settling in his thigh. Warren had already seen the Zapruder film several times, so Specter did not need to remind the chief justice what happened next, when a second bullet struck the president in the back of the head.

"When I finished my discourse, the Chief Justice remained silent," Specter recalled. "He turned on his heel and stepped away, still saying nothing." Specter was annoyed that Warren could not be bothered to say anything, if only to compliment him on the quality of the presentation. But Warren's silence, Specter decided, probably signaled that he had accepted, in full, the single-bullet theory.

From the book depository, the group was taken across the street to the Dallas county jail, where they would use the sheriff's kitchen to take Ruby's testimony. Ford remembered the room as relatively small, about ten feet by eighteen feet, and "very austere." A table, about three feet by eight feet, had been placed in the middle of the room, with chairs around it for Ruby and his questioners.

Specter remembered that Warren had specifically requested a small room for Ruby's testimony, to limit the number of people who could witness

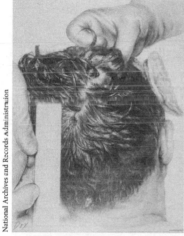

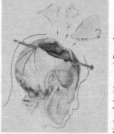

The evidence. CLOCKWISE FROM TOP: Oswald's Italian-made Mannlicher-Carcano rifle; two artist's reconstructions of the fatal head wound; the president's bloodied shirt; the bullet that, the commission's staff was convinced, hit both Kennedy and Connally; an artist's reconstruction, based on autopsy photos, of the president's head wound, the skull open to the right.

Chief Justice Earl Warren and Gerald Ford visited Dallas on June 7, 1964, to inspect Dealey Plaza and take the testimony of Jack Ruby. They are shown leaving the Texas School Book Depository, followed by general counsel J. Lee Rankin and staff lawyer Joseph Ball. BELOW: In September, Senator Richard Russell (*center*) organized his own visit to Dallas to see Dealey Plaza and interview Marina Oswald. He was joined in front of the Texas School Book Depository by fellow commission members (*far left*) Hale Boggs and (*far right, in hat*) John Sherman Cooper.

© Bettmann/CORBIS

AP Photo/Ferd Kaufman

the event. "A swarm of Washington and Texas bigwigs had descended" on Dallas in hopes of being part of this moment of history, Specter said. But not all could get in. There was so little space that Warren could see he would have to leave a member of his own delegation out of the room. "As the Chief Justice studied the roster, he found only one person he could exclude—me," Specter said. "So I sat in the sheriff's office watching the Philadelphia–San Francisco baseball game on national television. At the time, I didn't mind too much. In retrospect, I should have."*

At about eleven forty-five a.m., Ruby was brought in by sheriff's deputies. He was wearing a white prison-issue jumper. His feet were covered in thong sandals, which were given to prisoners on suicide watch in place of shoes with laces. Ford remembered that Ruby took a seat and fumbled with a small piece of paper tissue and a rubber band. He was "clean-shaven, balding, hawk-nosed, big hands and feet for a small, slight person," Ford said. One of Ruby's trial lawyers, Joe Tonahill, joined them. At first, Ruby appeared "surprisingly rational and quite composed—certainly far different acting than psychiatric reports I had read before the trip," Ford said. But Ruby was also inscrutable. He had a "habit to look right at you for a period" before looking away, so it was "hard to know what he is thinking."

Even before Ruby was sworn in by Warren, he had an urgent question for the chief justice: "Without a lie detector on my testimony, my verbal statements to you, how do you know if I am telling the truth?"

"Don't worry about that, Jack," Tonahill said.

Warren stepped in: "You wanted to ask something, did you, Mr. Ruby?"

Ruby: "I would like to be able to get a lie detector test, or truth serum, on what motivated me to do what I did. . . . Now, Mr. Warren, I don't know if you have any confidence in the lie-detector test and the truth serum, and so on."

Warren would later admit that he did not think fast enough, and he found himself agreeing to Ruby's request. "If you and your counsel want any kind of test, I will arrange it for you. I would be glad to do that, if you want it."

Ruby was pleased. "I do want it."

Warren: "We will be glad to do it."

---

* Specter had other reasons to be agitated that afternoon, since his hometown Phillies were defeated by the San Francisco Giants, 4–3, in ten innings, allowing San Francisco to hold on to first place in the National League.

That settled, Ruby wanted to be certain he would have time, on this visit, to tell his full story.

"Are you limited for time?" he asked.

Warren: "No, we have all the time you want."

The testimony had only begun, but Ruby already wanted to know: "Am I boring you?"

Warren: "Go ahead, all right, Mr. Ruby, tell us your story."

Ruby's account of the two days that began November 22, with news of Kennedy's murder, and ended November 24, with Ruby gunning down Oswald in police headquarters, would be long and convoluted. He said he heard about the shooting in Dealey Plaza seconds after it occurred; he had been a few blocks away at the *Dallas Morning News*, placing weekend advertisements for the Carousel Club. He was shattered by the news of Kennedy's death, he said. "I became very emotional. . . . I couldn't stop crying." He immediately decided to close his club for the weekend.

That night, he took advantage of his friendship with Dallas police officers to slip into police headquarters to watch the news conference in which Oswald was paraded in front of reporters. Ruby told strangers in the pressroom that night that he was an Israeli journalist; if anyone had challenged his presence, he could always drop in a few words of the Yiddish he had learned in childhood.

At that point, his testimony quickly became so disjointed that it was almost impossible for Warren to follow. Ruby threw out names—of friends, of family members, of strippers, and of other employees at the Carousel Club—and places and dates that meant nothing to the chief justice and the others. In moments of coherence, however, he consistently denied that he had been part of any conspiracy to silence Oswald. He insisted that he had not known Oswald and that he had no thought of killing him until he read a newspaper article that Sunday morning that suggested Mrs. Kennedy might have to return to Dallas to testify. "I felt very emotional and carried away for Mrs. Kennedy, with all that the strife she had gone through," Ruby said. "Someone owed it to our beloved president that she shouldn't be expected to come back to face this heinous trial."

Killing Oswald was an impulsive act, he said. He was aware of the many rumors that some of his organized-crime contacts might have put him up to it, but he said that "no one else requested me to do anything. . . . I never spoke to anyone about attempting to do anything. No subversive organization gave me any idea. No underworld person made any effort to contact me."

Ford recalled that Ruby's testimony went reasonably well for about forty-five minutes, until Ruby and his lawyer began arguing for reasons that were not clear and the court reporter stopped recording the session. The scene then became "terribly tense," Ford said. It was "touch and go" whether Ruby would be able to continue. Warren, he said, "tried to be reassuring and was very patient in his cajoling" of Ruby.

Down the hall, Elmer Moore, a Secret Service agent assigned to the trip to protect the chief justice, found Specter in the sheriff's office watching the baseball game. He announced that Specter was needed, as quickly as possible, in the kitchen. "They want you," he said. "Ruby wants a Jew in the room." Specter knew enough about Ruby to know how he valued his Jewish heritage and how he had become fixated on the idea that Jews were being massacred because of him.

Specter followed Moore down the hall. As he entered the kitchen, Specter could see that Ruby was studying him. "Looking straight at me, he silently mouthed the words, 'Are you a Yid?'"

Specter said nothing. Again, Ruby mouthed the words: "Are you a Yid?" And then a third time.

Specter said he tried to remain stone-faced, not even to nod his head. He wanted none of this taken down by the court reporter. "I didn't flinch or respond in any way."

At just that moment, Specter recalled, the court reporter ran out of paper, and Ruby jumped up and pulled the chief justice into a corner, motioning for Specter to join them. Joe Ball, the other commission staff lawyer, stood up and tried to enter the conversation.

"Are you Jewish?" Ruby asked.

"No," Ball replied.

"Well, go away," Ruby told him.

Ruby then turned to Warren. "Chief, you've got to get me to Washington. They're cutting off the arms and legs of Jewish children in Albuquerque and El Paso."

"I can't do that," the chief justice said.

Ruby urged Warren to talk to Abe Fortas, the well-known Washington lawyer who was close to President Johnson and would soon be named to the Supreme Court—and who was Jewish. "Get to Fortas," Ruby said. "He'll get it worked out."

Ford could see that Ruby relaxed at the acknowledgment—it was not clear by whom—that Specter was indeed Jewish. "This seemed to give him confidence to continue testifying."

When the stenographer was ready to resume, Ruby, Warren, and Specter returned to their seats. Ruby noticed his lawyer, Tonahill, pass a note to Ford. Ruby insisted that he be allowed to read it, and the conversation stopped while the note was handed to Ruby, who was farsighted and struggled to make out the words on the page. The chief justice handed Ruby his glasses.

"You see," Tonahill had written. "I told you he was crazy."

Ruby put the note aside, seemingly untroubled by his lawyer's insult, and turned back to the chief justice. He wanted Warren to confirm again that he would allow him to take a polygraph test or be injected with truth serum—"Pentothal," he said, referring to Sodium Pentothal, the depressant sometimes referred to as a "truth serum." He asked again to be taken to Washington.

"Do I sound dramatic? Off the beam?"

Warren tried to keep him calm: "No, you are speaking very, very rationally."

"I want to tell the truth, and I can't tell it here," Ruby said, using words that would sound ominous when read by conspiracy theorists in years to come.

This was the first time that Specter, who had missed the start of Ruby's testimony, had heard about his request for a polygraph—and about Warren's agreement to give him one. Specter said he understood instantly that the chief justice had made a terrible mistake. He knew Warren, like most serious-minded law-enforcement veterans, gave little credence to polygraphs; the chief justice, in fact, had already vetoed the idea of giving one to Marina Oswald. Yet he had just promised one—on the record—to Oswald's seemingly delusional killer.

Ruby tried to step up the pressure on Warren, claiming that his life was in danger if he remained in Dallas. He was convinced that "other people"—he suggested members of the right-wing John Birch Society—were trying to tie him to a conspiracy to kill Kennedy. And because he was Jewish, Jews everywhere were being murdered in retaliation for the president's assassination. "The Jewish people are being exterminated at this moment," he said. "I am used as a scapegoat. I am as good as guilty as the accused assassin of President Kennedy. How can you remedy that, Mr. Warren?" If he could get to Washington and testify, Ruby said, "maybe my people won't be tortured and mutilated."

Specter could see how flustered Warren was. The chief justice told Ruby: "You may be sure that the president and his whole commission will do anything that is necessary to see that your people are not tortured."

After more than three hours of this, Warren decided to stop the testimony, insisting he was doing it for Ruby's own good. "I think we have tired Mr. Ruby," the chief justice said. "We appreciate your patience and your willingness to testify in this manner for us."

Ruby: "All I want to do is tell the truth, and the only way you can know it is by the polygraph."

Warren: "That we will do for you."

Still hoping to get out of Dallas by day's end, the chief justice left for a late lunch at the Dallas apartment of Robert Storey, a former president of the American Bar Association. The end of the lunch produced what was, for Specter, another astonishing display of the chief justice's awkwardness when called on to make quick decisions. After leaving Storey's apartment, Warren noticed a group of reporters and photographers at the end of the hall eager to hear his thoughts about his day in Dallas. "Instead of turning left and facing the pack," Specter remembered, "the Chief Justice ran down a corridor to the right and down a flight of stairs to avoid talking to them." It would have been easy enough for Warren to smile and offer a polite "no comment" to the reporters. Instead, he had created a baffling scene in which the chief justice of the United States could be seen fleeing, almost in panic, from a group of reporters who wanted to ask him a few simple questions.

On the plane home that night, Warren told Specter how unhappy he was that he had promised a polygraph test to Ruby. "I don't believe in polygraphs," he said. "I don't believe in Big Brother."

Specter told Warren that he had no choice but to go through with the test, unless Ruby changed his mind about wanting one. "Mr. Chief Justice, you promised him a polygraph," Specter said. It "would look awful if the commission reneged on an on-the-record promise." If Ruby was denied a polygraph now, "at best, it would look as though the commission was not exhausting every lead." At worst, it would look like a cover-up designed to prevent Ruby from exposing a conspiracy. Warren might not believe in polygraph tests, but opinion polls suggested that the American public did. "Mr. Chief Justice," Specter said, "you can't turn him down."

41

Secret Service director James Rowley had reason to fear for his job when he testified before the Warren Commission; certainly he had cause to fear that his ninety-nine-year-old agency might not survive the commission's investigation. The Bronx-born, fifty-six-year-old Rowley was the first director of the Secret Service to have a president assassinated on his watch, and he would face the toughest questioning of any senior government official who came before the commission. Other law-enforcement agencies—the FBI, in particular—might have intentionally tried to hide information from the investigation. In the case of the Secret Service, however, the cover-up seemed indisputable. Warren had evidence of what he considered outrageous misconduct—the decision by several Secret Service agents in the president's motorcade in Dallas to go out drinking the night before the assassination—and of how Rowley had tried to hide the details of the episode from the public. Some of the chief justice's anger may have been stoked by his friendship with Drew Pearson, who had broken the story about the agents' drinking on the radio program that he used to promote his newspaper column. Whatever the reasons for his outrage, Warren walked into the commission's hearing room on the day of Rowley's testimony with the attitude of a prosecutor.

Shortly after nine a.m. on June 18, Rowley was sworn in, and he was immediately hit with questions about the drinking incident. It was Rankin's first substantive question, in fact: "Did you learn in connection with the trip when the assassination occurred that certain of the Secret Service agents had been in the Press Club and what is called the Cellar, in Fort Worth, the night before?"

Rowley: "Well, that came to my attention through a broadcast that Mr. Pearson made—that agents were inebriated the night before." He said he immediately dispatched a Secret Service inspector to Texas to investigate.

Rankin: "What did you learn?"

Rowley admitted that much of what Pearson had reported was true, although Rowley said he did not believe that any agent was drunk, as Pearson had claimed. The internal investigation showed that a total of nine agents had been out drinking; three had each downed a scotch, while "the others had two or three beers" each. The next day, at least four of those agents were assigned to the motorcade, including Clint Hill, the agent who appeared to have saved Jacqueline Kennedy's life.

Rankin asked: "Did you learn whether or not there were any violations of the regulations of the Secret Service by these men?" It was a question to which Rankin—and Warren—already knew the answer.

Rowley: "Yes, there was a violation."

To make the commission's point as clearly as possible, Rankin then asked Rowley to cite the specific regulation in the Secret Service manual that barred drinking on duty, and then to read it out loud. Rowley was handed a copy of the employee manual; he turned to the first chapter of Section 10: "Employees are strictly enjoined to refrain from the use of intoxicating liquor during the hours they are officially employed at their post of duty or when they may reasonably expect that they may be called upon to perform an official duty."

The rules were stricter for agents assigned to the president's personal detail. Rowley was asked to read those out, as well: "The use of intoxicating liquor of any kind, including beer and wine, by members of the White House detail and special agents cooperating with them, or by special agents on similar assignments while they are in a travel status, is prohibited." It was a firing offense, Rowley admitted, reading out the rest of the regulation: "Violation or slight disregard of the above paragraphs or the excessive or improper use of intoxicating liquor at any time will be cause for removal."

Rankin asked the next question with what was, for him, uncharacteristic aggressiveness: How could Rowley be sure that his agents might not have saved the president's life? "How can you tell that the fact that they were out as they were the night before . . . had nothing to do with the assassination?" Rankin asked. "Have you done anything to discipline these men for violations of the regulations of the Secret Service?"

Rowley defended himself and the agents. He said he believed that the agents in the motorcade had performed in "an exemplary manner," whatever the aftereffects of the alcohol. "I did consider what type of punishment would be provided," he said. "Then I also considered the fact that these men in no way had—their conduct had no bearing on the assassination." To punish them might lead the public to believe "they were responsible for the assassination of the president. I didn't think this was fair, and that they did not deserve that. . . . I did not think in the light of history that they should be stigmatized with something like that, or their families or children."

Warren was having none of it: "Don't you think that if a man went to bed reasonably early, and hadn't been drinking the night before, he would be more alert than if they stayed up until 3, 4 or 5 o'clock in the morning, going to beatnik joints and doing some drinking along the way?" Warren was using Pearson's description of the Cellar, an all-night club, as a "beatnik joint."

As the president's motorcade traveled through Dallas, Secret Service agents were supposed to be scanning the crowd and the buildings along the route for threats, Warren noted. The commission had heard testimony from witnesses who said they saw a rifle barrel pointing out of the sixth-floor window of the Texas School Book Depository before the shots rang out, yet the Secret Service agents missed it entirely. "Some people saw a rifle up in that building," the chief justice said. "Wouldn't a Secret Service man in this motorcade, who is supposed to observe such things, be more likely to observe something of that kind if he was free from any of the results of liquor or lack of sleep than he would otherwise? Don't you think that they would have been much more alert, sharper?"

"Yes, sir," Rowley conceded. "But I don't believe they could have prevented the assassination."

Warren was not done. The misconduct went beyond the agents, he suggested; it went to Rowley's own performance, since the Secret Service director was apparently willing to ignore misconduct by his own employees. "It seems to me that they were all given a complete bill of health," Warren said. "I just wonder if that is quite consistent with the facts that the commission should have."

Rowley: "As I said earlier, we don't condone their actions, nor do we try to belittle the violation. But in the circumstances, I took the decision that I thought right. . . . I don't think that these people should be blamed for the tragedy."

Weeks later, Warren was dismayed when he read draft chapters of the commission's final report dealing with the Secret Service and its performance in Dallas. The drafts, written by Sam Stern, Warren's former clerk at the court, did not include any direct criticism of the agents who had gone out drinking. Nor did Stern offer any harsh criticism in the draft chapter of the failure of FBI agent James Hosty to alert the Secret Service to Oswald's presence in Dallas. After months of turning himself into the commission's in-house expert on the Secret Service, Stern still could not muster any outrage over the drinking incident, and he continued to be impressed that so many Secret Service agents and their supervisors seemed genuinely to grieve over what happened in Dallas, and to accept some responsibility for the assassination. It came as an awkward surprise for Stern to discover how differently the chief justice felt. Warren ordered Stern's drafts rewritten to make direct attacks on the Secret Service agents and on Hosty. "We would have looked silly if we hadn't mentioned the Secret Service agents going out the night before the assassination," Warren said later. "We would have looked bad if we failed to point out that the FBI had had reason to look up Oswald before the event, knowing all that it did."

Much as Warren wanted to be tough on the Secret Service, Gerald Ford wanted to be tough on the State Department. The department was a traditional foe for Ford and other conservative Republicans in Congress who saw it as a bastion of liberal Ivy Leaguers all too eager to reach accommodation with nations behind the Iron Curtain. Many department officials were still traumatized over the attacks that had been made on their loyalty by Senator Joseph McCarthy in the 1950s.

Ford told aides he believed there was evidence of incompetence, if not worse, at the department in its dealings with Oswald over the years, beginning with its decision in 1962 to allow him to return home from Russia. Why should Oswald have been allowed to reclaim his full rights as a citizen after he announced to American diplomats in Moscow, shortly after he arrived there in 1959, that he wanted to renounce his citizenship? The department had not only allowed Oswald to return to the United States, bringing with him a new Russian wife; it had provided him with a loan of about $400 to cover his travel costs. Ford was also outraged, he said, over the public statements issued by the State Department in Washington, within hours of Kennedy's murder, that there was no evidence of a foreign conspiracy in the assassination—a judgment made before any real investigation had begun.

Secretary of State Dean Rusk was called before the commission on Wednesday, June 10, to answer questions about his department's performance. David Slawson was the staff lawyer responsible for preparing the list of questions for Rusk. He had always found the dour, fifty-five-year-old Georgian to be a remarkably unimpressive figure—a view widely shared, it turned out, inside the Kennedy administration. "Rusk seemed to be a deliberate non-thinker," Slawson decided.

Kennedy had chosen Rusk, a career diplomat, to run the State Department over several more high-profile, certainly more charismatic candidates because the president "intended to be his own Secretary of State," according to Kennedy's friend and adviser Arthur M. Schlesinger Jr. As time went on, the president despaired of Rusk's meekness and his unwillingness to voice an opinion. "It was generally impossible to know what he thought," Schlesinger wrote. "His colorlessness of mind appeared almost compulsive." Jacqueline Kennedy told Schlesinger shortly after the assassination that her husband had intended to replace Rusk in a second term. "Dean Rusk seemed to be overtaken by that apathy and fear of making the wrong decision," she said. "It used to drive Jack crazy."

Rusk had been kept on at the department by Johnson to show continuity with Kennedy's foreign policy, and Rusk, seemingly more comfortable with a fellow southerner in the White House, became more assertive. He would go on to become a public champion of Johnson's plans to escalate the military commitment in Vietnam.

In his testimony to the commission, Rusk had little to offer beyond what the State Department had been saying consistently since Kennedy's death—that it did not believe the Soviets or Cubans were involved. "It would be an act of rashness and madness for Soviet leaders to undertake such an action," he said. "It has not been our impression that madness has characterized the actions of the Soviet leadership in recent times." As for Cuba, "it would be even greater madness for Castro or his government to be involved."

Rankin stepped in, asking Rusk if he had read the cables sent to Washington immediately after the assassination from then U.S. ambassador to Mexico Thomas Mann, who was convinced that Castro was behind the murder. Rusk acknowledged that he had read the cables and that they had "raised questions of the most far-reaching character involving the possibility" of a foreign conspiracy, "so I had a very deep personal interest in that at the time." But the investigation of those allegations by the CIA and the FBI in Mexico and elsewhere had since "run its course," as Rusk put it, without proof of Cuban involvement.

Ford pressed his criticism that the department had been too quick to make public statements immediately after the assassination that seemed to rule out a foreign conspiracy. Rusk defended the statements: "We did not then have evidence of that sort, nor do we now, and the implications of suggesting evidence in the absence of evidence would have been enormous."

Ford: "I don't understand that."

Rusk: "Well, for us to leave the impression that we had evidence that we could not describe or discuss, when in fact we didn't have the evidence on a matter of such overriding importance, could have created a very dangerous situation in terms of—"

Ford interrupted: "Wouldn't it have been just as effective to say 'no comment'?"

Rusk: "Well, unfortunately, under the practices of the press, no comment would have been taken to confirm that there was evidence."

For the questioning of Rusk, Ford was, as usual, well briefed, and he decided to quiz Rusk on whether the secretary of state had ever bothered to acquaint himself with evidence that might still point to a Communist conspiracy. He asked Rusk if he had been aware of news reports that Castro, just weeks before the assassination, had warned publicly that he would retaliate with violence against American leaders who had targeted the Cuban dictator and his colleagues for assassination.

Rusk said he recalled reading nothing, before or after the president's murder, about Castro's threats.

* * *

After Rusk's testimony, Ford was convinced that the State Department should not "get off scot-free" in the commission's final report. Two days later, he telephoned Rankin to make the point. Rankin was out of the office, so Ford instead talked to Slawson, who was then drawing up lists of questions for others from the department. "We cannot afford to be light or easy on the witnesses," Ford told him. "The burden to prove that they acted properly is on them. We should make it as tough as possible for them. Our proper role is the 'devil's advocate.'"

Ford asked Slawson what he thought of the State Department's contacts with Oswald over the years and whether the department could have done more to stop him from getting his chance to kill the president. Slawson said he could not see how the department bore any responsibility for the assassination. The decision to allow Oswald to return to the United States "seemed to have been correct"; other Americans who had defected behind the Iron Curtain and then changed their minds had been treated much the same way, Slawson said.

It was not the answer that Ford was looking for. He thought the State Department's decision to allow Oswald to return had been made "much too glibly and routinely." If Slawson was not going to get tough on Rusk's deputies, Ford made clear, he would.

The commission's staff lawyers staged several reenactments in Dealey Plaza. David Belin is shown at the fifth-floor window of the Texas School Book Depository, during an experiment to determine what would have been seen and heard there as rifle shots were fired from the sixth-floor window above. BELOW: Arlen Specter explains the single-bullet theory, with government agents positioned in a limousine at the spots where President Kennedy and Governor Connally had been seated.

LEFT: Although CIA and FBI officials ruled out Cuban involvement, the American ambassador to Mexico and others were convinced the assassination was connected to the government of Fidel Castro, shown after capturing a Marlin in the Caribbean. BELOW: In a photo taken September 7, 1963, Castro is shown making a point to Associated Press correspondent Dan Harker (with arms crossed) during an encounter in Havana. Harker reported in a resulting article that Castro threatened to retaliate against American officials who had targeted Cuban leaders for violence.

AFP/Getty Images

AP Photo

42

THE OFFICE OF THE DIRECTOR
THE FEDERAL BUREAU OF INVESTIGATION
WASHINGTON, DC
WEDNESDAY, JUNE 17, 1964

J. Edgar Hoover insisted on reviewing every important FBI document before it was sent to the commission. If the FBI uncovered new evidence related to the assassination, or if the bureau had a response to questions posed by one of the commissioners or the staff, the information was passed to the commission in the form of a letter on bureau stationery signed by Hoover. He sent hundreds of letters to the commission during the course of the investigation—often several a day—and they had a standard format. Each was addressed directly to Lee Rankin ("Dear Mr. Rankin") and dispatched by armed couriers to the commission's offices on Capitol Hill. Many of Hoover's letters were classified TOP SECRET, the words typed across each page.

When FBI documents arrived, Rankin would share them with Redlich. And if Hoover's letters were particularly interesting or important, Redlich would in turn show them to his deputy, Mel Eisenberg; the two men, both proud New Yorkers, had become close friends over the months of the investigation. "We shared an office and talked all the time," Eisenberg said. By June, Eisenberg had returned to his New York law firm part-time, but he was still in Washington two or three days a week. When Hoover's letters involved questions about possible foreign involvement in the assassination, they were routinely directed to David Slawson.

On Wednesday, June 17, according to Hoover's files, the FBI director prepared an especially sensitive, top secret letter to Rankin. The contents were explosive, or at least they had the potential to be. According to Hoover's letter, it appeared that Cuban diplomats in Mexico City had advance knowledge of Oswald's plan to kill the president—because Oswald had talked openly about it. If the information gathered by the FBI was correct, Oswald had marched into the Cuban embassy in Mexico in October 1963 and announced, "I'm going to kill Kennedy."

Hoover might have feared the commission's reaction to his letter. What did it mean that Cuban diplomats in Mexico had known weeks in advance about Oswald's plans to murder the president? Was this evidence of the foreign conspiracy that Hoover had seemed so determined to rule out? More to the point for the FBI, did this information suggest that the bureau had bungled its investigation in Mexico City and that there might still be people there who needed to be tracked down because they had known about, or even encouraged, Oswald's plans?

The ultimate source of the information in the letter was, remarkably enough, Fidel Castro himself. The Cuban dictator's words had been relayed to the FBI from a "confidential" bureau informant who "had furnished reliable information in the past," Hoover wrote. According to the informant, Castro had recently been overheard in Havana talking about what his diplomats in Mexico City had known about Oswald. "Our people in Mexico gave us the details in a full report of how he acted when he came to Mexico," Castro was quoted as saying.

According to Castro, Oswald became infuriated when he was told that he would not be granted, on the spot, a travel visa for Cuba. He turned his rage not against the Cuban government but against Castro's nemesis— Kennedy. Oswald seemed to blame the American president for the breakdown in relations with Cuba that was now making it so difficult for him to begin his new life in Havana. "Oswald stormed into the embassy, demanded the visa, and, when it was refused to him, headed out saying, 'I'm going to kill Kennedy for this,'" Castro was quoted as saying. He said the Cuban diplomats in Mexico had not taken Oswald seriously and ignored his threat against the president's life, believing that the young American might be some sort of CIA provocateur. The Cuban government, Castro continued to insist, had nothing to do with the assassination of the president.

In the letter, Hoover offered no clue to the identity of the bureau's confidential source in Havana. Years later, the FBI would reveal that it was Jack Childs, a Chicago man who posed as a devoted member of the American Communist Party but was, in fact, working for the FBI. Childs visited Castro in Havana in June 1964, the same month that Hoover prepared his letter to Rankin. Childs's brother, Maurice, a fellow Communist Party member, also spied for the FBI. The work of the Childs brothers—Operation Solo, the bureau called it—would be considered one of the bureau's greatest Cold War accomplishments. Under the cover of promoting the cause of Communism, the brothers traveled throughout the Communist world, meeting Khrushchev, Mao, and Castro, among others, and then feeding what they had learned back to the FBI. The bureau's records showed that the information from the Childs brothers proved remarkably accurate.

But commission lawyers would never have the chance to ponder the implications of this—including the possibility that Oswald had announced loudly in Mexico that he intended to kill the president—because Hoover's June 1964 letter to Rankin appears never to have reached staff members who should have seen it. What happened to the document would remain a mystery decades later. There is a reference to the letter in the commission's correspondence logs. But the letter itself could not be found in the commission's paper files stored at the National Archives or in Rankin's personal files, which his family donated to the archives after his death. Former staff members were perplexed when they heard about the existence of the letter. Eisenberg had no recollection of ever seeing it or of being told about it by Redlich or anyone else. He said he was convinced he would have heard about it if Redlich had seen it, since it was so obviously important. David Slawson was convinced he never saw it either; he said he would have remembered such a "bombshell" document. Although Hoover's letter disappeared from the commission's files, assuming it ever reached the commission, it did land in the files of another agency: the CIA. Decades after the Warren Commission completed its investigation, the letter turned up in the agency's files that were declassified as a result of continuing debate over Kennedy's death.*

---

* At the request of the author in 2012, the National Archives researched the question of why a copy of Hoover's June 17, 1964, letter was found in the CIA's declassified files but not in the commission's. The National Archives said it was unable to determine the answer.

*   *   *

As spring turned to summer in Mexico City in 1964, CIA station chief Winston Scott and his deputies in the U.S. embassy could begin to relax. It appeared they would escape any criticism in the Warren Commission's final report. The station might have failed to detect the threat that Oswald posed, but the word inside the spy agency was that the Warren report would find no fault in Scott's operation.

Most of his key deputies had come under no direct scrutiny at all during the investigation. When the commission's lawyers visited Mexico City in April, their questions for the CIA were answered almost exclusively by Scott himself; there was no record that they interviewed most of Scott's deputies, including Anne Goodpasture—Scott's "right-hand woman"—and David Atlee Phillips, one of Scott's most trusted covert operatives.

Phillips, a forty-one-year-old Texan who had been recruited by the agency while working as a newspaperman in Chile in 1950, was in charge of all espionage operations directed against the Cuban embassy. He had long experience in dealing with Cuba; he had been posted undercover in Havana twice in the 1950s and was part of CIA planning for the Bay of Pigs. Scott would describe Phillips as "the finest covert action officer" he had ever worked with. At a time in the early 1960s when James Bond was a new cultural phenomenon, he even looked the part. Strikingly good-looking as a younger man, Phillips had originally sought a career in New York as an actor; after World War II, he was drawn to a very different career, albeit one that would require an actor's skill, in the newly created CIA.

In his many years operating undercover, Phillips might have been forgiven for losing track of the false names he was supposed to call himself. He had two formal CIA pseudonyms (Michael C. Choaden and Paul D. Langevin), and he estimated that, over the years, he used as many as two hundred other names and aliases.

He believed he had an unusually important job in Mexico. The Cuban embassy there was a staging post for Castro "in exporting his ideas of revolution in Latin America," Phillips said years later. "I was to know what the Cubans were doing in Mexico City, specifically in their embassy, and to try to obtain as much information as possible about their intentions." He was responsible for recruiting agents to spy against Cuba—most importantly from within the Cuban embassy—as well as to monitor

Americans who made contact with the embassy and might offer themselves up as spies for Castro's government.

The CIA was not authorized to watch American citizens in Mexico or in any other foreign country "unless they are clearly engaged in the espionage game," Phillips said later. But if an American visited the Cuban embassy and seemed suspicious, "it would be imprudent not to observe them long enough to find out what they are up to." In some cases, he recalled, he tried to intercept potential American traitors in Mexico before they had a chance to hand over secrets to the Cubans. He would boast about one particular success in the early 1960s—how he foiled the traitorous plans of a "middle-grade United States military officer" who showed up in Mexico City with plans to sell defense secrets to Cuba. In that case, Phillips dispatched a Mexican agent who "spoke fluent English and could pass for a Cuban intelligence type" to meet with the officer. Pretending to be a Cuban spy ready to pay for the American's secrets, the Mexican agent told the officer to return home to the United States to await further instructions from Havana. The investigation was then turned over to the FBI. "I don't know how the case turned out," Phillips wrote. "But it must have been a shock to the disloyal military man when, eventually, there was a knock on his door" and the caller was the FBI.

After the assassination, Phillips insisted that Oswald had never fallen into the category of somebody worth paying much attention to, even after he was seen at both the Cuban and Soviet embassies in Mexico; he was just a "blip on the station's radar screen." At the time of Oswald's visit, he said, Oswald seemed to be no more than an adventurous American tourist who wanted a visa that would give him a chance to see life in a Communist country. His past exploits, including his failed defection to the Soviet Union, would only be learned later, after Oswald had left Mexico and it was too late for the CIA to act, Phillips said. Before the assassination, Phillips acknowledged, he had known the name of Silvia Duran. The CIA's Mexico City station was well aware of her tangled romantic life, including her reported affair with the former Cuban ambassador to Mexico. Phillips said he believed he had read a transcript—in October, before the assassination—of a wiretapped telephone conversation between Duran and Soviet diplomats about visa requests involving an American man who would later turn out to be Oswald. But the conversation "didn't mean anything to me, I'm sorry to say, until after the assassination."

Phillips said years later that he came to the conclusion that Oswald was "kind of a loony fellow who decided to shoot the president—and he did" and that there was "no evidence to show that the Cubans or the Soviets put him up to it."

Phillips thought he met with some of the Warren Commission staff members when they visited Mexico, although the commission's paperwork made no mention of his name. His actions would not draw intense scrutiny until years later, when congressional investigators and others questioned whether Phillips had lied about his knowledge of Oswald. In the years to come, Phillips grew angry over conspiracy theories that suggested he and his CIA colleagues might have tried to recruit Oswald to spy against Cuba or that they had bungled an operation—similar to the one with the traitorous American military officer—in which they tried to intercept Oswald in Mexico City before he made contact with the Cubans. Phillips said the idea that he had been part of "a cover-up of the murder of one of my presidents disturbs me a great a deal, and my children."

But it is possible that no one—in the CIA or anywhere else in the government—did more to confuse the record about Lee Harvey Oswald and what the government had known about him before Kennedy's assassination. At times, Phillips's effort to muddy the record about what had happened in Mexico seemed almost pathological. He was, by profession, a man who traded in deception. It seemed, at times, that he was simply unable to tell the truth, if he knew it, about Oswald's visit to Mexico. Even as he continued to insist that Oswald had been only a "blip" on the CIA's radar, the agency eventually declassified cables showing that Oswald had in fact been closely tracked in the streets of the Mexican capital and that the CIA had alerted the FBI, the State Department, and other agencies—before the assassination—to his activities there.

More significant, perhaps, were Phillips's repeated misstatements under oath about his own whereabouts in September and October of 1963, when Oswald was in Mexico. While he initially claimed that he had been in Mexico throughout Oswald's visit, CIA records showed that Phillips was out of the country for much, if not all, of the period. He was, at the time, either in Washington or in Miami. During his visit to Miami, he worked out of a CIA office that was helping mobilize groups of anti-Castro Cuban exiles—including at least one of the groups that Oswald had tried to infiltrate earlier in the year.

Toward the end of his life, Phillips appeared ready to capitalize on the conspiracy theories about Oswald. He seemed to want to tantalize others about the possibility that the CIA had been lying about Oswald and that the agency actually bore some responsibility for Kennedy's death. When he died in 1988, Phillips left behind a typewritten, eight-page outline for a novel that would be a fictionalized account of his work in Mexico. The outline referred to characters based on himself and on Winston Scott, identified in the novel as Willard Bell, as well as on a conspiracy theorist resembling Mark Lane. Oswald was identified by his actual name, as was former director of Central Intelligence—and Warren Commission member—Allen Dulles.

The outline included a passage in which the character based on Phillips told his son:

I was one of the two case officers who handled Lee Harvey Oswald. After working to establish his Marxist bona fides, we gave him the mission of killing Fidel Castro in Cuba. I helped him when he came to Mexico City to obtain a visa, and when he returned to Dallas to wait for it, I saw him twice there. We rehearsed the plan many times: In Havana, Oswald was to assassinate Castro with a sniper's rifle from the upper floor window of a building on the route where Castro often drove in an open jeep. Whether Oswald was a double-agent or a psycho I'm not sure, and I don't know why he killed Kennedy. But I do know he used precisely the plan we had devised against Castro. Thus the CIA did not anticipate the President's assassination but it was responsible for it. I share that guilt. Allen Dulles gave the other CIA agent and me $800,000 in cash to finance the operation and set up Oswald for life after Castro's death. When the scheme went so horribly awry, Dulles told us to keep the money—he feared that an effort to give it to the Agency's operational funds would cause problems.

You can imagine how this sad history has troubled me. Many times I have thought of revealing the truth, but somehow couldn't. Perhaps you, reading this, will decide it's time for the truth.

OFF THE COAST OF CUBA
SUMMER 1964

William Coleman wrote nothing down about the riskiest assignment he undertook in a long career in the law and public service. He said he was told he should not say anything—ever—about the
assignment, other than to brief Chief Justice Warren, Lee Rankin, and
possibly President Johnson about the results. No paperwork was retained
in the commission's files, at least not in the files released to the National
Archives.

The mission that summer began on Florida's Atlantic coast, where
Coleman said he had been flown from Washington. Once there, he was
transferred to a U.S. government boat—"I don't know if it was a CIA boat
or a Navy boat"—for the trip to the waters off Cuba. About twenty miles
from the coast, he said, the boat stopped when it caught sight of a yacht—
Fidel Castro's. On the boat was Castro himself. He was waiting there to
answer the question that Coleman had been dispatched to ask: Had the
Cuban leader ordered President Kennedy's assassination?

Coleman had been selected for the assignment, he thought, because
he was the senior lawyer on the "conspiracy" team and, more important,
because it was known on the commission that he had met Castro before.
They had first been introduced in the 1940s or 1950s in Harlem, when
Castro was in New York on one of several visits he paid to the United
States before he came to power. Whatever his later complaints about the

capitalist decadence that the city might represent, Castro said he loved New York. He had spent much of his honeymoon in the city in 1948 and returned several times over the next decade. Like Coleman, the future Cuban leader was partial to the late-night music and dance clubs of Harlem.

As a black man, Coleman was not allowed into the nightclubs of midtown Manhattan in that era, so he, like his friends, would wait until one a.m. or so, when some of the most popular black entertainers of the time would finish their evening performances in midtown and head uptown to Harlem to entertain black audiences. The singer Lena Horne became a good friend of Coleman's. It was a magical time, he said. "Lena and all these talented people, they would come up to Harlem and the clubs, and you would have them all in same room together," Coleman said. "You would give your right arm to be in there at 4 o'clock the morning." It was in those clubs up along 125th Street where Coleman, a lifelong Republican, made a friend of Nelson Rockefeller, the future GOP governor of New York State and a fellow jazz-lover.

Coleman remembered that he had been impressed by Castro, who spoke some English. "I never thought he'd be the head of that country," Coleman said. "But he was an impressive guy. He had legal training. He was a very attractive guy, smart."

Now, all these years later, Castro was the feared dictator of Communist Cuba, the man who had brought the world to the brink of nuclear war two years earlier, and who John Kennedy had so desperately wanted to oust from power. Coleman considered it "irony upon irony" that he had been selected to undertake a secret mission to see his old acquaintance from the jazz clubs of Harlem and ask if he had killed the president.

As it was explained to Coleman, Castro had sent word to Washington that he wanted to offer testimony to the commission—to convince the investigation that he had nothing to do with Kennedy's murder. "Castro indicated he wanted to see somebody, and I was the guy to do it," Coleman said.

Years later, Coleman said he remembered discussing the mission only with Rankin and possibly with Warren. "I'm pretty sure I talked to the Chief Justice about it," he said. "The whole thing was hush-hush." He was told to say nothing about the assignment to Slawson, his junior partner.

There was good reason for the secrecy, he recalled; if his meeting was mishandled or became public, it could create a scandal, or worse. "If I screwed up, if I said the wrong thing," Castro might seize on it as an official exoneration in Kennedy's killing. "The next day, he could have a press conference and say, 'Even Mr. Coleman said I didn't do it.'"*

Still, Coleman recalled, he felt the mission was worth the risk: "I decided we had to do it."

Coleman's ability to keep the trip secret from most of his colleagues for decades was entirely in character. William Thaddeus Coleman Jr., born and raised in Philadelphia, prided himself on being a "Philadelphia Lawyer," a term once widely used around the country to describe an especially capable, discreet lawyer—a lawyer's lawyer. That the forty-three-year-old Coleman had risen so far in the profession by 1964 against such long odds was a tribute to just how talented he was. Only a dozen years earlier, despite graduating at the top of his law school class at Harvard and having worked as a Supreme Court clerk to the legendary Felix Frankfurter, he could not find a job at any firm in his hometown. He made it a point rarely to complain to other lawyers about the discrimination he had faced in his career; instead he spoke proudly about all that he had accomplished despite his skin color. His inability to find a job in Philadelphia early in his career was the one instance of ugly, obvious racism that did gnaw at him. "That really bothered me."

He finally found a job in 1949 at a fast-growing New York firm, Paul Weiss, where he became the first black associate in the firm's history—and one of the first black associates at any sizable firm in the country. Although he worked in New York, he remained devoted to Philadelphia and made his home there, requiring him to commute two and a half hours each day, each way, by train to and from Manhattan. For years, his alarm went off at five fifty every weekday morning, and he would not return home for dinner until eight thirty p.m., at the earliest. At Paul Weiss, Coleman began

---

* Coleman said the author of this book was the first journalist he had ever told about the secret mission, although it appears he confirmed a similar but less detailed account in response to questions from the writer and broadcaster Anthony Summers in the mid-1990s. Former commission staff members told the author of this book they had long heard rumors about Coleman's meeting with the Cuban leader. Asked about the rumors, Coleman confirmed to the author that they were true. He said he made no mention of the Castro meeting in his own memoirs, published in 2010, because he understood the information was still classified.

to earn his place in the history of the civil rights movement. In 1949, he was asked by Thurgood Marshall—then chief counsel of the NAACP Legal Defense Fund and later a justice of the Supreme Court—to become involved in court challenges to end segregation of the nation's public schools. Before long, Coleman was asked to help write briefs to be presented to the court on behalf of black families in Kansas who were seeking to desegregate the public schools of Topeka, the case that became *Brown v. Board of Education*. When it came time for Marshall to argue the case in front of the Supreme Court in December 1953, he invited Coleman, then thirty-three, to sit next to him at the counsel's table.

In 1952, Coleman finally realized his dream of going to work for a large Philadelphia law firm. His hiring as an associate by the firm of Dilworth, Paxson, Kalish & Green led a group of white secretaries to threaten to resign at the thought of working with a black man. As Coleman recalled it, the firm's senior partner ended the protest by telling the secretaries that they could leave if they wanted, because "we can find someone almost as good to replace you." Coleman, he said, could not be easily replaced. "Once you get to know him, you'll find he's a decent human being." The secretaries stayed.

Years later, Coleman said he had forgotten many of the details of his trip to meet Castro's yacht—whether the American captain and the sailors were armed, for example—but he did remember stepping onto the Cuban's boat and catching his first glimpse in years of the bearded Castro. The Cuban leader recognized Coleman at once and greeted him as a friend. "He certainly knew I'd met him up in New York. . . . It was a pretty animated conversation."

The meeting lasted for about three hours, with Coleman pressing Castro on every possible scenario in which the Cuban government might have been involved in Kennedy's assassination, even indirectly. Castro denied any Cuban tie to the president's murder. In fact, Coleman recalled, "he said he admired President Kennedy." Despite the Bay of Pigs invasion and all of the Kennedy administration's other efforts to force him from power, even to kill him, Castro insisted that he "still didn't think ill" of Kennedy.

Ever the careful lawyer, Coleman did not accept Castro's denials as the truth, and he said he left the meeting unsure of anything. On returning to Washington, all he could offer Rankin and Warren was his judgment that he had heard nothing that undermined Castro's declaration of his innocence in Kennedy's death. "I'm not saying he didn't do it," Coleman said. "But I came back and I said that I hadn't found out anything that would cause me to think there's proof he *did* do it."

Earl Warren insisted to his colleagues on the commission that he never leaked information about the investigation. By late spring, however, somebody was leaking, and in detail, about the likelihood that the commission would conclude that Oswald had acted alone. The leaks first went to Anthony Lewis, the Supreme Court correspondent of the *New York Times*, who was close to Warren and Rankin from his years of covering them at the court. In 1963, Lewis won a Pulitzer Prize for his coverage of the court; in June 1964, his book *Gideon's Trumpet*, a history of the landmark Supreme Court case *Gideon v. Wainwright*, was published. The book was effusive in its praise of the chief justice and Rankin for their roles in the case, in which the Warren Court ruled that indigent criminal defendants had to be provided with free lawyers.

Within days of the book's publication, the *Times* carried a front-page story by Lewis about the Warren Commission, with the headline: PANEL TO REJECT THEORIES OF PLOT IN KENNEDY DEATH. The article said the commission's final report, still months from completion, was expected "to support the original belief of law-enforcement authorities in this country that the president was killed by one man acting alone, Lee H. Oswald." Much of the story was written without attribution, as if the information was unquestioned fact. Lewis reported that "a spokesman for the commission," unnamed in the article, confirmed that the commission would debunk the many conspiracy theories about the assassination, especially those being spread by Mark Lane. Although it was impossible to identify the "spokesman" with certainty, Rankin's personal calendars show he met with Lewis in the commission's offices for nearly forty minutes, three days before the article appeared. Similar leaked articles quickly appeared in other newspapers.

The stories outraged Ford. He saw the leaks as an effort by someone within the commission to manipulate the outcome of the investigation before all the facts were in. It had become a constant complaint among Ford's behind-the-scenes advisers, who worried that the commission—Warren, in particular—was still ignoring evidence that might point to a Communist conspiracy. Ford requested an urgent meeting to make his protests known, and Warren scheduled it for Thursday, June 4. The leaks were the only item on the agenda. Warren, Dulles, and McCloy attended the meeting, along with Ford.

Warren immediately turned the meeting over to Ford, who warned somberly that there appeared to be a mole among them. "In my judgment, somebody somewhere is planting or leaking these stories," he said, adding that he thought he knew who the leaker was. "I have some personal conclusions, but I cannot prove them, so I don't want to make any allegations." He said the leaks were designed to prejudge the commission's findings. "They are creating an atmosphere throughout the country that will, I think, create a predetermined public opinion of what we may or may not have come to," he said. "I don't like being quoted when I have not made any final judgment."

Warren tried to reassure Ford. "As far as I am concerned, I share your feelings exactly," he said. "I am inclined to think that most of this comes from thin air and from speculation. I have no knowledge of anybody talking to anybody." Ford urged that the commission release a public statement denying it had reached any conclusions. Warren and the others quickly agreed. A brief statement went out to reporters the next day, saying that the commission was nearing the end of its investigation but "is giving thought to the content and form of the report" and had reached no findings.

One more round of witnesses would be called to testify in Washington before the investigation ended. Some who had already appeared needed to be called back after it became clear that their credibility was in doubt. Few faced more doubts about their truthfulness than Marina Oswald and Mark Lane; both were recalled to explain gaps in their earlier sworn appearances.

In the four months since she had first testified, the perception of Marina's honesty and her larger character had shifted dramatically among the commissioners, and for the worse. Since her appearance in February, the commission had heard the many unflattering reports about her seemingly carefree romantic life and her hard drinking. (The FBI had continued to bug her house, including her bedroom.) "She became a chain-smoker and a drinker of straight vodka," William Manchester would later write in his book. The commissioners had more substantive concerns about whether she had perjured herself in her earlier testimony, especially in her denial that she had known in advance about her husband's plans to kill the president. That denial was now in question with the discovery that she had told both her business manager and her brother-in-law—but not the commission—about her husband's plot to kill Nixon. Staff lawyers on the commission now suspected that if Oswald had told his wife about his plans to kill Nixon and Walker, he would also have told her about his plan to kill Kennedy.

Marina Oswald returned to the commission's offices on Thursday, June 11. This time, there was no statement from Warren to welcome her or to express gratitude for her testimony. There was no grandfatherly concern for her welfare and that of her children. The questioning, led by Rankin, often bordered on hostile.

Rankin: "Mrs. Oswald, we would like to have you tell about the incident in regard to Mr. Nixon."

Marina seemed to understand how much trouble she was in. "I am very sorry I didn't mention this before," she began, speaking through a Russian translator. "I had forgotten entirely about the incident with Vice President Nixon when I was here the first time. I wasn't trying to deceive you."

Ford pressed her: "Can you tell us why you didn't mention this incident?"

Marina: "I was very tired and felt that I had told everything."

She then offered what she said was the full story about the Nixon threat—how in mid-April 1963, several days after her husband's assassination attempt on Walker, Oswald told her that he was about to go to the street in search of Richard Nixon. Oswald, she said, claimed that Nixon was visiting Dallas that day. He grabbed the pistol he kept in the house and said, "I will go out and have a look and perhaps I won't use my gun. But if there is a convenient opportunity, perhaps I will." She said she was terrified by the threat and attempted to lock her husband in the bathroom to prevent him from leaving. "We actually struggled for several minutes and then he quieted down," she said. "I remember that I told him that if he goes out, it would be better for him to kill me."

Even as she tried to explain away the gaps in her earlier testimony, Marina was creating new confusion, especially since the commission's staff determined that Nixon did not visit Dallas in April 1963. Some of the commissioners questioned whether she was confusing former vice president Nixon with then vice president Lyndon Johnson, who had been in Dallas that month. She was certain she was not confused, however. "I remember distinctly the name Nixon," she said. "I never heard of Johnson before he became president."

Allen Dulles put the question to her: If her husband had tried to kill Walker and threatened to kill Nixon, "didn't it occur to you then that there was danger that he would use these weapons against someone else? He never made any statement against President Kennedy?"

"Never," she replied. "He always had a favorable feeling about President Kennedy."

She made a new plea for the commission's sympathy. She tried to explain away her failure to warn the police—or anyone else—that her husband was capable of political violence. She had remained silent, she said, because she had been terrified that her husband might someday be arrested and jailed, abandoning her in a country in which she had no family and few friends. She wanted to remain in the United States and worried that she might be deported to Russia if she turned her husband in. "Lee was the only person who was supporting me," she said. "I didn't have any friends, I didn't speak any English and I couldn't work and I didn't know what would happen if they locked him up."

Her husband had been taunting her for months with the possibility that she would be forced to return to Russia without him, she said. He had a "sadistic" streak and made her "write letters to the Russian embassy stating that I wanted to go back to Russia," she said. "He liked to tease me and torment me in this way. . . . He made me several times write such letters." Over her protests, he then mailed the letters. She said she had resigned herself to the possibility of a bleak return to her homeland. "I mean if my husband didn't want me to live with him any longer and wanted me to go back, I would go back," she said. "I didn't have any choice."

By Thursday, July 2, the date of Mark Lane's second and final appearance before the commission, he was as well known to the American public as most of the commissioners. At the age of thirty-seven, Lane was now a celebrity, with admirers around the world eager to hear him explain how Lee Harvey Oswald had been framed and how the chief justice was covering up the truth. When the commission forced Lane to return to Washington under threat of a subpoena, he had to cut short a tour of Europe, where he was giving speeches and raising money.

The commission's stated reason for calling him to testify a second time was to demand that he reveal the source of some of his more shocking allegations, especially his claim of a meeting in Ruby's Carousel Club a week before the assassination that was attended by Officer J. D. Tippit and a prominent anti-Kennedy activist. The commission's staff had found nothing to back up the rumor, nor had any of the reporters in Dallas who had all heard it from the same drunken Texas lawyer who had been peddling the story for months. The commission was also still trying to resolve the confusion over Lane's claim that Dallas waitress Helen Markham, one of the witnesses to Tippit's murder, had backed away from her identification of Oswald as the killer.

After taking his seat at the witness table, Lane wasted no time: he made it clear that he would answer none of the commission's central questions and declared that there was no way to force him to.

Warren appeared to struggle to contain his anger. Unless Lane offered up his sources, "we have every reason to doubt the truthfulness of what you have heretofore told us," the chief justice told Lane, effectively accusing the young lawyer of perjury. Lane felt free to conduct his own "inquisition" into the assassination and repeat any outrageous rumor he came across, Warren said. "You have done nothing but handicap us."

Lane was defiant: "I have not said anything in public, Mr. Chief Justice, that I have not said first before this commission. . . . When I speak before an audience, I do hold myself out to be telling the truth, just as when I have testified before this commission, I have also told the truth." With Lane, the commission would get no further.

PART 3
THE REPORT

Chief Justice Warren delivers the
commission's report to President Johnson,
September 24, 1964

44

Warren's devoted wife, Nina, worried most of all. She said that the chief justice, who had turned seventy-three in March, was working so hard that he had put his health at risk. Through the spring, the commission's work had soaked up every free minute of his day and night away from the court. Late each evening, before sleeping, he sat up in bed and tried to make his way through a growing stack of transcripts of the testimony of recent witnesses before the commission.

In the decade since he had arrived in Washington, Warren tried to stay in good shape. He liked to swim for exercise. Drew Pearson thought the beefy, white-haired chief justice resembled an aging but contented sea lion as he glided through the water. For most of 1964, though, Warren had to give up his late-afternoon visits to the pool at Washington's University Club; there was simply no time. "The Warren Commission was a drag on him," said Bart Cavanaugh, the former city manager of Sacramento, California, and one of Warren's closest friends. "It was an awful strain." Cavanaugh visited the Warrens in Washington that spring. "Mrs. Warren said he was awfully worn down, that he'd lost considerable weight." She urged Cavanaugh to help take her husband's mind off his work by getting him out of town. "Mrs. Warren said, 'Why don't the two of you sneak off and go to New York for the weekend?' and we did," Cavanaugh said. "We drove up to New York, went to the ball game." But the next week, back in Washington, the pressure of Warren's two full-time jobs returned.

His aggravation rose as each of the deadlines he set for the commission's work slipped. He had begun to worry that he would not get any summer vacation at all that year. As of early June, only the ever-efficient Arlen Specter—operating without help or hindrance from his long-departed senior partner, Francis Adams—had finished a draft of his portion of the report, outlining the events of the day of the assassination. Most of the other teams had known for weeks that the deadlines were hopeless.

The chief justice had stopped hiding his anger over the delays. Slawson remembered Warren's fury when his initial June deadlines were not met. On May 29, the last Friday in May, Rankin realized that Warren would have to be told, once and for all, that the staff would fail to meet the deadline the following Monday—June 1—for completing draft chapters of the report. As Rankin prepared to go home for the weekend, he asked Willens to break the news: "You had better tell the chief it won't be ready." The chief justice was "furious," Slawson recalled. Willens said he thought Warren's anger was understandable. For most of his life, after all, the chief justice had controlled his own schedule, as well as the schedule of the people who worked for him. Now, his schedule was at the mercy of a group of young lawyers, most of whom he barely knew. He felt he was "a prisoner of the staff," Willens said.

Warren, who normally escaped Washington every July and August to avoid the capital's swamp-like heat, shortened his vacation to a month. He planned to leave on July 2 to go fishing in his beloved Norway, his family's ancestral home, and to return in early August, in time to oversee the final writing of the report. Before departing, he got around to answering some of the scolding letters he had been receiving all year from prominent lawyers around the country who wanted to tell him how wrong he had been to accept the job of running the commission. In his belated replies, Warren told his critics that they were right and that he had taken the assignment only because President Johnson insisted. "I share your view that it is not the business of members of the Court to accept outside assignments," Warren wrote to Carl Shipley, a Washington securities lawyer. "I had expressed myself both in and out of Court circles to that effect." In explaining why he had taken the job, Warren cited a favorite quotation from President Grover Cleveland: "Sometimes, as you know, we are faced with—as Grover Cleveland said—a condition and not a theory. In this situation, the President so impressed me with the gravity of the situation at the moment that I felt in good conscience I could not refuse."

The Supreme Court had just completed another eventful term, with the justices deciding several landmark cases, including *New York Times v. Sullivan*, a unanimous decision announced in March in which the court struck a blow for both free speech and civil rights. The ruling weakened the ability of public officials to use libel laws to punish journalists; at the time, the laws were being used to bankrupt news organizations reporting on civil rights abuses in the South. On June 22, in *Escobedo v. Illinois*, the court held that criminal suspects had a right to counsel during police interrogations—an extension of the protections granted to criminal defendants in the unanimous *Gideon v. Wainwright* decision the year before. Unlike the Sullivan and Gideon cases, Escobedo had been a close call: the ruling had a bare 5-4 majority. The one-vote margin suggested to some lawyers that Warren's campaign to expand the rights of criminal defendants was losing momentum.

Warren said later that he had always understood it would be difficult to achieve unanimity on the commission—to bridge differences among seven men who, in other circumstances, would agree on almost nothing. "Politically, we had as many opposites as the number of people would permit," he recalled. "I am sure that I was anathema to Senator Russell because of the court's racial decisions." He was struck by how much hostility there was between Democratic congressman Boggs and Republican congressman Ford: "They were not congenial—there was no camaraderie between them." The chief justice had much more respect for Boggs than for Ford, even if Boggs was far less active in the investigation. "Boggs was a good commissioner," the chief justice said. "He approached things objectively. I found him very helpful." Boggs also had the nicer disposition, he thought. "Boggs was friendly and Ford was antagonistic." Warren said he came to have great respect for the common sense of John McCloy, who seemed always to rise above partisanship. "He was objective and extremely helpful." And despite Allen Dulles's eccentricity and tendency to nap during meetings, he was "also very helpful . . . he was a little bit garrulous, but he worked hard and was a good member."

By late spring, Warren thought he had won over most of the commissioners to his conviction that Oswald acted alone. "The non-conspiracy theory was probably the basic decision of the case." The most outspoken holdout, he said, was Ford, who continued to suggest the possibility that Oswald had been part of a conspiracy, probably somehow involving Cuba. "Ford wanted to go off on a tangent following a Communist plot," Warren remembered. He also could not be sure where Russell would come out, given how little the senator had been involved in the investigation.

The work of drafting the report was left almost entirely to the staff, which was typical for a federal blue-ribbon commission. Warren and the commissioners decided they would weigh in after they were presented with draft chapters. As he had long planned, Redlich, now secure in his job thanks to the chief justice, assumed the role of the report's central editor, working with Willens and Alfred Goldberg. Rankin reserved for himself the final decisions about the editing, at least until the drafts reached the commissioners. His goal, he said, was to edit the report for a uniform, sober style and to stick as much as possible to the facts of the case against Oswald, without overstating them. "I wanted everything to be as precise as possible," he recalled. Staff members who wanted to complain about the way their chapters had been rewritten would automatically be granted an audience, Rankin announced.

Among the lawyers, the broad outlines of the report had been known for weeks: the commission would conclude that Oswald had assassinated President Kennedy and probably acted alone. The principal debate was over how forcefully to state those conclusions and whether the commission should acknowledge that there was evidence that was inconclusive about Oswald's guilt. The lawyers would have to decide, for example, how and whether to mention testimony from witnesses at Dealey Plaza who were convinced that bullets had been fired at Kennedy's limousine from the front instead from the Texas School Book Depository to the rear.

For the first time, Rankin began to worry seriously about the budget and how the commission would pay for the publication of what was likely to be a mammoth final report, accompanied by several additional volumes of witness testimony. For the first several months of the investigation, President Johnson had been true to his word: the White House had provided whatever money and other resources the commission needed. Tens of thousands of dollars would be transferred to the commission's bank accounts on the basis of little more than a brief phone call to the White House from one of Rankin's secretaries. "We received any money we needed, and we were never at any time told that we were to limit ourselves," Rankin recalled with gratitude.

But after meeting with the Government Printing Office that spring, Rankin was startled by the estimate of the cost of publishing the full report and the additional volumes: at least $1 million. "When I told the Chief Justice that, he was very much shocked," Rankin said.

"My, we can't spend money like that," the notoriously frugal Warren said.

Rankin reminded Warren of the commission's vow of transparency. It was important, Rankin said, for the commission to publish not only its final report, but as much of the testimony and evidence as possible.

"Well, that is up to Congress," Warren replied, refusing to approve the budget by himself. "I don't know whether they will approve anything like that or spend the money." He directed Rankin to talk to the four members of Congress on the commission and ask if they could convince their colleagues in the House and Senate to approve the expenditure.

Rankin began with Russell, who, as chairman of the Senate Armed Services Committee, oversaw billions of dollars a year of federal spending on military programs.

"How much is it going to cost?" Russell asked.

Rankin told him $1 million.

Russell promised to come up with the money. "You go right ahead," he told Rankin. "We will get that money for you." To a senator who oversaw the budget of the Defense Department, $1 million was barely a rounding error.

Rankin asked Russell if he needed to consult separately with the other lawmakers: Boggs, Ford, and Cooper. "I will talk to them," Russell said. "We will get the money."

Rankin was also anxious that spring about all the empty desks in the commission's offices. David Belin had returned home to Iowa in late May, and Leon Hubert was gone days after that. Arlen Specter would stop working full-time in Washington in June, after finishing his draft chapter. Among the junior lawyers who had been there from the start, only

Griffin, Liebeler, and Slawson would still be at their desks most days that summer, along with a dozen or so secretaries and other clerical workers. If the final report was ever going to get done, Rankin knew, he needed to hire more lawyers, and fast. Warren agreed to dispatch several Supreme Court clerks to help out, and to begin the process of double-checking information and preparing footnotes for the report. Justice Arthur Goldberg allowed one of his clerks, twenty-five-year-old Harvard Law School graduate Stephen G. Breyer, to join the commission's staff temporarily.*

Rankin wanted a new, full-time assistant, given how busy he assumed Redlich and Willens would be with the actual writing of the report. On May 12, his twenty-fourth birthday, Columbia Law School student Murray Laulicht got a phone call in New York, asking him to report to Washington immediately for a job interview. Laulicht, a third-year student who was just about to graduate, first in his class, was free to go, he remembered; that same day he had taken his last law-school exam—on trusts and estates. He was in Rankin's office the next morning and was offered a job on the spot. "Rankin wanted me to start that day," he said, recalling his shock at the abruptness of the offer. He "begged" Rankin for an additional few days. "I didn't bring any clothes," he remembered telling Rankin. "I promise you the night I graduate from law school, I will come down here."

They compromised. Laulicht agreed to start work on June 4, the day after he was handed his diploma. "So literally the night I graduated from Columbia, I went back down there" to Washington. His new colleagues welcomed Laulicht; he brought fresh eyes to the evidence about the assassination they had been analyzing for months. And what he told them was reassuring. After reviewing several draft chapters of the report, he sensed the commission was right to conclude that Oswald acted alone. He listened to the debates about the single-bullet theory, and the theory sounded logical to him.

He was excited to be working in Washington, if also daunted—as an observant Jew—for cultural reasons. The city did not make it easy for anyone who followed a kosher diet; he recalled ordering a fruit salad at a restaurant near the commission's office and discovering it was served with Jell-O, which was barred under Jewish dietary laws, since the gelatin was made with animal by-products. For the rest of the summer, "I ate

---

* Breyer would join the Supreme Court as an associate justice in 1994.

a lot of potato chips and things like that." In the commission's offices, he was amazed by the discovery of a machine straight out of science fiction—"a phenomenal new technology called a Xerox machine." He was so impressed that he urged his family back in New Jersey to invest in the company. "My mother bought some Xerox stock and she did very well with it."

Rankin had an early assignment for Laulicht. He was asked to help Burt Griffin complete the investigation of Jack Ruby—specifically, to write Ruby's biography, which would then be included in the report. From what he read of the evidence, Laulicht said he had no trouble believing that Ruby's murder of Oswald was impulsive and that he had acted alone. "He was just hot-headed enough to do this." Ruby was so obsessed with avenging Kennedy that he might be compared to a Holocaust survivor, Laulicht thought. "It's what a survivor might do if he saw a Nazi."

Laulicht's knowledge of Jewish culture came in helpful in resolving a lingering mystery about Ruby. Griffin and Hubert, who were not Jewish, had been unable to understand the origins of Ruby's childhood nickname—"Yank," or something that sounded like that when uttered by Ruby's Yiddish-speaking neighbors back in Chicago. Was it short for Yankee, a reference to some strong pro-American views that Ruby held as a child? No, Laulicht could see. Ruby's real nickname was "Yunk," a shortened version of the Yiddish translation for the name Jack—"Yunkle." Mystery solved, Laulicht said.

Another late arrival to the staff, twenty-seven-year-old Lloyd Weinreb, two years out of Harvard Law School, was much less excited than Laulicht to be there. After completing a term as a Supreme Court clerk to Justice John Marshall Harlan, Weinreb had been hired that summer at the Justice Department's Criminal Division, and assigned to work for Howard Willens. Since Willens was still on assignment to the commission, he asked Weinreb to come help out on the investigation. "He asked me if I would come over there for a few weeks, which I very much did not want to do," Weinreb remembered. But because Willens "was going to be my boss, I thought it would be injudicious to say no."

Weinreb was alarmed from the moment he arrived in the VFW building. He could see all the empty desks, and he quickly learned from the remaining lawyers how much work remained to be done. "I remember having a sense of an office where everyone was springing for the hills," with these few "poor suckers left behind," he recalled. It would prove to be a "perfectly awful job," with the staff expected to work fourteen- or fifteen-hour days, seven days a week, throughout the summer until the report was finished. He was startled to discover that the offices were not air-conditioned on weekends, despite temperatures that could sometimes reach one hundred degrees in Washington at the height of summer. "It was a lousy building," he said. "It was miserable. I think a lot of the poor quality of the Warren reports comes from these very banal things."

He was given the assignment of writing Oswald's biography, which would then be published in the final report. The biography had originally been the responsibility of Albert Jenner, but Jenner had proved incapable of finishing it, given his obsession with confirming the tiniest details of Oswald's life story. "Jenner was still tracking down utterly remote leads," Weinreb said. "He could not let go of it." Jenner, he said, "simply had no conception of what doing history was. His idea was that anyone mentioned anywhere—maybe a fifth cousin whom Oswald had never seen—had to be checked out."

Weinreb had a strong sense that, by midsummer, it was Willens who was holding the investigation together, taking on responsibilities that should have been Rankin's. "Howard was essentially in charge of the staff at that point," he said. "Willens was a vastly more powerful person intellectually than Rankin," he said. "Rankin seemed to be a middle-level bureaucrat." Weinreb had no contact with Warren, which was no surprise given what he already knew of the chief justice's "protective perimeters" in dealing with his clerks and clerical staff back at the court.

Weinreb did find the job of writing the biography interesting. He said he first went in search of all of the background reports on Oswald's life, including the top secret files from the CIA about his time in Russia. It was the first time Weinreb had seen classified national-security documents. "I remember having a sense of wow, this is cloak and dagger stuff." Most of the biographical material on Oswald was found in large files—four or five inches thick—that had been compiled from FBI and CIA reports. As he started to page through them, though, Weinreb detected a problem. Much of the paperwork he expected to find was missing, apparently taken by other staff members while writing their own parts of the report. "There was absolutely no order to the evidence," he said. Some staff lawyers appeared to be hoarding files for fear they might otherwise disappear into someone else's desk. "You literally walked around the halls to see if you could get a hold of something and then you hid it in your bottom drawer to maintain possession. You put it in your bottom drawer because you didn't want anybody else to take it."

Weinreb did not agonize over the actual writing of the biography; he had been known to his fellow Supreme Court clerks as an elegant, and quick, writer. He prided himself on not needing to rewrite his work; his first draft was usually his final draft. And he did not agonize, he said, over the question of whether Oswald had killed the president and whether Oswald had been part of a conspiracy. From all that he could see in the commission's files, Oswald appeared to be the lone assassin. Weinreb could understand why the conspiracy theories had developed, but the evidence against Oswald was overwhelming, he said. "It would have taken a lot to make me think otherwise."

Richard Mosk began making plans to leave the commission's staff in mid-August; he had been called back to duty by the air national guard. Before departing, he completed a detailed study of Oswald's marksmanship skills. He did not have trouble believing that Oswald had the ability to fire the shots that killed Kennedy and hit Connally. The Mannlicher-Carcano rifle was "a very accurate weapon," Mosk wrote.

Mosk reviewed the testimony taken from four expert marksmen, including that of Major Eugene Anderson, assistant head of the Marksmanship Branch of the U.S. Marine Corps. He testified that the shots that struck Kennedy's neck and head were not "particularly difficult," especially given how slowly the president's motorcade was moving. An FBI firearms specialist, Robert Frazier, told the commission that Oswald would "not have any difficult hitting" his targets, especially since his rifle had been equipped with a telescopic sight. "I mean it requires no training at all to shoot a weapon with a telescopic sight," Frazier said. A gunman would simply "put the crosshairs on the target" and pull the trigger. "That is all that is necessary."

45

THE HOME OF SILVIA ODIO
DALLAS, TEXAS
JULY 1964

That summer, Silvia Odio was trying to get on with her life. The twenty-seven-year-old Cuban refugee said she had mostly kept quiet about what had happened back in December, when two FBI agents showed up unannounced at the offices of the chemical company where she worked. They wanted her to tell them the story that she had told a few friends, about how Oswald and two young Latino men had appeared on the doorstep of her Dallas apartment before the assassination. Odio had been alarmed by the way the FBI agents had contacted her—by sending agents to her office instead of her home—and the visit had upset her boss. "It brought a lot of problems in my work," she said later. "You know how people were afraid at the time. My company, some officials of it, were quite concerned that the FBI should have come to see me." And after the December interview, she said she heard nothing from the FBI. For the bureau then to completely dismiss her story—the one also told by her teenage sister, Annie—was perplexing and insulting.

In June, however, she learned that the Warren Commission might be taking her account more seriously. Wesley Liebeler called from Washington and asked if she would be available to give sworn testimony when he visited Dallas later that summer. She agreed, although she told him she continued to worry that her story, if it became public, might somehow endanger her parents, who remained in custody in Cuba as political prisoners. Her father, Amador, had been a prominent businessman there in the 1950s—he was described by *Time* as his country's "transport tycoon"—and become an outspoken opponent of Castro. He had been a leader of a relatively moderate anti-Castro group known as JURE, or Junta Revolucionaria Cubana. In exile, Silvia remained a member of JURE.

Liebeler planned to set off on his trip to see Odio and other witnesses in Dallas and New Orleans as soon as he completed his draft chapter of the commission's report—an analysis of Oswald's possible motives for killing the president. He turned in the ninety-eight-page draft on June 23. In it, he offered his judgment that Oswald had not begun to think about killing Kennedy until shortly before the assassination, maybe only hours earlier, and probably not before Tuesday, November 19, the day Kennedy's motorcade route was first announced in Dallas newspapers.

He acknowledged in the report that no one could say with certainty why Oswald killed Kennedy. Instead, he offered a list of possible motives, tying together Oswald's troubled childhood, his oft-stated desire for global fame, and his commitment to Marxism and to Castro's revolution in Cuba. "Lee Harvey Oswald was a man profoundly alienated from the world in which he lived," Liebeler wrote. "He never seemed to be able to relate meaningfully to any part of it. His life was characterized by isolation, frustration, suspicion, failure at almost everything he ever tried to do, and, increasingly, by a system of delusion and fantasy designed to protect himself from his own failure and impotence." Oswald's Marxism made him hostile to American government leaders and "increased his alienation from society around him."

Even as he wrote those words, however, Liebeler admitted to colleagues on the commission's staff that he could be wrong and that there might be evidence of a conspiracy that they had missed. He was especially troubled, he said, by the many gaps in the commission's knowledge about Oswald's activities in the months before the assassination. He knew how troubled Slawson was about the inability of the FBI and CIA to account for whole days of Oswald's trip to Mexico; there were similar gaps in the time line of his activities in New Orleans and in Dallas. And Silvia Odio's account, if true, meant that Oswald was traveling in the company of anti-Castro exiles weeks before the assassination and that he might have talked openly of his desire to see President Kennedy dead.

* * *

Liebeler went first to New Orleans, where he was welcomed with the blast of heat and humidity that explained the common wisdom that only the crazy, the poor, and the air-conditioned wealthy remained in "the Big Easy" in the summertime. The city, Oswald's birthplace, had been his home again for several months beginning in April 1963; Marina thought he went there because he feared arrest in Texas as a result of his failed attempt to assassinate Edwin Walker.

It was in New Orleans that Oswald had first tried to make a name for himself as a public champion of Castro's revolution and to identify himself with the Fair Play for Cuba Committee. That spring, Oswald purported to set up the committee's New Orleans branch. He used one of his aliases—Lee Osborne—to print up membership forms, as well as pamphlets bearing the slogan "Hands Off Cuba."

At the same time, it appeared that Oswald was making attempts in New Orleans to infiltrate anti-Castro groups, possibly to gather intelligence that he could later share with the Cuban government in a demonstration of his loyalty to Castro. On August 5, the FBI determined, Oswald visited Carlos Bringuier, a Cuban-born lawyer who was active in the anti-Castro movement, and asked to join the exiles' struggle.* Bringuier told the FBI that Oswald identified himself as a former marine who had guerrilla training. The day after their first meeting, he gave Bringuier his Marine Corps handbook as proof of his military background.

If Oswald was in fact attempting to infiltrate anti-Castro groups, that mission came to a violent end a few days later, when Bringuier and two other Cuban exiles encountered him on a street corner as he handed out Fair Play for Cuba flyers. A fight broke out, leading to Oswald's arrest. Oswald, who spent the night in jail, asked to speak to an FBI agent, seemingly to create an official record at the bureau of what he was doing. He told the agent that he belonged to the Fair Play for Cuba Committee and that the president of the local chapter was a man he identified as A. J. Hidell—the alias that he would use to purchase his Mannlicher-

---

* Members of Bringuier's militant anti-Castro group, the Directorio Revolucionario Estudiantil ("Revolutionary Student Directorate"), or DRE, participated in the Bay of Pigs operation. Although its leaders were known to be especially bitter toward President Kennedy for his failure to oust Castro, the group continued to accept money and other support from the U.S. government, most of it funneled through the CIA. (House Select Committee on Assassinations, vol. X, "Anti-Castro Activities," March 1979).

Carcano rifle. Marina Oswald said she thought her husband used the alias Hidell because it rhymed with Fidel. Liebeler had taken Bringuier's testimony in New Orleans in April and found him credible.

During his return in July, Liebeler met with others in New Orleans who, he believed, had far less credibility but who still needed to be interviewed to be certain that the commission's record was complete. This included Dean Andrews Jr., a colorful, small-time lawyer who seemed to live in a perpetual state of Mardi Gras. Even in exotic New Orleans, he was hard to miss, both because of his appearance—he was obese and wore sunglasses constantly, including indoors—and from his unusual speaking style. He talked in the language of a Cajun hipster; a stylish man was a "swinging cat" and a good bar was a "freaky joint."

Within days of the Kennedy assassination, Andrews had contacted the FBI to report that Oswald had visited his law office in the summer of 1963, seeking help in reversing his "undesirable" discharge from the Marine Corps. That part of Andrew's story made sense to the FBI and to the Warren Commission, since they knew Oswald had been agitated over the less-than-honorable discharge. Andrews's tale to the FBI went well beyond that, however. Oswald, he said, had visited his office in the company of a trio of young homosexual Latinos—"three gay boys"—and appeared to be a homosexual himself. "He swang with the kids," Andrews said. "He didn't swish, but birds of a feather flock together."

And Oswald appeared to have a mysterious patron in New Orleans. Only hours after the assassination, Andrews claimed, he received a phone call from a local lawyer he knew by the name of Clay Bertrand, who was somehow connected to the "three gay boys" and who was himself known to be bisexual, and who asked Andrews to go to Dallas immediately to defend Oswald. The commission had pressed the FBI to follow up on Andrews's account, especially to track down Bertrand, but the bureau said it could find no evidence to suggest that Bertrand even existed. Also, Andrews's description of Bertrand had kept changing, including on Tuesday, July 21, when he gave sworn testimony to Liebeler.

Liebeler asked him, once again, to give a physical description of Bertrand.

"He is about 5 feet 8 inches. Got sandy hair, blue eyes, ruddy complexion," Andrews replied.

Liebeler looked back at the FBI reports of its interviews with Andrews and could see that he had initially described Bertrand's height as six foot one or six foot two. How could Bertrand be half a foot shorter than Andrews had originally estimated?

"I am guessing now," Andrews conceded.*

Liebeler took what he thought of as more useful testimony that same day from a Cuban-American bartender, Evaristo Rodriguez, who had told the FBI that Oswald had visited his bar on Decatur Street, the Habana Bar, sometime in 1963. Oswald had been in the company of two other men, one of them clearly a Latino. Rodriguez recalled that Oswald appeared to be drunk and "draped himself" over the bar before ordering a lemonade. The Latin man ordered tequila. "So I told him the price of the tequila was 50 cents," Rodriguez said. "The man protested at the price, thought it was too high, and he made some statement to the effect that he was a Cuban . . . and words to the effect that surely the owner of this bar must be a capitalist."

Although other witnesses insisted that Oswald never drank heavily after his return from Russia, Liebeler was struck that he might have been in the bar in the company of a Cuban who was so outspoken in sharing Oswald's anticapitalist views. He asked for a physical description of the Cuban. Rodriguez said he thought the man was in his late twenties and that he had an irregular hairline; he was balding in an unusual way at the front of his head. Liebeler remembered that in her earlier interviews with the FBI, Silvia Odio had described one of the Latin men traveling with Oswald—"Leopoldo"—as having an unusual bald spot at the front of his head.

---

* Dean Andrews's testimony might have been easily ignored had it not been for New Orleans district attorney Jim Garrison, who would claim in 1967 that Clay Bertrand was an alias used by a respected local businessman, Clay Shaw, who was then prosecuted by Garrison for involvement in Kennedy's assassination. Long before Shaw's acquittal, the case was seen as a shocking display of prosecutorial misconduct. Even so, Garrison, as portrayed by the actor Kevin Costner, was the hero of Oliver Stone's 1991 film *JFK*, about the Kennedy assassination. Andrews would be portrayed by the comedian John Candy.

46

For months, the FBI had been aware of reports that the commission was mishandling classified documents. Gerald Ford had been the first to come under suspicion, with the rumors that he was leaking secret files, and maybe even selling them, all of which he furiously denied. The first documented case of a serious security breach by a commissioner centered on Congressman Boggs, who left a copy of a top secret White House document about the assassination on the front seat of his government-issued Mercury sedan in April. Boggs had parked the car, which had markings to show that it was assigned to his House office, at Baltimore's Friendship International Airport, not far from Washington. A Pennsylvania man who parked in front of the car noticed the document in the front seat, clearly stamped TOP SECRET, and he called the FBI. The car doors were unlocked, the man could see.

Wesley Liebeler's breach was far more serious than Boggs's, however, because it was so brazen—and because it was brought directly to the attention of J. Edgar Hoover. The FBI chief learned of the security violation in a letter sent to him by name in June from a retired U.S. naval officer from Wilmette, Illinois, James R. David, who wanted to report what he had witnessed aboard a Northeast Airlines flight from Keene, New Hampshire, to New York, on May 31, the Sunday of the Memorial

Day weekend. David was seated in one of two seats at the far rear of the plane. The flight was full, and the last seat was taken a man who had "red hair, a red face and a rather full red beard." David was unable to determine the man's name, but he "carried a slim black attaché case" embossed with the initials W.J.L.

Almost as soon as the red-haired man took his seat, David wrote, he opened the case and pulled out a report with a cover identifying it as "U.S. Department of Justice, Copy No. 10 of 10, The President's Commission on the Assassination of President Kennedy." David said he was astonished as the man then began—"indiscreetly"—to page through what was clearly a highly classified document. "Each page was identified at the top and bottom in large block red letters TOP SECRET," David wrote. "Without too much difficulty I could have read most of this report. However, because of the security classification of this document, I had no interest in doing so—with the exception that for further identification, I attempted to memorize one sentence which occurred at the top of page 412 and read, to the best of my memory, as follows:

"Mr. Rankin: 'Did he take money from the wallet from time to time?'
"Mrs. Oswald: 'No.'"

It took the FBI no time to determine that the red-haired man was Liebeler, who was on the flight, returning to New York from his country home in Vermont.

Hoover passed on the information to Rankin, apparently leaving it to the commission—at least for the moment—to decide how to deal with Liebeler. And Hoover sent a personal thank-you note to David for alerting the FBI to what he had seen in the plane. Hoover's files show that a background check was conducted on David to be certain he was not himself a security risk. The check found no derogatory information.

Other staff lawyers said they were only vaguely aware of the incident, which Rankin appeared eager to keep quiet for fear that it could become a scandal; certainly he might have feared that Hoover would leak news of the security breach at an opportune moment for the bureau. Slawson said he understood that Liebeler was "just bawled out, very, very strongly" by Rankin and that "Warren let him know, through Rankin, he was extremely displeased." None of the staff lawyers remembered Liebeler as being especially alarmed over the incident.

He would be far more anxious, his colleagues said, about how the commission intended to rewrite, or even to scrap, his draft chapter about

Oswald's motives in killing the president. He had slaved over the draft for weeks, and now—largely at Redlich's insistence, he thought—most of his hard work would be edited out of the final report. Redlich and Rankin agreed that Liebeler's draft amounted to an effort to psychoanalyze a dead man and that it would be impossible for the commission to conclude, as Liebeler had, that Oswald's Marxism and support for Castro might have had something to do with his decision to assassinate Kennedy. Rankin thought that Oswald's quest for fame—not his Marxism—was a much more likely explanation of his motives, a view shared by some of the commissioners. Rankin worried that Liebeler's suggestion that Oswald's pro-Castro views led him to kill Kennedy might be seized on by conservative lawmakers who wanted to blame Cuba for the assassination.

Liebeler's draft was circulated among some of the commissioners. Ford passed his copy to Francis Fallon, the young Harvard Law School student from Michigan who was reviewing commission documents at Ford's request. In late July, Fallon returned Liebeler's draft with a note suggesting that Ford not bother to read it. The draft "is very poorly done and . . . is being completely rewritten."

Liebeler's summer trip to New Orleans and Dallas gave him a chance to turn his mind to something other than his internal struggles on the commission. After completing his interviews in New Orleans, he flew to Texas, where he would meet with Silvia Odio and Marina Oswald. He dedicated most of the day on July 22, a Wednesday, to take Odio's testimony in the offices of the United States attorney. He set aside Friday for testimony from Marina, who would be asked follow-up questions about the Walker shooting and about her life with her husband in New Orleans.

Odio said she was nervous about her session, which began at nine a.m., and she made sure to be on time. She turned heads as she walked into the building. She was as lovely as the photographs that Liebeler had seen back in Washington suggested.

"We want to ask you some questions about the possibility that you saw Lee Harvey Oswald," Liebeler began.

Odio: "Before you start, let me give you a letter of my father's which he wrote me from prison. You can have it."

She handed him a one-page handwritten letter, dated December 25 and written in Spanish, that her father had sent jointly to Silvia and his other nine children to wish them a Merry Christmas. Castro's government mostly barred political prisoners from sending out mail, apart from a single letter to family to mark the holidays.

The letter was significant, she explained, because in it, her father replied to a question she had asked him in a letter that she had sent to him in October—a month before the Kennedy assassination. In her letter, she had mentioned the strange encounter on her doorstep with the American man she now believed to be Oswald and with his two Latino companions. She asked her father if it was true that he knew the three men. Writing back, her father replied that he did not know them and that she should be cautious. "Tell me who this is who says he is my friend," he wrote. "Be careful." His reply lent credibility to her account since it seemed to provide additional proof that the encounter at Odio's apartment, or something like it, had indeed happened.

In hours of testimony, Odio came off as an intelligent, sophisticated woman who believed that what she was saying was true. "Odio might be right," Liebeler said to himself, wondering why the FBI had been so insistent that she was mistaken. The bureau had dismissed her story because it believed that Oswald was in Mexico at the time Odio placed him at her apartment. After dealing with the FBI for months, though, Liebeler knew better than to accept anything its agents said at face value. He wondered if the bureau had misread the calendar or misunderstood Oswald's itinerary to and from Mexico. When he got back to Washington, he decided, he would ask Rankin's permission to press the FBI to look again at the time line of Oswald's travels. He would also ask that the FBI begin to search in earnest for "Leopoldo" and the other Latin man.

What happened in Dallas on the evening of Odio's testimony would remain her secret for years, she said. She chose not to tell anyone because it might mean a scandal that could damage her and her family, pitting her word against Liebeler's.

Liebeler, she said, tried to seduce her.

The trouble began immediately after she finished her testimony, when Liebeler asked her out to dinner. "That surprised me, but I was afraid, and I went." They ate at the Sheraton hotel in downtown Dallas, where Liebeler was staying, and were joined at the table by a man she remembered as one of Marina Oswald's lawyers; years later, she could not recall his name.

"There was a kind of double-talk at the table between the lawyer and him," Odio recalled. "I wasn't sure they wanted me to hear the conversation." Soon, however, the conversation became bizarrely confrontational, with Liebeler turning to Odio and demanding to know if she had lied in her testimony. He suggested that she was hiding information, perhaps about her involvement in other anti-Castro groups. "I wasn't hiding anything," she said. It seemed to her that Liebeler was engaged in "a little game" to test her credibility. Liebeler "kept threatening me with a lie-detector test."

The three were drinking, she said. Liebeler seemed to hope that "maybe if I had a few drinks and the conversation became very casual, I would go ahead and volunteer information he thought I was hiding." Odio was thankful, she said, that she had limited herself to a single drink—a Bloody Mary. She recalled being relieved at the thought that, "My God, I'm not that drunk." She also remembered thinking: "Silvia, the time has come for you to keep quiet. They don't want to know the truth."

Liebeler kept pressing her, trying to bait her with what seemed to be outrageous statements about the commission's investigation. She remembered him telling the other man, "If we do find out that this is a conspiracy, you know that we are under orders from Chief Justice Warren to cover this thing up." (Years later, Odio was asked by a congressional investigator if Liebeler had used those exact words. "Yes, sir, I could swear on that.")

After the dinner, the other lawyer went home, and Liebeler asked her to join him in his hotel room to review some photographs related to the investigation. "He invited me to his room upstairs," she said, acknowledging that she had not been naive about this; she suspected that Liebeler's invitation had nothing to do with the commission's work and that he was trying to seduce her.

"I did go," she said. "I went to his room. I wanted to see how far a government investigator would go and what they were trying to do to a witness." When they were in the room, "he made advances," she said. "Of course nothing happened because I was in my right senses. . . . I told him he was crazy."

She said Liebeler tried to flatter her, telling her that his colleagues in Washington were jealous. "He mentioned that they had seen my picture and that they had even joked about it at the Warren Commission—saying like what a pretty girl you are going to see, Jim, and things like that."

Odio said she was shocked to find herself, supposedly a significant witness in the investigation of the president's murder, turned into the sexual target of one of the investigators. "I was expecting the highest respect," she said. "I wasn't expecting any jokes in the investigation of the assassination of a president." To Liebeler, she said, "it was a game. . . . I was being used in this game."

When Liebeler returned to Washington, he said nothing to the other lawyers about an awkward encounter with Odio. He did, however, make an odd boast about what had happened when he met with Marina Oswald in Dallas on July 24, two days after Odio's testimony.

He announced that he had tried—and failed—to seduce Oswald's widow. He "had a smile on his face" as he described the encounter, said Slawson, who recalled that he and his colleagues had no doubt of the truth of the story. That was Liebeler's nature; he could not help himself if a pretty woman was nearby.

Years later, some of his former colleagues were embarrassed to admit that—at the time, in the summer of 1964—they found it amusing, not offensive, that Liebeler would try to have sex with the widow of the president's assassin. On reflection, Slawson said, "it was, of course, reckless and stupid." He was more horrified to imagine Liebeler's attempted seduction of Odio. On the staff, it had been Slawson, more than anyone else, who had seen her potential importance as a witness, and understood how she might link Oswald to a conspiracy involving anti-Castro Cuban exiles. He knew of Odio's struggles as a young refugee in Dallas and her decision to seek psychiatric help. It would have been "just cruel" for Liebeler to prey on her, Slawson said. He thought how lucky Liebeler had been that Odio's allegations did not surface publicly at the time; it could have ended his career.

47

During the trip to Dallas, Liebeler interviewed several other witnesses, including Abraham Zapruder, the local women's wear manufacturer whose home-movie camera had captured the essential, nightmarish moments of the assassination. Zapruder—under oath and between bouts of sobbing as he recalled the scene in Dealey Plaza—came close to perjuring himself as he was questioned.

Warren, in particular, had been alarmed for months about the fact that Zapruder had sold the rights to the film to *Life* magazine, and Liebeler had been directed to press Zapruder on how much money he had been paid. Warren said he thought the film's sale had set a terrible precedent for the marketing of trial evidence.

"I would like to ask you if you wouldn't mind telling us how much they paid you for the film," Liebeler asked Zapruder. "The commission feels it would be helpful."

Zapruder resisted. "I just wonder whether I should answer it or not because it involves a lot of things and it's not one price."

Liebeler tried the question again.

"I received $25,000," Zapruder replied, explaining that all of that money had been given to a local benevolence fund for Dallas police officers and firemen, with a suggestion that it go to the widow of Officer J. D. Tippit.*

"You gave the whole $25,000?" Liebeler asked.

"Yes," Zapruder replied. "I am surprised that you don't know it. I don't like to talk about it too much."

Liebeler seemed impressed by Zapruder's generosity. "We appreciate your answer very much,'" he said. "I want to tell you that your film has been one of the most helpful things to the work of the commission." He explained to Zapruder how the film had been used to determine "with a fair degree of accuracy" the facts about the ballistics evidence.

Zapruder insisted modestly, "I haven't done anything."

What he hadn't done, in fact, was tell Liebeler the whole truth about the sale of the film. Years later, *Life* would acknowledge that it agreed, within days of the assassination, to pay Zapruder at least $150,000 for the rights to the film, in annual installments of $25,000. (In 2009, the federal government would purchase the rights from Zapruder's heirs for $16 million, after rejecting the family's initial request for $30 million.) Zapruder had sold the film to *Life* after screening it for several news organizations—including CBS News, the *Saturday Evening Post*, and the Associated Press—and weighing rival bids. Richard B. Stolley, *Life*'s Los Angeles bureau chief and the man who negotiated the deal, said Zapruder was worried about "exploitation" and obtained the magazine's promise to treat the images as respectfully as possible. But Zapruder also clearly "understood its value to his family's financial future," Stolley said.

In Dallas, Liebeler also took testimony from Edwin Walker, the retired army general apparently targeted for assassination by Oswald seven months before Kennedy's murder. Walker, an outspoken segregationist and a prominent member of the ultraconservative John Birch Society, had been forced out of the military by President Kennedy in 1961 after it was learned that he had distributed Birch Society materials to troops under his command in Germany. Walker recalled how he had narrowly escaped being shot in the head when a bullet was fired into his Dallas home on the evening of Wednesday, April 10. "I was sitting behind my desk," he testified. "It was right at 9 o'clock and most of the lights were on in the house and the shades were up." He was crouched over the desk,

---

* Given the effects of inflation, $25,000 in 1963 would be equivalent to about $190,000 in 2013.

working on his income taxes, when he heard a blast over his head. He turned around to see a bullet hole in the wall.

Marina Oswald had told the commission that her husband admitted to her that same night that he had been responsible. According to Marina, Oswald called Walker a "fascist" and compared him to Adolf Hitler, saying Walker's assassination was justified because of his political views. Photos of Walker's home were found among Oswald's possessions.

Although Marina said she was convinced her husband had acted alone in trying to kill Walker, the retired general was not sure. Walker said he had been conducting his own investigation to try to determine if Oswald had coconspirators, including Jack Ruby. Walker, whose anti-Semitism was well known, would refer to Ruby only by his birth name, Rubenstein. "The indications seem to be not only mine, but all over the country, that Rubenstein and Oswald had some association." Pressed by Liebeler, Walker admitted that he had no evidence of any conspiracy, beyond the theories of Mark Lane and others.

Walker's testimony to the commission was his idea. He had demanded it in a telegram to Warren weeks earlier; he said he wanted to testify in part because he wanted to end speculation that he and his right-wing supporters in Texas had something to do with Kennedy's death. "I am tired of them blaming the right wing, and I have had enough of this, and it is about time that the commission cleared the city of Dallas," he told Liebeler.

A few days earlier, Arlen Specter had also been in Dallas on commission business, overseeing Ruby's polygraph examination. Specter was annoyed that the task had been handed to him by the chief justice, who—to Specter's mind—had made such a "stupid blunder" six weeks earlier in agreeing to Ruby's request. The polygraph was scheduled for Saturday, July 18, which meant that Specter would have to spend yet another stifling summer weekend in Texas.

The FBI had been reluctant to administer the polygraph. Aides to Hoover told the commission that it might be improper to subject a man on death row, especially one who appeared to be mentally ill, to the test. The commission insisted, however, and in the end the bureau sent one of its most experienced polygraph specialists, Bell Herndon, to Dallas. The setting was the county jail, and Specter opened the session at eleven a.m. with a discussion of whether Ruby really wanted to go through with it. If

Ruby had changed his mind, Specter said, the commission was ready to cancel the test on the spot. "That will conclude the issue, so far as the commission is concerned."

One of Ruby's defense lawyers, Clayton Fowler, had advised him against the polygraph, and he left the room to discuss the question with Ruby one last time. "If he insists on it, I can't and won't hold him back," Fowler warned as he stepped outside. He and Ruby returned a few minutes later. "He's says he's going to take the test, regardless of his lawyers," Fowler announced.

Specter turned to Ruby, reminding him that the results of the polygraph could be used by prosecutors to undermine his appeal. Ruby, however, was certain of his decision; he said he welcomed the test. "I will answer anything, without reluctance," he said. "There's no punches to be pulled. I want to answer anything and everything."

He sat down in the chair that had been rigged with the polygraph equipment. Herndon, the examiner, pulled a rubber tube around Ruby's chest to monitor his breathing. Small sensors were attached to his fingers to measure electrical patterns in his skin; a blood-pressure cuff was placed on his left arm. Strapped to the devices, Ruby repeated what he had told Warren the month before—that he had killed Oswald on impulse. "There was no conspiracy," he said. "I felt so carried away—that at that particular time of the great tragedy, I felt somehow in my little bit of a way I could save Mrs. Kennedy the ordeal of coming back for trial here."

"Is everything you told the Warren Commission the truth?" Specter asked.

"Yes," Ruby replied.

Specter had two lists of questions for Ruby—one that he had drawn up, another that Ruby and his lawyers had prepared. The combined lists were so long, and Ruby's answers were so disjointed, that an examination that would normally take about forty-five minutes lasted nearly nine hours, Specter remembered; he said he exaggerated only slightly in describing it as "the longest polygraph test in the history of the world." The questioning would not end until nine p.m. The next day, Specter and Herndon flew back to Washington together. Herndon told Specter that Ruby "had passed the test with flying colors and clearly was not involved in the assassination." While Specter was still skeptical about the accuracy of polygraph exams, he was also convinced that Herndon was right.

* * *

The FBI and the commission were trying to tie up other loose ends in Dallas. There was still confusion about why the city's police department and its hapless chief, Jesse Curry, had not done more to protect Oswald on the morning of his murder, especially since both the department and the FBI had received scores of phone threats against Oswald's life in the hours before his death.

The fifty-year-old Curry was already a target of the commission's ridicule. It was Curry who had allowed Dallas police headquarters to become a circus in the days after the assassination, with an armed Jack Ruby wandering the halls virtually at will. Curry and the city's district attorney, Henry Wade, had made repeated errors in their statements to reporters in the hours after Kennedy's murder—statements that complicated the work of the commission and provided Mark Lane and others with the opportunity to allege a cover-up. One of the worst of the misstatements came on the night of the assassination, when Wade told reporters that the police had recovered a German-made Mauser rifle from the book depository; in fact, the weapon was Oswald's Italian-made Mannlicher-Carcano. Wade later admitted the error, but it was too late to stop Lane, who would argue for decades that a Mauser had been found in the assassin's perch, more proof that Oswald was not the president's killer.

The commission had not been able to resolve a serious discrepancy between accounts given to the FBI by Curry and one of his officers, Captain W. B. Frazier, about events in the early morning hours before Oswald's death. Frazier had worked the overnight shift beginning Saturday night and was alarmed when he was told of a seemingly credible report that a mob of as many as one hundred people would gather downtown on Sunday to kill Oswald. He consulted with the head of the department's Homicide Division, who said that Curry should be notified immediately, so that the department could beef up security for Oswald that morning. Frazier repeatedly tried to call Curry's home telephone between five forty-five and six a.m. The line was constantly busy, and Frazier said he asked an operator for help. She told him that the phone appeared to be out of order. When he finished his shift at six, Frazier said the call had still not gone through, and he left it in the hands of the relief officer to try to contact the police chief to warn him that Oswald's life appeared to be in danger.

Questioned by the FBI after Oswald's murder, Curry insisted that his home telephone had worked fine and that he received no call about threats to Oswald. Frazier's account, he said, was wrong.

In July, the commission asked the FBI to try to work out the discrepancy between the accounts. And in an interview with the bureau on July 17, Curry announced that he needed to correct the record. It turned out, he said, that his wife had taken the phone off the hook that Saturday night to allow the couple to get some sleep. He acknowledged what that meant: on the last night of Lee Oswald's life, and only two nights after the president of the United States was gunned down in the streets of Dallas, the city's police chief was unreachable.

48

The commission suffered from public-relations stumbles throughout the year. None was more damaging, it was clear to the commission's staff, than Warren's statement to reporters in February that the full truth about the assassination might not be known "in your lifetime." David Belin, back at his law firm in Iowa that summer, wrote Willens in August to say that Warren's "lifetime" comment was so damaging that it needed to be addressed—and formally repudiated—in the commission's report. The report needed to make clear that the chief justice had seriously misspoken, he said. "There is no other way that I know of to take away the fears of so many people that we are glossing over matters and not letting the people know the true facts."

But that recommendation, like so many others offered by Belin, had no effect on the final report, which would make no reference to Warren's blunder. And while Belin and the other young staff lawyers appeared to have no way of knowing the extent of it, the commission did in fact begin to censor its records heavily that spring. Most significantly, it abruptly stopped keeping a verbatim record of its own deliberations.

For the first six months of the investigation, closed-door meetings of the commission had been carefully transcribed by a court reporter, with the understanding that the transcripts would be classified as top secret and not released publicly for years, if ever. The approach was designed to give the commissioners confidence that they could speak openly but also to give assurance to the public that there was a complete record that future investigators could consult. Warren hired Ward & Paul, a respected private court-reporting company in Washington that often worked for the CIA and FBI when the agencies needed to take testimony involving classified material. The company employed a number of court reporters who themselves had high-level security clearances.

That changed in June, however, when the commission, for reasons it did not explain, ended the arrangement with Ward & Paul and stopped keeping transcripts of its internal deliberations. The commission's files do not reveal who made the decision, but it meant that the public would forever be deprived of knowing exactly what was said among the commissioners in their final and most important deliberations, and of how close the commission had come to producing a divided final report.

The commission's last fully transcribed meeting took place on the afternoon of Tuesday, June 23, with three members—Warren, Ford, and Allen Dulles—in attendance. It focused on a question of censorship: Should the commission strip the final report of references to Yuri Nosenko, the Russian defector? The CIA's lobbying campaign to censor the Nosenko material had been effective, and there was little debate among the three commissioners. "I have been led to believe, by people who I believe know, that there is a grave question about the reliability of Mr. Nosenko being a bona fide defector," Ford said. "I would have grave questions about the utilization of what he says concerning Oswald." Warren agreed: "I am allergic to defectors, and I just think we shouldn't put our trust in any defector unless it is known absolutely and positively that he is telling the truth—unless it can be corroborated in every respect. And we cannot corroborate this man at all."

The next executive session was scheduled for Monday, June 29, when the commission would begin to debate, in earnest, the conclusions of the final report. All seven commissioners attended. Instead of a transcript, the commission prepared a nine-page summary of what was discussed at the session, and even that summary would disappear from the commission's files. A copy was uncovered decades later in Rankin's personal papers.

According to the summary, most of the meeting was taken up by a discussion of a checklist of seventy-two questions that the commission's staff believed the report would need to address, including the all-important question of whether there was evidence of a conspiracy. As they went down the list, the commissioners mostly sided with the staff about the conclusions they should reach. Although the debate continued over the single-bullet theory, they agreed that the evidence suggested that the three shots were probably fired at the motorcade from behind the president's limousine (and that at least two of them hit); that all of the shots came from the sixth floor of the book depository; and that Oswald was the lone gunman.

The commissioners hesitated, however, when they came to Question 48: "Is there evidence of any foreign conspiracy?" According to the summary, the commission "reserved its answer on this question—and said this would be answered later."

The commissioners rejected, once and for all, the draft chapter by Liebeler on Oswald's motives. According to the summary, the commissioners "were unwilling to assign any particular motive or get involved in psychiatric theories or terminology." The draft "was too soft and sympathetic about Oswald."

There was a different type of censorship under way at the commission, much of it aimed at presenting a final report that would not make delicate readers blush. Rankin wanted it scrubbed clean of anything that might be considered distasteful, scurrilous, or a violation of privacy—even of Oswald's privacy.

David Slawson urged one last time that the commission reveal in the report that Oswald had been stricken with venereal disease while in the marines. In a memo to Rankin, he wondered if Oswald's gonorrhea had been properly treated and if that could have affected his mental health: "It is worthwhile at least to inquire confidentially of a competent physician who specializes in this kind of disease or a related area to find out whether gonorrhea in particular can have this kind of serious aftereffect?" In fact, as Slawson learned later, untreated gonorrhea could lead to devastating physical complications, but not directly to mental illness. As Rankin had already decreed, there would be no mention of Oswald's venereal disease in the report.

Stuart Pollak, the young Justice Department lawyer detailed to the commission, was given the task of reviewing the draft chapters, as well as some of the witness transcripts that would be published later, for other instances of bad taste or violations of privacy. In memos, he went page by page through the drafts, citing every instance in which someone named in the report was accused of a crime, a sexual indiscretion, or some other character flaw. He was not surprised by several examples of off-color material involving Ruby's Carousel Club and witness descriptions of his strippers and their onstage performances. In a memo, Pollak questioned whether the report should retain a witness's descriptions of one of Ruby's most popular strippers, Janet "Jada" Conforto, who was said to be "just a little indecent about her act," requiring Ruby to "turn off the lights every once in a while and tell her to clean it up a little."

Pollak cited every instance of profanity. "The record includes several mild profanities, such as reference to a 'goddamn,'" he wrote. He also questioned whether the report needed to include some of the grislier details about the president's corpse and his bloodied clothing. Pollak asked: Was it really necessary "to include a description of the president's underclothing?"

As for the alleged assassin, Pollak wrote: "I take it that everything about Lee Harvey Oswald is fair game and essential to a complete evaluation of the individual." Still, he wondered if the commission should cite every distasteful detail it had learned about Oswald's private life, especially about his sexuality. "Attention should perhaps be directed to the references to him as a possible homosexual . . . and to his unsatisfactory sexual relations with Marina."

Rankin also asked the staff to censor out some of more graphic descriptions of the army experiments that had been conducted, at the commission's request, to try to replicate Kennedy's and Connally's wounds. The commissioners were squeamish, Rankin suggested, over how to describe the tests in which live goats were shot. He asked that "the words 'animal flesh' be substituted for the term 'goat' wherever it appears." Similarly, Rankin said, the commissioners did not want to reveal that the army had fired shots at human cadaver wrists in trying to duplicate Connally's wrist wounds. The commission, Rankin wrote, "directed that where there were references to 'cadaver wrist,' there be substituted 'bone structure' or some other expression."

* * *

That summer, senior government witnesses who appeared before the commission were given the right to request changes to the written record of their testimony. Few took up the offer, although there was a last-minute editing request by Secret Service director James Rowley. In a brief note to the commission in late June, Rowley requested a subtle, but telling, change to his answer to a question about the Secret Service agents who had gone out drinking the night before the assassination. It came in a passage of the transcript in which a clearly agitated Warren asked whether the agents could have better protected the president if they had not been out drinking hours earlier.

Rowley's original answer was: "Yes sir, but I don't know of anything they could have done that they did not do."

In his note, Rowley asked that those words be replaced with: "Yes sir, but even so, I still do not believe this would or could have prevented the tragedy."

With his revision, Rowley was qualifying his defense of his agents. He seemed now to be suggesting that the agents might have been able to do something more to save the president if they had remained fully sober the night before. After consulting with Warren, Rankin agreed to revise the transcript using slightly different words, so that Rowley's answer for posterity would read: "Yes, sir, but I don't believe they could have prevented the assassination."

49

The Polish man looked nervous as he stood to ask Robert Kennedy what he described as "a personal question." The young Pole, a local Communist Party official in Krakow, the country's second-largest city, said his countrymen wanted to hear Kennedy's "version of the assassination."

Kennedy appeared taken aback. For nearly seven months, he had managed to avoid any public comment about his brother's murder. The creation of the Warren Commission had given the attorney general an excuse for his silence; he could insist he did not want to prejudge the investigation or influence Warren's findings. But Kennedy's triumphant trip to Europe in June—first to Germany, where he had unveiled a plaque honoring his brother in the newly named John F. Kennedy Platz in Berlin, and now to Poland—had appeared to lift his spirits. The crowds in Communist Poland had repeatedly cheered the mention of his brother's name.

So he decided to answer the young Pole's question.

President Kennedy, he said, had been assassinated by a "misfit" named Lee Harvey Oswald who had been motivated by his anger against American society. "There is no doubt" about Oswald's guilt, Kennedy declared. "He was a professed Communist, but the communists, because of his attitude, would have nothing to do with him." Kennedy continued: "What he did he did on his own and by himself. . . . Ideology, in my opinion, did not motivate his act. . . . It was the single act of one person protesting against society." His remarks made for instant headlines back in the United States, since the attorney general seemed to be endorsing what the Warren Commission was expected to conclude in its final report.

For much of 1964, Kennedy had been beyond grief, it seemed; he had effectively gone into hiding. He had accepted Johnson's offer to stay on as attorney general, saying he was committed to pursuing his late brother's agenda at the Justice Department, especially on civil rights. But he then largely ignored his responsibilities at the department, staying away from the headquarters building on Pennsylvania Avenue for days at a stretch. He spent his time instead at Hickory Hill, the Civil War–era mansion that he and Ethel had bought from Jack in 1957, or in Georgetown with Jacqueline and her children. He seemed to find real comfort only from the company of family, especially his eight children; Ethel was pregnant with their ninth.

Kennedy literally wrapped himself in evidence of his despair; he had taken to wearing his dead brother's clothes. When he made his regular nighttime visits to the gravesite at Arlington National Cemetery, he was sometimes seen wearing either Jack's favorite leather jacket or the slain president's old overcoat. Before his trip to Europe, when the subject of his brother's assassination came up, Kennedy insisted that he was paying no attention to the work of the Warren Commission and that he had little interest in the question of whether Lee Harvey Oswald had acted alone. "Why should I care?" was the answer he offered routinely when asked about the commission's work. "None of it is going to bring Jack back."

But as his aides and closest friends knew, those comments were meant largely for public consumption. They would admit years later that Kennedy had never stopped suspecting that there had been a conspiracy to kill his brother. Throughout 1964, some of his Justice Department deputies—and friends elsewhere—continued to search, at his request, for evidence that might point away from Lee Oswald as the lone gunman. Kennedy appeared worried, in particular, about the possibility that Castro or the Mafia was behind the assassination.

Kennedy would have known that there was a terrible logic to theories about a Cuban connection to his brother's murder, since the United States had been trying for so long to assassinate Castro, sometimes with the help of the Mafia. By 1964, he had known for at least two years about the plots to kill the Cuban strongman, government records would later show. After the debacle at the Bay of Pigs in April 1961, his brother placed him in charge of the administration's secret war against Castro, known at the CIA as Operation Mongoose. Among officials who took part in Mongoose, there was little doubt that the operation was intended to bring about Castro's violent death.

Kennedy had been aware of the Mafia's involvement in CIA plots against Castro since at least May 1961, only four months after he was sworn in as attorney general, when he was warned by J. Edgar Hoover in a memo that the CIA was involved in "dirty business" in Cuba with Chicago Mafia boss Sam Giancana. Kennedy clearly read the FBI memo because he wrote a note in the margin: "I hope this will be followed up vigorously." A year later, he was told explicitly that the "dirty business" included CIA plots to assassinate Castro. In a meeting in May 1962 that he requested, Kennedy was told by CIA briefers the names of the organized crime figures involved in the plots, including Giancana. According to a CIA summary of the briefing, he claimed to his briefers from the spy agency that the Mafia's involvement in the schemes came as an unwelcome surprise: "I trust that if you ever try to do business with organized crime again—with gangsters—you will let the attorney general know." But was it a surprise, given Hoover's report to him a full year earlier? And while Kennedy's friends would later insist that he would never have approved of an order to assassinate a foreign leader, the fact is that the CIA's efforts to murder Castro would continue until the final hours of the Kennedy administration, at a time when Robert Kennedy was running the secret war against Cuba. The CIA's inspector general, the agency's internal watchdog, would determine years later that on November 22, 1963, the day of President Kennedy's murder, a CIA officer was meeting in Paris with a Cuban agent to hand him a poison pen—a ballpoint pen rigged with a hypodermic needle that could be filled with a deadly, commercially available poison known as Blackleaf 40—to take back to Havana. The inspector general wrote that "it is likely that at the very moment President Kennedy was shot, a CIA officer was meeting with a Cuban agent . . . and giving him an assassination device for use against Castro." Even after his brother's murder, Kennedy continued to receive reports about ongoing efforts by the Mafia, with or without the CIA's backing, to kill Castro. In June 1964, at about the time of the attorney general's trip to Germany and Poland, the CIA forwarded a detailed memo to his office about reports of a new offer by "Cosa Nostra elements," working with anti-Castro Cubans, to murder the Cuban leader. "They have offered to assassinate Castro for $150,000," the agency's memo said.

Whether President Johnson knew in 1964 about the Castro plots could never be determined with certainty, although the long-secret recordings of his White House telephone calls suggest that the CIA told him nothing about the plots, and the Mafia's involvement, until 1967. Still, in the first months of his presidency, Johnson appeared to have a strong suspicion that the assassination was somehow an act of revenge by a foreign government. That winter, Johnson told his press secretary, Pierre Salinger, who held the same job under Kennedy, that the assassination had been "divine retribution" for reported American involvement in the deaths of Rafael Trujillo, the dictator of the Dominican Republic, and of President Ngo Dinh Diem of South Vietnam; the Vietnamese leader had been killed less than three weeks before Kennedy, during an American-backed coup d'état.

Johnson's remark was quickly relayed to Kennedy, as the president might have suspected, and the attorney general was furious. "Divine retribution?" Kennedy asked in astonishment. In a conversation in April 1964 with his friend, the historian Arthur M. Schlesinger Jr., Kennedy described it as "the worst thing that Johnson" had ever said.

But was Johnson wrong? Whatever his fury toward the new president, Kennedy had his own suspicions that a foreign leader targeted for assassination by the Kennedy administration had simply struck first: Castro. According to Schlesinger, he asked Kennedy that fall—"perhaps tactlessly"—if he really believed that Oswald had acted alone. "He said that there could be no serious doubt that Oswald was guilty, but there was still argument if he had done it by himself or as part of a larger plot, whether organized by Castro or by gangsters."

So Kennedy faced a dilemma that June, when he received the letter from Chief Justice Warren, writing on behalf of the commission, asking if the attorney general had "any information suggesting that the assassination of President Kennedy was caused by a domestic or foreign conspiracy."

Should Kennedy reveal what he knew about the Castro plots and his suspicions of a conspiracy that might involve Cuba? What would be the impact of the disclosure that he had been aware, for years, that the CIA had not only tried to kill Castro but had recruited Mafia chieftains to do it—the same mobsters who were supposedly targeted for prosecution by his Justice Department?

Kennedy's political strategists would certainly not have welcomed any of that information becoming public, especially in the summer of 1964, when they were—sometimes bizarrely, it seemed—trying to whip up speculation that the attorney general was the obvious choice to be Johnson's running mate that November. Although he did little to hide his loathing for Johnson, Kennedy also did not dampen the speculation about his candidacy. Opinion polls showed him, by a wide margin, the most popular choice for number-two on the Democratic ticket.

Kennedy delayed responding to Warren's letter. "What do I do?" he wrote in a tiny, undated handwritten note to an aide who reminded him weeks later that the commission was awaiting his response.

Ultimately, though, on August 4, he signed a one-page letter to the chief justice that hinted at none of what he really knew or what he suspected:

> I would like to state definitely that I know of no credible evidence to support the allegations that the assassination of President Kennedy was caused by a domestic or foreign conspiracy. I would like to assure you that all information relating in any way to the assassination of President John F. Kennedy in the possession of the Department of Justice has been referred to the President's Commission for appropriate review and consideration. I have no suggestions to make at this time regarding any additional investigation which should be undertaken by the Commission prior to the publication of its report.

Given what would later be learned about Kennedy's suspicions, the letter was, at best, evasive and, at worst, an attempt to throw the commission off the trail of evidence of a possible conspiracy. The wording of the letter might be literally true, but it masked his dark fears that Oswald had not acted alone. Kennedy might have no "credible evidence" of a conspiracy, but he had plenty of suspicion. He might not be aware of evidence "in the possession of the Department of Justice" to suggest a conspiracy, but it might exist elsewhere—at the CIA, especially.

Although the commission had already ruled out the need for his testimony, Kennedy closed the letter with an offer to appear before the panel and answer questions; it was an offer he could be confident would not be accepted. Other than President Johnson, the attorney general was the highest-ranking government official not required to give sworn testimony to the investigation.

50

THE OFFICE OF THE DIRECTOR
THE FEDERAL BUREAU OF INVESTIGATION
WASHINGTON, DC
AUGUST 1964

Lee Rankin was genuinely embarrassed over the demands that the commission made on the FBI, he said. The requests for information and assistance continued nonstop throughout the summer of 1964, even as the commission was moving to finish its report. On August 18, Rankin telephoned Alex Rosen, head of the bureau's General Investigative Division, to thank the FBI for its willingness to carry out requests "regardless of how ridiculous the request might have seemed."

In the final weeks of the investigation, FBI agents in Texas and across the border in Mexico fanned out to chase the commission's new leads. Agents in Mexico City were asked to contact every silver store in that massive city in search of one that might have sold Oswald the bracelet he had given to Marina. The commission wanted the search conducted, even though its staff was convinced the bracelet was actually made in Japan and bought by Oswald after he returned to the United States. The FBI's Mexico City office was asked to conduct a similar investigation of every photo shop where Oswald might have had passport photos taken for his visa application to Cuba.

More significantly, the commission wanted the FBI to conduct a thorough reinvestigation of the allegations of Silvia Odio. "Mrs. Odio's reliability has been vouched for by several reputable people who know her," Rankin wrote to Hoover on July 24, adding that the commission wanted Annie Odio, Silvia's sister, to be reinterviewed as soon as possible. Hoover wrote back on August 12 to report that the FBI had interviewed Annie Odio and that, although she supported her sister's account, the FBI was still convinced that the investigation was at a dead end. "No further action is contemplated in this particular matter in the absence of a specific request from the commission," Hoover wrote.

Wesley Liebeler said that he was astonished by the letter. Why did the FBI have so little interest in following up on a seemingly credible witness whose account might point to conspirators in the president's murder? He began his own detailed review of Odio's claims, matching her account against what was known of the chronology of Oswald's trip to Mexico. The outcome suggested to Liebeler that although time would have been extraordinarily tight, Oswald could have made the trip to Dallas in late September. If he had had access to a private car or had flown, he could have slipped into Dallas, if only for a matter of hours, before crossing the border into Mexico.

In late August, Liebeler drafted a detailed letter for Rankin to sign in which the commission would, effectively, demand that the FBI reopen and reinvestigate every part of the Odio story. Rankin could be sure the letter would not be well received by Hoover, but he sent it anyway. "It is a matter of some importance to the commission that Mrs. Odio's allegations either be proved or disproved," the letter said. "Would you please conduct the investigation necessary to determine who it was that Mrs. Odio saw in or about late September or early October 1963?" The letter offered Liebeler's detailed analysis of the timetable of Oswald's travels, and it noted the similarities between Odio's description of one of the two Latino men at her door—"Leopoldo"—and a man who was reportedly seen in Oswald's company in a New Orleans bar.

The commission's request was passed on to the FBI's Dallas field office, and the task of following up was handed to Special Agent James Hosty, the same agent who had investigated—and dismissed—Odio's claims back in December. Hosty said later that he rolled his eyes at the assignment; he would be reviewing exactly the same evidence that he had gone over eight months earlier. At what point, he wondered, "would this nightmare end?" Hosty was a public figure in Dallas for all the wrong reasons that summer, he said. Anyone in the city who closely read a newspaper knew his name; all of his neighbors knew he was the belea-guered FBI agent who had investigated Oswald before the assassination and failed to see the threat he posed. Hoover and his deputies in Wash-ington seemed determined to prove that Oswald had acted alone in kill-ing Kennedy, and nothing Hosty had discovered since the assassination undermined their argument. It would take a "brave, if not foolhardy" FBI agent to dare suggest that Hoover was wrong. "How much longer do I have to hear the name Lee Harvey Oswald?" Hosty asked himself. "I was sick of this."

By late summer, Hoover's contempt for Warren and several of the other commissioners was all but total, even as he continued to fear how their final report would treat the FBI. Hoover's internal files had become a running, venomous commentary on the commission and its work. His views were often expressed in brief notes, written in his distinctive, loop-ing cursive, at the bottom of his deputies' memos.

Many of his angriest comments were prompted by press coverage. From a reading of his handwritten notes, Hoover seemed to assume any article in a major newspaper or magazine that criticized the FBI for its actions before or after the assassination had been planted by the com-mission—in some cases, by the chief justice himself. After the magazine the *Nation* questioned that winter whether Oswald had ever been an FBI informant, Hoover wrote to aides that he wanted a thorough analysis of who was feeding information to the magazine. He guessed the chief jus-tice: "*The Nation* is Warren's Bible," he wrote. When the *Dallas Times-Herald* revealed details of the commission's investigation of whether Oswald had been prone to violence while serving in the marines, an aide to Hoover prepared a summary of the article, writing that it appeared to be based on a "leak on the part of a commission member." At the bottom of the memo Hoover wrote: "Sounds like Warren."

Hoover thought the commission, far from ending rumors about Oswald and a possible conspiracy to kill Kennedy, was continuing to fuel them, especially after Warren's statement to reporters about not knowing the full truth about the assassination "in your lifetime." "If Warren had kept his big mouth shut about this, these conjectures would not have arisen," Hoover wrote.

He became convinced that the FBI was also the victim of the incompetence—and, he said, the venality—of the Dallas police department and the Dallas district attorney's office. He believed the city's law-enforcement officials were continuing to feed disparaging information about the FBI to the commission in hopes of more lenient treatment in the final report. For a time earlier that year, Hoover had quietly ordered the FBI's Dallas field office to cut off all contact with the city's chief homicide prosecutor, William Alexander, because Hoover believed Alexander was spreading the rumor that Oswald had been an FBI informant. He was also suspicious of Alexander's boss, district attorney Henry Wade. "This fellow is just a low s.o.b.," Hoover wrote of Alexander. "Instruct our Dallas office to have no contact with him and to be most circumspect with Wade."

As the commission's investigation began to wind down, Hoover admitted to aides that the bureau had mishandled its dealings with the commission, often creating suspicion where he believed none had been justified. After an incident in which midlevel FBI officials gave a narrow reading to a request for background information about Jack Ruby, leading to protests from the commission about why some documents had been withheld, Hoover wrote that he was "becoming more and more concerned about our failure to properly handle this matter." He said in a later memo: "I don't understand why we give narrow interpretations to the commission's requests."

In March, a top Hoover aide, William Branigan, wrote to recommend that the FBI reject the commission's request for closer surveillance of public appearances by Mark Lane and Marguerite Oswald. He suggested the potential for a scandal if it became known that Warren's investigation was having its critics followed. "The requests of the commission are extremely broad and, if literally interpreted, could pose a serious investigative burden on us which would also be of great potential embarrassment," Branigan wrote. Hoover, however, was wary of turning the commission down. "I do not like this constant reluctance on our part to comply fully with the commission's requests. I realize how impractical and absurd many of them are," he wrote. "But it is a fact that at least Warren is hostile to the Bureau & we are furnishing him ammunition by our equivocation."

Rankin would later say that much of his energy that year had to be directed to trying to salvage some sort of relationship with the bureau. Behind the scenes, the investigation was faced with repeated threats by Hoover and the bureau to shut off the FBI's assistance. There was a showdown that spring over the commission's decision to have outside experts review some of the physical evidence that had already been inspected by the FBI Laboratory, including the bullets and bullet fragments from Dallas. The move was seen by senior aides to Hoover as an affront to the bureau, suggesting that the commission did not trust the lab's findings. Hoover seemed to be offended, too: "I concur it is getting to be more and more intolerable to deal with this Warren Commission."

At one point, he appeared to authorize Assistant Director Alex Rosen to threaten to cut off the laboratory's assistance to the commission entirely. "I pointed out to Mr. Rankin that our Laboratory was greatly burdened with a large volume of work and that if the examinations that we made were not going to be accepted, it would appear there would be no reason for our Laboratory experts to be tied up on these examinations," Rosen wrote.

Rankin tried to make amends. He repeatedly spoke by phone with Rosen and apologized for the many "unreasonable requests" the commission had made. Rankin tried to be conciliatory, praising the FBI Laboratory and insisting that the outside experts would simply confirm the accuracy of the bureau's findings. After more pleas from Rankin, including more statements of "my respect for the FBI and the work of its laboratory," the bureau lifted its threat. Still, Hoover felt the dispute was a useful moment to remind his deputies to ignore any words of praise or other "sweet-talk" they heard from Rankin and his colleagues at the commission. "I place no credence in any complimentary remarks made by Warren or the commissioners," Hoover wrote on a copy of one of Rosen's memos. "They are looking for FBI 'gaps' and, having found none, they try to get 'syrupy.'"

Whatever his hostility toward Warren, Hoover worked to maintain a good relationship with the commissioner who, he felt, would defend the FBI in the writing of the report: Gerald Ford. His files show that he met Ford at a party given at the home of Cartha DeLoach in April. The next day, Hoover followed up with a note to Ford: "I want to let you know how much I enjoyed talking to Mrs. Ford and you during the party at DeLoach's home last night. Particularly, I was very pleased to discuss in this informal manner some vital matters of interest to you, as well as the FBI." The letter did not reveal what the "vital matters" were. "It is always encouraging to know that we have alert, vigorous Congressmen, such as you, who are aware of the needs and problems confronting our country," he continued. "Whenever you have an opportunity, I would be happy to have Mrs. Ford and you drop by FBI headquarters for a special tour of our facilities. And of course, I would like you to feel free to call on me any time our help is needed or when we can be of service."

The bureau also kept tabs throughout the year on William Manchester, as he gathered research for his book. DeLoach asked for a background check on the writer, and the results were encouraging. As a Washington correspondent for the *Baltimore Sun*, Manchester had dealt with the bureau occasionally, and a review of FBI files showed that "our relations with him in the past have been most cordial," DeLoach reported. That spring, Robert Kennedy asked Hoover to meet with Manchester; the request came to the FBI director through Edwin Guthman, Kennedy's press secretary, whose office was helping schedule the author's appointments. Hoover, who was rarely in a mood to do favors for the attorney general, initially refused to be interviewed for the book. Instead, Manchester was invited to speak with DeLoach, and Kennedy's office organized the meeting for April 22.

While outlining his research plan for DeLoach, Manchester pressed for the chance to speak directly with Hoover; he said he wanted a full understanding of what happened in Washington in the hours after the president's murder, including the exact sequence of phone calls between the FBI director and Robert Kennedy in which Hoover broke the news of the assassination. (Kennedy had already told Manchester how appalled he had been at Hoover's cold, almost robotic tone during the calls.) Manchester signaled to DeLoach that Hoover took a risk if he chose not to tell his side of the story because the other side of the story—as told by Kennedy—might be very unflattering. The writer made clear how much he already knew. According to DeLoach, Manchester said that he had "visited the Attorney General's home and the swimming pool where the Attorney General had been standing at the time the Director had called him."

Hoover gave in and agreed to the interview, setting aside an hour for Manchester in early June. As expected, much of the interview focused on Hoover's telephone calls with Robert Kennedy on the day of the assassination. Hoover portrayed his tone in those calls as professional, not cold, and he appeared to suggest that it was Kennedy who had drawn the initial conversations to an end, not him. After telling Kennedy in the first call that his brother had been shot and was being rushed to a hospital, Hoover recalled, "the Attorney General had been quiet for a few moments and had then requested" that the FBI "keep him informed of any further facts" before ending the call. The attorney general, he said, was "not the explosive type" and seemed reasonably calm during the call, given the circumstances.

Hoover offered Manchester his long-standing defense of the FBI's failure to alert the Secret Service to Oswald's presence in Dallas—"we did have some information regarding Oswald; however, it was quite flimsy in nature"—while repeating his attack on the competence of the Dallas police. "If the FBI had taken custody of Lee Harvey Oswald . . . he never would have been killed by Jack Ruby," he said. "All of this could have been avoided had the Dallas police taken proper action."

The interview ended with what Hoover and his deputies might have seen as an odd question from Manchester: Why had Hoover not attended the president's funeral services or burial, which were conducted only a few minutes' drive from FBI headquarters in downtown Washington? It would have been impossible, Hoover replied; there was too much work to be done, both in managing the investigation in Dallas and Mexico City— "leads had spread to Mexico"—and in overseeing the security arrangements for the many foreign dignitaries who traveled to Washington that weekend for the funeral ceremonies. As Hoover explained it, he had "been at his desk constantly."

51

For much of the summer, John McCloy, like most of the commissioners, dealt with the investigation from a distance. He worked from his luxurious offices in One Chase Manhattan Plaza, the sixty-story white-steel skyscraper in lower Manhattan that was home both to Chase Manhattan Bank, which he had run as chairman from 1953 to 1960, and the white-shoe law firm that bore his name, Milbank, Tweed, Hadley & McCloy. His name was so synonymous with the bank and the law firm that there was no suite or floor number on his office stationery; it was unnecessary. There were hundreds of offices and thousands of workers in the building, but a letter addressed simply to John McCloy, One Chase Manhattan Plaza, New York, would reach him.

After reading through some of the draft chapters sent up from Washington, McCloy decided that the commission should just admit it: Oswald might have been trained by the KGB to spy. That did not mean there was a Russian conspiracy to kill Kennedy—not at all. McCloy had told the other commissioners he agreed that Oswald had been the lone gunman and that it was hard to imagine that the Soviet Union had anything to do with the assassination. But it was possible that the Russians might at some point have considered using Oswald as a "sleeper" agent who, after returning to the United States, would lie in wait, maybe for years, to carry out an operation on Moscow's behalf. The fact that Oswald seemed to know some spycraft—using false names to open post-office boxes, for example—suggested that he might have undergone KGB training. The commission's report would only be stronger, McCloy said, if it acknowledged that there were still many mysteries about Oswald's past.

On July 21, McCloy dictated a letter for Lee Rankin and asked his secretary to mark it PERSONAL. He wrote to praise the latest draft of the chapter in which the commission addressed—and ruled out—the possibility of a foreign conspiracy. "I think this draft is much better than the earlier one," McCloy told Rankin. But he had a suggestion. "Somewhere," he wrote, "I feel there should be added something like this":

> The Commission has noted that Oswald did exhibit some tendency toward the use of undercover practices which raises a suspicion that he did receive some rudimentary instruction in undercover activities. . . . It is not beyond the realm of possibility that the Soviet authorities may have considered using him as a sort of "sleeper" in the United States, on whom they might call at some future time, but our more considered view is that even in this capacity they would have had serious doubts regarding his reliability.

In other words, the KGB might have considered using Oswald as a spy but, ultimately, the Russians were too smart to have anything to do with "that punk," as McCloy often referred to him.

The letter effectively disappeared after it reached Washington. If McCloy's suggestion inspired debate within the commission, it would not be reflected in its records or in the final report. The letter, which several of the staff lawyers say they never saw, was filed away in Rankin's personal papers at the National Archives, apparently forgotten. Years later, the lawyers were not surprised that the chief justice would have resisted McCloy's suggestion to leave open the possibility of ties between Oswald and the KGB. By that summer, Warren seemed determined to produce a final report that ended speculation about Oswald as anything other than a delusional, violent young man who was alienated from all people and institutions—certainly not someone who would be seen by the Kremlin as a potential spy.

* * *

David Slawson had written much of the draft that McCloy had just read, and the young lawyer was pleased with the way his material in the report had taken shape. As the writing had begun in earnest, Slawson felt convinced that there was no foreign conspiracy, or at least no credible evidence of one. He reserved final judgment on the question until the FBI completed its late-summer review of the claims of Silvia Odio in Dallas. If her account of meeting Oswald proved to be true, everything changed, and the question of a conspiracy would have to be reopened. If Odio's allegations proved false, however, Slawson felt comfortable with the conclusion, as stated in a July 15 draft, that the commission had investigated "all rumors and allegations" and "found no credible evidence indicating that the Soviet Union, Cuba or any other foreign nation was involved in the assassination. All of the facts on Lee Harvey's life, literally from his birth to his death, have been examined for evidence of subversive foreign connections."

Not that he was completely satisfied, Slawson admitted. He was still troubled that so much of the information about Oswald's Mexico trip would be attributed directly—on the commission's orders—to the central witness he had not been permitted to interview: Silvia Duran. She would be identified by name more than thirty times in the report, with reference to the statements she had made—under duress and possibly even under threat of torture—to the Mexican police. The staff settled on the final wording about her credibility. She would be labeled "an important source of information" whose account had been confirmed by "sources of extremely high reliability," a cryptic reference to the CIA's wiretapping and bugging operations in Mexico City. "Her testimony was truthful and accurate in all material respects," the report would conclude.

William Coleman took on the assignment of writing the report's chronology of Oswald's Mexico trip. His draft made sweeping statements suggesting that he, even more than Slawson, was confident that the CIA and the FBI had shared all they knew. "I did trust the CIA especially," Coleman said later.

According to his twenty-five-page draft on the Mexico trip, dated July 20:

The commission undertook an intensive investigation to determine what Oswald did on this trip and its purpose. As a result, it has been able to reconstruct and explain most of Oswald's actions during this time. . . . The Commission is confident that what it does know about Oswald's activities in Mexico is representative of all his actions there, and that while in Mexico, Oswald made no contacts having any relation to the assassination.

As the summer wore on, the staff began to fall into two camps: those who were content with the way their drafts were being edited by Rankin and his deputies, and those who were unhappy, or even furious. There seemed to be no middle ground. Arlen Specter felt his summary of the events of the day of the assassination, and his explanation of much of the medical evidence, had been edited carefully and respectfully by Redlich. Others might still find Redlich testy and territorial, but Specter only had praise; the two would be lifelong friends. "Norman was the architect of the report, and he essentially let my work stand," Specter recalled. "You've got to remember that the report was put together lickety-split. I give Redlich a lot of credit."*

Specter would become aware only later, after the drafts were edited, how reluctant some of the commissioners had been to accept the single-bullet theory, or at least the way he had presented it. After reading through draft chapters about the ballistics, McCloy wrote to Rankin in June to warn that the commission should be wary of overstating its confidence in the theory. "I think too much effort is expended on attempting to prove that the first bullet which hit the president was also responsible for all of Connally's wounds," he said. "In many respects, this chapter is the most important chapter in the report and it should be the most convincing." McCloy attached an eight-page typewritten memo to his letter in which he proposed sixty-nine other editing changes in the report, many intended to tone down what he considered its overheated language.

---

* As a United States senator, Specter suggested that his respect and fondness for Redlich was a factor in his decision in 1987 to join Senate colleagues in rejecting the Supreme Court nomination of Robert Bork, a federal appeals court judge and former law professor at Yale. In a previously unpublished 1996 interview, Specter said that he had been offended by reports of an incident years before the nomination in which the conservative Bork ridiculed the very liberal Redlich during a dinner speech in New York, with Redlich in the audience. "Redlich had been very ill and came out to the dinner as a matter of courtesy" to Bork, Specter said. "When Redlich told me what happened between him and Bork, I really had a very negative view of Bork, which didn't help Bork any" at his Senate confirmation hearings (Specter interviews).

He said he was alarmed by the use of needlessly dramatic turns of phrase, including a reference to the "fateful day" of the assassination. "If this is to be an historical document, there is no need and indeed it would appear to be improper to use phrases such as 'fateful day.'" The phrase was removed. A more direct attack on the single-bullet theory came from Senator Cooper, who had otherwise been such a secondary figure in the investigation. On August 20, he sent a memo to Rankin in which he suggested that the theory was, simply, wrong. Cooper had been impressed by Connally's testimony. "On what basis is it claimed that one shot caused all the wounds?" Cooper asked. "It seemed to me that Governor Connally's statement negates such a conclusion. I could not agree with this statement."

No one seemed angrier about the way the report was being edited than David Belin. Now back at his law firm in Des Moines, he said he seethed as he read through the drafts sent to him from Washington. In letters back to Rankin, he complained that the report was raising needless questions about the commission's confidence in its own findings. The report, he said, was written defensively, focusing too much on rebutting the conspiracy theories being spread by Mark Lane and others. Belin was shocked, he said, to discover that a full chapter would be devoted to proving that all the shots fired at Kennedy's motorcade had come from the Texas School Book Depository and not, as the conspiracy theorists argued, from the grassy knoll. "The evidence of the source of the shots is among the strongest evidence there is to show that Oswald was the assassin," Belin wrote. "To set it aside in a separate chapter by itself is a case of gilding the lily." The conspiracy theorists "have succeeded in steering the commission onto a false course," he continued. "There can be absolutely no doubt about the source of the shots, and it does not take 69 typewritten pages to prove it."

Belin was angered, as well, to discover that the commission intended to ignore his one-man investigation that spring of a mystery that had nagged at him from the start of the investigation: Where was Oswald heading after the shooting? It was known that Oswald had left the book depository minutes after the assassination and made his way to his rooming house across town—first by bus, then by taxi after the bus was stopped in the suddenly chaotic traffic. At the rooming house, he collected his .38 Smith & Wesson revolver and began walking east; it was then that he encountered and killed Officer Tippit before hurrying on. The question was: To where? The absence of any obvious escape route fed rumors that Oswald knew Ruby and was heading in the direction of Ruby's apartment, which was about two-thirds of a mile away in the direction he was walking. Belin, however, was convinced that the rumors were wrong. "We made every effort to uncover credible evidence of a possible link between Oswald and Ruby," Belin said. "None was found."

Was it possible that Oswald had no escape route? Some of Belin's colleagues suspected that Oswald had no destination in mind and always intended to be captured or killed. That might explain why he had left the money in his wallet—$170—for Marina that morning; he had also left behind his wedding ring. But Belin was convinced that Oswald was fleeing, and to somewhere specific, and that there were clues to his destination in a small slip of paper found in his pockets: a bus transfer, issued in the minutes after the assassination. To Belin, the transfer slip suggested that Oswald—who routinely traveled by public bus in Dallas and knew the schedules by heart—planned to connect to another bus that would take him out of town. "There must have been a reason for him to keep that bus transfer."

Belin thought Oswald's most likely destination was Mexico, and then Cuba. Liebeler reminded him of testimony from one of Oswald's fellow marines, who had said that Oswald had talked about going to Cuba through Mexico if he ever got in trouble with the law. It was significant, Belin thought, that Oswald had lied so blatantly to the Dallas police about the Mexico trip when he was interrogated after the assassination, claiming that he had never been to Mexico. "Is it not reasonable to assume that the denial of his trip to Mexico is strong circumstantial evidence, pointing to someone in Mexico who was in some way involved, directly or indirectly, with the assassination?" Belin asked. "Who would that person be?" He suspected those questions led back to Oswald's visit that fall to the Cuban embassy in Mexico, where he almost certainly would have encountered Cuban diplomats and others who saw the Kennedy administration as a mortal threat. Belin thought there was at least a possibility then that while in Mexico, "Oswald had a conversation with a Castro agent or sympathizer about getting back at Kennedy and was promised financial and other support if he was ever able to succeed" in killing the president. Someone might have been waiting for Oswald on the border to help him—by definition, it seemed, a coconspirator in the assassination. It was "pure speculation," Belin admitted, but it sounded logical.

With the FBI's help, he analyzed bus routes out of Dallas to see if Oswald had an easy way of getting to Mexico. After days with maps and timetables spread out on his desk, Belin thought he had identified Oswald's likely route, and it was not so complicated. With the transfer slip, Oswald could have reached a pickup point for Greyhound bus lines, which that day had a bus leaving Dallas at three fifteen p.m. headed for Laredo, Texas, on the Mexican border.

Belin laid out his theory in a detailed memo to Rankin and Redlich. He offered an explanation for why Oswald had left the money behind for Marina instead of saving it for bus fare; he had not needed the money because he had his handgun. "Even if he did not have enough money to get to Mexico, the pistol would have helped him obtain same," he said. After Tippit's vicious murder, Oswald would seemingly have had no qualms about using the gun again to rob passersby, or even a bank. Belin acknowledged that he could not prove Mexico was Oswald's destination, but he thought it was important for the commission report to at least suggest where Oswald was headed, if only to dampen the rumors about a rendezvous with Ruby.

It was Norman Redlich, above all, who objected to any mention of the theory in the report. The commission should not raise questions about Oswald's route—especially to suggest that he was headed to Mexico, where so many questions had already been raised and left unanswered—without proof, he declared. "Norman argued that because it was a theory and not a fact, no mention of it should be made in the final report," Belin remembered. "Norman won the argument."

Alfred Goldberg was stunned that summer when he learned what the chief justice intended to do with the commission's internal files—he wanted them shredded or incinerated. "Warren wanted to destroy all the records," Goldberg recalled. "He thought these records would stir up more than they should," providing conspiracy theorists with evidence about internal disputes on the commission's staff, which Mark Lane and others would then use selectively to raise doubts about Oswald's guilt. Warren had other reasons for destroying the files, Goldberg recalled. He worried that much of the paperwork turned over by government agencies, and the CIA in particular, revealed national-security secrets only tangentially related to the president's murder. "He thought the country and the world would be better off with those things never being made public," said Goldberg, who decided that he had to move fast—and quietly—to convince Warren to change his mind. As a historian, Goldberg was appalled at the idea that so much raw evidence about a turning point in American history would be lost to future scholars. Worse, he was convinced that if the public ever learned what had happened, the conspiracy theories would spin out of control; Lane and the others would seize on the document destruction as proof of a cover-up.

Goldberg thought that if anyone could change Warren's mind, it was Richard Russell. Whatever the differences between Warren and the senator, the Georgian was one of the most respected men in the capital, and the chief justice would listen to him. "No one in Washington dared to ignore the advice of Senator Richard Russell," Goldberg said. So he went to Alfredda Scobey, Russell's representative on the staff, and asked her for help. She, in turn, went to Russell, who agreed to talk to the chief justice. And the senator convinced Warren that, whatever the risk of the disclosure of government secrets, "it would be a whole lot worse if we destroyed the documents," Goldberg said. Warren quickly reversed his order. Russell, Goldberg said, had "saved the day."

That summer was the busiest of Goldberg's life. In the final weeks of the investigation, he promised himself that he would always get home each night for at least a few hours of sleep, but beginning in June, fourteen-hour workdays were the rule, and he worked seven days a week. He had one day off that summer—the Fourth of July, which Rankin insisted that the staff honor by staying home. Typically Goldberg would not leave the offices until well after midnight. "Most of us were there until 1, 2, 3 o'clock in the morning."

Especially during those late-night hours, he and the other lawyers were thankful for the commission's increasingly loose rules for handling classified documents. "We could just pile things on tables," Goldberg said. "I thought it was great." FBI agents who visited the offices in mid-September reported back to headquarters that they found "a complete lack of organization insofar as records are concerned," with "no document control whatsoever and no accountability for such documents, classified or not." The commission's two Xerox photocopiers "are used constantly by any member of the staff or any employee" to copy files, including many stamped TOP SECRET.

Goldberg took on several writing assignments. He wrote the special chapter that listed—and rebutted—every major rumor and conspiracy theory. He divided the rumors into ten categories, ranging from the source of the bullets that struck the motorcade to the events at the scene of Officer Tippit's murder, and the many allegations about ties between Oswald and Ruby. He whittled down the list to 122 "speculations and rumors," and then answered each one with the "commission finding" that spelled out the truth, as determined by the investigation. In his introduction to the chapter, he noted that every major assassination had produced conspiracy theories and that they began to circulate almost instantly. "The rumors and theories about the assassination of Abraham Lincoln that are still being publicized were for the most part bruited within months of his death."

As part of his research, Goldberg tried to read every one of the hundreds of magazine and newspaper articles that suggested an alternative explanation for Kennedy's murder. "There was so much literature," he recalled. "There was an underground network operating already—all kinds of allegations, speculations, rumors." He was outraged after reading the first of the major conspiracy books—*Who Killed Kennedy?* by Thomas Buchanan, the expatriate American writer for *L'Express*. The book, released in the United States by the publishing house G. P. Putnam's Sons, alleged that there had been at least two gunmen in Dealey Plaza. Buchanan hinted that the conspiracy was underwritten by right-wing Texas businessmen. "I thought it was nonsense, the way most of those books were," Goldberg said. He was offended by the way so many supposedly legitimate scholars and journalists did not trouble themselves to research the basic facts of the assassination before rushing garbled conspiracy tales into print. "It was a good money-making thing for a lot of people," Goldberg said. The conspiracy theorists "were, in the main, either ignorant, crazy or dishonest." Goldberg believed that Buchanan, Mark Lane, and others were preying on the confusion of millions of Americans who found it difficult to accept that the most powerful man in the world could be brought down by "such a pathetic little man" as Lee Harvey Oswald. "They'd be much more comfortable knowing it was the result of some conspiracy, that some major figures were involved," Goldberg said. "How could this pipsqueak do all this?"

He was proud that his own detective work put to rest one specific, well-publicized set of rumors. For months, Lane and others raised an alarm about the disappearance of a Texas man named Darryl Click who had been identified as the cabdriver who drove Oswald back to his rooming house after the assassination. The *New York Times*, the *Washington Post*, and other newspapers had published a transcript of a news conference on November 24 at which Dallas district attorney Henry Wade had referred to the taxi ride and seemed to identify Click by name. But Lane and others could find no record of Click in phone books or other public records. The confusion about Click and his whereabouts was "seized on by all the conspiratorial people," Goldberg recalled. "There were hints of a dark mystery." To try to resolve it, Goldberg obtained a tape recording of Wade's news conference. "I listened to it over and over again," he said. "I went thru it 75 times." And he found the error. It had been made by the transcriptionist, who had obviously been baffled by Wade's deep Texas drawl. The transcript published in the *Times* and elsewhere quoted Wade as saying that Oswald "caught a taxicab driver, a Darryl Click," and was driven to his rooming house. Wade had actually said that Oswald "caught a taxi to Oak Cliff" and then went home. The rooming house was in the city's Oak Cliff neighborhood. To an ear unaccustomed to a Texas accent, "Oak Cliff" sounded like "Darryl Click." There was no Darryl Click.

In preparing the "rumors" appendix, Goldberg made use of the final report of staff lawyer Richard Mosk and IRS supervisor Philip Barson, an accountant who had been loaned to the commission to complete the investigation of whether Oswald had income from unexplained sources, possibly from coconspirators. Goldberg was impressed. In their report in July, Mosk and Barson had been able to account—almost to the penny—for the money that went in and came out of Oswald's pockets in the final weeks of his life, beginning on September 25, the day he reportedly left New Orleans for Mexico. His income, including salary and unemployment insurance, totaled $3,665.89, while his expenses, including the cost of the Mexico trip, totaled $3,497.79. It was a difference of $168, and that money was apparently accounted for, since Oswald left the $170 in cash for Marina in a drawer in the bedroom dresser.

After figuring that he had spent almost every waking hour of his life since January thinking about the troubled life of Jack Ruby, Burt Griffin was finally willing to accept the conclusion that the commission seemed likely to adopt—that Ruby had not been part of any conspiracy in the killing of Oswald. He bristled, though, at the early draft chapters that focused on Ruby. He thought they went too far in suggesting that the commission had answered every significant question about Ruby's past. "I think it is a mistake for the Commission to make any statement which indicates that its investigation in that regard has been exhaustive," Griffin wrote to Willens on August 14.

That month, Griffin and the other lawyers who remained in Washington were asked to take on the additional duty of reading through the draft chapters that they had not written, acting as editors and fact-checkers on one another's work. Characteristically, no one approached the job more eagerly—and at times, aggressively—than Liebeler. He became, in many ways, the commission's principal in-house contrarian. As Griffin described it, Liebeler was "the cross-examiner who was looking for the weaknesses" that the commission's critics would otherwise find. "He wanted the report to be so well written and the evidence to be so accurate that a lawyer on the other side could not say that the commission staff had done an inadequate job or had drawn unwarranted conclusions."

Griffin and his colleagues said they had no inkling of it at the time, but by establishing himself as their chief internal critic, Liebeler was about to create an angrily worded paper trail that conspiracy theorists would cite decades later in order to argue that the commission—and Liebeler himself—had been part of a monstrous cover-up.

52

Norman Redlich's energy was almost superhuman. He existed on little sleep, often less than four hours a night, and could wolf down a meal at his desk in the few minutes it took for one of the secretaries to change a typewriter ribbon. He was honored to have the job of the principal writer and editor of the report. The document was likely to be read and studied centuries into the future—by his grandchildren and their children "and on and on," he told his family. More than anything else he might do in a long career, Redlich—thirty-eight years old and younger than most of his colleagues on the faculty back at NYU law school—understood that this might be what he would be remembered for.

His wife, Evelyn, recalled that, reasonably early in the investigation, her husband had become convinced that Oswald had acted alone. "Norman never entertained any conspiracy notions," she said. "None." And so it was that much easier for Redlich to do what Warren wanted him to do that summer: complete the report as quickly as possible and put to rest the swirling rumors about the assassination.

The pressure to finish was not only coming from Warren. Although the chief justice insisted that President Johnson had imposed no deadlines, the commission's lawyers heard differently. Repeatedly that summer, word reached them that the president, through his top aides, was demanding that the report be completed before the end of August, when the Democratic National Convention would be held in Atlantic City, New Jersey, and Johnson would receive his party's nomination to run for a full four-year term as president; his Republican challenger in November would be Barry Goldwater, the Arizona senator. Johnson, the lawyers were told, did not want to be blindsided by anything in the report before the campaign. "Every once in a while, someone would say to us, 'Johnson just sent over a message,'" Lloyd Weinreb remembered. "And the message is, 'Where's the fucking report?'"

The staff felt the pressure. Weinreb said an aunt, visiting Washington and seeing how exhausted he was, demanded that he take a weekend off with his wife. "She said, 'Lloyd, you've simply got to go away,'" he said. "She gave us some money to do it." He planned a single Sunday night away in the nearby seaport of Annapolis, Maryland. "So midday on Sunday we drove to Annapolis to a motel and we were going to stay for the night," he said. But almost as soon as they arrived, the phone rang. "We got a call from Lee Rankin saying that we had better come back to Washington." There was no time for even a single night away; the couple returned home immediately. "I was pissed," Weinreb said. He was blessed, he said, with a spouse who was slow to anger. "My wife is a very agreeable person."

For the first time, tempers began to flare among some of the lawyers. Weinreb recalled several blowups that summer with Wesley Liebeler, especially over how the report should describe Oswald's self-proclaimed Marxism and whether it would have motivated him to kill Kennedy. "That was a source of great controversy between us," Weinreb remembered. "Liebeler was a right-wing guy" who argued that Oswald's motivation "was all political, that it was something about Castro." Weinreb was convinced Liebeler was wrong. "I didn't think it was political, I still don't."

Liebeler's battles with Redlich were far nastier. Beyond the stark differences in their political views, the two men had never gotten along, and now they argued over the writing of the report. Liebeler warned that Redlich might be so eager to finish the report and please Warren that he was maneuvering to shut down important, last-minute lines of investigation that might still point to a conspiracy. There were a number of examples, Liebeler said. Several staff members were alarmed, for instance, by the discovery that summer that the FBI had never determined the sources of fingerprints on cartons found on the sixth floor of the Texas School Book Depository; they were the cartons that Oswald had apparently stacked around his sniper's perch. At least eleven of the fingerprints belonged to someone other than Oswald.

No matter how little time remained in the investigation, Liebeler and other staff lawyers felt that the FBI had to determine whose fingerprints they were. Redlich, however, resisted and tried to write around the issue, as if it was unimportant. Griffin joined with Liebeler in protesting to Redlich: "You can't dismiss 11 fingerprints. You've got to find out whose prints those are." It was possible that the prints would identify coconspirators in the assassination. "Hell, there could be a whole football team up there," Griffin warned. Murray Laulicht, the new arrival on the staff, remembered that Redlich felt it was too late to worry about the prints, especially if it meant holding up the report. "What, you want to fingerprint the whole city of Dallas?" he remembered Redlich asking with annoyance.

Redlich also resisted asking the FBI about a conflict over whether Oswald's palm print had been identified on the barrel of the rifle found at the book depository. A Dallas police fingerprint expert claimed the print appeared to be Oswald's, while an FBI expert who inspected the rifle later found no print at all. Liebeler believed both issues—the source of the fingerprints on the cartons and the discrepancy over a print on the rifle—had to be resolved. "The record could not be left in the condition it was in," he declared.

Rankin sided with Liebeler, and he signed letters to J. Edgar Hoover in late August pressing for answers about the prints. The responses came back in the final days of the investigation: the bureau reported that most of the previously unidentified fingerprints were those of an FBI clerk and a Dallas police officer who had handled the cartons as evidence. The FBI concluded that Oswald's palm print had in fact been on the rifle barrel, as the Dallas police had found. The FBI expert who inspected the rifle had been unaware that the Dallas police preserved the palm print by lifting it off the barrel with a piece of adhesive tape.

Liebeler had a more sweeping complaint: he felt that Redlich was writing the final report like a "prosecutor's brief," leaving no question at all about Oswald's guilt. Liebeler told his colleagues he agreed that Oswald was the lone assassin. Even so, he said, the report should state clearly that there was evidence that might have pointed away from Oswald if there had been a trial.

In late August, Liebeler's frustration boiled over in conversations with Redlich and Willens in which they seemed to suggest that Liebeler was to blame if the commission had missed evidence of a domestic conspiracy. "I personally cannot be held responsible for the present condition of the work on conspiracy," Liebeler wrote in an angry memo in late August to both of them. "I am more than willing, if able, to accept my full share of responsibility for the work of this staff. I cannot, however, leave myself in the position implied by the . . . oral statements made by both of you which I hope you will both admit upon reflection are false and unfair."

With only days supposedly left in the investigation, Liebeler was astonished at how much work was left to be done. He was startled by the news in August that Marina Oswald had—she claimed—only just recalled that there were still mementoes from Oswald's Mexico trip inside a small brown suitcase that she had kept after the assassination. The FBI, she said, had never bothered to inspect the case. It raised a new, last-minute alarm for the commission's staff about the bureau's basic competence; Liebeler wondered what other evidence the FBI might have missed due to the bungling or laziness of its agents. Several items were found inside the suitcase, including a bus-ticket stub from Oswald's Mexico trip.

On Friday, September 4, as Liebeler was preparing to leave Washington to spend Labor Day weekend at his country home in Vermont, he was given galley proofs of Redlich's edited version of Chapter 4—the chapter that focused on evidence establishing that Oswald was the assassin. There would be little time for Liebeler to enjoy the holiday because, as he read, he became more and more agitated over what Redlich had done—or more precisely, what Redlich had allowed to remain in the chapter from earlier drafts.

Liebeler was troubled, first, by the many factual errors, large and small, that he detected. He thought some of the mistakes were understandable given the large number of people involved in "an extremely painful process" of writing and editing. He was more upset, he recalled, about the overall tone of the report and the way it was still being "overwritten" to suggest that Oswald was so clearly guilty that there was no need to trouble readers with facts that might contradict that conclusion. "It made statements that could not really be supported," Liebeler said. There was a tendency "to downplay or not give equal emphasis to contrary evidence."

Liebeler decided to do something dramatic to protest. And so he sat down at a typewriter he kept in the Vermont house and batted out a twenty-six-page memo, finally totaling more than sixty-seven hundred words, that deconstructed the chapter, paragraph by paragraph. He pointed to dozens of instances of what he described as errors or exaggerations. The memo was, in its own way, a masterwork, proof of Liebeler's keen intelligence and his phenomenal memory; he could recall even the tiniest details of the evidence and witness testimony and match them up against what he was reading in the draft.

In perhaps the most contentious part of the memo, Liebeler said he disagreed fiercely with Redlich and other staff members who believed that Oswald's weapons training in the marines meant that he had an easy shot in Dealey Plaza. Liebeler felt that the report needed to point out that Oswald had been mocked at times by fellow marines during target practice and that he barely passed at least one marksmanship test. The evidence, he said, tended "to indicate that Oswald was not a good shot and that he was not interested in his rifle while in the Marine Corps," yet that conflicting evidence was missing from the draft. "To put it bluntly, that sort of selection from the record could seriously affect the integrity and credibility of the entire report." He continued: "The most honest and the most sensible thing to do given the present state of the record on Oswald's rifle capability would be to write a very short section indicating that there is testimony on both sides of several issues. The commission could then conclude that the best evidence that Oswald could fire his rifle as fast as he did and hit the target is the fact that he did so. It may have been pure luck. It probably was to a very great extent. But it happened."

When he returned from Vermont that weekend, Liebeler placed the memo on Redlich's desk. Initially he heard back nothing. "There was really no response to it for a considerable period of time," Liebeler recalled.

Then, several days later, new page proofs for the chapter arrived in the commission's offices, and Liebeler began to read to see what, if anything, had changed as a result of his memo. The answer, he recalled, was almost nothing; his most serious complaints had been ignored. He marched into Rankin's office to protest. Seeing how angry Liebeler was, Rankin agreed to review the chapter with him—that minute. He asked Liebeler to get a copy of his memo and a set of the galleys and come back to his office. "We sat down, the two of us, and started going through the chapter," Liebeler said. Willens joined them, but apparently not before calling Redlich, who was home in Manhattan that day and at his desk at NYU.

Realizing that his editing was being undone, Redlich dashed to LaGuardia Airport to catch a flight to Washington. He was in the commission's offices that same afternoon. The four of them then "spent the rest of that day and long into the night going over this memorandum and the page proofs, and my recollection is that we considered and discussed all the issues," Liebeler recalled. He got some, but far from all, of the changes he requested. Over the next two weeks, he bombarded Rankin and the others with more memos, totaling an additional eight thousand words.

Liebeler knew his voluminous memos that summer had created a permanent record of how strongly he had fought, over what he considered matters of principle, in the writing of the report, so at some point, he decided to keep copies of his memos for himself. He began to slip the copies out of the commission's offices, putting them in his attaché case, and then filing them away at home, initially at his apartment in Washington. If there ever came a time when the commission's legacy was under attack and he needed to defend his own reputation, Liebeler would have all of his memos and files available; he could make them all public.

Senator Richard Russell was always apologetic about how many of the commission's meetings he missed. As he had predicted from the start, 1964 had turned out to be an awful year in his long career in the Senate. He spent most of the first six months of the year trying, and ultimately failing, to block the momentous civil rights legislation that Johnson had offered as a tribute to Kennedy, most important the Civil Rights Act of 1964. Some of Russell's fellow segregationists had hoped his close friendship with Johnson might convince the White House to weaken the act. Russell, however, had sensed from the start that it was hopeless. He described the Senate vote on the bill on June 19 as "the final act of the longest debate and the greatest tragedy ever played out in the Senate of the United States." It passed overwhelmingly, 73 to 27, and was signed into law by Johnson on July 2. Russell was praised by the president after the Georgian repeatedly urged fellow southerners to comply peacefully with the law. "Violence and defiance are no substitute for the campaign of reason and logic we must wage," Russell said.

Russell's absence from the commission meant that he had mostly forfeited his ability to control how the investigation was conducted, including how the staff was chosen and what they were assigned to do. The controversy over Norman Redlich that spring had created trouble for Russell with conservative constituents back home. Russell drafted a letter that could be sent out to Georgians who wrote in to complain. "Let me tell you again that I did not know that Redlich was working for the commission until the hearings were practically concluded," he wrote, blaming the hiring on Lee Rankin. "When the matter was before the commission, I made it clear that had I known of his employment and background, I would have vigorously opposed his employment, and I told Mr. Rankin that I thought he had been derelict." In May, he had complained directly to Johnson about Redlich. "I sat up last night until 11:30 readin' the FBI reports on some son-of-a-bitch that this fellow Rankin hired over here on the Warren Commission," he told the president in a recorded phone call. "Everybody's raisin' hell about him bein' a Communist and all . . . a left-winger."

But even while he participated little in the day-to-day work of the commission, Russell continued to monitor the investigation with the help of Alfredda Scobey. Every night, he insisted, he took home transcripts of the commission's witness testimony. He read through the commission's paperwork "until I thought my eyes were going to burn up," he complained to an aide. And from a distance, he did not like what he was reading. He repeatedly told his Senate staff that he was disturbed by the way Warren was running the "assassination commission." (Russell's former press secretary, Powell Moore, said later that the senator refused to call it the Warren Commission. "Senator Russell always insisted on calling it the assassination commission.") While the commission might be moving toward a conclusion that Oswald had acted alone, Russell was never certain of it; he said he found it hard to believe that Oswald "could have done all this by himself." He was troubled by what he was reading about Oswald's visit to Mexico and about his friendship while he lived in the Russian city of Minsk with a group of young Cubans.

The passage of the Civil Rights Act allowed Russell to become involved—reluctantly, he said—in the commission's work. He announced that he wanted to see the scene of the assassination for himself and to interview Marina Oswald. He asked Rankin to organize a trip to Dallas. The other two southern lawmakers on the commission—Senator Cooper of Kentucky and Congressman Boggs of Louisiana—agreed to join him. Cooper recalled that Russell hoped he might be able to break Oswald's widow and convince her to tell him secrets that she was still keeping from the commission. Warren, Russell complained, had treated her too gently, even after all her lies had been exposed. The chief justice "was all too grandfatherly," he told his Senate secretary. "She should have been given something closer to a third-degree type of questioning."

Russell's delegation arrived in Dallas on Saturday, September 5, and toured the book depository the next day. Russell nearly created a panic on the streets outside the warehouse. The *Dallas Morning News* reported that about 150 sightseers were startled when they looked up and noticed an elderly man with a rifle standing at the window of the sixth floor, seeming to take aim at them. It was explained to them that it was Senator Russell, holding the weapon as he tried to imagine what Oswald would have seen. "Well, I just hope he's not using real bullets," said a woman scurrying for cover.

That afternoon, the delegation went to a nearby military base to meet Marina Oswald. Russell arrived with a long, handwritten list of questions. The session lasted more than four hours, with the congressmen learning almost nothing that had not been revealed before. Russell focused his questions on the relationship between Mrs. Oswald and her husband; he goaded her, suggesting that Oswald had actually been a "very devoted husband" who had been entitled to her loyalty.

"No," Mrs. Oswald replied. "He was not a good husband."

Russell reminded her that she had testified that Oswald had helped her with the housework and was good with his daughters.

"Well, I also testified to the fact that he beat me on many occasions," she replied. "He was not good when he beat me."

Russell: "He beat you on many occasions?"

Marina: "Many."

Russell pressed her on aspects of her life in Russia before meeting Oswald, including her ties there to the Communist Party and about an uncle who worked for the Russian interior ministry. She could see where the questions were heading; he seemed to be suggesting that she was herself some sort of spy. "I want to assure the commission that I was never given any assignment by the Soviet government," she declared.

The only surprising development in her testimony came when Mrs. Oswald volunteered her new theory that her husband had not intended to kill the president but had instead aimed his rifle at Governor Connally. The governor was the target, she said, because he, as navy secretary, had refused to intervene to overturn her husband's less-than-honorable discharge from the Marine Corps.

Russell doubted she was right: "I think that you have your evidence terribly confused."

Mrs. Oswald readily acknowledged that it was only speculation. "I have no facts whatsoever," she said.

Her appearance that day reflected a seemingly newfound confidence. At her earlier appearances before the commission, she had always brought a lawyer along. This time she did not. "The attorney costs me too much," she said.

During the questioning, Russell, like Warren before him, seemed to soften in the presence of the pretty young widow. He said he was glad that she was writing her memoirs and had found so many other ways to sell her story to newspapers and magazines, since it offered her a way to support herself and her daughters. "I was hoping that you had found some means of commercializing on it either to the moving picture people or to the publishing world."

On matters of national security, Russell was almost certainly the best-informed man in Congress, and it had been that way for years. In 1965, he would mark his tenth year as chairman of the Senate Armed Services Committee. In that job, he was privy to the most highly classified national-security information gathered at both the Pentagon and the CIA; at the time, the budgets of both agencies came under his oversight.

After Fidel Castro came to power in Havana in 1959, Russell would have known many secrets about Cuba, especially. He knew how the Kennedy administration had struggled since its first days in power to oust the Cuban government. That appeared to explain why, in his conversations with President Johnson and others after the assassination, Russell sensed, almost immediately, that Castro might have been involved, and if not Castro personally, some element of the Cuban government that believed it was operating on his behalf. He offered no similar dark suspicions about Soviet leaders.

Russell also sensed that, whatever the truth about the assassination, the CIA and the FBI were not necessarily eager to find it, if only to protect themselves from the discovery that there had been a conspiracy that the two agencies should have been able to disrupt. In his office files, Russell kept a small, ominous note that he had written to himself after the first meeting of the commission back in December. "Something strange is happening," he wrote, referring to the investigation by the CIA and

FBI of Oswald's visit to Mexico. The investigation was only just getting under way, yet there already seemed to be a rush to demonstrate that Oswald was the lone assassin, whatever the evidence—to show that Oswald was the "only one ever considered" as the assassin, Russell wrote. "This to me is an untenable position."

He knew that the CIA and the FBI had insisted from the start that they could find no evidence of a foreign plot. But through long experience, he also knew that the agencies were capable of lying—or so muddying the facts that no one would ever be able to figure out the truth. Also alarming to Russell was the possibility that Warren was being privately briefed—by the CIA? the White House? the president himself?—regarding sensitive elements of the investigation. At that first December meeting, he wrote, the chief justice seemed to know more about the possibility of Cuban involvement than he was telling. Warren appeared to know, for example, about the unconfirmed report from the CIA that Oswald might have received thousands of dollars at the Cuban embassy in Mexico. It surprised Russell that Warren had already been told that. The chief justice "knew all I did and more about [the] CIA."

Russell's last-minute trip to Dallas had not ended his suspicion of a conspiracy. Nor had the trip ended his skepticism about the single-bullet theory. He respected Governor Connally, and if Connally believed he had been hit by a separate bullet, Russell was not going to doubt him. So after returning to Washington, he knew he faced a dilemma as the commission prepared to meet to approve a final report. He needed to ask himself if he could put his name to conclusions that he could not accept. In mid-September, he called in a secretary and began dictating his formal dissent—a document that would remain secret in his Senate files until years after his death.

He began by rejecting the single-bullet theory: "I do not share the finding of the Commission as to the probability that both President Kennedy and Governor Connally were struck by the same bullet. . . . . Reviewing the Zapruder film several times adds to my conviction that the bullet that passed through Governor Connally's body was not the same bullet as that which passed through the President's back and neck."

He then moved on to questions about whether Oswald acted alone: "While I join with my colleagues in the finding that there is no clear and definite evidence connecting any person or group in a conspiracy with

Oswald to assassinate the President, there are some aspects of this case that I cannot decide with absolute certainty." He said he was still alarmed by reports about Oswald's association with the Cuban students in Minsk and by the lack of a "detailed account of all of Oswald's movements, contacts and associations on his secret visit to Mexico." He wrote that he could not share "in a categorical finding that Oswald planned and perpetrated the assassination without the knowledge, encouragement or assistance of another person."

In the final days of editing the report, the staff at last heard back from the FBI about Silvia Odio and her claim of meeting Oswald on her doorstep in Dallas. The bureau said it had new information to prove that the young Cuban woman was wrong. FBI agents had finally identified the three men who were seen at Odio's door—and Oswald was not among them. The news arrived on September 21 in a letter from J. Edgar Hoover. According to Hoover, the bureau had tracked down a thirty-four-year-old Cuban-American truck driver named Loran Eugene Hall who claimed he was one of the anti-Castro militants who went to see Odio. Hall identified himself as a professional mercenary who turned against Castro after serving in his guerrilla army.

In September 1963, Hall said, he had been traveling in Dallas with two fellow anti-Castro guerrillas—Lawrence Howard, who was Mexican-American, and William Seymour, who was not a Latino and spoke only a few words of Spanish—to raise money for the cause, and they had gone to the home of a woman he believed was Odio. Hall thought she might have mistaken Seymour for Oswald.

Hoover acknowledged that the investigation was ongoing and that FBI agents were still searching for Howard and Seymour. Still, there was a sense of relief at the commission about the last-minute news from the FBI. Now the final report could rule out what had previously seemed to be the strongest testimony from any witness suggesting that Oswald might have had coconspirators.

David Slawson, who had pressed so vigorously to pursue Odio's claims, could not recall years later if he had read Hoover's letter, nor did he remember the details of how the bureau had apparently resolved Odio's claims. Like his colleagues, Slawson was simply too busy with the task of completing his part of the report. There was no discussion, or at least none that Slawson could recall, about having someone from the commission interview Hall; there was no time for it. "We could only assume that the FBI had it right."

With Hoover's letter in hand, the portions of the report that dealt with Odio were hurriedly rewritten to explain—and rebut—what she had claimed. In the report, the commission saluted itself for pushing the FBI to revisit Odio's story: "In spite of the fact that it appeared almost certain that Oswald could not have been in Dallas at the time Mrs. Odio thought he was, the Commission requested the FBI to conduct further investigation to determine the validity of Mrs. Odio's testimony." The report noted the FBI's success in tracking down Loran Hall and how it was Hall and his two companions who had appeared at Odio's door. "While the FBI had not yet completed its investigation into this matter at the time the report went to press, the Commission has concluded that Lee Harvey Oswald was not at Mrs. Odio's apartment in September of 1963."

Although the commission was about to close its doors and could no longer monitor the FBI investigation in Dallas, the bureau did continue to pursue the Odio inquiry, and the account it had provided to the commission fell apart almost instantly. Over time, Loran Hall would change his story more than once, eventually insisting—under oath to congressional investigators—that the FBI had misrepresented him and that he had never visited Odio's apartment. He thought the FBI agents who had initially interviewed him might have concocted a false story to appease the commission. Seymour and Howard were also located; both insisted that they did not know Odio and had never been to her apartment. There was evidence to support their denials. The FBI was able to confirm that Seymour had been working in Florida on the night that he was supposedly in Texas.

FBI agents in Dallas paid another visit to Odio on October 1, a week after the commission's report was issued, and showed her photographs of Hall, Howard, and Seymour. She recognized none of them, and she insisted again—as she would insist for decades to come—that it was Lee Harvey Oswald she had seen at the door of her Dallas home in September 1963.

53

THE OFFICES OF REPRESENTATIVE GERALD R. FORD
THE HOUSE OF REPRESENTATIVES
WASHINGTON, DC
SEPTEMBER 1964

Gerald Ford's book project was becoming harder to keep a secret. A fast-growing circle of editors in the publishing industry in New York were aware of his plans to write a book that would be an inside account of the investigation, with publication soon after the commission's report was made public. Ford and his friend and coauthor, Jack Stiles, had lined up the William Morris talent agency to negotiate a deal with the publishing house Simon and Schuster.

The final contract called for Ford to be paid an advance of $10,000, and up to 15 percent of the retail price on each book sold after the advance was recouped; a contract for the paperback rights to the book would be negotiated later. The advance alone was equivalent to nearly half of Ford's $22,500 annual salary in the House.* The book, which would center on Oswald's life story and his possible motives for assassinating Kennedy, was given the title *Portrait of the Assassin*, although Ford had initially suggested *Kennedy's Killer*. Ford had been introduced to the publisher by

---

* The salary of members of the House of Representatives in 1963—$22,500 a year—would be equivalent to about $168,000 in 2013, given inflation. Ford's $10,000 book advance would be equivalent, in 2013, to about $75,000.

the editor of *Life* magazine, Edward K. Thompson, who wanted to publish an excerpt of the book in conjunction with the release of the commission's final report.

Simon and Schuster decided to go ahead with the book despite internal qualms, both about the quality of the sample chapters they were reading—"effortful, awkward suspense writing," one editor said—and the propriety of Ford taking on the project at all. "I am still disturbed by the idea of one member of this august body writing a one-man 'behind-the-scenes story,'" another editor wrote.

Ford had worked throughout the summer to keep *Life* and Simon and Schuster interested in the project, even inviting editors from the magazine and the publishing house to come down to Washington to read through internal commission documents stored in his office. He made the offer even at a time when he knew he was facing questions from the FBI about whether he had leaked Oswald's "Historic Diary" to *Life*. "Got Jerry Ford on the telephone," Thompson, the magazine editor, wrote on July 8 to an executive at Simon and Schuster. "He suggested that someone might want to see some of the basic documents in his Washington office . . . and if you think that ought to be done, let me know." Thompson put his own journalistic curiosity aside and passed up the offer to see the secret files. He had reminded Ford, he wrote, that documents by themselves would not sell books. Readers would instead want to read Ford's "personal contribution"—his private thoughts about the investigation and about Oswald. "I didn't see much purpose to be served by going over the documents, which so far are strictly from the commission."

In the face of later criticism that he was trying to profit off the assassination, he insisted that the book was a valuable contribution to the historical record. Ford also saw nothing wrong, he said, with his decision to allow Stiles and his other informal advisers—including John Ray, the retired congressman, and Francis Fallon, the Harvard Law student—to review classified documents. "They made a good team," he said of his circle of advisers. "Jack was a writer, John a lawyer. They prepared questions for me to ask at commission hearings, they analyzed the transcripts, looking for discrepancies." Without them, he said, he might have fallen far behind on his work for the commission.

The year had proved unusually busy anyway for Ford. He was always swamped with work as a result of his membership on the House

Appropriations Committee, and in 1964 he was drawn deeply into national politics. That summer, it was widely reported that he was on the short list of vice presidential candidates being considered by Barry Goldwater. Fallon, who turned twenty-three that year, came away impressed with Ford's commitment to the investigation, despite his heavy duties in Congress. He thought Ford's only failing as a commissioner was his tendency to assume the best about the FBI and J. Edgar Hoover.

As the summer wore on, Fallon urged Ford to press the commission to keep looking for evidence of a conspiracy. In a memo on July 31, he told Ford he was worried that the report was being written to gloss over evidence suggesting that Oswald had been trained for espionage in the Soviet Union. "Don't allow a whitewash job," Fallon told Ford. "In too many areas, we just don't have enough information. Try to get more info if possible. Be sure you see sources for statements attributed to 'confidential sources.'" Ford's friend Stiles expressed even stronger suspicions. On September 4, with the investigation nearly at an end, he urged Ford to consider again the possibility that Oswald had been someone's spy. "Do we have any real proof that Oswald was not an agent? We have no proof that he was, but it is a different matter to totally close the door on the subject."

Ford was closing no doors prematurely, he insisted. He said later he carefully weighed all of the conspiracy theories, including some that had not been widely shared with the public. In May, a reporter for the *Detroit Free Press*, the largest morning newspaper in Ford's home state, contacted him to ask what he made of rumors that Oswald had been part of a conspiracy to kill Kennedy that was launched in New Orleans when he lived there in 1963. The rumors were complicated to follow and they had elements of the salacious, which explained why many reporters outside Louisiana had declined to pursue them.

The rumors focused on a New Orleans man who was involved in right-wing groups seeking Castro's overthrow: a former Eastern Airlines pilot named David Ferrie, who had been questioned by both New Orleans police and the FBI shortly after the assassination. As a teenager, Oswald had belonged to a Louisiana squadron of the Civil Air Patrol, or CAP—a volunteer group sponsored by the United States Air Force to encourage aviation enthusiasts. Records showed that Oswald had been a member of the local squadron at a time when Ferrie was helping run it; Ferrie would adamantly deny knowing Oswald, although a photograph would emerge years later that seemed to show them together at a CAP meeting.

Ford scribbled down notes to himself as he heard the increasingly bizarre story about Ferrie (he misspelled the name as "Ferry"), who had been dismissed by the airline "for homosexual activity" involving teenage boys and who—the reporter said—"wears a wig and false eyebrows." (Ferrie suffered from alopecia, an ailment that causes the loss of body hair.) According to the Detroit reporter, Ferrie was also tied to organized crime figures; he worked as a part-time investigator for a New Orleans lawyer who represented local mob chief Carlos Marcello, and it was rumored that he had flown Marcello back into the United States after a Justice Department attempt to deport him during the Kennedy administration.

"Probably knew O in CAP," Ford wrote in his notes, referring to Oswald and the Civil Air Patrol. "Lee Harvey Oswald—Homosexual?" He tried to imagine how these details might come together. If Oswald was tied to Ferrie, possibily through a shared sexual orientation or through Cuban exile groups, could that mean that he was also tied to a Mafia boss who might have wanted revenge against Kennedy?

On the commission's staff, the investigation of the rumors about Ferrie—and about the possibility of other ties among Oswald and organized-crime figures in New Orleans—was assigned to Wesley Liebeler. During his New Orleans trip in July, Liebeler found nothing to support the idea of any larger conspiracy involving Ferrie or the Mafia. As a result, there was no mention of the rumors about Ferrie at all in the commission's final report. "The FBI did a very substantial piece of work on Ferrie," Liebeler said later. "It just did not lead anywhere."*

By the end of the investigation, Ford said he had come to accept that conspiracy theories about the assassination were unavoidable given "the complexity of events, the freakish coincidences of facts" that the commission was uncovering. "In retrospect, the unbelievable coincidences that took place couldn't happen—and yet they did." In conversations with Stiles, Ford tried to talk through all of the possible conspiracies. They found useful ways of framing the discussion, especially after they realized that most conspiracy theories required that Oswald be a "plant" at

---

* Liebeler also investigated allegations that Oswald was connected to Marcello through an uncle who lived in New Orleans, Charles "Dutz" Murret, a New Orleans bookie alleged to be tied to Marcello's crime network. The commission found no evidence of any link between Murret and the assassination.

the Texas School Book Depository. Could that be true? They reviewed the facts of how he had gotten the job in October—how at Marina Oswald's urging, Ruth Paine had phoned a supervisor at the book depository, who agreed to meet with Oswald and then hired him. The book depository had two warehouses in Dallas. Unless the supervisor was somehow in on the conspiracy, it was only chance that led him to assign Oswald to the building that overlooked Dealey Plaza.

Ford found another effective way to frame the debate—by analyzing calendars for the final months of 1963. If Oswald and his coconspirators had somehow arranged for him to get a job at the book depository, they would have needed to know that Kennedy's motorcade would pass in front of the building. Ford reviewed the chronology of Kennedy's Texas trip and how it had been organized by the White House. The timelines showed that Kennedy's plans to visit Texas on November 21 and 22 had been known publicly since late September. But the inclusion of Dallas in the itinerary was not confirmed until November 9—three weeks after Oswald had been hired at the book depository. And it was not until November 19, only three days before Kennedy's arrival, that the motorcade route past the book depository was made public. It was "sheer coincidence" that put Oswald in a building where he would have a clear shot at the president, Ford could see. "Fate put him in the right place at the right time to play his black role."

Similarly, Ford felt that the timeline of the events of Sunday, November 24, the day Oswald was killed, proved that Ruby had not been part of a conspiracy. It was "pure happenstance" that had given Ruby the time he needed to get to the basement of police headquarters to gun down Oswald. The transfer of Oswald to the county jail had been held up at the last minute at the request of a federal postal inspector who wanted the chance to ask a few questions of the accused assassin; the inspector had been at Sunday church services and could not get there earlier. That brief delay gave Ruby—who had been across the street at a Western Union office, wiring $25 to one of his strippers—the time he needed. If Oswald's transfer had been moved up just two or three minutes, Ruby would have arrived too late.

Ford was frustrated by the commission's failure to reach a judgment about Oswald's motives. In his book with Stiles and in his later comments on the assassination, he offered his best guess about what drove

Oswald to kill President Kennedy, and it would prove to be the most detailed, and in many ways the most thoughtful, explanation offered by any of the commissioners.

In Ford's view, many of the answers could be found in Oswald's "Historic Diary." Oswald was not motivated principally by politics in anything he did, Ford thought. His "so-called Marxism" was "a mishmash of revolutionary dialectics and dreams of a better society he could not put his finger on." Instead, Ford believed, Oswald was motivated by a desperate craving for attention and a childlike stubbornness that blocked his ability to call off an act to which he had committed himself. Ford was the father of four young children, three of them boys, and he thought he knew enough about child psychology to sense that Oswald had not outgrown the impulses of a juvenile. The "Historic Diary" was a "vivid self-portrait of a young man, who, when he couldn't have his own way, resorted to melodramatic and rash actions to call attention to himself," he wrote. "When thwarted by circumstances, an ordinary person might beat his fists on the table or, better yet, learn a lesson. But not Lee Harvey Oswald. . . . He was like a child who, failing to gain the attention he wants, finds that smashing a toy or making a mess is the easiest way to obtain recognition."

Ford thought something else had motivated Oswald, although he did not put it in his book or say it publicly. It involved Oswald's sexuality. The commission had heard from witnesses, several times, about the Oswalds' sexual problems. Ford guessed that Oswald was impotent and that Marina's mocking of his sexual performance had left him so humiliated that he set out to prove his masculinity with a rifle. "I have a feeling, and I think others shared it, that he, Oswald, was being prodded by his wife on his impotence," Ford said in a 2003 interview published after his death. "He had to do something to display his bravado."

As Ford and his advisers read through draft chapters of the report, they pulled together long lists of editing suggestions that Ford then submitted to the commission. His editing changes were easy to track, since he submitted them—for each draft chapter—in a letter on House stationery addressed to Rankin. Many of his suggestions were welcome, since he often caught errors, reflecting the close reading that his advisers had given the drafts. On September 2, he wrote Rankin to insist that the commission correct a statement suggesting that Oswald rarely drank alcohol, an assertion that would undermine possibly credible witnesses who had claimed to see him in bars in New Orleans and Dallas. "The record is clear that he drank liquor, sometimes to excess, while he was in Russia, and also in New Orleans in 1963." As Ford had recommended, the passage was deleted.

He urged another change that would later become controversial, asking that a key sentence about the medical evidence be rewritten to clarify the location of the entrance wound on Kennedy's body from the first bullet to hit him—the one that had apparently also hit Connally. The draft had originally said that "a bullet had entered his back at a point slightly above the shoulder and to the right of the spine." On his copy, Ford crossed out those words and changed them to: "A bullet had entered the base of the back of his neck slightly to the right of the spine." The change was made. Ford explained years later that he was only trying to clarify the wound's location. "To any reasonable person, 'above the shoulder and to the right' sounds very high and way off to the side—and that's the way it sounded to me." Conspiracy theorists would later claim that Ford was instead trying to deceive readers about the bullet's trajectory in an effort to bolster the single-bullet theory. In fact, Ford's change appeared to reflect the commission's continuing confusion about exactly where the bullets had landed.

Decades later, a congressionally authorized review by a team of independent medical experts determined that the navy pathologists who conducted the autopsy at Bethesda Naval Hospital had made astonishing errors, including misstating the location of both entrance wounds in Kennedy's body. When outside pathologists were finally shown the autopsy photos, they concluded that the first shot struck lower in the back than the autopsy report suggested and that the entrance wound in the head was a full four inches higher.

Warren said it was alarming for him to look at the calendar in September and realize how few days remained until the first Monday in October— that year, Monday, October 5—and the start of a new term for the Supreme Court. He and Rankin announced a schedule for the completion of the commission's work. The final executive session was set for Friday, September 18, at ten a.m., in the hearing room at the VFW building, with the full day set aside for the commissioners to debate and approve the report. The final edited galleys would then be transferred to the Government Printing Office, with a copy of the bound report ready to be hand-delivered to President Johnson the following Thursday, September 24, at the White House.

Warren was more determined than ever to produce a unanimous report; anything less might lead the public to conclude that the facts about the president's murder were still uncertain or that they were being hidden. "It would have been disastrous if we hadn't been unanimous," he told Drew Pearson. To Pearson, he recalled again, with pride, the behind-the-scenes campaign he had mounted to achieve a unanimous decision in *Brown v. Board of Education* in 1954. He remembered the satisfaction he felt at the moment the Brown ruling was read out, by him, in the court: "When the word 'unanimously' was spoken, a wave of emotion swept the room," he said. It was an "instinctive emotional manifestation that defies description."

But to obtain a unanimous verdict in an important Supreme Court case, Warren often needed months of planning—and coaxing. In the Brown decision, he mounted what was, in effect, an aggressive lobbying campaign over several months to convince colleagues to sign on to the ruling, even appearing at one justice's hospital bedside to press the case. To obtain unanimity on the assassination report, however, the chief justice would have only weeks, or even days. If Warren intended to adhere to the deadlines he had set, the final executive session on September 18 would be his last and only chance to convince the commissioners that they needed to speak with one voice about the president's death.

Since the commission was no longer keeping transcripts of its deliberations, at least none that would ever be made public, there would be no way of saying with certainty how Warren achieved the unanimous report or how close he might have come to failure. Over the years, however, some of the commissioners would give accounts of what happened that day.

Russell revealed later that he had gone into the meeting ready to sign a dissent—he had already written one, after all—and he suspected other commissioners would join him in defying Warren. He had been saying for weeks that he did not believe, or at least could not support, the single-bullet theory. Yet the draft chapters he was shown before the meeting concluded that the theory had to be true. Russell felt almost as strongly, he said, that the commission had to leave open the possibility that Oswald had been part of a conspiracy. But the draft chapters, as he read them, stated flatly that Oswald had acted alone.

Russell told aides after the meeting that Warren had, at first, stubbornly refused to alter the report to raise any questions about the single-bullet theory. "Warren just wouldn't give in," he told his longtime Senate secretary. "He was adamant that this was the way it was gonna be." According to Russell's account, Warren explained the necessity for a unanimous report and then urged the commission to adopt the findings as they had been laid out by the staff: Russell recalled that Warren looked around the room at the other commissioners and declared, before inviting any discussion, "We're all agreed and we're going to sign the report."

That was when Russell spoke up to correct—and to challenge—the chief justice. They were *not* in agreement. There would be a dissent, he warned, especially about the single-bullet theory. "I'll never sign that report if this commission says categorically that the second shot passed through both" Kennedy and Connally, he declared. He was offended, he said, by the idea that the commission would challenge Connally's certainty that he had been hit by a separate bullet. Senator Cooper spoke up to support Russell, saying he also believed Connally and would sign the dissent. Russell remembered Congressman Boggs suggested that he, too, was not fully convinced by the single-bullet theory.

On what he expected would be the final substantive day of the commission's work, Warren was suddenly faced with a rebellion, and the possibility of a divided report. Two, and perhaps three, commissioners were prepared to dissent.

Warren said consistently in the years after the investigation that he believed, strongly, in the single-bullet theory and that he understood the argument made passionately by the staff that the theory had to be true if Oswald had acted alone. But Warren had spent most of his career not on the bench but in politics. He knew—probably as well as anyone in that room—that while compromise could be distasteful when it meant shading the truth, it could also be the price of getting something done. So he agreed to negotiate.

The result was language, approved by both Warren and Russell, that watered down the original text and left open the possibility that Connally had been hit by a separate bullet—an assertion that the commission's staff believed simply made no sense. The awkward compromise language inserted into the report read:

> Although it is not necessary to any essential findings of the commission to determine just which shot hit Governor Connally, there is very persuasive evidence from the experts to indicate that the same bullet which pierced the President's throat also caused Governor Connally's wounds. However, Governor Connally's testimony and certain other factors have given rise to some difference of opinion as to this probability, but there is no question in the mind of any member of the Commission that all the shots which caused the President's and Governor Connally's wounds were fired from the sixth floor window of the Texas School Book Depository.

Russell wanted other changes in the report. He announced that he was again prepared to dissent if the commission did not leave open the possibility of a conspiracy. He said he agreed that Oswald appeared to be the lone gunman. But he declared it wrong to suggest that there was not even a remote possibility that Oswald had coconspirators in Dallas or elsewhere. "I agree wholly with the facts before us, but we cannot say that at some point in the future there may not be some other evidence," Russell told Warren. "We cannot categorically close the door to the facts that may arise."

This time, Ford said, he stepped forward to support Russell, and the rewriting on this point was less tortured. Rather than make an unqualified statement that there had been no conspiracy, the report was rewritten to say that instead, the commission had found "no evidence" of a conspiracy, leaving open the possibility that the evidence might emerge someday. And with that, the chief justice had what he wanted: a unanimous report that, he hoped, would forever end the dark rumors about the assassination of a president he had so admired, even loved. Warren announced that the seven commissioners would meet again in six days' time at the White House to present the report to President Johnson.

Lee Rankin came out of the meeting to explain to his deputies, Howard Willens and Norman Redlich, what had happened. Willens was appalled. By backing away from full support for the single-bullet theory, the commission was being dishonest, several staff lawyers agreed. "Rankin made an effort to explain the commission's decision to Redlich and me, but we could not accept the excuses that he offered," Willens recalled. The changes had obviously been made "out of deference to Connally," not because of any commitment to the truth. The Texas governor's mistake in insisting that he was hit by a separate bullet was understandable, but it still was a mistake. Yet the commission was now suggesting that Connally might be right, which left open—forever—the possibility of a second gunman. "The compromise was indefensible and endangered the credibility of the report," Willens said later. "It raised more questions than it answered and gave comfort to conspiracy theorists for decades to come."

None of the commissioners reported any serious debate at the meeting about the harshness of the wording of the report's criticism of the FBI and the Secret Service. The agencies would be castigated for their failure to share information about possible threats to the president; in particular, the bureau's Dallas office and FBI agent James Hosty would be singled out for having failed to share Oswald's name with the Secret Service ahead of Kennedy's visit. "The FBI took an unduly restrictive view of its role in preventive intelligence work prior to the assassination," the report concluded. "A more carefully coordinated treatment of the Oswald case by the FBI might well have resulted in bringing Oswald's activities to the attention of the Secret Service."

The Secret Service was more harshly criticized, with the commission calling for the agency to "completely overhaul" the way it gathered information about potential threats to the president. The report called on President Johnson to set up a cabinet-level committee to monitor the performance of the Secret Service. As Warren had insisted, the report recounted how agents in the Dallas motorcade had gone out drinking the night before the assassination; the report seemed to suggest, but did not say explicitly, that the agents could have saved the president's life: "It is conceivable that those men who had little sleep, and who had consumed alcoholic beverages, even in limited quantities, might have been more alert."

Despite his outspoken support for Hoover, Ford said later that he did not seek to soften the report's criticism of the FBI; he thought Hoover would be comforted to see that the Secret Service was the far bigger target. From his reading of the findings, Ford said, "roughly 80 percent of our criticism" was directed at the Secret Service. "We found fault with the FBI only to a minor degree."

Nor was there any debate, the commissioners recalled, about the report's harsh criticism of municipal law-enforcement officials in Dallas, especially the city's police department and the incompetence that had allowed Oswald to be murdered on live national television. As Russell said later, apparently facetiously, "It appeared to me that the Dallas police department was determined to let Oswald be executed without a trial."

One prominent federal agency escaped criticism: the CIA. The report did not say it directly, but the commission seemed to accept the spy agency's assessment that it had performed competently in its occasional surveillance of Oswald over the years, including in Mexico City. The CIA appeared to come out of the investigation with the respect of most of the commissioners, as well as of the staff, if only because the agency—in such sharp contrast to the FBI—had appeared willing to cooperate.

The only official record of the commission's last executive session was a drily written, seven-page summary that said nothing about the heated debates later described by Russell and Ford. In purporting to explain what had happened in the meeting, the summary was fundamentally dishonest. The typewritten document—its author is not identified—made no mention of the dispute over the single-bullet theory, nor did it describe the debate that led the commission to leave open the possibility of a conspiracy. The summary made no reference at all to Russell's threats of a dissent. The record would only show that the final report was approved and that it was approved unanimously.

54

President Johnson wanted to talk to his old friend Richard Russell, and he had the White House switchboard track Russell down at his home in Georgia, where the senator had gone for the weekend. The final meeting of the Warren Commission to approve its report had taken place earlier in the day, and Russell—exhausted, he said—fled Washington within hours.

If Johnson was even aware of the commission's meeting that day, it was not clear from the recording that was made of the phone call. He seemed far more eager to talk with Russell in his old mentor's role as chairman of the Armed Services Committee. Johnson had been consumed with reports throughout the day of a clash in the South China Sea between a pair of American destroyers and four North Vietnamese patrol boats. Just a month earlier, a skirmish between American and North Vietnamese warships in the Gulf of Tonkin had led Johnson to order bombing raids on North Vietnamese military compounds and prompted Congress to pass the so-called Gulf of Tonkin Resolution, granting Johnson broad powers to respond to threats from the Communist North. The resolution would eventually enable Johnson to order the first large deployments of American troops to Vietnam.

By day's end Friday, Johnson was relieved by news that the initial reports of the clash with the North Vietnamese that morning were overstated. Still, with the presidential election six weeks away and Vietnam a potential flashpoint in the campaign, Johnson wanted to discuss the situation in Southeast Asia—and its political implications—with Russell, whose support he would want for any move to escalate the fight in Vietnam.

Johnson reached Russell just before eight p.m.

"Well, you're always leavin' town," Johnson told the senator in a joking tone. "You must not like it up here."

"Well, you left," Russell replied, referring to a trip that Johnson had made to the West Coast a few days earlier. "No, that dang Warren Commission business has whupped me down so."

He explained that the commission had approved the final report that afternoon. "You know what I did? I went over, got on the plane, came home. I didn't even have a toothbrush I got a few little things here. I didn't even have my antihistamine pills to take care of my emphysema."

Johnson: "Why did you get in such a rush?"

Russell: "Well, I was just worn out, fightin' over that damn report."

Johnson: "Well, you oughta taken another hour and gone to get your clothes."

"No, no," Russell replied. "Well, they were trying to prove that same bullet that hit Kennedy first was the one that hit Connally . . . went through him and through his hand, his bone, into his leg and everything else."

Johnson: "What difference does it make which bullet got Connally?"

Russell: "Well, it don't make much difference. But they believe . . . the commission believes that the same bullet that hit Kennedy hit Connally. Well, I don't believe it!"

"I don't either," Johnson replied, a comment that seemed to reflect his respect for Russell, not any detailed understanding of the single-bullet theory.

"And I couldn't sign it," Russell continued. "And I said that Governor Connally testified directly to the contrary, and I'm not gonna approve of that. So I finally made 'em say there was a difference in the Commission, in that part of 'em believed that that wasn't so."

Johnson wanted to know what the rest of the report would say: "What's the net of the whole thing? What's it say? That Oswald did it, and he did it for any reason?"

Russell: "Well, just that he was a general misanthropic fella that . . . had never been satisfied anywhere he was on earth, in Russia or here, and that he had a desire to get his name in history and all. I don't think you'll be displeased with the report. It's too long, but . . ."

Johnson: "Unanimous?"

Russell: "Yes, sir."

Johnson: "Hmmm."

Russell: "I tried my best to get in a dissent, but they'd come round and trade me out of it by giving me a little old thread of it." (Russell appeared to be referring to Warren's concession to rewrite the report to leave a "thread" of doubt, both about the single-bullet theory and a possible conspiracy.) With that, the conversation moved on to the developments in Vietnam.

The last days before publication were a frenzy, with the remaining staff lawyers—and the team of Supreme Court clerks, called in to help—checking and double-checking the text. "I just worked like a dog the last days," David Slawson remembered. His law firm in Denver was desperate to have him return to work on a major antitrust case—the firm's partners had originally been assured that Slawson would return by mid-spring—and so Slawson declared that Friday, September 18, would be his last day in the office. It was the same day the commissioners approved the report.

In his final hours at his desk, Slawson began to feel ill. "I thought, 'Oh Christ, I'm coming down with the flu,'" he said. But it was not the flu. Instead, he was exhausted to the point of collapse. "When I left on Friday night, I went to bed and . . . I didn't get up until Sunday. I didn't eat anything for two days. I just slept." On Sunday, he felt well enough to begin the three-day drive back to Denver.

John McCloy said he was disturbed, slightly, by the hurry to complete the investigation. He thought the commission had reached the right conclusions but that the report could have been better, more clearly written. "We had no rush to judgment," he recalled, but "there were some questions of style. . . . I had a feeling at the end we were rushing a little bit." That helped explain several sloppy errors in the report, including a number of misattributed footnotes and misspelled names, and many instances in which information in one chapter was repeated, almost word for word, in another.

In preparing to close down the office, the commission determined which staff lawyers had worked the hardest—as measured by the workdays for which they had billed the commission—and who had done almost no work at all. To no one's surprise, the records showed that Frank Adams, Specter's long-absent partner, had worked the least—a total of 16 days, five hours. Coleman came in second, although he worked four times as many days as Adams, for a total of 64 days. Among the junior lawyers, Burt Griffin had worked the most days—225—followed by Liebeler with 219 and Slawson with 211. The senior staff lawyer with the most workdays was Lee Rankin: 308, which meant that he had, effectively, worked more than a full workday every day, including weekends, since he was hired in December. Few on the staff doubted it was true.

In the final weeks of the investigation, the trio of women who, more than any other, had held the panel's attention—Jacqueline Kennedy, Marina Oswald, and Marguerite Oswald—made contact with the commission. Mrs. Kennedy sent word through intermediaries that she wanted to take custody of her husband's blood-soaked clothes. In their final executive session, the commissioners gave their consent, so long as she agreed to make the clothes available to later investigations "to support the work the commission has done."

Warren said later he refused to turn over the clothing unconditionally. "Little Mrs. Kennedy asked me for the president's clothing," he told Drew Pearson, according to Pearson's diary. "I suspected she wanted to destroy it, but I declined. We couldn't be in the position of suppressing or destroying any evidence." Ultimately, she did not take the clothes. "In the end, we sent his clothing, the X-rays and the photographs to the Justice Department with instructions that they should not be shown to the public," Warren said. The clothes were later turned over to the National Archives for preservation in perpetuity.

Oswald's widow and mother would also be left unsatisfied. Until the final days of the commission's work, Marina Oswald asked for the return of all of her husband's belongings, including both the Mannlicher-Carcano rifle and Smith & Wesson pistol. The request for the weapons was denied, a decision made easier by the discovery that she was trying to sell them to collectors.

The staff lawyers said they were not surprised when a letter arrived in mid-August from a Manhattan literary agent representing Marguerite Oswald. Mrs. Oswald, the agent said, was insisting that the commission be blocked from making any use of her testimony or any of the material she had given to the investigation—"photographs, documents or any other kind of property of hers"—without her permission. The commission needed her "written consent, which you do not presently have," the agent warned. For good measure, the agent sent copies of the letter to the White House, the Speaker of the House, and the president of the Senate; Mrs. Oswald, he made clear, wanted to put everybody in the federal government on notice of her demands. To no avail, however: the commission ignored the letter and published her testimony in full.

Like her daughter-in-law, Mrs. Oswald was busy selling off souvenirs of her son's life. Earlier that year, she had sold *Esquire* magazine sixteen letters that her son had written to her from Russia, for a reported $4,000; the letters were published along with photos of Mrs. Oswald taken for the magazine by the celebrated photographer Diane Arbus. Mrs. Oswald also recorded a phonograph album that year in which she read from the letters.

On Thursday morning, September 24, Chief Justice Warren lifted the navy-blue box that contained a copy of the final report—four inches thick, 888 pages, 296,000 words—and handed it to President Johnson in the White House Cabinet Room. A swarm of reporters and photographers recorded the scene. "It's pretty heavy," the president said—the only words he spoke that reporters could make out clearly. The White House released a letter that day that the president had written to Warren: "The Commission, I know, has been guided by a determination to find and tell the whole truth of these terrible events."

Warren was joined for the ceremony by the other six members of the commission. Under an agreement with the White House press corps, the report was not released to the public that day. Johnson planned to take it with him to his ranch in Johnson City, Texas, to read over the weekend. On Saturday, news organizations would be given copies with the understanding that their stories would be embargoed for release at six thirty p.m. Sunday, Eastern time. The three television networks announced plans for live programs that night to reveal the report's conclusions. CBS News planned a two-hour special that would include interviews with many of the eyewitnesses to the murder of either President Kennedy or Officer Tippit. "We ended up with 26 witnesses, all of whom had appeared before the commission and all of whom told us the same story they told the commission," said Leslie Midgley, the show's producer. The *New York*

Times announced plans to publish the entire report in Monday's edition and, two days later, to publish the full report as a softcover book in conjunction with Bantam Books, with a retail price of $2. For readers in Washington who did not want to wait, the official report published by the Government Printing Office would be available for sale at eight thirty Monday morning—$3.25 for the hardcover edition, $2.50 for the softcover. The commission announced plans to release the twenty-six volumes of the appendix—containing much of the evidence of the investigation, as well as witness testimony—later that year.

The headline in the *New York Times* that Monday ran across the entire front page in black type only slightly smaller than the font size used ten months earlier for the headline reporting Kennedy's death:

> WARREN COMMISSION FINDS OSWALD GUILTY
> AND SAYS ASSASSIN AND RUBY ACTED ALONE;
> REBUKES SECRET SERVICE, ASKS REVAMPING

Anthony Lewis of the *Times*, the recipient of so many of the commission's leaks, wrote a sweeping, three-thousand-word article on the front page that—in its opening paragraph—stated the report's findings as fact, without attribution, as if there was no question about the truth of what the investigation had found:

> WASHINGTON, Sept. 27—The assassination of President Kennedy was the work of one man, Lee Harvey Oswald. There was no conspiracy, foreign or domestic.

The article praised the report for its "painstaking detail, fairness and neutrality" and "genuine literary style." The article continued: "Few who loved John Kennedy, or this country, will be able to read it without emotion." In an editorial, the *Times* declared that the report was "comprehensive and convincing," adding: "The facts—exhaustively gathered, independently checked and cogently set forth—destroy the basis for the conspiracy theories that have grown weedlike in this country and abroad."

Time magazine was also full of praise: "In its final form, the Commission's report was amazing in its detail, remarkable in its judicious caution and restraint, yet utterly convincing in its major conclusions."

There were a few discordant notes in the nation's major newspapers. James Reston, the respected Washington columnist for the *Times*, suggested that while the commission had "tried, as a servant of history, to discover truth," the report was disappointing because it had left many questions unresolved. "The central mystery of who killed the President has been answered by the commission only in the process of raising a new catalogue of mysteries," including why Oswald had done it; his motives were only guessed at in the report. On that question, Reston concluded, "the distinguished members of the commission and their staff obviously gave up."

Warren was pleased with the response from the Kennedy family. Just weeks before the report's release, Robert Kennedy had stepped down as attorney general to join the race for a Senate seat in his newly adopted home state of New York. On the day of the release, he provided reporters with a written statement in which he said he believed the Warren Commission had established the truth about his brother's murder. His praise was unqualified. He noted that he had "not read the report, nor do I intend to." It would simply be too painful, his friends said. "But I have been briefed on it and I am completely satisfied that the commission investigated every lead and examined every piece of evidence. The commission's inquiry was thorough and conscientious. . . . As I said in Poland last summer, I am convinced Oswald was solely responsible for what happened and that he did not have any outside help or assistance. He was a malcontent who could not get along here or in the Soviet Union."

At his request, his surviving brother, Senator Edward Kennedy of Massachusetts, did read through the report and arranged a meeting with the chief justice in the commission's offices to discuss how the panel had reached its conclusions. "Bobby asked me . . . because he emotionally couldn't do it," Kennedy recalled later in his memoirs. "When I reached him by telephone, Warren told me he would be glad to give me a briefing and go over the parts of the report that were particularly contentious." The chief justice "gave me a full briefing, as I requested," he said. "I asked many questions. The whole process took about four hours." He recalled that Warren "told me quite persuasively that he felt a responsibility to the nation to get it right." And Kennedy said he came away convinced that the commission had gotten it right, and that Oswald had acted alone. "I reported to Bobby that I accepted the commission's report and thought he should, too. Bobby agreed readily." According to Edward Kennedy, at least, his brother "did not want to continue to investigate Jack's death."

For Warren there was also a heartening initial response from the public. Opinion polls suggested that the investigation had convinced millions of Americans that there had been no conspiracy. The Harris Survey conducted polls in September 1964, just before release of the report, and in October, just after it was issued. The polls showed that after the report, 87 percent of respondents believed that Oswald had killed the president, up from 76 percent days before. The share of the polls' respondents who believed that Oswald had accomplices fell to 31 percent, from 40 percent just before the report's release. It would be the last time a major national poll showed that a plurality of Americans accepted the idea that Oswald acted alone.

Some of the commissioners reveled in the early praise. Congressman Boggs was quoted in the weekly newspaper the *National Observer* on October 5 as saying he should write a book because he had kept such extensive notes. "It was he who wrote many of the 300,000 words in the final report," the newspaper declared, a statement that drew chuckles from staff lawyers who knew the truth.

One commissioner, however, wanted to distance himself almost immediately from the report: Richard Russell. He gave an interview to the *Atlanta Constitution*, his state's largest newspaper, for an article published two days after the report's release. Although he described the report as "the very best we could have submitted," he expressed skepticism that the commission knew the full truth. It was still unknown, he said, if Oswald acted "with the encouragement or knowledge of anyone else," adding that speculation about Kennedy's death would "continue for hundreds of years or longer."

J. Edgar Hoover got his copy of the report on September 24, the same day as President Johnson, and he immediately turned it over to Assistant Director James Gale, the head of the FBI's internal affairs department. Hoover attached a note: "I want this carefully reviewed as it pertains to FBI shortcomings. Chapter 8 tears us to pieces."

For Hoover, the news was as bad as he had long feared. As he saw it, the bureau had been disgraced, and it might even be dismantled, as a result of the report, given the suggestion that the FBI had missed a chance to prevent the president's assassination. The commission did not accuse Hoover himself of any personal misconduct, although it would later become clear from his own files that he had lied repeatedly—and under oath. His most obvious lie was his repeated statement that FBI agents had not mishandled the investigation of Oswald before the assassination, even as he was quietly disciplining those same agents.

After reading the report, Gale urged Hoover on September 30 to begin a second round of punishments of FBI employees. The report, Gale wrote, "has now set forth in a very damning manner some of the same glaring weaknesses for which we previously disciplined our personnel, such as lack of vigorous investigation after we had established that Oswald visited the Soviet Embassy in Mexico." Gale said it was "appropriate at this time to consider further administrative action against those primarily culpable for the derelictions in this case, which have now had the effect of publicly embarrassing the bureau." Hoover agreed. In the new wave of disciplinary action, seventeen FBI agents and others would be demoted or otherwise punished; all but three of them had been disciplined in the first round, as well. Agent James Hosty was demoted and immediately transferred to Kansas City. "There is no question in my mind but that we failed in carrying through some of the most salient aspects of the Oswald investigation," Hoover wrote to a group of his senior aides on October 12. "It ought to be a lesson to us all, but I doubt if some even realize it now."

As with the first round of punishments, some of Hoover's inner circle feared that the news would leak. "I think we are making a tactical error by taking this disciplinary action in this case at this time," Assistant Director Alan Belmont wrote Hoover in October. "The Warren Commission report has just been released. It contains criticism of the FBI. We are currently taking aggressive steps to challenge the findings of the Warren Commission insofar as they pertain to the FBI. It is most important, therefore, that we not provide a foothold for our critics or the general public to say, in effect, 'See, the Commission is right.'"

Hoover angrily disagreed; there would be no delay. "We were wrong," he replied to Belmont. "The administrative action approved by me will stand. I do not intend to palliate actions which have resulted in forever destroying the Bureau as the top level investigative organization." In a separate note to a deputy on October 6, he wrote that "the FBI will never live down this smear, which could have been so easily avoided if there had been proper supervision and initiative."

Even as he was effectively, if secretly, agreeing with much of the commission's criticism of the bureau, Hoover lashed out against the report. In a series of letters to the White House and Acting Attorney General Nicholas Katzenbach, Hoover complained that the report was "seriously inaccurate insofar as its treatment of the FBI is concerned." He offered a detailed list of what he said were errors in the commission's portrayal of the bureau.

Hoover's office instructed FBI inspector James Malley, the bureau's day-to-day liaison with the commission, to telephone Rankin on Hoover's behalf. Malley was instructed to inform Rankin that he "did the bureau a great disservice and had out-McCarthy-ed McCarthy." Hoover also prepared himself to strike back, if necessary, against members of the commission's staff. After reading a flattering article in the *Washington Post* in late September that profiled Rankin and the staff lawyers ("Praise Is Voiced for Staff Engaged in Warren Report"), Hoover ordered that FBI files "be checked" for background information on all eighty-four people on the commission's official staff roster, including secretaries and clerks—a move that was understood by Hoover's aides to be an order to search for derogatory information. On October 2, Hoover's office was informed that the background searches were complete and that "bureau files contain derogatory information concerning the following individuals" who had worked for the commission—sixteen of them—"and their relatives."*

The commission's offices on Capitol Hill were closed down once and for all in December, the two floors of office space returned to the Veterans of Foreign Wars. Alfred Goldberg was one of the last staff members to leave. He had remained to compile the twenty-six volumes of evidence, witness statements, and hearing transcripts that were released to the public in November.

Before leaving Washington, Rankin had one last confrontation with Hoover, and some of the staff lawyers laughed out loud when they heard about it. On October 23, as the twenty-six volumes of the appendix were being prepared for publication, Hoover sent an angry letter to Rankin, expressing alarm that the commission was ready to violate the privacy of so many people who were identified in raw FBI files that the commission would make public in the volumes. Suddenly, it seemed, J. Edgar Hoover

---

* The author has chosen not to list all those names, since most of the "derogatory" information appeared to be not that at all. The longest entry in the memo was, not surprisingly, for Norman Redlich. Joseph Ball was on the list, in part, because the FBI considered him a "civil rights libertarian" who had "consistently injected himself in support of the civil rights movement."

had become a champion of personal privacy. The files "contain considerable information of a highly personal nature which was furnished to our agents during the investigation of these cases," Hoover warned. "I again want to specifically call this matter to your attention and point out the responsibility which must be assumed by the Commission in the event these documents are made available to the public."

Rankin replied on November 18. He told Hoover that the commission intended to "minimize the use of information of a highly personal nature" while providing the public "with the fullest possible record of the investigation."

That same day, Rankin sent another letter to Hoover—one that may have given him some pleasure to write. Hoover had pledged publicly that he would pursue the investigation of the president's murder indefinitely, with the bureau aggressively following up new leads. And so Rankin's second letter on November 18 amounted to the commission's last assignment to the FBI—one final tip that the bureau would need to chase.

"In view of your continuing investigation of the assassination of President Kennedy, I wish to draw your attention to the following," Rankin wrote. As the commission's officers prepared to close, a staffer had received a telephone call from a New York man, identified as Louis Kleppel, who reported that he needed to share "information of vital importance concerning the assassination of the President," Rankin wrote.

"Mr. Kleppel stated he was a mental case, specifically a schizophrenic, but that he felt that the government had nothing to lose by taking his statement."

Rankin would leave it to Hoover's men to investigate.

Senator Russell had one last way in 1964 to show how much he disapproved of the commission's report. It might bear Russell's name, but that did not mean the report had to bear his actual signature, in fresh ink.

As a memento of the investigation, Warren had wanted to give each of the commissioners—and every member of the staff—a copy of the final report that was hand-signed by all seven of them. (The report's cover-page bore a printed version of their signatures.) He also wanted to give everyone an autographed copy of the official joint portrait of the commissioners. So more than one hundred copies of the report and the photo were set aside for that purpose, and the commissioners were invited to stop by the office at their convenience to do the signings.

On December 7, after all the other commissioners had turned up to sign copies of the report and the photograph, Julia Eide, Rankin's secretary, told him that she was giving up on Russell. The senator had refused to sign, insisting for weeks that he was too busy with Senate business to cross the street to the commission's offices. She called Russell's office that day and spoke to one of his secretaries, who said the senator had just left for Georgia and did not intend to return until the new year.

"I guess they will have to be sent out without his signature," Eide wrote to Rankin, hinting that she knew just how close the commission had come to a divided report because of Russell. "And what's the difference?" she wrote. "It didn't seem to me that he did anything except cause us some trouble, so perhaps the books don't deserve his 'John Henry.'"

PART 4
AFTERMATH

View from the U.S. Embassy in Mexico City, 1964

Almost immediately after the Warren Commission released its report in September 1964, information began to appear in classified government files that suggested that the history of the assassination would need to be rewritten. Most of that information would remain secret for decades. But in the swirl of unanswered questions about the president's murder, the conspiracy movement would grow stronger in the 1960s, quickly convincing a majority of Americans that Lee Harvey Oswald had not acted alone. The commission's legacy would come under siege from critics who would, over time, include some of the men who wrote the commission's report.

55

There was relief—delight, even—at the CIA in the days after the release of the Warren report. The fear that the CIA would be accused of bungling its supposedly aggressive surveillance of Oswald in Mexico a year earlier—that the agency might somehow have prevented the assassination—had been misplaced. The outcome was a credit, the agency thought, to Mexico City station chief Win Scott, who had taken such a personal role in convincing the commission that the CIA had done its job properly.

In a cable to the Mexico City station on September 25, the day after the commission's report was presented to President Johnson, CIA headquarters offered its congratulations and thanks to Scott: "All Headquarters components involved in the OSWALD affair wish to express their appreciation to the Station for its effort in this and other facets of the OSWALD case." The name of Scott's old friend James Angleton, who had quietly controlled what information was shared with the commission, was not on the congratulatory cable from Langley. That would have been entirely in character for Angleton, who seemed to prefer always to lurk in the shadows, even within the hallways of the CIA itself.

So after all the good news from Washington and the pats on the back from his friends at Langley, the report that landed on Scott's desk just two weeks later must have come as a surprise.

Dated October 5, it was from a CIA informant whose information, if true, meant that Scott and his colleagues—and through them, the Warren Commission—had never known the full story about Oswald's trip to Mexico City. The informant, June Cobb, an American woman living in Mexico, had a complicated background. A Spanish-language translator, the Oklahoma-born Cobb had lived in Cuba earlier in the 1960s and had actually worked in Castro's government; she was apparently sympathetic at the time to the Cuban revolution. Now in Mexico City, she was renting a room in the home of Elena Garro de Paz, the Mexican writer whose fame had grown with the 1963 publication of her much praised novel *Los Recuerdos del Porvenir* (*Recollections of Things to Come*). Scott knew the talented, opinionated Garro from the diplomatic party circuit.

Cobb described listening in on a conversation among Garro, her twenty-five-year-old daughter, Helena, and Elena's sister, Deva Guerrero, that was prompted by the news from Washington about the just-released Warren Commission report. The three Mexican women told a remarkable story: they recalled how they had all encountered Oswald and his two "beatnik-looking" American friends at a dance party thrown by Silvia Duran's family in September 1963, just weeks before the assassination. The Garros were cousins, by marriage, of Duran.

When Elena and her daughter "began asking questions about the Americans, who were standing together all evening and did not dance at all, they were shifted to another room," Cobb reported. Elena said she continued to ask about the Americans and was told by Silvia's husband that he "did not know who they were," except that Silvia had brought them. When Elena pressed again to meet the Americans, she was told there was no time for an introduction. "The Durans replied that the boys were leaving town very early the next morning," according to Cobb. They did not depart the city so quickly, as it turned out; Elena and her daughter saw the young Americans the next day walking together along a major Mexico City thoroughfare called Insurgentes.

The three women then described their astonishment when they saw photographs of Oswald in Mexican newspapers and on television in the hours after Kennedy's assassination; they instantly remembered him from the "twist party." The next day, they learned that Duran and her husband, Horacio, had been taken into custody by the Mexican police; the arrests "underlined" their certainty that it had been Oswald at the party. According to Cobb, Elena said she did not report any of her information about Oswald to the police out of fear that she and her daughter might be

RIGHT: Commission staff lawyer Wesley "Jim" Liebeler's decision to grow a beard outraged Chief Justice Warren, who ordered that it be shaved off. Over time, Liebeler would establish himself as the commission's in-house contrarian and most determined rule-breaker. Although married, he boasted of his many female conquests while working on the commission staff. BELOW: Silvia Odio, a Cuban refugee in Dallas who seemed credible in her insistence that she saw Oswald in the company of anti-Castro activists weeks before the assassination, complained to congressional investigators years later that Liebeler had invited her to his hotel room and tried to seduce her.

ABOVE: In December 1965, American diplomat Charles Thomas (*far right*) was told by noted Mexican author Elena Garro de Paz (*center*) that she had encountered Oswald at a dance party in Mexico City weeks before the assassination. Garro claimed that her cousin, Silvia Tirado de Duran, a Cuban embassy employee, was also at the party and had briefly been Oswald's mistress. At left is Garro's daughter, Helena, who also reported seeing Oswald at the party. The man between Garro and her daughter is unidentified. BELOW LEFT: Thomas and his wife, Cynthia, at a party in Mexico City in the mid-1960s BELOW RIGHT: Charles and Cynthia Thomas on the steps of their Mexico City hacienda, with Charles holding the couple's daughter Zelda, who was born in Mexico in 1965.

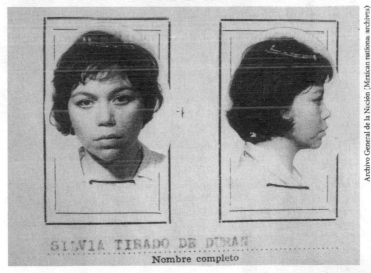

SILVIA TIRADO DE DURAN

Nombre completo

Silvia Duran, a self-proclaimed Socialist who was a Mexican employee of the Cuban consulate in Mexico City, had been under surveillance by both the CIA and the Mexico government for months before the Kennedy assassination. TOP: In a police surveillance photo, Duran (*center*) is seen with her husband, Horacio, a Mexican journalist, and an unidentified woman. CENTER: Duran's mug shot, taken after she was arrested by the Mexican police at the request of the CIA. BOTTOM: A smiling Duran in the 1970s in a photograph obtained by the House Select Committee on Assassinations, which interviewed Duran.

Dolph Briscoe Center for American History, The University of Texas at Austin

TOP: CIA "mole hunter" James Jesus Angleton pushed aside an agency colleague to take control of information shared with the Warren Commission. CENTER: CIA Mexico City station chief Winston "Win" Scott, in a home movie of his 1962 wedding, which was attended by Mexican President Adolfo López Mateos, shown far left with Scott. In next photo, CIA operative David Phillips is shown left of López Mateos; shown right of Scott is future Mexican president Gustavo Díaz Ordaz. BOTTOM: American ambassador to Mexico Thomas Mann, in conversation with President Johnson, was convinced that Cuba was involved in the assassination.

arrested, too. They did act immediately to distance themselves from the Durans, however. The Garros were "so sickened" at the thought that Silvia Duran and her family might have had some sort of connection to the president's assassin that "they broke off their relations with the Durans."

Scott might have hoped that the release of the Warren Commission's report meant he had put the questions about Oswald—and the threat they had once seemed to pose to Scott's career—behind him. But given the potentially explosive information from June Cobb, he knew the embassy had to follow up. The job was given to FBI legal attaché Clark Anderson. He was the same FBI agent who, in the immediate aftermath of Kennedy's assassination, had been in charge of the local investigation of Oswald's activities in Mexico. If anyone should have tracked down the Garros earlier, it was Anderson.

The story that the Garros told Anderson was consistent, down to small details, with the account that Cobb had overheard. Elena Garro said she thought the party had taken place on Monday, September 30, 1963, or on one of the two following days: Tuesday, October 1, or Wednesday, October 2; she recalled thinking how unusual it was to have a dance party on a weekday. There had been about thirty people at the party, which was held at the home of Ruben Duran, Silvia's brother-in-law. It was at about ten thirty p.m., she said, that "three young, white Americans arrived at the party. They were greeted by Silvia Duran and spoke only to her. They more or less isolated themselves from the rest of the party and, insofar as she observed, they had no conversation with anyone else." Garro said the Americans "appeared to be between 22 and 24 years of age." (Oswald was twenty-three at the time.) Oswald, she said, was dressed in a black sweater and appeared to be about five foot nine inches in height. (That was exactly Oswald's height.) One of his two American companions was "about six feet tall, had blond, straight hair, a long chin, and was a bit 'beatnik' in appearance." Anderson asked Garro if she recalled anyone else at the party. She did: a young Mexican who had flirted with her daughter. The man was contacted by the FBI and confirmed some elements of the Garros' story, although he insisted he saw no one who looked like Oswald.

Anderson sent his report to Washington on December 11 and, his files suggest, did nothing more. There was no recorded effort to contact Garro's sister, who had also been at the party. Anderson drew no final conclusion in the report but suggested that the Garros were simply mistaken about seeing Oswald. It was a judgment based largely on the fact that Oswald would not have been in Mexico City on two of the three possible dates offered by Elena Garro for the party, assuming that he was also seen on the street the next day. "It is noted that investigation has established that Lee Harvey Oswald departed Mexico City by bus at 8:30 a.m. on Oct. 2, 1963, and could not have been identical with the American allegedly observed by Mrs. Paz at the party if this party were held on the evening of Oct. 1 or Oct. 2," Anderson reported. He did not point out the obvious: that on the first date offered by Garro, September 30, Oswald was in Mexico City and could have been seen on the street the next day.

It was not clear from Scott's files that he notified CIA headquarters about any of this at the time. A later internal CIA chronology of the actions of the CIA Mexico City station suggested that none of the material reached Langley in 1964. If true, that would mean that CIA headquarters would learn nothing about the Garros—and the "twist party"—for another year.

As always, it seemed, Wesley Liebeler could not resist making trouble.

In the summer of 1965, he had agreed to meet a Cornell University graduate student, Edward Jay Epstein, who wanted to interview him about the Warren Commission. The thirty-year-old Epstein was writing a master's thesis in government, using the commission as a case study in answering a question posed by one of his professors: "How does a government organization function in an extraordinary situation in which there are no rules or precedents to guide it?" Liebeler invited Epstein up to his vacation home in Vermont, where he had always found it easier to think.

In the ten months since the release of the commission's report, Liebeler, now thirty-four, had made many changes in his life. Instead of resuming his promising career at a Manhattan law firm, he had moved west, accepting an appointment to teach law at the University of California at Los Angeles, specializing in antitrust law. The Southern California lifestyle was enticing to Liebeler, as were all the pretty young women on campus.

Liebeler was intrigued by Epstein's Ivy League credentials. Here was a scholar, not a scandal-mongering reporter, and Liebeler thought Epstein's research might help blunt the army of conspiracy theorists who were continuing to attack the commission's findings. Several new books promoting conspiracy theories in Kennedy's death, including one by Mark Lane, were in the works. Liebeler knew he was not alone in talking to Epstein, who also requested interviews with the seven commissioners. The young graduate student eventually talked to five of them—all except Warren, who declined, and Senator Russell, who was forced to cancel an interview because of illness. Epstein also interviewed Lee Rankin, Norman Redlich, and Howard Willens.

Liebeler told Epstein that, although he stood by the conclusions of the commission's report, he was critical of the investigation. His comments were characteristically pithy—and indiscreet—and he would be quoted by name throughout Epstein's thesis. Liebeler explained how the commission's staff lawyers had done virtually all of the real detective work. Asked by Epstein how much work was done by the seven commissioners, Liebeler replied: "In one word, nothing." (He would later say he did not recall making the comment to Epstein, although he did not dispute its accuracy.) Epstein would later recall how—in comments that were not published in his thesis—Liebeler "ridiculed the seven commissioners, saying the staff called them 'Snow White and the Seven Dwarfs' because of their refusal to question the claims of Oswald's Russian wife, Marina, who was 'Snow White.'" Liebeler had a slightly different roster than some of his colleagues in identifying which dwarf was which. He thought that "'Dopey' was Warren, who dismissed any testimony that impugned Marina's credibility," while "Sleepy" was Allen Dulles "because he often fell asleep during the testimony of witnesses and, when awakened, asked inappropriate questions." John McCloy was "Grumpy" because "he became angry when staff lawyers did not pay sufficient attention to his theories about possible foreign involvement."

Liebeler revealed the intense time constraints faced by the staff, a situation made worse by the FBI's incompetence; he described the bureau's investigation of the assassination as "a joke." He told Epstein about Rankin's ill-chosen comment at the end of the investigation regarding the need to draw the work to a close, even if there were still unanswered questions: "We are supposed to be closing doors, not opening them." That quotation, when published by Epstein, would be cited regularly by conspiracy theorists as proof that the investigation had been rushed to a preordained conclusion.*

Liebeler went one step further to help Epstein: he turned over copies of most, if not all, of the internal files he had taken from the commission, including the memos he had written to protest that the report was being written as a "brief for the prosecution" against Oswald. In his thesis, a grateful Epstein did not identify Liebeler by name as the source of the files, offering thanks only to an unnamed "member of the staff." Years later, Epstein would recall his excitement when Liebeler agreed to give him two large cardboard boxes crammed with "staff reports, draft chapters . . . and two blue-bound volumes of preliminary FBI reports, which had not been released to the public."

Liebeler told friends that he did not foresee what was about to happen. Epstein, it turned out, had found a respected publisher, Viking Press, to turn his thesis into a book, *Inquest: The Warren Commission and the Establishment of Truth*, with publication set for June 1966, just two months after he submitted his thesis to his advisers at Cornell. The publication date meant that his book would reach bookstores ahead of Lane's *Rush to Judgment*, which was scheduled for release later that summer. Before publication, Epstein was coy about what would be in *Inquest*, telling the *New York Times*, "It may be dull—let's wait and see." Reviewers were intrigued that the book's introduction would be written by Richard Rovere, the Washington correspondent for the *New Yorker*. Whatever was in the book, it would apparently be a serious work.

Inquest turned out to be a fierce attack on the Warren Commission, alleging that it had ignored evidence that pointed to a second gunman in Dealey Plaza. In his most alarming charge, Epstein suggested that Kennedy's autopsy report had been altered to fit the single-bullet theory and that the theory itself might be fiction. His allegations centered on the discrepancies between the autopsy report and a pair of FBI memos, prepared within weeks of the assassination, about what had happened to the first bullet to hit the president; it was the bullet that the commission's staff

---

* Liebeler would later tell Vincent Bugliosi, the author and Kennedy assassination historian, that Rankin's comment was actually "not inappropriate at the time" since Rankin made it on the very day that the final draft of the commission's report was being distributed among the commissioners. "From the beginning, we were all after the truth, and there were no limitations on that," Liebeler told Bugliosi. (Bugliosi, *Reclaiming History*, p. 358.)

was certain had also struck Connally. The FBI memos stated that the bullet penetrated only a short distance into the president's body from behind, possibly before falling out. The commission's lawyers, especially Arlen Specter, had been convinced early on in their investigation that the FBI memos were wrong and reflected the initial confusion among the pathologists at Bethesda Naval Hospital about the bullet's path; two FBI agents who witnessed the autopsy had taken down the doctor's faulty speculation as fact. To Epstein, however, the differences between the FBI memos and the autopsy report were possible evidence of a cover-up. If the FBI reports were right, the bullet could not have hit Connally.

Epstein said he found other gaps in the commission's investigation; he identified seemingly important witnesses who were never questioned by the commission. And he seemed to have the best possible evidence to back up his attacks—previously unpublished commission records, especially Liebeler's detailed, harshly critical internal memos.

The book was a sensation, prompting respectful news articles, as well as glowing reviews, in major newspapers and magazines. In his introduction, Rovere praised Epstein as a "brilliant young academician" who had proved that the Warren Commission investigation "fell far short of being exhaustive" and that evidence supposedly showing Oswald to be the sole gunman was "highly vulnerable." *Inquest* would be remembered as the book that gave credibility to the conspiracy-theory movement. Under the headline "Pandora's Box," Eliot Fremont-Smith, a critic for the *New York Times*, described it as "the first book to throw open to serious question, in the minds of thinking people, the findings of the Warren Commission." For the paperback edition of *Inquest*, the cover was redesigned to make it more eye-catching, with a silhouette of a man with a rifle standing behind a photograph of Oswald beneath the words, in red: "Is one of the murderers of John F. Kennedy still on the loose?"

Liebeler's obvious cooperation with Epstein infuriated some of his former colleagues; it was now one of their own, they thought, who was fueling the conspiracy movement. Albert Jenner, who already loathed Liebeler from their time together on the commission, wrote to David Belin that he "glanced through those portions of Epstein's odious screed in which Herr Liebeler is copiously quoted" and could see that "Jim is still a frustrated, envious, inferiority-complex plagued man," and went on: "I might forgive him this if he had exhibited good taste." He thought that

"Epstein and his Harvard Ph.D. supervisors should be, but very likely are not, thoroughly ashamed." (Epstein had gone on to a doctoral program at Harvard.) Norman Redlich wrote to Epstein's thesis adviser at Cornell to protest the book, which he described as a "wholly specious work." He said he had been wildly misquoted. "Frankly," he wrote, "I am appalled by the inaccuracies of the book and the statements which he had attributed to me which I never made." Belin said he had sensed, during the investigation, that Liebeler would do something like this. "When I left Washington, I was sure on the basis of conversations I had with Jim Liebeler that he was going to talk to someone," Belin said later. "The fact that he did and the fact that he tried to make himself out as the real hero of the investigation is not surprising." In the months after publication of *Inquest*, Liebeler tried, futilely, it seemed, to distance himself from the book, insisting in letters to friends that he did not question the commission's central findings. He described Epstein's book as a "shallow, superficial and poorly thought-through piece of work."

The damage, however, was done. In late July, Richard Goodwin, a former Kennedy speechwriter, became the first member of the slain president's senior staff at the White House to call for an official reexamination of the findings of the Warren Commission. "*Inquest*," Goodwin said, "not only raises questions but demands explorations and answers."

At the Supreme Court, Warren refused to be drawn into any new debate, telling the court's press office to make no comment to reporters about the book. Still, the questions came at the chief justice—to his face. He appeared startled in late June 1966 when, minutes after stepping off a plane in Israel, where he had gone to participate in the dedication of a memorial to President Kennedy, he was confronted by a reporter with questions about *Inquest*. "I would not care to comment," Warren said. "We wrote our report—it was the best we could do after 10 months of intensive research.... It was unanimous."

In August, *Rush to Judgment* was released. Lane's book did not receive the overwhelming critical praise that Epstein had enjoyed; Lane was just too controversial, and too many reporters said they had learned from experience not to trust what he said. But there was praise. The *Houston Post* described it as "a compelling, powerful and patriotically impassioned plea in behalf of the unvarnished truth." The *New York Times Times* said that while the book suffered from "bias and shrillness," it was "an eloquent summary of the defense." And the book became a massive bestseller, much larger than *Inquest*, and rose to number one on the *New York Times* nonfiction bestseller list. It would remain on the list for twenty-six weeks.*

After the commission, David Slawson had returned to work at his law firm in Denver, but he stayed only briefly in Colorado before turning around and heading back to Washington. Like Liebeler, who would remain a lifelong friend, Slawson decided that he did not want to spend the rest of his career behind a desk at a law firm. He, too, wanted a career in teaching. He decided to begin applying for faculty jobs at major law schools while taking another brief detour into public service. In the summer of 1965, he was delighted with an offer to join the staff of the Justice Department's elite Office of Legal Counsel in Washington.

Slawson felt some regret that he had missed the chance to work at the department under Robert Kennedy, who had since been elected to the Senate; the Kennedy years at the department had obviously been a thrilling time. Slawson was also disappointed that he had so little chance to resume contact with a treasured old friend from Denver who now worked for Kennedy—Joseph Dolan. "I just loved Joe," Slawson said. "A wonderful guy, with a big Irish sense of humor."

Slawson and Dolan had both been active in Democratic politics in Colorado. They met when they worked together in John Kennedy's 1960 presidential campaign; they were introduced by Kennedy's campaign manager in the state, Byron "Whizzer" White, Slawson's mentor at his law firm. After Kennedy's victory, White and Dolan both left for jobs at the Justice Department in Washington. White had first worked as deputy attorney general under Robert Kennedy, and was then nominated to the Supreme Court. Dolan had emerged as one of Robert Kennedy's "Irish mafia" of trusted aides in the attorney general's office, and he then followed Kennedy to Capitol Hill, where he ran Kennedy's Senate staff.

In his first months at the Justice Department, Slawson usually faced a sea of anonymous faces on the side streets of Pennsylvania Avenue when he left work for the day. As efficient as ever, he could usually get all of his work done by five p.m. and join the crush of federal workers heading

---

* Gerald Ford's 1965 book on Oswald, *Portrait of the Assassin*, had disappointing sales, never recouping Ford's $10,000 advance from Simon and Schuster. Under terms of the contract, he was allowed to keep all of the advance.

home in the afternoon rush. So it was a happy surprise for Slawson when he left the office one afternoon and saw a face he instantly recognized.

It was Dolan, standing off in the distance on the sidewalk. He quickly began walking toward Slawson, his arm outstretched.

"Joe? Here? What's he doing here?" Slawson thought to himself.

He said he realized almost instantly that this encounter was no coincidence; Dolan was not the sort of person you found loitering on a sidewalk in the middle of the afternoon, at least not anymore. Dolan, it seemed, had been standing there, waiting for Slawson to exit the building.

That this was no coincidence was reflected on Dolan's face. If this had been a surprise, he would have been all smiles. Instead, as he walked toward Slawson, "he was somber, purposeful."

"Dave, great to see you," Dolan said. "Have you got a minute? Can we talk?"

"Of course," Slawson replied.

"The senator has sent me over to ask a few questions."

"Sure, Joe, sure," said Slawson, trying to imagine what Kennedy might want to know from him and why the senator might want the information gathered in this cloak-and-dagger fashion—near a busy street at rush hour, with no formal record that the conversation had ever occurred.

Dolan got straight to the point. "Dave, it's about his brother's assassination. It's about the Warren Commission."

Slawson said he was taken aback.

"Dave, this needs to remain between us, but the senator is still concerned about a conspiracy. I've told the senator about your duties on the commission—that you investigated the whole conspiracy question. And he wants me to ask you: Are you sure the Warren Commission got it right? Are you sure that Oswald acted alone?"

Slawson tried to imagine what had prompted this. Kennedy had insisted publicly, more than once, that he believed the commission's findings. Had Kennedy learned something that had changed his mind?

"Joe, I still think we got it right," Slawson told Dolan. "I think Oswald did it alone."

As they stood there, the afternoon traffic whizzing by, Slawson offered a shorthand version of how he and the commission concluded there had been no conspiracy.

Dolan listened closely and nodded in what seemed to be agreement.

"Thanks, Dave," he said. "I'll take this back to the senator. He'll be glad to hear it." The two men shook hands, and Dolan walked off, seemingly satisfied.

Charles Thomas and his wife, Cynthia, had come to love Mexico City, where Charles was posted in April 1964 as a political officer in the U.S. embassy. "We felt like the luckiest people in the world," said Cynthia, who was twenty-seven when the couple arrived in Mexico as newlyweds. They had married two months earlier after a whirlwind romance that began with a chance meeting at a party thrown by a mutual friend, a Broadway costume designer, in New York; Cynthia had been working in Manhattan as a researcher for *Time* magazine and attempting to launch an acting career. After the wedding, her well-to-do parents held a candlelit reception for the couple at the Plaza hotel in New York. Their first child, Zelda, named for his late mother, was born in Mexico in 1965.

For American diplomats in the mid-1960s, Mexico City was considered an important—and pleasant—assignment. The city then had a relatively manageable population of about four million people, a figure that would explode in decades to come. The Thomases found a gracious, airy, high-ceilinged hacienda not far from the embassy. Through a friend, Guadalupe Rivera, daughter of the famed artist Diego Rivera, they hired one of the city's best cooks—"our guests knew we served the most exquisite Mexican food in the city," Cynthia said. Ambassador Fulton Freeman considered Thomas one of his most talented deputies, and Freeman often attended parties in the Thomas home. The ambassador was enchanted by Cynthia—"in addition to being an uncommonly attractive and accomplished actress, she is an excellent hostess" who had "opened doors for the embassy to dramatic, cultural and intellectual groups of young Mexicans where we had enjoyed few if any contacts."

The couple made good friends at the embassy, although Cynthia found herself "a little wary" in her encounters with Win Scott; it was well known among diplomats' families that Scott was "the CIA man" in the embassy, operating undercover as a State Department political officer. Scott could be charming, and he often praised Charles to his wife. "Charles should really be in Paris and could do a lot of good work with his extraordinary knowledge of French," he told her at a party. But she found it disquieting when Scott asked if she could be of help gathering intelligence for him in her contacts with prominent Mexicans. She felt she was being recruited to work for the CIA. "I found it very awkward," she said.

The Thomases were favorites among local writers and artists. "Charles was an extraordinary man," said Elena Poniatowska, a Mexican writer of both fiction and nonfiction who would become one of her country's most celebrated investigative journalists. "He was an intellectual. He could speak about anything." The Thomases became especially close to another talented Mexican writer—Elena Garro. Cynthia remembered Garro as an "intelligent, charming, thoughtful woman. So full of life."

It was at a party in December 1965 that Garro took Charles Thomas aside and told him the astonishing story about Oswald and the "twist party." She explained how she had shared the story a year earlier with the American embassy and had heard nothing since. She offered Thomas an additional, startling bit of information that she had not told the embassy; it was about her cousin Silvia Duran. Garro said there had been a sexual relationship between Oswald and Duran and that others in Mexico City were aware of it. She had been the assassin's "mistress."

Thomas wondered if this could be true. He knew Garro to be unusually intelligent and well informed, but what would it mean if the man who killed Kennedy had an affair, just weeks before the assassination, with an employee of Castro's government, at a time when Oswald was supposedly under close surveillance by the CIA in Mexico?

He recorded Garro's account in a memo dated December 10, 1965, that was presented to Scott and others in the embassy. "She was very reluctant to discuss the matter, but finally imparted" the story, Thomas wrote. In the memo, he also noted Garro's strange account of what had happened to her in the days after the assassination. After learning of Oswald's arrest, she said, she immediately assumed that Cuba was involved, given what she knew about Oswald's contacts at the Cuban embassy. Outraged, she and her daughter drove to the embassy on Saturday, the day after the president's murder, and stood outside the compound and shouted, "Assassins," at the Cubans inside. Later that day, she and her daughter received a visit from a friend who was an official in Mexico's Interior Ministry. The friend, Manuel Calvillo, broke the news to them about the arrest of Silvia Duran—it had not been announced publicly—and warned them that they were in danger from "Communists." Calvillo told them they needed to go into hiding. "He had orders to take them to a small and obscure hotel in the center of town," Thomas wrote.

Garro tried to protest. "She told Calvillo she wanted to go to the American Embassy and explain what she knew of Oswald's connections here with the Mexican Communists and Cubans," Thomas reported. But Calvillo warned that the embassy "was full of Communist spies." Frightened that not even the U.S. embassy could be trusted, Garro and her daughter agreed to go into hiding and to say nothing. They were escorted to a small, nondescript hotel across town, where they remained for eight days.

After reading Thomas's report, Win Scott immediately began to create a paper trail that would mock Elena Garro and dismiss her story. Scott wanted it to be established—for the official record—that he was accusing Garro of making this all up.

"What an imagination she has!" he wrote on Thomas's memo.

Scott would take a risk by ignoring the memo entirely, given the suggestion—again—that the CIA might have missed so much information about Oswald's contacts in Mexico. He invited Thomas to a meeting at his office along with Nathan Ferris, the FBI's new legal attaché. Scott and Ferris "pointed out that there had been a great many rumors about Oswald at the time of the assassination and that some could not be verified and others had proved false," Thomas wrote later. "They asked me, however, to try and get a more detailed replay of Miss Garro's story."

At a gathering on Christmas Day, Thomas talked with Garro again, and he followed up with a detailed five-page memo—typed up that same day—for his embassy colleagues. In the new conversation, Garro talked about how frustrating it had been to try to tell her story about Oswald to the embassy the year before. "The embassy officials did not give much credence to anything they said," which explained why she "did not bother to give a very complete story," Thomas wrote.

Garro tried to remember more details about the small hotel where she had gone into hiding. She could not remember its name, but she remembered roughly where it was. She took Thomas on a driving tour until they found it: the Hotel Vermont in the Mexico City neighborhood known as Benito Juarez. (In 1966, the FBI confirmed that part of her story to Scott; she was indeed registered at the hotel from November 23 to November 30, 1963.) Garro also explained why her sister, Deva, had never come forward to confirm the sighting of Oswald at the party. According to Elena, Deva had been visited by two "Communists" after the assassination who threatened her and warned her never to reveal that she had seen Oswald.

Thomas's Christmas Day memo went to Scott and Ferris—and both said they were unimpressed. Ferris sent a memo to Ambassador Freeman on December 27, in which he said he did not intend to reopen the investigation. "In view of the fact that Mrs. Garro de Paz's allegations have been previously checked out, without substantiation, no further action is being taken concerning her recent repetition of those allegations." Scott sent a separate cable to Langley to report on the FBI's decision not to pursue the Garros' story. One of his deputies, Alan White, attached a note to Scott's cable. He questioned whether the embassy had done enough to follow up on Elena Garro's claims. "I don't know what the FBI did in November 1964, but the Garros have been talking about this for a long time, and she is said to be extremely bright," White wrote.

"She is also 'nuts,' " Win Scott wrote back.

56

In the fall of 1966, Lyndon Johnson worried that his presidency was being tarnished by the growing attacks on the Warren Commission— that they might even do damage to his reelection hopes for 1968. He saw the hand of his political enemies in the conspiracy theories about the Kennedy assassination, especially since some of the theories continued to point to him as a suspect. He told aides he was convinced that Robert Kennedy and his political strategists were trying to keep the conspiracy theories alive. Johnson was outraged by an October 1966 opinion poll, conducted after publication of the books by Epstein and Lane, in which 2 percent of the respondents said they believed he was somehow responsible for Kennedy's death. While 2 percent might represent only a small fringe of the people who were polled, Johnson was astonished that anyone could still suspect him of such a terrible thing. The poll was conducted by the survey company run by Louis Harris. "Lou Harris is just owned by Bobby," Johnson told a friend.

Johnson wanted Warren to speak out to defend the commission. He dispatched a White House aide, Jake Jacobsen, to the Supreme Court to urge the chief justice to respond publicly if the attacks on the commission became more serious.

The president also asked for help from Warren's newest colleague on the bench: Associate Justice Abraham "Abe" Fortas, who had been nominated to the court by Johnson the year before. Fortas, a former law professor at Yale who had founded a powerhouse Washington law firm, had been a friend and political adviser to Johnson for years. To the dismay of some of his court colleagues who knew about it, Fortas had continued to offer political counsel to Johnson, even helping write the president's 1966 State of the Union address.

Fortas saw the problem created by the attacks on the Warren Commission. In October 1966, he told Johnson in a phone call that he had gone to the chief justice and urged him to write a book defending the commission. "I told him I thought somebody ought to . . . do it right away," Fortas said. "He thinks the best man to do that is Lee Rankin." Warren was in a "slow burn" over the criticism of the commission.

Johnson told Fortas that he was also alarmed by the impending release of the long-awaited book that the Kennedy family had authorized, *The Death of a President*, by William Manchester. It was scheduled for publication sometime in 1967. After being permitted to read the book ahead of publication, *Look* magazine agreed to pay a record $665,000 for the right to publish excerpts. That suggested to Johnson that Manchester must have bombshell disclosures. His aides heard—and confirmed—that it had an unflattering, boorish portrayal of Johnson, especially about his interactions with Jacqueline and Robert Kennedy on the day of the assassination.

The book was published the following spring, but only after Jacqueline and Robert Kennedy filed suit in New York to try to block publication. They claimed that Manchester needed, but did not have, their approval of the manuscript. Although she never fully explained what so offended her, Mrs. Kennedy, who was portrayed in the book in an almost saintly light, appeared to feel it revealed too much painful, gory detail about her husband's murder and too much personal information about her. (It revealed, for instance, that she smoked, something she had tried as First Lady to keep secret.)

Manchester's book was not nearly as damaging to Johnson as he had feared. And the court showdown, which ended with an agreement between Manchester and the Kennedys to edit out the equivalent of 7 pages from a 654-page manuscript, worked to the president's political advantage, since the court fight was perceived as a heavy-handed effort by the Kennedy family to censor the historical record. Opinion polls showed that the popularity of both Jacqueline and Robert Kennedy was damaged as a result. In an unfortunate choice of words, Johnson expressed his delight to a friend over the polls: "God, it's murderin' Bobby and Jackie both. It just murders 'em."

The chief justice, too, had reason to be pleased with *Death of a President*, since Manchester embraced the commission's findings about Oswald as the lone gunman. Still, as with all of the other books, Warren wanted to say nothing publicly. "I can't be in the position of answering these books," he told Drew Pearson. "And I'm not going to. The report is going to stand or fall on what's in it."

In January 1967, Drew Pearson asked to speak with the chief justice in person. It was urgent, and Warren readily agreed to see his old friend. Pearson was sitting on one of the biggest scoops of his career. Unfortunately for the chief justice, it was a scoop that also threatened to damage Warren's legacy.

It was about the Kennedy assassination, and about the possibility that Castro was behind the president's murder. As Warren listened, Pearson explained that he had been told by a trusted source that the Kennedy White House had ordered the CIA to kill Castro; that the order had been given directly to the agency by Robert Kennedy; and—perhaps most astonishingly—that the CIA had recruited the Mafia to carry out the murder. Pearson's source understood that Castro became aware of the plots against him, rounded up the potential assassins in Cuba before they could act, and then retaliated by dispatching a team of assassins to kill Kennedy.

If only elements of the story were true, it proved that the CIA and Kennedy had withheld information from the Warren Commission that would have offered a clear motive for Castro to kill Kennedy, since the Cuban dictator knew that Kennedy was trying to kill him. It also meant that a member of the commission, Allen Dulles, who was running the CIA at the time of the plots, had probably joined in the cover-up. Pearson revealed his source to Warren: an influential Washington lawyer named Edward Morgan, who was then representing Teamsters leader Jimmy Hoffa. Morgan had learned about the Castro plots—and the possibility that Kennedy had been killed in retaliation—from another of his clients, Robert Maheu, a former FBI agent turned private investigator who had been hired by the CIA to organize Castro's murder.*

---

* The CIA would eventually acknowledge publicly that Maheu, who had done other work for the spy agency, had been asked to organize Castro's murder. It was Maheu who then recruited Mafia figures, including a West Coast mobster named John "Handsome Johnny" Roselli, to carry out the assassination. Edward Morgan would eventually represent Roselli as well. (*New York Times*, August 6, 2008.)

Morgan said he agonized about whether to tell Pearson—and through him, the chief justice. "I wrestled with this for a long time," he recalled. As a trial lawyer, he said, he didn't lose much sleep about the awful secrets he was sometimes told by his clients in criminal cases. "If you do, you don't live long. But this bothered me terribly." He said he finally decided to act because he was desperate to protect Warren, a personal hero. "I finally said to myself, how do I at least get this information to the Chief Justice?"

Morgan recalled visiting Pearson at his palatial town house several blocks from the White House. "I said, 'Drew, I have got to talk to you about something that I want sealed in blood.' . . . We went in the back room, and I told him essentially what I knew" about the CIA plots. The columnist's reaction, he said, "was one of absolute disbelief." He "went through the ceiling." Morgan did not want Pearson to write about any of this in his column, at least not immediately, but he did want him to warn that "poor devil" Warren that he risked being humiliated by the disclosure that the commission had been wrong and that there had been a conspiracy in Kennedy's death. "I will sleep better if I know that the Chief Justice . . . knows this," Morgan told Pearson. "It could undercut the validity of the report, and even his reputation." Warren was a "sitting duck" for scandal.

Pearson did as he was asked. At his meeting with the chief justice on Thursday, January 19, he laid out the complicated story about the CIA's plots against Castro, and how Kennedy might have been killed by Castro in retaliation. Warren, he said, "was decidedly skeptical," insisting that it would not have made sense for the Cuban leader to order Kennedy's death and then have only one assassin in Dallas, especially one as volatile as Oswald. "It would not have been a one-man job," the chief justice said.

Warren declined to meet with Morgan, but he was willing to pass the information to law-enforcement agencies. He asked Pearson which agency should be alerted. Pearson said Morgan, who had a tangled relationship with Hoover, preferred that the information go to the Secret Service instead of the FBI. The chief justice contacted Secret Service director James Rowley, asking to meet with him privately at the Supreme Court. The meeting took place at eleven fifteen a.m. on Tuesday, January 31, Rowley's records showed. It was the first time he had met with Warren in an official capacity since Rowley's awkward testimony before the commission. The Secret Service director recalled years later that the January 1967 meeting with Warren at the court lasted about half an hour and that the chief justice thought the allegations about the Castro plots needed to be taken seriously, even if they sounded far-fetched. "He said he thought this was serious enough and so forth, but he wanted to get it off his hands."

Pearson had shared news of the CIA assassination plots with someone else: President Johnson. Whatever their differences in the past, Pearson had generally been supportive of Johnson's presidency, and the columnist had easy access to the Oval Office.* On January 16, three days before meeting with Warren, Pearson visited Johnson at the White House to tell him about the Castro plots and how they might be linked to Kennedy's assassination. "Lyndon listened carefully and made no comment," Pearson recalled in his diary. "There wasn't much he could say." The secret recordings of his Oval Office telephone calls would suggest that at the time of Pearson's visit, more than three years into his presidency, Johnson was still ignorant of exactly how the CIA had schemed for years to kill Castro.

On Monday, February 20, Johnson alerted Acting Attorney General Ramsey Clark to the "rumors." Their phone conversation began with a discussion of an alarming article published three days earlier in a New Orleans newspaper about how the city's district attorney, Jim Garrison, had opened a local investigation of the Kennedy assassination. In Washington, the reasons for Garrison's investigation were a mystery. Clark speculated that the investigation must involve something that happened when Oswald lived briefly in New Orleans in 1963. From what he knew of the eccentric Louisiana prosecutor, Clark said there was the possibility that Garrison was "just completely off his rocker."

Johnson then mentioned what he had heard about the Castro plots. "You know this story going around about the CIA and they're trying to get—sendin' in the folks to get Castro?"

Clark: "No."

Johnson offered a summary of what he had heard from Pearson, suggesting he did not believe that the CIA had tried to murder Castro. "It's

---

* Although Pearson and other journalists and Congressional investigators had continued to pursue allegations of wrongdoing involving Johnson and the Washington lobbyist Bobby Baker, the former Senate aide known as "Little Lyndon," the scandal quieted for a time after the Kennedy assassination, and Johnson was never directly implicated in any of Baker's crimes. In 1967, Baker was sentenced to up to three years in prison after his conviction on charges of tax evasion, theft, and fraud in an unrelated corruption case. (*New York Times*, April 8, 1967.)

incredible," he said. "I don't believe there's a thing in the world to it, and I don't think we oughta seriously consider it. But I think you oughta know about it."

Days later, Garrison made headlines around the world with the announcement that he had uncovered a conspiracy in Kennedy's assassination. On March 1, 1967, Garrison formally charged that a respected local businessman and philanthropist, Clay Shaw, was at the heart of the plot.

In Washington, the headlines from New Orleans worried Jack Anderson, Pearson's junior reporting partner on the Washington Merry-Go-Round column. Even more than Pearson, it seemed, the forty-four-year-old Anderson treasured a scoop, and he feared that he and Pearson were about to be scooped by Garrison about the CIA-Mafia plots.* Anderson could not discuss any of this with Pearson, at least not easily, since Pearson was thousands of miles away, touring South America with his friend the chief justice; Warren was on an official visit to Andean nations. The two men had just arrived in Lima, Peru, when word reached them of what Anderson had published in the Merry-Go-Round on March 3. It was written in the column's always-breathless style:

> WASHINGTON—President Johnson is sitting on a political H-bomb—an unconfirmed report that Senator Robert Kennedy, (D-N.Y.), may have approved an assassination plot which then possibly backfired against his late brother.
>
> Top officials, queried by this column, agreed that a plot to assassinate Cuban Dictator Fidel Castro was "considered" at the highest levels of the Central Intelligence Agency at the time Bobby was riding herd on the agency. The officials disagreed, however, over whether the plan was approved and implemented.
>
> One version claims that underworld figures actually were recruited to carry out the plot. Another rumor has it that three hired assassins were caught in Havana where a lone survivor is still supposed to be languishing in prison. These stories have been investigated and discounted by the FBI.

---

* Anderson, once memorably described by J. Edgar Hoover as "lower than the regurgitated filth of vultures," inherited the column after Pearson's death in 1969. In 1972, he won a Pulitzer Prize for his reporting about secret diplomacy between the United States and Pakistan during the Indo-Pakistani War of 1971.

Yet the rumor persists, whispered by people in a position to know, that Castro did become aware of an American plot upon his life and decided to retaliate against President Kennedy.

This report may have started New Orleans's flamboyant District Attorney Jim Garrison on his investigation of the Kennedy assassination.

Pearson was unhappy that Anderson had published the column. "It was a poor story in the first place, and violated a confidence in the second," Pearson wrote in his diary on March 20, after returning home. "Finally it reflected on Bobby Kennedy without actually pinning the goods on him." But the article had set events in motion that would quickly prove to Pearson and to Warren and Johnson—that many of the essential elements of the story were true. The CIA had plotted for years to kill Castro, even recruiting the Mafia to help. Robert Kennedy was clearly aware of the plots, and he may have been responsible for some of them. And the Warren Commission had apparently been told none of it.

Someone else had known about the Castro plots—J. Edgar Hoover. On March 6, three days after the column appeared, the FBI presented the White House with a classified report that bore an eye-popping title: "Central Intelligence Agency's Intentions to Send Hoodlums to Cuba to Assassinate Castro." The report summarized what the FBI had known— for years—about the CIA's plots. It noted that Hoover had personally alerted Robert Kennedy in 1961 to the Mafia's involvement.

In April, President Johnson called in Pearson to congratulate him on the scoop. "We think there's something to" the CIA-Mafia plots, Johnson said. "There were some attempts to assassinate Castro through the Cosa Nostra, and they point to your friends in the Justice Department."

Pearson understood what Johnson was getting at. "You mean *one* friend in the Justice Department," Pearson said. The president was referring to Robert Kennedy. Johnson would later be quoted as saying that he was appalled to discover that during the Kennedy administration, "we had been operating a damned Murder Inc. in the Caribbean."

The impact of Pearson's scoop was limited at first, given the inability of other Washington reporters to confirm such highly classified information and because Pearson's reporting was so often flawed that other news organizations found it easy to ignore him. And if Warren was angry that the commission that bore his name had been told nothing about the Castro plots, he said nothing about it publicly. There is no suggestion in his correspondence or datebooks from the court to show that he contacted Dulles to ask what the former spymaster knew of the plots and why Dulles might have withheld the information from his fellow commissioners. Dulles died in 1969.

Warren's apparent calm was not shared by many of the commission's former staff members, who began to allege publicly that they had been lied to and that the commission had been denied information that could have pointed to a conspiracy in Kennedy's death. Lee Rankin, normally so slow to anger, told congressional investigators years later that he had been outraged to discover what had been hidden—both by the CIA, which organized the Castro plots, and the FBI, which knew about them. He regretted he had been "naive enough" while on the commission to "think that when the president of the United States told everybody to cooperate with us, they would understand that was an order and a mandate." The commission "made a mistake by believing that the FBI would not conceal. It made a mistake by believing that the CIA would not withhold information."

John Whitten, the veteran CIA officer who had been the agency's first liaison to the Warren Commission, said he was furious to learn about the Castro plots—because he, too, had been told nothing about them in 1964, when he was supposedly providing the commission with every bit of intelligence out of the CIA's files that might be related to the president's murder. "Had I known, my investigation would have been entirely different," Whitten complained years later. "It might indeed turn out that the Cubans had undertaken this assassination as retaliation for our operations to assassinate Castro."

Whitten was angry, in particular, with Richard Helms, who had been promoted to director of Central Intelligence in 1966 by President Johnson. It would eventually be determined by Congress that Helms had personally approved the Castro plots, including the schemes involving the Mafia. Whitten said later that he believed Helms withheld the information from the Warren Commission because "he realized it would reflect very poorly on the agency, and very poorly on him." Helms's decision, he said, "was a morally reprehensible act, which he cannot possibly justify under his oath of office."

Helms saw things very differently when called before Congress in the 1970s to justify the Castro plots and explain why he had not told the commission about them. In his career as a spy, Helms had been responsible, above all, for keeping secrets. He said he determined, in his own mind, that the CIA's Castro plots had nothing to do with Kennedy's assassination, and therefore there was no reason to tell the commission—or his deputy Whitten, for that matter—about them. "It never occurred to me," he explained. "We never talked to anybody outside the agency about covert operations of any kind." Besides, Helms asked later, why had it been his responsibility to tell the commission about the Castro plots since he was certain that one of the commissioners—Dulles—knew all about them, as had Robert Kennedy? "All kinds of people knew about these operations high up in the government," Helms said angrily. "Why am I singled out as the fellow who should have gone up and identified a government operation to get rid of Castro?"

Hugh Aynesworth, the former *Dallas Morning News* reporter, would never really get off the "assassination beat," as it came to be known among journalists in Dallas. Year after year, he would keep getting pulled back to the story. By January 1967, he had moved on to a new job as a national correspondent at *Newsweek*, expected to take on every sort of assignment from his new base in Houston. But he had barely settled in at the magazine when the phone rang, with an urgent call from New Orleans. It was district attorney Jim Garrison. He invited Aynesworth to come to New Orleans to talk about the new information he had gathered on the Kennedy assassination.

"I keep running into your name, and I think you have information that could help me," Garrison said. "I want to share some stuff with you. You need to come down here." Naturally intrigued, Aynesworth went to New Orleans to meet Garrison at his home, and it was "one of the strangest days of my life." With his booming voice, the six-foot-four-inch Garrison could have moments of impressive lucidity, but they were fleeting. Garrison was "unhinged," Aynesworth quickly concluded. The conversation was "both nutty and disturbing for the fact that a high-level elected official could believe the nonsense that Garrison professed to believe."*

Over the years, Garrison was never able to settle on exactly who was

---

* In Oliver Stone's 1991 film *JFK*, which suggested that Garrison had come close to exposing the truth about a vast conspiracy in the assassination, the role of Chief Justice Earl Warren was played by the real-life Jim Garrison.

responsible for the assassination. His list of suspects included—at one time or another and in no particular order—gay, sadomasochistic "thrill killers," narcotics traffickers, anti-Castro and pro-Castro Cuban exiles, the Defense Department, the Justice Department, Texas oilmen who had backed President Johnson's political career, as well as the president himself. Garrison accused Chief Justice Warren and other members of the assassination commission of orchestrating the cover-up. The CIA figured as a coconspirator in many of Garrison's theories, as did "queers"; he claimed that at least six men involved in the plot were gay. Oswald, he said, was "a switch-hitter who couldn't satisfy his wife . . . that's all in the Warren report." The assassination, he said, was carried out by a "precision guerrilla team" of at least seven gunmen positioned around Dealey Plaza.

At their first meeting, Garrison offered to introduce Aynesworth to a key prosecution witness. "You're lucky you're in town," he said. "We've just verified this guy and believe me, it's dynamite." An assistant district attorney arrived at Garrison's home with the witness—"a slight little guy from Houston, a piano player who proceeded to relate how he knew that Ruby and Oswald were longtime gay lovers." The piano player recalled how Oswald and the man who would later kill him had been thrown out of a Houston club because they had been "groping each other all evening long." Aynesworth did not tell Garrison, but he had seen this man before—back in Dallas in the days just after Kennedy's murder. "He had come forward within three days of the assassination, telling exactly the same story to the Dallas police." It was clear to Aynesworth back then, just as it was clear to him now, that the piano player was another of the desperate, delusional attention-seekers determined to pretend that they had some personal role in the great drama. "The last I'd seen of the piano man, he was crying and scrambling out the police station door in Dallas."

Garrison's other prosecution witnesses would include a man who called himself Julius Caesar, a former resident of a psychiatric hospital who dressed, appropriately, in a red toga and sandals. Caesar claimed to have seen Oswald and Ruby in the company of the man would become the focus of the district attorney's investigation: Clay Shaw, who had come into Garrison's sights largely because he was known to be gay. The district attorney's targets included another gay Louisianan, David Ferrie, the former Eastern Airlines pilot who may—or may not—have known Oswald in the 1950s. Hounded by the district attorney's office, Ferrie would be found dead in his New Orleans apartment on February 22, 1967; the coroner ruled out foul play or suicide, although Ferrie had left behind notes that suggested he was under so much pressure that he was contemplating whether to kill himself.

In its issue dated May 15, 1967, *Newsweek* published a devastating article under Aynesworth's byline, the first major exposé of the possibly illegal tactics of the New Orleans district attorney. The article cited evidence that Garrison had offered a bribe to a witness for perjured testimony that would tie Ferrie to Shaw. The article, which appeared under the headline "The JFK 'Conspiracy,'" began:

> Jim Garrison is right. There has been a conspiracy in New Orleans—but it is a plot of Garrison's own making. It is a scheme to concoct a fantastic "solution" to the death of John F. Kennedy and to make it stick; in this case, the district attorney and his staff have been indirect parties to the death of one man and have humiliated, harassed and financially gutted several others.

Aynesworth said a furious Garrison called after the article appeared, accusing the reporter of trying to undermine the "search for truth" and warning that he risked arrest if he dared to return to New Orleans. "I hope *Newsweek* has good lawyers and you may have a surprise when you come back to town."

On March 1, 1969, two years after Clay Shaw's arrest on charges of conspiring in the Kennedy assassination, a New Orleans jury took less than an hour to acquit him.

57

In June 1967, Win Scott was eager—desperate even—to downplay the significance of a new informant's report about Silvia Duran. A second source had come forward to report that Oswald had a sexual relationship with Duran during his visit to Mexico City.

It had been nearly three years since the CIA had first heard the story from the "nut" Elena Garro. This time, it would be much harder for Scott to attack the credibility of the source, since this new information was coming from one of the CIA's own trusted informants, identified in the agency's files by the code name LIRING/3 (all of the agency's informants in Mexico City had code names that began "LI"). In June 1967, LIRING/3 reported that he had heard about Oswald's brief affair with Duran from the best possible source—Duran herself.*

The informant, a Mexican painter whose circle of friends included Cuban diplomats and who had been friendly with Duran in the past, told his CIA handler that he had recently spoken to Duran by phone and then visited her home. During those conversations, he said, she revealed her affair with Oswald in 1963, adding that she had admitted the relationship

---

* LIRING/3's name was identified in CIA records that were declassified decades later. Since there is no way to confirm that the CIA records are accurate, the author has chosen not to publish the informant's name here. Contacted by phone in 2013, the painter confirmed that he knew Duran, although he denied he had any relationship with the CIA. He also denied that Duran had ever told him that she had a sexual relationship with Oswald.

to the Mexican police during the brutal interrogations in the days after Kennedy's assassination.

According to the debriefing report prepared by LIRING/3's CIA handler:

> Silvia Duran informed him that she had first met Oswald when he applied for a visa and had gone out with him several times since she liked him from the start. She admitted that she had sexual relations with Oswald.... When the news of the assassination broke, she was immediately taken into custody by the Mexican police and interrogated thoroughly and beaten until she admitted she had had an affair with Oswald. She added that ever since that she has cut off all contact with the Cubans, particularly since her husband Horacio, who was badly shaken by the whole affair, went into a rage and has forbidden her to see them.

She continued to insist that she "had no idea" of Oswald's plans to kill Kennedy.

The informant's report came at an anxious moment for the CIA, given the global media furor created by Garrison's investigation in New Orleans—and his claim that the agency was involved in Kennedy's murder. Within days of LIRING/3's debriefing, Scott received a letter from a colleague at Langley that directed the Mexico City station to remain silent:

> The Garrison investigation of the Kennedy assassination has prompted a rash of spectacular allegations and charges, some against the CIA. Although Garrison's "case" is flimsy indeed and apparently largely made up of unsubstantiated rumors by an odd assortment of disreputable characters, every effort is being made to turn down all such charges and have the facts in hand. In this situation you understand, of course, that it is essential that all of us be particularly careful to avoid making any statement or giving any indication of opinion or fact to unauthorized persons which could somehow be seized upon by any party, innocently or otherwise.

Scott pondered what to do. What would be the effect of a long-delayed disclosure that Oswald, supposedly monitored by the CIA in Mexico, had in fact slipped out from under the agency's surveillance and into the bed of a local employee of Castro's government? What would Garrison do if he learned that the agency had known—but failed to pursue, for years—claims of the affair? How would critics react to a disclosure that the CIA had never attempted to identify two young "beatnik" Americans who were reported to be traveling with Oswald in Mexico?

Scott and his colleagues were required under agency rules to file a report that summarized every significant encounter with paid informants, so they would need to forward a report to Langley on the latest debriefing with LIRING/3. Scott faced the question of how—and whether—to note Duran's apparent confession of the affair. He hit on a solution; he mentioned Duran's confession deep in his debriefing report, and without context, dismissing its importance. It would be the sixth paragraph of his eight-paragraph report:

> The fact that Silvia DURAN had sexual intercourse with Lee Harvey OSWALD on several occasions when the latter was in Mexico is probably new, but adds little to the OSWALD case. The Mexican police did not report the extent of the DURAN-OSWALD relationship to the Station.

That was it. CIA analysts back at the agency's headquarters who had not read anything else on the subject might assume that "the fact" of an affair between Oswald and Duran was old, unimportant news. Certainly, it appeared, that was what Scott wanted them to believe.

There was more troubling news for Scott that spring. In May 1967, an American diplomat working in the U.S. consulate in the Mexican port city of Tampico reported an encounter with a local newspaper reporter, Oscar Contreras, who claimed that he had spent several hours with Oswald in September 1963. At the time, Contreras was a law student at Mexico City's National Autonomous University. He said he and a group of leftist friends, all of them known on campus as Castro sympathizers, were approached by Oswald, who asked for help in convincing the Cuban consulate to give him a visa. Contreras said he was unable to help, although he and his friends spent that evening and much of the next day with the young American. It was not clear who had sent Oswald to speak with the students, although Contreras said he had many friends at the Cuban embassy.

The account, if true, offered another belated example of gaps in the

CIA's surveillance of Oswald in Mexico—or, alternatively, how little Scott and his colleagues chose to tell CIA headquarters about what they had actually known. If the Mexican reporter's account was accurate, Oswald had ducked CIA surveillance for at least a day and a half—about a quarter of his time in Mexico City.

It was at about that same time in 1967 that Scott began talking openly to his colleagues of his plans to retire from the CIA. After twenty years at the agency, most of them in Mexico, he said he wanted to leave the government and make some real money. He intended to remain in Mexico and set up a consulting firm, allowing him to profit from his many contacts in the Mexican government. He also intended to write his memoirs, including his account of what had happened with Oswald.

Scott had always considered himself a writer. He especially loved poetry and had self-published a collection of his own love poems under a pseudonym in 1957. It might have been an obvious thought, then, to put his life story, especially his many exciting adventures as a spy, on paper. In what appeared to be a grave violation of CIA security rules, he sent a detailed outline for his memoirs—through regular mail—to a friend in New York who was an editor at *Reader's Digest*. He told the editor that the book would follow his spying career from its start in World War II, when he formed an early friendship with Allen Dulles, and reveal how he and Dulles had written a study of British intelligence agencies that was used in 1947 as the blueprint for the creation of the CIA. Much of the book would focus on Mexico. "During my 13 years in Mexico, I had many experiences, many of which I can write about in detail," Scott told the editor. "One of these pertains to Lee Harvey Oswald. . . . I know a great deal about his activities from the moment he arrived in Mexico."

Scott's initial title for the book, *It Came to Little*, was drawn from a passage of the Bible—"Ye looked for much, and lo, it came to little"—and reflected his disenchantment with the CIA. "My theme is that with all our work, the dollars spent and the thousands of hours put into the battle against communism, we who were and those who are still in the CIA would have to admit that 'it came to little,' if we are honest," he wrote. "The United States is getting more and more timid about confronting communism" even as "we are more and more deeply penetrated by communists." He eventually settled on a different title—*The Foul Foe*—and decided on a pen name, "Ian Maxwell." It was the same one he had used for his love poems.

When he decided to run for president in 1968, Robert Kennedy knew he might face questions about his brother's murder. The prospect, as always, seemed agonizing.

His last substantive public comment about the Warren Commission came that March, while he was on the campaign trail in California. In a raucous meeting near Los Angeles with college students, he was asked if he would make the commission's records public in response to the flood of conspiracy theories about the assassination. Reporters said that Kennedy tried at first to ignore the question but, after a moment's hesitation, reconsidered. "If I became president, I would not reopen the Warren report," Kennedy declared. "I have seen everything that's in there. I stand by the Warren Commission." He added that "nobody is more interested than I in knowing who was responsible for the death of President Kennedy."

Three months later, on June 6, the night he won the California primary for the Democratic nomination, Kennedy was assassinated in Los Angeles. He was gunned down by a twenty-four-year-old Palestinian, Sirhan Sirhan, who said he wanted to punish Kennedy for his support for Israel.

The assassination had immediate ramifications at the Supreme Court. Within a week, a shaken Chief Justice Warren asked for a meeting with President Johnson and announced that he intended to retire, allowing Johnson time to put a successor in place before the presidential elections that fall. Johnson had not sought reelection and, with Robert Kennedy's death, the chances that the Republican nominee, former vice president Richard Nixon, would win the presidency had grown much stronger. Warren clearly did not want Nixon, his old nemesis, to have the chance to replace him.

The situation did not work out as Warren had hoped. Johnson nominated Abe Fortas as Warren's successor, but Fortas ran into strong opposition, much of it tied to allegations of conflicts of interest from his continuing political counsel to the president. The nomination was withdrawn in October, and Johnson announced that he had asked Warren to remain at the court until Johnson's successor, Democrat or Republican, was in place to make a new nomination. After Nixon's election, the new president announced his selection of Warren Burger, a conservative appeals court judge from Minnesota, as chief justice. Burger was confirmed by the Senate in June 1969.

Warren gave few interviews in retirement, and when he spoke to reporters and historians, he preferred always to focus on his legacy on the court and as California's governor—not on the commission. When pressed about the assassination, he said he had never wavered in his view that Oswald acted alone. He said he was not disturbed by polls that showed that a growing share of the public doubted the commission's findings. "People are still debating the Lincoln assassination," he said. "It's understandable."

In retirement, he made a decision that pleased former staff members of the commission: he decided to cooperate on a book that Lee Rankin and Alfred Goldberg planned to write as a formal defense of the commission. He granted an extended, tape-recorded interview to Goldberg on March 26, 1974. It would be one of his last interviews on any subject; he died in Washington less than four months later, on July 9, at the age of eighty-three. In the interview, Warren suggested that he regretted nothing about the way he conducted the investigation, apart from wishing that the commission had a face-to-face interview with President Johnson. He stood by his decision to block access to Kennedy's autopsy photos and X-rays. "For good or ill, I take full responsibility for it," he said. "I couldn't conceive permitting these things being sent around the country and displayed in museums." He said he was still convinced that the single-bullet theory was correct and that Governor Connally had been wrong to think he was hit by a separate bullet. "A shot can deaden one's emotions or reactions." He remained convinced that all of the bullets fired at Kennedy's limousine had come from the Texas School Book Depository, not from the so-called grassy knoll or the railway overpass, as so many conspiracy theorists alleged. "No one could have fired from the knoll or the overpass without having been seen."

Rankin and Goldberg abandoned plans for the book after they were unable to interest major publishers. "The publishing houses only wanted a book about a conspiracy to kill Kennedy," Goldberg said. "That's not what we were writing."

In October 1968, with the election to choose his successor only a month away, Johnson granted a wide-ranging valedictory interview to veteran

ABC News anchorman Howard K. Smith. Off camera, Johnson offered to tell the newsman a secret that, for now, Smith could tell to no one else. Smith agreed.

"I'll tell you something that will rock you," Johnson said. Fidel Castro, he said, was responsible for the Kennedy assassination. "Kennedy was trying to get to Castro, but Castro got to him first."

Smith, who knew that Johnson was capable of "blarney," pleaded for more information. "I was rocked all right," he said. "I begged for details. He refused, saying it will all come out someday."

In September 1969, in retirement at his vast ranch outside Austin, Texas, Johnson was interviewed by CBS News anchorman Walter Cronkite for a planned series of programs about his presidency. In discussing the Kennedy assassination, Cronkite asked if Johnson still believed the Warren Commission was right and that there had been no conspiracy in Kennedy's death.

"I can't honestly say that I've ever been completely relieved of the fact that there might have been international connections," Johnson said.

"You mean you still feel there might have been a conspiracy?" Cronkite asked.

"I have not completely discounted that."

Cronkite sounded startled. "Well, that would seem to indicate that you don't have full confidence in the Warren Commission."

Johnson: "No, I think the Warren Commission study . . ." He paused. "I think first of all, it was composed of the ablest, most judicious, bipartisan men in this country. Second, I think they had only one objective, and that was the truth. Third, I think they were competent and did the best they could. But I don't think that they or me or anyone else is always, absolutely sure of everything that might have motivated Oswald, or others that could have been involved."

Cronkite knew he had a scoop, and a historic one. But before the interview could be aired, Johnson insisted that his comments about the commission and his fears of a conspiracy had to be cut from the interview on "national security" grounds. After a fierce internal battle, CBS agreed to edit out the material, although word of what Johnson had said leaked to other news organizations, including both the *New York Times* and the *Washington Post*.

What led Johnson to doubt the Warren Commission so profoundly would never been entirely clear. Joseph Califano, his domestic policy aide at the White House from 1965 until 1969, recalled how Johnson often said privately to deputies that he was convinced that Oswald had been part of a conspiracy. It was a view shared by Califano, who had been the general counsel of the army during the Kennedy administration and was one of a small team of advisers to Robert Kennedy asked to dream up plots to oust Castro—and, if possible, to kill him—as part of Operation Mongoose. "Robert Kennedy was absolutely determined to assassinate Castro," Califano said years later. "The Kennedys were obsessed with it." Califano always suspected there was truth in the rumor that Castro, once he became aware of the assassination plots targeting him, retaliated by ordering Kennedy's assassination. Califano said he believed Robert Kennedy assumed the same thing. "I have come to believe that Robert Kennedy experienced that unbelievable grief after his brother's death because he believed it was linked to his—Bobby's—efforts to kill Castro."

Cynthia Thomas was more shocked than her husband at the news that his career at the State Department was over. Certainly she was angrier. Charles had always been the fatalist between them. It did not make sense, they both knew. Charles had been uniformly—and enthusiastically—praised by the ambassadors he had worked under during his eighteen years in the Foreign Service. The bad news reached him while he was back in Washington in 1969. Since he had failed to win a promotion in time, he was being dismissed—"selected out." "It seemed nonsensical," Cynthia said. "Charles was the best sort of American diplomat."

It was then, in his final act as a State Department employee, that Thomas typed up his July 1969 letter to Secretary of State William Rogers, with a last plea that someone review the allegations made by Elena Garro. "A careful investigation of these allegations could perhaps explain them away," Thomas wrote. "Until then, however, their public disclosure could reopen the debate about the true nature of the Kennedy assassination and damage the credibility of the Warren Report."

In the letter, Thomas speculated, apparently for the first time on paper, why the CIA had not wanted to get to the bottom of the story in Mexico City: "Some of the people appearing in the Elena Garro scenario may well be agents of the CIA." He did not identify who the possible CIA agents might be or how they might have interacted with Oswald in Mexico.

A month later, on August 28, the State Department's Division of Protective Security passed on his letter to the CIA, with a cover memo asking for the spy agency to consider pursuing the allegations. The CIA's response to the State Department was dated September 16. At forty-six words, the memo could not have been much shorter:

SUBJECT: Charles William Thomas

Reference is made to your memorandum of 28 August 1969. We have examined the attachments, and see no need for further action. A copy of this reply has been sent to the Federal Bureau of Investigation and the United States Secret Service.

The memo was signed by CIA counterintelligence director James Angleton and his deputy, Raymond Rocca. Angleton's name meant nothing to Cynthia Thomas and, decades later, she said she thought it had never meant anything to her husband, either. "I don't think we had any idea who Angleton was," she said. "Why should we?"

That summer, Thomas began a difficult job search that would only end with his suicide two years later. The search was much harder than he could have imagined, Cynthia said. When prospective employers asked Thomas why he left the State Department short of the retirement age, he felt compelled to tell them the truth: he had been forced out. He tried, but failed, to find work elsewhere in the government, including at the CIA, Cynthia said. She remembered that Win Scott in Mexico City had offered "to write recommendation letters for him" but "never did." She came to understand that there was a "concerted effort by the State Department" to block her husband from getting a job on Capitol Hill. Money became a problem almost immediately. The family had no real savings. The Thomases and their two young daughters lived in a rented house in Washington. To provide at least a small income, Thomas put his law degree to work part-time to defend indigent criminal defendants in Washington's municipal criminal courts. The pay was $7.50 an hour. He was "too proud" to ask for anyone's help in finding a permanent job, Cynthia said.

Even though the State Department and the CIA had refused his request to reopen the investigation in Mexico, Thomas tried to follow up himself. Late in 1969, he began to search for Garro. She had left Mexico City the year before as a result of the furor she created with public comments in which she alleged that left-wing intellectuals bore responsibility for instigating large antigovernment protests that fall; the protests were put down brutally by the Mexican government, resulting in the death of scores, if not hundreds, of protesters and bystanders. Thomas eventually located Garro in New York, where she was living—destitute—with her daughter.

His handwritten notes of his phone conversations with Garro—placed in a file folder labeled KENNEDY that was found after his death in his black leather briefcase—suggest that Garro had nothing new to say about the long-ago encounter with Oswald. She was too confused—and paranoid. "She has been in hiding," apparently fearing that she was in danger in Mexico, Thomas wrote. "She said 'they' were coming after her again." At Thomas's request, a friend of his in New York invited Garro and her daughter to dinner. The friend reported back that she "had never seen anyone as frightened."

On April 12, 1971, the day he committed suicide by putting a gun to his head in the family's second-floor bathroom, three more rejection letters arrived in the mail, including one for a job as staff director of the House Foreign Affairs Committee. Thomas was told that the committee had decided on a younger man. He killed himself with a gun he had bought years earlier as a souvenir of a visit to Cuba in the 1950s.

In his briefcase, after his death, Cynthia found the KENNEDY folder, although she said she did not understand its significance at the time. The file was also stuffed with yellowed newspaper and magazine clippings about the continuing disputes over the findings of the Warren Commission. He had clipped out articles about Richard Russell—and Russell's belief that the commission's report was wrong. Years later, Cynthia Thomas would say she knew "almost nothing at all" about Garro's allegations about Oswald and Silvia Duran. It was typical that her husband would not have shared such sensitive information with her at the time, Cynthia said. "He was right not to tell me," she said. "This was embassy work, and it was sensitive. My goodness, it was about President Kennedy's assassination. Charles was not supposed to bring something like this home to share with his family."

After the suicide, she began a one-woman campaign to prove that her husband was the victim of injustice within the State Department's promotion system and to fight for his posthumous reinstatement to the Foreign Service, as well as his back salary and pension. It was a campaign prompted, in part, by her family's desperate financial condition. At the age of thirty-five, with two young children, she had been left with a single physical asset of any value—a used 1967 Plymouth sedan worth $500—and $15,000 in debts, including $744.02 she owed to a Washington funeral home for her husband's burial.

She began hearing rumors, almost immediately, that there was more to her husband's forced departure from the government than the family had been told—that the CIA was involved and that it somehow related to his posting in Mexico. Her notes from the time show that a well-connected European journalist in Washington told her that "high sources" in the U.S. government believed that Thomas was ousted because someone had spread false rumors connecting Thomas to "the Mexican left." More specifically, she was alerted that Stanley Watson, Scott's deputy in the CIA's Mexico City station, had somehow "damaged" Charles's career prospects behind the scenes.* It had been reported in diplomatic circles in Mexico that Watson, possibly at Scott's urging, had begun a whispering campaign aimed at Thomas, suggesting that he was too close to Mexican Socialists. Decades later, the Thomases' friend Guadalupe Rivera, a law professor who would later be elected to the Mexican Senate, recalled hearing the news in 1971 of Thomas's suicide and immediately assuming it was linked to Watson's rumor campaign, which had reached her, too. She was overheard at a party in Mexico City discussing the suicide and blurting out, "It was that pig, Stanley Watson." Cynthia said she could not understand why Watson, or Scott, or anyone else at the CIA, would have been so determined to see her husband forced out of the government.

After his suicide, former colleagues at the State Department said they were astonished to learn that Thomas's career might also have been derailed by what the department claimed was an innocent clerical error—the misfiling of a glowing job evaluation prepared in 1966, while Thomas was in Mexico. It was the evaluation that described Thomas as "one of the most valuable officers" in the Foreign Service and recommended his immediate promotion. The department said that the report had been mistakenly placed in the file of the other diplomat who had the name Charles Thomas. The report was placed in the proper file two days after the pro-

---

* In light of the allegations against Mr. Watson, the author of this book attempted to reach him through both the CIA and the Association of Former Intelligence Officers, a Washington-area group that represents retired agency employees. Both said they had no information about Watson, including whether he is still alive. "We haven't been able to find anyone who maintains a relationship with Mr. Watson and/or his family," a CIA spokesman said.

motion board had turned Thomas down. The board chose not to reconsider its decision, since it was not the board's mistake that resulted in the misfiling.

Cynthia Thomas's campaign, combined with the internal furor at the State Department over the treatment of her late husband, forced the department to overhaul its promotion policies for the diplomatic corps. In 1973, a federal judge in Washington ruled the department's promotion process unconstitutional as a violation of due process of law; the ruling came in a lawsuit that had been financed by donations from the Charles William Thomas Defense Fund, which had been established by his widow and some of Thomas's old colleagues.

In January 1975, Congress provided Mrs. Thomas with some small amount of justice; it passed a so-called private bill that posthumously restored her husband to active duty in the Foreign Service, which meant that she and her two children would be entitled to the salary he had lost until the time of his death, as well as insurance benefits. The total compensation came to about $51,000. Mrs. Thomas was also hired by the State Department as a foreign service officer, and she went on to work as a diplomat in India and Thailand before retiring in 1993.

After passage of the bill in 1975, Mrs. Thomas received a letter from the White House—a formal apology for the government's treatment of her husband. "There are no words that can ease the burden you have carried over these years," the letter began. "The circumstances surrounding your husband's death are a source of deepest regret to the government he served so loyally and so well and I can only hope that the measures which came about as a result of this tragedy will prevent reoccurrences of this kind in the future." The letter was signed by President Gerald R. Ford.

Charles Thomas was not the only veteran of the United States embassy in Mexico to die in April 1971. Two weeks after Thomas's suicide, Winston Scott died at his home in the Mexican capital, at the age of sixty-two, after what was reported as an accidental fall. He appeared to have succumbed to internal injuries after tumbling from a ladder in his backyard.

News of Scott's death reached CIA headquarters almost immediately, and one of his former deputies in Mexico, Anne Goodpasture, now living in the United States, said she knew she had to act. Within hours, she said, she contacted Angleton to warn him that Scott had almost certainly kept classified documents at his house in Mexico City. It was well known among Scott's deputies that he took files home and did not always return them. Goodpasture recalled that Scott had at least one thick-walled safe in his house. She did not rule out the possibility that he had "squirreled away" at least one copy of a 1963 CIA surveillance tape of some of Oswald's telephone calls in Mexico.

Angleton flew to Mexico in time for the funeral. He recalled years later to congressional investigators that he had been dispatched to the funeral by Richard Helms, another old friend of Scott's. "I was appointed as an official by Dick to go down there" as a show of the agency's respect, Angleton said. The trip had a second purpose, he acknowledged. "Win was going to write a book, a manuscript," Angleton said. "It was sort of a last will and testament of an operator." Since Scott had not submitted the book to the CIA for the prepublication security review it would have needed, "my purpose was to go down and get all copies," Angleton said. "I was a close friend of his and I knew his wife and all that." Helms would later claim that he had only a vague memory of Angleton's trip—and the reasons for it. "There may have been some concern that maybe Scott had something in his safe that might affect the agency's work," Helms said, suggesting that the decision to enter Scott's home and empty out his safe was routine. "The agency just wanted to double-check and be sure there was nothing of that kind there."*

Scott's family recalled the unexpected knock at the door of their Mexico City home and how Scott's widow, Janet, discovered Angleton standing there. He announced that he had come to collect classified material that might be in the house. The family submitted to his inspection, and Angleton took several boxes of documents back to Langley, including two copies of the memoirs.

---

* Angleton had taken on a strangely similar assignment after the October 1964 murder of a Washington socialite and painter, Mary Pinchot Meyer, who was later identified as a former mistress of President Kennedy's. Hours after the murder, Angleton, a family friend, was found inside her locked home by Washington journalist Ben Bradlee, Meyer's brother-in-law and the future executive editor of the *Washington Post*. Angleton explained that he was looking for her diary, which she had told friends she wanted destroyed after her death. Angleton had apparently picked the lock, Bradlee said. When the diary was later found at Meyer's painting studio, Bradlee's wife gave it to Angleton to destroy. Bradlee saw the diary and said it contained "some handwritten descriptions" of what was "obviously an affair with the president." (Interview of Ben Bradlee, October 5, 1995, "Booknotes," C-SPAN.)

Much of Scott's manuscript would remain classified in the CIA's archives decades after his death, but a chapter focusing on the CIA's surveillance of Oswald in Mexico was quietly declassified in 1994 and released to Scott's family, part of the flood of millions of pages of government documents related to the Kennedy assassination that were declassified by the government in the 1990s, largely in response to the popularity of Oliver Stone's conspiracy-laden 1991 film *JFK*.

And what was in that chapter would shock former investigators for the Warren Commission when they finally saw it in 2012 and 2013.* Far from giving reassurance that the CIA had not hidden secrets, Scott's memoirs suggested just how much information had been intentionally withheld from the Warren Commission, often by Scott himself. There were startling differences between what Scott wrote in his book and what the CIA had told the commission years earlier.

Scott had assured the commission in 1964 that the government had come across no credible evidence, certainly nothing in Mexico, to suggest a conspiracy to kill the president. In his memoirs, however, Scott offered precisely the opposite view. What happened in Mexico, he wrote, raised the suspicion that Oswald was in fact an "agent" for a Communist government—Scott thought it was the Soviet Union—who might have been directed to kill Kennedy. "Above all, Oswald's visits at both the Communist Cuban Embassy and the Soviet Embassy in Mexico City during his brief five-day stay in September–October 1963 are, together with what is known of what took place during these visits, sufficient to make him a suspect agent, acting on behalf of the Soviets, in several things, possibly including the assassination of President Kennedy," Scott wrote. "It is evident that there are sufficient data for at least a suspicion that Oswald worked for the Soviets."

His memoirs revealed that, despite his insistence to the commission that there were no surveillance photos of Oswald in Mexico City, the CIA had in fact obtained photos of him outside both the Cuban and Soviet embassies. "People watching these embassies photographed Oswald as he entered and left each one, and clocked the time he spent on each visit," Scott wrote. He also suggested that there were reels of audiotapes from CIA wiretaps that had captured Oswald's voice in his phone calls to the embassies—tapes that Scott had claimed in 1963 and 1964 had all been

---

* They were shown it in 2012 and 2013 by the author of this book.

erased. "Oswald was of great interest to us," Scott wrote. "His conversations with personnel of these embassies were studied in detail."

In 1976, the House of Representatives established a special committee to reinvestigate the assassinations of both President Kennedy and civil rights leader Martin Luther King. Over the next two years, investigators for the House Select Committee on Assassinations tracked down at least three CIA officials who remembered seeing surveillance photos of Oswald in Mexico City. Among them was Stanley Watson, Scott's former deputy, who recalled a single surveillance photo of Oswald, alone, taken from the rear—"basically an ear and a back shot." Watson said he believed Scott had been capable of hiding or destroying material he did not want his CIA colleagues to see. He recalled how Scott had taken home contents of his embassy safe at his retirement; Watson also knew how Angleton had come to Mexico City to seize material from Scott's home after his death. He volunteered that he thought Scott was capable of "phonying" evidence. "I never believed Win Scott the first time he told me something."

In 1992, Congress established the Assassination Records Review Board to speed up the declassification of virtually all records related to the Kennedy assassination. The board forced the CIA to make public some of the records of the informants network maintained by Scott and his colleagues in Mexico City. On the list of Scott's informants was a former Mexican Interior Ministry official, Manuel Calvillo, and it was a name that would have been familiar to Elena Garro and her daughter. Calvillo was the family friend who, immediately after the assassination, contacted the Garros to urge them to go into hiding. If their account to Charles Thomas was true, it meant that the Mexican official who told Elena Garro and her daughter to say nothing to anyone about Oswald—about Silvia Duran, about the party, about Oswald's two "beatnik" traveling companions— was also working for the CIA.*

---

* CIA records identified Calvillo as an "unwitting" agent of the CIA, suggesting that he did not know that his handler worked for the agency. Investigators for the House Select Committee on Assassinations, working with the Mexican government, were unable to track down Calvillo in Mexico. He has since died.

58

In February 1975, David Slawson, now on the faculty of the law school at the University of Southern California, was thankful that he had turned down the job offer a decade earlier from Robert Kennedy. The proposal had come through Joe Dolan, then Kennedy's Senate aide, when Slawson was still at the Justice Department in Washington. Kennedy had wanted Slawson to sign on as legal counsel in his Senate office, with plans for Slawson to join Kennedy's presidential campaign in 1968. Slawson said he cringed at the thought that, had he joined the campaign, he might well have witnessed Kennedy's assassination at the Ambassador Hotel in Los Angeles. The hotel was just down the road from Slawson's office at USC.

He was also glad that he had not become associated with Kennedy's political entourage after all the ugly revelations about Kennedy's possible role in the CIA assassination plots targeting Castro. A special Senate committee chaired by Senator Frank Church of Idaho confirmed once and for all in the mid-1970s that the CIA had organized murder plots against several foreign leaders. The CIA's inspector general identified eight separate sets of plots directed at Castro alone in the Eisenhower and Kennedy administrations; the details of some of the schemes seemed drawn from a bad spy novel, with an arsenal of murder weapons to be smuggled into Cuba that included poison pens, poison pills, a fungus-infected scuba suit, and an exploding cigar.

James Angleton, a central witness before the Church Committee, was never directly tied to the Castro plots, although the committee turned up at least one well-placed CIA official who appeared convinced of a connection: John Whitten, the agency veteran who had been pushed aside by Angleton in the Oswald investigation in 1964. Whitten testified to congressional investigators that he understood Angleton "was one of several people in the agency who were trying to use the Mafia in the Cuban operations." Whitten recalled how, long before the Kennedy assassination, he had been forced to call off a CIA operation in Panama to search for the bank deposits of American mobsters because "Angleton vetoed it." Whitten said he was told at the time that "Angleton himself has ties to the Mafia and he would not want to double-cross them." Angleton was forced to resign from the agency in late 1974 as a result of the separate disclosure that, for years, he had overseen a massive, illegal domestic spy operation that had gathered information on American citizens, including opening their mail.

In Los Angeles in the 1970s, Slawson admitted that he could not follow every twist and turn of the congressional investigations of the misdeeds of the CIA. He was busy with his classes at USC, and there were times, he said, when Southern California seemed to exist in a different universe from Washington, DC. He was alarmed, though, every time he read some new disclosure about CIA activities that should have been revealed to him a decade earlier at the Warren Commission, especially about the Castro plots. While the plots did not necessarily have any connection to Kennedy's murder, the CIA had abdicated its responsibility to tell the commission about them. "The decision to withhold that information was morally wrong," Slawson said.

For a time, he was not so angry that he wanted to be drawn into "the circus" that had become the national debate about the assassination. For years, he was happy to leave the public debate to some of his old friends from the commission, especially David Belin, who became a fixture on radio and television programs in defending the Warren Commission's findings; Belin would write two books on the subject.

Slawson ended his silence once and for all, though, in February 1975, when he was contacted by a Washington correspondent for the *New York Times* who asked him to take a look at an intriguing FBI document that had just been unearthed in the National Archives. It was a memo to the State Department from J. Edgar Hoover in 1960, three years before the

Kennedy assassination, about Oswald, who would then have been living in Russia. The memo questioned whether an "imposter" might somehow be using Oswald's birth certificate; the issue had apparently first been raised with FBI agents in Dallas by Oswald's ever-excitable, conspiracy-minded mother, Marguerite.

As he read through the fifteen-year-old FBI memo, Slawson knew enough about Oswald's mother to know that there was almost certainly nothing to this. Slawson had heard no suggestion at all during his work on the Warren Commission that anyone had impersonated Oswald in Russia. Still, he was angry because he was certain that he had never seen Hoover's 1960 memo, and he should have seen it when he worked at the commission; he would have remembered it.

So he agreed to go on the record with the *Times*—both to attack the CIA and to join the growing calls for a new investigation of the Kennedy assassination, if only to determine why this document and so much other information, especially about the Castro plots, had been withheld. For former staff members on the commission, Slawson's comments represented a turning point—the Warren Commission's chief investigator on the question of whether President Kennedy had died in a foreign conspiracy now believed that the question needed to be asked again. "I don't know where the imposter notion would have led us—perhaps nowhere, like a lot of other leads," Slawson told the *Times*. "But the point is we didn't know about it. And why not?" He wondered if the CIA had been behind a decision to withhold the 1960 memo, just as the agency had withheld information about the Castro plots. The CIA "may have covered this up," he said.

Within days of the article in the *Times*, the phone rang in Slawson's home in Pasadena. It was a Sunday morning, he thought.

He had never heard the caller's voice before. It was plummy. At first, it sounded friendly.

"This is James Angleton," the caller said.

Slawson was not sure he knew exactly who Angleton was at the time. "I think I only knew he was high up at the CIA." Angleton's role in the CIA's domestic-spying operation, Operation Chaos, had been exposed by the *Times* only several months earlier, resulting in his resignation in December 1974.

Angleton would not physically depart his offices at CIA headquarters for months after resigning, however. And he made clear to Slawson that, even in his forced retirement, he was continuing to monitor how he and the agency were being depicted in the press, especially when it came to the Kennedy assassination.

Angleton wanted to talk about the article in the *Times* about Oswald and the Hoover memo. He briefly explained his background. "He really piled it on, how important and aristocratic he was," Slawson said.

Angleton then moved on to make it clear that he was an old friend of USC president John Hubbard, a former American diplomat and, by definition, Slawson's boss. "He asked how the president was getting along, as if I must be great buddies with the president," said Slawson, who in fact barely knew Hubbard.

It was then that the conversation took a menacing tone. Angleton wanted to know if Slawson had been accurately quoted in the article in the *Times*. He wanted to know exactly what Slawson had said to the *Times* reporter, and if it was true that Slawson wanted a new investigation of elements of the Kennedy assassination.

The threat was clearer in Angleton's sinister tone than in his words, Slawson said.

Angleton suggested that the CIA needed Slawson's help—his continuing help—as a "partner." As a partner in what? Slawson wondered.

"We want you to know how we appreciated the work you have done with us," Angleton said. Slawson reminded himself that he had never worked for the CIA; he had investigated the CIA.

"We hope you'll remain a friend," Angleton said. "We hope you'll remain a partner with us." Angleton spoke slowly, pausing to allow Slawson to take in what he was saying.

As he put down the phone, Slawson thought the message was obvious: "The message was: We know everything you're doing. We'll find it out. Just remember that. The CIA is watching you." He and his wife, Kaaren, were both alarmed by the call. What did it mean that this apparently powerful figure at the CIA would contact them out of the blue to suggest that Slawson was asking too many questions about the Kennedy assassination? Slawson was convinced that Angleton was giving him a warning: "Keep your mouth shut."

In Washington that summer, FBI director Clarence Kelley, beginning his third year in charge at the FBI, thought he was making progress in distancing the bureau from the increasingly dark legacy of his predecessor, the late J. Edgar Hoover. "We are truly sorry," Kelley would declare publicly, apologizing after the flood of posthumous revelations about Hoover's abuses of power, which included the FBI's illegal harassment for decades of civil rights leaders and antigovernment protesters; the abuses ended only with Hoover's death in 1972. "No FBI director should abide incursions upon the liberties of the people," Kelley said.

Still, in his years at the FBI, Kelley, the jut-jawed former police chief of St. Louis, Missouri, found himself dragged over and over again into internal investigations of the misdeeds, and often the crimes, of FBI agents and other bureau employees during the Hoover years. Those crimes, Kelley discovered to his astonishment in the summer of 1975, included the destruction of critical evidence about the Kennedy assassination by FBI agents in Dallas.

That July, Tom Johnson, the publisher of the *Dallas Times Herald*, the city's number-two newspaper, requested an urgent face-to-face meeting with Kelley. The FBI director agreed, and Johnson flew to Washington the next day. Ushered into Kelley's office, Johnson recalled later, he took a seat and wasted no time before revealing to Kelley why he was there: his newspaper was working on a story that suggested a massive cover-up in Dallas of what the FBI had known about Lee Harvey Oswald.

After years of hearing "so many nut stories, so many conspiracy theories" about the assassination, Johnson said, this "horrifying" story seemed to be true. The newspaper had learned that in early November 1963, just weeks before the assassination, a furious Oswald had arrived unannounced in the Dallas field office of the FBI, and that he left behind a threatening handwritten note. In the note, Oswald had apparently complained about the bureau's surveillance of his family, but the exact wording of his threats—and their target—was a mystery, since the note had vanished after the assassination. The FBI had covered up the note's existence and Oswald's visit, never telling the Warren Commission about any of it. It was the Texas publisher himself who had gotten the tip about the note and its disappearance—from an FBI official in Dallas he would refuse to name—and Johnson planned to write the story along with reporter Hugh Aynesworth, the longtime scoop artist of the *Dallas Morning News* who was now working at the rival *Times-Herald*.

"Kelley looked at me, and his expression was beyond being startled," Johnson recalled. "He looked bewildered." Kelley vowed to investigate. He asked Johnson "to send me the full story in writing, and give me some time to check on it."

It took little time for Kelley to determine "that the worst of it was painfully true." He was able to establish that Oswald had in fact delivered a handwritten note to the FBI field office in Dallas in early November 1963 and that it had been torn up and flushed down a toilet by Special Agent James Hosty, on orders of his supervisor, Gordon Shanklin, in the hours after Oswald's murder.

Kelley was appalled, he said. "Buried for 12 years was this FBI cover-up," he wrote later. "Why did the FBI people do this? The reason, at least in the beginning, was easy enough to understand: hide the news from Hoover." He could imagine how, after the assassination, Hosty and Shanklin had panicked at the note's existence. "To the world at large, they must have reasoned, it might look as if the FBI had the assassin within its grasp—and then let him get away. To J. Edgar Hoover in Washington, it most certainly would have looked that way." Kelley imagined how the disclosure "would have ignited an inferno of retribution in Hoover."

Kelley called Johnson in Dallas and told him he was free to run the story—because it was true. The article was published on August 31, 1975, and "was a sensation from coast to coast," Kelley said.

The incident led Kelley to step up what would be a personal, informal investigation of what had been hidden in the FBI's raw investigative files about the Kennedy assassination—what else the Warren Commission had never been allowed to see. The assassination was a subject on which he had always considered himself something of an armchair detective. "I regarded the Kennedy assassination as a piece of personal unfinished business," he said. Like most career law-enforcement officials, Kelley had "witnessed a considerable amount of heart-wrenching tragedy.... One becomes not necessarily immune to it, but in some ways, insulated against it." But not that one time in November 1963, he said. "President Kennedy's death staggered me."

He followed the many conspiracy theories about the assassination. "I read any number of the so-called 'assassination books,'" he wrote later. "The FBI file on the assassination is the largest ever created by the bureau on a single subject.... As director, I had access to all of it and, as time permitted, I reviewed portions of it."

Over the years, as he gathered up and paged through the bureau's raw files, he became particularly troubled, he said, by one subject: Oswald's visit to Mexico City. Kelley read about the CIA surveillance operation there that had targeted Oswald—and how the CIA's information had been mishandled after it was relayed to the FBI in the fall of 1963. Something important had happened in Mexico, Kelley decided. "Oswald's stay in Mexico City apparently shaped the man's thinking irrevocably."

Kelley came across Hoover's top secret June 1964 letter addressed to the commission—the letter that commission staff lawyers say never reached them—about Oswald's declaration in the Cuban embassy in Mexico City that he intended to kill Kennedy. From what Kelley was reading, there was no doubt that the incident had happened. "Oswald definitely offered to kill President Kennedy," he said. And from what he found elsewhere in the FBI's files, Kelley came to believe that Oswald had made an identical threat when he met with diplomats—and spies—at the Soviet embassy in Mexico, including the feared KGB agent Valeriy Kostikov. "The importance of Kostikov cannot be overstated," Kelley said. Well before Kennedy's assassination, Kostikov was known to both the CIA and to Soviet intelligence analysts at FBI headquarters as a specialist in assassinations.

That did not mean that the Cubans or the Soviets were behind Kennedy's murder, Kelley stressed. Kostikov also had routine diplomatic duties at the embassy as part of his cover. "I personally think the Soviets informed Oswald that they wanted no part of his scheme," Kelley said. As for Castro, the FBI had determined that "the dictator thought at the time that the offer might be a deliberate provocation by the U.S. government or that Oswald was simply a madman" and that Cuban diplomats in Mexico probably had nothing further to do with him.

Still, what was in the FBI's files—and never shared with the Warren Commission—was astonishing enough. It suggested that the Cuban and Soviet embassies in Mexico had known for weeks before the assassination that Oswald was talking openly of his intention to kill the president.

What followed Oswald's Mexico trip were a series of bureaucratic delays and blunders within the FBI that prevented much of the information, including the fact that Oswald had met in Mexico with a KGB assassinations expert, from reaching the FBI office in Dallas. In Washington, the FBI and CIA "had enough combined information on Oswald's trek to Mexico City to put his name in lights on a presidential security list of threats," Kelley said. But Hosty "was kept in the dark." The Dallas agent was given only sketchy information about the Mexico City trip; he was told nothing about Kostikov's true identity. "Apparently within the machinery of the bureau, those responsible just did not put two-and-two together fast enough," Kelley said.

After the assassination, Kelley learned, FBI supervisors in Washington—and, he believed, the Johnson White House—decided to keep those details away from Hosty and his colleagues in Dallas for fear of sparking a global crisis over the possibility of a Communist conspiracy in Kennedy's death. Kelley determined that at least two memos about the events in Mexico were removed from Oswald's case file in Dallas in the days after the assassination in the hope that Hosty had not yet read them. Kelley said he believed the order to remove the memos had come from the FBI's former number-three official, Assistant Director William Sullivan, and that Sulivan appeared to be acting on orders from the White House, which "seemingly considered the risk of a confrontation with the Soviet Union over the Kennedy assassination too great." In memoirs published in 1979, two years after his death in a hunting accident, Sullivan did not address Kelley's allegations, although he admitted that the FBI and the CIA had never gotten to the bottom of many of the mysteries about the president's murder, especially those connected to Oswald's trip to Mexico. "There were huge gaps in the case, gaps we never did close," Sullivan wrote. "We never found out what went on between Oswald and the Cubans in Mexico City."

Kelley came to see Hosty as a victim. He was convinced that if Hosty had been told everything that FBI headquarters knew about Oswald's Mexico trip, he would have alerted the Secret Service to the obvious threat that Oswald posed. The FBI, Kelley said, would have "undoubtedly taken all necessary steps to neutralize Oswald." And that was Kelley's larger conclusion—that President Kennedy's assassination could have been prevented, perhaps easily. Despite Hoover's insistence that Oswald was a lone wolf whose plans to kill the president could never have been detected by the bureau, the truth was different. If the FBI's Dallas office had been aware of what was known elsewhere in the FBI and CIA about Oswald at that moment, "without doubt JFK would not have died in Dallas on Nov. 22, 1963," Kelley said. "History would have taken a different turn."

ABOVE: New Orleans District Attorney Jim Garrison claimed in 1967 that he had un-covered a conspiracy in the Kennedy assassination that the Warren Commission had failed to detect—or had covered up. He is shown with Mark Lane in New Orleans on March 28, 1967. BELOW: Garrison's witnesses included colorful New Orleans lawyer Dean Andrews, who had earlier told the commission that he had been asked to go to Dallas to defend Oswald hours after the assassination. The request, he said, had been made by Oswald's mysterious patron—"Clay Bertrand." Andrews, shown being escorted by New Orleans sheriffs in August 1967, would later be convicted of perjury.

Alejandra Xanic von Bertrab

Jorge Vargas/Conaculta

Leticia Sánchez Medel

Alejandra Xanic von Bertrab

TOP LEFT: Silvia Duran, shown outside her home in 2013, still insists she never met with Oswald away from the Cuban consulate. TOP RIGHT: Helena Garro, daughter of Elena Garro, at a 2013 forum in Mexico City to honor her late mother; she says they saw Oswald at the Duran family party. CENTER LEFT: Duran's claims are also rebutted by her former sister-in-law Lidia Duran Navarro, who recalls distinctly that Silvia talked of going on a date with Oswald. CENTER RIGHT: Francisco Guerrero Garro, a prominent Mexican newspaperman, revealed in 2013 that he too had seen Oswald at the party. BELOW: In January 2013, Robert Kennedy Jr. revealed that his father had never accepted the Warren Commission's findings. He is shown being interviewed in Dallas with his sister Rory and TV host Charlie Rose.

Carter Rose, Courtesy of AT&T
Performing Arts Center, Margot and Bill
Winspear Opera House, Dallas

Author's Note

In 1977, the former American ambassador to Mexico, Thomas Mann, made an extraordinary demand of congressional investigators. Then in retirement in Texas, he told staff members of the House Select Committee on Assassinations that he would reveal the truth of what happened in Mexico City in the days after the assassination—information that he had withheld from the Warren Commission—but only if then president Jimmy Carter personally agreed to grant him immunity from prosecution. Like James Angleton, Mann seemed to know there was much more about Kennedy's murder that the government—the CIA, in particular—would want to keep hidden forever; he was not going to reveal it without direct approval from the Oval Office.

The report of the House investigators, which remained classified for years after they traveled to Texas to interview Mann, shows that the former ambassador hinted at what he was prepared to say under oath if he got immunity—that he had been personally ordered by Secretary of State Dean Rusk in the days after Kennedy's murder to shut down any investigation in Mexico that would "confirm or refute rumors of Cuban involvement in the assassination." Mann said he believed the same "incredible" order had been given to Winston Scott, the CIA station chief, and Clark Anderson, the FBI legal attaché, by their superiors back in the United States. "Mann did not believe that the U.S. government would stop the investigation solely on the grounds that it would create a flap with the Cubans," according to a long-classified summary of his interview. "Mann stated that . . . if he had to make a guess, there was a 99 percent chance that the investigation was stopped because it would have resulted in the discovery of covert U.S. government action" in Mexico that somehow targeted Castro. He concluded that Silvia Duran "was probably an agent for the CIA." He also said that Robert Kennedy "was heavily involved in counterintelligence activity in 1964," although there is no elaboration on that point in the summary.

Mann died in 1999, and the two House investigators who interviewed him are also no longer alive. Surviving staff members of the House Assassinations Committee say they cannot recall why the committee did not obtain immunity from the White House that would have allowed Mann to testify. Although he was briefly interviewed by the Warren Commission's staff, Mann was not called to give formal, sworn testimony to the commission, either. Instead, the principal State Department witness before the commission was Secretary Rusk, who swore that he knew of no evidence of a conspiracy involving Cuba or any other government. He died in 1994.

The House committee did take sworn classified testimony in 1978 from Ray Rocca, who—unintentionally—offered new evidence of the CIA's lies to the Warren Commission. Even as Win Scott was assuring the commission in 1964 that the CIA's Mexico City station had no serious suspicion about a conspiracy, he was apparently saying precisely the opposite to colleagues at the agency. It was not just in his never-published memoirs that Scott revealed his doubts that Oswald had acted alone; he told it to Rocca, too. "He was so firmly committed—Win was, personally—to the fact of Cuban involvement," said Rocca, who seemed unaware that Scott had said the opposite to the Warren Commission. "I can't believe—absolutely—that he would ever withhold it."

I spoke with James Angleton once in my life, as a young reporter in the Washington bureau of the *New York Times*. I don't remember the story I was working on, but it would have been in the early 1980s and somehow involved the CIA, and an editor in the bureau thought that Angleton, who had befriended a number of the more blue-blooded editors at the *Times* over the years, might offer some useful perspective. Like Angleton and so many others at the CIA, my editor was a proud graduate of Yale University. Angleton would then have been a few years into his forced retirement.

What I remember of the interview is that Angleton spoke in riddles, never answering any question I asked him, but suggesting that I needed to put myself on the path to some larger truth about protecting the United States from its adversaries behind the Iron Curtain. The conversation was perfectly bizarre (and not so different from the phone conversation that David Slawson described from 1975). The truth is that I thought Angleton might have been drunk; by the end of his career, his debilitating alcoholism was well known in intelligence circles. He died in 1987, at the age of sixty-nine.

In the years since that strange phone call, as more and more of the details of his thirty-year-long spying career have emerged, it has become clear that Angleton's legacy at the CIA was a uniquely disastrous one. He was the mole-hunter who never found a mole, but whose liquor-fueled, nicotine-stained paranoia about Communist infiltration of the spy agency and the rest of the government destroyed many lives, including those of agency colleagues he effectively accused of treason. There were others he suspected might be Soviet agents: Henry Kissinger, former British prime minister Harold Wilson, and Angleton's last boss at the CIA, Director of Central Intelligence William Colby.

The record shows Angleton delighted in creating an aura of menace and mystery about himself, and in promoting a sense of tragic romance about the work of counterintelligence, and at those labors he was undeniably successful. Since his death, he has become a figure in popular culture, portrayed on film by, among others, the actor Matt Damon in *The Good Shepherd*. Several major biographies have been written about Angleton, and more are coming. I suspect that he would have found it amusing, and probably satisfying, that half a century after the Kennedy assassination, a journalist like me could spend years in a "wilderness of mirrors" that he had created.

Going into this project, I had no idea—and I think many serious historians had no idea—that Angleton even had a role in the investigation of the Kennedy assassination. Nor did David Slawson and the other staff lawyers on the Warren Commission who were receiving information from the CIA only after it was filtered by Angleton and his staff. It was only when I shared the results of my research for this book with Slawson that he realized the control that Angleton, whose name he did not know in 1964, had exercised on the commission's work.

This is not speculation: Angleton and his colleagues, especially his old friend Win Scott in Mexico City, *did* muddy the facts about the

546 | AUTHOR'S NOTE

assassination, making it impossible today to know the full truth, especially in answering the all-important question of whether Oswald had been encouraged or even ordered to pick up that rifle in Dallas. There is example after example of how Angleton and Scott tried to shape—or rather, warp—the official history of the assassination. We know that:

- In early 1964, Angleton muscled aside a senior colleague to take control of the flow of information to the Warren Commission, even as he was maintaining discreet lines of communication to his friends at the FBI and to a commission member, Allen Dulles, who was his former boss at the CIA. John Whitten, the CIA colleague he pushed aside, was convinced that Angleton was tied to the CIA's plots with the Mafia to oust Castro.
- Angleton swooped down into Mexico City in the days after Scott's death in 1971 to seize Scott's memoirs, in which Scott revealed just how much information had been withheld from the commission, as well as his suspicion that there might well have been a foreign conspiracy behind Kennedy's murder.
- In 1969, Angleton signed the letter that dismissed the request by the diplomat Charles Thomas for a new investigation of the allegations made by Elena Garro about the "twist party" in Mexico and about a sexual relationship between Oswald and Silvia Duran. That single act by Angleton meant that Garro's claims would not be pursued again until after she—and most of the people who might support her account—were dead.

As for Scott, his former CIA colleagues in Mexico City recall those audiotapes and surveillance photos of Oswald that Scott would later insist did not exist. The record shows he repeatedly dismissed the evidence that Thomas brought to him from Elena Garro, even after Scott gathered intelligence independently that supported elements of her story, including what Scott would later describe as "the fact" of an affair between Oswald and Duran. All the while, Scott was establishing a written record in which he questioned Garro's mental stability, while Scott's former deputy launched a whispering campaign in Mexico City aimed at discrediting Charles Thomas.

Here is speculation that I clearly label as such: Is it possible that Angleton or Scott had a hand in the disappearance of J. Edgar Hoover's explosive letter to the Warren Commission in June 1964 in which he reported that Oswald had talked openly in Mexico City about his intention to kill President Kennedy—a story that supposedly came to the FBI straight out of the mouth of Fidel Castro? The letter from Hoover appears never to have reached key commission lawyers, although it turned up decades later in the archives of the CIA.

There is another eye-popping document, prepared at the CIA sometime after 1968, that deserves attention in trying to understand what was hidden by the agency. It is a meticulous, 132-page-long classified chronology of everything that was known about Oswald by the agency's Mexico City station, and when. The first entry is September 27, 1963, when Oswald was first detected at the Soviet embassy in Mexico. CIA records seem to suggest that the chronology was prepared by Anne Goodpasture, Scott's former deputy. The chronology documents the time line, at least as Scott presented it, of Garro's allegations about the "twist party" and her belief that Duran had been Oswald's "mistress." On one side of the chronology are brief typed commentaries by its author, who questions—despairingly, it seems—why the agency had been so skeptical of Garro, even after some of her allegations found support elsewhere. "How did Elena GARRO know about Silvia being the mistress of OSWALD?—This is 1965," one note reads, recalling that the CIA would then hear the same thing from one of its own informants in 1967. The chronology notes that the FBI was also eventually able to confirm Garro's claim that she had been hidden away—by a man later identified as a paid CIA informant—at a small Mexico City hotel for eight days after the assassination. "This is what Elena claimed and no one would believe her," a note attached to that entry reads. Elsewhere, the chronology's author writes: "The Warren Commission did not do an adequate investigative job. . . . It is hard to believe the Commission served the public well. Instead of ending all the rumors, they set the stage for a new and more serious era of speculation."

From other declassified CIA files, we know, for certain, another secret that Angleton would have been eager to keep: that his elite counterintelligence staff had kept an eye on Oswald—illegally—as far back as 1959, four years before the assassination. In November 1959, a month after Oswald arrived in Moscow and announced that he wanted to defect to the Soviet Union, Angleton's staff placed Oswald on a "SECRET EYES ONLY" watch list of about three hundred Americans targeted to have their overseas mail opened for inspection. That was a full year before the date that the CIA gave to the Warren Commission for the opening of the agency's first files on Oswald. Angleton's desire to keep the earlier surveillance a secret would make sense if only because the mail-opening program, known by the code name HK-LINGUAL, was known even within the CIA to be illegal; the agency had no court-approved warrants to open the mail of American citizens. (Over the years, others on the watch list included Martin Luther King, John Steinbeck, and former vice president Hubert Humphrey.) Why had Angleton's staff targeted Oswald almost immediately after his arrival in Russia, while other American military defectors were never put on that watch list? It is another question that cannot be answered with certainty.

I started work on this book in 2008, and I am writing this author's note in the late summer of 2013. During that time I have interviewed hundreds of people, many more than once, and traveled around the country and to several points abroad for my research. I have been allowed to see classified documents, private letters, court transcripts, photographs, films, and a variety of other materials that, to my knowledge, have not been shown to any other author. Every statement or quotation in this book has been sourced, which the footnotes and endnotes show in detail. What is clear to me is that over the last fifty years—actually more than fifty years, since parts of this narrative are set well before November 22, 1963—senior officials of the United States government, most especially at the CIA, have lied about the assassination and the events that led to it.

Several former officials bear special responsibility for the conspiracy theories that are likely to plague us forever. At the top of that list would be another CIA veteran, former director of Central Intelligence Richard Helms, who made the decision not to tell the Warren Commission about the agency's murder plots targeting Castro. And it was Helms, of course, who put the treacherous Angleton in control of what information reached the commission. At the FBI, J. Edgar Hoover and his deputies went out of their way—from the first hours after the assassination—to avoid pursuing evidence that might have led to the discovery that Oswald had coconspirators. It was far easier for Hoover to blame the assassination on a disturbed young misfit who had no recorded history of violence than to acknowledge the possibility that there had been a conspiracy to kill the president that the FBI might have been able to foil. It was Hoover's own successor, Clarence Kelley, who declared with certainty that President Kennedy would not have died if the FBI had simply acted on the information that existed in its files in November 1963.

There are two other names that belong on the list, and they are of men who are more often saluted for their accomplishments in public life: Chief Justice Earl Warren and Robert Kennedy. The chief justice was wise in initially refusing President Johnson's request that he lead the commission; Warren was right to fear that the commission's work might stain his legacy because it has, much to the disappointment of people like me who were raised to revere him for his accomplishments on the Supreme Court. What does it say about this presidential commission that its findings were ultimately rejected by the president himself? Warren has to be faulted above all for denying key evidence and witnesses to the commission's staff. Those monumental errors included his refusal to allow the commission to review the president's autopsy photos and X-rays—a decision that all but guaranteed the medical evidence would remain hopelessly muddled today—and his even more baffling order that blocked the staff from interviewing Silvia Duran.

I am left with nothing but admiration for most of the then young staff lawyers on the commission, who were clearly fighting to get to the truth about the assassination. That would include men like David Slawson, Burt Griffin, David Belin, Mel Eisenberg, and Sam Stern; I do believe they joined the investigation without any real sense of what they were up against. There can be no praise for Wesley Liebeler if there is even a hint of truth in the reports about his sexual advances on women witnesses, but I am convinced that he, too, would have been excited to find that Oswald had accomplices in killing the president, and then to track them down. Arlen Specter was willing to take the risk of standing up to—and often offending—the chief justice of the United States to insist on evidence that Specter felt he needed to do his job. If he had been allowed to inspect Kennedy's autopsy photos and X-rays, many of the debates about the medical evidence and the single-bullet theory might have been settled long ago.

And then, perhaps most surprisingly, it is clear that Robert Kennedy bears much responsibility for the fact that, half a century after the assassination, opinion polls show that most Americans are convinced today that they are still being denied the truth about the president's murder. No one had been better situated to demand the truth than Robert Kennedy—first as attorney general, then as a United States senator, and certainly as the slain president's brother. And yet, in the nearly five years between his brother's violent death and his own, Robert Kennedy kept insisting publicly that he fully supported the findings of the Warren Commission, all the while telling family and friends that he was convinced that the commission had it wrong. If anyone doubted Kennedy's lack of candor, those doubts were put to rest in January 2013, when his son and namesake, Robert Jr., appeared to stun an audience in Dallas—at a forum to honor his father's legacy—by revealing that his father thought the commission's report "was a shoddy piece of craftsmanship." He said his father believed the assassination might have been carried out by mobsters in retaliation for the Justice Department's crackdown on organized crime during the Kennedy administration, or that the murder might have been linked to Cuba, or even possibly to "rogue CIA agents."

Robert Jr. had an explanation for why his father had misled the public for years. His father, he said, felt he had no ability in the mid-1960s to pursue the investigation himself, and he worried that by raising his suspicions publicly about a conspiracy in his brother's assassination, he might divert attention from pressing national issues, especially the civil rights movement. "There was really nothing he could have done about it at that time," Robert Jr. explained. "As soon as Jack died, he lost all of his power."

I discovered that there is one place where there is still hope of resolving some of mysteries about the president's murder: Mexico City. I admit that I knew nothing—at all—about Oswald's Mexico trip until I began work on this book. In two lengthy reporting trips to the Mexican capital, I attempted to retrace Oswald's movements around that massive city. I was doing what the FBI and the CIA had apparently refused to do in the weeks after the assassination, including trying to track down and talk to Silvia Duran. I was also eager to locate people who had known the late Elena Garro, who died in 1998, from emphysema, at the age of seventy-seven.

In April 2013, my talented Mexico City stringer—Alejandra Xanic Von Bertrab, who shared in a Pulitzer Prize weeks later for her work for the *New York Times*—located Duran in Mexico City, where she still lives after having retired from Mexico's Social Security Administration. Duran will turn seventy-six on November 22, 2013; her birthday falls on the anniversary of the Kennedy assassination. She initially refused to be interviewed in any detail, declining to respond to telephone calls and letters. So I sent Duran a large package of the documentation that I had gathered about her from the declassified government archives of both the United States and Mexico. Among those papers: the detailed 1967 CIA report in which an agency informant—the Mexican artist who Duran acknowledges was a friend—described how Duran volunteered to him that she had a brief affair with Oswald. I also provided Duran with the surveillance records of the Mexican secret police that appear to document her extramarital relationships with other men in the year before the Kennedy assassination, including at least two other American visitors to Mexico. I also gave her the CIA reports that purport to document an affair between her and the former Cuban ambassador to Mexico. She appears to have come under surveillance by both the CIA and the Mexican Interior Ministry long before the assassination as a result of her work at the Cuban consulate and, earlier, at a Cuba-Mexico cultural institute. The surveillance reports were, by definition, distasteful and proved how Duran's privacy had been violated outrageously for years. But I thought it was only fair to Duran that she see what had so alarmed and intrigued me in the record. If she wanted to rebut any of this, I was eager to hear it.

As we waited to see if Duran would reply, Xanic and I tracked down Elena Garro's daughter, Helena Paz, now seventy-four years old and living in a medical care facility an hour's drive outside of Mexico City. Although reported to be mentally fit, Helena has been ailing for years as the result of a stroke. Through a cousin who serves as her legal guardian, she declined to be interviewed. We pressed the cousin to ask Helena if she stood by her account—and her mother's—that they had both encountered Oswald and the two American "beatniks," as well as Silvia Duran, at the "twist party." She did. "What she said in the 1960s is the truth," the cousin reported back to us. "It is still true."

I extended my stay in Mexico City for several days in the hopes of speaking with Duran, but she never replied to the package of documents. So in a last-ditch attempt to question her, Xanic and I drove to Duran's family home on Tuesday, April 9. Told by members of her extended family that she was out for the afternoon, we decided to wait in the street for her return. She finally arrived in a taxi, carrying shopping bags from the supermarket. She was angry at the sight of us, trying to open her tall iron gate and get inside without acknowledging us. But she relented after we pleaded for just a few minutes of her time. Scowling, she agreed to answer a few questions, perhaps hoping we would leave her alone after this.

Even after five decades, there was no doubt this was Silvia Duran. Her face was recognizable from the photos taken in the early 1960s. Her clothes now were comfortably fashionable, highlighted by a long pastel-colored checkered scarf around her neck; she wore Chanel-branded sunglasses. Although her once dark hair is now mostly gray, she wore it in essentially the same pixie cut she had in 1963. Her English was still good, although she frequently reverted to Spanish during what turned out to be nearly an hour of conversation outside the metal gates, her groceries placed on the ground. Even as she sparred with us, she was charming, funny, and smart. To our surprise, it took little coaxing to get her to allow us to take her picture.

She denied, as she had for so many years, that she had a sexual relationship with Oswald—if only, she claimed, because she had found him so unattractive. She said the suggestion that she would sleep with him was insulting. "Please!" she said in English in a mocking tone. "They say he was my lover? Please, please. Oswald was that size," she said, holding out her hand to suggest that Oswald was short. (He was five foot nine inches tall.) "How could I be a lover of this man who was so insignificant?" She denied the many reports and rumors, which were investigated but never proved by the Warren Commission and later U.S. government investigations, that she had worked as a spy for Cuba or Mexico, or possibly even for the CIA.

She said she remembered the dance party described by Elena Garro and that Oswald was not there. She recalled that there were Americans at the party, including an American "movie star" she would not identify, saying that she thought the actor was still alive and she did not want to create trouble for him. Asked why her cousin Elena would make up such an extraordinary story and claim that Duran and Oswald had an affair, Duran said that her cousin was "crazy—she was completely out of her mind. . . . I don't think she hates me so much. I think she was crazy." And why would Garro's daughter say the same thing? "She had a lot of psychological problems," Duran replied. Elena and her daughter "were both pretty crazy, always."

I pointed out that it was not just the Garros who alleged the affair between Duran and Oswald. The interrogation reports prepared by the Mexican secret police show that she was questioned repeatedly after the assassination about whether she had "intimate relations" with Oswald, as if the police had evidence of it. Why had her friend the artist claimed in

1967 that she had told him about an affair? She replied that she might have been a victim of the lies of jealous men who had wanted to sleep with her—but whom she refused. "I was married," she said. "That's why I get so mad when I read all of this. It's all gossip. . . . They want to say everybody was my lover—the ambassador, the consul." She insisted again—as she had been insisting for years—that she saw Oswald only within the confines of the Cuban consulate during two visits on a single day in September 1963. "I didn't do anything beyond the normal" in trying to help him with his visa application, she said. "I only saw him inside the consulate. I never saw him outside the consulate—never, never, never."

It was only a few weeks later that we tracked down a new witness who contradicted an important element of the story that Duran had just told us—her former sister-in-law, Lidia Duran Navarro, a renowned Mexican choreographer. Lidia is eighty-five and her memory has faded on many of the details of the weeks before and after Kennedy's assassination. Although her late brother and Silvia Duran divorced decades ago, Lidia expressed only fondness for Silvia. Lidia said she had always doubted that Silvia would have had an affair with Oswald. Her reasoning was the same as her former sister-in-law's: Oswald, Lidia said, was too physically unattractive to be taken as a lover. "It's absurd," Lidia said. "He was a weakling puppet, with a fool's face."

But Lidia did have a clear memory of something that Silvia had told her in confidence decades ago—that, despite all of Silvia's claims to the contrary, she had gone out on at least one date in Mexico City with Oswald. According to Lidia, a smitten Oswald invited Silvia to a lunch date at a Sanborns restaurant close to the Cuban consulate. (She distinctly remembered it was a Sanborns, part of a popular Mexican chain of restaurants with that name.) And Silvia, she said, accepted. "She should not have accepted an invitation coming from an American," Lidia recalled. Diplomats at the Cuban embassy were furious when they discovered that Duran had dared to be seen on a date with an American, even one who claimed to be a devoted supporter of Castro's revolution. "The Cubans scolded her," Lidia recalled.

If Lidia's account is correct, Silvia has never told the truth in her central assertion that she "never, never, never" met Oswald outside the Cuban consulate and that she and Oswald discussed only his visa application. In fact, according to Lidia, Silvia Duran went out on a date—at least once—with a man who appeared eager to impress her with his support for Cuba's revolution and who, less than two months later, would kill the president of the United States.

In June 2013, Xanic and I located two men—both prominent Mexican newspapermen, both friendly with Silvia Duran in the 1960s—who would blow much larger holes in her story. The first, Oscar Contreras, a columnist for the Mexican newspaper *El Mañana*, was the same journalist who came forward in 1967 to report that, while he was a law student and prominent Castro sympathizer at a Mexico City university four years earlier, he had spent time with Oswald, who had wanted his help to obtain a Cuban visa. That much of the story Contreras had told many years before.

But what he said in 2013 went much further and suggested far more extensive contacts between Oswald and Cuban agents in Mexico— contacts that Duran said never occurred. Contreras said that he not only encountered Oswald at the university; he also saw him again at a reception a few days later at the Cuban embassy. "I saw him at a distance, talking to people," said Contreras, who said he did not approach Oswald at the reception because of warnings from Cuban friends that he might be some sort of CIA plant. Why had Contreras not told American officials in Mexico about Oswald's mysterious appearance at a Cuban diplomatic reception? There was a simple answer, Contreras said: the diplomats never asked.

And then we found arguably the most important, most credible witness of all: Elena Garro's nephew Francisco Guerrero Garro, a prominent Mexican newspaperman who had been a twenty-three-year-old university student at the time of the Kennedy assassination and who has kept his silence for half a century about what he knew about Lee Harvey Oswald.

Guerrero, now seventy-three, a founder and retired senior editor of *La Jornada*, a major left-wing newspaper in Mexico, said he had said nothing about Oswald for decades out of fear that what he knew would put his family in danger. "I had never wanted to tell," he said. "We did get scared back then when we realized many of the people involved in the Kennedy case died" in mysterious circumstances.

Guerrero's secret? He said he had been at the party where his aunt had encountered Oswald and Silvia Duran. In fact, he had driven his aunt and his mother—Deva Guerrero, Elena's sister—to the party. And he said he is certain that he saw Oswald, too. "He was standing there, next to the chimney," Guerrero said. "His face was unmistakable . . . he was very gloomy. He was just standing there, looking at the people, like scrutinizing people. . . . I can swear that he was there."

In the hours after the Kennedy assassination and the first images of Oswald were made public, he recalled, there was a panicked telephone conversation between his mother and his aunt, Elena Garro.

"I heard my mom say on the phone: 'It's not possible! It's not possible! Really, Elena, it's not possible! Are you sure? . . . I'll be right there.'" Guerrero said his mother ordered him to get the family car. "She then tells me, 'Take me to Elena's house.'" Guerrero said he protested that he needed to leave for class and his mother replied, "Doesn't matter. Take me to Elena's house."

They drove straight to the home of Elena Garro, who had a television, and together they watched the first reports from Dallas, and saw the first flickering images of Oswald under arrest. Guerrero remembered that his mother and Elena turned to each other and became hysterical as they realized that they had seen the president's assassin at a family party a few weeks earlier. "Yes, yes, that's him, that's him!" he remembered everyone yelling out. "His face appeared on TV again and again," he said. "My mom would insist: 'It is him! It is him!'"

He remembered asking out loud if the Mexican secret police would somehow try to implicate his family in the Kennedy assassination if it became known that they had attended a party where Oswald had been. "What the hell do we have to do with this? We only went to a party where this man was. We didn't take him there."

His mother vowed to keep her silence forever about what she had seen, Francisco said. She was a dedicated Communist—the political opposite of her sister, Elena—and she knew how to keep secrets at a time when being a declared Marxist in Mexico could be dangerous. Everyone else at the party decided to keep silent too, Francisco said. "There was consensus that it was him [Oswald]," he said. "But nobody wanted to talk about this. I think they were afraid. I was afraid myself."

The subject became "taboo," he said. "No one spoke about it."

He said the one person who did tell authorities about the party and about Oswald was his aunt, Elena, and that she went to talk to someone at the United States embassy—"with whom, I do not know"—either the day after the assassination or the following day. She was driven there, he said, by one of his uncles, Albano Garro, Elena's brother, who has since died. Francisco remembered that his uncle was angry because Elena, who only intended to stay fifteen minutes at the embassy, did not leave for nearly four hours. He heard from his mother that Elena Garro then received telephone calls "several times" from someone at the embassy "as if it was an important matter."

There is no absolute proof in the archives of the CIA or the Mexican government that Silvia Duran was anyone's spy, although there was clearly plenty of suspicion about it in 1963 and 1964. Duran insists today, as she has in the past, that she spent no time with Oswald outside of the four walls of the Cuban consulate. But if Duran has been telling the truth all these years, many, many people must have lied, including people who were her relatives and once close friends, some of whom are still alive today. And half a century later, why would they still be lying?

The credibility of the people I have tracked down in Mexico for this book is enhanced by the fact that they have not tried, like so many in the United States and elsewhere, to profit from what they knew about the president's assassin. They have not written tell-all books or attempted to sell interviews. The same is true for the survivors of Charles William Thomas. His widow, Cynthia, and other members of his family have refused for decades to talk to journalists about what happened to a fine man whose cherished career, and then whose life, ended so cruelly for reasons they have never fully understood. I am honored that all of these people would take the risk of talking to me, with no promise of anything but my commitment to try to determine if what Elena Garro told Charles Thomas all those years ago was true—that Lee Harvey Oswald was invited by Silvia Duran to a dance party in Mexico City attended by Cuban diplomats and spies, as well as Mexican supporters of Castro's government, and that some of the guests had spoken openly of their hope that someone would assassinate President John F. Kennedy, if only to ensure the survival of the revolution in Cuba that Kennedy had been so desperate to crush. "The fact is we saw Oswald at the party," Francisco Guerrero Garro insists today. "We met and saw and spoke with someone who then went and killed the president of the United States."

Washington, DC
September 2013

Afterword to the 2015 Edition

WASHINGTON, DC
AUGUST 2014

Exactly half a century ago this summer, working from a cramped, paper-strewn temporary office on Capitol Hill, a fresh-faced thirty-three-year-old Denver lawyer named David Slawson was earning his place in modern American history.

It was the Kennedy assassination that brought him to Washington, as readers of this book will know. In January 1964, two months after President Kennedy's murder in Dallas, Slawson was part of that small group of hotshot young lawyers recruited to Washington to join the hastily organized staff of the Warren Commission and to do the bulk of the commission's detective work. He had an extraordinary assignment on the staff, which explains why his story became central to *A Cruel and Shocking Act: The Secret History of the Kennedy Assassination*. Although he had no background in foreign affairs or law enforcement, the Harvard-educated Slawson was responsible—at times, almost single-handedly—for the search for evidence of a foreign conspiracy in Kennedy's death. When the commission issued a final report in September 1964 that identified Lee Harvey Oswald as the assassin and effectively ruled out any conspiracy, foreign or domestic, Slawson was satisfied. "I was convinced—then—that we had it right," he said.

And for most of the next five decades, Slawson, who went on to a distinguished teaching career in California, tried to put his work on the commission behind him, even as the national debate about the Kennedy assassination and the legacy of the Warren Commission raged on. He was dragged into the debate sporadically in the 1970s, joining with other former commission lawyers to protest over the disclosure that the CIA, the FBI, and other parts of the government had kept important secrets from the commission, especially about the Kennedy administration's plots to kill Fidel Castro. But those protests were more than thirty years ago. Since then, Slawson has been content mostly to keep his silence, continuing to believe that nothing had undermined the commission's essential finding that Oswald was a "true lone wolf" who had acted without the knowledge or encouragement of others—that there was no conspiracy. Slawson and his wife, Kaaren, say that years could go by with barely a mention between them of the Warren Commission.

In 2014, however, Slawson's silence has ended once and for all, he says. Half a century after the commission's investigation concluded with an 888-page report that was supposed to convince the America people that they were being given the full truth about their president's death, Slawson is now convinced that the nation is far from the full truth. With the fiftieth anniversary of the Warren report this fall, Slawson, now eighty-three and retired from the law school at the University of Southern California, says he has been shocked by the recent, belated discovery of just how much more evidence was withheld from the commission—from him, specifically—and how that rewrites the history of the Kennedy assassination.

He is now wrestling with the question he thought he would never have to confront: Was the commission's final report, in fundamental ways, wrong? "It's amazing—it's terrible—to discover all of this fifty years late," said Slawson, whose health is still good and whose memories of his work on the commission remain sharp. The commission, he says, was the victim of a "massive cover-up" by senior government officials who wanted to hide the fact that, had they simply acted on the evidence in front of them in November 1963, the assassination would have been prevented.

His most startling conclusion: Slawson now believes that other people probably knew about Oswald's plans to kill the president and encouraged him—raising the possibility that there was a conspiracy in Kennedy's death, at least according to the common legal definition of the word conspiracy. "I now know that Oswald was almost certainly not a lone wolf," he said.

Slawson is not describing the sort of elaborate, far-flung assassination plot that this nation's army of conspiracy theorists tends to dwell on; their roster of suspects usually includes the Mafia, Texas oilmen, anti-Castro Cuban exiles, southern segregationists, elements of the CIA and FBI, and even President Lyndon Johnson. Slawson did not believe in 1964, and does not believe now, that Fidel Castro and the leaders of the Soviet Union or any other foreign government were involved in the president's murder. He is certain that Oswald was the only gunman in Dealey Plaza.

What he does suspect is that Oswald, during that long-mysterious trip to Mexico City that began in late September 1963, only weeks before the assassination, encountered Cuban diplomats and Mexican civilians who were supporters of Castro's revolution and who probably urged Oswald to kill the American president if he had the chance. "I think it's very likely that people in Mexico encouraged him to do this," Slawson told me. "And if they later came to the United States, they could have been prosecuted under American law as accessories" in the conspiracy.

Slawson said he has also come to believe—again, only recently—that the CIA doctored evidence, including tapes of the spy agency's wire-tapped phone calls in Mexico, that would have shown the CIA knew before the assassination about the danger that Oswald posed. Although Slawson readily admits he cannot prove it, he suspects that the agency knew in October 1963, the month before Kennedy's murder, that Oswald had spoken openly in Mexico about his intention to kill the president. Slawson suspects the spy agency had—and later erased—tapes of intercepted phone calls to and from the Cuban and Soviet embassies in Mexico in which Oswald's threat on the president's life was discussed. (The CIA insisted that all tapes that captured Oswald's voice in phone calls in Mexico City were routinely erased before the assassination, a claim that many later government investigators have always found difficult to believe.)

What has changed Slawson's mind so dramatically on questions that he thought were settled half a century ago?

This book did. Slawson says he has been inspired to speak out after cooperating with me closely on *A Cruel and Shocking Act*. "It was because of your book—and our conversations about what you discovered—that my mind has been changed," Slawson told me. "It never occurred to me until you interviewed me and I read your book that the commission's investigation had been blocked like this." It never occurred to him, he said, "that they tried to sabotage us like this."

It was clear to me from the earliest days of my research on this book, back in 2008, just how much I would want Slawson's cooperation. It is hard to overstate his significance in the work of the commission—and in the investigation's finding that Oswald acted alone. Although he had been the junior member of the two-lawyer team that focused on a possible foreign conspiracy, the work of the "conspiracy team" fell almost entirely to Slawson, as I report in the book. His senior partner, William Coleman, continued to live in Philadelphia and made clear from the start of the investigation that he could work only part time, and so Slawson finished up doing "ninety percent of the work," he told me. "Maybe ninety-five percent."

In 2010, after two years of gathering up tens of thousands of declassified documents from the National Archives and elsewhere, I made the first of several transcontinental reporting trips to meet with Slawson at his home on a beautiful, isolated, heavily wooded island off the Pacific coast of Washington state. Each time, I would bring with me the latest batch of documents and witness statements that I had retrieved out of once-secret government files. And during each of my trips, Slawson would grow more and more alarmed to discover how much evidence about the assassination—and specifically, about Oswald and the possibility of a conspiracy—had not been shared with him in 1964.

He was outraged, in particular, when I showed him the top-secret June 1964 letter from FBI Director J. Edgar Hoover to the Warren Commission that described how Oswald, during his Mexico trip, had apparently vowed to kill the president—an FBI document, written in the middle of the commission's work, that Slawson was certain he had never seen before. I explained to him that I had found the two-page Hoover letter in the declassified files of the CIA—if it ever existed in the commission's files, the physical copy had disappeared—and that I sensed instantly it was a bombshell. I showed it to Slawson because I could not understand why he had not followed up on it in 1964.

"Obviously somebody intercepted that letter before it could reach me," Slawson told me. If he had seen it, he says, he would have raised "many, many questions" about who else knew that Oswald—a former Marine with rifle training, a self-proclaimed Marxist looking for a dramatic way to demonstrate his loyalty to Castro—was talking openly about killing the president. Slawson would have insisted that the FBI and CIA try to track down anyone in Mexico who might have known about the threat on Kennedy's life. "I never had the chance to follow up because I never knew any of this."

He says he feels betrayed by several senior government officials, especially at the CIA, whom he trusted in 1964 to tell the truth. He is most angry with one man in particular—former Attorney General Robert Kennedy, who assured the commission during the investigation that he knew of no evidence of a conspiracy in his brother's death. As this book documents, Robert Kennedy withheld vital information from the investigation. While he publicly and unconditionally supported the commission's findings, Kennedy's family and friends have confirmed in recent years that he was in fact harshly critical of the commission's report and believed that the investigation had missed evidence that might have proved the assassination was the work of Cuba, the Mafia, or some rogue group of CIA officials.

"What a bastard," Slawson says today of Robert Kennedy. "This is a man I once had admiration for." What Kennedy described as "the alleged incompetence of the commission" in its failure to get to the full truth about the assassination "was in fact clearly his fault."

Slawson said he is now convinced Kennedy and the CIA worked together to hide information from the commission, especially about Oswald's Mexico trip, because they feared that the investigation might stumble onto the fact that the Kennedy administration had been trying, for years, sometimes with the help of the Mafia, to assassinate Castro. Mexico had been a staging area for elements of the Castro plots. Public disclosure of the plots, Slawson said, could have derailed, if not destroyed, Robert Kennedy's political career; he had led his brother's secret war against Castro and, it would later be shown, had known much about the Mafia's involvement in the CIA's often harebrained schemes to murder the Cuban dictator. "You can't distinguish between Bobby and the CIA on this," Slawson said. "They were working hand in glove to hide information from us."

Slawson's suspicions about Robert Kennedy were bolstered by the recent disclosure—by intelligence scholar Brian Latell—of the existence of the never-published memoirs of the late Thomas C. Mann, who was the U.S. ambassador to Mexico at the time of the assassination. In the memoirs, completed in 1982 and later donated to the University of Texas, Mann recounted the shocking order from the State Department that he was given in the days after the assassination—to shut down any investigation in Mexico that might point to Cuban involvement in Kennedy's murder. (That portion of the memoirs expands on the comments that Mann made to investigators for the House Select Committee on Assassinations in 1977, as mentioned in my Author's Note.) Mann wrote that after the State Department refused to withdraw its order, he told his embassy colleagues that "Washington must have known something we did not know" and that "our instructions could not have been sent without the knowledge and consent of Robert Kennedy, who was then Attorney General." Mann, who strongly believed Cuba was involved in the Kennedy assassination and that the plot might have been hatched in Mexico City, offered no further details in his book to support his assertion that Robert Kennedy must have been behind the decision to shut down the investigation in Mexico.

Slawson also now suspects—but admits again, cannot prove—that Chief Justice Earl Warren was an unwitting participant in the cover-up, agreeing with the CIA or Robert Kennedy to make sure that the commission did not pursue certain evidence and witnesses, especially in Mexico. Warren, he suspects, was given few details about why the commission's investigation had to be limited. "He was probably just told that vital national interests" were at stake. "He was probably told this was all national security."

"It was a different time," Slawson said. "We were more naïve. Warren would have believed what he was told."

That would explain what Slawson always saw as Warren's most baffling decision—the Chief Justice's refusal to allow the commission's staff to interview Silvia Duran, the young Mexican woman who worked for the Cuban consulate in Mexico and had dealt face-to-face with Oswald. Slawson had viewed her in 1964 as perhaps his most important witness. Why would the CIA try to block her testimony? After reading my book, Slawson now suspects that Duran had probably overheard Oswald's threat to kill the president, or at least she knew about it from her colleagues in the Cuban embassy, and that she might have revealed it if she had testified. That disclosure might in turn have led to the discovery that the CIA's Mexico City station, which wiretapped all of the Cuban embassy's phone lines and had bugging devices planted inside the embassy itself, had also known about the threat—and failed to alert the FBI and Secret Service, perhaps assuming that Oswald was just a harmless malcontent whose threat on the president's life could be ignored.

Despite all that he has learned in recent years, Slawson is not hard on his "naïve" thirty-three-year-old self. He said he still remains proud of his own contribution to the Warren Commission and its final report. "I know I did the best I could," he said. "I had no way of knowing what I wasn't being told."

It has got him thinking about how the government should investigate national tragedies like the Kennedy assassination, and how it might be possible to avoid the sorts of "terrible mistakes" that were made in 1964. He says the commission would obviously have benefited from a more varied, experienced staff, including more career prosecutors, as well as physicians, scientists, historians, and scholars with a background in Soviet and Cuban affairs. Certainly the outcome might have been different if there had been a "total commitment" to pursue evidence wherever it led. "How is it possible we didn't interview Silvia Duran?" Slawson asks today, shaking his head. "How is it possible that I wasn't allowed to interview my most critical witness?"

He said he has some confidence that the mistakes of fifty years ago would probably not be repeated, if only because the American public is so much more cynical today about the government and its truthfulness. The national traumas and political scandals that followed the Kennedy assassination—the Vietnam War, Watergate, the Iran-contra affair, the 9/11 terrorist attacks, and the huge intelligence failures that preceded both 9/11 and the disastrous American invasion of Iraq in 2003—have all seen to that. That is probably why the legacy of the 9/11 Commission, which was modeled in part on the Warren Commission, has not been tarnished, at least not so far, with the same widespread allegations of cover-up and incompetence that were leveled at the Warren Commission almost as soon as it finished its work. The 9/11 Commission brought in outside, independent experts, including several historians and scholars with a background in intelligence work, and it had much more time to complete its work. Unlike the Warren Commission, the 9/11 Commission frequently clashed with the White House and CIA over access to government secrets, and it demanded public, sworn testimony from senior officials.

In 1964, "we assumed that government officials would tell us the truth," Slawson said. Half a century later, "no one makes that assumption anymore."

Biographical Notes on Principal Characters

Information about people not listed here can be found by referring to the index and footnotes.

Francis W. H. Adams (born June 26, 1904 in Mount Vernon, New York) Assistant counsel on the Warren Commission. Police commissioner of New York City in the 1950s. Largely abandoned his duties on the commission.

Jack Anderson (born October 19, 1922 in Long Beach, California) Drew Pearson's reporting partner on the syndicated Washington Merry-Go-Round column.

Dean Andrews Jr. (born October 8, 1922 in Louisiana) New Orleans lawyer who claimed he encountered Lee Harvey Oswald before the assassination.

James Jesus Angleton (born December 9, 1917 in Boise, Idaho) CIA counterintelligence chief who quietly controlled the flow of information to the Warren Commission.

Hugh Aynesworth (born August 2, 1931 in Clarksburg, West Virginia) Reporter for the *Dallas Morning News* whose exclusive stories repeatedly complicated the work of the Warren Commission.

Joseph A. Ball (born December 16, 1902 in Stuart, Iowa) Assistant counsel on the Warren Commission. Prominent defense lawyer in southern California.

David W. Belin (born June 20, 1928 in Washington, D.C.) Assistant counsel on the Warren Commission. Lawyer from Des Moines, Iowa.

Alan Belmont (born 1907 in New York City) Assistant FBI director.

Representative Hale Boggs (born February 15, 1914 in Long Beach, Mississippi) Member of the Warren Commission. Louisiana Democrat and Majority Whip of the House of Representatives.

Commander J. Thornton Boswell M.D. (born November 26, 1922 in Enid, Oklahoma) Navy pathologist who participated in the president's autopsy.

Howard Brennan (born March 20, 1919 in Oklahoma) Witness in Dealey Plaza who testified he saw Oswald in the window of the Texas School Book Depository.

Thomas G. Buchanan (born 1920 in Maryland) Paris-based journalist and author of the first major book suggesting a conspiracy in the assassination.

Rear Admiral George Burkley M.D. (born August 29, 1902 in Pittsburgh, Pennsylvania) President Kennedy's personal physician in the White House.

Fidel Castro (born August 13, 1926 in Birán, Cuba) Cuban leader.

William T. Coleman Jr. (born July 7, 1920 in Germantown, Pennsylvania) Assistant counsel on the Warren Commission. Prominent lawyer in the civil rights movement. Would later report he had met secretly with Fidel Castro.

Governor John Connally (born February 27, 1917 in Floresville, Texas) Governor of Texas. Seriously injured while riding in President Kennedy's limousine.

Idanell "Nellie" Connally (born February 24, 1919 in Austin, Texas) Wife of Governor Connally, also traveling in the president's limousine.

Senator John Sherman Cooper (born August 23, 1901 in Somerset, Kentucky) Member of the Warren Commission. Kentucky Republican and former U.S. Ambassador to India.

Jesse Curry (born October 3, 1913 in Hamilton, Texas) Dallas police chief.

Cartha "Deke" DeLoach (born July 20, 1920 in Claxton, Georgia) Assistant FBI director and the bureau's liaison to Congress.

George de Mohrenschildt (born April 17, 1911 in Russia) Russian-born oil engineer who befriended Lee and Marina Oswald in Texas.

Allen W. Dulles (born April 7, 1893 in Watertown, New York) Member of the Warren Commission. Director of Central Intelligence in the Eisenhower and Kennedy administrations. Forced to resign in 1961.

Silvia Duran (born November 22, 1937 in Mexico) Mexican employee of the Cuban consulate who met with Oswald during his visit to Mexico weeks before the assassination.

Melvin A. Eisenberg (born December 3, 1934 in New York City) Assistant counsel on the Warren Commission. Researched criminal science. Recruited from New York law firm.

John Hart Ely (born December 3, 1938 in New York City) Staff member of Warren Commission. Later a Supreme Court clerk to Chief Justice Warren.

David Ferrie (born March 28, 1918 in Cleveland) Former airline pilot accused by New Orleans District Attorney Jim Garrison of involvement in the assassination. Died before charges could be brought.

Lieutenant Colonel Pierre Finck M.D. Army pathologist who participated in the president's autopsy.

Representative Gerald R. Ford (born Leslie Lynch King, Jr. on July 14, 1913 in Omaha, Nebraska) Member of the Warren Commission. Michigan Republican and member of the powerful House Appropriations Committee.

Abraham "Abe" Fortas (born June 19, 1910 in Memphis, Tennessee) Prominent Washington lawyer and longtime Johnson adviser. Named by Johnson to the Supreme Court.

Jim Garrison (born November 20, 1921, in Denison, Iowa) New Orleans district attorney who claimed to uncover a vast conspiracy in the assassination.

Elena Garro de Paz (born December 11, 1916 in Puebla, Mexico) Prominent Mexican writer who told American diplomat Charles Thomas in 1965 that she encountered Lee Harvey Oswald at a party in Mexico City in the company of Silvia Duran.

Alfred Goldberg (born December 23, 1918 in Baltimore) Staff member of the Warren Commission. Air Force historian.

William Greer (born September 22, 1909 in Stewartstown, County Tyrone, Ireland) Secret Service agent who drove the president's limousine in Dallas on the day of the assassination.

Burt W. Griffin (born August 19, 1932 in Cleveland, Ohio) Assistant counsel on the Warren Commission. Former Justice Department prosecutor. Researched background of Jack Ruby.

Richard Helms (born March 30, 1913 in St. Davids, Pennsylvania) Deputy Director for Plans at the CIA in the Kennedy administration. Named Director of Central Intelligence by President Johnson.

Clint Hill (born January 4, 1932 in Larimore, North Dakota) Secret Service agent who jumped onto the president's limousine and pushed Mrs. Kennedy back into the vehicle.

J. Edgar Hoover (born January 1, 1895 in Washington, DC) FBI Director.

James P. Hosty (born August 28, 1924 in Chicago) FBI special agent in Dallas who had conducted surveillance of Oswald before the assassination.

Leon D. Hubert Jr. (born July 1, 1911 in New Orleans) Assistant counsel on the Warren Commission. Former federal and city prosecutor in New Orleans. Would investigate background of Jack Ruby.

Commander James Humes M.D. (born in 1925 in Philadelphia) Navy pathologist who oversaw Kennedy's autopsy at the Bethesda Naval Hospital.

Albert E. Jenner Jr. (born June 20, 1907 in Chicago) Assistant counsel on the Warren Commission. Oversaw research on background of Lee Harvey Oswald.

Claudia Alta "Lady Bird" Taylor Johnson (born December 22, 1912 in Karnack, Texas) First Lady.

President Lyndon Baines Johnson (born August 27, 1908 in Stonewall, Texas)

Nicholas Katzenbach (born January 27, 1922 in Philadelphia) Deputy Attorney General in the Kennedy administration. Attorney General in the Johnson administration.

Roy Kellerman (born March 14, 1915 in Macomb County, Michigan) Secret Service agent in the president's limousine in Dallas.

Jacqueline Kennedy (born July 28, 1929 in Southhampton, New York) First Lady.

President John F. Kennedy (born May 29, 1917 in Brookline, Massachusetts) Assassinated in Dallas, Texas, on November 22, 1963.

Robert F. Kennedy (born November 20, 1925 in Brookline, Massachusetts) Attorney General and younger brother of President Kennedy. Later, United States Senator from New York.

Valeriy Kostikov (born March 17, 1933 in Moscow) KGB agent undercover at Soviet embassy in Mexico.

Mark Lane (born February 24, 1927 in New York) New York lawyer and leading conspiracy theorist.

Murray J. Laulicht (born May 12, 1940 in Brooklyn, New York) Staff lawyer on Warren Commission.

Wesley J. Liebeler (born May 9, 1931 in Langdon, North Dakota) Assistant counsel on Warren Commission. Recruited from a New York law firm. Gathered background information on Lee Harvey Oswald.

William Manchester (born April 1, 1922 in Attleboro, Massachusetts) Journalist recruited by the Kennedy family to write an authorized history of the assassination.

Thomas C. Mann (born November 11, 1912 in Laredo, Texas) U.S. Ambassador to Mexico at the time of the assassination. Later a senior State Department official and adviser to President Johnson. Suspected Cuban involvement in the assassination.

Helen Markham (born in Dallas) Witness to Tippit's murder. Restaurant waitress.

James "Jim" Martin Dallas motel manager who became Marina Oswald's business manager.

John J. McCloy (born March 31, 1895 in Philadelphia) Member of the Warren Commission. Prominent New York lawyer. Former president of the World Bank and former chairman of Chase Manhattan Bank.

John A. McCone (born January 4, 1902 in San Francisco) Director of Central Intelligence in the Kennedy and Johnson administrations. Former California industrialist.

Richard M. Mosk (born May 18, 1939 in Los Angeles) Staff member of the Warren Commisison. Attorney.

Silvia Odio (born May 4, 1937 in Havana, Cuba) Cuban refugee living in Dallas who says Oswald and two anti-Castro activists appeared at her door weeks before the assassination.

Lee Harvey Oswald (born October 18, 1939 in New Orleans) Charged with assassination of President Kennedy and Dallas police officer J. D. Tippit. Killed by Jack Ruby in Dallas on November 24, 1963.

Marguerite Oswald (born July 19, 1907 in New Orleans) Lee Harvey Oswald's mother.

Marina Oswald (born July 17, 1941 in Molotovsk, Soviet Union). Lee Harvey Oswald's Russian-born wife.

Robert Oswald (born April 7, 1934 in New Orleans) Lee Harvey Oswald's older brother.

Michael Paine (born June 25, 1928 in New York City) Estranged husband of Ruth Paine.

Ruth Paine (born September 3, 1932 in New York City) Russian-speaking American friend of Marina Oswald who invited Marina and her children to live in her home in Irving, Texas, before the assassination.

Andrew "Drew" Pearson (born December 13, 1897 in Evanston, Illinois) Muckraking newspaper columnist who was close to Chief Justice Warren.

Malcolm Perry M.D. (born September 3, 1929 in Allen, Texas) Chief doctor at Parkland Hospital to attend to President Kennedy.

David Atlee Phillips (born October 31, 1922 in Fort Worth, Texas) CIA covert officer in Mexico City, responsible for surveillance of the Cuban embassy in Mexico.

Stuart R. Pollak (born August 24, 1937 in San Pedro, California) Staff member of the Warren Commission. Justice Department lawyer.

J. Lee Rankin (born July 8, 1907 in Hartington, Nebraska) General counsel of the Warren Commission. Solicitor General of the United States in the Eisenhower administration.

Norman Redlich (born November 12, 1925 in New York City) Assistant counsel on the Warren Commission. Key editor of the Warren report. New York University law professor. His appointment to the commission would create turmoil after it was discovered that he was a member of civil liberties and civil rights groups labeled by the FBI as subversive.

Raymond Rocca (born February 22, 1917 in California) Top deputy to CIA counterintelligence director James Angleton. CIA liaison to the Warren Commission.

James J. Rowley (born October 14, 1908 in New York City) Director of the Secret Service at the time of the assassination.

Jack Ruby (born Jacob L. Rubenstein in March 1911 in Chicago) Dallas nightclub operator who killed Lee Harvey Oswald on November 24, 1963.

Senator Richard B. Russell Jr. (born November 2, 1897 in Winder, Georgia) Member of the Warren Commission. Georgia Democrat, chairman of the Senate Armed Services Committee.

Bob Schieffer (born February 25, 1937 in Austin, Texas) Reporter for the *Fort Worth Star Telegram* who was the first journalist to encounter and interview Marguerite Oswald after the assassination.

Alfredda Scobey (born October 15, 1912 in Kankakee, Illinois). Staff member of the Warren Commission. Hired specifically to assist Senator Richard Russell.

Winston "Win" Scott (born March 30, 1909 in Jemison, Alabama). CIA Station Chief in Mexico City.

Charles N. Shaffer Jr. (born June 8, 1932 in New York City) Staff member of Warren Commission. Justice Department lawyer.

J. Gordon Shanklin (born December 10, 1909 in Elkton, Kentucky) Special agent in charge of the FBI Dallas field office.

Clay Shaw (born March 17, 1913 in Kentwood, Louisiana) New Orleans businessman charged in 1967 with involvement in the assassination. Acquitted by a jury.

W. David Slawson (born June 2, 1931 in Grand Rapids, Michigan) Assistant counsel on the Warren Commission. Led search for evidence of a possible foreign conspiracy in the assassination. Recruited from Denver law firm.

Arlen Specter (born February 12, 1930 in Wichita, Kansas) Assistant counsel on the Warren Commission. Assistant district attorney in Philadelphia. Oversaw reconstruction of the events of the day of the assassination.

Samuel A. Stern (born January 21, 1929 in Philadelphia) Assistant counsel on the Warren Commission. Reviewed the performance of the Secret Service. Washington attorney. Former Supreme Court clerk to Chief Justice Warren.

Charles William Thomas (born June 20, 1922 in Orange, Texas) American diplomat at the U.S. embassy in Mexico who was given information in 1965 suggesting possible Cuban involvement in the assassination.

J. D. Tippit (born September 18, 1924 in Red River County, Texas) Dallas police officer gunned down shortly after Kennedy. Witnesses identify Oswald as Tippit's killer.

Henry Wade (born November 11, 1914 in Rockwall County, Texas) Dallas district attorney.

Edwin Walker (born November 10, 1909 in Center Point, Texas) Retired Army general in Dallas who led an ultraconservative political movement. Victim of April 1963 assassination attempt blamed by the Warren Commission on Lee Harvey Oswald.

Chief Justice Earl Warren (born March 19, 1891 in Los Angeles) Chairman of the Warren Commission. Chief Justice of the United States and former governor of California.

Lloyd L. Weinreb (born October 9, 1936 in New York City) Staff member of the Warren Commission. Justice Department lawyer.

John Whitten (born 1920) CIA covert operations officer. Pushed aside by CIA counterintelligence director James Angleton as the agency's liaison to the Warren Commission.

Howard P. Willens (born May 27, 1931 in Oak Park, Illinois) Assistant counsel to the Warren Commission. Justice Department lawyer who also served as the department's liaison to the commission.

Abraham Zapruder (born May 15, 1905 in Kovol, Ukraine) Womens-wear manufacturer whose home movie camera captured key images of the assassination.

Notes

The Warren Commission (the President's Commission on the Assassination of President Kennedy) published a final 888-page report, as well as a twenty-six-volume appendix of hearing transcripts and evidence reports. For the purposes of simplicity, they are identified in these endnotes as Warren Report (for the central volume) and Warren Appendix (volumes 1–26). There were two major congressional investigations in the 1970s that reviewed the work of the Warren Commission, one by the Senate Select Committee to Study Governmental Operations with Respect to Intelligence Activities (better known as the Church Committee, named for its chairman, Senator Frank Church, Democrat of Idaho), the other by the House Select Committee on Assassinations. They are identified in these notes as the Church Committee and HSCA. In 1992, largely in response to conspiracy theories fueled by the Oliver Stone film *JFK*, Congress created the Assassination Records Review Board, to review and release assassination-related records. In these notes, the board is referred to as ARRB. Most Warren Commission records are stored by the National Archives and Records Administration (hereafter NARA). Other valuable records about the commission's work are found at the Library of Congress (hereafter LOC), the Gerald R. Ford Presidential Library in Ann Arbor, Michigan (hereafter Ford Library), the Lyndon Baines Johnson Presidential Library in Austin, Texas (hereafter LBJ Library), the John F. Kennedy Presidential Library in Boston (hereafter JFK Library), and the Richard B. Russell Library at the University of Georgia Library at the University of Georgia in Athens, Georgia (hereafter Russell Library).

In the decades after the assassination, virtually all of the FBI's internal files regarding the Warren Commission and the Kennedy assassination have been declassified and made public. Most are maintained electronically, largely in chronological order, by the Mary Ferrell Foundation and other private assassination-research organizations, as well as by the National Archives. The FBI archives of assassinated-related documents (hereafter FBI) are to some degree searchable online on the Mary Ferrell Web site: http://www.maryferrell.org/wiki/index .php/JFK_Documents_-_FBI.

I was the first outside researcher to have access to the uncensored transcripts of interviews conducted with the late senator Arlen Specter for his 2000 memoir, *Passion for Truth*. The transcripts are stored at the Arlen Specter Center for Public Policy at Philadelphia University, which opened in 2013. In the full interviews, Specter offered opinions that he chose not to share in his book, including harsh criticism of Chief Justice Warren and of elements of the commission's work. I interviewed Specter myself. For the purposes of these notes, Specter's interviews for his memoirs are identified hereafter as Specter memoir transcripts. Material from my interviews is identified as Specter interviews.

PROLOGUE

1   **On Monday, April 12:** Death certificate, District of Columbia Department of Health; Cynthia Thomas interviews.

1   **And since he had:** The description of the term "selected out" described in unsigned article, "Undiplomatic Reforms," *Time*, November 15, 1971.

1   **At first, he thought:** Thomas interviews.

2   **And on July 25:** Copies of Thomas's memos were obtained from his widow, Cynthia. Copies are also found in the archives of the House Select Committee on Assassinations, NARA.

2   **He wanted to be remembered:** Thomas interviews.

3   **Thomas was a self-made man:** State Department personnel records on Charles Thomas were obtained from Cynthia Thomas; Thomas interviews.

4   **In September 1964, the presidential commission:** Warren Report, pp. 21, 24.

5   **In the body of the memo:** Biographical material on Garro is available from several sources, including: Cypess, *Uncivil Wars*, and from Garro's obituary in the *New York Times*, August 28, 1998.

8   **He made sure:** Biographical material on Scott and information on his friendship with Angleton are available in Morley, *Our Man in Mexico*, the definitive biography of Scott.

9   **After his suicide two years later:** *Washington Post*, April 14, 1971.

9   **"I always thought it":** Interview with former House of Representatives investigator, who spoke on condition of anonymity.

9   **Former senator Birch Bayh of Indiana:** Bayh interview.

10   **The caller was someone I had never met:** Interview with former Warren Commission staff lawyer, who spoke on condition of anonymity.

11   **In interviews shortly:** Hosty interviews.

11   **The title of this book:** Warren Report, p. 1.

12   **The records of the Warren Commission:** "Introduction to the Records of the Warren Commission," NARA Web site, http://www.archives.gov/research/jfk/warren-commission-report/intro.html (accessed June 10, 2013).

12   **The rose-pink suit worn:** *Washington Post*, February 5, 2011. President Kennedy's comment is reported in "Remembering Jackie," *New Yorker*, May 30, 1994.

12   **A separate vault:** Associated Press, April 2, 1997.

12   **Much of Warren's personal paperwork:** "Collection Summary: Earl Warren, 1891–1974," LOC Web site, http://lccn.loc.gov/mm82052258.

CHAPTER 1

17   **Navy Commander James Humes:** Deposition of Dr. James Joseph Humes, ARRB, February 13, 1996, p. 138 (hereafter Humes Deposition). Humes gave testimony or interviews about the autopsy to several government investigations, including an interview with a panel of medical experts to the HSCA on September 16, 1977, in Washington (hereafter Humes interview) and less detailed testimony to the HSCA on September 7, 1978 (hereafter Humes Testimony).

17   **At about eleven that night:** Humes Deposition, p. 135. Description of home in interview with Humes's son James Jr.

18   **"It *doesn't* have to be done":** Jacqueline Kennedy, as quoted by Burkley in an interview for the JFK Library, October 17, 1967, p. 8.

18   **He reminded her:** The most authoritative account of the conversation aboard Air Force One was obtained by William Manchester for his book *The Death of a President*, the history that was originally authorized by the Kennedy family, pp. 349–50. Also see Burkley interview with JFK Library, passim.

18   **Commander J. Thornton Boswell:** Deposition of J. Thornton Boswell, ARRB, February 26, 1996, p. 15 (hereafter Boswell Deposition).

18   **Neither Humes nor Boswell:** Ibid., p. 18.

19   **What might recommend:** Humes Deposition, p. 51.

19   The autopsy room: Ibid., p. 57.
19   The president's body arrived: Boswell Deposition, p. 14.
19   The autopsy was: Ibid., p. 46. Also see Humes Deposition, interview.
20   "Those people were in": Boswell Deposition, p. 101.
20   He knew the Kennedy family: Ibid., p. 24. Also see Burkley interview with JFK Library.
20   "Let them see": Manchester, *Death*, p. 348.
20   Burkley had another: Humes Deposition, p. 29.
21   "He promised George Burkley": Boswell Deposition, p. 11.
21   Days after the autopsy: Humes Deposition, p. 38.
21   "He told me": Ibid., p. 148.
21   The doctors began to worry: Boswell Deposition, p. 109.
22   "There was no way we could": Humes interview, p. 243.
22   "I x-rayed the president": Humes Deposition, pp. 34, 113.
23   "The minute he said": Humes interview, p. 257.
23   That Saturday night: Humes Deposition, pp. 125, 126; Boswell Deposition, p. 111.
23   "I sat down": Humes Testimony, p. 5.
23   "When I noticed": Humes Deposition, p. 126.
24   Humes gave the original notes: Ibid., pp. 133–35.
24   On Friday, hours after: Testimony of Mrs. Lee Harvey Oswald, February 5, 1964, Warren Appendix, Vol. 1, p. 79. Also see commission exhibit 1788 from Warren Appendix, Vol. 23, "FBI report setting forth circumstances surrounding the publication in *Life* magazine and other publications of Oswald holding rifle," pp. 400–401.
25   Her mother-in-law would later insist: Testimony of Mrs. Marguerite Oswald, February 10, 1964, Warren Appendix, Vol. 1, p. 152.
25   At about six p.m. Sunday: Hosty interviews; Hosty, *Assignment: Oswald*, pp. 59, 29.
26   Hosty had a lot to protect: Hosty, *Assignment*, pp. 16, 83.

CHAPTER 2

27   The knock on the heavy oak door: Warren, *The Memoirs of Chief Justice Earl Warren*, p. 351.
28   "The President was shot": The text of the note is as it is found in Warren, *Memoirs*, p. 351. (Obituaries of McHugh offer a slightly different text: "It was reported that the President has been shot while riding in a motorcade in Dallas, Texas.")
28   The members of the court: Warren, *Memoirs*, p. 352.
28   Warren and the other justices: Ibid., pp. 351–52.
28   During the 1960 campaign: *New York Times*, November 5, 1960.
29   At the White House reception: Ibid.
29   The assassination was "like": Warren, as quoted in Weaver, *Warren, the Man, the Court, the Era*, p. 300.
29   "The days and nights": Undated letter from Warren to journalist Jim Bishop, Warren Commission correspondence files, Earl Warren papers, LOC.
29   After receiving confirmation: Manchester, *Death*, p. 205.
30   It was the fulfillment: Warren, *Memoirs*, p. 260.
30   Eisenhower came to regret: The "biggest damned fool" remark has been repeatedly attributed to Eisenhower, including in the *New York Times* obituary of Earl Warren, July 10, 1974. Although friends and advisers to Eisenhower say the comment reflected his views about Warren, there has been debate about whether the former president actually uttered those specific words.
31   Within hours of the assassination: Warren statements, November 22, 1963, Warren papers, LOC.
31   Later that day: Warren, *Memoirs*, p. 352; Johnson, *The Vantage Point*, p. 26.
32   At about nine that evening: Warren, *Memoirs*, pp. 352–53.

33   "John Fitzgerald Kennedy—a good": as published in Warren, *Memoirs*, pp. 353–54.

34   **Robert Kennedy told friends:** Schlesinger, *Robert Kennedy and His Times*, p. 611. (Schlesinger suggests he was given access to a transcript of Kennedy's interviews with William Manchester for his book *The Death of a President*. The Manchester transcripts have not been made public by the JFK Library in Boston.)

34   **Senator Richard Brevard Russell:** Russell note, December 5, 1963, Russell Library.

34   **On the afternoon:** Mudd, *The Place to Be*, p. 127.

35   **Soon, however, Russell would have cause:** Holland, *The Kennedy Assassination Tapes*, pp. 196–206.

35   **In a horrible twist of fate:** Thomas, *Robert Kennedy: His Life*, p. 276.

35   **Seconds after receiving word:** Manchester, *Death*, p. 196.

35   **Morgenthau recalled later:** Manchester, *Death*, p. 196.

35   **Years later:** Schlesinger, *Robert Kennedy*, p. 608.

36   **"There's been so much hate":** Guthman, *We Band of Brothers*, p. 244.

37   **After the debacle:** *New York Times*, April 25, 1966. The article reported: "President Kennedy, as the enormity of the Bay of Pigs disaster came home to him, said to one of the highest officials of his administration that he wanted 'to splinter the CIA in a thousand pieces and scatter it to the winds.'"

37   **"I asked McCone":** Walter Sheridan, RFK Oral History Project, JFK Library, June 12, 1979. As quoted in Schlesinger, *Robert Kennedy*, p. 616.

38   **Rather than wait for others to investigate:** Thomas, *Robert Kennedy*, p. 277. (Thomas's book provides the richest, most authoritative history of what happened at Hickory Hill on the afternoon the assassination.)

CHAPTER 3

39   **He had often felt humiliated:** The use of "Uncle Cornpone" by Kennedy aides described in several places in Caro, *The Passage of Power*, passim.

39   **Now, in his first panicky minutes:** As recounted by Johnson in phone conversation with aide Bill Moyers, December 26, 1966, as published in Holland, *The Kennedy Assassination Tapes*, p. 363.

40   **One of Johnson's first orders:** Manchester, *Death*, p. 220.

40   **Fearful of snipers:** Johnson, *The Vantage Point*, p. 12.

41   **Although Secret Service agents:** Elements of this scene are captured in Johnson, *The Vantage Point*; Manchester, *Death*; and Caro, *Passage*.

41   **The White House photographer who captured:** Manchester, *Death*, p. 320.

41   **After a seven-minute helicopter:** Elements of this scene are captured in Johnson, *The Vantage Point*; Manchester, *Death*; Caro, *Passage*.

42   **"I need you more":** Caro, *Passage*, p. 410.

42   **He privately described Johnson as "mean":** Guthman and Shulman (eds.), *Robert Kennedy, in His Own Words*, pp. 417, 411.

43   **On the afternoon of Thursday:** Pearson diaries, November 1963, Pearson papers, LBJ Library. (Pearson misstated the date of the entry, identifying November 21 as Friday. It was actually a Thursday.)

44   **In 1942, he bought:** Woods, *LBJ: Architect of American Ambition*, p. 533. See also Caro, *Master of the Senate*.

44   **"He was my close":** Johnson remarks honoring Hoover, May 8, 1964, accessed from the American Presidency Project, http://www.presidency.ucsb.edu/ws/?pid=26236. Also see "President Johnson's Dogs," essay on the Web site of the LBJ Library, http://www.lbjlib.utexas.edu/johnson/archives.hom/faqs/dog/doghouse.asp.

45   **Johnson's motives were:** *Time*, February 5, 1973.

45   **"You're more than the head":** Telephone conversation between Johnson and Hoover, November 29, 1963, in Holland, *The Kennedy Assassination Tapes*, p. 147.

45   Johnson asked President Kennedy's: Caro, *Passage*, p. 374.
45   At about ten a.m., Johnson: Holland, *The Kennedy Assassination Tapes*, pp. 68–73.
48   Among the tens of millions: Ibid., pp. 87–89.
49   He told a friend: Telephone conversation between Johnson and columnist Joseph Alsop, November 25, 1963, in Holland, *The Kennedy Assassination Tapes*, p. 98.
49   With Oswald dead: Johnson, *The Vantage Point*, p. 26.

CHAPTER 4

51   Two of her three husbands: The history of the Oswald family, including that of Margue rite Oswald, is offered in detail in the Warren Report, pp. 69–80.
51   At the age of three: Robert Oswald, *Lee: A Portrait of Lee Harvey Oswald*, pp. 32–33.
51   "It seemed to me": Ibid., p. 33.
51   On the afternoon: Bob Schieffer, "A Ride for Mrs. Oswald," *Texas Monthly*, January 2003.
53   "That's how it would": Oswald, *Lee: A Portrait*, p. 178.
54   "Nothing really to put my finger": Testimony of Robert Edward Lee Oswald, February 20, 1964, Warren Appendix, Vol. 1, p. 346.
55   She remembered that on: Statement of Marina Oswald, February 19, 1964, in Dallas, Texas, FBI transcript, as reproduced in Aynesworth, *JFK: Breaking the News*, p. 146.
56   Mrs. Martin introduced: Lewis, *The Scavengers and Critics of the Warren Report*, p. 65.
56   "Mrs. Oswald called": Lane interview; also, Lane as quoted in Lewis, *Scavengers*, p. 24.

CHAPTER 5

57   Clare Booth Luce: Martin, *A Hero for Our Times*, p. 159, as cited in Caro, *Passage*, p. 115.
58   The night of the assassination: Johnson, *The Vantage Point*, pp. 26–27.
58   On the afternoon of Friday: Warren, *Memoirs*, pp. 355–56.
58   Cox described Warren: *Time*, November 17, 1967.
58   "I told them I thought": Warren, *Memoirs*, p. 356.
58   Former chief justice Harlan Fiske Stone: Conot, *Justice at Nuremberg*, p. 63.
59   "Early in my life": Johnson, *The Vantage Point*, p. 27.
59   At about three thirty that afternoon: Warren, *Memoirs*, p. 356.
59   The chief justice was about to be: For an explanation of the "Johnson Treatment," see Tom Wicker, "Remembering the Johnson Treatment," *New York Times*, May 9, 2002.
59   "I was ushered in": Warren, *Memoirs*, p. 357.
59   The president said he needed: Johnson, *The Vantage Point*, p. 27; Warren, *Memoirs*, p. 357.
60   According to Warren: Warren, *Memoirs*, p. 357.
60   He explained his reasoning: Johnson, *The Vantage Point*, p. 27; Warren, *Memoirs*, p. 358.
60   Johnson told the chief justice: Warren, *Memoirs*, p. 358.
61   "If Khrushchev moved on us": Telephone conversation between Johnson and Senator Thomas Kuchel, November 29, 1963, as cited in Holland, *The Kennedy Assassination Tapes*, p. 193. See also published interview of Johnson by Drew Pearson, Pearson papers, LBJ Library. In the undated Pearson interview, Johnson says he warned Warren about reports of a $6,500 payment to Oswald.
61   "You were a soldier": Warren, *Memoirs*, p. 358.
61   "The President of the United States says": Johnson, *The Vantage Point*, p. 27.
61   The truth was that: Ibid.
61   In that first call: Holland, *The Kennedy Assassination Tapes*, pp. 153–59.
61   He would be delivering: Holland, *The Kennedy Assassination Tapes*, pp. 196–206.
62   "Dick?": Ibid., pp. 196–206.
64   At the Supreme Court the next day: Warren, *Memoirs*, p. 356.
64   He later told his friend: Pearson diaries, November 1963, Pearson papers, LBJ Library.

CHAPTER 6

67   **Warren's children:** Interviews with Robert Warren (January 28, 1971) and Earl Warren Jr. (July 8, 1970), conducted for the Regional Oral History Office of the Bancroft Library, University of California at Berkeley, found on the library's Web site: http://archive.org/stream/warrengovfamilywaooearlrich/warrengovfamilywaooearlrich_djvu.txt.

69   **Hoover had come to consider:** Hoover memo to Tolson et al., June 22, 1964 ("Re: Justice Edward Tamm"), FBI.

70   **When Governor Warren traveled:** Gentry, *J. Edgar Hoover: The Man and the Secrets*, p. 410.

70   **Warren later told Drew Pearson:** "The 'Chief,' " unpublished profile of Warren by Drew Pearson based on extensive interviews with Warren, found in Pearson papers, LBJ Library.

70   **It would be:** Telephone conversation between Johnson and Hoover on November 25, 1963, from Holland, *The Kennedy Assassination Tapes*, p. 95.

71   **It was Warren's selection of Olney:** Memo from DeLoach to Mohr, February 7, 1964, "Subject: Assassination of the President—allegations that Oswald was an FBI Informant," FBI. Although Hoover would deny that the FBI was responsible for undermining the choice of Olney, DeLoach's memos and other paperwork show otherwise.

71   **Warren scheduled the first meeting:** Warren Commission Executive Session transcript, December 5, 1963, NARA.

71   **The FBI argued:** Memo from Belmont to Tolson, December 3, 1963, FBI.

71   **On December 3:** Associated Press, "FBI Report on Oswald Nearly Ready," as published in the *Star News* of Pasadena, California, December 3, 1963 (accessed through newspaperarchive.com).

72   **"It almost has to":** Warren Commission Executive Session, December 5, 1963, NARA.

72   **Deputy Attorney General Katzenbach:** Warren Commission Executive Session, December 6, 1963, p. 8.

72   **The meeting that Thursday:** Warren Commission Executive Session, December 5, 1963, p. 8.

72   **"This is a very sad":** Ibid., p. 1.

72   **He then set out:** Ibid., pp. 1–3.

72   **"I think our job here":** Ibid., pp. 1–2.

73   **If the commission:** Ibid., p. 2.

73   **"If we have the subpoena power":** Ibid., p. 40.

73   **If the commission:** Ibid., pp. 40, 2.

73   **Warren's mailbag:** Ibid., p. 2.

73   **McCloy, a sixty-eight-year-old:** *Esquire*, May 1962. Although the article was written tongue in cheek, there was little doubt that McCloy deserved the title.

73   **McCloy did not:** Warren Commission Executive Session, December 5, 1963, p. 37.

74   **"There is potential":** Ibid.

74   **Warren was wrong:** Ibid.

74   **The investigation had:** Ibid.

74   **Boggs and Ford:** Ibid.

74   **"If the rest of you":** Ibid., p. 39.

74   **Next, Russell objected:** Ibid., p. 53.

74   **He reminded Warren:** Ibid.

74   **McCloy suggested:** Ibid., p. 39.

74   **The chief justice spent:** Ibid., pp. 43–46, 55.

74   **Olney, he said:** Ibid., p. 45.

75   **Olney might be:** Ibid., pp. 46–47.

75   **"I don't want":** Ibid., p. 46.

75   **"I have a feeling":** Ibid., p. 48.

75   "I think the chairman": Ibid., p. 50.
75   The chief justice said: Ibid., pp. 55, 62.
75   He put the plea: Ibid., p. 62.
75   The meeting ended: Ibid., p. 68.
75   Ford, Dulles, and McCloy: Warren Commission Executive Session, December 6, 1963, p. 21.
76   "I would not want": Ibid., pp. 4–6.
76   Overnight, McCloy: Ibid., p. 4.
76   The mention: Ibid., p. 6.
76   As solicitor general: Ibid., p. 6.
76   Most notably: *Brown v. Board of Education*, 347 U.S. 483 (1954).
76   "We saw": Warren Commission Executive Session, December 6, 1963, p. 6.
76   Rankin, he said: Ibid., p. 10.
76   Russell recommended that: Ibid., p. 20.
76   Before the meeting ended: Ibid., p. 12.
76   "No, I have not": Ibid.
76   "They have": Ibid.
76   "Of course we do": Ibid.

CHAPTER 7

77   Gerald Ford asked: Memo from DeLoach to Mohr, December 12, 1963, FBI. After public release of the DeLoach memo decades later, Ford did not dispute the contents of the memo, although he said he had no substantive contacts with the FBI over commission work after December 1963.
77   Fifty-year-old "Jerry": Gerald R. Ford Biography, Ford Library, http://www.fordlibrary museum.gov/grf/fordbiop.asp.
78   He used one of his: Ford speech, July 8, 1949, Congressional Record, House of Representatives. A salary of $17,500 a year in 1949 would be equal to about $171,000 in 2013.
79   "Ford told me": Memo from DeLoach to Mohr, December 12, 1963, FBI.
79   The FBI's former number-three official: Sullivan, *The Bureau*, p. 53.
80   On Sunday, November 24: Jenkins memo for the files, November 24, 1963, four p.m., as cited in the Church Committee, Vol. 5, pp. 32–43.
80   On Tuesday, November 26: Hoover, as recorded in HSCA final report, p. 244.
80   Three days later, on November 29: Ibid.
80   That estimate proved: The full FBI report, "Investigation of Assassination of President John F. Kennedy," December 9, 1963, is available online through the Mary Ferrell Foundation Web site, http://www.maryferrell.org/mffweb/archive/viewer/showDoc.do?docId=10402 &relPageId=4.
81   Warren and the other commissioners: Warren Commission Executive Session, December 16, 1963, NARA.
81   "He's been with me": Ibid., pp. 1–2.
81   "We're in business": Ibid., p. 2.
82   "The grammar is bad": Ibid., p. 12.
82   "Gentlemen, to be very": Ibid., p. 11.
82   "This bullet business": Ibid., p. 12.
82   "There are all kinds": Ibid.
82   Even Ford: Ibid., p. 33.
83   "It will take quite a while": Ibid., pp. 19–20.
83   Warren was also now ready: Ibid., p. 22.
83   Someone on the staff: Ibid., p. 24.
84   "This is a serious concern": Ibid., pp. 25–26.
84   Boggs suggested that: Ibid., p. 10.
84   McCloy had questions: Ibid., pp. 35, 55.

85   **Warren hesitated:** Ibid., p. 54.
85   **"Your mind plays tricks":** Ibid., p. 55.
85   **"You have to feed":** Ibid., p. 57.
85   **"You understand that reports":** Ibid., p. 59.
86   **The next day, Hoover called:** Memo from Hoover to Tolson, December 22, 1963, FBI.
86   **The day after the meeting:** Memo from Tolson to Mohr, December 17, 1963, FBI.

CHAPTER 8

88   **His teenage son:** James Rankin interview.
88   **"He never expressed":** Sara Rankin interview.
89   **J. Lee Rankin:** *New York Times*, June 30, 1996.
90   **Rankin, a graduate:** James and Sara Rankin interviews.
90   **"If you made a typo":** Sara Rankin interview.
90   **"The substantive decisions":** Deposition of J. Lee Rankin, HSCA, August 17, 1978 (hereafter Rankin Deposition), NARA.
90   **Within hours of Warren's:** James and Sara Rankin interviews.
91   **Willens arrived at the commission's:** Testimony of Howard P. Willens, HSCA, November 17, 1977, p. 312.
92   **"No one could seriously":** Ibid., p. 327.
92   **"I do concede":** Ibid., p. 322.
93   **Rankin thought that Redlich:** Redlich conceded his lack of background on criminal law and investigative work in HSCA testimony, November 8, 1978, p. 109.
93   **His involvement in social justice:** See eulogy for Redlich prepared by Dean Richard Reversz of New York University's law school, June 13, 2011, as published by the law school online: https://www.law.nyu.edu/ecm_dlv3/groups/public/@nyu_law_website__news__media/documents/documents/ecm_pro_069050.pdf.

CHAPTER 9

94   **The sealed envelope:** Warren, *Memoirs*, p. 371.
94   **An FBI inventory:** "Autopsy of Body of President John Fitzgerald Kennedy," FBI, November 26, 1963. Accessible through history-matters.com Web site: http://www.history-matters.com/archive/jfk/arrb/master_med_set/md44/html/Image0.htm.
94   **"I saw the pictures":** Warren, *Memoirs*, pp. 371–72.
98   **Arlen Specter was a young man:** Specter interviews. Also see Specter, *Passion for Truth*, p. 36. See also "Court Refuses Appeal of 6 Convicted for Union Fraud," *New York Times*, November 10, 1964.
98   **The recruiting call:** Specter interviews; Specter, *Passion*, pp. 43–45.
99   **"They were all very excited":** Specter interviews, Specter memoir transcripts. See also Specter, *Passion*, passim.

CHAPTER 10

100   **In the first days of January 1964:** Slawson interviews.
101   **There was no second-guessing:** Slawson interviews.
105   **"At the beginning, I really thought":** Coleman interviews. See also Coleman, *Counsel for the Situation*, pp. 171–78.
105   **"He dealt with his":** Guthman and Shulman, *Robert Kennedy*, p. 252.
105   **He still resembled:** Helms, *A Look over My Shoulder*, pp. 59–60.
106   **Robert Kennedy recalled:** Schlesinger, *Robert Kennedy*, p. 446.

CHAPTER 11

107   **In the first hours after the assassination:** Particulars of the meeting are found throughout Whitten's testimony to the Church Committee on May 7, 1976 (hereafter Whitten

Senate Testimony) and his testimony to the HSCA, May 16, 1978 (hereafter Whitten House Testimony), NARA.

107 **Whitten's real name:** Whitten Senate Testimony, passim.

107 **When President Johnson created:** Description of Whitten's personality and background comes from Jefferson Morley, "The Good Spy," *Washington Monthly*, December 2003, pp. 40–44; description of Whitten's job and responsibilities at the CIA comes from Whitten Senate Testimony.

108 **Like so many of his colleagues:** That Whitten reviewed Oswald's agency file comes from Whitten House Testimony and Whitten Senate Testimony, passim.

108 **At the meeting on November 23:** That Helms told the others that Whitten would have "broad powers" comes from Whitten House Testimony, passim.

108 **"was to be in charge":** Whitten Senate Testimony, p. 76000140417.

108 **Whitten thought:** Whitten House Testimony, p. 1–136/001918.

108 **"I had investigated":** Whitten House Testimony, p. 1–112/001894.

108 **Among the others in Helms's office:** Who was at the meeting comes from Whitten Senate Testimony, p. 76000140429.

108 **The two men had clashed:** Whitten Senate Testimony, p. 76000140459; Whitten House Testimony p. 1–71/001852.

108 **"None of the senior officials":** Whitten House Testimony, p. 1–74/001855.

109 **Whitten thought of Angleton as a sinister force:** Angleton was paranoid. Whitten House Testimony, p. 1–167/001949.

109 **Angleton had a:** Whitten House Testimony, p. 1–167/001949.

109 **The Yale-educated Angleton:** Martin, *Wilderness of Mirrors*, p. 10.

109 **"Everything that Angleton did":** Whitten House Testimony, p. 1–71/001852.

109 **"He had enormously influential":** Whitten House Testimony, p. 1–169/001951.

109 **"One of the reasons":** Whitten Senate Testimony, p. 76000140472.

109 **"The FBI could be extremely clannish":** Ibid., p. 76000140473.

110 **"Angleton's influence also extended":** That Angleton was close to Allen Dulles can be found in Whitten Senate Testimony, p. 76000140469; Whitten House Testimony p. 1–73/001854.

110 **Whitten admitted he took some pleasure:** Whitten Senate Testimony, p. 76000140459.

110 **"We were flooded":** Whitten House Testimony, p. 1–131/001913.

110 **"We dropped almost everything else":** Ibid.

110 **Much of it was:** Ibid., p. 1–135/001917.

110 **Whitten said he knew nothing:** Whitten Senate Testimony, p. 76000140473; Whitten House Testimony, pp. 1–30/001811 and 1–47/001828.

110 **That was not surprising:** Whitten House Testimony, pp. 1–15/001796 and 1–103-A/001885.

110 **They were detected:** Ibid., p. 1–50/001832.

111 **Whitten shared Hoover's admiration:** Ibid., p. 1–18/001799.

111 **According to Whitten:** Whitten Senate Testimony, p. 76000140458.

111 **Whitten said that every:** Whitten House Testimony, pp. 1–51/001833 and 1–56/001837.

111 **Whitten recalled:** Ibid., pp. 1–129/001911 through 1–131/0013.

111 **"We were sure to give them":** Ibid., p. 1–163/001945.

111 **"We wondered":** Ibid., p. 1–161/001943.

111 **"There was no nefarious":** Ibid.

112 **The station had secretly:** Whitten House Testimony, pp. 1–61/001837 through 1–68/001849.

112 **Scott was a force unto:** See Morley, *Our Man in Mexico*, for the definitive biography of Scott.

112 **Among his deputies:** Interview of Anne Goodpasture, HSCA, November 20, 1978, JFK Records, RIF: 180–10110–10028, NARA (hereafter Goodpasture House interview).

112 **She had also begun:** Morley, *Our Man*, p. 84.

112 **In later years, Goodpasture denied:** Deposition of Anne Goodpasture, ARRB, p. 36, NARA (hereafter Goodpasture Deposition). See also Morley, *Our Man*, for the definitive biography of Goodpasture.

112　**Goodpasture was sometimes confused for:** Goodpasture House interview, p. 31.
113　**She was not a street spy:** Goodpasture Deposition, p. 14.
113　**"He maintained his own":** See Morley, *Our Man*, passim. See Goodpasture Deposition, Goodpasture House interview, passim.
113　**"Win never trusted":** Morley interview with Goodpasture, May 2–3, 2005, cited in *Our Man*, p. 257.
113　**Over time:** Memo from CIA officer Scott Breckinridge, "Memo for the Record: Conversation with Ann [*sic*] Goodpasture," July 18, 1978, NARA (document: 1993.08.09.10:37:28:500060). Also see Goodpasture Deposition, pp. 27, 32. See also Morley, *Our Man*, passim.

CHAPTER 12
115　**Whitten put together:** Testimony of John Scelso (pseudonym for John Whitten), Whitten Senate Testimony, p. 76000140416, NARA, available from www.maryferrell.org (accessed May 13, 2013).
115　**By this point:** Testimony of John Scelso, Whitten House Testimony, pp. 1–114/001896 through 1–116/001898.
115　**Whitten saw no evidence:** Whitten Senate Testimony, pp. 76000140443 and 76000140446.
115　**As he finished the report:** Whitten Senate Testimony, p. 76000140417; Whitten House Testimony, p. 1–73/001854.
115　**He confronted Angleton:** Whitten House Testimony, p. 1–74/001855.
116　**Without Whitten's knowledge:** Whitten Senate Testimony, p. 76000140469; Whitten House Testimony, pp. 1–73/001854 through 1–74/001855.
116　**"You go tell him":** Whitten House Testimony, p. 1–74/001855.
116　**Whitten began to worry:** Whitten House Testimony, pp. 1–74/1855 and 1–114/001896 through 1–116/001898; Whitten Senate Testimony, pp. 76000140417 through 76000140418.
116　**Whitten was also startled to discover:** Whitten House Testimony, p. 1–114/001896.
116　**As he read on:** "vast amount of information," Whitten Senate Testimony, p. 76000140473; "simultaneously outdated," ibid., p. 76000140469; "useless," ibid., p. 76000140470. This episode is also covered in Whitten House Testimony, pp. 1–115/001897 through 1–116/001898.
116　**The situation:** This episode is outlined in Whitten House Testimony, pp. 1–115/001897 through 1–116/001898; "so full of errors . . ." and "it was never," Whitten Senate Testimony, p. 76000140470.
117　**Angleton urged:** Whitten Senate Testimony, p. 76000140472.
117　**Whitten was struck that:** Ibid.
117　**Within the CIA:** Testimony of Richard Helms, HSCA, 1978, JFK Assassination Files, CIA NARA, record number: 104-10051–10025, p. 9 (hereafter Helms House Testimony). Also see Whitten Senate Testimony, pp. 76000140471 through 76000140471 and Whitten House Testimony, pp. 1–115/001897 through 1–116/001898.
117　**Whitten's specialty:** Whitten House Testimony, pp. 1–4/001784 and 1–5/001785; investigation had expanded, Whitten Senate Testimony, pp. 76000140471 through 76000140472 and Whitten House Testimony, pp. 1–135/001917 through 1–138/001920.
117　**Years later:** That Whitten was outraged, ibid., pp. 76000140441, 76000140466, and 76000140495; Whitten House Testimony, pp. 1–137/001918 and 1–153/001935.
118　**He typically ended:** Powers, *The Man Who Kept the Secrets*, p. 3.
118　**"The whole thrust":** Helms House Testimony, p. 10.
118　**"It is an untidy":** Ibid., September 22, 1978, HSCA, p. 172.
118　**David Slawson, still new:** Slawson interviews. See also Testimony of W. David Slawson, November 15, 1977, HSCA. Text from *HSCA Security Classified Testimony*, available from the Assassination Archives and Research Center (accessed May 22, 2013).
118　**He was struck:** Slawson interviews.
118　**The CIA had done:** Slawson interviews. See also Testimony of Raymond Rocca, July 17,

1978, HSCA. Text from *HSCA Security Classified Testimony*, available from the Assassination Archives and Research Center (accessed May 22, 2013).

119   **Rocca, a San Franciscan:** See obituary of Rocca, "Raymond Rocca, CIA Deputy and Specialist on Soviets, 76," *Washington Post*, November 14, 1993.

119   **Slawson said he found:** Slawson interviews.

121   **The SAS had its own:** Church Committee, "The Investigation of the Assassination of President John F. Kennedy," Vol. 5, pp. 57–58.

121   **On February 20:** "Memorandum for Chief, Subject; Documents Available in Oswald's 201 file," February 20, 1964, as reproduced in the transcript of the Helms House testimony, September 22, 1978.

CHAPTER 13

122   **"The only thing":** Warren interview with Alfred Goldberg, March 26, 1974, as found in Warren Commission files, Warren papers, LOC.

122   **"I never put any faith":** Ibid.

123   **"I never heard":** Rankin Deposition.

123   **"I assumed conspiracy":** Belin, *Final Disclosure*, p. 50.

123   **"I felt it was highly":** Belin, *November 22, 1963; You Are the Jury*, p. 4.

123   **"My initial reaction":** Griffin interviews.

124   **When he entered:** Griffin interviews.

124   **"I thought the FBI":** Griffin interviews. See also Griffin testimony to the HSCA, November 17, 1977.

125   **Their office:** Griffin interviews.

125   **As he introduced:** Griffin interviews.

125   **It was like:** Eisenberg interviews.

126   **The odd man out:** Griffin, Slawson, Specter interviews. Also see Specter memoir transcripts.

126   **He told Specter:** Specter interviews; Specter memoir transcripts.

127   **Slawson remembered a few:** Slawson interviews.

127   **According to memos:** Memo from Eisenberg to files, "First Staff Conference (January 20, 1964)," February 14, 1964, staff files, Warren Commission, NARA. Also see memo from Willens "for the record," "Staff Meeting of Jan. 20, 1964," January 21, 1964, staff files, Warren Commission, NARA.

CHAPTER 14

129   **Hugh Aynesworth:** Aynesworth interviews. See also Aynesworth, *JFK: Breaking the News*, passim.

129   **At first, Aynesworth:** Aynesworth interviews.

130   **Aynesworth understood:** Aynesworth interviews; Aynesworth, *JFK: Breaking*, p. 7.

130   **"I felt badly":** Aynesworth interviews; Aynesworth, *JFK: Breaking*, pp. 6–7.

130   **The paper was controlled:** History of the *Dallas Morning News* available on the Web site of the Texas State Historical Association, http://www.tshaonline.org/handbook/online/articles/eed12 (accessed June 15, 2013).

130   **Jacqueline Kennedy:** Manchester, *Death*, p. 121.

130   **Aynesworth had many gifts:** Description of Aynesworth taken from William Broyles, "The Man Who Saw Too Much," *Texas Monthly*, March 1976.

132   **He had no notepad:** Aynesworth interviews; Aynesworth, *JFK: Breaking*, p. 22.

132   **"I knew he was":** Aynesworth interviews; Aynesworth: *JFK: Breaking*, p. 29.

133   **Helen Markham:** Aynesworth, *JFK: Breaking*, p. 33.

133   **Aynesworth watched:** Aynesworth interviews; Aynesworth, *JFK: Breaking*, p. 47.

134   **"He was a nut":** Aynesworth interviews; Aynesworth, *JFK: Breaking*, pp. 104–16.

134   **Aynesworth was horrified:** Aynesworth interviews.

134 The first, he said: Aynesworth, *JFK: Breaking*, pp. 69, 216.
135 In that category: Ibid., p. 217; Aynesworth interviews.
135 "He told me": Aynesworth interviews; Aynesworth, *JFK: Breaking*, pp. 222–23.
136 Among the most persistent: Aynesworth, *JFK: Breaking*, pp. 126–27.
137 The byline was: *Houston Post*, January 1, 1964.
137 In his column for: Washington Merry-Go-Round, December 2, 1963, available in the Drew Pearson archives maintained by American University, http://dspace.wrlc.org/doc/bitstream/2041/50086/b18f09–1202zdisplay.pdf#search=".
138 Any move to discipline: Testimony of James Rowley, Warren Appendix, Vol. 5, June 18, 1964, passim.
138 In his diary: Pearson Diaries, December 1963, Pearson papers, LBJ Library.
138 Later in December: Washington Merry-Go-Round, December 14, 1963, http://dspace.wrlc.org/doc/bitstream/2041/50099/b18f09–1214zdisplay.pdf#search=".

CHAPTER 15

140 Before Christmas: Memo from Willens to Rankin, "Outline of Commission's Work," December 30, 1963, staff files, Warren Commission, NARA.
140 "We have an important": Memo from Rankin to staff, January 13, 1964, staff files, Warren Commission, NARA.
141 Warren opened: Warren Commission Executive Session, January 21, 1963, NARA, p. 8.
141 Gerald Ford: Ibid., pp. 34–35.
142 "It is not too early": Ibid., p. 12.
142 He asked Russell: Ibid., pp. 24–25.
143 Hoover said he: Church Committee, Vol. 5, p. 47.
143 "To have them just lie": Rankin Deposition, pp. 15–16.
144 Rankin recalled: Ibid., p. 129. See also Warren Commission Executive Session, January 22 and January 27, 1964, NARA.
144 Ford was in a hearing: Ford, *Portrait of the Assassin*, pp. 15–16.
144 He was struck: Ibid., p. 21.
145 "You wouldn't pick up": Warren Commission Executive Session, January 22, 1964, NARA, p. 6.
145 "They found their": Ibid.
145 "You would have people think": Ibid., p. 12.
146 *Time* magazine: Warren Commission Executive Session, January 27, 1964, NARA, p. 152.
146 "We do have a dirty": Ibid., p. 139.
146 Warren and Rankin had: Ibid., pp. 160, 137.
147 "I would be frank": Ibid., p. 137.
147 The chief justice said: Ibid., pp. 152–54.
148 "There is no man": Ibid., p. 158.
148 Warren: "If you tell": Ibid., p. 164.
148 "They have tried the case": Ibid., p. 171.

CHAPTER 16

149 Rankin was ushered: Hoover appointment calendar, January 24, 1964, FBI, accessed through Mary Ferrell Foundation, http://www.maryferrell.org/mffweb/archive/viewer/showDoc.do?docId=141177&relPageId=16.
149 Assistant Director Cartha: DeLoach, *Hoover's FBI*, p. 12.
149 In an outer office: Ibid., p. 29.
149 The effect: Ibid., p. 13.
149 FBI employees: Ibid., p. 24.

150   Like Chief Justice Warren: Testimony of J. Lee Rankin, HSCA, September 21, 1978 (hereafter Rankin Testimony), p. 19.
150   "I told Rankin": Memo from Hoover for Mr. Tolson, January 31, 1964, FBI.
150   The bureau's attitude: Rankin Deposition, p. 19.
151   It was a skill: See Hoover biography at Web site of the J. Edgar Hoover Foundation, http://www.jehooverfoundation.org/hoover-bio.asp (accessed June 15, 2013).
151   "There was nothing up": Testimony of J. Edgar Hoover, May 14, 1964, Warren Appendix, Vol. 5, p. 112.
151   In late November: Church Committee, Vol. 5, p. 50.
151   The answer came on: Description of Gales as "Barracuda" from Hosty interviews. See also Hosty, Assignment: Oswald, p. 179.
151   He would go forward: Church Committee, Vol. 5, pp. 50–51.
152   "Rain clouds had formed": DeLoach, Hoover's FBI, p. 149.
152   The failure to do so: Church Committee, Vol. 5, pp. 51 52.
152   As he told the commission: Testimony of J. Edgar Hoover, Warren Appendix, Vol. 5, p. 159.
153   The FBI's Domestic Intelligence: Church Committee, Vol. 5, p. 37.
153   He had no memory: "Castro Blasts Raids on Cuba," New Orleans Times Picayune, September 9, 1963.
154   Anderson had received: Testimony of Clark Anderson, February 4, 1976, Church Committee (hereafter Anderson Testimony).
154   On October 18: Ibid., p. 15.
155   "I don't think": Anderson Testimony, p. 59.
155   "I don't think there was ever": Ibid., p. 24.
155   "I don't recall that": Ibid., p. 22.
155   His agents did determine: Name and room rate of Hotel del Comercio, Warren Report, p. 433.
155   Anderson, who had: Anderson Testimony, p. 32.
155   Almost from the moment: Cable from Mann to State Department, "AMEMBASSY MEXICO CITY to SECSTATE," November 28, 1963, RIF: 104–10438–10208, NARA (hereafter Mann cable).
156   The ambassador told colleagues: Ibid.
156   Anderson reported Mann's belief: Church Committee, Vol. 5, p. 40.
156   A twenty-three-year-old: For background on Alvarado, see Bugliosi, Reclaiming History, p. 1286.
156   In an urgent cable: Mann cable.
157   "She denied all of that": "Cable: Translation of a Transcript of Telephone Conversation Between Cuban President and Cuban Ambassador," November 26, 1963, CIA, RIF: 14–10429–10227, NARA.
157   In a cable to Washington: Mann cable.
157   Back in Washington: Church Committee, Vol. 5, p. 42.
157   Keenan, who had been: Keenan interview. Many of Keenan's allegations were detailed in a 2006 German documentary film, "Rendezvous with Death," by filmmaker Wilfried Huismann, which was broadcast on the German channel ARD in January 2006. See Financial Times, January 6, 2006. Also see Anthony and Robbyn Summers, "The Ghosts of November," Vanity Fair, December 1994.
158   He was given: Testimony of Laurence P. Keenan, April 8, 1976, Church Committee, Vol. 1, p. 7, RIF: 157–10014–10091, NARA.
158   First, he would try: Ibid., pp. 42, 9, 10, 83, 61.
159   On November 30, the Mexican: "Cable: Re Gilberto Alvarado Story re Lee Oswald Received Money in Cuban Embassy Being False," November 30, 1963, RIF: 104–10404–10098, NARA.

159   **With Alvarado's reversal:** Keenan testimony, Church Committee, Vol. 1, p. 58.

159   **Waiting in Keenan's office:** Ibid., pp. 71, 53.

160   **Mann also left Mexico:** *New York Times*, December 15, 1963.

160   **In one of his final:** "Telegram: Mexican Authorities Have Informed Us That the Nicaraguan," Mann to State Department, November 30, 1963, RIF: 104–104380–10210, NARA.

160   **He was quoted:** Thomas Mann interview with author Dick Russell, July 5, 1992, as cited in Morley, *Our Man*, p. 334. See also Russell, *The Man Who Knew Too Much*.

CHAPTER 17

161   **And Arlen Specter, his junior:** Specter interviews; Specter, *Passion*, pp. 49–58.

162   **During his tumultuous:** see *New York Times* obituary of Adams, April 21, 1990.

162   **Specter remembered:** Specter, *Passion*, pp. 49–58.

163   **"He was one of the finest":** Joseph Ball and Judith Fischer, "A Century in the Life of a Lawyer," *California Western Law Review*, Fall 1999.

163   **Specter, however, would:** Specter interviews.

164   **"Adams should have":** Belin, *You Are the Jury*, p. 15.

164   **Specter remembered Ball:** Specter, *Passion*, pp. 57, 76–78.

165   **He outlined hundreds:** "Proposed Questioning of Marina Oswald," undated document found in chronological staff files of the Warren Commission, NARA.

166   **In a memo attached to:** Memo from Specter to Rankin, "Subject: Suggestions on Questioning of Marina Oswald," January 30, 1964, staff files, Warren Commission, NARA.

166   **Warren asked the director:** Goldberg interviews.

168   **"They were incompetent":** Slawson interviews.

CHAPTER 18

170   **At the news conference:** *New York Times*, January 15, 1964.

170   **James Martin, her business:** *New York Times*, January 8, 1964.

171   **Reporters got wind:** *Time*, February 14, 1964.

171   **"Mrs. Oswald, did you have":** All quotations from Testimony of Marina Oswald, February 3, 1964, Warren Appendix, Vol. 1, pp. 1–126.

175   **On February:** See "Telephone Conversation between Mr. Norman Redlich and Mrs. Margaret [*sic*] Oswald," February 4, 1964, staff file on Marguerite Oswald, Warren Commission, NARA.

176   **Rankin called her:** "Conversation between Mr. Rankin and Mrs. Margaret [*sic*] Oswald," February 5, 1964, staff file on Marguerite Oswald, Warren Commission, NARA.

177   **On Monday morning:** "Testimony of Mrs. Marguerite Oswald," February 10, 1964, Warren Appendix, Vol. 1, pp. 127–264.

177   **Congressman Ford recalled:** Ford, *Portrait*, pp. 61–62.

179   **"I have to have something":** *Time*, February 21, 1964.

179   **Lane and Mrs. Oswald:** *New York Times*, February 19, 1964.

180   **Back in Washington:** See McCloy comments in Warren Commission Executive Sessions transcripts from December 1963 and January 1964, NARA.

180   **It had begun:** See obituary for Jacqueline Kennedy, *New York Times*, May 20, 1994.

180   **On January 9, Kennedy:** Telegram from Kennedy to Warren, correspondence files, Earl Warren papers, LOC.

181   **On February 5, the journalist:** Manchester, *Controversy and Other Essays in Journalism*, p. 5.

181   **Manchester remembered:** Ibid., pp. 6–7.

182   **A few days later:** See unsigned staff note to Warren at the Supreme Court, May 21, 1964. "Mr. Rankin apparently did not share your views in regard to making available to Mr. Manchester some of the Commission material. Manchester says in view of that

development he will drop the matter unless he hears from you or Mr. Rankin to the contrary." Warren Commission files, Earl Warren papers, LOC.

CHAPTER 19

183   **Away from the commission:** See Russell letter to Paul R. Eve, January 17, 1967, in personal correspondence files, Russell Library.

183   **"For some reason":** Russell note, January 7, 1964, Russell Library.

184   **He began to draft:** Draft of letter from Russell to President Johnson, February 24, 1964, found in Russell office files at Russell Library.

185   **"The only person":** Oral history of Chief Justice Earl Warren, September 21, 1971, LBJ Library, p. 13. See also Alfred Goldberg interview of Warren, March 26, 1974, in Earl Warren papers, LOC.

185   **If Russell stepped down:** Rankin Deposition, p. 6.

185   **Scobey was a lawyer:** See the Scobey obituary in *Atlanta Constitution*, December 9, 2001.

186   **Columnist Murray Kempton:** "Boy, Don't You Know I'm on Camera?" *New Republic*, February 29, 1964.

186   **The lowest moment:** *New York Times*, March 6, 1964.

186   **Ruby was represented:** Belli, *Dallas Justice*, passim.

187   **Belli used an insanity defense:** Ibid. See also Brown, *Dallas and the Jack Ruby Trial*, p. 60.

187   **"A village idiot".** Associated Press, February 19, 1964.

187   **"May I thank this":** *New York Times*, March 15, 1964.

188   **"The fact that":** Griffin interviews.

188   **Phone records obtained:** Memo from Hubert and Griffin to "Members of the President's Commission," March 20, 1964, staff files, Warren Commission, NARA.

189   **"That's the first moment":** Griffin interviews.

189   **In mid-March, Hubert:** Memo from Hubert and Griffin to members of the commission, March 20, 1964, staff files, Warren Commission, NARA.

190   **"Hubert and I were totally":** Griffin interviews.

191   **Hubert locked in:** Memo from Hubert to Rankin, "Checking persons who left or entered the United States," February 19, 1964. Also see Hubert memo to Rankin, February 27, 1964, staff files, Warren Commission, NARA.

191   **"He was demoralized":** Griffin interviews.

CHAPTER 20

192   **"Pure fabrication":** Earl Warren Oral History for the LBJ Library, September 21, 1971, p. 14.

193   **The bureau had already:** Memo from Willens to Rankin, "Re: Mark Lane," February 26, 1964, staff files, Warren Commission, NARA.

193   **In a separate memo:** Memo from Willens to Rankin, "Re: Interrogation of Mark Lane," February 27, 1964, staff files, Warren Commission, NARA.

194   **When he was promised:** Belin, *You Are the Jury*, p. 79.

194   **"Could you just give me a moment":** Lane telephone interview with Helen Markham as published in Warren Appendix, Vol. 20, p. 571.

195   **"She gave to me a more detailed":** Testimony of Mark Lane, March 4, 1964, Warren Appendix, Vol. 2, p. 51.

195   **David Belin thought:** Belin, *You Are the Jury*, p. 471.

195   **Jim Liebeler compared:** Bugliosi, *Reclaiming History*, p. 1001.

197   **"It would be ridiculous":** Eisenberg interviews. See also Eisenberg memos on criminology science, March 4, 1964 (ballistics) and March 7, 1964 (value of witness testimony), staff files, Warren Commission, NARA.

CHAPTER 21

200 **The commission:** Memo from Willens to Rankin, March 9, 1964, staff files, Warren Commission, NARA.

201 **In February, he wrote:** Letter from Rankin to McCone, February 12, 1964, staff files, Warren Commission, NARA.

201 **The commission received:** Memo from Willens to Rankin, March 9, 1964, staff files, Warren Commission, NARA.

202 **If the CIA had nothing:** Slawson memo for the record, "Conference with the CIA," March 12, 1964, staff files, Warren Commission, NARA.

203 **Slawson read them:** Memo from Coleman and Slawson for the record, "Mexico: Questions Raised by Ambassador Mann," April 2, 1964, staff files, Warren Commission, NARA.

204 **Stern was handed:** Stern interviews; memo from Stern to Rankin, "CIA file on Oswald," March 27, 1964, staff files, Warren Commission, NARA.

204 **"They let it be known":** Slawson interviews.

205 **Yuri Ivanovich Nosenko:** For background on Nosenko, see *New York Times* obituary on August 28, 2008. See also Martin, *Wilderness.*

205 **Nosenko's defection:** *New York Times*, February 15, 1964.

206 **He worried, especially:** Martin, *Wilderness*, passim.

206 **Rocca insisted to Slawson:** Slawson interviews.

207 **He was given nothing:** *Washington Post*, September 1, 2008.

207 **The request would have to go:** Testimony of W. David Slawson, HSCA, November 15, 1977, passim.

CHAPTER 22

209 **It was sometime early that month:** Testimony of Norman Redlich, HSCA, November 8, 1977.

210 **"Of course we thought":** Slawson interviews.

210 **"It was self-protection":** Specter, *Passion*, p. 93; Specter interviews.

210 **Griffin saw it:** Griffin interviews. Also see Griffin testimony to the HSCA, November 17, 1977.

210 **"Needless to say":** Letter from Rankin to Hoover, February 20, 1964.

211 **As Hosty described it:** Hosty interviews; Hosty, *Assignment: Oswald*, p. 234.

211 **In December, he:** Letter from Hoover to Hosty, December 13, 1963, as reprinted in Hosty, *Assignment: Oswald*, p. 101.

211 **"You're going to be":** Hosty, *Assignment: Oswald*, p. 118.

212 **"I didn't know":** Ibid., p. 36.

212 **In the months after:** Ibid., p. 83.

213 **Hosty interviewed Odio:** Ibid., pp. 132–34.

213 **As Odio described:** Testimony of Silvia Odio, July 9, 1964, Warren Appendix, Vol. 11, p. 367 and passim.

214 **During the interview with Hosty:** Memo from Griffin to Slawson, July 12, 1964, staff files, Warren Commission, NARA. Also see Hosty, *Assignment: Oswald*, p.132 and passim.

214 **He contacted Odio's psychiatrist:** Testimony of Dr. Burton Einspruch, HSCA, July 11, 1978, passim.

215 **In the weeks after:** Hosty, *Assignment: Oswald*, p. 133.

CHAPTER 23

216 **The reports were not:** Slawson interviews.

218 **In the United States, a more serious:** Memo from Redlich to Rankin, February 11, 1964, staff files, Warren Commission, NARA.

219 **On February 12:** See photocopy of *Tocsin* front page found in congressional correspondence files, Ford Library.

219 **Within days, Congressman:** Letter from Baldwin to Ford, February 12, 1964, congressional correspondence files, Ford Library.

219   He contacted the House Un-American Activities: See letter from Francis J. McNamara of the House Un-American Affairs Committee to Ford, February 27, 1964, congressional correspondence files, Ford Library.

220   Asked by reporters: *New York Times*, February 5, 1964; Associated Press, February 4, 1964. See also Newton, *Justice for All*, p. 434.

220   Arlen Specter said: Specter interviews; Specter, *Passion*, p. 59.

220   The *Columbus Enquirer*: Attached to a letter from Harold Callaway to Ford, February 10, 1964, congressional correspondence files, Ford Library.

221   The chief justice was: See transcript of Johansen remarks, February 6, 1964, found in congressional correspondence files, Ford Library.

221   A senior editor at *Newsweek*: Letter from Graham to Warren, February 18, 1964, and Bernstein letter to Warren, February 14, 1964, correspondence files, Warren papers, LOC.

222   On Monday, February 17: Letter from Hoover to Rankin, February 17, 1964, staff files, Warren Commission, NARA.

222   Rankin reacted instantly: Letter from Rankin to Hoover, February 18, 1964, staff files, Warren Commission, NARA.

222   As Rankin watched: See memo from Charles N. Shaffer, "Memorandum for the Record," February 17, 1964, staff files, Warren Commission, NARA.

222   "I took a bath": Statement of Marina Oswald to the FBI, February 19, 1964, as reprinted in Aynesworth, *JFK: Breaking*. See also letter from Hoover to Rankin, February 20, 1964, staff files, Warren Commission, NARA.

223   "Could it be possible": Ford, *Portrait*, p. 511.

224   Robert testified: Testimony of Robert Oswald, February 20, 1964, Warren Appendix, Vol. 1, pp. 264–502.

224   "Mr. Rankin said": Memo from Hoover to Tolson et al., February 24, 1964, FBI.

225   Within days, eight: Memo from FBI Dallas field office to FBI headquarters, "Recommendations for Installation of Telephone and Microphone Surveillance," March 2, 1964, FBI.

225   The next witness before the commission: Testimony of James Herbert Martin, February 27, 1964, Warren Appendix, Vol. 1, pp. 469–502.

226   "As Martin's testimony": Memo from Redlich to Rankin, February 28, 1964, staff files, Warren Commission, NARA.

227   Two days later: Memo from DeLoach to Ford, February 14, 1964, congressional correspondence files, Ford Library.

CHAPTER 24

228   As the commission's chief: Stern interviews.

229   It was darkly: For the history of the Secret Service, see Kessler, *In the President's Secret Service*, passim. Also, Blaine, McCubbin, and Hill, *The Kennedy Detail*, passim.

229   The limousine used: For background on the Kennedy limousine, see the Web site of the Henry Ford Museum, www.thehenryford.org/research/kennedylimo.aspx.

229   "It was not designed": Stern interviews; memo from Stern to Rankin, "Report on Security Measures to Protect the President," February 17, 1964, staff files, Warren Commission, NARA.

230   "It was horrible": Stern interviews.

230   Within the agency: Warren Report, p. 430; memo from Stern for the record, February 17, 1964, and Stern's "Memorandum of Interview," March 20, 1964, staff files, Warren Commission, NARA.

231   Stern felt sorry: Stern interviews.

232   Stern had a sense: Stern interviews. A description of the Metropolitan Club party is found in Peppers and Ward, *In Chambers: Stories of the Supreme Court Law Clerks and Their Justices*.

CHAPTER 25

234 **In March, Ford wrote:** Letter from Ford to Rankin, March 28, 1964, staff files, Warren Commission, NARA.

235 **The chief justice was never:** Specter, *Passion*, p. 56.

235 **John Stiles:** For background on Stiles, see obituary in the *Grand Rapids (Michigan) Press*, April 15, 1970.

236 **In March, Ford was:** "Checklist of Questions Raised by Mark Lane," March 6, 1964, congressional correspondence files, Ford Library.

236 **Representative James D. Weaver:** Letter from Weaver to Ford, April 23, 1964, congressional correspondence files, Ford Library.

237 **A memo to Ford:** Unsigned memo to Ford, "Memorandum for Honorable Gerald R. Ford," March 17, 1964, congressional correspondence files, Ford Library.

237 **"How did it happen":** Letter from Poff to Ford, April 20, 1964, congressional correspondence files, Ford Library.

237 **A Texas doctor:** Note from George H. Kakaska, MD, to Ford, April 23, 1964, congressional correspondence files, Ford Library.

237 **On April 3, Rankin wrote to Ford:** Letter from Rankin to Ford, April 3, 1964, congressional correspondence files, Ford Library.

237 **Ford wrote Rankin:** Letter from Ford to Rankin, April 7, 1964, congressional correspondence files, Ford Library.

237 **In a separate letter to Rankin:** Letter from Ford to Rankin, April 24, 1964, congressional correspondence files, Ford Library.

238 **He prepared a handwritten:** Undated memo from Ray to Ford, undated, congressional correspondence files, Ford Library.

238 **An unsigned staff memo to Ford:** "Observations: Re: Mr. R," April 7, 1964, congressional correspondence files, Ford Library.

239 **In January, Ford's Washington:** Letter from H. L. Hunt to Ford, January 25, 1964, congressional correspondence files, Ford Library.

239 **"When I heard about this":** Goldberg interviews.

239 **In his hard work:** See background material about Ford's book, *Portrait of the Assassin*, in Ford's correspondence files, Ford Library. A copy of Ford's book contract is also in the files.

CHAPTER 26

242 **"I have had to somewhat":** Letter from Belin to colleagues at Herrick, Langdon, Sandblom & Belin, January 27, 1964, Belin's Warren Commission files, Ford Library.

242 **Raised in a music-loving:** *Des Moines Register*, June 15, 2000.

242 **Another letter to Des Moines:** Letter from Belin to colleagues at Herrick, Langdon, Sandblom & Belin, February 11, 1964, Belin's Warren Commission files, Ford Library.

243 **"When there are":** Belin, *You Are the Jury*, p. 175.

243 **Asked how Oswald dressed:** Ibid., pp. 4–5.

243 **There were far more:** Ibid., pp. 5–8.

244 **"I really was not":** Letter from Belin to colleagues at Herrick, Langdon, Sandblom & Belin, March 26, 1964, Belin's Warren Commission files, Ford Library.

246 **Friends on the police force:** See *New York Times*, November 25, 1963, as well as extensive biographical material on a Tippit family memorial Web site: www.jdtippit.com.

247 **For the test, Belin:** Belin, *You Are the Jury*, pp. 139–40.

247 **Belin conducted another:** Ibid., pp. 261–63.

247 **"I could hardly believe":** Ibid., p. 42.

248 **"I heard this crack":** Testimony of Howard Brennan, March 24, 1964, Warren Appendix, Vol. 3, pp. 140–211.

249 At about the time: Belin, *You Are the Jury*, p. 136.

250 Holland's testimony was: Stern interviews. Also see testimony of S. M. Holland, April 8, 1964, Warren Appendix, Vol. 6, pp. 239–48.

250 If Howard Brennan was: Belin, *You Are the Jury*, p. 69.

251 Warren passed a handwritten: The undated, handwritten note is found in Ford's congressional correspondence files, identified as having been written by the chief justice and handed to Ford during Markham's testimony.

251 Markham admitted that she: Testimony of Helen Markham, March 26, 1964, Warren Appendix, Vol. 3, pp. 304–22.

252 Could Lane have impersonated: Belin, *You Are the Jury*, pp. 340–42.

253 In late February, *Life*: Ibid., pp. 302–5.

CHAPTER 27

255 Of the ninety three: Specter interviews; Specter, *Passion*, p. 107.

256 He divided them into: Memo from Specter to Rankin, "Outline of Suggested Questions for Mrs. Jacqueline Kennedy," March 31, 1964, staff files, Warren Commission, NARA.

256 "The Chief Justice had taken": Specter interviews. Also see Specter, *Passion*, passim.

257 Kellerman struck Specter: Specter interviews; Specter, *Passion*, pp. 66–69.

257 When Jacqueline Kennedy learned: Gallagher, *My Life with Jacqueline Kennedy*, p. 341, Mary Barelli Gallagher had been Mrs. Kennedy's personal secretary in the White House.

257 Later, when William: Manchester, *Death*, p. 290.

258 Specter thought: Specter, *Passion*, pp. 63, 69. Also see Hill, Clint, and McCubbin, *Mrs. Kennedy and Me: An Intimate Memoir*, p. 281.

259 Hill offered Specter a convincing: Testimony of Clint Hill, March 9, 1964, Warren Appendix, Vol. 2, pp. 132–43.

260 An alarmed reporter from: Manchester, *Death*, p. 222.

260 No news organization: Ibid., pp. 165, 345.

260 "He was very suspicious": Specter, *Passion*, p. 77.

261 An FBI report issued in December: The initial FBI report on the autopsy, the source of the essential information republished in the reports in December and January, was prepared by agents Francis X. O'Neill and James W. Sibert, who observed the autopsy. The full report, dated November 26, 1963, was released by the ARRB and is available online at http://www.history-matters.com/archive/jfk/arrb/master_med_set/md44/html/Imageo.htm.

261 It was then, Specter: Specter, *Passion*, p. 78. Also see Humes Testimony, Humes interview.

262 Specter later remembered: Specter, *Passion*, p. 80.

263 "I see that Governor Connally": Testimony of James J. Humes, March 16, 1964, Warren Appendix, Vol. 2, pp. 347–76.

265 "It was dangerous": Belin, *You Are the Jury*, pp. 345–46.

265 The Kennedy family: Specter, *Passion*, p. 84.

CHAPTER 28

266 "The Chief Justice did not": Specter interviews; Specter, *Passion*, pp. 90–99.

267 The error had been: Testimony of Dr. Ronald Coy Jones, March 24, 1964, Warren Appendix, Vol. 6, pp. 51–57.

269 The key testimony: Testimony of Darrell Tomlinson, March 20, 1964, Warren Appendix, Vol. 6, pp. 128–34.

270 One strong possibility: Warren Report, pp. 111–112.

270 The clothes were: Specter interviews; Specter, *Passion*, pp. 69–75.

270 "I couldn't bear": Nellie Connally, *From Love Field*, p. 119.

271 Nellie Connally found it: Ibid., pp. 120–21.

272 **Specter recalled that:** Specter interviews; Specter, *Passion*, p. 72.

272 **Mrs. Connally had the film:** Belin, *You Are the Jury*, pp. 308–9.

272 **"Even 'magic' bullets":** Connally, *From Love Field*, p. 120.

273 **"Russell was immaculately dressed":** Specter interviews.

273 **"I heard a noise":** Testimony of Governor John Connally, March 16, 1964, Warren Appendix, Vol. 4, pp. 131–46.

274 **The scene produced:** Specter interviews.

275 **Connally, Warren decided:** Warren interview with Alfred Goldberg, March 26, 1974, as found in Warren Commission files, Warren papers, LOC.

CHAPTER 29

276 **"I must have watched":** Pollak interviews.

277 **"There he was":** Goldberg interviews.

278 **"The Chief Justice was":** Pollak interviews.

278 **Mosk's first assignment:** Mosk interviews.

279 **In late April, Mosk wrote a memo:** Memo from Mosk to Slawson, April 23, 1964, staff files, Warren Commission, NARA.

280 **Two years earlier:** See obituary of Ely in *New York Times*, October 27, 2003.

280 **Ely had been assigned:** Memo from Ely to Jenner and Liebeler, "Lee Harvey Oswald's Marine Career," April 22, 1964, staff files, Warren Commission, NARA.

280 **The seemingly prudish:** Memo from Ely to Rankin, May 5, 1964, staff files, Warren Commission, NARA.

CHAPTER 30

281 **Dean had told a number of seemingly:** Testimony of Patrick T. Dean, March 24, 1964, Warren Appendix, Vol. 12, pp. 415–49. Also see *Dallas Morning News*, March 25, 1979.

282 **Griffin was not the only:** Aynesworth, *JFK: Breaking*, pp. 176–79. Also see Huffaker, *When the News Went Live*, passim.

283 **When Griffin took Dean's:** Testimony of Patrick T. Dean, March 24, 1964, Warren Appendix, Vol. 12, pp. 415–49.

284 **Dean said later:** *Dallas Morning News*, March 25, 1979.

284 **"No member of our staff":** Testimony of Patrick T. Dean, June 8, 1964, Warren Appendix, Vol. 5, pp. 254–58.

285 **Immediately after a staff:** Memo from Griffin to Willens, April 4, 1964, staff files, Warren Commission, NARA.

285 **"We do not think":** Ibid.

285 **"We should proceed as":** Memo from Willens to Rankin, April 6, 1964, staff files, Warren Commission, NARA.

285 **"We believe that":** Memo from Hubert and Griffin to Rankin, "Adequacy of Ruby Investigation," May 14, 1964, staff files, Warren Commission, NARA.

286 **The memo essentially:** Memo from Willens to Griffin, "Re: Adequacy of Ruby Investigation," June 1, 1964, staff files, Warren Commission, NARA.

286 **He told Rankin he needed:** Memo from Hubert to Rankin, June 1, 1964, staff files, Warren Commission, NARA.

286 **According to David Belin:** Belin, *Final Disclosure*, p. 46.

286 **On April 26:** Letter from Dr. Louis West to Henry Wade, May 7, 1964, staff files, Warren Commission, NARA.

288 **Ruby readily acknowledged:** Letter from Dr. Robert Stubblefield to Judge Joe B. Brown, May 15, 1964, staff files, Warren Commission, NARA.

CHAPTER 31

289 "Duran could be": Slawson interviews.

289 The day before their departure: Memo from Slawson for the record, "Trip to Mexico City," April 22, 1964, staff files, Warren Commission, NARA.

290 "The CIA told me": Slawson interviews. Also see testimony of W. David Slawson, HSCA, November 15, 1977.

293 The commission lawyers: Memo from Slawson for the record, "Trip to Mexico City," April 22, 1964, staff files, Warren Commission, NARA.

295 "We still have the": Slawson interviews.

296 Coleman added to the confusion: Coleman interviews.

298 On Saturday night: Slawson interviews.

CHAPTER 32

299 "Mr. Manchester": Manchester, Controversy, pp. 11–15.

300 Four days after: Manchester, Death, pp. x–xiii.

301 The chief justice raised: Statement of President Lyndon B. Johnson, July 10, 1964, Warren Appendix, Vol. 5, pp. 561–64.

301 "I think it would have been": Oral history of Chief Justice Earl Warren, September 21, 1971, LBJ Library, p. 12.

301 "I cast one last": Statement of Mrs. Lyndon B. Johnson, July 16, 1964, Warren Appendix, Vol. 5, pp. 564–65.

302 Warren agreed to be interviewed: Manchester, Death, pp. x–xi.

302 Manchester was given a tour: Manchester, Controversy, p. 10.

303 "Jackie has been reigning": Pearson diaries, November and December 1963, Pearson papers, LBJ Library.

304 "TV viewers of the Kennedy": Washington Merry-Go-Round, December 10, 1963, available in the Drew Pearson archives maintained by American University. The actual column can be found at http://dspace.wrlc.org/doc/bitstream/2041/50094/b18f09-1210zdisplay.pdf#search=".

305 The column produced: Pearson diaries, November and December 1963, Pearson papers, LBJ Library.

305 Under his contract: Manchester, Controversy, p. 8.

305 Warren always felt: Goldberg interviews.

305 Much of the report: Memo from Goldberg to Rankin, "Proposed Outline of Report," April 13, 1964, staff files, Warren Commission, NARA.

306 On March 16: Memo from Goldberg to Rankin, March 16, 1964, staff files, Warren Commission, NARA.

306 "They had all been": Goldberg interviews.

307 "From an overall standpoint": Letter from Belin to Willens, March 19, 1964, staff files, Warren Commission, NARA.

307 On April 24, he: Memo from Goldberg to Rankin, April 28, 1964, staff files, Warren Commission, NARA.

CHAPTER 33

308 He heard that: Slawson interviews.

310 Warren, for his part: Warren interview with Alfred Goldberg, March 26, 1974, as found in Warren Commission files, Warren papers, LOC.

312 In June, Warren met privately: Ibid.

313 "If the suicide incident": Memo from Slawson to Specter, March 13, 1964, staff files, Warren Commission, NARA.

313 In a memo to his colleagues: Memo from Slawson to Hubert and Griffin, "Re: Silvia Odio," April 6, 1964, staff files, Warren Commission, NARA.

314 "Einspruch stated that": Memo from Griffin to Slawson, "Interview with Dr. Burton C. Einspruch," April 16, 1964, staff files, Warren Commission, NARA.

CHAPTER 34

315 **Rankin remembered Liebeler:** Rankin Deposition, passim.

315 **"Mr. Redlich and I have":** Testimony of Wesley Liebeler, HSCA, November 16, 1977 (hereafter Liebeler Testimony).

315 **Slawson recalled him:** Slawson, Griffin, Specter interviews. See also Specter memoir transcripts.

316 **"It was a great, beautiful":** Rankin Deposition.

317 **Over the years, his younger:** Eric Liebeler interview.

317 **"I finally decided to":** Liebeler Testimony.

317 **While Liebeler was:** Specter interviews; Specter memoir transcripts.

317 **Back in Chicago:** For background on Jenner, see *New York Times* obituary, June 25, 1974.

318 **Alfred Goldberg recalled:** Goldberg interviews, Specter interviews, Slawson interviews.

318 **If there was any:** Memo from Ely to Jenner and Liebeler, March 9, 1964, staff files, Warren Commission, NARA.

319 **Ely was next asked:** Memo from Ely to Jenner and Liebeler, "Lee Harvey Oswald's Military Career," April 22, 1964, staff files, Warren Commission, NARA.

321 **A Dallas homicide detective:** Testimony of Guy Rose, April 8, 1964, Warren Appendix, Vol. 7, pp. 227–31.

321 **"We were very close":** Testimony of George S. de Mohrenschildt, April 22, 1964, Warren Appendix, Vol. 9, pp. 166–264.

323 **"Mrs. Paine, are you":** Testimony of Ruth Hyde Paine, March 18, 1964, Warren Appendix, Vol. 2, pp. 430–517.

324 **"All sorts of speculation":** Testimony of George S. de Mohrenschildt, April 22, 1964, Warren Appendix, Vol. 9, pp. 166–264.

325 **The commission later determined:** Although Moore was not identified by name in the central volume of the commission's final report, apparently in deference to the CIA, his name does appear in the commission's internal paperwork and in the official public transcript of de Mohrenschildt's testimony.

CHAPTER 35

326 **They joked about:** Specter interviews; Specter memoir transcripts.

326 **Slawson, the staff lawyer:** Slawson interviews, Specter interviews.

327 **The FBI agent who attended:** Specter, *Passion*, pp. 83–84.

327 **"I don't think the commissioners":** Specter interviews.

329 **"I raised hell with Rankin":** Specter, *Passion*, p. 87; Specter interviews.

329 **The Kennedys, Belin said:** Belin, *You Are the Jury*, p. 347.

329 **"It wasn't a":** Specter interviews; Specter memoir transcripts.

329 **The memo, dated April 30:** Memo from Specter to Rankin, "Autopsy Photographs and X-Rays of President John F. Kennedy," April 30, 1964, staff files, Warren Commission, NARA.

330 **"The staff feels that":** Warren Commission Executive Session, April 30, 1964, pp. 5860–92.

333 **Thomas Kelley, the Secret Service:** Specter, *Passion*, pp. 88–89; Specter interviews.

333 **Back in Washington, Alfred:** Goldberg interviews.

CHAPTER 36

334 **In a speech on the House:** For Gurney quotations, see nationally syndicated column by Fulton Lewis Jr., as published in the *Lebanon Daily News*, Lebanon, Pennsylvania, May 8, 1964 (accessed through www.newspaperarchive.com).

334 **"It is absolutely":** See republication of *St. Louis Globe-Democrat* editorial in the *News Tribune* of Jefferson City, Missouri, May 10, 1964 (accessed through www.newspaperarchive.com).

335 **"The commission knows of no":** Eisenberg interviews.

335 **A script was prepared:** Undated copy of the script is found in the staff files, Warren Commission, NARA.

335 **The FBI's background:** For additional background, see obituary of Redlich in the *New York Times*, June 11, 2011.

336 **Eisenberg, as close to:** Eisenberg interviews, Slawson interviews.

336 **Redlich's wife, Evelyn:** Evelyn Redlich interview.

336 **Warren opened the meeting:** Warren Commission Executive Session, May 19, 1964.

340 **Redlich's gratitude was:** Griffin interview.

CHAPTER 37

341 **The phone rang:** Hosty interviews; Hosty, *Assignment: Oswald*, pp. 117–20.

343 **Hosty spent much of:** Hosty, *Assignment: Oswald*, pp. 139–56.

344 **"Did it occur":** Testimony of James Hosty, May 5, 1964, Warren Appendix, Vol. 4, pp. 440–76.

346 **On May 5, Rankin:** Letter from Rankin to Hoover, May 5, 1965, staff files, Warren Commission, NARA.

347 **On Thursday, May 14:** Testimony of J. Edgar Hoover, May 14, 1964, Warren Appendix, Vol. 5, pp. 97–119.

348 **That same day:** Testimony of John A. McCone and Richard M. Helms, May 14, 1964, Warren Appendix, Vol. 5, pp. 120–29.

348 **In Dallas, Hugh:** *Dallas Morning News*, June 27, 1964.

348 **Two weeks after:** *Life*, July 10, 1964.

348 **Slawson worried, in particular:** Memo from Slawson to Rankin, "Publication of Oswald's Historic Diary," September 6, 1964, staff files, Warren Commission, NARA.

349 **Life insisted:** *Life*, July 10, 1964.

349 **In a July 8:** Letter from Hart to Captain W. P. Gannaway of the Dallas police department, July 8, 1964, Dallas Municipal Archives, Office of the City Secretary.

350 **The statement was drawn:** Memo from DeLoach to Mohr, "Lee Harvey Oswald," August 24, 1964 (referring to interview with Ford on August 17, 1964), FBI.

350 **The truth:** Aynesworth interviews; Aynesworth, *November 22, 1963: Witness to History*, pp. 134–135.

CHAPTER 38

351 **"Warren was dead-set":** Specter interviews; Specter memoir transcripts.

352 **Specter got other welcome:** Warren Report, p. 95.

352 **The army's Edgewood Arsenal:** Olivier and Dziemian, *Wound Ballistics of 6.5-MM. Mannlicher-Carcano Ammunition*, May 1964, published by Edgewood Arsenal, Department of the Army, found in staff files, Warren Commission, NARA.

353 **Like his colleagues:** Specter interviews; Specter memoir transcripts.

353 **There was "frustration":** Letter from Belin to Willens, October 20, 1966, Belin correspondence files, Belin papers, Ford Library.

354 **"If she would":** Memo from Belin to Rankin, "Examination of Marina Oswald," January 29, 1964, staff files, Warren Commission, NARA.

355 **Belin thought it was:** Belin, *You Are the Jury*, pp. 431–33.

CHAPTER 39

357 **David Slawson knew:** Slawson interview.

357 **After consulting with:** Memo from Willens to Rankin, "Proposed Exchange of Letters," June 4, 1964, and memo from Willens to Katzenbach, "Proposed letters to the President's Commission," June 12, 1964, staff files, Warren Commission, NARA.

357 **Warren's letter:** Letter from Warren to Robert Kennedy, June 11, 1964, staff files, Warren Commission, NARA.

358 **Other than the attorney general:** Specter, *Passion*, pp. 120–22.

358   O'Donnell's account: Testimony of Kenneth P. O'Donnell, May 18, 1964, Warren Appendix, Vol. 7, pp. 440–57.

359   Specter guessed that O'Donnell: Specter, *Passion*, pp. 120–22.

360   In conversations behind: Ibid., p. 107.

360   Shortly after four p.m.: Testimony of Mrs. John F. Kennedy, June 5, 1964, Warren Appendix, Vol. 5, pp. 178–81.

361   "I'll share him": The quotation appeared in the original manuscript of Manchester's *Death*, but was cut out during negotiations in 1966 between Manchester and the Kennedy family. Manchester interviewed Ethel Kennedy in April 1964. See Thomas, *Robert Kennedy*, pp. 278, 451.

364   The transcript of: For a description of how the exact wording from the transcript was obtained through a Freedom of Information Act request by a Canadian filmmaker, see *Ottawa Citizen* (Ottawa, Canada), August 14, 2001.

CHAPTER 40

365   "I could smile at it": Oral history of Chief Justice Earl Warren, September 21, 1971, LBJ Library, p. 12. Also see Warren, *Memoirs*.

365   However reluctantly, Warren: Specter, *Passion*, pp. 105–8.

368   From the book depository: Ford report on trip and Ruby testimony, "Dallas Trip, June 7, 1964," as found in congressional correspondence files, Ford Library.

369   "As the Chief Justice": Specter, *Passion*, p. 112.

369   "Without a lie detector": Testimony of Jack Ruby, June 7, 1964, Warren Appendix, Vol. 5, pp. 181–213.

371   Down the hall: Specter interviews; Specter, *Passion*, p. 113.

372   Ford could see that: Ford report on trip, "Dallas Trip, June 7, 1964," as found in congressional correspondence files, Ford Library.

372   "You see," Tonahill: Specter, *Passion*, p. 114.

373   "Instead of turning left": Specter interviews; Specter memoir transcripts.

373   On the plane home: Specter, *Passion*, p. 115.

CHAPTER 41

374   The Bronx-born: See the *New York Times* obituary of Rowley, November 3, 1992.

374   Shortly after nine a.m.: Testimony of James Rowley, June 18, 1964, Warren Appendix, Vol. 5, pp. 449–85.

378   The department had not only: Warren Report, p. 113. The exact amount was $435.71.

378   Secretary of State Dean Rusk: See the *New York Times* obituary of Rusk, December 22, 1994.

378   "Rusk seemed to be": Slawson interviews.

378   Kennedy had chosen Rusk: Schlesinger, *A Thousand Days*, p. 435.

378   Jacqueline Kennedy told: Michael Beschloss, ed., *Jacqueline Kennedy: Historic Conversations on Life with John F. Kennedy*, p. 112.

380   After Rusk's testimony: Memo from Slawson to Rankin, "Subject: Taking Testimony of Remaining State Department Witnesses," June 12, 1964, staff files, Warren Commission, NARA.

CHAPTER 42

381   When FBI documents arrived: Eisenberg interviews, Slawson interviews, Griffin interviews.

382   On Wednesday, June 17: Letter from Hoover to Rankin, June 17, 1964, CIA, NARA. (This document appears in declassified files of the CIA, not in the paper files of the commission stored at the National Archives.)

382   If the information: In his letter, Hoover said that, according to Castro's account, Oswald had made the threat in "their embassy" and that it was "unclear" from the Cuban leader's remarks "whether he means Cuban or Russian Embassy." According to FBI officials who

have reviewed other documents involving the informant's encounter with Castro in 1964, the Cuban dictator was clearly referring to the Cuban embassy.

383 **Years later, the FBI would reveal:** Barron, *Operation Solo*, pp. 112–14. The FBI has declassified many of its internal documents involving Operation Solo, and they are available online at the FBI's Web site, http://vault.fbi.gov/solo.

383 **Former staff members:** After publication of this book in October 2013, Howard Willens, the Justice Department lawyer who helped direct the commission's staff, told the author that he had seen Hoover's letter in 1964 and that he was certain it had been shared with others on the staff. He said he had no explanation for why David Slawson and others were equally certain they had not seen it. Willens had declined to be interviewed by the author before this book's publication. In an article published on February 23, 1975 ("Data on Oswald Apparently Withheld from Key Warren Commission Aides"), the *New York Times* reported a similar instance in which Willens remembered seeing an FBI document about Oswald that Slawson and other staff members did not recall having seen. In an interview with the author of this book in May 2014, Willens denied any suggestion that he had hidden documents from other commission lawyers. In his 2013 book *The JFK Assassination Diary: My Search for Answers to the Mystery of the Century*, the author Edward Jay Epstein wrote that he had interviewed commission member John McCloy in June 1965 and that McCloy had said that Attorney General Robert Kennedy had placed "his own man, Howard Willens, on the staff, to deal with 'inappropriate revelations'" and that Willens had "locked away material in his desk." Epstein continued: "According to McCloy, Willens did not believe the staff had any need to see" material concerning "a 'national security issue' he was not free to discuss." The "national security issue" and the "inappropriate revelations" were not described further by McCloy. Willens told the author of this book that he had no idea what McCloy or Epstein were referring to. "I did not hide documents," he said in May 2014. "I do not recall that my desk had a drawer that locked. I know that I never had a key to any such drawer." He added that it was wrong for the author of this book to focus on discrepancies in the memories of former Warren Commission staff members about whether they saw certain documents in 1964: "I think relying on any single person's memory, including mine, about events some fifty years ago is not a sound practice. There is an extensive written record of our investigation, and our mistakes and accomplishments, without searching for conflicting memories among members of the staff on matters which today have virtually no importance."

384 **Phillips, a forty-one-year-old:** See the *New York Times* obituary of Phillips, July 10, 1988.

384 **He had two formal:** Testimony of David Atlee Phillips, April 25, 1998, HSCA.

384 **The Cuban embassy there:** Testimony of David Atlee Phillips, November 27, 1976, HSCA.

385 **The CIA was not authorized:** Phillips, *The Night Watch*, pp. 162–64.

385 **Before the assassination:** Testimony of David Atlee Phillips, November 27, 1976, HSCA, pp. 103–35.

386 **More significant, perhaps:** Testimony of David Atlee Phillips, April 25, 1978, HSCA, pp. 51–53.

387 **"I was one of the two case officers":** Morley, *Our Man*, p. 336. Also see Kaiser, *The Road to Dallas*, p. 288 (who reported that he had obtained the outline from Morley), and Anthony and Robbyn Summers, "The Ghosts of November," *Vanity Fair*, December 1994. The author obtained a copy from a source who insisted on anonymity.

CHAPTER 43

388 **William Coleman wrote nothing:** Coleman interviews.

388 **They had first been introduced:** Coleman, *Counsel*, p. 58.

390 **There was good:** After publication of this book in October 2013, the journalist Anthony Summers, author of the 1980 book *Conspiracy*, about the Kennedy assassination, reported

that Coleman had offered him a similar account in the mid-1990s and that it was mentioned in later editions of the book (with a new title, *Not in Your Lifetime*) over protests
from Coleman about its accuracy. Coleman offered the story to the author of this book in
on-the-record interviews, suggesting that he only now felt comfortable that the information be public.

390 **At Paul Weiss, Coleman began:** Coleman interviews; Coleman, *Counsel,* passim.

391 **When it came time:** Coleman, *Counsel,* p. 149.

391 **In 1952, Coleman finally:** Coleman, *Counsel,* passim.

392 **The leaks first went:** See the *New York Times* obituary for Lewis, March 25, 2013.

392 **Within days of the book's:** *New York Times,* June 1, 1964.

392 **Although it was impossible to identify:** Julia Eide phone and appointment logs for
Rankin, May 29, 1964, 2:00–2:40 p.m., staff files, Warren Commission, NARA.

393 **Warren immediately turned:** Warren Commission Executive Session, June 4, 1964.

393 **"She became a chain-smoker":** Manchester, *Death,* p. 635.

394 **Marina Oswald returned:** Testimony of Mrs. Lee Harvey Oswald, June 11, 1964, Warren
Appendix, Vol. 5, pp. 387–408.

395 **By Thursday, July 2:** Testimony of Mark Lane, July 2, 1964, Warren Appendix, Vol. 5, pp.
546–61.

CHAPTER 44

399 **"The Warren Commission was a":** Transcript of interview with Cavanaugh found in Fry,
Hunting and Fishing with Earl Warren, pp. 1–69. Available online through www. openli-
brary.org, http://openlibrary.org/books/OL7213177M/Hunting_and_fishing_with_Earl
_Warren.

400 **On May 29, the last Friday:** Testimony of Howard Willens, November 17, 1977, HSCA.

400 **"I share your view":** Letter from Warren to Carl L. Shipley, July 6, 1964, personal correspondence files, Warren papers, LOC.

401 **The Supreme Court:** *New York Times Co. v. Sullivan,* 376 U.S. 254; *Escobedo v. Illinois,* 378
U.S. 478.

401 **Warren said later that he:** Warren interview with Alfred Goldberg, March 26, 1974, as
found in Warren Commission files, Warren papers, LOC.

402 **Rankin reserved for himself:** Testimony of J. Lee Rankin, August 17, 1978, HSCA.

403 **But after meeting with:** Given the effects of inflation, $1 million in 1964 would equal
about $7.5 million in 2013.

404 **On May 12:** Laulicht interviews.

405 **Another late arrival:** Weinreb interviews.

407 **Before departing, he completed:** Memo from Mosk to Redlich, June 7, 1964, staff files,
Warren Commission, NARA.

407 **Mosk reviewed the testimony:** Testimony of Eugene D. Anderson, July 24, 1964, Warren
Appendix, Vol. 11, pp. 301–4.

407 **An FBI firearms:** Testimony of Robert A. Frazier, Warren Appendix, Vol. 3, pp. 390–441,
and Vol. 5, pp. 58–74.

CHAPTER 45

408 **"It brought a lot of problems":** Testimony of Silvia Odio, July 22, 1964, Warren Appendix, Vol. 11, pp. 367–89.

409 **Her father, Amador:** *Dallas Morning News,* May 5, 1962.

409 **He turned in the ninety-eight:** Liebeler draft chapter, "Possible Personal Motive," June
23, 1964, staff files, Warren Commission, NARA.

410 **At the same time, it appeared:** Warren Report, pp. 407, 727–29.

410 **On August 5, the FBI determined:** Testimony of Carlos Bringuier, April 7–8, 1964, Warren
Appendix, Vol. 10, pp. 32–50.

411 **This included Dean Andrews:** Testimony of Dean Adams Andrews Jr., July 21, 1964, Warren Appendix, Vol. 11, pp. 325–39.

412 **Liebeler took what he thought of:** Testimony of Evaristo Rodriguez, July 21, 1964, Warren Appendix, Vol. 11, pp. 339–45.

412 **Liebeler remembered that in her:** Testimony of Silvia Odio, July 22, 1964, Warren Appendix, Vol. 11, p. 383.

CHAPTER 46

413 **The first documented case:** Memo from FBI Baltimore field office to FBI Headquarters "TO: DIRECTOR FBI, FROM SAC BALTIMORE, RE: ASSASSINATION OF PRESIDENT JOHN FITZGERALD KENNEDY," April 7, 1964, FBI. Also, memo from FBI Washington, DC, field office to FBI Headquarters, "TO DIRECTOR FBI, FROM SAC WFO," April 8, 1964, FBI.

413 **The FBI chief learned:** Memo from Belmont to Rosen ("Subject: James R. David, Information Concerning Security Violation"), June 9, 1964, FBI.

414 **And Hoover sent a personal:** Letter from Hoover to James R. David, June 9, 1964, FBI.

414 **Other staff lawyers said they:** Slawson interviews.

415 **He had slaved:** Testimony of Wesley J. Liebeler, November 13, 1977, HSCA.

415 **Ford passed his copy:** Memo from Fallon to Ford, July 31, 1964, congressional correspondence files, Ford Library.

415 **"We want to ask you":** Testimony of Silvia Odio, July 22, 1964, Warren Appendix, Vol. 11, pp. 367–89.

415 **She handed him a one-page:** Letter from Hoover to Rankin, August 7, 1964, staff files, Warren Commission, NARA.

416 **What happened in Dallas:** Notes by HSCA investigator Gaeton Fonzi from his interview with Silvio Odio, January 16, 1976, staff files, HSCA, RIF: 180–10001–10132, NARA.

418 **He announced that he had tried:** Slawson interviews; staff interviews with other staff members on condition of anonymity.

CHAPTER 47

419 **"I would like to ask you":** Testimony of Abraham Zapruder, July 22, 1964, Warren Appendix, Vol. 7, pp. 569–76.

420 **Years later, *Life* would:** *Los Angeles Times*, August 4, 1999.

420 **Richard B. Stolley, *Life*'s:** Richard Stolley, "Shots Seen Round the World," *Entertainment Weekly*, January 17, 1992.

420 **Walker, an outspoken:** See the *New York Times* obituary of Walker, November 2, 1993.

420 **"I was sitting behind":** Testimony of Major General Edwin A. Walker, July 23, 1964, Warren Appendix, Vol. 11, pp. 404–28.

421 **Specter was annoyed:** Specter interviews; Specter memoir transcripts.

422 **"That will conclude":** Testimony of Jack Ruby, July 18, 1964, Warren Report, pp. 807–13.

422 **The combined lists were:** Specter interviews; Specter, *Passion*, pp. 116–17.

423 **The commission had not been:** Report of interview with Captain W. B. Frazier by FBI Special Agents James W. Bookhout and George W. H. Carlson in Dallas, December 7, 1963, FBI; Letter from Hoover to Rankin, July 30, 1964, staff files, Warren Commission, NARA.

CHAPTER 48

425 **"There is no other way":** Letter from Belin to Willens, August 25, 1964, staff files, Warren Commission, NARA.

426 **"I have been led":** Warren Commission Executive Session, June 23, 1964.

427 **A copy was uncovered decades:** Summary was found in J. Lee Rankin papers donated to the National Archives in 1999, box 22, folder 350, Warren Commission, NARA.

427 **David Slawson urged one last:** Memo from Slawson to Rankin and Willens, "Re: Possible Medical Testimony on Oswald," June 2, 1964, staff files, Warren Commission, NARA.

428 **He was not surprised:** Memo from Pollak to Rankin, "Subject: Comments on Volumes 1–4, 6, 7," June 18, 1964, staff files, Warren Commission, NARA.

428 **He asked that "the words":** Memo from Rankin to Willens, August 17, 1964, staff files, Warren Commission, NARA.

429 **In a brief note to the commission:** Memo from Rankin to Stern, June 30, 1964, staff files, Warren Commission, NARA.

CHAPTER 49

430 **The Polish man looked:** *New York Times*, June 30, 1964.

431 **Kennedy literally wrapped:** See Thomas, *Robert Kennedy*, pp. 282, 333.

432 **Kennedy had been aware:** Church Committee report, "Alleged Assassination Plots Involving Foreign Leaders," November 20, 1975, pp. 98, 126–34.

432 **The CIA's inspector general:** Ibid., pp. 88–89.

433 **In June 1964:** Associated Press, October 12, 2012.

433 **In the spring of 1964:** Schlesinger, *Robert Kennedy*, pp. 649, 615. Also, Califano interview.

434 **"What do I do?":** Thomas, *Robert Kennedy*, p. 284. Based on memo from Justice Department aide Harold Reis to the attorney general, June 12, 1964.

434 **"I would like to state":** Letter from Kennedy to Warren, August 4, 1964, staff files, Warren Commission, NARA.

CHAPTER 50

436 **"Mrs. Odio's reliability":** Letter from Rankin to Hoover, July 24, 1964, staff files, Warren Commission, NARA.

437 **Hoover wrote back:** Letter from Hoover to Rankin, August 12, 1964, staff files, Warren Commission, NARA.

437 **"It is a matter of some importance":** Letter from Rankin to Hoover, August 23, 1964, staff files, Warren Commission, NARA.

437 **The commission's request:** Hosty interviews.

438 **After the magazine the *Nation*:** Hoover's handwritten note found on cable from Dallas field office to FBI headquarters, "TO DIRECTOR FBI, FROM DALLAS," March 14, 1964, FBI.

439 **"This fellow is just a low":** Hoover's handwritten note found on memo from FBI Dallas field office to Sullivan, February 13, 1964, FBI.

439 **After an incident:** Hoover's handwritten note on a letter from Rankin to Hoover, March 3, 1964, FBI.

439 **In March, a top Hoover aide:** Hoover's handwritten notes on memo from Branigan to Sullivan, "RE: LEE HARVEY OSWALD INTERNAL SECURITY," March 3, 1964, FBI.

439 **He said in a later memo:** Memo from Rosen to Belmont, March 16, 1964. Also see memo from Rosen to Belmont, "Subject: President's Commission," April 4, 1964, FBI.

440 **Hoover seemed to be:** Hoover's handwritten notes on memo from Jevons to Conrad, "RE: ASSASSINATION OF PRESIDENT JOHN F. KENNEDY," March 12, 1964, FBI.

440 **"I place no credence":** Hoover's handwritten notes on memo from Rosen to Belmont, "Subject: President's Commission," April 4, 1964, FBI.

440 **"I want to let you know":** Letter from Hoover to Ford, April 17, 1964, FBI.

441 **DeLoach asked for a background check:** Memo from DeLoach to Mohr, April 22, 1964, FBI.

441 **Hoover gave in and agreed to the interview:** Memo from DeLoach to Mohr, "Subject: William Manchester, Author of Kennedy Book," June 4, 1964, FBI.

CHAPTER 51

443 **He worked from his:** See the *New York Times* obituary for McCloy, March 12, 1989. For background on One Chase Manhattan Plaza, see *New York Times*, June 6, 2013.

443 **But it was possible:** Letter from McCloy to Rankin, July 21, 1964, staff files, Warren Commission, NARA.

445 **David Slawson had written:** Slawson interviews.

445 **If Odio's allegations:** Unsigned draft chapter entitled "Foreign Conspiracy," July 15, 1964, staff files, Warren Commission, NARA. Also see undated memo from Coleman and Slawson to Rankin, "Subject: Suggested Changes in the Foreign Conspiracy [*sic*], Dated July 15, 1964," staff files, Warren Commission, NARA.

445 **The staff settled:** Warren Report, p. 305.

445 **"I did trust the CIA":** Coleman interviews.

445 **"According to his twenty-five":** Coleman memo, "Oswald's Trip to Mexico City September 26, 1963, to October 3, 1963," July 20, 1964, staff files, Warren Commission, NARA.

446 **Arlen Specter felt:** Specter interviews. Also see Specter, *Passion*, passim.

446 **After reading through:** Letter from McCloy to Rankin, June 24, 1964, staff files, Warren Commission, NARA.

447 **On August 20, he sent:** Letter and memo from Cooper to Rankin, August 20, 1964, staff files, Warren Commission, NARA

447 **"The evidence of the source":** Letter from Belin to Rankin, July 7, 1964, staff files, Warren Commission, NARA

448 **"We made every effort":** Belin, *Final Disclosure*, pp. 213–16. Also see Belin, *You Are the Jury*, pp. 425–40.

449 **Alfred Goldberg was stunned:** Goldberg interviews.

450 **FBI agents who visited:** Memo from the FBI's Washington field office to FBI headquarters, "SAC WFO TO DIRECTOR, FBI RE: LEE HARVEY OSWALD," September 17, 1964, FBI. Also see memo from Rosen to Belmont, "SUBJECT: LEE HARVEY OSWALD," September 21, 1964, FBI.

451 **As part of his research:** Goldberg interviews.

452 **The *New York Times*, the *Washington Post*:** *New York Times* and *Washington Post*, November 26, 1963.

452 **In July, Barson said he:** Memo from Barson and Mosk to Rankin, July 9, 1964, staff files, Warren Commission, NARA.

452 **After figuring that he had spent:** Griffin interviews.

453 **"I think it is a mistake":** Memo from Griffin to Willens, "Re: Memo on Ruby Conspiracy Portion of Chapter VI," August 14, 1964, staff files, Warren Commission, NARA.

CHAPTER 52

454 **His wife, Evelyn, recalled:** Evelyn Redlich interview.

455 **"Every once in a while":** Weinreb interviews.

455 **Liebeler's battles with Redlich:** Testimony of Wesley Liebeler, HSCA, November 15, 1977, pp. 209–61.

456 **Rankin sided with Liebeler:** Memo from Liebeler to Rankin, August 28, 1964, staff files, Warren Commission, NARA. Also see Liebeler testimony, HSCA, November 15, 1977, passim.

457 **In late August:** Memo from Liebeler to Willens and Redlich, "Subject: Conspiracy," August 27, 1964, staff files, Warren Commission, NARA.

457 **He was startled by the news:** Memo to Rankin from Hoover, September 3, 1964, staff files, Warren Commission, NARA. Also see memo from Liebeler to Willens, "Re: Relevant Property Remaining in Possession of Marina Oswald," September 2, 1964, staff files, Warren Commission, NARA.

457 **There would be little:** Liebeler memo, "Memorandum re: Galley Proofs of Chapter IV," September 6, 1964, staff files, Warren Commission, NARA.

458 **"There really was no response":** Testimony of Wesley Liebeler, HSCA, November 15, 1977, pp. 209–61.

459 **He described the Senate vote:** Associated Press, June 18, 1964.

459 **"Violence and defiance":** Fite, *Richard B. Russell, Jr., Senator from Georgia*, p. 46.

460 **"Let me tell you again":** Letter from Russell to C. R. Nichols, June 30, 1964, correspondence files, Russell Library.

460 **In May, he had complained:** Holland, *The Kennedy Assassination Tapes*, p. 240.

460 **He read through:** *Atlanta Constitution*, September 28, 1964.

460 **Russell's former press secretary:** Interview with Powell A. Moore, "Oral History Interview #7," March 6, 1971, Russell Library.

461 **The chief justice:** Interview of Barboura G. Raesly, "Oral History Interview #157," June 16, 1974, Russell Library.

461 **The *Dallas Morning News*:** *Dallas Morning News*, September 7, 1964.

461 **Russell focused his questions:** Testimony of Marina Oswald, September 6, 1964, Warren Appendix, Vol. 5, pp. 588–620.

463 **The investigation was only just:** Handwritten note by Russell on United States Senate notepaper, December 5, 1963, personal files, Russell Library.

463 **In mid-September:** Draft dissent by Russell, "Assassination Commission," September 16, 1964, Russell Library.

464 **The news arrived on September 21:** Letter from Hoover to Rankin, September 21, 1964, staff files, Warren Commission, NARA.

464 **David Slawson, who had pressed:** Slawson interviews.

465 **"In spite of the fact":** Warren Report, pp. 322–24.

465 **Over time, Loran Hall:** Testimony of Loran Hall, October 5 and 6, 1977, HSCA, RIF: 180–10118–10115, NARA.

465 **FBI agents in Dallas:** See Appendix to Hearings, Vol. 10, "Anti-Castro Activities and Organizations," March 1979, HSCA, pp. 19–35.

CHAPTER 53

466 **The final contract:** "Publishing Agreement between Simon and Schuster and Gerald R. Ford," October 9, 1964, Warren Commission files, Ford Library. The entire contract and other paperwork related to the book are found at the Ford Library.

467 **Simon and Schuster decided:** "Editorial Department Report, Simon and Schuster," July 29, 1964, Warren Commission files, Ford Library.

467 **"Got Jerry Ford on the telephone":** Letter from Thompson to Peter Schwed, Simon and Schuster executive, July 8, 1964, Warren Commission files, Ford Library.

468 **That summer, it was:** *New York Times*, July 7, 1964.

468 **In a memo on July 31:** Memo from Fallon to Ford, July 3, 1964, Warren Commission files, Ford Library.

468 **Ford's friend Stiles:** Memo from Stiles to Ford, September 4, 1964, Warren Commission files, Ford Library.

468 **In May, a reporter:** Ford's handwritten notes, "Gene Roberts, *Detroit Free Press*, 5/9/64," Warren Commission files, Ford Library.

469 **"The FBI did a very substantial piece":** *New York Times*, February 23, 1967.

469 **By the end of the investigation:** Ford, *Portrait*, pp. 53–60.

470 **The timelines showed:** Ibid., pp. 335, 483, 301–14, 90–99.

471 **Ford guessed that Oswald:** Interview of Gerald R. Ford, "Oral History Interview by Vicki Daitch," July 18, 2003, JFK Library.

471 **On September 2, he wrote:** Letter from Ford to Rankin, September 2, 1964, staff files, Warren Commission, NARA.

472　The draft had originally said: Associated Press, July 2, 1997.

472　Decades later, a congressionally: Testimony of Dr. Michael Baden, September 17, 1978, HSCA.

473　"It would have been disastrous": Pearson Diaries, October 1966, Pearson papers, LBJ Library.

473　"When the word": Warren, *Memoirs*, p. 3.

474　"Warren just wouldn't": Interview of Barboura G. Raesly, "Oral History Interview #157," June 16, 1974, Russell Library.

475　Although it is not necessary: Warren Report, p. 19.

475　"Rankin made an effort": Proposal by Howard Willens for a book to be entitled *The Assassination*, undated. Willens announced in 2013 that he planned to write a book about his experiences on the Warren Commission, with a new title: *History Will Prove Us Right: Inside the Warren Commission Investigation into the Assassination of John F. Kennedy*.

476　"The FBI took an unduly": Warren Report, p. 24.

476　The Secret Service: Ibid., p. 26.

476　"It is conceivable": Ibid., p. 451.

476　From his reading of the findings: Article submitted by Ford to the California State Chamber of Commerce, "Why the President Died," December 30, 1964, Warren Commission files, Ford Library. The article was based on a speech that Ford had given to the chamber.

477　The only official record: Warren Commission Executive Session, September 18, 1964, NARA.

CHAPTER 54

478　President Johnson wanted: Holland, *The Kennedy Assassination Tapes*, pp. 247–51

480　"I just worked like a dog": Slawson interviews.

480　John McCloy said he was: Interview of John McCloy, "*Face the Nation*, July 2, 1967," CBS News.

481　To no one's surprise: "The Warren Commission," Appendix to Hearings, Vol. 11, March 1979 HSCA, p. 78.

481　Warren said later he refused: Pearson Diaries, October 1966, Pearson papers, LBJ Library.

481　The staff lawyers said they were: Letter from Oscar Collier to the commission, August 14, 1964, staff files, Warren Commission, NARA.

482　Like her daughter-in-law: *Esquire*, May 1964.

482　"It's pretty heavy": *New York Times*, September 25, 1964.

482　"We ended up with 26 witnesses": Ibid.

483　The headline in the *New York Times*: *New York Times*, September 28, 1964.

483　*Time* magazine was also: *Time*, October 2, 1964.

484　"The central mystery of who": *New York Times*, September 28, 1964.

484　On the day of the release: Ibid.

484　At his request, his surviving brother: Kennedy, Edward M., *True Compass: A Memoir*, pp. 211–212.

485　The polls showed that after: *Public Perspective*, October–November 1998.

485　Congressman Boggs: *National Observer*, October 5, 1964.

485　He gave an interview: *Atlanta Constitution*, September 27, 1964.

485　Hoover attached a note: Hoover's handwritten note on memo from DeLoach to Mohr, "Subject: THE PRESIDENT'S COMMISSION," September 25, 1964, FBI.

486　Gale said it was: Memo from Gale to Tolson, "Subject: SHORTCOMINGS IN HANDLING LEE HARVEY OSWALD MATERIAL BY FBI PERSONNEL," September 30, 1964, FBI.

486　"I think we are making": Memo from Belmont to Tolson, October 1, 1964, FBI.

486 **"We were wrong":** Hoover's handwritten note on memo from Belmont to Tolson, October 1, 1964, FBI.

486 **In a separate note:** Hoover's handwritten note on memo from DeLoach to Mohr, "SUBJECT: CRITICISM OF THE FBI," October 6, 1964, FBI.

487 **Hoover complained that the report:** Letter from Hoover to Walter Jenkins, Special Assistant to the President, September 30, 1964, FBI.

487 **Hoover's office instructed:** Memo from Rosen to Belmont, "SUBJECT: PRESIDENT'S COMMISSION," October 2, 1964, FBI.

487 **After reading a flattering:** *Washington Post*, September 29, 1964.

487 **On October 2, Hoover's office:** Memo from Rosen to Belmont, "SUBJECT: PRESIDENT'S COMMISSION," October 2, 1964, FBI.

488 **The files "contain considerable":** Letter from Hoover to Rankin, October 23, 1964, staff files, Warren Commission, NARA.

488 **He told Hoover that the:** Letter from Rankin to Hoover, November 18, 1964, staff files, Warren Commission, NARA.

489 **On December 7, after all:** Memo from Eide to Rankin, December 7, 1964, staff files, Warren Commission, NARA.

CHAPTER 55

495 **"All Headquarters components":** "SILVIA TIRADO BOZAN DE DURAN," undated, Russ Holmes Work File, CIA, RIF: 104–10404–10123. See also "Mexico City Chronology," undated, CIA, RIF: 104–10086–10001, NARA.

495 **The report, dated October 5:** "MEXICAN COMMUNISTS WHO HAD CONTACT WITH OSWALD," October 5, 1964, CIA, RIF: 104–10404–10332. Also see "SILVIA TIRADO BOZAN DE DURAN," undated, Russ Holmes Work File, CIA, RIF: 104–10404–10123; "Mexico City Chronology," updated, CIA, RIF: 104–10086–10001. June Cobb was identified as the informant by the House Select Committee on Assassinations in its "Report on Lee Harvey Oswald's Trip to Mexico City" by staff members Dan Hardway and Edwin Lopez, undated, HSCA, RIF: 180–10110–10484 (hereafter Lopez Report, as it was known by House staff members).

497 **There had been about thirty:** Memo by Legal Attaché FBI, "Lee Harvey Oswald," December 11, 1964, RIF: 104–10404–10330.

498 **It was not clear from Scott's files:** also "Mexico City Chronology," updated, CIA, RIF: 104–10086–10001, NARA. The note by the author of the chronology in reference to this material: "WHY WAS THIS NOT SENT TO HQ??"

498 **The thirty-year-old Epstein:** Epstein, *Inquest*, p. 3.

499 **Asked by Epstein how much:** Ibid., p. 20.

500 **Epstein would recall:** "Wesley Liebeler: The File Keeper, June 30, 1965," essay available on Epstein's Web site: http://edwardjayepstein.com/liebeler.htm.

500 **Before publication, Epstein:** *New York Times*, April 24, 1966.

501 **In his introduction:** Epstein, *Inquest*, pp. ix–xiv.

501 **Inquest would be remembered:** *New York Times*, July 6, 1966.

501 **Albert Jenner, who already:** Letter from Jenner to Belin, July 13, 1966, Belin's Warren Commission files, Ford Library.

502 **"Frankly," he wrote:** Letter from Redlich to Andrew Hacker, Cornell University, June 2, 1966, as attached to letter from Redlich to Belin, July 15, 1966, Belin's Warren Commission files, Ford Library.

502 **He described:** In an email exchange with the author in 2013, Epstein said that despite Liebeler's reported complaints about *Inquest*, the two men remained in contact and that he "saw Liebeler many times after publication of my book." Asked about criticism of his book by other members of the commission's staff, Epstein said that he would "fully dis-

cuss the background of my investigation" in his "assassination diary," which he said was scheduled for publication in September 2013.

502 **Richard Goodwin, a former Kennedy:** *New York Times*, July 24, 1966.

502 **He appeared startled in late June:** *New York Times*, July 1, 1966.

502 **The *New York Times* said that:** *New York Times*, August 16, 1966.

503 **After the commission, David Slawson:** Slawson interviews.

503 **Slawson was also disappointed:** See *Denver Post* obituary of Dolan, September 5, 2008.

505 **Charles Thomas and his wife:** Cynthia Thomas interviews.

506 **"Charles was an extraordinary man":** Poniatowska interview.

506 **He recorded Garro's account:** Copies of Thomas's memos were obtained from his widow, Cynthia. Copies are also found in the archives of the House Select Committee on Assassinations, NARA.

507 **Garro tried to remember:** Lopez Report, p. 225.

508 **Ferris sent a memo:** Memo from Ferris to Freeman, "INTERVIEW WITH MRS. ELENA GARRO DE PAZ," December 27, 1965, as found in CIA report entitled "SILVIA TIRADO BOZAN DE DURAN," undated, Russ Holmes Work File, CIA, RIF: 104-10404-10123.

508 **One of his deputies:** Cable to CIA Mexico City to CIA, "CABLE RE; LEGAL ATTACHE MEXI INTERVIEW ELENA GARRO DE PAZ," December 29, 1965, CIA, RIF: 104-10404-10320, NARA.

CHAPTER 56

509 **Johnson was outraged:** *Washington Post*, October 3, 1966.

509 **"Lou Harris is just owned":** Holland, *The Kennedy Assassination Tapes*, pp. 312–13.

510 **After being permitted to read:** *New York Times*, December 17, 1966.

510 **Manchester's book was not:** "A Clash of Camelots," *Vanity Fair*, October 2009.

511 **"I can't be in the position":** Pearson Diaries, October 1966, Pearson papers, LBJ Library.

511 **In January 1967:** Pearson Diaries, January 1967, Pearson papers, LBJ Library.

512 **Morgan said he agonized:** Testimony of Edward P. Morgan, March 19, 1976, Church Committee, RIF: 157-10011-10040.

512 **Warren, he said, "was decidedly":** Pearson Diaries, January 1967, Pearson papers, LBJ Library.

512 **The meeting took place:** Testimony of James J. Rowley, February 13, 1976, Church Committee, RIF: 157-10014-10011.

513 **"Lyndon listened carefully":** Pearson Diaries, January 1967, Pearson papers, LBJ Library.

513 **On Monday, February 20:** Holland, *The Kennedy Assassination Tapes*, pp. 389–98.

514 **On March 1, 1967:** *New York Times*, March 2, 1967.

514 **WASHINGTON—President Johnson:** Washington Merry-Go-Round, March 3, 1967, available in the Drew Pearson archives maintained by American University. The actual column can be found at: http://dspace.wrlc.org/doc/bitstream/2041/53102/b20f02-0303zdisplay.pdf#search=".

515 **Pearson was unhappy:** Pearson Diaries, March 1967, Pearson papers, LBJ Library.

515 **On March 6:** "Central Intelligence Agency's Intentions to Send Hoodlums to Cuba to Assassinate Castro," March 6, 1967, FBI, as cited in "SUMMARY OF FACTS: INVESTIGATION OF CIA INVOLVEMENT IN PLOTS TO ASSASSINATE FOREIGN LEADERS," undated, found in the staff files of Richard Cheney, White House chief of staff in the Ford administration, Ford Library. The document is available online at the Ford Library Web site: http://www.fordlibrarymuseum.gov/library/document/0005/7324009.pdf.

515 **In April, President Johnson:** Pearson Diaries, April 1967, Pearson papers, LBJ Library.

515 **"We had been operating":** *New York Times*, June 17, 1973.

516 **He regretted he had been:** Testimony of J. Lee Rankin, September 21, 1978, HSCA. Also see Executive Session Deposition of J. Lee Rankin, August 17, 1978, HSCA.

516 **John Whitten, the veteran CIA:** Whitten House Testimony, May 16, 1978. Also see Whitten Senate Testimony, May 7, 1976.

517 **"It never occurred to me":** Helms House Testimony, September 22, 1978.

517 **By January 1967:** Aynesworth interviews.

517 **"I keep running into your name":** Aynesworth, *JFK: Breaking*, p. 232.

518 **The CIA figured:** Phelan, *Scandals, Scamps, and Scoundrels*, pp. 150–51.

518 **"You're lucky you're in town":** Aynesworth, *JFK: Breaking*, p. 234.

518 **Garrison's other prosecution:** Ibid., p. 235.

518 **Hounded by the district attorney's offices:** *New York Times*, February 23, 1967.

519 **"I hope *Newsweek*":** Aynesworth, *JFK: Breaking*, p. 244.

519 **On March 1, 1969:** *New York Times*, March 2, 1967.

CHAPTER 57

520 **This time, it would be much harder:** Cable from Scott to Chief, Western Hemisphere Division, CIA, "The LIRING/3 Operation," June 13, 1978, CIA, RIF: 104–10437–10102.

521 **The Garrison investigation of the Kennedy:** Letter from Thomas W. Lund, CIA, to Scott, "LETTER: AS YOU ARE AWARE, THE GARRISON INVESTIGATION OF THE KENNEDY ASSASSINATION HAS PROMPTED A RASH OF SPECTACULAR ALLEGATIONS AND CHARGES," June 14, 1967, CIA, RIF: 104–10247–10418, NARA.

522 **The fact that Silvia DURAN:** Cable from Scott to Chief, Western Hemisphere Division, CIA, "The LIRING/3 Operation," June 13, 1978, CIA, RIF: 104–10437–10102.

522 **In May 1967, an American diplomat:** Letter from Benjamin Ruyle, U.S. Consulate, Tampico, to Wesley Boles, Department of State, May 11, 1967, CIA, RIF: 104–10433–10011.

523 **He told the editor:** Letter from Scott to John Barron, *Reader's Digest*, November 25, 1970, found in "INFORMATION FOR HSCA FROM WIN SCOTT'S PERSONAL FILE," HSCA, RIF: 1993.08.12.15:08:41:650024.

523 **Scott's initial title:** "Ye looked for much and lo, it came to little," *Haggai* 1:9.

523 **He eventually settled on a different title:** Morley, *Our Man*, p. 276.

524 **"If I became president, I would not":** *Los Angeles Times*, March 25, 1968. Also see United Press International, March 25, 1968.

524 **The assassination had immediate ramifications:** Newton, *Justice for All*, p. 490.

525 **He granted an extended, tape-recorded:** Warren interview with Alfred Goldberg, March 26, 1974, found in Warren Commission files, Warren papers, LOC.

525 **On July 9, at the age:** *New York Times*, July 10, 1974.

526 **After a fierce, internal battle:** *New York Times*, April 29, 1970; *Washington Post*, April 28, 1970.

526 **Joseph Califano, his domestic policy aide:** Califano interview. See also Califano, *Inside: A Public and Private Life*, pp. 124–27.

527 **Cynthia Thomas was more shocked:** Thomas interviews.

527 **"A careful investigation":** Copies of Thomas's memos were made available by his widow, Cynthia. Copies are also found in the archives of the House Select Committee on Assassinations, NARA.

527 **A month later, on August 28:** Letter from Bert M. Benningham, State Department, to Deputy Director Plans, CIA, August 28, 1969, as found in "CHARLES THOMAS," undated, CIA, RIF: 1993.06.22.19:24:22:430330.

528 **SUBJECT; Charles William Thomas:** Memo from Angleton to Deputy Assistant Secretary of State, "SUBJECT; Charles William Thomas," September 16, 1969, CIA, RIF: 1993.08.11.19:02:46:030031.

528 **Angleton's name meant:** Thomas interviews.

528 **He tried, but failed:** A handful of conspiracy theorists have tried to suggest that Charles Thomas himself worked for the CIA, operating undercover in the guise of a State Depart-

ment employee. Thomas's personnel records, however, make clear that he was a Foreign Service officer. The allegation that he worked for the spy agency is undermined by long-classified testimony of others who worked in the Mexico City embassy, notably Anne Goodpasture, Win Scott's deputy, who readily identified her CIA colleagues in the embassy by name, making clear that Thomas was not among them. The reports of CIA efforts to harm Thomas's reputation in Mexico would also strongly argue against any idea that he worked for the agency.

528 **Even though the State Department:** Thomas's handwritten notes, as found in the "KEN-NEDY" file in his briefcase. Cynthia Thomas granted the author access to the file and other material.

529 **On April 12, 1971:** Death certificate, District of Columbia Department of Health.

531 **Cynthia Thomas' campaign:** *Washington Post*, December 12, 1973.

531 **In January 1975, Congress provided:** "Private Bill for the Relief of Charles William Thomas," January 2, 1975, 93.18-JAN. 2 1975.

531 **"There are no words":** Letter from Ford to Cynthia Thomas, January 2, 1975. Cynthia Thomas provided a copy of Ford's letter to the author.

531 **Two weeks after Thomas's suicide:** Morley, *Our Man*, pp. 256–57.

532 **Within hours, she said:** Testimony of Ann [*sic*] Goodpasture, November 20, 1978, HSCA, RIF: 180–10110–10028.

532 **"I was appointed as an official":** Testimony of James Angleton, October 5, 1978, HSCA, RIF: 180–10110–10006.

533 **Scott had assured the commission:** "CHAPTER XXIV FROM DRAFT MANUSCRIPT OF 'THE FOUL FOE,'" CIA, RIF: 1993.08.12.15:27:41:250024, NARA.

534 **Over the next two years:** Lopez Report, pp. 90–100.

534 **On the list of Scott's informants:** "CALVILLO, MANUEL (LICHANT-1)," undated, CIA, RIF: 104–10174–10067.

CHAPTER 58

535 **In February 1975:** Slawson interviews.

536 **Whitten testified to congressional investigators:** Whitten House Testimony.

536 **Slawson ended his silence:** *New York Times*, February 23, 1975; Slawson interviews.

538 **In Washington that summer:** See *New York Times* obituary of Kelley, August 6, 1997.

538 **"We are truly sorry":** *Washington Post*, May 9, 1976.

539 **That July, Tom Johnson:** Johnson interviews.

540 **It took little time:** Kelley and Davis, *Kelley: The Story of an FBI Director*, pp. 249–97.

542 **In memoirs published in 1979:** Sullivan, William, and Bill Brown, *The Bureau: My Thirty Years in Hoover's FBI*, p. 51.

AUTHOR'S NOTE

543 **Then in retirement:** Interview of Thomas C. Mann, November 29, 1977, HSCA, RIF: 180–10142–10357, NARA.

544 **"He was so firmly committed":** Deposition of Raymond C. Rocca, July 17, 1978, HSCA.

545 **Since his death, he has become:** *The Good Shepherd* (2006), http://www.imdb.com/title/tt0343737/.

546 **Here is speculation:** Letter from Hoover to Rankin, June 17, 1964, FBI, RIF: 104–10095–10412, NARA.

547 **There is another eye-popping:** "Mexico City Chronology," undated, CIA, RIF: 104–10086–10001, NARA.

547 **In November 1959, a month:** "MISCELLANEOUS ISSUES—HTLINGUAL INDEX CARDS," December 26, 1976, HSCA, RIF: 180–10142–10334, NARA. For the definitive account of Oswald's surveillance by HT-LINGUAL program, see Newman, *Oswald and the CIA*, pp. 52–57. Also see Martin, *Wilderness*, pp. 68–72.

550 **If anyone doubted:** *Dallas Morning News*, January 13, 2013; *Washington Post*, January 13, 2013.

551 **Through a cousin who serves:** Ruben Garro interviews.

552 **She denied, as she had:** Silvia Duran interview.

553 **Lidia is eighty-five:** Lidia Duran Navarro interviews.

554 **The first, Oscar Contreras:** Contreras interviews.

554 **Guerrero, now seventy-three:** Guerrero interviews.

Bibliography

BOOKS

Anson, Robert Sam. *"They've Killed the President!" The Search for the Murderers of John F. Kennedy*. New York: Bantam Books, 1975.

Arévalo, Juan José. *The Shark and the Sardines*. New York: Lyle Stuart, 1961.

Aynesworth, Hugh. *JFK: Breaking the News*. Richardson, TX: International Focus Press, 2003.

———. *November 22, 1963: Witness to History*. Dallas, TX: Brown Books, 2013.

Baden, Michael M., M.D. *Unnatural Death: Confessions of a Medical Examiner*. New York: Random House, 1989.

Bagley, Tennent H. *Spy Wars: Moles, Mysteries and Deadly Games*. New Haven, CT: Yale University Press, 2007.

Barron, John. *Operation Solo: The FBI's Man in the Kremlin*. Washington, DC: Regnery Publishing, 1995.

Belin, David. *Final Disclosure: The Full Truth About the Assassination of President Kennedy*. New York: Charles Scribner's Sons, 1988.

———. *November 22, 1963; You Are the Jury*. New York: Quadrangle, 1973.

Belli, Melvin M., with Maurice C. Carroll. *Dallas Justice: The Real Story of Jack Ruby and His Trial*. New York: David McKay Company Inc., 1964.

Benson, Michael. *Who's Who in the JFK Assassination*. New York: Citadel Press, 1993.

Beschloss, Michael R. *Taking Charge: The Johnson White House Tapes, 1963–1964*. New York: Simon & Schuster, 1997.

Bird, Kai. *The Chairman: John J. McCloy and the Making of the American Establishment*. New York: Simon & Schuster, 1992.

Bishop, Jim. *The Day Kennedy Was Shot*. New York: Funk & Wagnalls, 1968.

Bissell, Richard. *Reflections of a Cold Warrior: From Yalta to the Bay of Pigs*. New Haven, CT: Yale University Press, 1996.

Blaine, Gerald, with Lisa McCubbin. *The Kennedy Detail*. New York: Gallery Books, 2010.

Blakey, G. Robert, and Richard N. Billings. *Fatal Hour: The Assassination of President Kennedy by Organized Crime*. New York: Times Books, 1992. (Also published as *The Plot to Kill the President*. New York: Berkley Books, 1992.)

Brennan, Howard L., and J. Edward Cherryholmes. *Eyewitness to History: As Seen by Howard Brennan*. Waco, TX: Texian Press, 1987.

Brinkley, Douglas. *Cronkite*. New York: HarperCollins, 2012.

————. *Gerald R. Ford*. New York: Times Books, 2007.

Brown, Joe E. Sr., and Diane Holloway, eds. *Dallas and the Jack Ruby Trial*. Lincoln, NE: Authors Choice Press, 2001.

Brownell, Herbert, and John P. Burke. *Advising Ike: The Memoirs of Howard Brownell*. Lawrence: University Press of Kansas, 1993.

Buchanan, Thomas G. *Who Killed Kennedy?* New York: G.P. Putnam, 1964. (Also published as *Who Killed Kennedy?* New York: MacFadden Books, 1965.)

Bugliosi, Vincent. *Reclaiming History: The Assassination of President John F. Kennedy*. New York: W. W. Norton & Company, 2007.

Burden, Wendy. *Dead End Gene Pool: A Memoir*. New York: Gotham Books, 2012.

Burleigh, Nina. *A Very Private Woman: The Life and Unsolved Murder of Presidential Mistress Mary Meyer*. New York: Bantam Books, 1998.

Califano, Joseph A. Jr. *Inside: A Public and Private Life*. New York: PublicAffairs, 2004.

Cannon, James. *Time and Chance: Gerald Ford's Appointment with History*. Ann Arbor: University of Michigan Press, 1998.

Caro, Robert A. *Master of the Senate*. New York: Alfred A. Knopf, 2002.

————. *The Passage of Power*. New York: Alfred A. Knopf, 2012.

Colby, William, and Peter Forbath. *Honorable Men: My Life in the CIA*. New York: Simon & Schuster, 1978.

Coleman, William T. Jr., and Donald T. Bliss. *Counsel for the Situation: Shaping the Law to Realize America's Promise*. Washington, DC: Brookings Institution Press, 2010.

Compston, Christine. *Earl Warren: Justice for All*. New York: Oxford University Press, 2011.

Connolly, John, and Mickey Herskowitz. *In History's Shadow: An American Odyssey*. New York: Hyperion, 1993.

Connally, Nellie, and Mickey Herskowitz. *From Love Field: Our Final Hours with President John F. Kennedy*. New York: Rugged Land, 2003.

Conot, Robert. *Justice at Nuremberg*. New York: Harper & Row, 1983.

Cornwell, Gary. *Real Answers: The True Story*. Spicewood, TX: Paleface Press, 1998.

Corry, John. *The Manchester Affair*. New York: G. P. Putnam's Sons, 1967.

Cray, Ed. *Chief Justice*. New York: Simon & Schuster, 1997.

Cronkite, Walter. *A Reporter's Life*. New York: Alfred A. Knopf, 1996.

Cypess, Sandra Messinger. *Uncivil Wars. Elena Garro, Octavio Paz, and the Battle for Cultural Memory*. Austin: University of Texas Press, 2012.

Dallek, Robert. *Lyndon B. Johnson: Portrait of a President*. New York: Oxford University Press, 2004.

————. *An Unfinished Life: John F. Kennedy*. Boston: Little, Brown, 2003.

Davison, Jean. *Oswald's Game*. New York: W. W. Norton & Company, 1983.

DeFrank, Thomas M. *Write It When I'm Gone: Remarkable Off-the-Record Conversations with Gerald R. Ford*. New York: G. P. Putnam's Sons, 2007.

DeLillo, Don. *Libra*. New York: Viking, 1988.

DeLoach, Cartha ("Deke"). *Hoover's FBI*. Washington, DC: Regnery Publishing, 1995.

DiEugenio, James and Lisa Pearse, eds. *The Assassinations: Probe Magazine on JFK, RFK, MLK and Malcolm X*. New York: Feral House, 2012.

Dulles, Allen. *The Craft of Intelligence*. New York: Signet Books, 1965.

Epstein, Edward Jay. *The Assassination Chronicles: Inquest, Counterplot and Legend*. New York: Carroll & Graf, 1992.

————. *Inquest: The Warren Commission and the Establishment of Truth*. New York: Bantam, 1966. (Also published as *Inquest: The Warren Commission and the Establishment of Truth*, New York: Viking, 1966.)

Feldstein, Mark. *Poisoning the Press: Richard Nixon, Jack Anderson, and the Rise of Washington's Scandal Culture*. New York: Farrar, Straus and Giroux, 2010.

Fenster, Mark. *Conspiracy Theories: Secrecy and Power in American Culture.* Minneapolis: University of Minnesota Press, 1999.

Fite, Gilbert C. *Richard B. Russell Jr., Senator from Georgia.* Chapel Hill: University of North Carolina Press, 1991.

Fonzi, Gaeton. *The Last Investigation: A Former Federal Investigator Reveals the Man Behind the Conspiracy to Kill JFK.* New York: Thunder's Mouth Press, 1994.

Ford, Gerald R. *A Time to Heal: The Autobiography of Gerald R. Ford.* New York: Harper and Row, 1979.

Ford, Gerald R., and John R. Stiles. *Portrait of the Assassin.* New York: Ballantine Books, 1965. (Also published as *Portrait of the Assassin,* New York: Simon & Schuster, 1965.)

Fox, Sylvan. *The Unanswered Questions about President Kennedy's Assassination.* New York: Award Books, 1965.

Fuhrman, Mark. *A Simple Act of Murder: November 22, 1963.* New York: William Morrow, 2006.

Gallagher, Mary Barelli. *My Life with Jacqueline Kennedy.* New York: Paperback Library, 1970.

Garrison, Jim. *On the Trail of the Assassins: My Investigation and Prosecution of the Murder of President Kennedy.* New York: Warner Books, 1988.

Gentry, Curt. *J. Edgar Hoover: The Man and the Secrets.* New York: W. W. Norton & Company, 1991.

Goldberg, Robert Alan. *Enemies Within: The Culture of Conspiracy In Modern America.* New Haven, CT: Yale University Press, 2001.

Goldsmith, John A. *Colleagues: Richard B. Russell and His Apprentice, Lyndon B. Johnson.* Macon, GA: Mercer University Press, 1998.

Groden, Robert J. *The Killing of a President.* New York: Viking Penguin, 1993

Grose, Peter. *Gentleman Spy: The Life of Allen Dulles.* New York: Houghton Mifflin, 1994.

Guthman, Edwin. *We Band of Brothers: A Memoir of Bobby Kennedy.* New York: Harper & Row, 1971.

Guthman, Edwin O., and Jeffrey Shulman, eds. *Robert Kennedy, in His Own Words.* New York: Bantam Books, 1988.

Helms, Richard, with William Hood. *A Look over My Shoulder: A Life in the Central Intelligence Agency.* New York: Random House, 2003.

Hersh, Seymour M. *The Dark Side of Camelot.* Boston: Little, Brown, 1997.

Hill, Clinton. *Mrs. Kennedy and Me: An Intimate Memoir.* New York: Gallery Books, 2012.

Hofstadter, Richard. *The Paranoid Style in American Politics.* New York: Alfred A. Knopf, 1965.

Holland, Max. *The Kennedy Assassination Tapes.* New York: Alfred A. Knopf, 2004.

Hosty, James, with Thomas Hosty. *Assignment: Oswald.* New York: Arcade Publishing, 1996.

Huffaker, Bob, and Bill Mercer, George Phenix, and Wes Wise. *When the News Went Live.* Lanham, MD: Taylor Trade Publishing, 2007.

Hurt, Henry. *Reasonable Doubt: An Investigation into the Assassination of John F. Kennedy.* New York: Holt, Rinehart & Winston, 1985.

Hutchinson, Dennis J. *The Man Who Once Was Whizzer White: A Portrait of Justice Byron R. White.* New York: Free Press, 1998.

Isaacson, Walter, and Evan Thomas. *The Wise Men.* New York: Simon & Schuster, 1986.

Joesten, Joachim. *Oswald: Assassin or Fall Guy?* New York: Marzani & Munsell, 1964.

Johnson, Lyndon Baines. *The Vantage Point: Perspectives of the Presidency, 1963–1969.* New York: Holt, Rinehart & Winston, 1971.

Kaiser, David. *The Road to Dallas: The Assassination of John F. Kennedy.* Cambridge, MA: Belknap Press of Harvard University Press, 2008.

Kantor, Seth. *The Ruby Cover-Up.* New York: Kensington Publishing, 1978.

———. *Who Was Jack Ruby?* New York: Everest House, 1978.

Kearns, Doris. *Lyndon Johnson & the American Dream.* New York: Signet, 1977.

Kelley, Clarence M., and James Kirkpatrick Davis. *Kelley: The Story of an FBI Director.* Kansas City, MO: Andrews McMeel Publishing, 1987.

Kelley, Kitty. *His Way: The Unauthorized Biography of Frank Sinatra.* New York: Bantam Books, 1986.

Kennedy, Edward M. *True Compass: A Memoir.* New York: Twelve, 2009.

Kennedy, Jacqueline (in conversation with Arthur M. Schlesinger Jr.). *Historic Conversations on Life with John F. Kennedy.* New York: HarperCollins, 2011.

Kessler, Ronald. *The Bureau: The Secret History of the FBI.* New York: St. Martin's Press, 2002.

Kirkwood, James. *American Grotesque: An Account of the Clay Shaw–Jim Garrison Affair in the City of New Orleans.* New York: Simon and Schuster, 1968.

Kluckhorn, Frank, and Jay Franklin. *The Drew Pearson Story.* Chicago: Chas. Halberg & Company, 1967.

Klurfeld, Herman. *Behind the Lines: The World of Drew Pearson.* Englewood Cliffs, NJ: Prentice-Hall, 1968.

Lambert, Patricia. *False Witness: The Real Story of Jim Garrison's Investigation and Oliver Stone's Film JFK.* New York: M. Evans and Company, 1998.

Lane, Mark. *Citizen Lane.* Chicago, Lawrence Hill Books, 2012.

———. *A Citizen's Dissent: Mark Lane Replies.* New York: Holt, Rinehart & Winston, 1968.

———. *Rush to Judgment.* New York: Holt, Rinehart & Winston, 1966.

Latrell, Brian. *After Fidel.* New York: Palgrave Macmillan, 2005.

———. *Castro's Secrets: The CIA and Cuba's Intelligence Machine.* New York: Palgrave Macmillan, 2012.

Lewis, Anthony. *Gideon's Trumpet.* New York: Random House, 1964.

Lewis, Richard Warren, and Lawrence Schiller. *The Scavengers and Critics of the Warren Report.* New York: Dell, 1967.

Lifton, Davis S. *Best Evidence: Disguise and Deception in the Assassination of John F. Kennedy.* New York: Macmillan, 1980.

McAdams, John. *JFK Assassination Logic: How to Think About Claims of Conspiracy,* Washington, DC: Potomac Books, 2011.

McMillan, Priscilla Johnson. *Marina and Lee.* New York: Harper & Row, 1977.

Mailer, Norman. *Oswald's Tale: An American Mystery.* New York: Random House, 1995.

Mallon, Thomas. *Mrs. Paine's Garage and the Murder of John F. Kennedy.* New York: Pantheon Books, 2002.

Manchester, William. *Controversy and Other Essays in Journalism.* Boston: Little, Brown, 1975.

———. *The Death of a President.* New York: Harper & Row, 1967.

———. *Portrait of a President.* Boston: Little, Brown, 1962.

Mangold, Tom. *Cold Warrior: James Jesus Angleton.* London: Simon and Schuster, 1991.

Marrs, Jim. *Crossfire: The Plot That Killed Kennedy,* New York: Carroll & Graf, 1989.

Martin, David C. *Wilderness of Mirrors.* Guilford, CT: Lyons Press, 1980. (Also published as *Wilderness of Mirrors: How the Byzantine Intrigues of the Secret War Between the CIA and KGB Seduced and Devoured Key Agents James Jesus Angleton and William King Harvey.* New York: Harper & Row, 1980.)

Martin, Ralph G. *A Hero for Our Times: An Intimate Story of the Kennedy Years.* New York: Scribner, 1983.

McKnight, Gerald. *Breach of Trust: How the Warren Commission Failed the Nation and Why.* Lawrence: University of Kansas Press, 2005.

Meagher, Sylvia. *Accessories After the Fact: The Warren Commission, the Authorities and the Report.* New York: Vintage, 1976.

Mellen, Joan. *Our Man in Haiti: George de Mohrenschildt and the CIA in the Nightmare Republic.* Walterville, OR: Trine Day, 2012.

Morley, Jefferson. *Our Man in Mexico: Winston Scott and the Hidden History of the CIA.* Lawrence: University Press of Kansas, 2008.

Mudd, Roger. *The Place to Be: Washington, CBS and the Glory Days of Television News.* New York: PublicAffairs, 2008.

Newman, Albert H. *The Assassination of John F. Kennedy.* New York: Clarkson N. Potter Inc., 1970.

Newman, John. *Oswald and the CIA.* New York: Carroll & Graf, 1995.

Newton, Jim. *Justice for All: Earl Warren and the Nation He Made.* New York: Riverhead Books, 2006.

O'Donnell, Kenneth P., and David F. Powers with Joe McCarthy. *Johnny, We Hardly Knew Ye: Memories of John Fitzgerald Kennedy.* Boston: Little, Brown, 1972.

O'Neill, Francis X. Jr. *A Fox Among Wolves: The Autobiography of Francis X. O'Neill Jr., Retired FBI Agent.* Brewster, MA: Codfish Press, 2008.

O'Reilly, Bill, and Martin Dugard. *Killing Kennedy.* New York: Henry Holt and Company, 2012.

Oswald, Robert L., with Myrick Land and Barbara Land. *Lee: A Portrait of Lee Harvey Oswald by His Brother.* New York: Coward-McCann, 1967.

Pearson, Drew. *Diaries: 1949–1959.* New York: Holt, Rinehart & Winston, 1974.

Phelan, James. *Scandals, Scamps and Scoundrels: The Casebook of an Investigative Reporter.* New York: Random House, 1982.

Philby, Kim. *My Secret War: The Autobiography of a Spy.* New York: Modern Library, 2002. (Also published as *My Secret War.* London: MacGibbon & Kee, 1968.)

Phillips, David Atlee. *The Night Watch.* New York: Ballantine Books, 1977. (Also published as *The Night Watch: 25 Years of Peculiar Service.* New York: Atheneum, 1977.)

Pilat, Oliver. *Drew Pearson: An Unauthorized Biography.* New York: Pocket Books, 1973.

Popkin, Richard H. *The Second Oswald.* New York: Avon Books, 1966.

Posner, Gerald. *Case Closed: Lee Harvey Oswald and the Assassination of JFK.* New York: Anchor Books, 1994. (Also published as *Case Closed: Lee Harvey Oswald and the Assassination of JFK.* New York: Random House, 1993.)

Powers, Thomas. *The Man Who Kept the Secrets: Richard Helms and the CIA.* New York: Alfred A. Knopf, 1979.

Rather, Dan, with Mickey Herskowitz. *The Camera Never Blinks: Adventures of a TV Journalist.* New York: William Morrow, 1977.

Reston, James. *Deadline: A Memoir.* New York, Random House, 1991.

Russell, Dick. *The Man Who Knew Too Much: Hired to Kill Oswald and Prevent the Assassination of JFK.* New York: Carroll & Graf, 1992.

Russo, Guy, and Stephen Molton. *Brothers in Arms: The Kennedys, the Castros, and the Politics of Murder.* New York: Bloomsbury, 2008.

Schieffer, Bob. *This Just In: What I Couldn't Tell You on TV.* New York: Putnam, 2003.

Schlesinger, Arthur M. Jr. *Robert Kennedy and His Times.* New York: First Mariner Books, 2002. (Also published as *Robert Kennedy and His Times.* Boston: Houghton Mifflin, 1978.)

———. *A Thousand Days: John F. Kennedy in the White House.* Boston: Houghton Mifflin, 1965.

Schorr, Daniel. *Clearing the Air.* Boston: Houghton Mifflin, 1978.

Scott, Peter Dale. *Deep Politics and the Death of JFK.* Berkeley: University of California Press, 1993.

Semple, Robert B., ed. *Four Days in November: The Original Coverage of the John F. Kennedy Assassination by the Staff of* The New York Times. New York: St. Martin's Press, 2003.

Shesol, Jeff. *Mutual Contempt: Lyndon Johnson, Robert Kennedy, and the Feud that Defined a Decade.* New York: W. W. Norton & Company, 1997.

Specter, Arlen, and Charles Robbins. *Passion for Truth: From Finding JFK's Single Bullet to Questioning Anita Hill to Impeaching Clinton.* New York: William Morrow, 2000.

Stafford, Jean. *A Mother in History: Three Incredible Days with Lee Harvey Oswald's Mother.* New York: Farrar, Straus and Giroux, 1966.

Stone, Oliver, and Zachary Sklar. *JFK: The Book of the Film.* New York: Applause Books, 1992.

Sullivan, William C., and Bill Brown. *The Bureau: My Thirty Years in Hoover's FBI*. New York: W. W. Norton & Company, 1979.

Summers, Anthony. *Conspiracy*. New York: Paragon House, 1989.

——. *Not in Your Lifetime*. New York: Marlowe, 1998.

Talbot, David. *Brothers: The Hidden History of the Kennedy Years*. New York: Free Press, 2007.

Thomas, Evan. *Robert Kennedy: His Life*. New York: Simon & Schuster, 2000.

——. *The Very Best Men*. New York: Simon & Schuster, 1995.

Thompson, Josiah. *Six Seconds in Dallas: A Micro-study of the Kennedy Assassination*. New York: Bernard Geis Associates, 1967.

Toruño-Haensly, Rhina. *Encounter with Memory*. Bloomington, IN: Palibrio, 2011.

Waldron, Lamar, with Thom Hartmann. *Ultimate Sacrifice: John and Robert Kennedy, the Plan for a Coup in Cuba and the Murder of JFK*. New York: Carroll & Graf, 2005.

Warren, Earl. *The Memoirs of Chief Justice Earl Warren*. Langham, MD: Madison Books, 2001. (Also published as *The Memoirs of Earl Warren*. Garden City, NY: Doubleday, 1977.)

Weaver, John Downing. *Warren, the Man, the Court, the Era*. Boston: Little, Brown, 1967.

Weisberg, Harold. *Case Open*. New York: Carroll & Graf, 1994.

——. *Never Again! The Government Conspiracy in the JFK Assassination*. New York: Carroll & Graf, 1995.

——. *Whitewash: The Report on the Warren Commission*. Hyattstown, MD: Self-published, 1965.

Weiner, Tim. *Enemies: A History of the FBI*. New York: Random House, 2012.

——. *Legacy of Ashes: The History of the CIA*. New York: Random House, 2007.

White, G. Edward. *Earl Warren: A Public Life*. New York: Oxford University Press, 1982.

Widmer, Ted, and Caroline Kennedy. *Listening In: The Secret White House Recordings of John F. Kennedy*. New York: Hyperion, 2012.

Woods, Randall B. *LBJ: Architect of American Ambition*. Cambridge, MA: Harvard University Press, 2007.

GOVERNMENT REPORTS

Alleged Assassination Plots Involving Foreign Leaders, An Interim Report of the Select Committee to Study Governmental Operations with Respect to Intelligence Activities, United States Senate, Together with Additional Supplemental and Separate Views. 94th Congress, 1st session, Senate Report No. 94-465. Washington: Government Printing Office, 1975. (Church Committee)

Final Report of the Assassination Records Review Board. Washington: Government Printing Office, 1998. (ARRB)

Final Report of the Select Committee on Assassinations, U.S. House of Representatives, Ninety-fifth Congress, Second Session, Summary of Findings and Recommendations. House Report 95-1828. Washington: Government Printing Office, 1979. (HSCA)

Hearings Before the President's Commission on the Assassination of President Kennedy, Volumes 1-26. Washington: Government Printing Office, 1964. (Warren Appendix Volumes 1-26)

The Investigation of the Assassination of President John F. Kennedy: Performance of the Intelligence Agencies. Book V. Final Report of the Select Committee to Study Governmental Operations with Respect to Intelligence Activities. 94th Congress, 2nd session, Senate Report No. 94-755. Washington: Government Printing Office, 1976. (Church Committee)

Report of the President's Commission on the Assassination of President Kennedy. Washington: Government Printing Office, 1964. (Warren Report)

Report to the President by the Commission on CIA Activities within the United States. New York: Manor Books, June 1975. (Rockefeller Commission)

Acknowledgments

I began this project reluctantly. The Kennedy assassination is the most written about—and without doubt, most misunderstood—event in modern history, and I now know that many of the mysteries that surround November 22, 1963, will likely never be solved. As I explain elsewhere in these pages, I was led to this project because my first book was a history of the 9/11 Commission. It seemed logical to consider doing my next book on the Warren Commission, the other landmark federal investigation of a national tragedy in my lifetime. Still, I worried: Was I going to fall down the rabbit hole, pursuing the ultimate unknowable story? As a reporter, I usually begin an investigation with confidence that I will end up with the answers to most of my questions. I had no such confidence here, although five years later, I am convinced that *A Cruel and Shocking Act* does reveal startling new evidence about the assassination.

As I set to work on the research for this book, I was hit almost immediately by the realization that, by comparison, the terrible story of the 9/11 attacks was downright straightforward. The debate about the Kennedy assassination is an absolute morass, in part because of the failings of the Warren Commission, which clearly rushed its investigation and left so many questions unanswered despite the eagerness of its young staff investigators to get to the truth. (I am struck by the fact that the 9/11 Commission had twenty months to complete its work and did not begin investigating until after Congress had completed its own exhaustive inquiry. The Warren Commission was "finished" in half that time; it was established just seven days after the shots rang out in Dealey Plaza.) Some of the conspiracy theories about the Kennedy assassination are not so far-fetched, especially given the legal definition of conspiracy, which requires only that two people plot wrongdoing. If only one other person aided Oswald in a plot to kill Kennedy, there was by definition a conspiracy.

So I begin these acknowledgments by thanking a handful of writers, researchers, and historians whose books and other work gave me an all-important head start in trying to make sense of what is easily the most complicated story I have ever pursued. Since I am reaching for superlatives, I start by crediting the authors of what may be the single most intriguing government report I have ever seen—by Dan Hardway and Edwin Lopez-Soto, two then very young Cornell University law students who were recruited in the 1970s as staffers for the House Select Committee on Assassinations. Their report, entitled "Oswald, the CIA and Mexico City," would not be declassified until the 1990s, and it gave me the essential road map that led me to the story of Charles Thomas, Elena Garro, and the "twist party" in Mexico City. Dan and Ed were generous with their time in interviews for this book.

Of the more than two thousand books published about the assassination, only a handful will still be read generations from now. And while I might fundamentally disagree with the conclusions of a few of these authors, I know that the essential library will always include Jefferson Morley's remarkable *Our Man in Mexico*, which opened my eyes even wider to the unanswered questions about Oswald's Mexico trip; *The Last Investigation* by Gaeton Fonzi; *Case Closed* by Gerald Posner; *Brothers in Arms* by Gus Russo and Stephen Molton; *Castro's Secrets* by Brian Latell; *Conspiracy* by Anthony Summers; *Inquest* by Edward Jay Epstein; *Oswald and the CIA* by John Newman; *Brothers* by David Talbot; and Evan Thomas's gracefully written and revealing *Robert Kennedy: His Life*. I deeply admire the work of the nation's two great historians on the assassination—Max Holland, whose book *The Kennedy Assassination Tapes* is perhaps the best starting point for anyone who conducts research on this subject, and Vincent Bugliosi, whose 1,612-page masterwork, *Reclaiming History*, has sat on my desk for most of the last four years. I have read and reread Don DeLillo's brilliant *Libra* and I marvel at how close I think his work of fiction might have come to the truth.

I've had a real partner in this undertaking: Kathy Robbins, who is my cherished friend and my literary agent, in that order. She is a born editor and has shaped this book in countless invaluable ways, all the while keeping my spirits up when the project threatened to overwhelm me. She is backed up at home and in life by another magnificent editor, her husband, Richard Cohen, whose suggestions have made this a much better, more readable book.

I am grateful to the legendary Stephen Rubin, president and publisher of Henry Holt and Company, for seeing the promise in this project, and for his patience. Steve is that rare thing: a true gentleman. There are many people at Holt or associated with Steve to thank, including Maggie Richards, Phyllis Grann, Pat Eisemann, Kenn Russell, Muriel Jorgensen, Emi Ikkanda, Meryl Levavi, and Michael Cantwell.

At the Robbins Office, I am thankful for the wise counsel of David Halpern, Louise Quayle, Katherine DiLeo, and their former colleagues Micah Hauser and Mike Gillespie. Thanks to photo researcher Laura Wyss and photo restorer Matthew Brazier for helping organize such a strong lineup of images. Laura and I are both grateful to Rex Bradford of the Mary Ferrell Foundation and Mark Davies of the Sixth Floor Museum in Dallas for all their assistance with the photos. JoAnne Hakala-Applebaugh was an intelligent, thoughtful research assistant and voice of good cheer.

My biggest stroke of luck was the discovery—through my friend and former New York Times colleague Ginger Thompson—of Alejandra Xanic Von Bertrab. Xanic, who often works for the Times out of Mexico City, is a phenomenal journalist and managed to track down many of the central characters in the tangled story of Oswald's visit to Mexico; these are the people the FBI and the CIA ignored or missed fifty years ago. It was no surprise to me—but it was a delight—when Xanic won a Pulitzer Prize in 2013 for her part at the Times in exposing how Walmart used bribery to take control of much of Mexican retailing.

The talented Washington author Charles Robbins generously agreed to talk me through his understanding of some of the inner workings of the Warren Commission—knowledge he had gained as a former top aide to Senator Arlen Specter and as coauthor of the senator's memoirs, Passion for Truth. Charles helped me arrange two of the last interviews that Specter, who died in 2012, would ever give to discuss his key role on the commission. Charles also graciously helped me track down some of the commission staff lawyers and others he had interviewed for the senator's book.

I was fortunate to come across talented archivists and librarians to guide me through a mountain of evidence related to the assassination:

Mary Kay Schmidt at the National Archives in College Park, Maryland; William H. McNitt at the Gerald Ford Presidential Library in Ann Arbor, Michigan; Karen M. Albert at the Arlen Specter Center for Public Policy at Philadelphia University; Sheryl B. Vogt at the Richard B. Russell Library at the University of Georgia; Brian C. McNerney at the Lyndon Baines Johnson Library in Austin, Texas; and also in Austin, Stefanie Lapka, Margaret L. Schlankey, and Aryn Glazier of the Briscoe Center at the University of Texas. Marie Fonzi, Gaeton's widow, has a valuable collection of material gathered by her late husband from his work on the House Assassinations Committee.

I was relieved to discover the existence of private research groups that have created digital libraries of declassified material about the assassination, notably the Mary Ferrell Foundation (www.maryferrell.org), which has a searchable archive of more than a million documents related to the deaths of both John and Robert Kennedy, as well as of Martin Luther King. The foundation's ninety-nine-dollar-a-year research fee was among the wisest investments I made for this book. Among the other groups with impressive electronic archives on this subject are the Assassination Archives and Research Center (www.aarclibrary.org) and History Matters, (www.history-matters.com).

The families of several of my sources have been unfailingly gracious as I have intruded into their lives, especially Kaaren Slawson, David's wife; Paula Aynesworth, Hugh's wife; and Laura and Tom Belin, David's daughter and son. Laura and Tom's loving devotion to their father's legacy is an inspiration. I owe a special debt to the family of Charles William Thomas—especially to his widow, Cynthia, who took such a risk by talking with me after talking to no other reporter or author for decades about the most traumatic events of her life. I have huge admiration for Cynthia's daughter, Zelda Thomas-Curti, who has the instincts of a reporter and who sensed years ago that the true story about her father was being hidden. I was delighted to be introduced to Charles's other daughter, Jeanne-Marie Thomas Byron, in the final stages of writing this book and to learn that she, too, has been searching for the truth.

While I know he will disagree with my portrayal of him in these pages, I do thank Mark Lane for welcoming me into his home in Virginia and giving me an extended interview for this book. Whatever our disagreements, I know now that the title of his most famous, bestselling book about the Warren Commission, *Rush to Judgment,* was an appropriate one.

To my mother, Philippa Shenon, and the rest of my family in California and elsewhere, I apologize for my long absences from the dinner table because of the book project—this one—that I tried to keep a secret for so many years. To my friends Desmond Davis, Darnell Harvin, Betty Russell, Dino Sciulli, and Julian Wells in Washington, DC, thank you for keeping me company during so many long days and nights of writing.

Index

To buy any of our books and to find out
more about Abacus and Little, Brown, our authors
and titles, as well as events and book clubs,
visit our website

www.littlebrown.co.uk

and follow us on Twitter

@AbacusBooks
@LittleBrownUK

To order any Abacus titles p & p free in the UK,
please contact our mail order supplier on:

+ 44 (0)1832 737525

Customers not based in the UK should contact
the same number for appropriate postage
and packing costs.